I0131708

Robust Cloud Integration with Azure

Unleash the power of serverless integration with Azure

Mahindra Morar
Abhishek Kumar
Martin Abbott
Gyanendra Kumar Gautam
James Corbould
Ashish Bhambhani

Pack<t>

BIRMINGHAM - MUMBAI

Robust Cloud Integration with Azure

Copyright © 2017 Packt Publishing

All rights reserved. No part of this book may be reproduced, stored in a retrieval system, or transmitted in any form or by any means, without the prior written permission of the publisher, except in the case of brief quotations embedded in critical articles or reviews.

Every effort has been made in the preparation of this book to ensure the accuracy of the information presented. However, the information contained in this book is sold without warranty, either express or implied. Neither the authors, nor Packt Publishing, and its dealers and distributors will be held liable for any damages caused or alleged to be caused directly or indirectly by this book.

Packt Publishing has endeavored to provide trademark information about all of the companies and products mentioned in this book by the appropriate use of capitals. However, Packt Publishing cannot guarantee the accuracy of this information.

First published: March 2017

Production reference: 1170317

Published by Packt Publishing Ltd.
Livery Place
35 Livery Street
Birmingham
B3 2PB, UK.
ISBN 978-1-78646-557-3

www.packtpub.com

Credits

Authors
Mahindra Morar
Abhishek Kumar
Martin Abbott
Gyanendra Kumar Gautam
James Corbould
Ashish Bhambhani

Reviewers
Jeff Hollan
Bill Chesnut
Glenn Colpaert
Howard S. Edidin
Riaan Gouws

Commissioning Editor
Kartikey Pandey

Acquisition Editor
Prachi Bisht

Content Development Editors
Juliana Nair
Rashmi Suvarna

Technical Editor
Mohd Riyan Khan

Copy Editor
Dipti Mankame

Project Coordinator
Judie Jose

Proofreader
Safis Editing

Indexer
Pratik Shirodkar

Graphics
Kirk D'Penha

Production Coordinators
Shantanu N. Zagade
Shraddha Falebhai

Foreword

As the world becomes ever more connected to the cloud, integration is more relevant and important than ever. Also, as enterprises trust the cloud to run more and more workloads, robustness is a core non-negotiable requirement. With the diversity of services and applications both in the cloud and on premises, the need to provide the connective tissue that gets systems and services talking in a clean and efficient way is paramount. Let's not forget that everyone also wants to achieve and improve the reuse and manageability as well as implementing their solutions quicker. Enterprise integration skills and experience are core competencies for this generational shift. As a practitioner for more than 20 years, I've seen this evolving firsthand, and the pace of innovation has not only been dramatic, but it's also accelerating.

Keeping up with everything has become a challenge in itself and the goal of this book is to get you success in your projects as fast as possible. It covers everything from basic introductions to services to complex integration solutions all underpinned with practical and easy-to-understand scenarios that help consolidate your learning. Whether it is creating a simple Logic App or a more complex hybrid integration solution that spans both cloud and on premises, this book delves deep into all the key technologies that are part of the current integration landscape in Microsoft Azure.

Mahindra, Abhishek, Martin, James, Gautam, and Ashish have accumulated over 50 years of integration knowledge between them, and they use this experience to great effect to tell the story of cloud and hybrid integration in a way that is accessible and easy to learn. Using a fictional company, Sunny Electricals, they stitch together solutions that are immediately relevant and usable. I'm sure you'll enjoy reading this book as much as I did and gain valuable insights from these experts that will help you be a great integration professional as well.

There's never been a more exciting time to be working in the integration space. It's time for you to take your first steps into the world of Robust Cloud Integration with Azure!

Jon Fancey

Principal Program Manager

Pro Integration, Microsoft Corporation

About the Authors

Mahindra Morar has been working in the IT sector from 1997, developing Windows and website enterprise applications. In 2009, he has been focusing primarily on integrating systems as a principle integration consultant.

Having come from an electronics engineering background, he is able to use this knowledge to design solutions that integrate between wetware, software and hardware. He has worked in many industries, including manufacturing, financial institutions, insurance, retail/wholesale and power utilities.

His interests are exploring new technologies and deciding how to use them in the integration world.

You can view Mahindra's blog at `https://connectedcircuits.wordpress.com`.

This is Mahindra's second book he has co-authored; the first book was called *SOA Patterns with BizTalk Server*, and was published in 2015.

> *I would like to thank my co-authors, Abhishek, James, Martin, Gautam, and Ashish, who also dedicated their time in writing this book. Without them this book would not have created. The last 9 months writing this book has been a great learning experience; I now truly appreciate the hard work and dedication authors endure. I take my hat off to you all. For the readers of this book, I hope you find it interesting and beneficial to your career in IT. Finally, I would like to thank the three precious people in my life: Vanita, my lovely wife, and my two joyful boys, Ameesh and Jayan, who gave me the time to co-author this book.*

Abhishek Kumar is working as Integration Consultant with Datacom New Zealand and has more than 8 years of experience in the fields of designing, building, and implementing integration solution.

He is a Microsoft Azure MVP and worked with multiple clients worldwide on modern integration strategies and solutions. He started his career in India as a BizTalk Consultant with Tata Consultancy Services before taking up consultant roles at Cognizant Services and Robert Bosch GmbH.

Abhishek has published multiple articles on modern integration strategy on the Web and the Microsoft TechNet wiki. His areas of interest include technologies such as Logic Apps, API Apps, Azure Functions, Cognitive Services, PowerBI, and Microsoft BizTalk Server.

His Twitter username is @Abhishekcskumar.

I would like to thank my co-authors, Mahindra, James, Martin, Gautam, and Ashish, who also dedicated their time and effort in writing this book. It has been a fabulous 9 months of work by all of us as a team. Thanks to our exceptional technical reviewers, Jeff Hollan, Bill Chesnut, Riaan Gouws, Glenn Colpaert, and Howard S. Edidin for their efforts in reviewing each chapter and providing valuable insights for the authors. I would also like to take this opportunity to thank Datacom and my manager, Brett Atkins, for their guidance and support throughout our write-up journey.

Martin Abbott is a Microsoft Azure MVP living in Perth, Western Australia. He started his career developing subroutines for commercial computational fluid dynamics software, eventually moving on to more mainstream development and systems integration.

He has been working with BizTalk Server since the early days of the product, has spent a lot of time with WCF, but more recently has moved in to providing his customers with integration solutions spanning both on-premises and cloud workloads.

Most recently, his interests and work have led him to the Internet of Things, where he has been actively involved in the development of products and solutions for customers across a range of industries.

Martin is a regular speaker, runs the Perth MS Cloud Computing User Group, and is a member of the admin teams that organize Global Azure Bootcamp and Global Integration Bootcamp.

His blog can be found at: `http://martinabbott.com`, and his Twitter username is `@martinabbott`.

I would first like to thank my co-authors, James, Abhishek, Mahindra, Gautam, and Ashish, for their support and tireless effort during the development of this book. It has been a pleasure to work with you all and I look forward to our next collaboration. We managed to secure some great reviewers for the book, and I would like to thank them for their dedication to making sure this book hits every mark, and for providing great constructive feedback. Thank you to you, the reader of this book. You are the reason we do this, and having you thumb through the pages, either physically or electronically, makes this all worthwhile. Finally, no acknowledgement would be complete without me thanking the most important people in my life. I want to thank my wife, Leigh, and my three wonderful sons, Joel, Noah, and Aaron, for their support and the sacrifices they have made over many weekends and evenings as this book has taken shape. I love you all and I could not have done it without you.

Gyanendra Kumar Gautam is a BizTalk consultant, specialized in integration solutions across enterprise and cloud with Microsoft's suite of tools and services. He is currently working with Synegrate as Sr. Cloud Integration Architect in the San Francisco Bay Area, helping customers to hook their stuff together within their enterprise by providing unified integration solutions, both on-premise and on the cloud.

Gautam began his career in 2005 at a start-up consulting firm in Bangalore, India. Since this startup company was primarily focused on the healthcare industry, he worked on multiple projects to develop healthcare software such as Practice Management System (PMS), Electronic Medical Records (EMR), and a few HL7 integrations. He also worked for a global IT consulting firm and a global mutual fund company, which gave him exposure to SOA/BPM technologies.

Prior to Synegrate, Gautam was with Microsoft as a PFE (Premier Field Engineer). In this role he was responsible for ensuring the success of enterprise integration solution using Microsoft BizTalk Server within customers' IT operations by providing deep technical skills for proactive and reactive delivery that involved technically complex or politically sensitive situations in large, enterprise-scale environments.

Gautam holds certifications in developing Microsoft Azure Solution and Microsoft BizTalk Server (MSTS). He also maintains a blog as learning web-log from his day-to-day work experience about enterprise integration with BizTalk Server and Azure Cloud Platform at: `http://gautambiztalkblog.com/`.

I would like to thank my co-authors, Abhishek, Mahindra, James, Martin, and Ashish, for all the hard work they did on their chapters, as well as for helping me out with the reviewing process of my chapters. I also want to thank my exceptional technical reviewers, Riaan Gouws, Glenn Colpaert, Howard S. Edidin, and Bill Chesnut. They made significant contributions in their role as technical reviewers. This book is of a higher caliber as a result of their insight, wisdom, and real-world experience. I would also like to thank my mentor, John Sonmez, for inspiring and guiding me to pursue my goals with hard work and dedication. Most of all, I would like to thank my lovely wife, Shilpa, for being so patient with me and understanding me while I was working on this book. I couldn't have gotten this task done without her support. Finally, thank you, dear readers, for reading this book. It makes all the effort worthwhile.

James Corbould has been working in the IT sector since 2003, developing and supporting applications in New Zealand and the United Kingdom. Since 2010, James has been working in the software integration field, designing and building integration solutions using Microsoft technologies such as BizTalk, SQL Server, WCF, .NET, and now Azure, for a wide range of different customers. Recently, he has been working in the health insurance sector and in the building supplies sector.

Living and working in Auckland, New Zealand, James currently works for Datacom Systems as a consultant and team lead.

James seeks to contribute to the community through his blog (`https://jamescorbould.wordpress.com`) and is a technical reviewer for a couple of publications: *The A-Y of running BizTalk Server in Microsoft Azure* and *BizTalk Server Extensibility*, both available from the BizTalk360 website. This is James' first foray as an author. You can follow him via his Twitter username: `@jamescorbould`.

I would like to thank my fellow co-authors, Abhishek, Mahindra, Martin, Gautam, and Ashish, for their commitment to this project, through all the challenges and good times. It was a pleasure to work with you all and to make new friends. Many thanks too to our reviewers and the excellent feedback and comments that we received. Thanks also to my employer, Datacom, to my colleagues and managers, for the mentorship, assistance, opportunities, and the trust placed in me over the years. Last, and by no means least, to my beautiful wife, Bronwyn, and my two wonderful boys, Ben and Lachlan, for their support and encouragement while writing this book. I would also like to thank my parents, Nigel and Linda, for such wonderful support over the years. I hope that all readers find something useful in this book, as an introduction to the brave new world of integration using the Azure platform.

Ashish Bhambhani is an Integration Sr. Premier Field Engineer working for Microsoft. He lives in the Seattle region. He has been working in the integration space for more than a decade. In his current role he helps Microsoft's enterprise customers by architecting, designing, building, and maintaining their integration solutions. He has worked with some of the world's biggest customers for Microsoft in the integration space. Recently, he has been able to roll out Azure technologies enterprise-wide for his clients and replace their legacy solutions. He is a content creator and master trainer for some of a Microsoft's training that is delivered to clients worldwide. Additionally, he was part of the team that wrote the BizTalk performance whitepaper for msdn.com.

I would like to thank my co-authors on the book (Abhishek, Mahindra, James, Martin, and Gautam) for putting in their time and effort into getting quality content created. Also, I would like to thank my family, especially my wife, Shruti, and my sons, Ekam and Meir, for inspiring me to do this and supporting along the way. Lastly, I would also thank my employer and my manager, Mark Edwards, for enabling me to write my parts for the book.

About the Reviewers

Jeff Hollan is a program manager for Azure Logic Apps at Microsoft. He has been with Microsoft for a number of years, initially working in Microsoft IT to integrate and gain real-time insights across sales, marketing, and development pipelines. For the past 3 years, he has been a part of the Microsoft Integration team, which focused on the development of the Azure Logic Apps service. Being a passionate presenter, he helps share Microsoft's vision for integration and serverless orchestrations at conferences and events around the world.

Bill Chesnut is a cloud platform and API evangelist for SixPivot based in Melbourne, Australia. Bill started his career in IT in 1983 with the US Defence Department as an IBM Mainframe Systems Programmer. In 1994, he switched to the Microsoft Windows platform, and he has been involved with Windows development ever since.

Bill has worked on numerous enterprise projects using the full suite of Microsoft technologies, specializing in systems integration. He started working with the first release of Microsoft BizTalk Server, BizTalk Server 2000, and has worked with every version of BizTalk, including the most recent BizTalk Server 2016. Bill has also been working with Azure since its initial release. In his current role as a cloud platform and API evangelist with SixPivot, Bill is helping clients streamline their adoption of cloud technologies, including Azure API Management, Azure Logic Apps, Azure App Services, and Azure Functions, with a focus on hybrid integration. Bill has been a Microsoft MVP since 2004, initially in BizTalk Server, then Microsoft Integration, and now Microsoft Azure. He has also been extensively involved in the Microsoft User Group Community as a leader of the Melbourne .NET User Group, Melbourne BizTalk User group, and assisting with the Melbourne Azure Meetup Group. Bill has presented at user groups in Australia, New Zealand, and the US. He has also presented at Microsoft TechEd/Ignite in Australia and New Zealand numerous times.

Glenn Colpaert is Azure and IoT Domain Lead at Codit, where he ensures the day-to-day operations of the Azure and IoT domain within Codit. Since 2014, he has been a Microsoft Azure MVP and Microsoft Azure Advisor.

Next to his day-to-day job, he also is a part of the Belgian BizTalk User Group (BTUG) board and the Belgian MEET Community.

Glenn has been integrating businesses with BizTalk, Cloud and Microsoft technologies for more than 8 years. He has gained a lot of hand-on experience during his projects and likes to share it with colleagues and the community.

You can find his blogposts on the Codit Blog (`http://www.codit.eu/blog/`) and follow his tweets via `http://twitter.com/GlennColpaert`.

Howard S. Edidin has over 25 years' experience in delivering enterprise integration solutions. For the past 15 years, Howard has been specializing in Healthcare and Life Sciences. He is a Microsoft MVP for the data platform and a P-TSP for Microsoft Healthcare and Life Sciences (BizTalk and Azure). Howard is also a DocumentDB Wizard and TechNet Ninja.

He has coauthored several books, the last one being *HL7 for BizTalk,* and has been a technical reviewer for two others.

Howard is very heavily involved with development and implementation of a new HL7 Standard, FHIR®.   He is considered the *go-to* person by Microsoft for HL7 integration on Azure.

Howard has been working directly with the Microsoft Product Managers to integrate FHIR on Azure. He has published two tutorials to the Microsoft Azure portal; Logging and Error Handling in Logic Apps (`https://docs.microsoft.com/en-us/azure/logic-apps/logic-apps-scenario-error-and-exception-handling`) and Notifying patients of HL7 FHIR healthcare record changes using Logic Apps and DocumentDB (`https://docs.microsoft.com/en-us/azure/documentdb/documentdb-change-feed-hl7-fhir-logic-apps`). Both tutorials are based on FHIR integration. Howard has also delivered several webcasts for the Integration User Group; Azure DocumentDB for Healthcare Integration – Part I (`http://www.integrationusergroup.com/azure-documentdb-and-biztalk/`) and Azure DocumentDB for Healthcare Integration – Part 2 (`http://www.integrationusergroup.com/azure-documentdb-for-healthcare-integration-part-2/`).

Howard is employed by VNB Consulting, Inc, a Microsoft Gold Partner for Integration and Azure Cloud Solution Provider (CSP), as a Sr. Azure Solutions Architect for Healthcare Integrations.

I would like to thank Mahindra, Gyanendra, James, Abhishek, Ashish, and Martin for giving me the opportunity to be a technical reviewer for this book.

Riaan Gouws, a seasoned integration architect, brings over 20 years of integration experience to the table. Riaan has a passion for technology, which is in turn complemented by his deep technical knowledge of integration, web, and data solutions.

Riaan cofounded Synegrate Inc, a consulting firm specializing in integration, web, and data workloads on the Microsoft Azure cloud platform. He holds the title of Chief Technology Officer. Synegrate is a Gold Partner, Application Integration, and shares Microsoft's strategic vision of cloud first, mobile first.

Riaan is also a member of the elite Microsoft Virtual Technology Specialist Program (VTSP) team, a small group of selected industry experts working as an extension to the Microsoft Technology Specialist teams. He has a strong relationship with Microsoft as a valued partner in implementing enterprise solutions on top of Microsoft Azure.

I would like to thank my wife, Selmarie, for being ever-supportive of my geekiness and Azure obsession.

www.PacktPub.com

For support files and downloads related to your book, please visit `www.PacktPub.com`.

Did you know that Packt offers eBook versions of every book published, with PDF and ePub files available? You can upgrade to the eBook version at `www.PacktPub.com` and as a print book customer, you are entitled to a discount on the eBook copy. Get in touch with us at `service@packtpub.com` for more details.

At `www.PacktPub.com`, you can also read a collection of free technical articles, sign up for a range of free newsletters and receive exclusive discounts and offers on Packt books and eBooks.

Mapt

`https://www.packtpub.com/mapt`

Get the most in-demand software skills with Mapt. Mapt gives you full access to all Packt books and video courses, as well as industry-leading tools to help you plan your personal development and advance your career.

Why subscribe?

- Fully searchable across every book published by Packt
- Copy and paste, print, and bookmark content
- On demand and accessible via a web browser

Customer Feedback

Thanks for purchasing this Packt book. At Packt, quality is at the heart of our editorial process. To help us improve, please leave us an honest review on this book's Amazon page at: www.amazon.com/dp/ASIN/B01KK6H3J4.

If you'd like to join our team of regular reviewers, you can e-mail us at customerreviews@packtpub.com. We award our regular reviewers with free eBooks and videos in exchange for their valuable feedback. Help us be relentless in improving our products!

Table of Contents

Preface

Microsoft is investing heavily in Azure, its cloud computing platform. It's tempting to view this trend as a fad, but it is obvious that Microsoft is committed to this endeavor, and businesses are realizing the benefits of a platform that abstracts and manages the complex tasks of infrastructure management and application lifecycle management on its behalf, to name just a couple of offerings.

As the platform matures, more enterprises move their systems and workloads to the cloud. Software as a Service (SaaS) providers now offer rich services that companies are attracted to, in order to provide a competitive edge to their operations. Although many SaaS solutions can be customized to fit particular use cases, this is often limited out of the box (regardless of what the sales literature says!); customization for specific use cases is sacrificed for the benefits of a shared feature platform.

Many companies have decades of investment in on-premises solutions that are often heavily customized, and it is difficult to justify migrating to a new platform. In addition, there may be privacy concerns with storing sensitive data in the cloud.

Within this landscape, companies wish to extend the reach of their IT systems to the cloud while often key systems remain on-premises. Typically, enterprises also wish to introduce a degree of smart business process automation too. In this book, we demonstrate, with a practical "hands-on" approach, how these aspirations may be achieved by integrating the various disparate cloud-based and on-premises systems using the technologies available in Azure.

The book also seeks to show how cloud and on-premises systems may be integrated in a "robust" fashion, by ignoring the hype and instead drawing on lessons learned from integrating systems in the past.

What this book covers

Chapter 1, *An Introduction to Systems Integration in the Cloud*, introduces the concept of cloud computing and modern integration using the Azure cloud platform.

Chapter 2, *What Is an Azure App Service?*, explores Azures Platform as a Service (PaaS) offering for a building and managing applications aka Azure App Service.

Chapter 3, *Getting Started with API Apps*, demonstrates how to build a robust, scalable, secure, and easy-to-use API backend to be consumed by your web, logic, or mobile app (or any third-party application hosted outside of App Service).

Chapter 4, *What is Azure API Management*, shows how to control and manage API assets using Azure API Management (APIM).

Chapter 5, *Trigger Your First Logic App in Azure*, is a first look at constructing workflows in the cloud using Logic Apps, to achieve smart business process automation quickly with no coding required.

Chapter 6, *Working with Connectors in Logic Apps*, provides an introduction to connectors that abstract away the complexities of directly interacting with a third-party API or data source, using prebuilt functionality provided by Microsoft. Learn how to create your own custom connector!

Chapter 7, *Azure Functions in Logic Apps*, looks into the hot topic of serverless computing by demonstrating how to build a function app and calling a function from a Logic App, to chain functionality and build complex workflows.

Chapter 8, *A Deep Dive into Logic Apps*, is a more in-depth look at Logic Apps, exploring advanced features such as control flow, looping, and exception handling.

Chapter 9, *Powerful Integration with SaaS Using Logic Apps*, shows how to hook up to Software as a Service (SaaS) providers using specialized Logic App connectors and how to leverage SaaS solutions in new and interesting ways to support unique business processes.

Chapter 10, *Advanced Integration with Powerful, Scalable Service Bus in the Cloud*, is a deep dive into Azure Service Bus, and this chapter demonstrates how to build loosely coupled and scalable integrations using this technology.

Chapter 11, *Connecting to Event Hubs and an Introduction to IoT Hubs*, provides an introduction to connecting disparate devices in Azure using IoT Hubs and processing large amounts of device data using Event Hubs.

Chapter 12, *EAI/B2B Integration Using Logic Apps*, introduces Enterprise Integration Pack, which is an Enterprise level set of features that extends Logic Apps to support common business scenarios such as B2B communication using XML, mapping between different message formats, and transmission protocols such as AS2.

Chapter 13, *Hybrid Integration Using BizTalk Server 2016 and Logic Apps*, introduces the reality that many businesses wish to not only leverage existing on-premises systems but also utilize SaaS applications (such as CRM Online). Using BizTalk Server 2016, this section demonstrates how to build a hybrid integration to do this, pairing with Logic Apps.

Chapter 14, *Tooling and Monitoring for Logic Apps*, looks into options after you have built your Logic App, to deploy your workflow in Azure and then ongoing monitoring and alerting features.

Chapter 15, *What's Next for Azure Integration?*, discusses Microsoft's future roadmap for integration using Azure and touches on Flow, the lightweight version of Logic Apps.

What you need for this book

The practical examples found in this book require an Azure subscription. It is possible to sign up for a free trial account via the Azure website, `https://azure.microsoft.com/`.

Other examples in the book may require a subscription to a particular SaaS provider; further details are provided in the relevant section.

Who this book is for

This book is for software developers, architects, and technical managers who wish to explore using Azure to connect cloud-based and on-premises systems. No prior knowledge of cloud computing and Azure is assumed.

It is expected that the reader has familiarity with the C# programming language and the JSON message exchange format. Code examples in this book use C# and JSON.

Conventions

In this book, you will find a number of text styles that distinguish between different kinds of information. Here are some examples of these styles and an explanation of their meaning.

Code words in text, database table names, folder names, filenames, file extensions, pathnames, dummy URLs, user input, and Twitter handles are shown as follows: "the code `PD30` specifies that payment was *past due by 30 days* and `COLL` indicates that the account was referred to a debt collection agency."

A block of code is set as follows:

```
public static string
SharedAccessSignatureTokenProvider.GetSharedAccessSignature(string keyName,
string sharedAccessKey, string resource, TimeSpan tokenTimeToLive)
```

When we wish to draw your attention to a particular part of a code block, the relevant lines or items are set in bold:

```
public static string
SharedAccessSignatureTokenProvider.GetSharedAccessSignature(string keyName,
string sharedAccessKey, string resource, TimeSpan tokenTimeToLive)
```

New terms and **important words** are shown in bold. Words that you see on the screen, for example, in menus or dialog boxes, appear in the text like this: "click on the **SQL databases** option and click on **Add** to create new SQL database instance."

Warnings or important notes appear in a box like this.

Tips and tricks appear like this.

Reader feedback

Feedback from our readers is always welcome. Let us know what you think about this book-what you liked or disliked. Reader feedback is important for us as it helps us develop titles that you will really get the most out of.

To send us general feedback, simply e-mail feedback@packtpub.com, and mention the book's title in the subject of your message.

If there is a topic that you have expertise in and you are interested in either writing or contributing to a book, see our author guide at www.packtpub.com/authors.

Customer support

Now that you are the proud owner of a Packt book, we have a number of things to help you to get the most from your purchase.

Downloading the color images of this book

We also provide you with a PDF file that has color images of the screenshots/diagrams used in this book. The color images will help you better understand the changes in the output. You can download this file from: `https://www.packtpub.com/sites/default/files/downloads/RobustCloudIntegrat ionwithAzure_ColorImages.pdf`.

Errata

Although we have taken every care to ensure the accuracy of our content, mistakes do happen. If you find a mistake in one of our books-maybe a mistake in the text or the code-we would be grateful if you could report this to us. By doing so, you can save other readers from frustration and help us improve subsequent versions of this book. If you find any errata, please report them by visiting `http://www.packtpub.com/submit-errata`, selecting your book, clicking on the **Errata Submission Form** link, and entering the details of your errata. Once your errata are verified, your submission will be accepted and the errata will be uploaded to our website or added to any list of existing errata under the **Errata** section of that title.

To view the previously submitted errata, go to `https://www.packtpub.com/books/content/support` and enter the name of the book in the search field. The required information will appear under the **Errata** section.

Piracy

Piracy of copyrighted material on the Internet is an ongoing problem across all media. At Packt, we take the protection of our copyright and licenses very seriously. If you come across any illegal copies of our works in any form on the Internet, please provide us with the location address or website name immediately so that we can pursue a remedy.

Please contact us at `copyright@packtpub.com` with a link to the suspected pirated material.

We appreciate your help in protecting our authors and our ability to bring you valuable content.

Questions

If you have a problem with any aspect of this book, you can contact us at `questions@packtpub.com`, and we will do our best to address the problem.

1
An Introduction to Systems Integration in the Cloud

Unity makes strength.
– Motto

This book is about building modern integration solutions in the cloud using **Microsoft Azure** technologies, enabling connectivity to **Software as a Service** (**SaaS**) applications such as **Salesforce** and **Dropbox**. Azure is Microsoft's premier cloud platform. It also looks at how to extend the reach of existing on-premises integration solutions and other legacy **Line of Business** (**LOB**) systems by connecting them to the cloud.

We also discuss important design patterns to build distributed systems in the cloud, such as the microservices pattern that builds on the principles of **service-oriented architecture** (**SOA**). We highlight some of the issues encountered when integrating traditional on-premises systems and how they can be solved, applying some of these learnings to the next generation of cloud-based applications.

We will discuss and demonstrate some of the Azure technologies using a full *turnkey* demonstration scenario as follows:

- **Azure App Service**: This is a new, fully managed **Platform as a Service** (**PaaS**) cloud solution in order to host web, mobile, and integration applications. In this book, we will be focusing primarily on API Apps, Logic Apps, and Web Apps (along with associated connectors):
    - **API Apps**: Build robust, scalable, and secure API backends for your web, mobile, and enterprise applications

- **Azure Service Bus**: Which comprises queues, topics, and relays
- **Logic Apps**: Automate business processes in a workflow and run them reliably in the cloud
- **API Management**: How to monitor APIs running in Azure and secure them using Azure Active Directory and OAuth
- **Azure Storage**: Blobs
- **Application Insights**: Get a view on how the various components comprising that your integration solution are working
- **Event Hubs/IoT Hubs**: Connect devices in the field and obtain valuable insights that can drive business automation and revenue
- **Azure Functions**: Trigger the execution of code on demand
- **ASP.NET Webhooks**: Notify subscribers that an event has occurred via an asynchronous callback
- **BizTalk Server 2016 Cloud Adapters**: Extend the reach of on-premises BizTalk into the cloud using the new Logic App adapter, for example

The cloud offering for on-premises systems will be examined, showing, for example, how to hook up BizTalk Server running in a local company data center to Azure using the new features of BizTalk Server 2016. Here, we will see how BizTalk on-premises can extend business capabilities into new territories not thought of before, well beyond the company firewall in a secure manner, reaching into third-party SaaS providers.

Businesses are realizing that with the right solutions in place, they can use the cloud to create extra competitive advantage, new business opportunities, and hence revenue by extending the capabilities of their IT, creating next generation solutions and also by enhancing existing applications. This is achievable through streamlined and responsive business automation in the cloud, which provides reliable and rich data to frontline applications. In this book, we seek to show how this can be done.

What is Azure?

Azure is Microsoft's cloud computing platform that comprises a collection of software services that can be hosted outside the traditional company IT infrastructure and provides an avenue to getting started quickly building and hosting software, in a *flexible pricing* business model.

A good place to learn more about Azure is via the Azure website:
`https://azure.microsoft.com`.

The following is a list of current service categories available in Azure:

- **Compute**: This is a high-level description of base services that provide a platform in order to run other applications and tasks, for example, virtual machines running Windows and Linux and platforms such as Service Fabric that act as a hosting platform within which applications can run.
- **Web and Mobile**: This includes services in order to run web and mobile applications, from the backend services required to the frontend web applications.
- **Data and Storage**: This includes relational and non-relational database systems including raw binary storage of data.
- Services focused on cognitive services and artificial intelligence.
- **Analytics**: This includes services in order to process large quantities of data using techniques such as machine learning as well as large-scale data transformation and movement.
- **Internet of Things**: This manages IoT assets on a big scale using IoT Hubs and processes real-time events and data using services such as **Stream Analytics**.
- **Networking**: This includes features such as load balancing, DNS, high-speed dedicated connections to Azure (ExpressRoute), and the configuration of private networks within Azure.
- **Media and CDN**: Robust content delivery through a distributed network of proxy servers deployed in multiple data centers across multiple regions.
- **Enterprise Integration**: This includes technologies in order to link on-premises and cloud-based systems, which encompasses Logic Apps, Service Bus, API Management, Functions, and BizTalk.
- **Identity and Access Management**: This includes authentication and authorization services using Active Directory in the cloud (with sync available to on-premises directories) and multifactor authentication.
- **Developer Services**: This includes services for the application developer including functionality such as Visual Studio Team Services for software development support and Application Insights that offers real-time monitoring of applications.
- **Management**: This assists with management tasks such as key management and offers task automation.

What is cloud computing?

There is little doubt that the concept of cloud computing is still in its infancy and as such, the definition of what cloud computing means is still much debated. This book doesn't seek to enter into the debate, instead prefers to focus on the services and capabilities that Azure can provide.

A good (and impartial) definition is available at `http://nvlpubs.nist.gov/nistpubs/Legacy/SP/nistspecialpublication800-145.pdf` provided by The **National Institute of Standards and Technology** (**NIST**), who defined cloud computing as follows:

> *"Cloud computing is a model for enabling ubiquitous, convenient, on-demand network access to a shared pool of configurable computing resources (e.g., networks, servers, storage, applications, and services) that can be rapidly provisioned and released with minimal management effort or service provider interaction."*

NIST go on to specify five essential characteristics of a cloud computing platform as follows:

1. **On-demand self-service**: Resources can be provisioned by the consumer at will and in a timely fashion, in a fully automated way. For example, it should be possible for a consumer to spin up a virtual machine as required with no service ticket needing to be raised with the provider; instead, the VM should be able to be provisioned in a self-serviced, automated way.
2. **Broad network access**: Resources should be available over the Internet and other networks via many different client devices, for example, laptop, mobile phone, and tablet.
3. **Resource pooling**: Consumers are provisioned computing resources via a common resource pool (multitenancy), which can be assigned dynamically, matching the highs and lows of consumer demand. Resource pools are geographically dispersed across different countries, states, and data centers.
4. **Rapid elasticity**: Resource utilization can go up or down automatically (or manually) to provide greater or lesser computing power based on current resource requirements.
5. **Measured service**: Feedback is readily available in regard to current resource usage and cost with metrics available (for example, storage and processing costs, bandwidth usage, the number of users). Billing is automated, transparent, consistent, and reliable.

Armed with these essential characteristics, it is apparent that there is a difference between a simpler hosting platform and a more fully featured cloud platform.

With a hosting platform, a company may employ VMware ESX hypervisor software on the private network to deploy and manage VMs. If a developer, for instance, requires a shared development VM on the company domain, it is usually not possible for the developer to start a VM in a **self-service model:** this would no doubt cause a few eyebrows to be raised by the IT infrastructure team! There is a finite limit on the total amount of resources assigned to the farm (disk, CPU, RAM, and so on), and this needs to be carefully managed. Also, there is a whole raft of questions and requirements around a regime of installing software patches, to mention just a few questions. In fact, in most organizations, a job ticket would need to be raised with the service provider (or internal IT infrastructure support team) for the VM to be provisioned. This proves a time-consuming and often onerous task.

Compare the description of a hosting platform with a cloud platform. With the cloud, the developer would be able to spin up a VM on a shared public platform, with the required supporting infrastructure and required specifications, on-demand. In Azure, for instance, this could be achieved via the web-based Azure Portal or using a scripting language such as **Windows PowerShell**. Costing would be *pay as you go*: as long as the VM is running, the developer will be charged a finely tuned fee based on the resource consumption of the VM (disk usage, CPU load, network usage, and so on). If the VM is switched off, the fee would just be for storing the VM image file. The VM can be spun up and shut down on-demand, as required, by the developer. If extra resources are required (for indicative software load testing, for instance), these can be assigned to the VM and the capacity is limitless. However, it would be the responsibility of the developer to install software and OS patches, so maintaining and supporting the VM.

So, we can see here that a hosting platform is missing many of the essential characteristics of a cloud platform. What many may regard as a cloud platform is in fact a hosting platform. Azure is firmly a cloud platform. A key difference is that in a cloud platform, computing power is a commodity and as such needs to be measured and easily provisioned.

Types of cloud platform

A cloud platform can be deployed in one of two modes:

1. **Private**: The platform is accessible by one organization only. A technology called **Azure Stack** running in a private company data center is an example of this. Stack is a version of the software and services provided by Azure that can be installed and run in a private data center.
2. **Public**: The platform is available on a public network, shared with multiple different organizations in multitenancy.

> At the time of writing, Azure Stack is currently in Technical Preview. More information on Azure Stack can be found at https://azure.microsoft.com/en-us/overview/azure-stack/.

Following on from this, an additional mode may be applied: *hybrid*. This typically describes a private or public cloud that is hooked up to one or more other, separate, cloud platforms (public or private). So this is an aggregation of at least two separate cloud platforms, each hosted on their own dedicated infrastructure, possibly providing extra capability to one or other cloud service provider in a way that is transparent to the user.

Azure is a public cloud owned, hosted, and operated by Microsoft, available to most organizations (and countries) across the globe. However, it is true that solutions can be built on Azure such that they are a hybrid. Consider, for example, a solution that is hosted primarily in Azure but leverages services in a company private data center running Azure Stack, a RESTful API. In this case, the solution can be considered a hybrid because it utilizes services provided by both a public and private cloud.

Another example hybrid solution may expose endpoints in Azure that forward requests to an endpoint in the local data center. Service Bus relays, for instance, provide this functionality. This is a pattern that is becoming more prevalent, as companies wish to leverage cloud solutions without opening wide the company on-premises firewall and proxy, relying instead on the security mechanisms offered by Azure.

Types of cloud service

Cloud providers typically break down their service offerings into three categories, which build on top of each other, as shown in the diagram here:

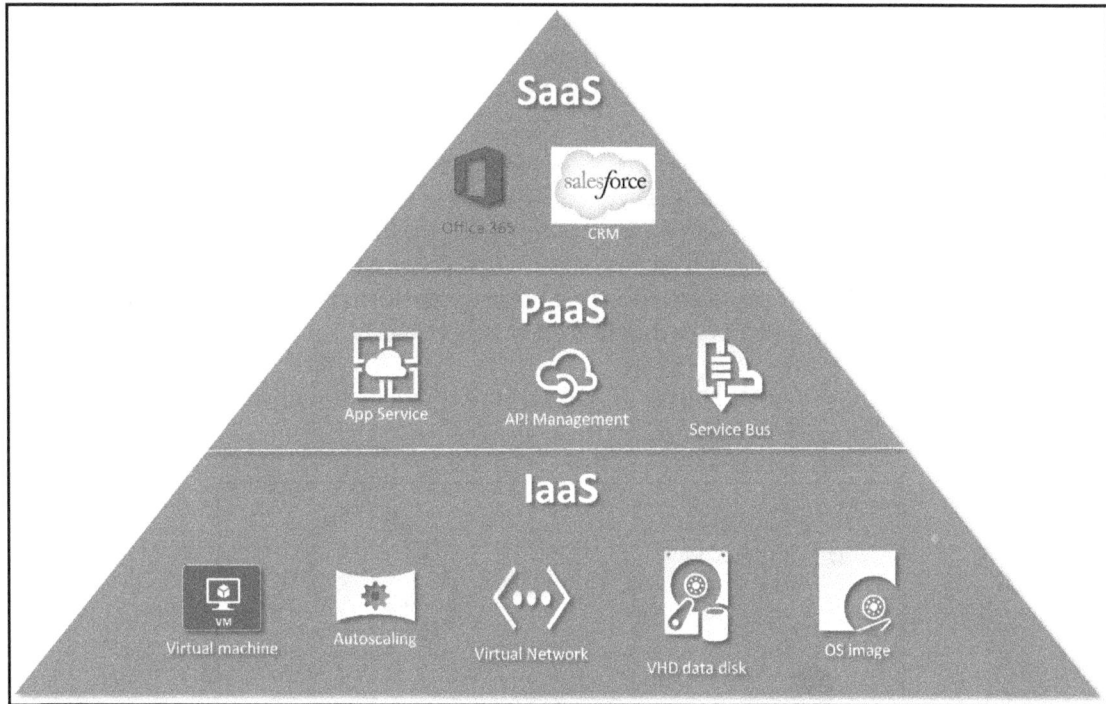

A diagram showing the relationships between Cloud Platform Services

1. **Infrastructure as a Service (IaaS)**: This layer describes the base hardware and software resources required to run application software in the cloud. This provides the ability to create and configure VMs and their hardware allocation (disk, CPU cores, RAM, and so on). Also, you can specify their base OS and configuration as required. With **Infrastructure as a Service (IaaS)** the cloud vendor supports the infrastructure as well, such as, network configuration (virtual switches, firewall configuration, and so on).

2. **Platform as a Service** (**PaaS**): This layer is built on top of the IaaS layer; in fact, the cloud provider is responsible for maintaining the IaaS layer and this is transparent to the end user. What is presented to the software provider (the *vendor*) is a readily scalable, configurable, and reliable application-hosting environment for its user base. Developers use development tools provided by the cloud vendor and deploy to the hosting platform. Deployments include the software developed to the specifications of the platform and associated configuration. Microsoft Azure App Services, discussed in this book, is there in this layer.

3. **Software as a Service** (**SaaS**): This is a term made famous by cloud applications such as `https://www.salesforce.com/in/?ir=1` (provider of CRM software). In this layer, application software runs transparently in the cloud. Via a web browser, for example, a user can use a word processing program via a tablet, not knowing that this program runs in a hosting platform (PaaS), which is in turn provisioned by various load-balanced servers (IaaS).

Inevitably, it has become a great source of amusement to hijack the phrase ... *as a service* in humorous ways!

Jokes as a Service (JaaS)

Cloud computing – something old or something new?

It will be apparent to some that the ideas presented here touch on a great many *old* paradigms (indeed computing *truths* if one may be so bold, that is, concepts that have been proven true time and time again through many implementations and as such are proven to be beneficial). Cloud computing is an agglomeration of a great many old ideas: for one, the concept of a shared pool of computing power invokes parallels with mainframes, running advanced time-sharing operating systems developed in the 1960s; also, the idea of software services that offer high cohesion provokes memories of SOA.

The base enabler for cloud computing is virtualization of computing resources and in many people's minds, this then puts Azure on par with an operating system that is essentially an abstraction of computing hardware for the purposes of ease of understanding and to ensure optimal use of the underlying hardware. But it is apparent that Azure is much more than an OS since it provides services typically in the area that would be considered application software, running on the OS.

Azure touches on so many aspects of computing, which is fascinating and at the same time overwhelming, in terms of effectively unlimited services that can be provided. But it is worth taking heart that core principles and characteristics exist that provide a jumpstart to learning about cloud platform services, which we hope to have introduced in this section of the book. So, all the old learnings are still relevant and provide a pattern for the future; rather, it is a case of *something old* for *something new!*

What is integration in the cloud?

Now that we have a good understanding of what cloud computing is and the benefits that it can offer, let's examine the heart of this book: integrating systems and applications using the cloud.

Software integration is the process of connecting disparate systems and applications together that would not normally talk to each other, allowing data and business rules to be shared to drive automated business processes that add value to the business.

Traditional on-premises integration is concerned with linking internal systems and applications together and communicating with other businesses. An **enterprise application integration** (**EAI**) product such as BizTalk Server is very good at this and provides useful features *out of the box* such as error handling and retry capability. However, it requires specialist knowledge, and also, it is now apparent that the demands of modern IT have changed the face of integration is several ways, as listed later, which has required new approaches to integration:

- The proliferation of mobile devices means greater demands in throughput requirements and the ability to scale to cope with peak demands. The microservices pattern (discussed in detail later on in this chapter) allows granular tuning and scaling of individual services to meet modern demands.

- Consumers expect to be able to use applications 24×7, and mobile applications are easily accessible and so promote this. It is therefore becoming increasingly unacceptable to have significant system downtime for software releases and patching. This has led to the development of new platform capabilities, where individual services can be brought offline without needing to disable an entire system or large sections of a system. These concepts are not easily adaptable to traditional integration platforms, which tend to be monolithic in nature.

- The rise of SaaS solutions hosted in cloud platforms means that it makes sense to host integration platforms in the cloud for performance reasons, and also the skillset required to enter the realm of the mainstream developer, where the platform can handle common integration tasks on behalf of the developer, removing the need for in-depth specialist integration knowledge.

- Society is now much more demanding in terms of new functionality, and this promotes rapid evolution of consumer demand. As a result, developers need to release new features rapidly to maintain a competitive edge (and also retire old or unsuccessful features equally as quickly): such rapid development is harder to achieve using the more traditional platforms (which require highly trained specialists), and this had led to the rise of Integration Platform as a Service (iPaaS) solutions that provide a hosting platform for integration solutions and reduce the time to market, by handling common integration development tasks automatically. Again, the microservices architectural style is a key enabler of building integration solutions that can support rapid change and versioning.

The nature of the cloud, with its elastic scalability and the investment of cloud providers in PaaS solutions that ease and speed up the development process (such as Azure App Service), are strongly positioned to solve these new integration problems of today.

The benefits of integration using the cloud

As touched upon in the previous section, the cloud is well positioned to solve the new integration challenges, as the list of following properties demonstrates:

- **Elastic scale**: As mentioned, a key benefit of the cloud is that a seemingly endless supply of computing power is available that can react in an automated way to peak demand. This is crucial in today's world, with the proliferation of devices available that can produce sudden spikes in load (network bandwidth, RAM, disk, and so on).

- **Granular service hosting**: The availability of application hosting platforms (such as the Azure App Service iPaaS) allows applications to be hosted such that they can be scaled and released independently. In this way, application downtime can be reduced since a complete solution does not need to be brought offline to enable new feature releases, for example. This is very relevant to the demands of today, where customers expect high availability of solutions in a 24×7 servicing fashion. This is particularly relevant for businesses with subsidiaries and customers in different time zones across the globe, matching the demands of a global market. An example of the benefits of platform hosting is a solution with services running in two data centers: by configuring the load balancer, it is possible to direct traffic to one data center only, thereby allowing services on the second data center to be updated. This procedure may then be reversed to allow the other data center services to be updated. In this way, consumers of the software experience zero downtime.

- **Simplified development with application platform hosting**: Customers demand a fast turnaround of new functionality, and sometimes, IT struggles to keep up with the consumer demand. The complexities of traditional EAI platforms (such as BizTalk Server) and the skillsets required are sometimes a bottleneck on new initiatives. The rise of PaaS solutions assists with reducing the time to market, by reducing the development effort, leading to greater customer satisfaction and loyalty, which in turn affects the bottom line positively. iPaaS solutions do this by offering *pre canned* components to developers for common integration tasks; in Azure App Service, for example, Logic Apps can make use of connectors that enable connectivity to popular SaaS solutions, such as Salesforce, SAP, and Twitter (to name a few). In this way, specialist knowledge is much reduced.

Design patterns for cloud integration

The risk associated with the new wave of cloud technologies is that the hype and excitement surrounding them lends too much focus on the technologies themselves and not enough consideration regarding how they can be used as part of the *integration toolbox*, to build robust (hence the name of this book, *Robust Cloud Integration with Azure*) and supportable solutions that are:

- **Maintainable**: It is easy to fix errors with existing components without impacting unrelated components.
- **Extensible**: It is straightforward to implement new features (and also to remove unused features) without affecting existing functionality.
- **Supportable**: In Production, it is easy to locate and troubleshoot application errors. Logging and tracking is readily available and accessible by the support staff.

These characteristics can be achieved through good design, which should not be forgotten.

One aim of this book is to show that integration design for the cloud is as important as ever, to prevent a proliferation of hard to maintain and fragile integration platforms that cannot be changed and expanded on in the future.

The evolution of integration design and how this applies to the cloud

Modern web based integration could be described as one of simplicity (for example, a single point-to-point solution), increasing to the complexities of the service-first approach associated with SOA, leading naturally to a fully decoupled integration layer with an inference engine, using technologies such as **Enterprise Service Bus** (**ESB**) and the simpler hub and spoke/publish and subscribe pattern of integration.

iPaaS solutions such as Azure App Service build on the service-first approach but to a more granular level (the *microservice* level). If a service represents a discrete function, the microservice idea goes one step further, breaking a service down into even more discrete *micro* functions.

The timeline here represents an example company's journey from no integration, to a complex mesh of many varied point-to-point solutions, to integration in the cloud over the course of a few years:

- **Year 0 – No integration**: There is no integration or sharing of data and business rules between the various systems. Data is siloed in each system, and where necessary, keyed manually into each system.
    - **Disadvantages**: Business processes are siloed and cannot be automated end to end, requiring costly manual steps. Since business rules are siloed, there are no common business processes across the business and hence no easy way to have a single view of the business. This leads to errors and lack of visibility of business flows across the enterprise.
    - **Repercussions**: Duplication of effort where lack of visibility of current processes leads to the retriggering of activities already in flight, bad data leading to incorrect business decisions (affecting the bottom line for example, *let's build a widget for customer x, even though they have a poor credit rating*), and poor customer satisfaction. In this scenario, IT is commonly seen not as an asset to the business, adding real value and driving business opportunities (like it should) but viewed as an operational overhead (a budget black hole, with no return on investment).

- **Years 1-3 – Costly and fragile point-to-point solutions**: Recognizing the need to break out from silos of data and business rules, the company exposes data using web services. Each system connects to each other, leading to a complex mesh of connections that prove hard to maintain over time (see the example diagram later). If one endpoint changes, for example, this affects all consumers, who each need to change their programs that consume the endpoint.

- **Disadvantages**: As can be seen in the diagram here, where each circle corresponds to a web service, there is a proliferation of connections between systems and tight coupling. A change to a system endpoint has a *ripple effect* on other consumers, so change becomes far-reaching, and the breadth of change increases the risk of a consumer connection no longer working, resulting in a fragile mesh of interconnections. The number of connections in this system is proportional to the number of endpoints, which can be represented by $c = n(n-1)$, where c is the number of connections and n is the number of endpoints.

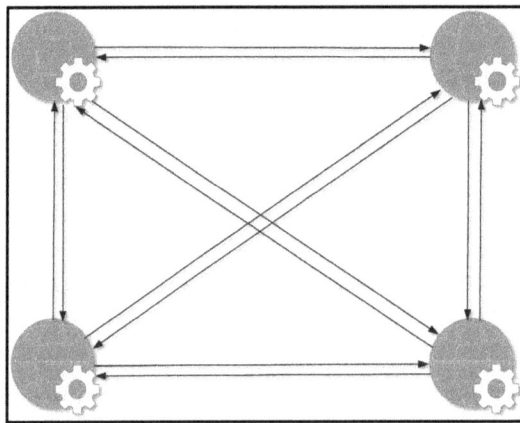

Diagram showing an example of point-to-point service connectivity

In this worst case scenario, each web service needs to connect every other, resulting in 4 x 3 = 12 connections in this system

- **Repercussions**: Change becomes costly and error-prone. It is difficult to support such a complex system; for example, tracing faults when so many connections exist is difficult. In the end, it becomes too difficult to implement changes and enhancements, resulting in stagnation with the resulting impact on business ventures. Again, IT is viewed as simply an operational expenditure with poor ROI.

- **Years 4-6 – Rationalization and manageability through a service-first approach using SOA principles and service decoupling using ESB**: In an effort to tackle the issues of point-to-point connectivity, the company decides to build an intermediary integration layer that decouples clients and endpoints. They implement and mandate the principles of SOA where the functionality is exposed as standalone, reusable services. Progressing from this, they implement ESB where a single endpoint is exposed and a Business Rules Engine infers what service should receive the client's request. The ESB routing slip pattern is also used to chain service functionality together, leading to service reuse across different users.

> Further information about the routing slip pattern is available at: `http://www.enterpriseintegrationpatterns.com/patterns/messaging/RoutingTable.html`.

   - **Advantages**: There is endpoint decoupling through an intermediary integration layer, which means that endpoints can be changed.
   - **Disadvantages**: Services are not easily scalable using traditional EAI platforms. As services are reusable, new projects make increasing use of them, but they prove difficult to scale to match demand. The processing overhead of ESB is also not suitable for real-time requests servicing mobile applications. Typically, an SOA governance team and a dedicated SOA development team determine what services should become *SOA services* and these are then built and maintained by the SOA team. However, these teams often become a bottleneck where they cannot analyze, design, and build services quickly enough to match demand, due to the workload. They also build up specialist knowledge that takes time to learn, meaning that it takes time to bring new team members up to speed to cope with the workload.
   - **Repercussions**: Over time, services become difficult to scale and the SOA team becomes a bottleneck to project delivery, resulting in a breakdown and stagnation of the *service-first* approach. This damages the foreseen benefits of SOA, and projects seek other ways to deliver services, desiring a more simplistic approach, so nonintegration developers can assist with the service development backlog. This often leads to a proliferation of services that are nothing more than simply point-to-point solutions mediated through the integration layer (which prompts discussion around the benefit of an integration layer).

- **Years 7-Now – Movement into the cloud**: The elastic scale of the cloud and the rise of iPaaS are two key drivers in order to adopt the cloud to maintain the benefits of good integration design (service decoupling and reuse). The company decides to progressively adopt cloud solutions to link with SaaS solutions such as Salesforce, using technologies such as Azure Service Bus Relay to permit access beyond the company firewall and using Logic Apps and its connectors to quickly build fine-grained services that talk to LOB SaaS systems. BizTalk Server is a key enabler as an on-premises platform that bridges connectivity between the on-premises and cloud-based LOB systems.

  - **Advantages**: Using the BizTalk Server cloud adapters, it is possible for the company to keep its current investment in on-premises integration while using the benefits of the cloud, expanding its LOB system line-up to include cloud-based solutions, such as Salesforce and SAP. The benefit of using an iPaaS solution such as Azure App Service is that specialist integration knowledge is not required, and it is easier to building loosely coupled and maintainable components by virtue of the platform design. The rise of simpler REST-based APIs (compared with the complex **WS*** Standards) also reduces the complexity of service interfaces, reducing the barriers to integration development.

More information about the WS* Standards are available at: https://msdn.microsoft.com/en-us/library/ms951274.aspx.

  - **Disadvantages**: The range of iPaaS connectors is limited, and solutions need to be built to fit the requirements of the platform: creativity is therefore constrained/sacrificed for the benefit of the standard approach offered by the platform. This may make integration with nonmainstream systems more difficult or simply not able to be supported (in the worst case). iPaaS offerings are also in their infancy and subject to intense work by cloud providers; it is therefore possible for frequent software releases to cause system outages and incompatibility issues with existing production solutions.

- **Repercussions**: It becomes increasingly obvious to the company that there is a dichotomy in their LOB systems: on-premises and cloud based. It may become increasingly the case that more and more functionality moves to the cloud such that eventually, the whole business IT architecture sits in the cloud and the on-premises solutions are disabled, and this proves more cost-effective and secure than hosting on-premises.

Introduction to the microservices architecture

Throughout this chapter, we have talked about Azure, PaaS, and the evolution of integration. The microservices architectural pattern has also been briefly touched upon and this will be fleshed out further in the following sections, because it is a pattern underpinning many of the current PaaS solutions.

In order to maximize the benefits of the cloud, it is essential to understand what architectural principles we should follow to maximize the use of cloud elasticity and also to be aware of the different design patterns that can provide increased granularity and isolation to a solution.

We have seen so far that cloud solutions are innovative: they have changed the way businesses are targeting potential customers today. If you have a product that is catering a large customer base, you can leverage cloud to have infrastructure and services running over multiple geographic regions and that too with no time. This was not the case a couple of years ago where you devote months to get hardware procurement and provisioning done. Cloud has eased the process of creating new customers and expanded the business horizon across multiple demographic boundaries.

As the business grows, the complexities around delivering services also increase. Today, businesses want to work with the SaaS approach to have continuous delivery along with continuous updates. No business house wants to shut down for a patching activity or any service feature enhancement.

We have seen business requirements where new features need to be added to a product, and this requires multiple updates to the hosted service within a single day. We also have seen use cases where a business needs to do scale up/scale down based on the current and future demand. How can this be done, whether the software solution is simple or complex? The answer is to follow correct design while building the software.

The evolution of architectures

In this decade, we have seen software design evolving. It has changed from desktop-based applications to applications running on the Internet and on devices. In the following diagram, we tried to summarize evolution stages:

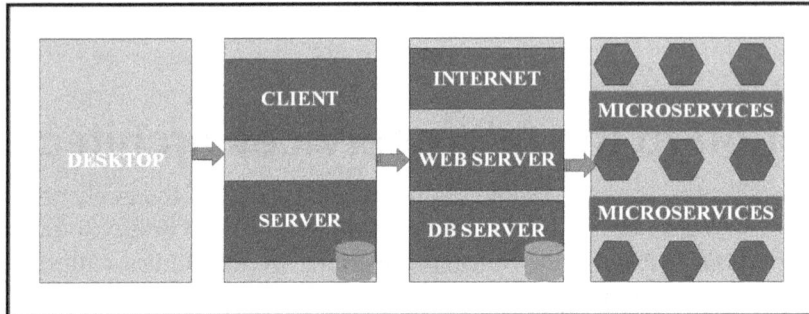

The evolution of software from the desktop to microservices architecture

From the earlier diagram, we can easily analyze the changes to software.

We started building software for desktops, and with immergence of networking and Internet, we started slicing software design vertically into layers or we can say divided the software into tiers. This is where we have all heard terms such as *client server architecture* or *two-tiered architecture, three-tiered architecture*, and *multi-tiered architecture*. The main objective of tiered architecture was to divide software responsibility into layers.

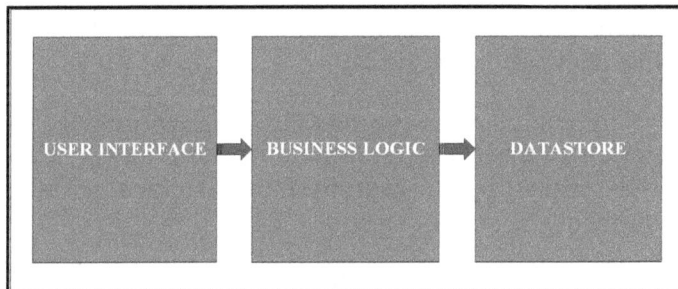

A simple diagram for three-tiered architecture

If we look at three-tiered architecture, every layer has to perform a certain set of functions. The UI layer is responsible for a user interaction; the business layer takes care of business logic, whereas the database layer is responsible for storing data.

With the emergence of cloud virtualization, infrastructure automation, continuous delivery, and domain-driven design, businesses started looking for SaaS-based approaches to provide services to end users. Tiered architecture has certain limitations to this and that's where microservices fits the overall concept to design distributed systems.

Limitation of monolithic application design

- **Autonomocity**: In the actual world, the application tiers or layers are not totally independent units or autonomous. The layers always overlap with each other to some extent, and this is one of the drawbacks in monolithic application design. For example, if you look at the diagram of three -tiered architecture earlier, you cannot change the UI layer without making similar changes to business or database layer.
- **Isolation**: As tiers are not autonomous, isolation is very difficult. It makes harder for a developer to make changes to one layer, test it, and deploy to the production. He needs to go through testing each connecting layer and make necessary modification to tiers if required.
- **Fault tolerance**: Monolithic Application Designs are not always fault-tolerant. If any of the layer/tiers started malfunction, then it can crash the whole application. This is one of the big drawbacks we see with the monolithic approach. If we take an example of three-tiered architecture and if the business layer or database layer starts giving exception or get corrupted, then it will halt the overall processing of application.
- **Technology-driven design**: With a monolithic approach, an organization is always divided in terms of technology. In every organization, you can see dedicated team for database administrators, networks, integration, UI, and so on. The division of team based on technology makes harder to make the business agile. No one holds entire business information, and changes are very difficult to make. For example, a database administrator does not have full knowledge of what is being implemented in the business layer or integration layer.

- **Frequent changes**: Technology is always business-driven, and if our business requires frequent change, then the technology should be in a position to accommodate those changes. Monolithic applications are not good candidates for frequent change; you cannot change your code base on an hourly basis and do a whole round of unit testing, regression testing, and the deployment *on-the-fly*. All these changes will take time, and it might halt your business to make frequent changes and updates to the service.

- **Security**: With a monolithic approach, a single component or framework will be responsible for the overall security of an application. For example, the same security mechanism will be used for the inventory and order modules of our application. We require a way to spilt this; there should be different security requirements for different modules.

- **Shared data**: In a monolithic or tiered design, the concept of shared data is being widely used. Data is stored in a database in a relational format (for example) and is being shared among other components involved in the service. If we make changes to one table design, it might break other components of the application; for example, as shown in the diagram later. If we try to change a single table schema of payment or rename a specific column in the table, it might break the code for the invoice component.

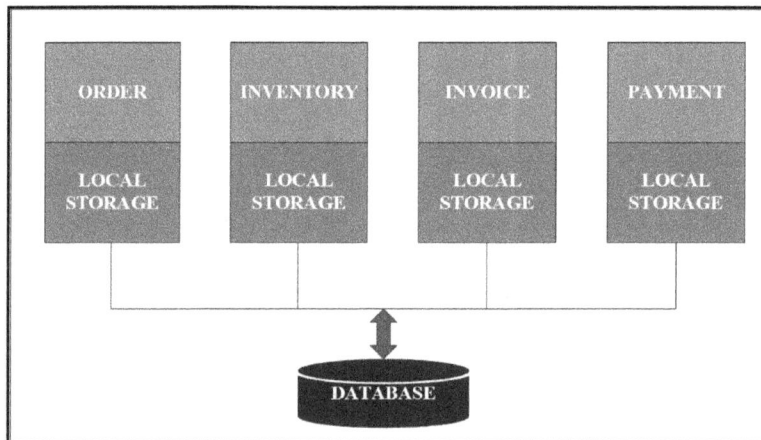

A Shared DATA model for Monolith Architecture

With a shared data approach, we have structured data, but it is not agile. Today, business is changing fast; to accommodate these fast-paced changes we need to move from the shared data approach.

The list does not end here: you can find multiple content over the Internet that discusses other limitations of the monolithic application design.

What is microservices?

Because of the limitations of Monolithic Architecture in designing distributed **system*** discussed earlier, James Lewis and Martin Fowler first came up with an application architecture model named microservices. It has gained popularity as the basis to build distributed systems.

So what is microservices and what are different characteristic of microservices?

Microservice can be explained as self-contained small unit of functionality, which will be used for specific business capability.

In simple words, microservices are an independent unit, and it follows the principle of single responsibility. Single responsibility means each microservice has a set of well-defined features and has a boundary and should run on a separate process.

This is the pattern where we divide an application into component parts, and each component is an independent unit of business. The basic principle of microservices is that it should not overlap with other services or share any common data storage. This way, microservices provide a layer of abstraction and isolation to other microservices in a distributed system.

While we are discussing the microservices architecture, it is very important to understand the set of common characteristics that each microservices will have.

A distributed system

A distributed system is a model in which component on the network communicate with each other by sending and receiving messages. The message format can be of multiple types such as flat files, XML, and JSON. To learn more about distributed computing, refer to the Wiki link, `https://en.wikipedia.org/wiki/Distributed_computing`.

The characteristics of microservices

The following points show the characteristics of the microservices architecture:

- **The Decentralization of data storage**: The decentralization of data storage means each microservice will be an independent service and does not share any data storage among themselves. The communication among microservices should only be done through a common set of protocols such as HTTP.

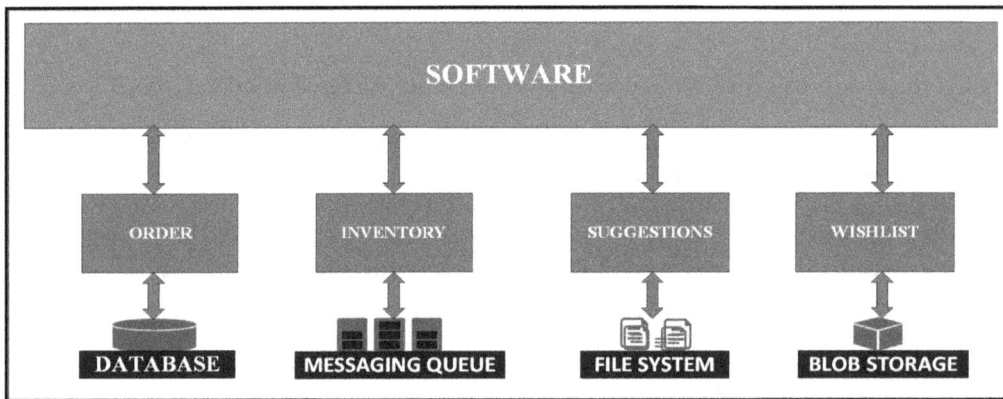

The decentralization of data storage

From the earlier diagram, we can easily see how microservices are independently structured and do not share any common data storage.

microservices should be independent to choose data source of its choice; some may choose a relational database, some may choose **NoSQL**, and another might use queues, a filesystem, and so on. This is the way we are removing dependency across multiple microservices.

- **Independent deployment and versioning**: As microservices are self-contained processes, any change to a microservices can be versioned, tested, and deployed independently. This is one of the key features of the microservice design pattern. You just need to concentrate on the business capability of a single microservice instead of thinking about the whole application. This provides the benefit of quick application enhancement, and you can update and add features to a service *on the fly*.

- **A Service broken into logical components**: When we talk about microservices characteristics, the basic principle is your services must be broken into multiple components. Each component should be independent and should have a well-defined capability via an interface. In this way, each component can be made language-agnostic, and we can choose any language of choice to build the microservice. One microservice can be a good candidate for .NET, whereas another can use the benefits of Java and Node.js, and so on.

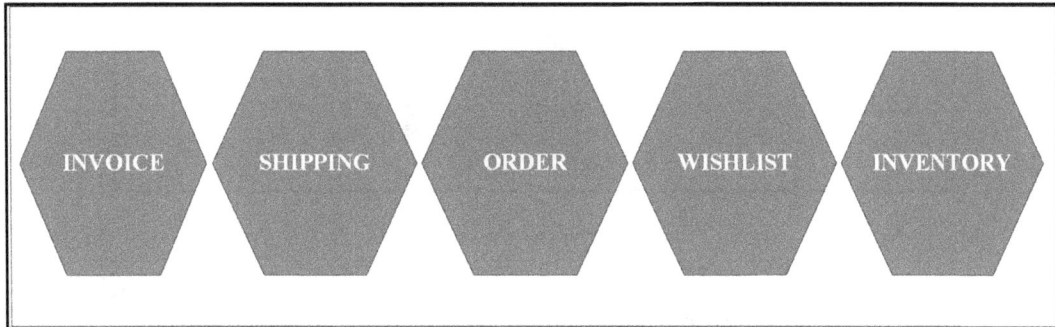

A component model with microservices

Each microservice has well-defined boundaries, and together, they make a complete service offering. While we think of microservices, we always ask how big the microservices should be. We would say divide services as independent chunks such that a small team can handle the overall responsibility. Another driving factor is how easily you can enhance, replace, or upgrade component without affecting functioning of other services.

- **Organize teams around business capability**: The concept has been taken from Melvin Conway's Law:

"Organizations which design systems are constrained to produce designs which are copies of the communication structures of these organizations".

Further information is available via
`https://en.wikipedia.org/wiki/Conway%27s_law`.

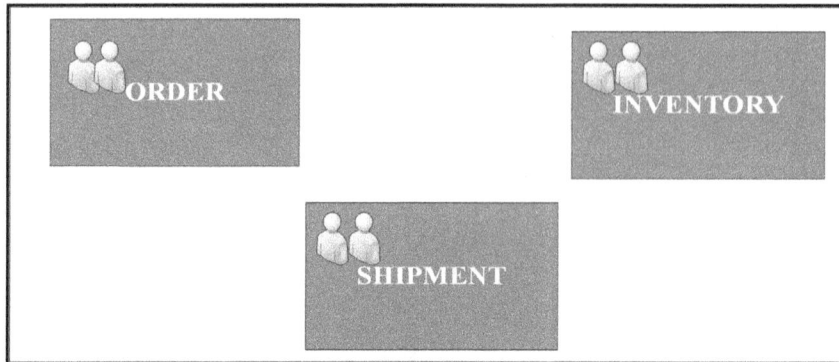

Conway's "Two Pizza Theory" of team distribution

Based on Conway's Law, Amazon came up with the *Two Pizza Theory*. It states that divide your team so small such that it is possible to feed them with two pizzas!

If we combine Conway's Law and Amazon's Two Pizza Theory and try to think in terms of the microservices pattern, we can say that to have an optimal output for the business, it is a good choice to have teams organized around business capabilities rather than teams driven by technology. This will give service ownership to a team and the team will have full control over service changes as long as it does not break consuming services.

If we take the example presented in the earlier diagram, a team dedicated to **SHIPMENT** will function better than a team responsible for the whole business. Make your team master of any specific business area instead of training them in everything. A team claiming to have knowledge of everything might not provide you the same output as a small dedicated business team can provide.

- **Infrastructure automation**: Microservices comes with a lot of complexity; with microservices design, you need to deal with lots of moving parts. A better IT infrastructure, supporting automation, is most important.

Automated testing, automated deployment, automated scale up/scale down of systems: all these are key aspect of microservices. When you design microservices, you should keep in mind where you want to run your services-on premises or cloud-based architecture. With cloud-based infrastructure, you have a lot of flexibility toward automation.

- **Hide internal details**: What microservices design states is that you should hide internal service implementation details from the consumer. If you expose internal service implementation it might cause you tight coupling between service consumers and your exposed service. You need to provide a layer of abstraction between your service and consumers.
- **Design to cope with failure**: We are human, we cannot predict the future, and for that reason, no design is 100% correct.

What you build today will need to be modified in future as per business requirements.

Keeping this into consideration, you design your microservices for failures. Failures can be technical failure, hardware failure, or implementation failure; your application design should gracefully handle these exceptions.

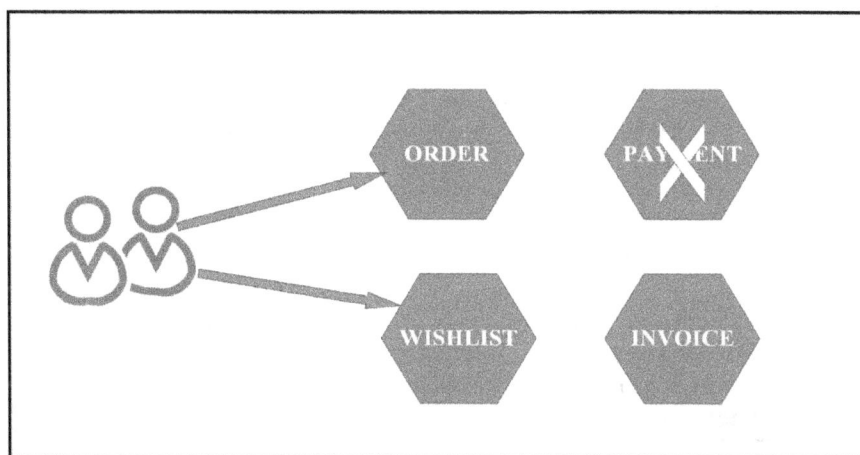

An Example Microservices Architecture with a Faulting Component (the Payment Service)

Consider the earlier diagram; if the **PAYMENT** module for the enterprise is not working, with the concept of microservice, it should not halt the whole business. Other modules should continue to work such as **Order**, Wish List, and so on. This way, each component execution is independent of the others.

- **Decentralize governance and monitoring**: With the microservices design pattern, you need to have smart governance in place. With microservices, you won't be dealing with a single point of failure; there will be small services that communicate with each other and come together to do a task.

In a real distributed system, you will be dealing with multiple servers, multiple log files, and maybe multiple network as well. So how will it go if some service starts troubling you, it will be a nightmare to monitor all the moving parts!

This is where the concept of smart monitoring and decentralized governance comes into place. If you are working on a cloud-first approach to design a distributed system, Azure provides you lot in the smart monitoring space. Throughout this book, we will discuss the concept of different monitoring techniques.

In the earlier sections, we have discussed a lot about monolithic design and microservices. The following table summarizes the key differences between the two architectures:

Monolithic	Microservices
In monolithic application, functional units are not autonomous	As the microservices concept is designed on the principle of single responsibility, each microservice is autonomous
The monolithic architecture approach is good when designing a small application as it hides the complexity	The microservices pattern is most useful when you try to build distributed applications
The monolithic approach is good when your application does not require regular features update	Microservices benefits maximum when your application required frequent updates and feature enhancement
If you have hardware limitation, it is better to go with the monolithic design approach	If you are looking for application design that you can easily scale up/scale down and hardware is not the consideration, then it will be better to have built it through a microservices design pattern
You can have a single version of software running on any specific hardware	You can have multiple versions of the same microservice running

| Monolithic applications are language dependent; you need to develop each layer in specific language | With microservices you can choose language of your choice; you may develop one microservice in Java another in Node.js and the rest in C# |

Differences between the Monolithic and microservices Architectural Styles

Types of microservices

Broadly speaking, there are two types of microservices:

- Stateless microservices
- Stateful microservices

Stateless microservices

Stateless services are good candidates as the building blocks of a distributed system. As the name suggests, stateless microservices do not maintain session state between requests, for example, if any of the service instance is being removed, it does not affect the overall processing logic for the service. Distributed systems do prefer stateless microservices.

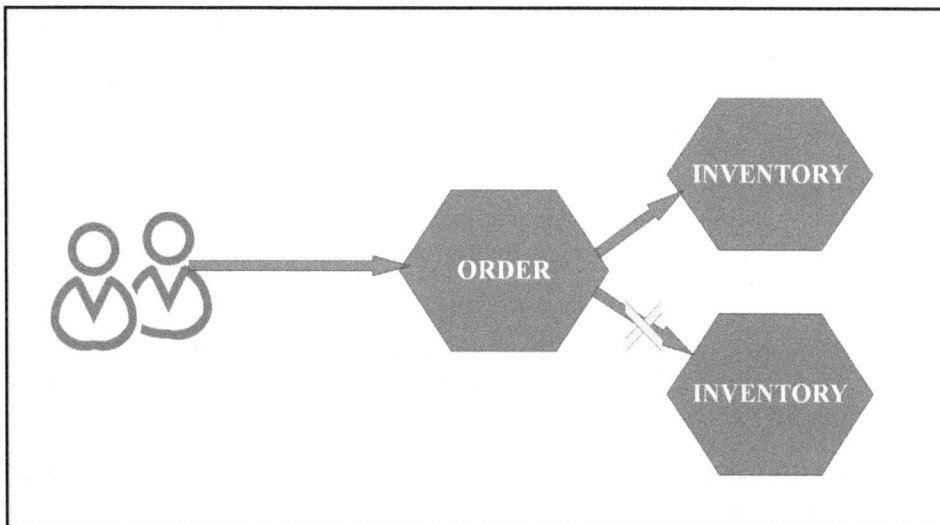

The ORDER diagram

If we look at the earlier diagram, a customer makes a request for a product through the **ORDER** service, and internally, the **ORDER** service checks for the product status through the **INVENTORY** service. Stateless means each request happens independently of the previous or future requests. One call to get product details would return the same result regardless of the previous context or requests. If one call to the **ORDER** service fails, then it should not halt whole business processing. There should be another instances of microservices running to take up the task.

Stateful microservices

Stateful microservices store session information in the code. When two or more microservices communicate, they maintain a service request state.

In the real world, stateless services are a good choice, but there are multiple use cases where you need to keep state information. If we think of a simple example, then transactions that require multiple database roundtrips require state to be stored.

To read more about stateful microservices, you can refer to the link: `https://docs.microso ft.com/en-us/azure/service-fabric/service-fabric-overview`.

Challenges with the microservices architecture

We have seen how microservices can be useful in creating distributed systems and can be optimized as per business requirement. As we progress through microservices concepts, it is also essential to discuss some of the following microservice challenges so that you can determine if it's the right design for your solution:

- **Application logic**: Unlike monolithic where you have all logic embedded inside the same solution package, application logic in microservices design pattern is distributed, and the whole logic behind your solution is distributed among multiple microservices.

  Various microservices calls with correct data and correct sequence of call makes your Application logic. This makes it harder for operational people to effectively manage and monitor the application.

- **Testing limitation**: While using microservices pattern, we are limited to testing scenarios. We cannot easily find all the possible interactions among microservices deployed, and it makes harder for us to come up with the exact test cases and results.

This makes change complex as we cannot predict whether a small change might break functionality of other dependent microservices.

- **Multiple technology**: The microservices architecture supports the use of multiple technology in developing stateful and stateless microservices. This concept finds some problem with real-life applications where you use third-party assemblies and libraries. It makes harder to organize your solution because of high dependency on third-party software.
- **Monitoring**: With microservices, organizations may find difficulty in monitoring the distributed environment as a whole. Technologies such as Docker and container concepts do ease the process of monitoring. They add one more layer of abstraction to your microservices.

SOA and microservices

Before we go into difference and similarities of SOA and microservices, it is better to move a step back and explain what is **Service Oriented Architecture** (**SOA**). What we understand from SOA: It is a design pattern or approach to build Application Architecture based on services. Each service has a specific set of functionality such as taking customer Order and Validating Order request.

With the definition of SOA, we can really see similarity between SOA and microservices. If we try to define microservices in terms of SOA, then we can say that *"microservices is a fine grained SOA Architecture style with a set of common features like decentralization, isolation, automation, overs able etc. We can also say that Microservices is subset of SOA"*.

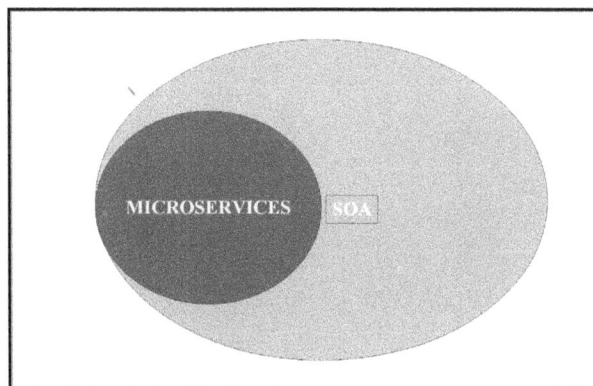

The diagram showing that Microservices is a subset of SOA

We have discussed microservices concepts in the earlier sections, and it is apparent that there is a lot of similarity with SOA design patterns. The preceding diagram shows how microservices and SOA are interrelated. We can say microservices is a subset of SOA based on the concept defined for SOA and microservices.

SOA is a wider concept; thus, the scope for problems with this style is larger. In SOA, defining a correct service boundary is always a problem; it is simple to how big or how small the service should be. Some useful concepts and technique of SOA, such as shared library and shared database, are totally been discarded from microservices.

Summary

In this chapter, we've given an overview of system integration in the cloud. We defined various components of the cloud such as **Platform as Service (PaaS)**, **Infrastructure as service (IaaS)**, and **Software as Service (SaaS)**. We described the evolution of integration and microservices architecture design principles and reasons why technology is moving toward better fine-grained design patterns using the microservices model.

In the next chapter, you will start the journey to learn the basics of Azure components such as resource group and app plan.

2

What Is an Azure App Service?

Change is the essential process of all existence.
— Mr. Spock, Star Trek

This chapter defines the details and capabilities of an Azure App Service. The chapter then explores the basics of the four building blocks of an App Service: the web app, mobile app, API app, and logic apps.

We will then introduce our sample solution for a fictional company named *Sunny Electrical Manufacturing*.

In this chapter you learn the following topics:

- What is an Azure App Service?
- Why you should consider developing applications using App Service
- What are Azure Resource Groups and how should we use them?
- What is an App Service Plan?
- An introduction to our hypothetical company

What is an Azure App Service?

An Azure App Service is a new composite PaaS service for developing web apps (websites and web applications), logic apps (data orchestration components), API apps (web services), and mobile apps (mobile backend services) all under the one service. Previously, these services were being offered as individual Azure services.

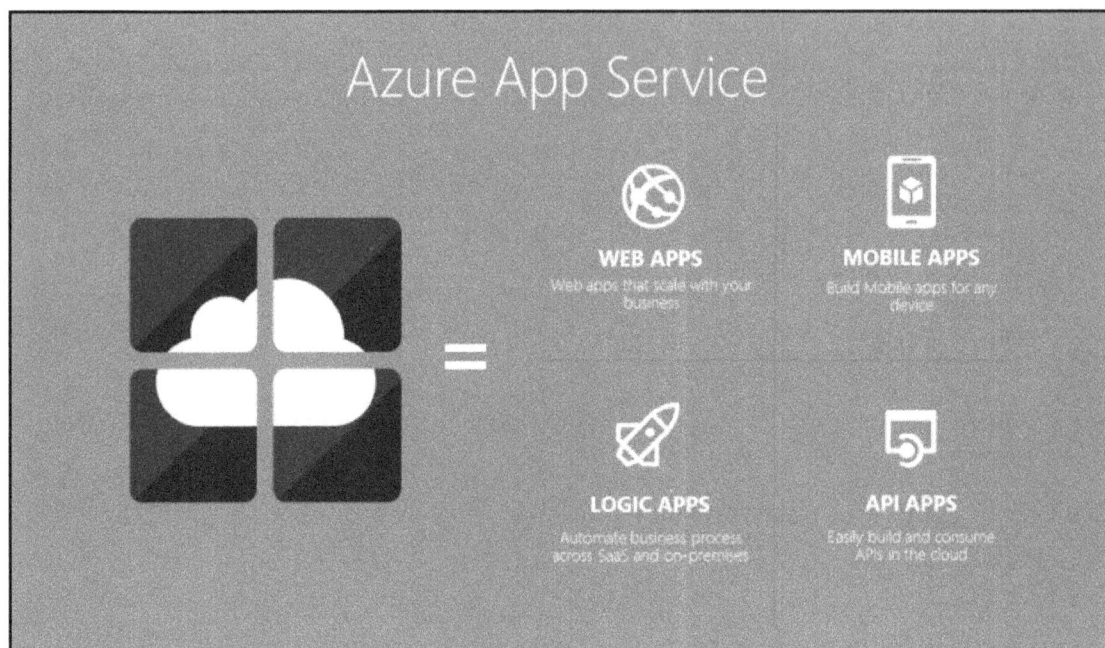

The table here describes the cross pollination between the old Azure services and the new App Service:

New name	Old name	Functionality
Web apps	Azure websites	The new name for Azure websites. The Web Hosting Plan now termed App Service Plans.
Mobile apps	Azure mobile services	A new app type that integrates previous mobiles services functionally. Can now integrate with on-premise and SaaS systems, WebJobs, and includes scaling options.

Enterprise Integration Pack	Azure BizTalk services	Allows users to perform enterprise application integration with App Service app types. Allows users to perform B2B integration scenarios with App Service App types.
API apps	New app type	Allows you to build and consume APIs in the cloud.
Logic apps	New app type	Allows you to automate business processes.

This integration of the services allows you to build enterprise systems and applications quickly and easily. The provided features and frameworks of Azure App Service allows an easier integration with on-premises or cloud applications using the built-in connectors and APIs. If you are an integration developer or architect, then logic apps, Azure functions, and API apps will be the key componets provided with Azure App Services.

Azure hosts your apps on a managed platform (virtual machines) that takes care of application deployment and management. You also have the choice of a shared VM resources or a dedicated VM, depending on your work load requirements and the selected pricing tier. There is also an **Azure App Service Environment** (ASE): `https://docs.microsoft.com/en-us/azure/app-service-web/app-service-app-service-environment-intro`. This is a premium Azure App Service (refer: `https://azure.microsoft.com/en-us/services/app-service/`) hosting environment that is dedicated, fully isolated, and highly scalable environment to run all your apps using virtual networks and security groups.

Also, unifying these artifacts into a single service allows for a simpler development experience by combining all these services into one solution. You may develop your solution in any of the common development languages, and target any platform and any device as before when developing for Azure websites. Developers now can deploy their code using methods such as GitHub and BitBucket, which allows you to deploy from any editor or any client that supports these repositories.

App Service also adds some new features that include logic/workflow apps and built-in connectors for the popular SaaS and on-premise applications, including Office 365, Salesforce, Facebook, Twitter, and Dynamics just to name a few, and is still growing. For a list of managed connectors, see this link: `http://aka.ms/logicapps-availableapi`.

The App Service can be broken down into the following application types described here. We will discuss these application types in detail in later chapters:

- **Web apps**: This is 100% compatible with previously supported Azure websites and is used to host websites and web applications.
- **Mobile apps**: This is the old Azure mobile service for building backend services plus a lot more features, including autoload balance, autoscale, Geo disaster recovery, virtual networks, and hybrid connections just to name a few. All the features that are bundled with web apps are now available in Mobile apps.
- **Logic Apps**: This is a new service offering business process automation and workflow using the web visual designer or Visual Studio for rapid creation or declaratively using a JSON file managed in source control. There are many templates available to help you get started building workflows to access your on-premises resources or popular SaaS applications.
- **API apps**: This develops and hosts REST-style web services using templates or the built-in APIs for the many popular SaaS applications.
- **Web jobs**: This provides the capability to execute background tasks either continuously, on demand, or scheduled. Previously, it was only available under Azure websites, now it is available for web apps and mobile apps.
- **Functions**: These are simple scripts created in any of the common languages or executable files that run on top of web apps similar to web jobs. Functions can be triggered by any number of events, such as blob storage, service bus, and HTTP requests.

App Service pricing is simpler now; the pricing has been changed so that you are no longer paying for two separate services. Previously, if you used a website and a mobile service, you were charged for two separate services. With the new pricing model, you can change the service tier at any time.

Turning off a service does not stop you from accruing charges.

Why use Azure App Service?

App Service allows a developer to focus on developing business requirements and not worry about compliance, operational overhead, and integration with other popular services. It allows a developer to target just about any platform or device, including Windows, iOS, and Android, with very little change to the source code.

As a developer, you can use existing services and APIs advertised in the Azure Marketplace as building blocks to build modern enterprise solutions quickly and simply, or you can contribute your own APIs for public or private use.

The agile software development methodology is supported using the features of continuous publishing and deployment slots that are available for a subset of App Service.

Security and resource contentions are the biggest concerns when hosting solutions in any cloud environment. Using **App Service Environment**, it provides a fully isolated and dedicated environment for your App Service. Security boundaries between your apps and backend services are possible using virtual networks and network security groups between different **App Service Environment** (**ASE**) that are in the same virtual network.

> Logic apps are not supported in the App Service Environment.

The key features and capabilities available as part of the Azure App Service framework are described here:

- **Multiple languages and framework support**: This provides first-class support for the following development languages: ASP.Net, Node.js, PHP, Python, Ruby, and Java. If you are an existing developer using one of these languages the development experience will become very familiar.
- **Service discovery**: The APIs you create can now be easily discoverable using metadata in Swagger 2.0 format. Swagger is machine-readable and language-agnostic.
  Using *Swashbuckle* available from Nuget:
  https://www.nuget.org/packages/Swashbuckle, it will dynamically generate the Swagger metadata and the Swagger UI page.

- **DevOps**: Using the new DevOps tools available for App Service allows for easier application life cycle management and agile methodologies.
  With the standard and premium App Service pricing models, you have the ability to publish to a staging deployment slot for any UAT testing before swapping to the production slot.
  Using repositories, such as GitHub, BitBucket, and **Visual Studio Team Services** (**VSTS**), you can set up continuous deployment for projects that involve frequent contributions.
  With **Azure Command-line Interface** (**Azure CLI**) installed on your local workstation, you can use open source shell-based command sets to manage resources in Azure.
  Perform A/B testing (a term for a `randomized experiment` with two variants as defined by Wikipedia `https://en.wikipedia.org/wiki/A/B_testing`). Using **traffic-routing**, you can direct a percentage of the live traffic to one or more deployment slots to provide real user traffic and interaction characteristics.

- **High availability:** App Service can use Microsoft's global data centers to provide high availability by replicating your App Service globally. Your apps can also be scaled to increase performance and throughput by increasing the number of cores and memory. This is referred to as scaling up or down. The number of instances can also be increased or decreased depending on the pricing tier. This is referred to as scaling out or in.

- **Connectors**: This allows your application to connect to other systems using APIs. These are grouped into several categories known as **Core Connectors** (Azure Service Bus, Bing, and Office 365), **Enterprise Integration** connectors (SAP, Oracle, Seibel, and so on), SaaS services (Salesforce, Concur, Demandware, and so on), and Internet services (Facebook, Twitter, and so on).
  Connectors are also available for hybrid connectivity between your on-premises resources, which are behind a corporate firewall, and those hosted in the Cloud.

- **Security**: There are basically two levels of security model:
  Infrastructure/platform, and Application security. Infrastructure/platform is handled by Azure conforming to industry standards and guidelines. However, at the application level, it is your responsibility. Options include using Azure Active Directory without having to add any authentication logic into your Web App or API App. Otherwise, use the built-in features of App Service that support OAuth 2.0 and OpenID Connect.
  Microsoft has also partnered with Tinfoil Security `https://www.tinfoilsecurity.com/`, which provides web penetration and vulnerability scanning.

- **Industry compliancy**: App Service is PCI DSS-compliant. This standard validates the processing or storing of payment card information is perform uncleared in a secure environment. More information is available at `https://azure.microsoft.com/en-us/support/trust-center`.

- **Application Templates:** These are templates available in the **Azure Marketplace** at: `https://azure.microsoft.com/en-us/marketplace` to speed up development by using these as building blocks.

- **Azure Resource Manager**: These are community-contributed templates to provision your applications using a declarative syntax written in JSON format. If your solution is fairly complex requiring multiple resources, you can use ARM to construct chain templates together to handle the deployments from a single-click deployment scenario.

- **Visual Studio integration**: The latest version of the Azure SDK for Visual Studio provides a rich set of development tools to develop cloud-based solutions using the new built-in templates. Deploying to Azure and debugging applications are seamless now that you can connect directly to your Azure subscription from within Visual Studio.

What are Azure Resource Groups?

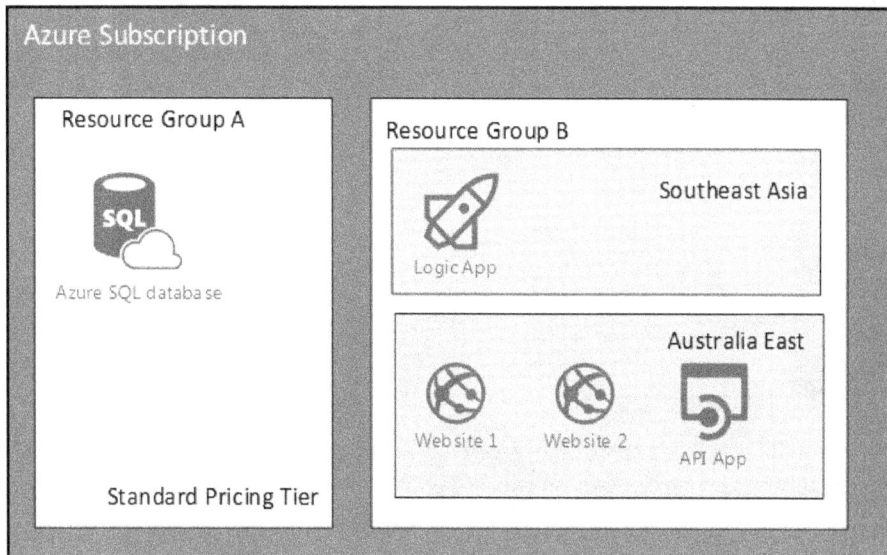

Developing complex Azure solutions normally consists of many resources, such as databases, storage artifacts, websites, and APIs. Managing the application life cycle, access control, and billing for these resources can be challenging at times.

Using resource groups which is only available in the Azure portal provides the capability to group the artefacts into a logical group. This gives you a much clearer picture of all the components that make up your solution and the ability to view the consumption and spending of the individual resources in a grouped manner.

Typically, you would group the resources according to your own requirements; this may be by region, capacity, business process, or administration, for example. All resources in the same group should share the same life cycle to deploy, update, or delete all together. If there is a need to manage the life cycle of a resource differently from the rest, then it should be placed in another resource group of its own.

Resources in a resource group can reside in different regions, but a resource cannot be shared across more than one resource group.

For our sample solution that we will be creating throughout this book, we have created three resource groups shown later, one for the business processing, another for predictive IoT monitoring and one for the product database.

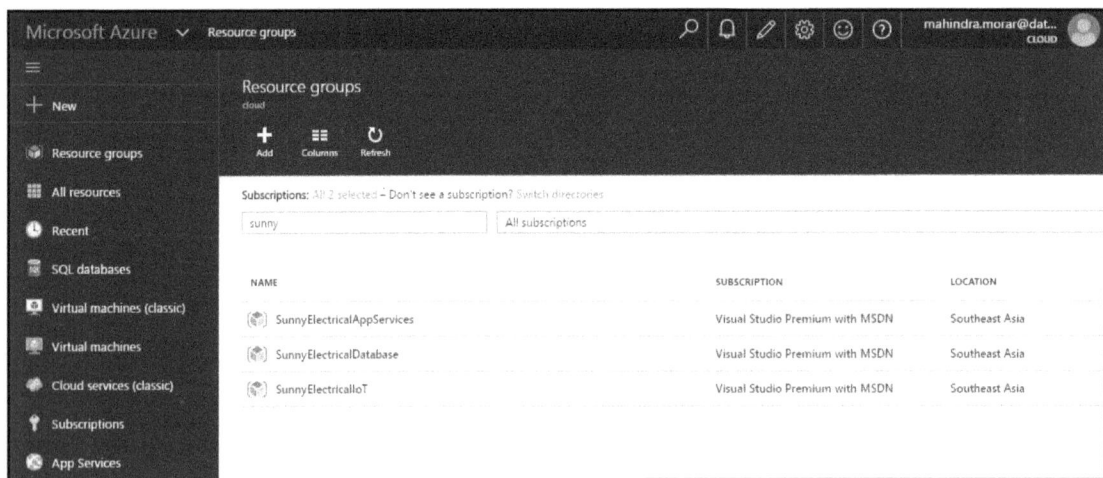

You can move most resources from one group to another. See this link here for more information on which resources can be moved around:
`https://azure.microsoft.com/en-us/documentation/articles/resource-group-move-re sources/`.

Deleting a resource group will delete all resources in that group.

There is no recovery option available to recover the resources that have been deleted by the deletion of the resource group. Fortunately, Azure provides an option to lock critical resource groups and resources from accidental deletion. There are two lock options provided, **CanNotDelete** or **ReadOnly**, that an administrator can set through the portal. The CanNotDelete lock provides the capability to add or modify an existing resource but cannot delete, whereas the ReadOnly lock sets the permission to the resource as the reader role only. Be careful when applying ReadOnly locks as some operations require additional actions, for example, listing the access keys for a storage account.

See this link here for more information:
https://azure.microsoft.com/en-us/documentation/articles/resource-group-lock-re
sources/.

App Service plans

An App Service plan determines the set of features and capacity you require for your apps and services to use. Also, it allows you to group several Azure resources together to share one pricing tier, thereby reducing costs.

There are five different pricing tiers: free, shared, basic, standard, and premium. The table here describes the overall features available for each type of pricing tier. For a more detailed list of the capabilities, see this link:

`https://azure.microsoft.com/en-us/pricing/details/app-service/plans/`.

	FREE Dev/test apps	SHARED Dev/test with higher limits	BASIC Go live with basic apps	STANDARD Go live with web, mobile, logic apps	PREMIUM Maximum scale, isolation and enterprise connectivity
Web, mobile, or API apps	10	100	Unlimited	Unlimited	Unlimited
Logic apps	10	10	10	25	100
Core connectors	200	200	200	10,000	50,000
Disk space	1 gigabits	1 gigabits	10 gigabits	50 gigabits	500 gigabits
Maximum instances			Up to 3	Up to 10	Up to 50
App Service Environments (require min 6 cores)					Supported
SLA			99.95%	99.95%	99.95%

- **Free**: This is a free model where your applications are run in a shared infrastructure. You are allowed to deploy up to 10 apps in this plan with a maximum of 60 CPU minutes per day. Also, there is no SLA provision available. This plan would suit **proof of concept** (**POC**) and testing scenarios.

CPU minutes is the amount of CPU time spent processing instructions for your application. As an example, a static web page will use less CPU time than a dynamically rendered web page.

- **Shared**: With this plan, there is SSL and custom domain support. This is still a shared infrastructure environment that provides up to 100 apps and up to 240 CPU minutes per day. As with the free plan, there is no SLA provision and would suit POC and testing scenarios.
- **Basic**: This is suitable for production applications with low traffic volumes and does not require advanced autoscale and traffic management features. This plan does provide an SLA of 99.95%. Your applications now run on dedicated instances. Pricing is based on the number of VM instances and capacity.
- **Standard**: This has all the features of basic but provides more storage and autoscale support for the number of instances to bring online depending on the traffic loads. This plan also provides two automated daily backups and deployment slots, and it supports **Traffic Manager** for geo availability.
- **Premium**: This is similar to the standard plan but provides improved performance by provisioning additional resources.
- **App Service Environment (ASE)**: This is aimed at enterprise customers that require a dedicated environment that is fully isolated from other tenants and is highly scalable. Environments can be created within a single Azure region or can span across multiple regions, but the applications are always deployed in a virtual network to provide isolation. Both inbound and outbound traffic may be controlled using security groups to provide secure network access. Connectivity to on-premise resources can be achieved using high-speed secure connections over virtual networks.

Within the Azure portal, you have the capability to move from one service plan to another, provided the resources are on the same resource group and geographic region.

If you require to move your app to a different geographic region, then cloning is an option. This will make a copy of your existing app and deploy it into a new or existing service plan in any region.

When developing and testing App Service, the recommended service plan is either free or shared. After testing is completed, then you would move your apps to either basic or standard. If you require a fully isolated environment, then the premium plan is the one you should choose.

An overview of our sample solution

Rather than giving you simple disparate samples of code for each chapter, we decided to develop a full-blown IT solution for a manufacturing and distribution company. This will show you how all the Azure artefacts can be integrated together to provide a working solution. By the end of this book, you should be able to appreciate how Azure services makes integration simpler and easier.

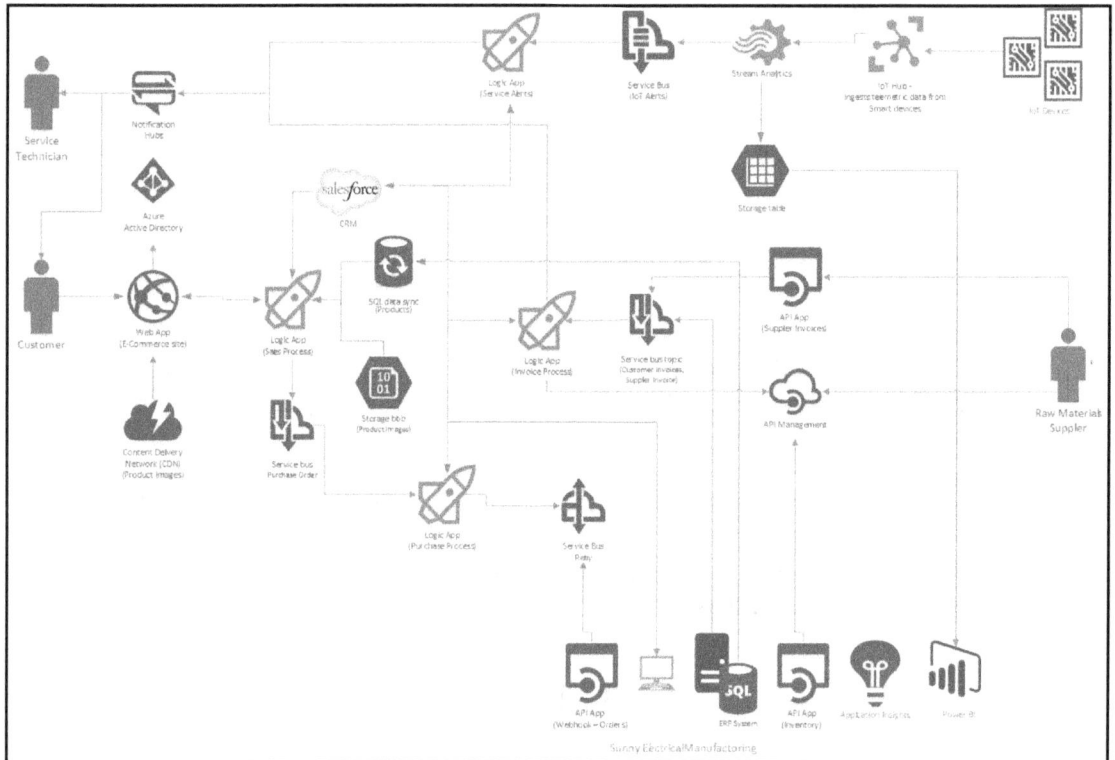

Our solution is based on a fictitious company named Sunny Electrical Manufacturing. This company manufactures electrical equipment for the electrical wholesale market. They source raw materials from suppliers around the world for their manufacturing division. Sunny Electrical Manufacturing encourages self-service for suppliers and customers. Suppliers are allowed to view stock levels of their products that they supply to automatically raise purchase orders.

Sunny Electrical Manufacturing wants to offer better serviceability by incorporating IoT devices in their products to provide predictive maintenance information to their technicians in the field.

Their CIO decided to use a hybrid technology solution for their backend systems. Their ERP system will be hosted on premise, and their CRM and ecommerce solution will be hosted in Azure.

Now, let's go through the high-level solution diagram:

1. Sunny Electrical Manufacturing has a public-facing website (e-commerce site) hosted in Azure. This is where customers can view products, raise purchase orders, and view invoices. To provide faster response times for the product catalog pages, we decided to use a **Content Delivery Network (CDN)** for the **Product images**.

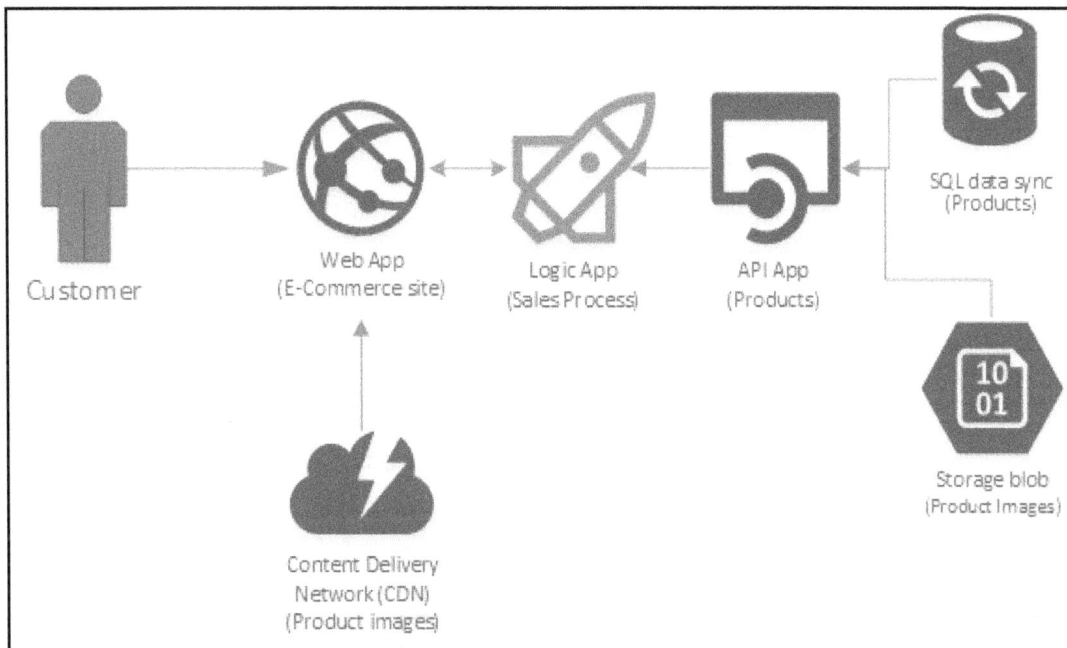

2. A **Logic App (Sales Process)** receives requests for product information from the website. This information is obtained from the **SQL data sync (Products)** database in Azure, which is kept in sync with the ERP system on premise. The same **Logic App (Sales Process)** also receives the sales request from the website and handles the workflow of checking **CRM** for customer details and credit validation before placing a purchase order on the **Service Bus Purchase Order**.

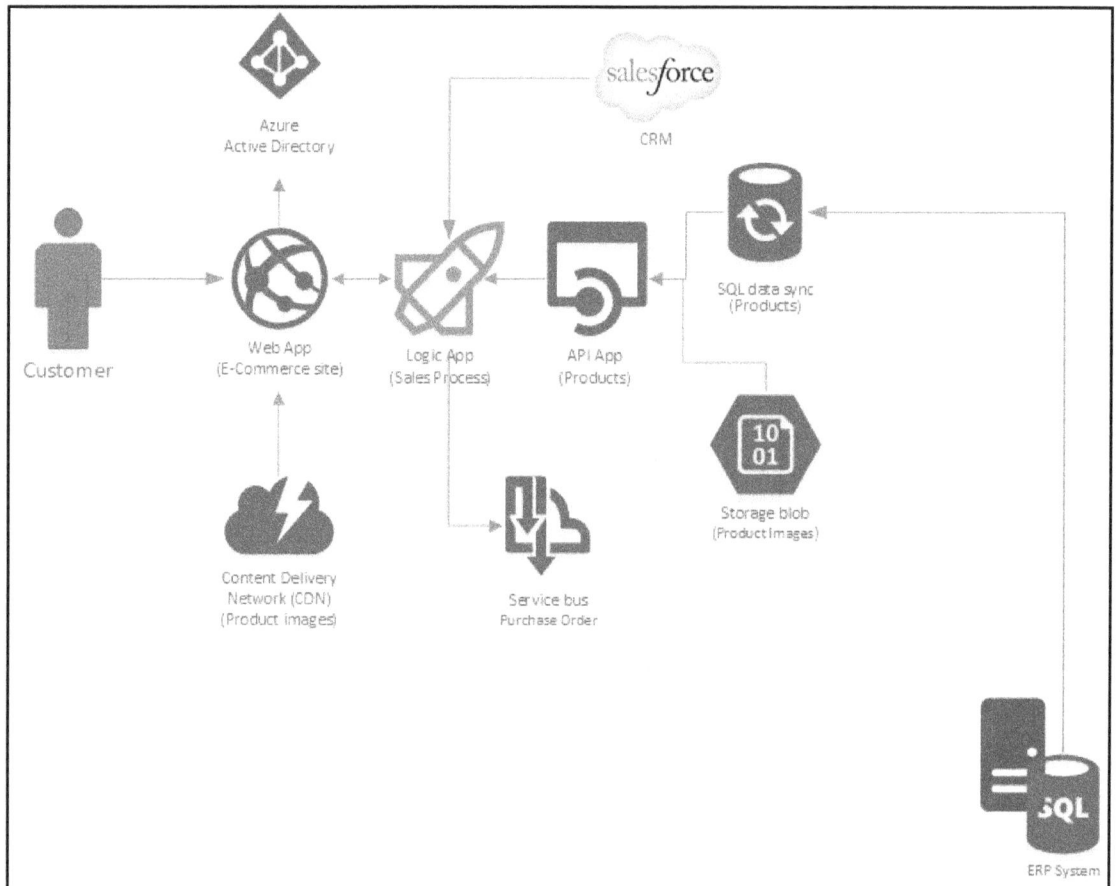

3. Another **Logic App (Purchase Process)** reads the purchase orders from the service bus queue and sends it to Sunny Electrical Manufacturing via an Azure Relay Service to an API web hook to receive orders. Before being sent, the purchase order is enriched with the customer's details obtained from **CRM**.

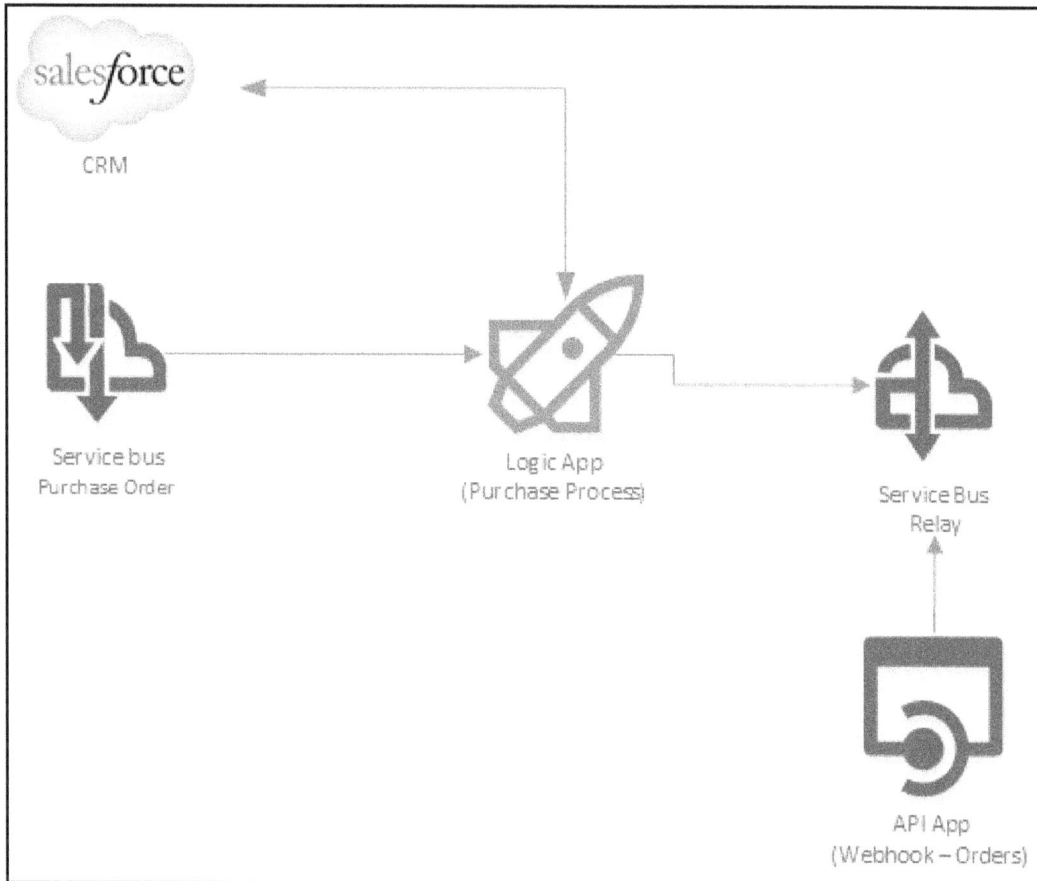

4. Customer invoices from Sunny Electrical Manufacturing are placed on a **Service Bus Topic (Customer Invoices, Supplier Invoice)** from the ERP system. A **Logic App (Invoice Process)** reads the customer invoices off the service bus topic and updates **CRM** before sending the customer a notification message.

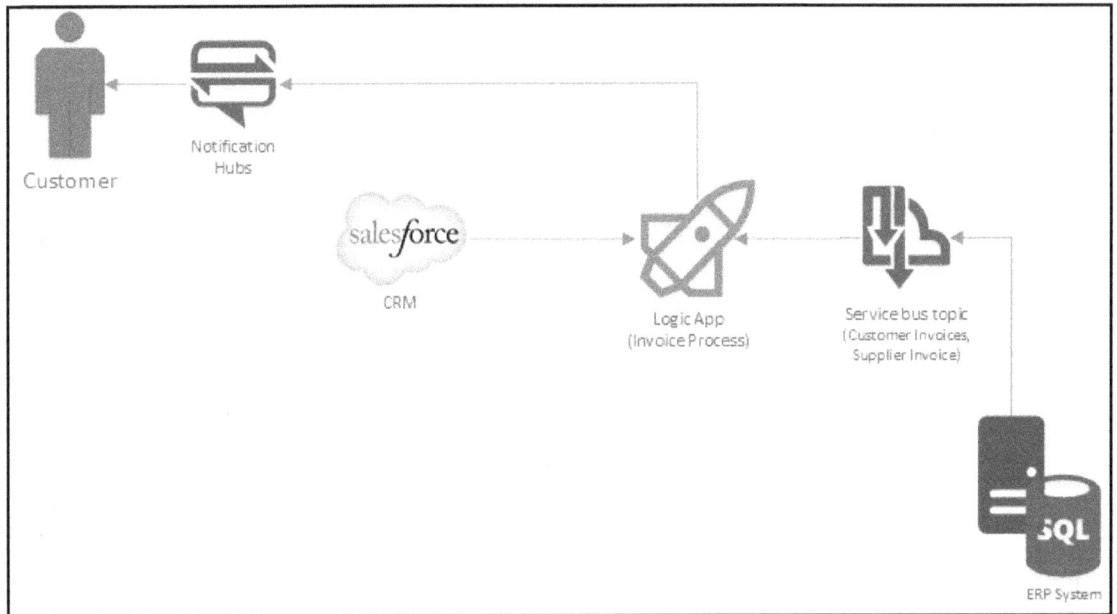

5. Suppliers have the capability to view Sunny Electrical Manufacturing stock levels through API's exposed via API Management. If stock levels are low, they have the authority to send more stock and upload the invoice to the API App (Supplier Invoices), which places it on the Service Bus Topic (Customer Invoices, Supplier Invoice). The Logic App (Invoice Process) reads the service bus topic and updates CRM and the ERP System.

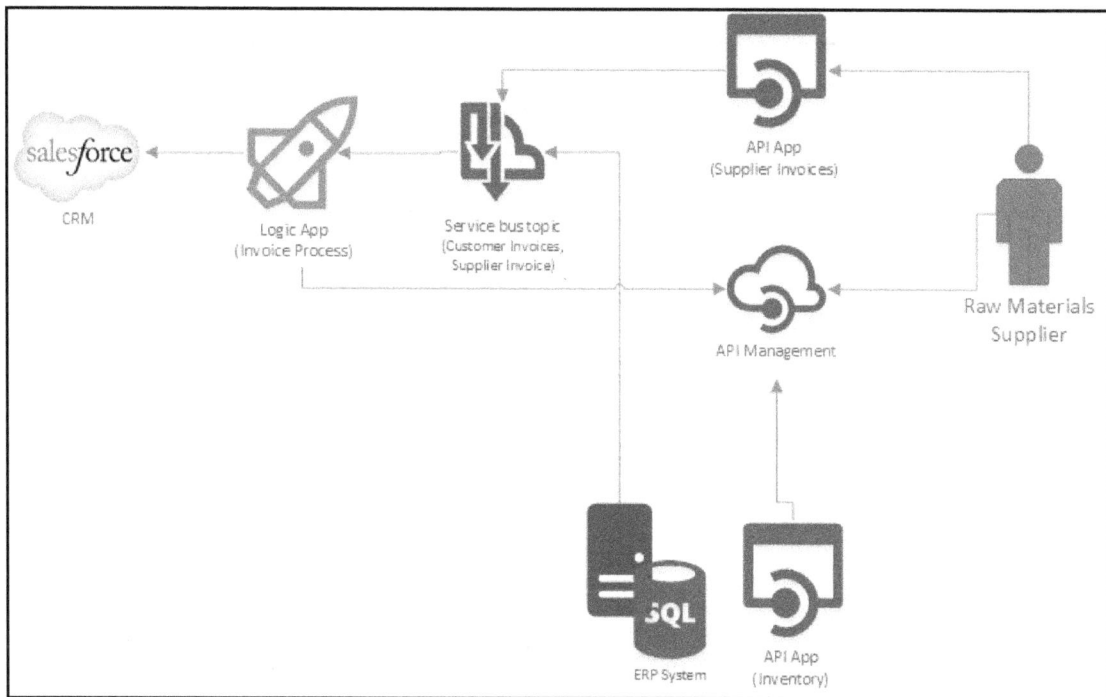

6. The IoT hub constantly receives telemetry data from the products sold by Sunny Electrical Manufacturing and uses **Stream Analytics** to interrogate the data for any alerts and to store the data in blob storage. Any alerts detected are placed on the **Service Bus (IoT Alerts)**. This queue is monitored by a **Logic App (Service Alerts)**. When an alert is detected on the queue, the logic app will retrieve the customers and technician details from **CRM** and place the alert on the **Notification Hubs** for the technician to respond.

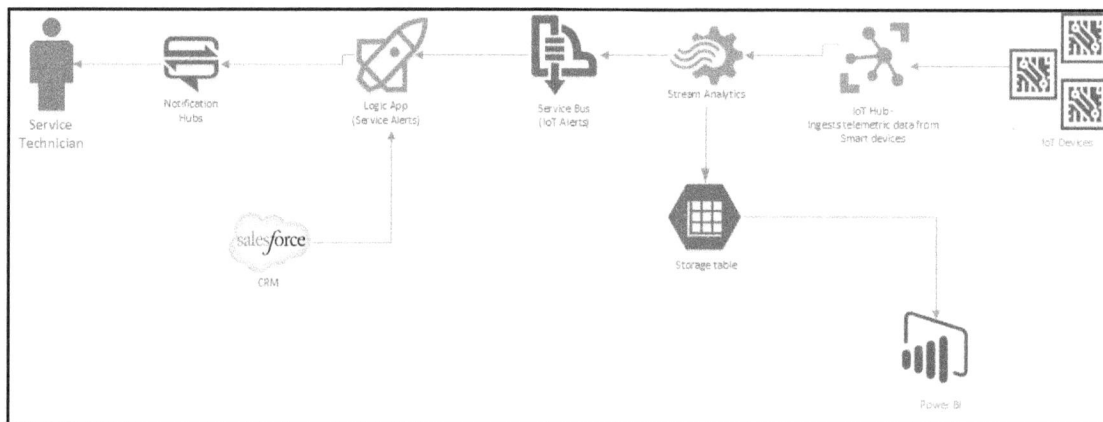

Summary

This chapter gave you an overview of Azure App Service and compared how the old Azure Services relates to the new Azure App Service. We covered the basic fundamentals of the different types of services and pricing tiers available.

We then introduced our fictitious company Sunny Electrical Manufacturing and described how Azure is used to integrate the components of the solution.

In the next chapter, we will describe how to get started building an API App.

3
Getting Started with API Apps

Insufficient facts always invite danger.
– Mr. Spock, Star Trek

Azure App Service is a fully managed **Platform as a Service** (**Paas**) for developers who makes it easier to build web, mobile, and integration apps. API Apps makes easy to build and consume your APIs in the cloud. It provides a rich platform and ecosystem in order to build, consume, and distribute APIs in the cloud and on-premise.

In this chapter, you will learn the following topics:

- How to build an API App and deploy it in Azure
- How to consume API Apps in different types of client application
- Different ways to secure your API App in Azure App Service

As discussed in the previous chapter, Azure App Service is a new fully managed PaaS platform in order to build web, mobile, and integration scenarios. API App is the big fundamental app type of four app types offered by Azure App Service (for more information, refer: `https://docs.microsoft.com/en-us/azure/app-service/app-servic e-value-prop-what-is.`).

It can help you build a robust, scalable, and secure API backend for your Enterprise Web, Mobile, and Logic Apps:

API Apps enable you to build your API in your preferred language and make it easy to use by automatically generating client SDK. In addition, it really easily integrates with API Management for a seamless integrated experience for managing, hosting, and developing of your API in Azure. We will learn more about API Management in the next chapter.

Why use API Apps?

API Apps in Azure App Service make it easy to develop, publish, and consume your APIs in cloud and on-premise. If you have some capability you want to expose as an API, you should deploy it as an API App to make use of these key benefits out of the box:

- A scalable RESTful API with enterprise-level security
- API discoverable using Swagger metadata
- Multiple language and framework support
- Automatic client SDK generation
- Visual Studio Integration

- Access on-premise data using Hybrid Connections
- Packaging and Marketplace support
- It can be used in a business process workflow by integrating it with Logic Apps:

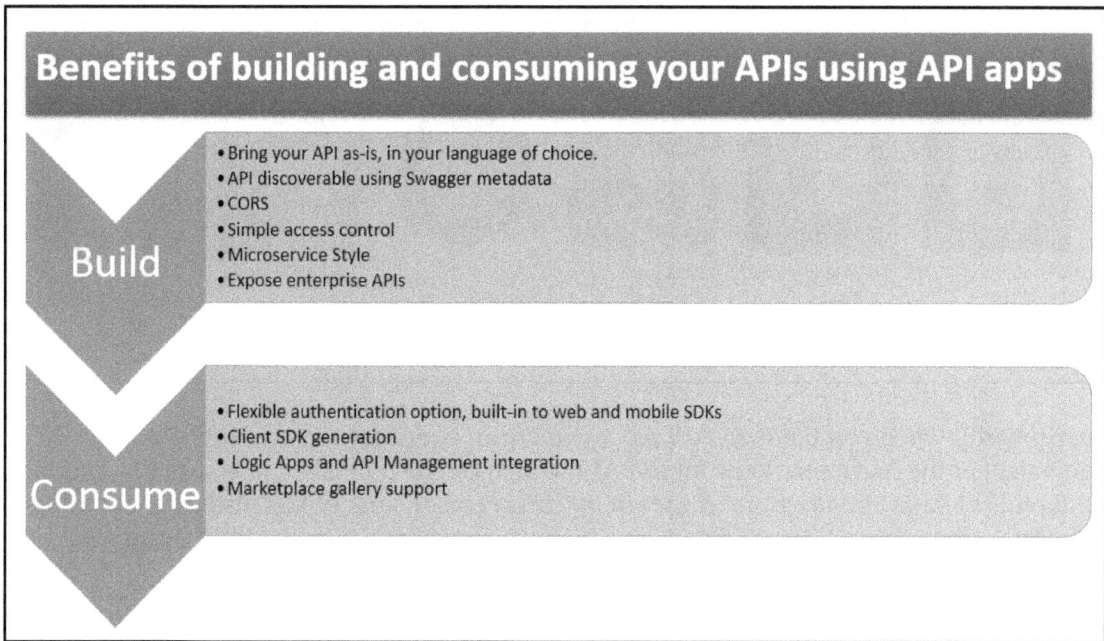

Benefits of building and consuming your APIs using API apps

Build
- Bring your API as-is, in your language of choice.
- API discoverable using Swagger metadata
- CORS
- Simple access control
- Microservice Style
- Expose enterprise APIs

Consume
- Flexible authentication option, built-in to web and mobile SDKs
- Client SDK generation
- Logic Apps and API Management integration
- Marketplace gallery support

The API App host takes care of managing authentication for the app, which helps developers get rid of the headache of implementing it themselves. They can now focus on developing the business logic and leverage API App features to secure it.

With enterprise-level security, you can use your secured API in any of your web app or mobile apps. API Apps also support the most popular and widely supported metadata format, Swagger, which makes your API easily discoverable.

You can also use your API capabilities in any business workflow to connect your apps to popular SaaS platforms. Azure App Service enables you to integrate your API App with Logic Apps, which makes it easy to connect to popular SaaS platforms, including Salesforce, Office 365, Twitter, Facebook, Dropbox, and many more.

You can also bring your API as is. If you have already built your API, you can bring your API in Azure App service platform to take the advantage of the features of the platform. You can use ASP.NET, Java, PHP, Node.js, or Python for your APIs. Your APIs can take advantage of the features of Azure App Service with no changes:

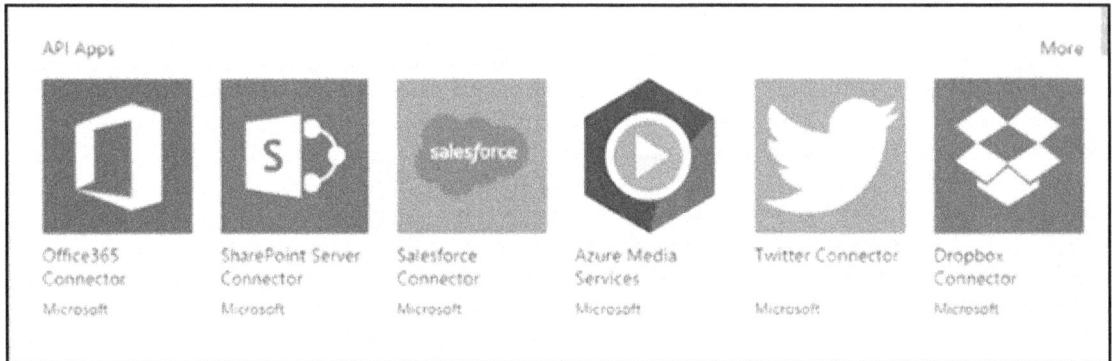

So, primarily when you build an API App, you cre an equivalent of the **NuGet** ate an equivalent of the NuGet package for the API, which can be published in Azure Marketplace with built-in APIs by Microsoft, as shown in the preceding image. You also get versioning support, automatic updates, and dependency deployment via an embedded Azure **Resource Management** (**RM**) template.

If you already have an existing web API, it can also be turned into an API App and then can be uploaded to Marketplace so that other developers can consume it in their application and business workflow using Logic Apps. More about Logic Apps is coming in later chapters.

> You can find the Azure documentation related to publishing your API App in the Azure Marketplace at: `https://docs.microsoft.com/en-us/a zure/marketplace-publishing/marketplace-publishing-getting-sta rted`.

Building, hosting, and consuming your first API App

Let's start with the app.

What is Swagger?

Swagger is open source software that provides powerful metadata representation of your RESTful API. It is a specification for documenting RESTful APIs. It is machine-readable and language agnostic, so there are different implementations for different platforms.

In Azure API Apps, Microsoft adapts **Swashbuckle** to implement **Swagger 2.0**. So, the API you create can be easily discoverable using metadata in Swagger 2.0 format, which is widely accepted and supported.

Support for Swagger 2.0 (Refer: `http://swagger.io/`) API metadata is built into Azure App Service. Each API App can specify a URL endpoint that returns metadata for the API in Swagger JSON format. The JSON metadata returned from that endpoint can be used to generate client code.

If you have a Web API project, then to add Swagger to the project you need to install Swashbuckle via NuGet. Swashbuckle enables the way Swagger metadata is generated for your API. Swashbuckle filters changes how Swagger metadata is generated so that it can include data from the attributes of the API operations.

Once you develop your APIs, they need to be documented so that other developers can quickly understand how to use them. Swagger solves this problem for you by doing a simple but very powerful thing; it generates the REST API descriptions (HTTP methods, URL path, parameters, responses message, HTTP error codes, and so on) and even provides a simple web UI to play with REST calls to your APIs:

SunnyElectricalProductAPI

Product   Show/Hide   List Operations   Expand Operations

`GET`   /api/Product

`POST`   /api/Product

`PUT`   /api/Product

`DELETE` /api/Product/{id}

`GET`   /api/Product/{id}

[BASE URL: , API VERSION: V1]

Developing and hosting RESTful API App

In this section, we will develop a simple Product API for Sunny Electrical (a fictitious company), which will list all the products from the**Product** table in Azure SQL database.

> In this scenario, we are using Azure SQL database as the data source for the API, but there are various other options for data sources such as on-premise SQL, Oracle, No-SQL database, and Excel. You can also have your API App without any data source.

To develop the RESTful API, there are a couple of prerequisites:

1. **Azure account:** You can create your free Azure account at: `https://azure.micro soft.com/en-us/free` or you can use *Try App Service* at: `https://tryappservic e.azure.com/`.

2. **Visual Studio 2015**: Visual Studio 2015 with the Azure SDK for .NET version 2.9 or higher at: `https://azure.microsoft.com/en-in/downloads/`.

Essentially, we would perform the following tasks:

- Make a SQL connection to the **Product** table in SQL database in Azure
- Use the **Entity Framework Database First Approach** to scaffold a CRUD operation
- Create an **ASP.Net Web Application** using the Azure API App template to expose the operations for the **Product** table
- Enable Swagger UI and API App testing locally
- Deploy the **Product API App** in Azure
- View and manage the **Product API App** in the Azure portal
- Consume a **Product API App** by generating client code in Visual Studio:

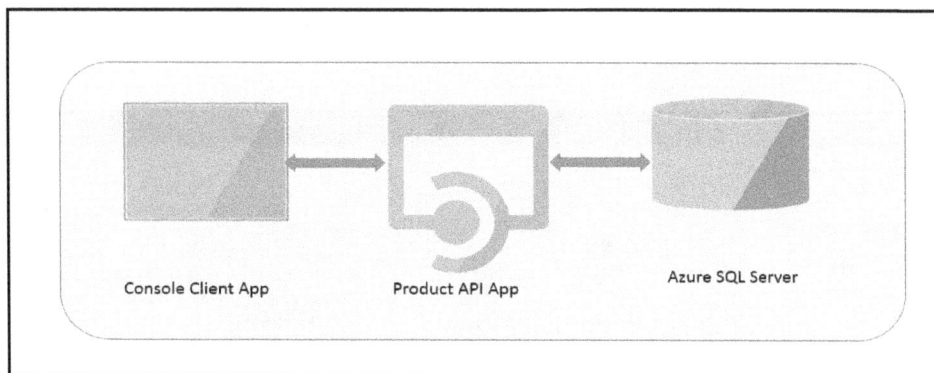

Once you have set up your development environment, you are ready to create your first Azure API App. Let's go ahead and create a new project by navigating to **New** | **Project** | **ASP.NET Web Application**:

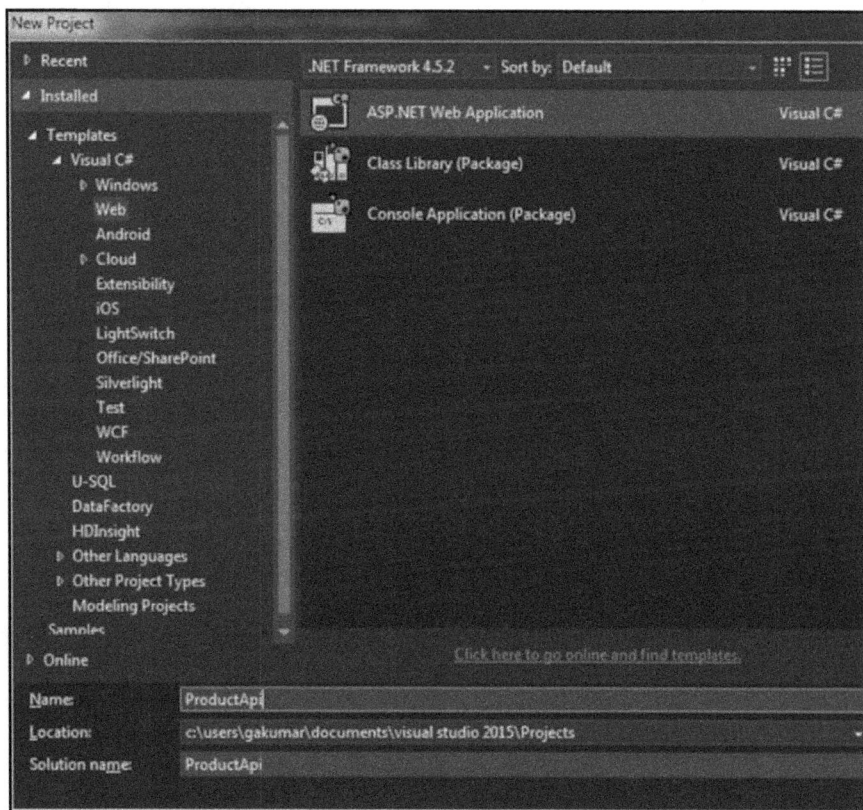

Give a suitable name to your **ASP.NET Web Application** and choose **Azure API App** from the template dialog box:

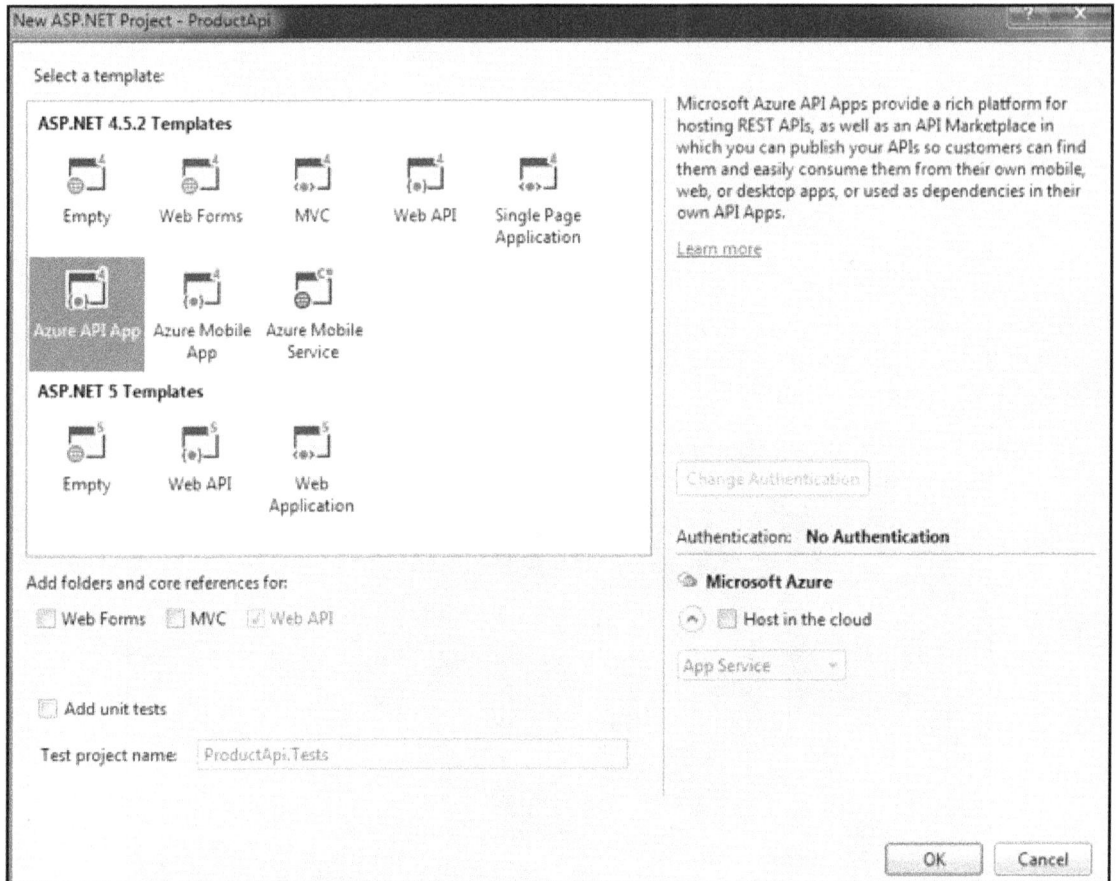

Click on **OK**, and Visual Studio creates your `ProductApi` project. Now you will see, by default, that the Swashbuckle NuGet package has been added to the reference. Swashbuckle seamlessly adds a Swagger to Web API projects. In our case, it uses ASP.NET Web API help methods to reflect our Web API automatically in Swagger.

Now we will connect to the **Product** table in the SQL Azure database, **AzureProductDb**, and use it as a model class for our `ProductApi`. You can refer to the azure documentation to create SQL database using an Azure portal
at: `https://azure.microsoft.com/en-in/documentation/articles/sql-database-get-st arted/`:

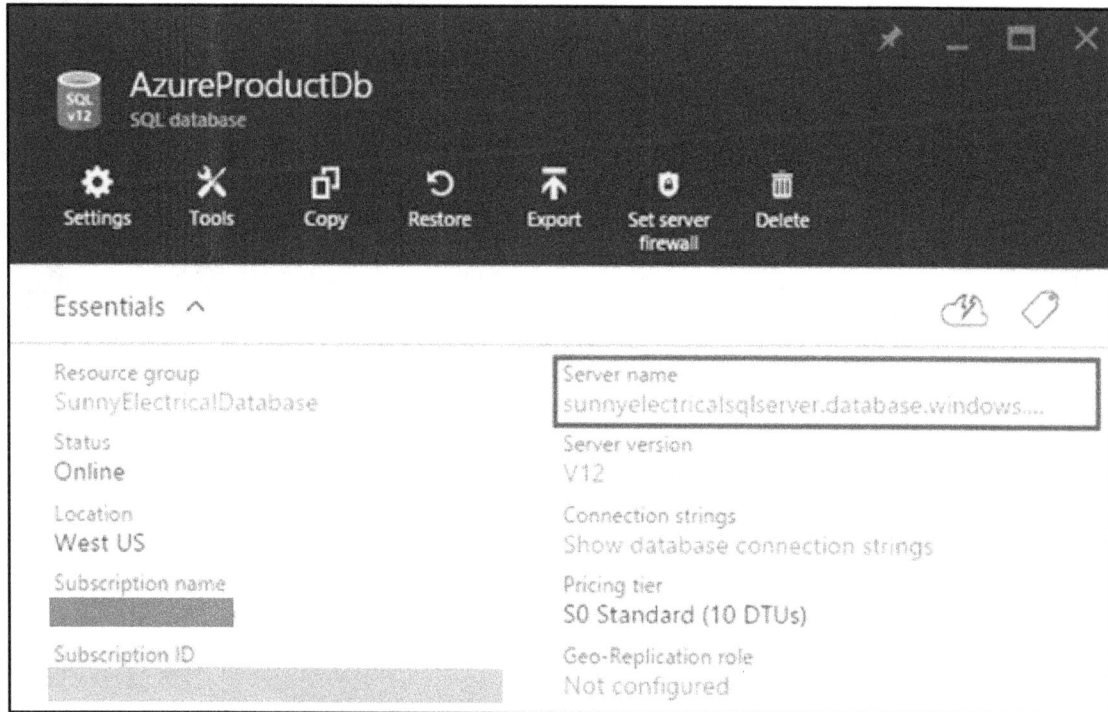

To connect to a SQL database in Azure, we need to perform the following tasks:

- Add a client IP to the database server firewall rule in the Azure portal
- Provide the database server name that hosts your SQL database in the following format: `<servername>.database.windows.net`
- Provide a username and password using SQL Server authentication
- Select the required database and click on **OK**

We will add **ADO.Net Entity Data Model** by right-clicking on the `Models` folder and selecting the **Data** tab. Enter the name for your model; in our case, it will be `Product`. Click on the `Add` button:

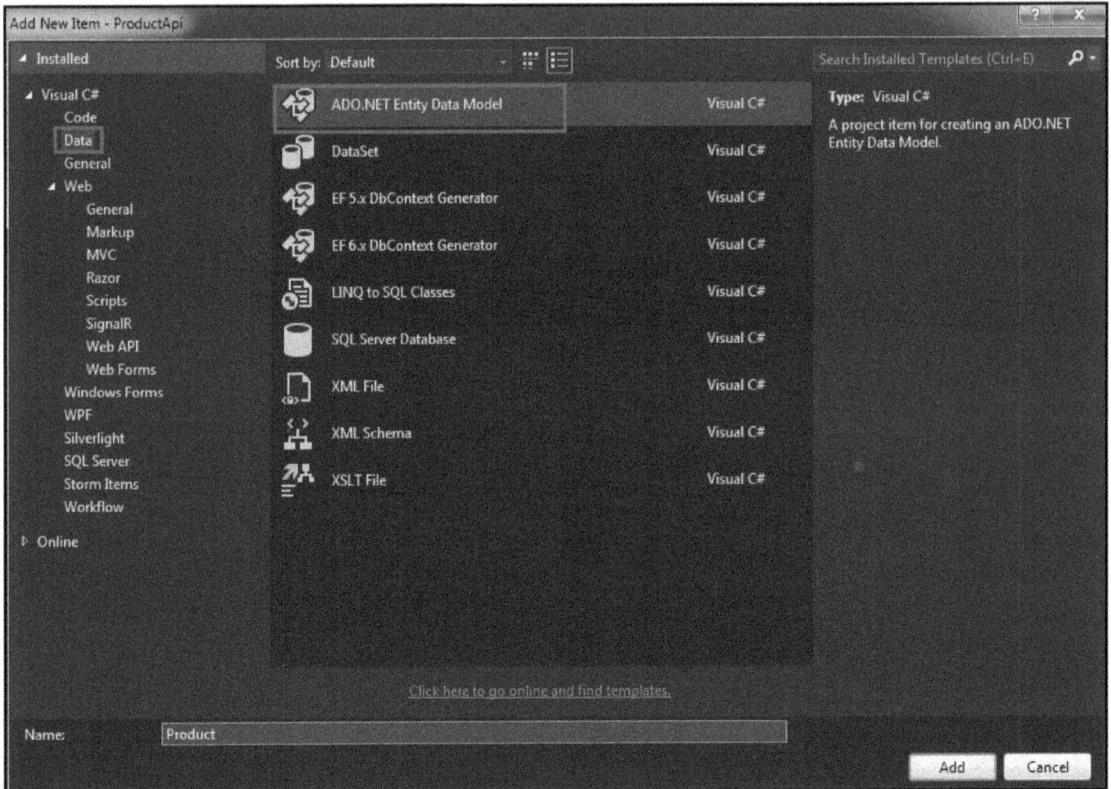

In the **Entity Data Model Wizard**, select the **EF Designer from database** option and click on**Next**, as shown in the following image:

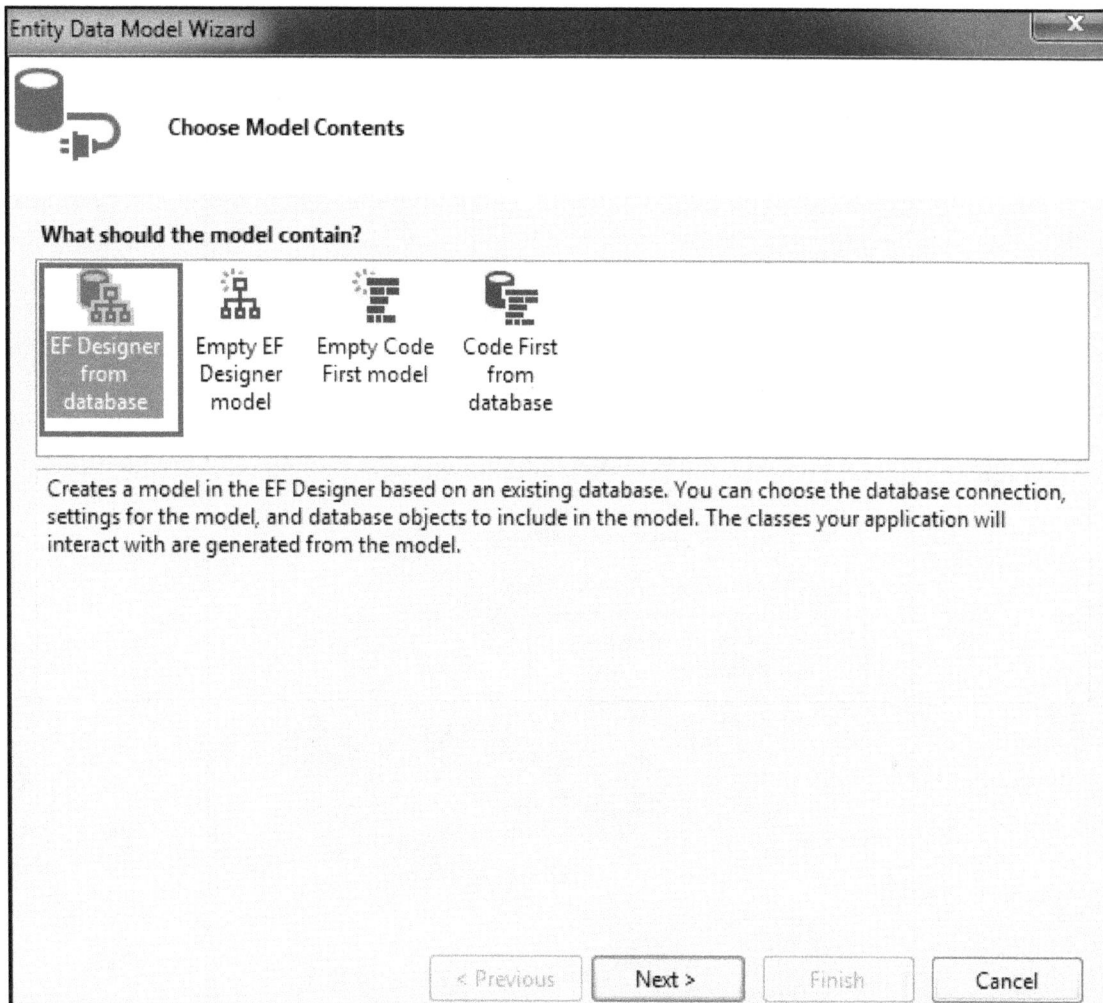

As discussed earlier, now we need to provide the Azure SQL Server name, database name, and credentials to make a successful connection:

Test the connection by clicking on the **Test Connection** button.

Since we have provided vital information, such as, username and password to connect to the Azure database server, the **Entity Data Model Wizard** provides an option to include sensitive data in the connection string or not. Here, we'll select the **Yes** radio button and click on **Next**. Also, if you want, you can change the connection string name here:

Now we need to select the entity to work with. In our case, it would be the Product table, as shown here:

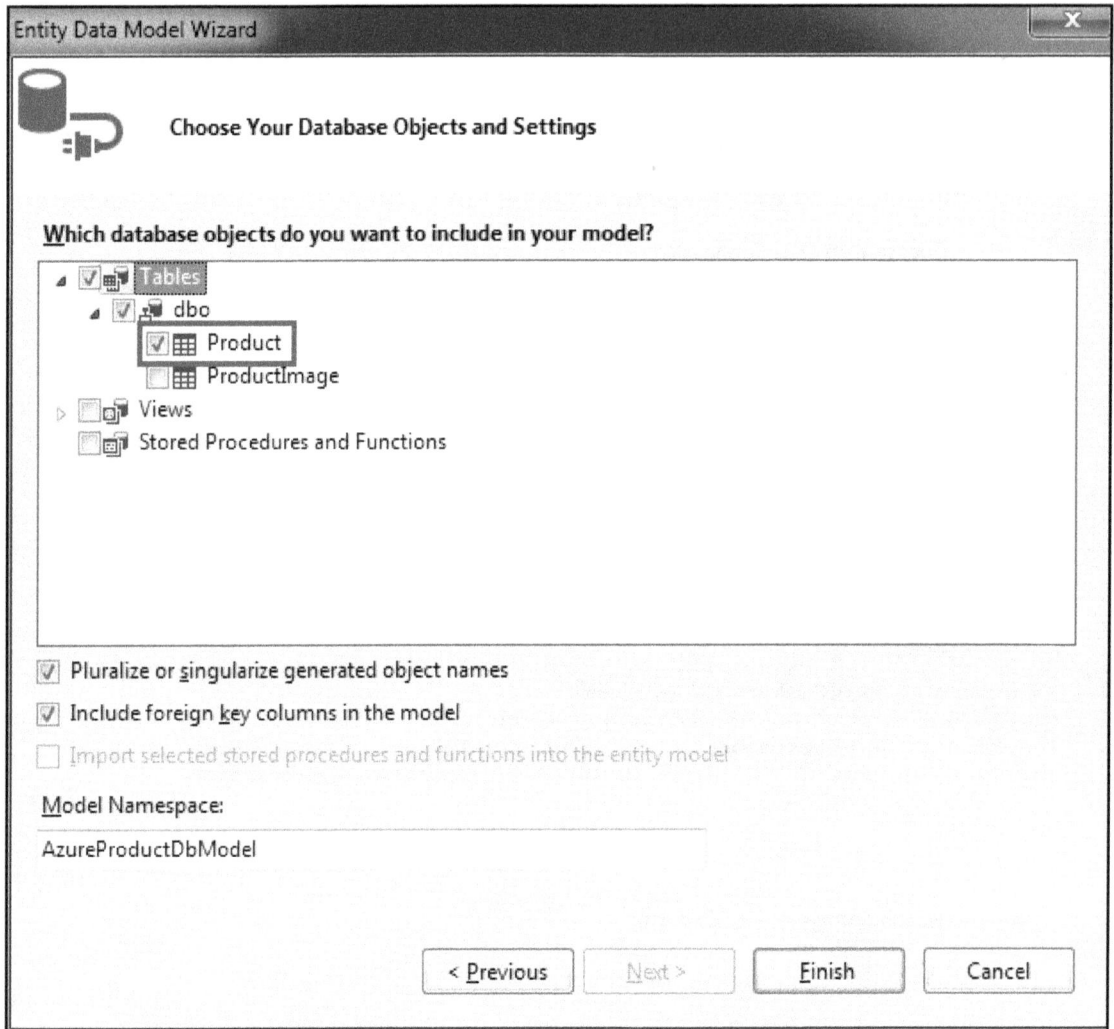

Next, to create the data model, click on **Finish** and we have added the `Product` model in the **Solution Explorer,** as shown in the upcoming image. The `Product` model is basically a class that models the shape of API inputs/outputs:

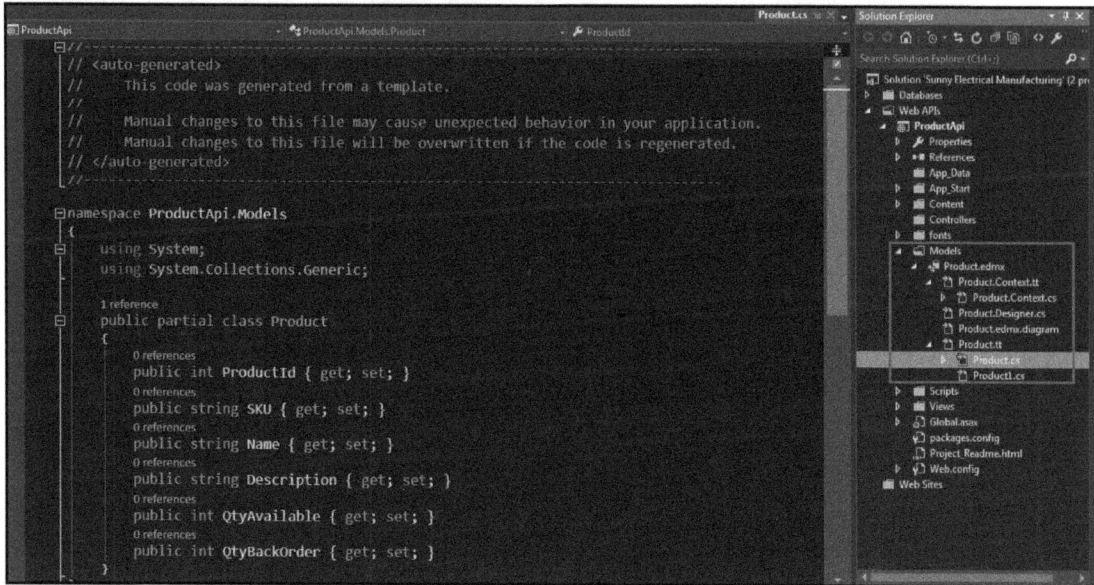

We will use this `Product` model to create the API App. Make sure that you have successfully built the project at this stage and then let's create a controller. Controllers are the classes where we implement the core logic within the methods to handle incoming HTTP requests.

Go to the `Controller` folder and delete the default `ValuesController` and add a new `Controller`.

In the scaffolding option,select **Web API 2 Controller with actions, using Entity Framework**, and click on the **Add** button:

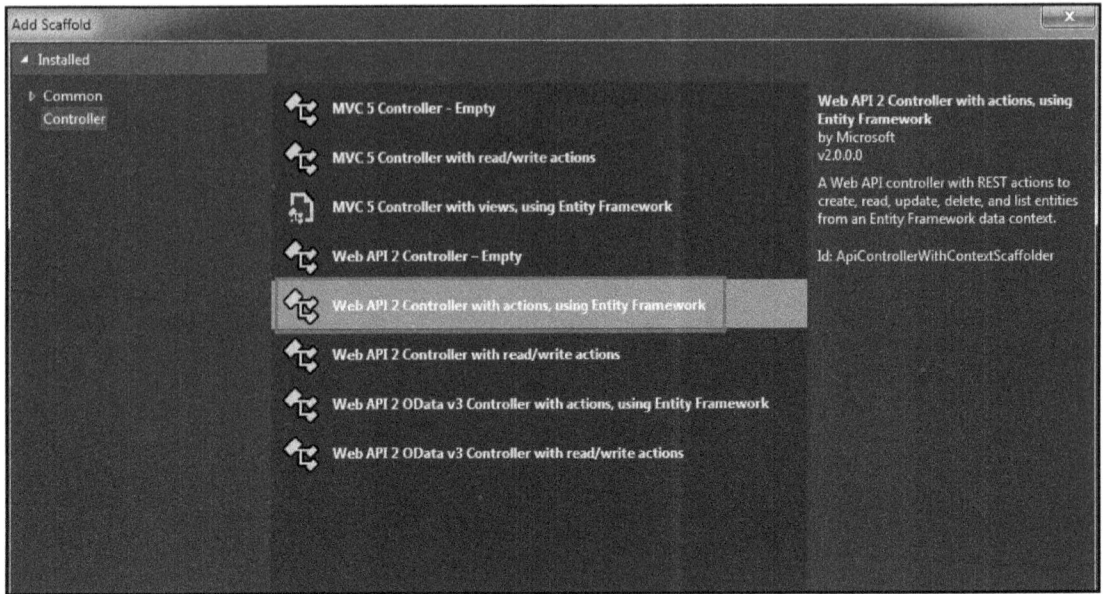

To add the Controller using the scaffolding, you need to select the following options:

- **Model class**: Choose **Product** from the drop-down
- **Data context class**: Choose **AzureProductDbEntities** from the drop-down

Either give your desired Controller a name or leave the suggested name that is based on the **Model class**:

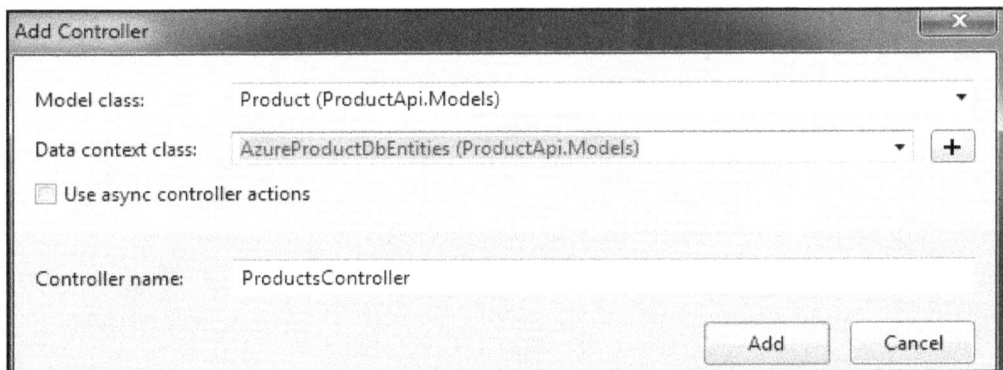

After clicking on **Add**, the `ProductsController` would be added to the project as shown here:

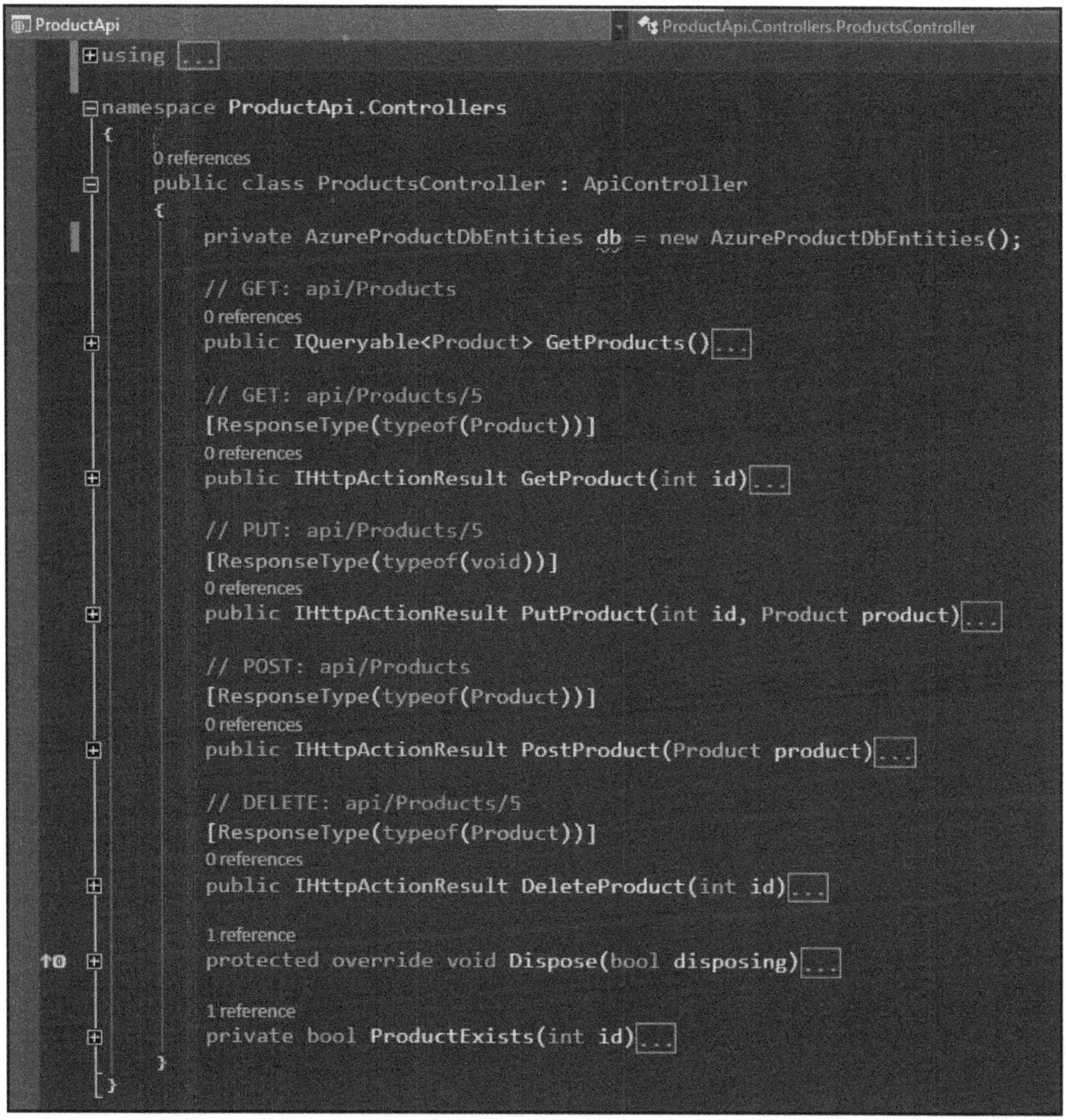

```csharp
ProductApi                                    ProductApi.Controllers.ProductsController

using ...

namespace ProductApi.Controllers
{
    0 references
    public class ProductsController : ApiController
    {
        private AzureProductDbEntities db = new AzureProductDbEntities();

        // GET: api/Products
        0 references
        public IQueryable<Product> GetProducts()...

        // GET: api/Products/5
        [ResponseType(typeof(Product))]
        0 references
        public IHttpActionResult GetProduct(int id)...

        // PUT: api/Products/5
        [ResponseType(typeof(void))]
        0 references
        public IHttpActionResult PutProduct(int id, Product product)...

        // POST: api/Products
        [ResponseType(typeof(Product))]
        0 references
        public IHttpActionResult PostProduct(Product product)...

        // DELETE: api/Products/5
        [ResponseType(typeof(Product))]
        0 references
        public IHttpActionResult DeleteProduct(int id)...

        1 reference
        protected override void Dispose(bool disposing)...

        1 reference
        private bool ProductExists(int id)...
    }
}
```

Essentially, we have created web API to perform CRUD operations on the **Product** table. In the next step, we have to enable the Swagger UI.

Enabling the Swagger UI

As mentioned earlier in the Swagger section, Swagger provides a simple web UI for the API descriptions such as HTTP methods, URL path, parameters, responses message, and HTTP error codes. In this section, we will see how to enable the Swagger UI for the Product API App.

If you build and run the project, the browser opens and shows the HTTP 403 error page:

HTTP Error 403.14 - Forbidden

The Web server is configured to not list the contents of this directory.

Most likely causes:

- A default document is not configured for the requested URL, and directory browsing is not enabled on the server.

Things you can try:

- If you do not want to enable directory browsing, ensure that a default document is configured and that the file exists.
- Enable directory browsing.

  1. Go to the IIS Express install directory.
  2. Run appcmd set config /section:system.webServer/directoryBrowse /enabled:true to enable directory browsing at the server level.
  3. Run appcmd set config ["SITE_NAME"] /section:system.webServer/directoryBrowse /enabled:true to enable directory browsing at the site level.

- Verify that the configuration/system.webServer/directoryBrowse@enabled attribute is set to true in the site or application configuration file.

Since API Apps supports Swagger, the REST API defines an endpoint URL that returns metadata for the API in the Swagger JSON format. To get JSON metadata for the API, in your browser address bar, add `swagger/docs/v1` to the end of the line (that is, `http://localhost:21862/swagger/docs/v1`) and then press **Return**:

{"swagger":"2.0","info":{"version":"v1","title":"ProductApi"},"host":"localhost:21862","schemes":["http"],"paths":{"/api/Product":{"get":{"tags":["Product"],"operationId":"Product_Get","consumes":[],"produces":["application/json","text/json","application/xml","text/xml"],"responses":{"200":{"description":"OK","schema":{"type":"array","items":{"$ref":"#/definitions/Product"}}}},"deprecated":false},"put":{"tags":["Product"],"operationId":"Product_Put","consumes":["application/json","text/json","application/xml","text/xml","application/x-www-form-urlencoded"],"parameters":[{"name":"product","in":"body","required":true,"schema":{"$ref":"#/definitions/Product"}}],"responses":{"204":{"description":"No Content"}},"deprecated":false},"post":{"tags":["Product"],"operationId":"Product_Post","consumes":["application/json","text/json","application/xml","text/xml","application/x-www-form-urlencoded"],"produces":[],"parameters":[{"name":"product","in":"body","required":true,"schema":{"$ref":"#/definitions/Product"}}],"responses":{"204":{"description":"No Content"}},"deprecated":false}},"/api/Product/{id}":{"get":{"tags":["Product"],"operationId":"Product_GetById","consumes":[],"produces":["application/json","text/json","application/xml","text/xml"],"parameters":[{"name":"id","in":"path","required":true,"type":"integer","format":"int32"}],"responses":{"200":{"description":"OK","schema":{"$ref":"#/definitions/Product"}}},"deprecated":false},"delete":{"tags":["Product"],"operationId":"Product_Delete","consumes":[],"produces":[],"parameters":[{"name":"id","in":"path","required":true,"type":"integer","format":"int32"}],"responses":{"204":{"description":"No Content"}},"deprecated":false}}},"definitions":{"Product":{"type":"object","properties":{"Id":{"format":"int32","type":"integer"},"Name":{"type":"string"},"Description":{"type":"string"},"Price":{"type":"string"}}}}}

This is the Swagger 2.0 JSON metadata for the `ProductApi`, which can be used to create the client code.

This metadata is also responsible for generating the Swagger UI. To enable the Swagger UI, go back to the project, open the `App_Start\SwaggerConfig.cs` file, then scroll down to the following code and uncomment it:

```
// ***** Uncomment the following to enable the swagger UI *****
/*
    })
.EnableSwaggerUi(c =>
    {
*/
```

Run the project again. In your browser address bar, add swagger to the end of the line (that is, `http://localhost:21862/swagger`) and then press **Return**:

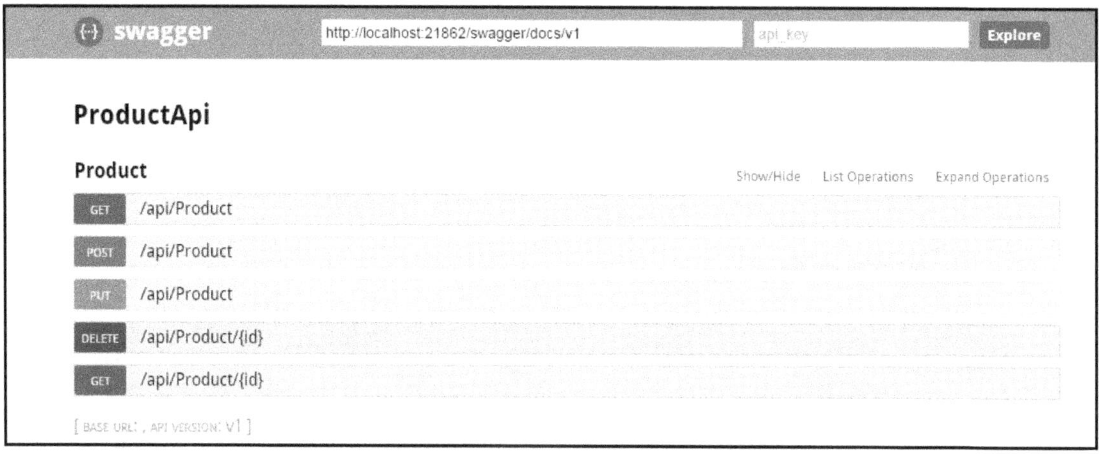

Testing your API

Using Swagger UI, we can test a `ProductApi` we created. Let's test the couple of things:

- **POST**: Create a product
- **GET**: List all the products

Click on **POST** and then click on the box under **Model Schema**. Clicking on **Model Schema** prefills the input box where you can specify the parameter value for the Post method. Change the JSON in the **product** parameter input box as shown here:

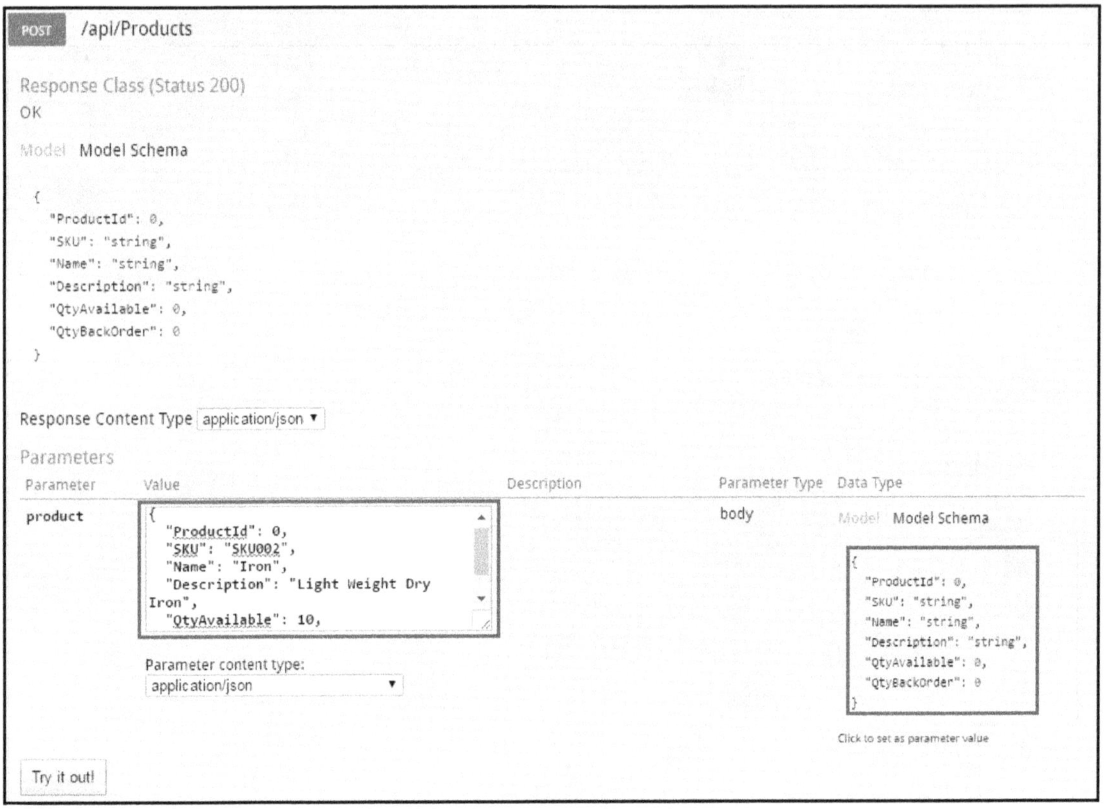

Click on **Try it out!**. The `ProductApi` returns an HTTP `201` response code that indicates success:

```
Request URL

  http://localhost:21862/api/Products

Response Body


  {
      "ProductId": 2,
      "SKU": "SKU002",
      "Name": "Iron",
      "Description": "Light Weight Dry Iron",
      "QtyAvailable": 10,
      "QtyBackOrder": 10
  }


Response Code

  201
```

Click on the first **GET** button and then, in that section of the page, click on the **Try it out!** button. The Get method response now includes the new product:

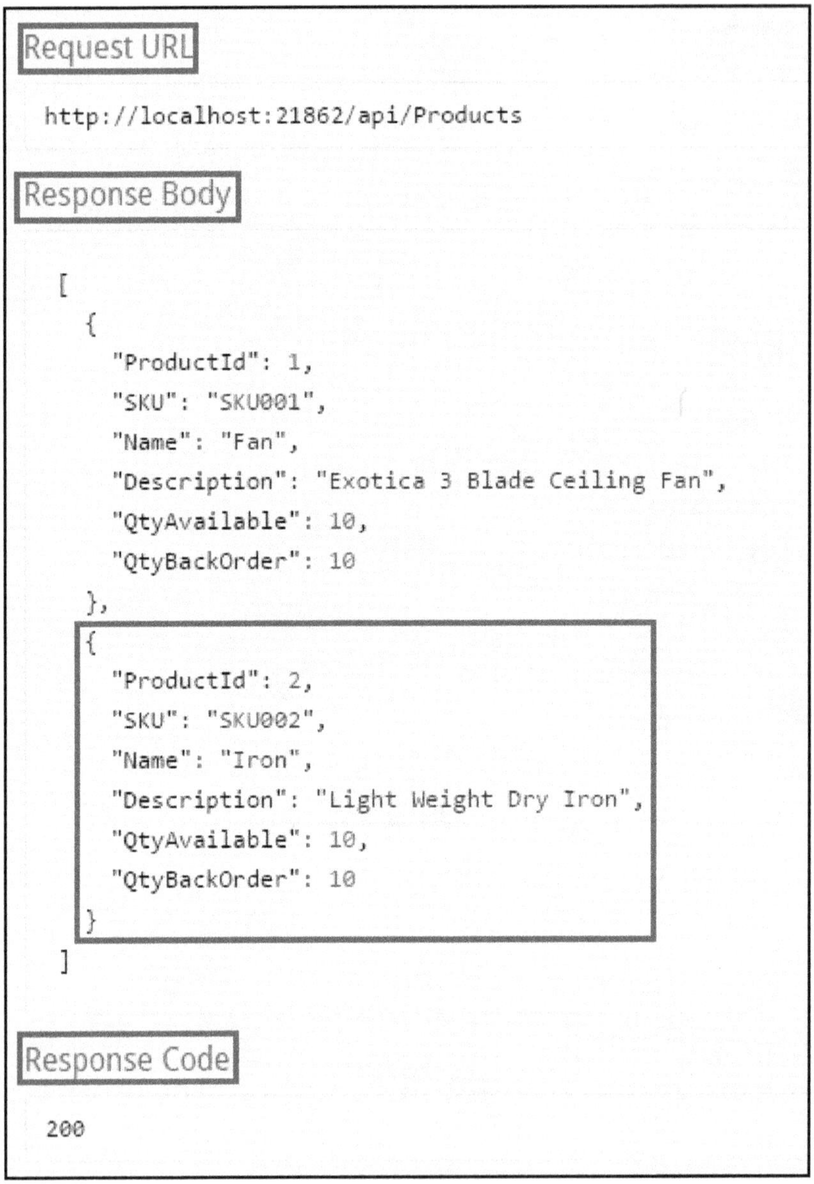

```
Request URL

  http://localhost:21862/api/Products

Response Body


  [
      {
          "ProductId": 1,
          "SKU": "SKU001",
          "Name": "Fan",
          "Description": "Exotica 3 Blade Ceiling Fan",
          "QtyAvailable": 10,
          "QtyBackOrder": 10
      },
      {
          "ProductId": 2,
          "SKU": "SKU002",
          "Name": "Iron",
          "Description": "Light Weight Dry Iron",
          "QtyAvailable": 10,
          "QtyBackOrder": 10
      }
  ]

Response Code

  200
```

Deploying ProductAPI to Azure

So far, we have developed our `ProductApi` locally and tested it using Swagger UI. Now we would use Visual Studio's integrated tool, the **Publish Web** wizard, to create a new API App in Azure and then deploy the `ProductApi` to a new API App.

> Make sure that you are using the latest SDK version. Refer to
> `https://azure.microsoft.com/en-us/downloads/` to download the latest
> SDK.

To open the **Publish Web** wizard, right-click on the `ProductApi` project in **Solution Explorer** and then click on **Publish**.

In the **Profile** step of the **Publish Web** wizard, click on **Microsoft Azure App Service**. Sign in to your Azure account:

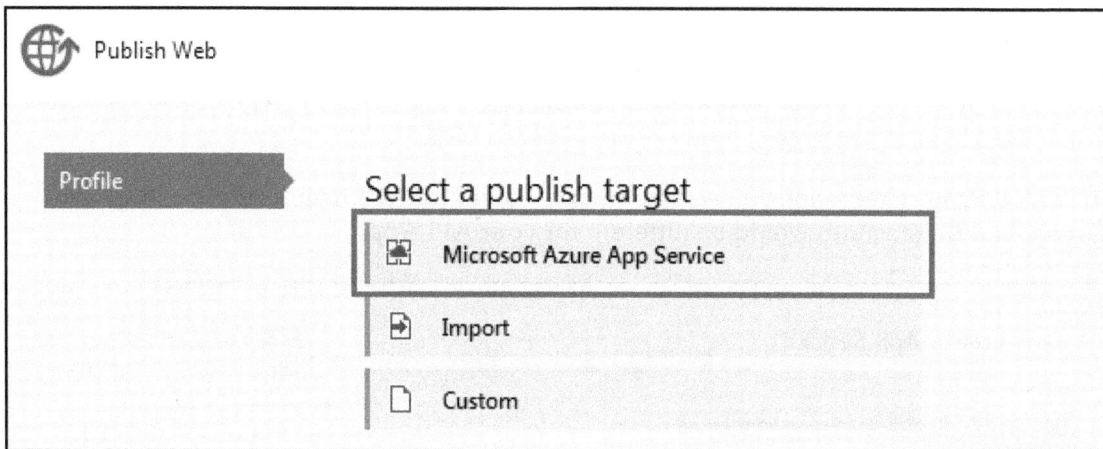

In the **App Service** dialog box, choose the Azure subscription you want to use and then click on **New:**

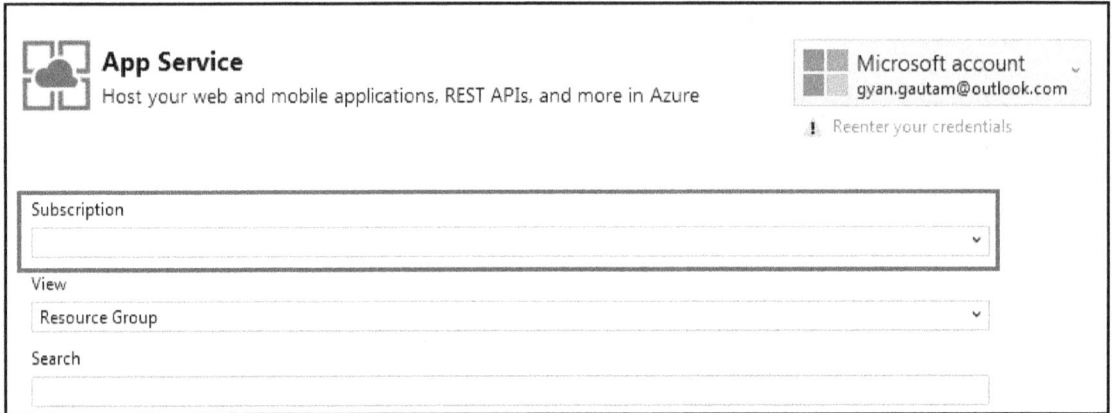

Select an API App type from the **Change Type** drop-down list to confirm that you are hosting the API App in the App Service. Now enter a unique name for your API App or accept the default name that Visual Studio proposes. The URL of the API App will be `{APi app name}.azurewebsites.net`.

In the following screenshot, you can see sample values for **API App Name** and **Resource Group**, and these values would be different for your API App:

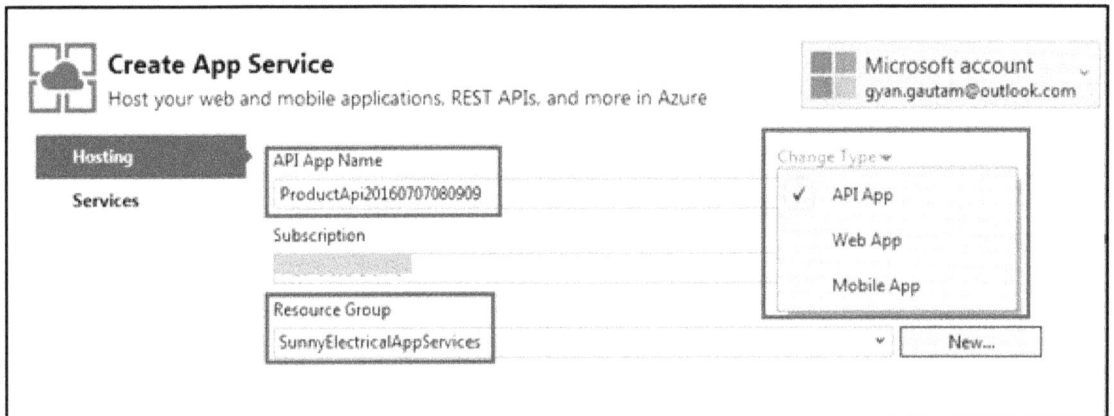

A Resource Group is a container for all your resources such as API Apps, Web Apps, databases, and VMs. It's good to create a new resource group to keep all related resources together according to your requirements. This may be by region, capacity, business process, or administration. All resources in the same group should share the same life cycle for deploying, updating, or deleting all together.

An **App Service Plan** determines the set of features and capacity you require for your apps and services to use. So, primarily an App Service Plan specifies the compute resources that your API App runs on.

Also, it allows you to group several Azure resources together to share a single pricing tier thereby reducing costs. For example, if you choose the free tier, your API App runs on shared VMs, whereas, for some paid tiers, it runs on dedicated VMs:

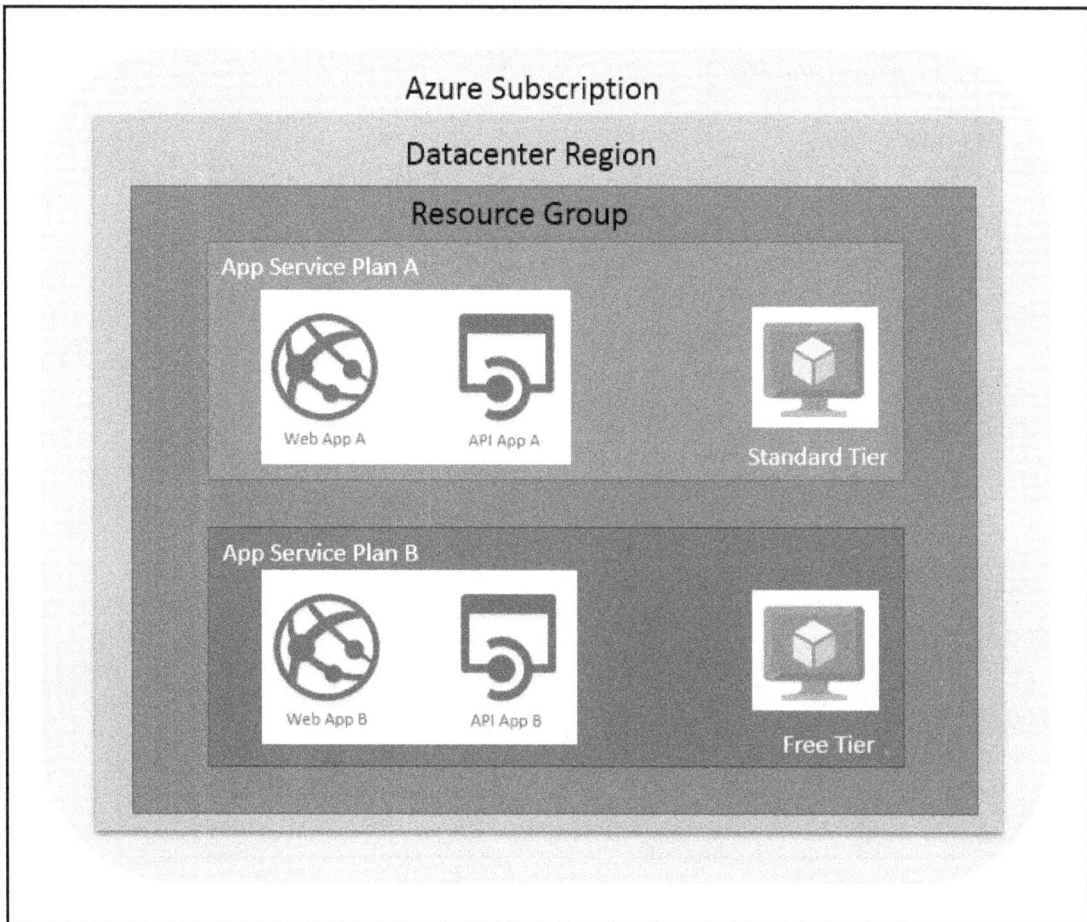

For further details about Resource Groups and App Service Plans, please refer to the previous chapter.

To create an App Service Plan for the Resource Group, SunnyElectricalAppServices, click on the **New** button next to the **App Service Plan** drop-down. In the **Configure App Service Plan** dialog, enter SunnyElectricalAppPlan or another name of your choice. In the **Location** drop-down list, choose the location that is closest to you. In the **Size** drop-down list, click on **Free** and then click on **OK**:

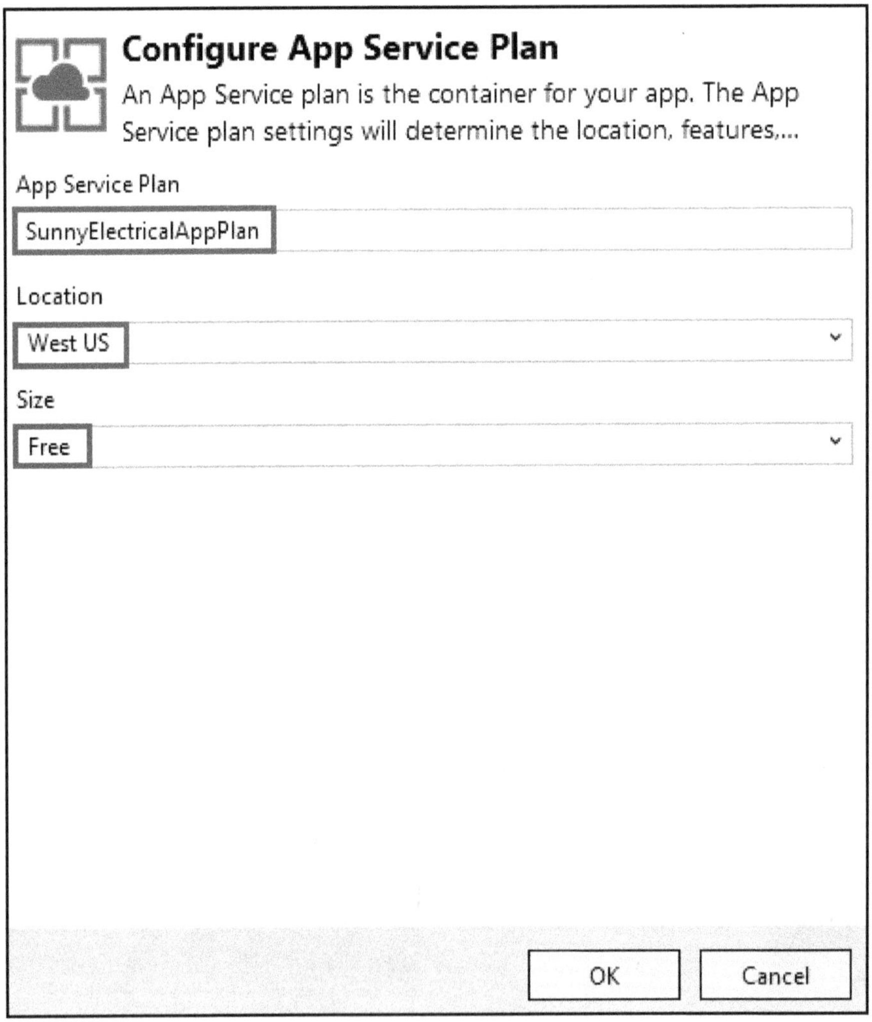

Configure App Service Plan

An App Service plan is the container for your app. The App Service plan settings will determine the location, features,....

App Service Plan

SunnyElectricalAppPlan

Location

West US

Size

Free

OK   Cancel

In the **Create App Service** dialog box, click on **Create**. In the background, Visual Studio reaches out to your Azure subscription to create the API App and downloads the publish profile that has all the required settings for the API App:

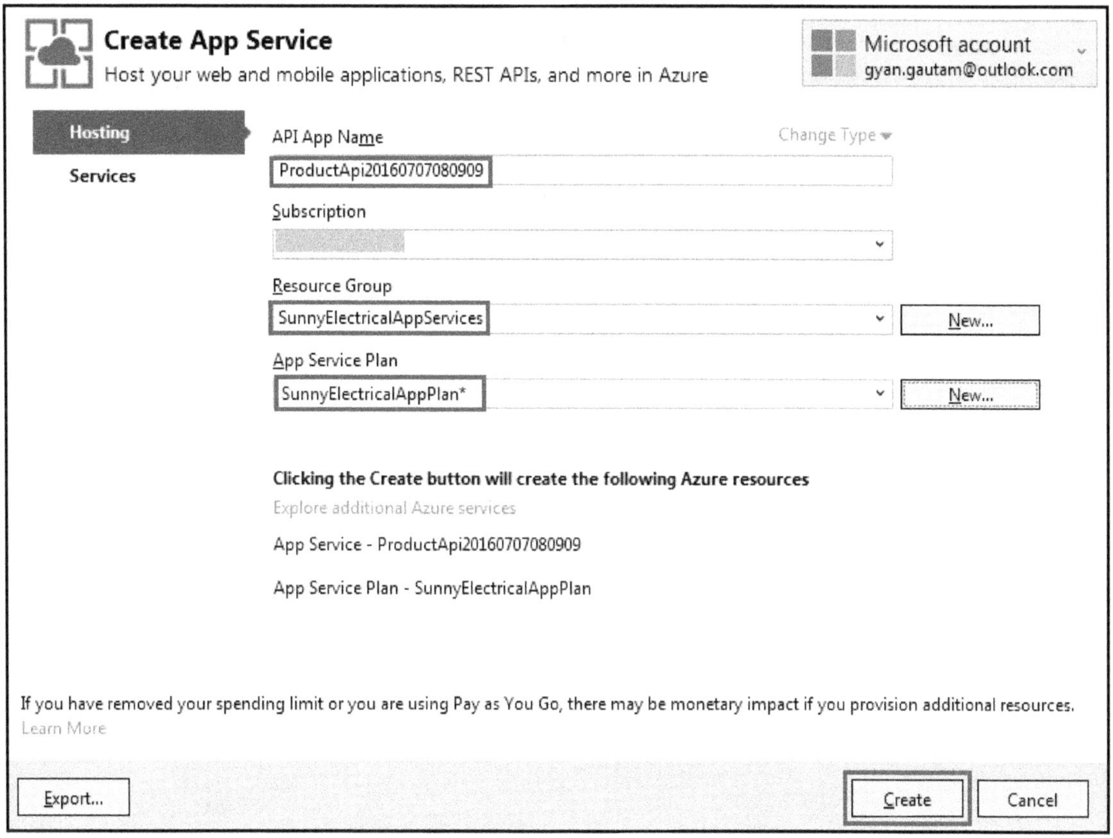

Create App Service
Host your web and mobile applications, REST APIs, and more in Azure

Microsoft account
gyan.gautam@outlook.com

Hosting

Services

API App Name

ProductApi20160707080909

Change Type ▾

Subscription

Resource Group

SunnyElectricalAppServices   ∨   New...

App Service Plan

SunnyElectricalAppPlan*   ∨   New...

Clicking the Create button will create the following Azure resources

Explore additional Azure services

App Service - ProductApi20160707080909

App Service Plan - SunnyElectricalAppPlan

If you have removed your spending limit or you are using Pay as You Go, there may be monetary impact if you provision additional resources. Learn More

Export...   Create   Cancel

The **Publish Web** wizard opens on the **Connection** tab, as shown later. The **Connection** tab shows the **Server** and **Site name** settings point to your API App along with the **User name** and **Password** are deployment credentials that Azure creates for you. Now click on **Next**:

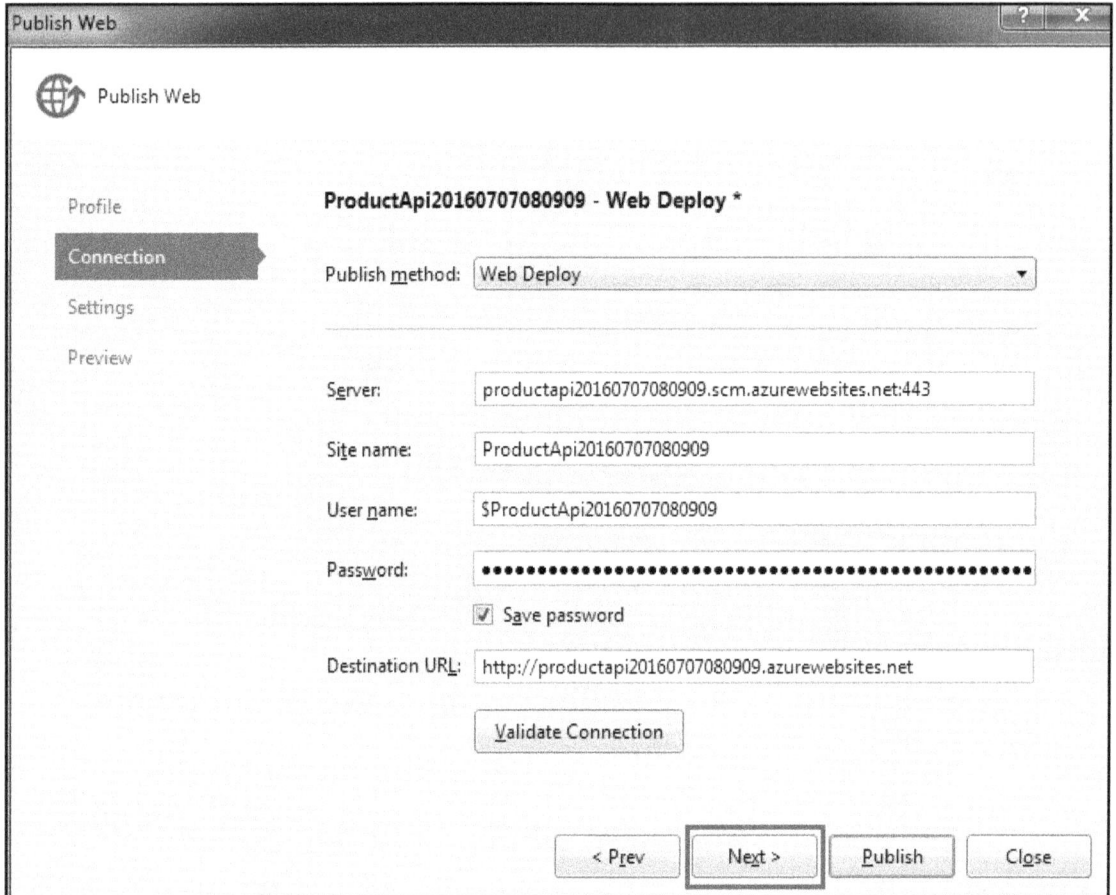

The **Settings** tab allows you to change the build configuration and several **File Publish Options**, as follows:

- **Remove additional files at destination**
- **Precompile during publishing**
- **Excludes files from the App_Data folder**

Here, you can also change the build **Configuration** tab to deploy a **Debug** build for remote debugging (refer to: `https://docs.microsoft.com/en-us/azure/app-service-web/web-sites-dotnet-troubleshoot-visual-studio#remotedebug`).

Click on **Next** to go to the**Preview** tab:

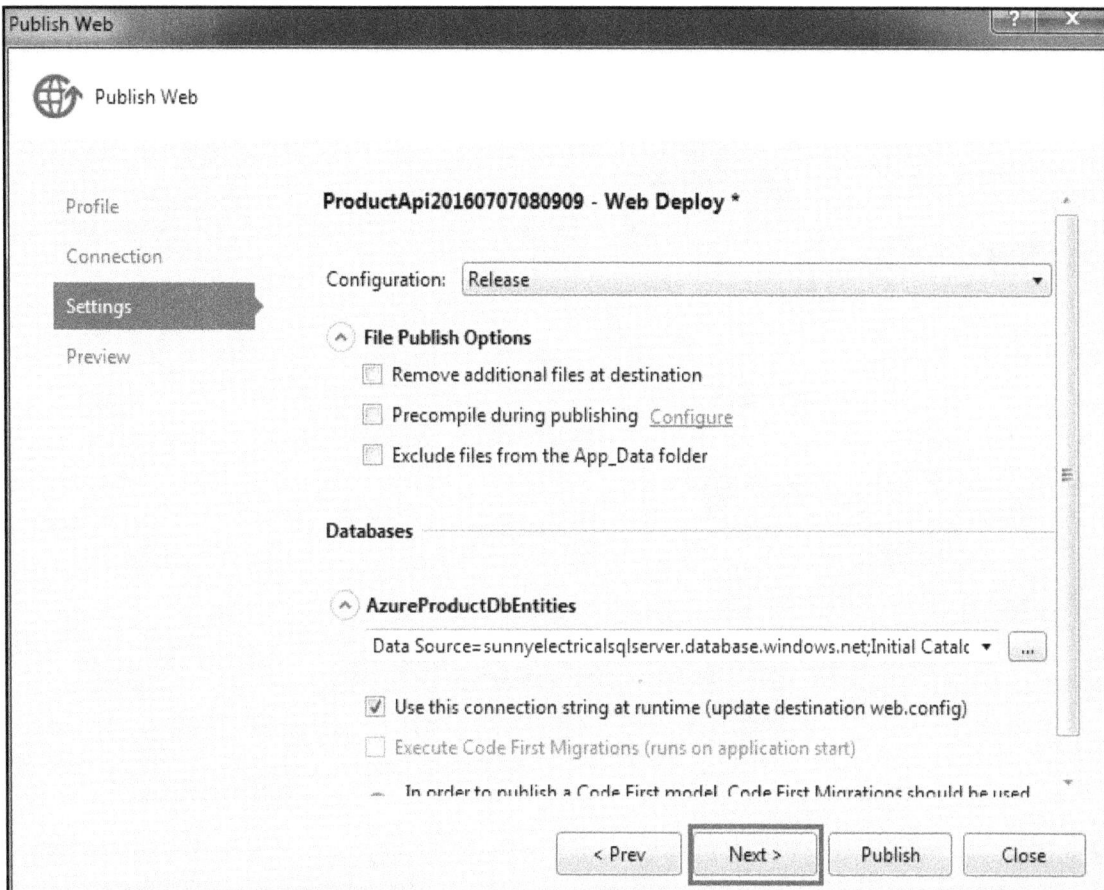

We are not using any of the **File Publish Options** here. For detailed explanations of what they do and other depolyments options, refer to `https://msdn.microsoft.com/library/dd465337.aspx`.

If you click on the **Start Preview** button on the **Preview** tab, it will list all the files that are going to be copied from your project to the API App. Now click on **Publish**:

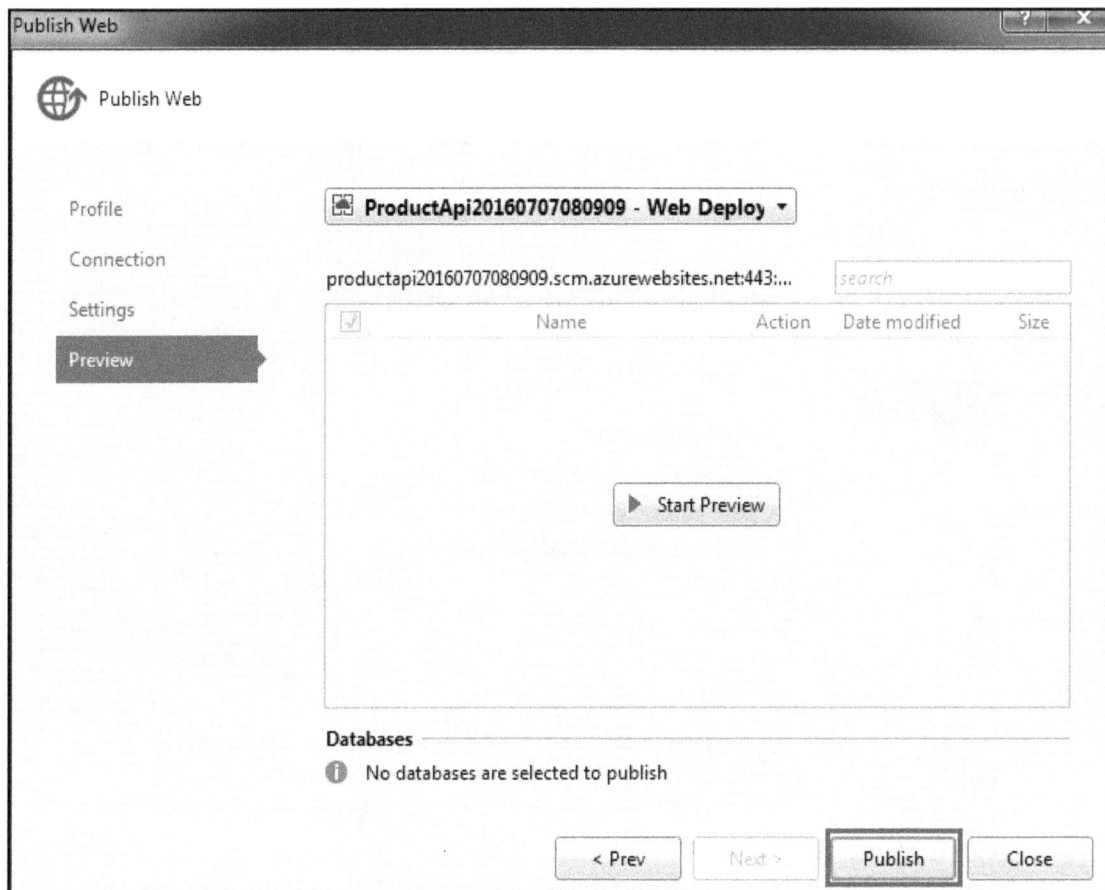

Visual Studio deploys the `ProductApi` project to the new API App in Azure. You can see the success message in the **Output** window logs once the deployment is completed successfully:

Also, a *successfully created* page would appear in a browser window opened to the URL of the API App:

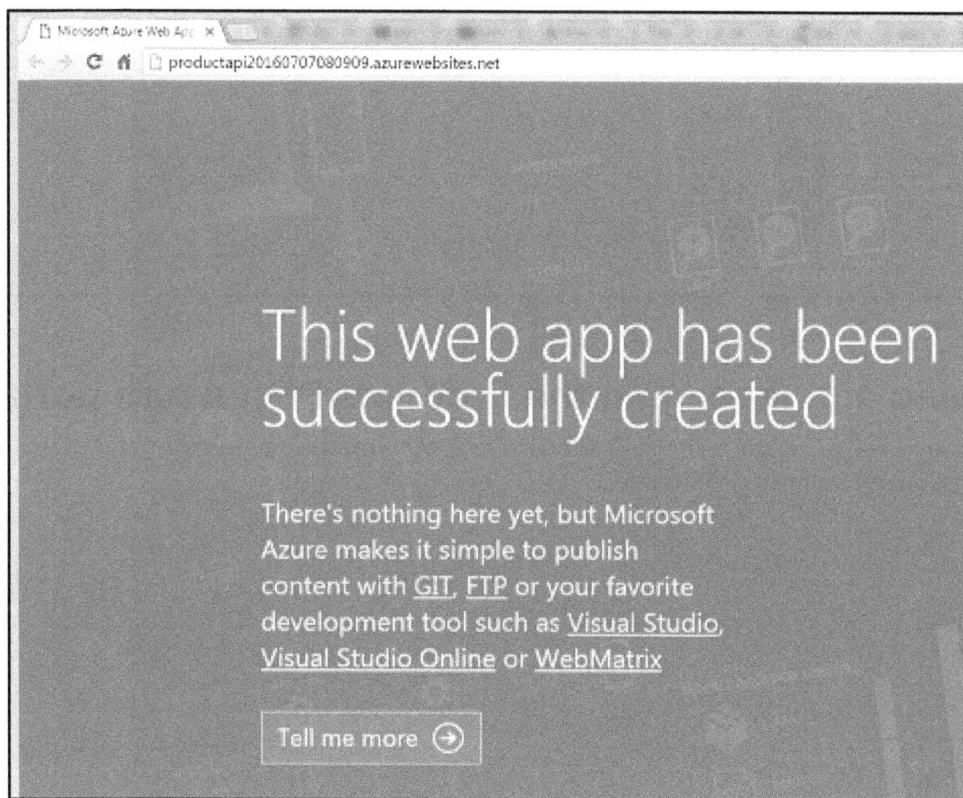

Add `swagger` to the URL in the browser's address bar (that is,
`http://{apiappname}.azurewebsites.net/swagger`) and then press *Enter.*

The browser displays the same Swagger UI that you saw earlier, but now it's running in the
cloud. Try testing a couple of scenarios that we previously tried locally.

- **GET**: List all the products
- **POST**: Create a product

You should see the same results, but the changes made now would be saved in Azure
instead your local machine:

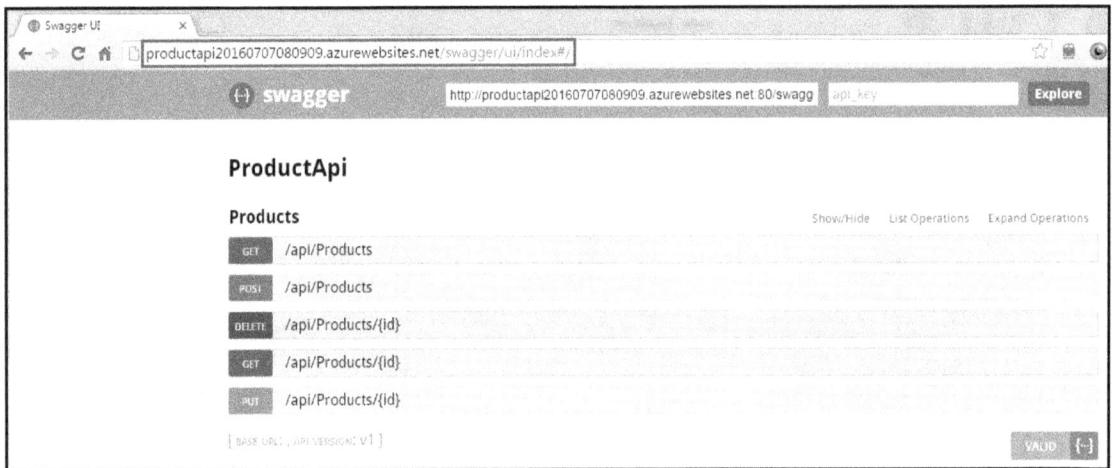

Viewing and managing the ProductAPI in Azure portal

An Azure portal provides a visual dashboard as a web interface to monitor and manage
Azure resources such as API Apps.

Open the Azure portal from`https://portal.azure.com`. Navigate to**Browse** | **App Services**:

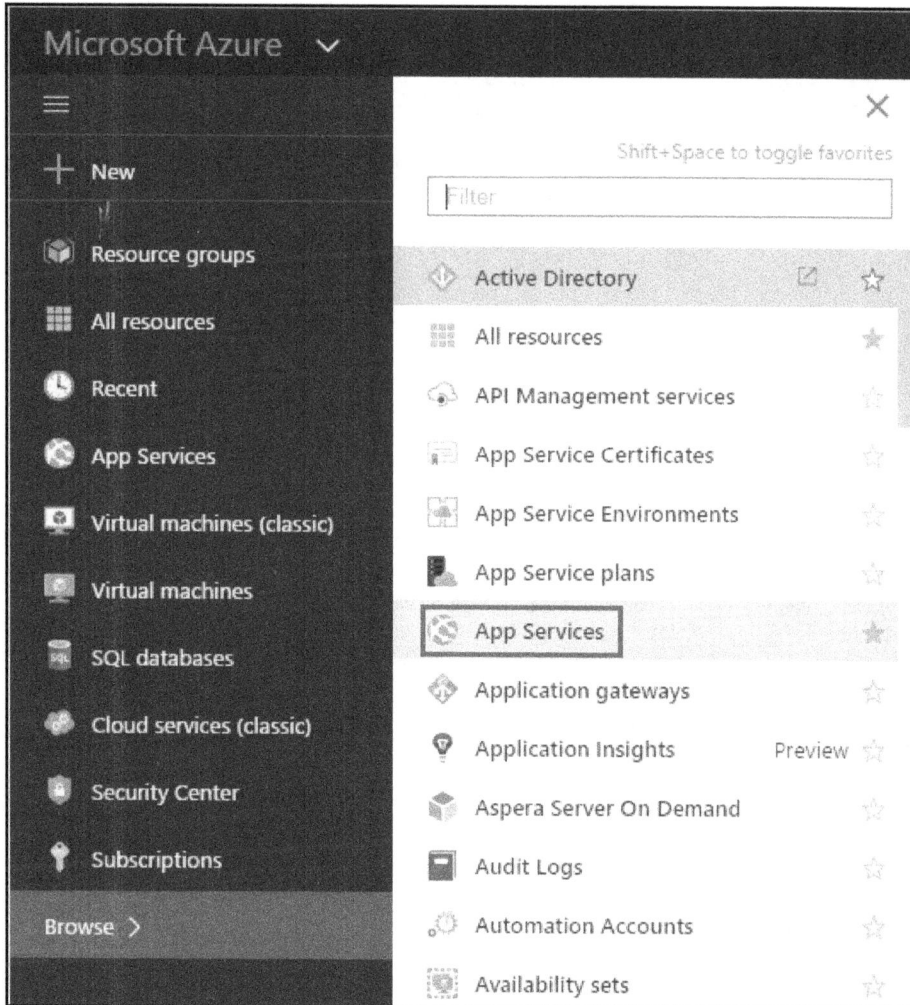

In the **App Services** blade (windows that open to the right are named **blades**), find and click on your new API App:

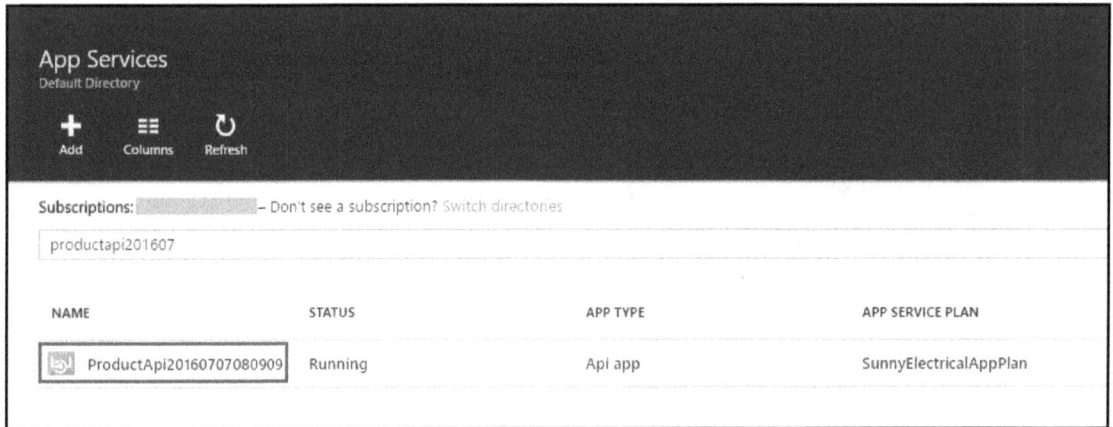

In the **Settings** blade, find the **API** section and click on **API definition**:

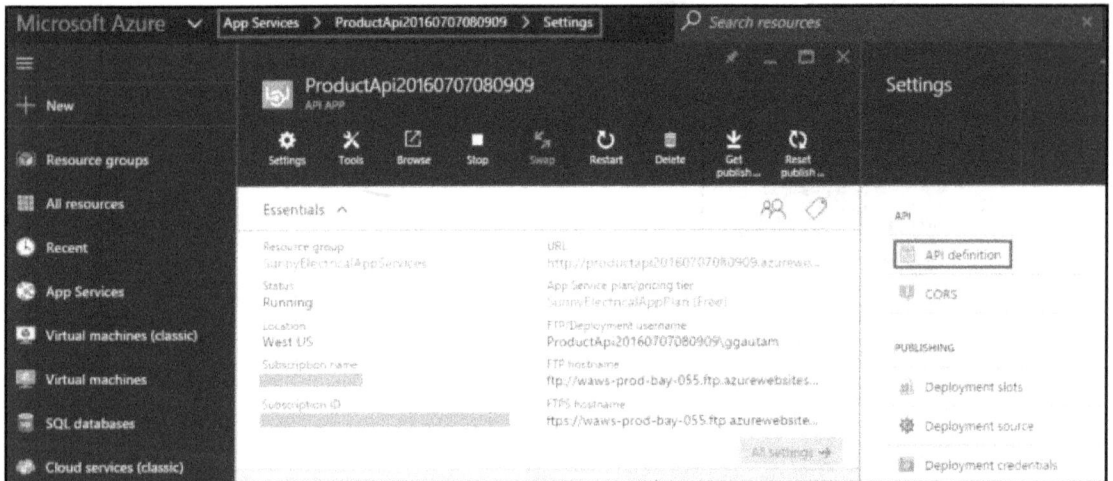

The **API definition** blade lets you specify the URL that returns Swagger 2.0 metadata in the JSON format. When Visual Studio creates the API App, it sets the **API definition** URL to the default value for Swashbuckle-generated metadata that you saw earlier, which is the API App's base URL plus `/swagger/docs/v1`:

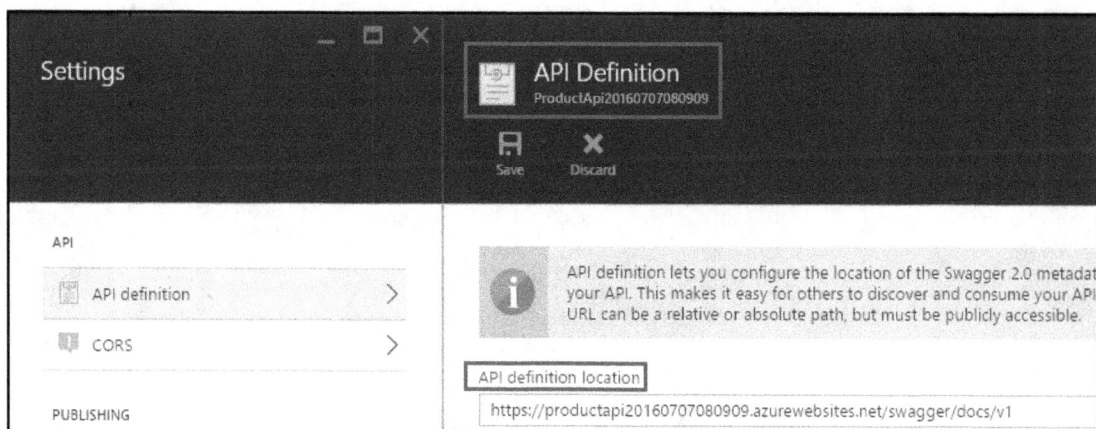

When you select an API App to generate client code for it, Visual Studio retrieves the metadata from this URL.

Consuming your API App by generating client code in Visual Studio

Integrating Swagger into Azure API Apps makes it very easy to generate built-in client code in Visual Studio. Generated client code makes it easier to write code that calls an API App.

In Visual Studio **Solution Explorer**, add a new console application project and give it a suitable name.

Now, right-click on the console (**ProductClient**) project and then navigate to **Add** | **REST API Client**:

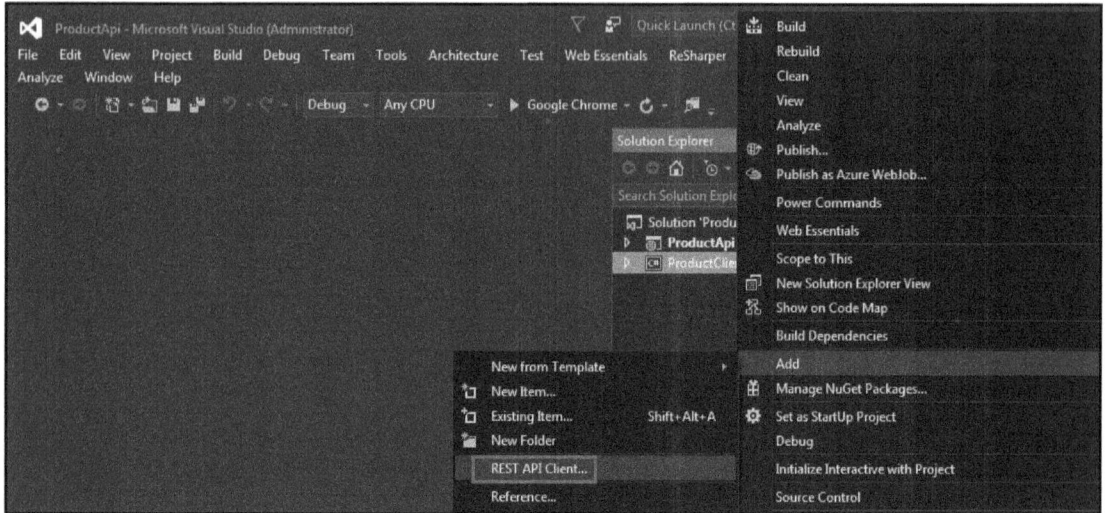

In the **Add REST API Client** dialog box, click on **Swagger Url** and then click on **Select Azure Asset**:

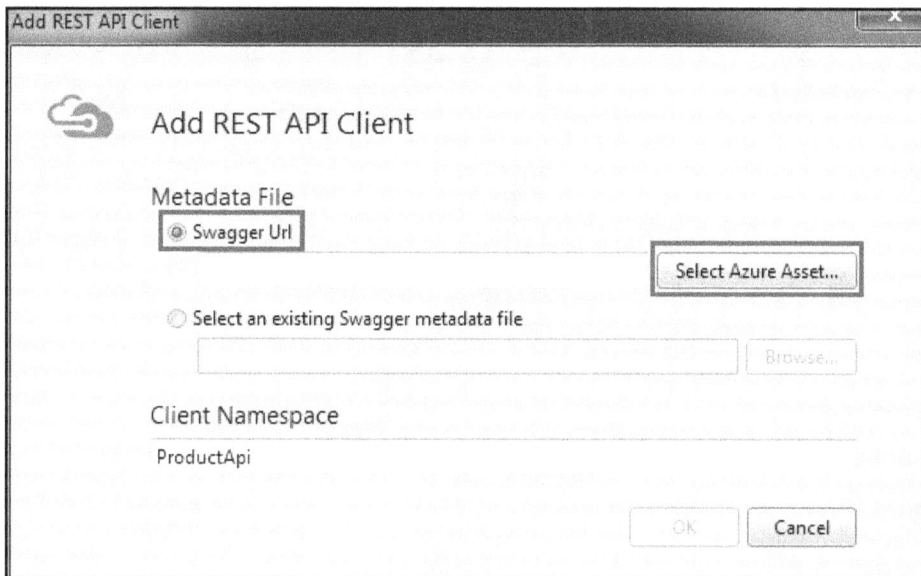

In the **App Service** dialog box, expand the **Resource Group**, select the one you're using for your API App, select the API App and then click on **OK**:

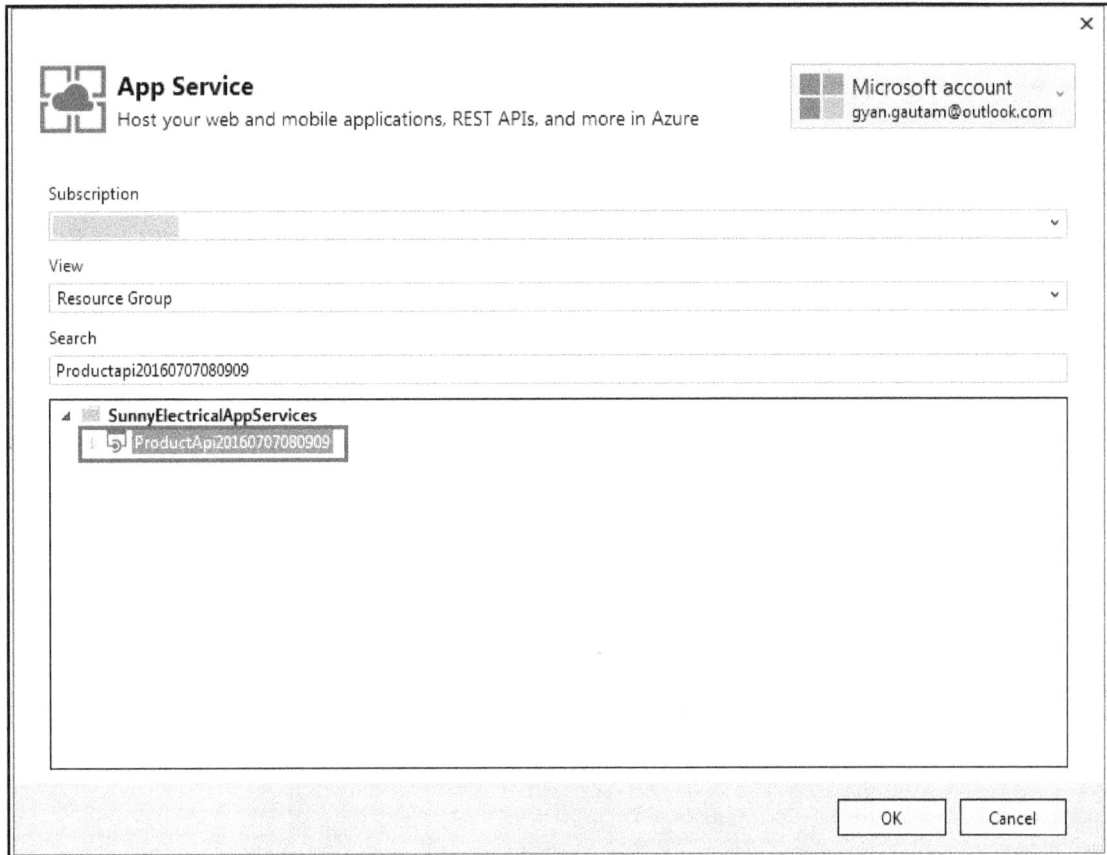

Note that when you return to the **Add REST API Client** dialog, the text box has been filled in with the API definition URL value that you saw earlier in the Azure Portal (mention the figure).

Alternatively, you can also use the Swagger JSON file, which you can get by going to the same URL, `http://productapi20160623.azurewebsites.net/swagger/docs/v1`.

Save the JSON file and use the **Select an existing Swagger metadata file** option:

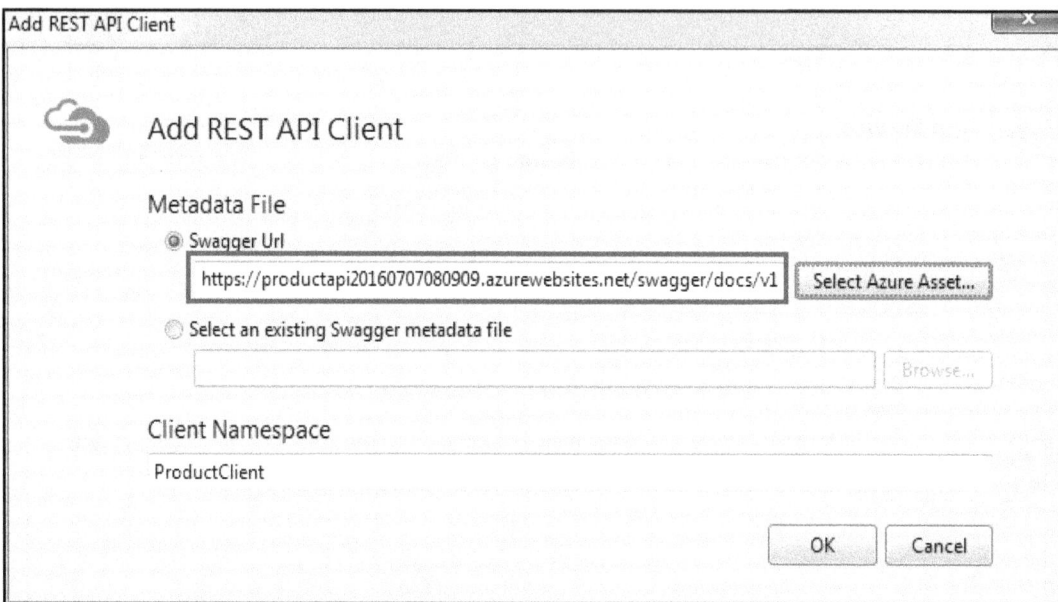

In the **Add REST API Client** dialog box, click on **OK**. Visual Studio creates a folder named after the API App and generates client classes, as shown here:

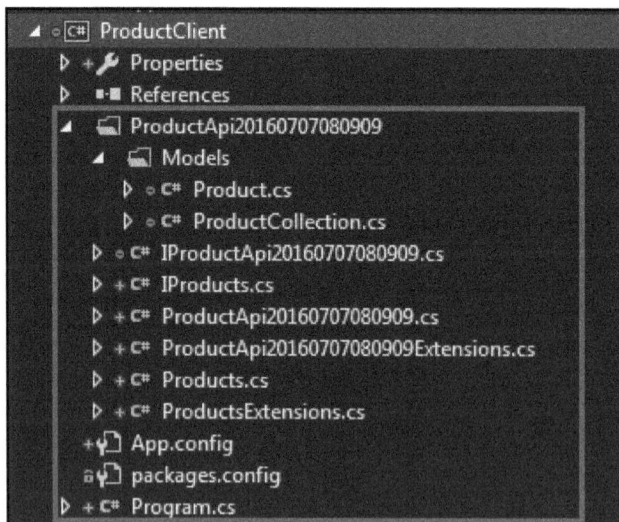

The following code snippet shows how to instantiate the client object and calls the Get method:

```csharp
using System;

namespace ProductClient
{
    0 references | 0 changes | 0 authors, 0 changes
    class Program
    {
        0 references | 0 changes | 0 authors, 0 changes
        static void Main(string[] args)
        {
            var client = new ProductApi20160707080909();
            foreach (var product in client.Products.GetProducts())
            {
                Console.WriteLine(product.Name + " - " + product.Description );
            }
            Console.ReadLine();
        }
    }
}
```

Run the client project to see the product details in the console:

```
file:///C:/GAUTAM/RobustCloudIntegration/Projects/Sunny Electrical Manufacturing/ProductClient...
Fan - Exotica 3 Blade Ceiling Fan
Iron - Light Weight Dry Iron
```

At this point, we have successfully created the Product API App using Visual Studio and then deployed it in Azure using the **Publish Web** wizard tool. We also generated client code for API Apps and consumed the Product API Apps from the .NET console client application.

The API App's architecture

In a nutshell, API Apps make it easy to build and consume your APIs in the cloud. It provides a rich platform and ecosystem for building, consuming, and distributing APIs in cloud and on-premise:

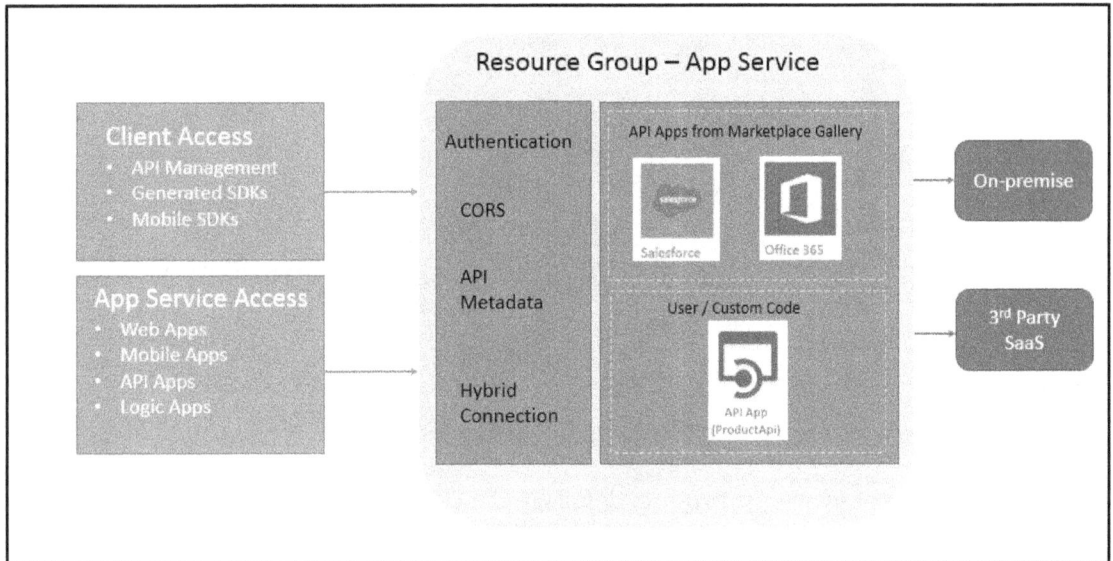

We already created a sample API (`ProductApi`), deployed it in Azure, and easily consumed it in visual studio using built-in automatic client code generation feature. We briefly touched the Resource Group concept, which is basically a container for your app. All things related to your app can live in the same resource group.

Along with our custom APIs, we also have managed APIs built by Microsoft in Marketplace gallery, which we can pull in our application to connect other SaaS application such as Salesforce and Office365. These managed APIs are also named connectors, which we will discuss in detail in `Chapter 6`, *Working with Connectors in Logic Apps.*

One of the design principles of API Apps allow you to bring your API as is, in the language of your choice. The other important feature is to turn on simple authentication that expands service-to-service and user authentication. It also expands to a number of identity providers including **Azure Active Directory (AAD)** as well as social providers such as Facebook and Google.

You can also enable **cross-origin resource sharing** (**CORS**) feature, which allows cross-domain browser access so that you can call your API in HTML and JavaScript web clients.

Because an API App is a part of App Service, it inherits the feature of **hybrid connectivity** and **virtual networks**. So, you can use the API App to build a cloud API, which is modern and REST on the top of the on-premise API that might not be REST and might be behind your enterprise firewall.

In the next sections of this chapter, we will explore all the key feature **Authentication** and **CORS**, and it will also see how you can bring your API as is and deploy it as an API App.

The CORS support

Understanding CORS

As defined on Wikipedia,

> *"CORS allows many resources on a web page to be requested from another domain outside the domain from which the resource originated."*

In other words, CORS defined a way that a browser application can interact safely with a service that originates in a different domain or even a different server.

CORS enables HTML and JavaScript web clients to make cross-domain calls to APIs that are hosted in API Apps.

To understand more clearly, let's create a simple AngularJS website that lists all the products by calling our `ProductApi`.

```javascript
(function () {
    "use strict";

    var app = angular.module("productManagement",
                            ["common.services"]);

}());
(function () {
    "use strict";

    angular
        .module("common.services",
                    ["ngResource"])
        .constant("appSettings",
        {
            serverPath: "http://productapi20160623.azurewebsites.net"

        });
}());
(function () {
    "use strict";

    angular
        .module("common.services")
        .factory("productResource",
                    ["$resource",
                     "appSettings",
                        productResource])

    function productResource($resource, appSettings) {
        return $resource(appSettings.serverPath + "/api/product/:id");
    }
}());
```

Now when I run this website locally, it will not show up the list because the `ProductApi` call will fail. The browser's developer tool's **Console** window shows a cross-origin error message, as shown here:

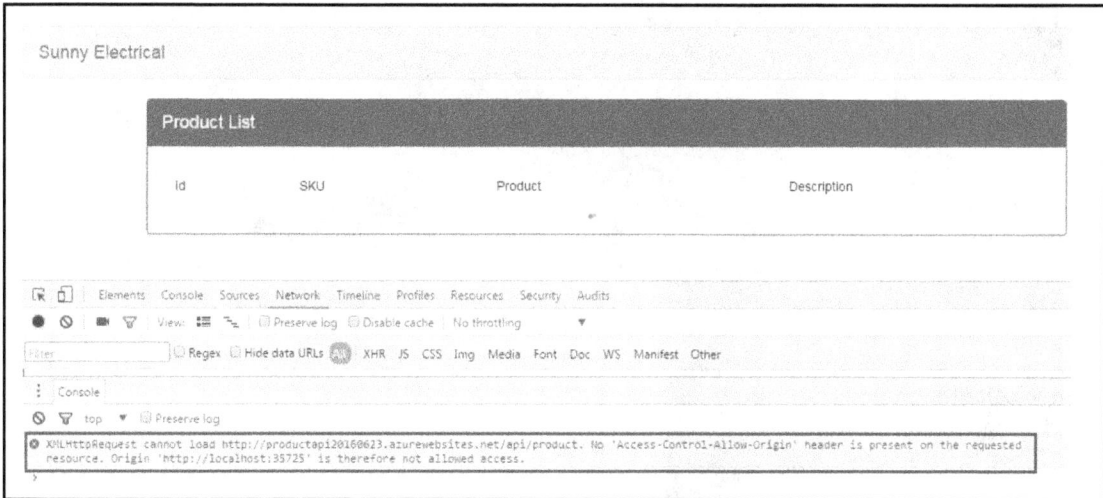

The reason for failure is that the frontend is running in a different domain (`http://localhost:35725/`) than the backend (`http://productapi20160623.azurewebsites.net/`).

Enabling CORS in Azure App Service

Now we will configure CORS settings in Azure for `ProductApi`, which will allow JavaScript calls from the website.

In a browser, go to the Azure portal at `https://portal.azure.com`. Click on `App Service` and then click on the **ProductApi** App.

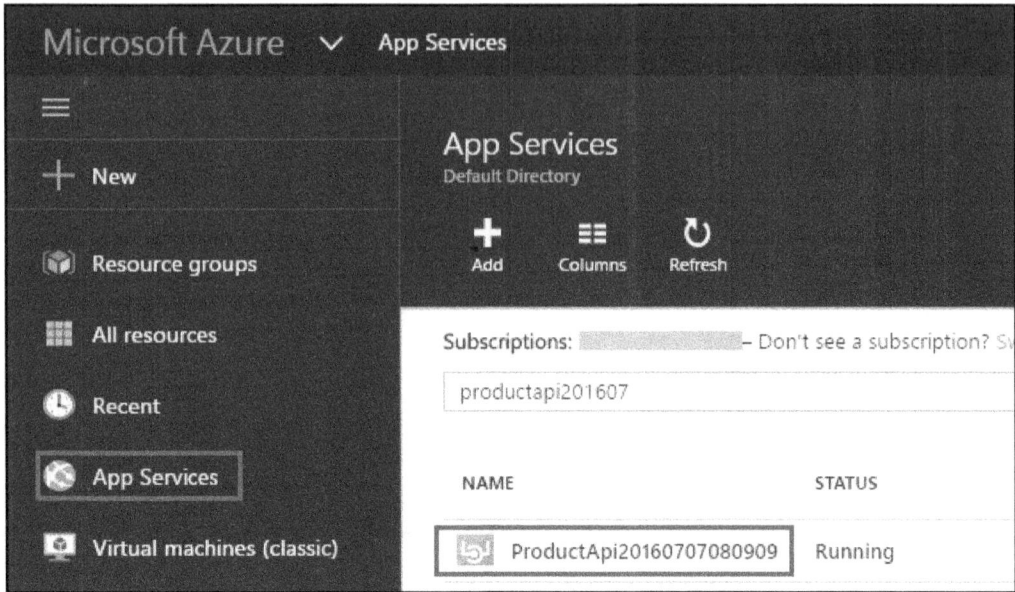

In the **Settings** blade that opens to the right of the **API App** blade, find the **API** section and then click on **CORS**.

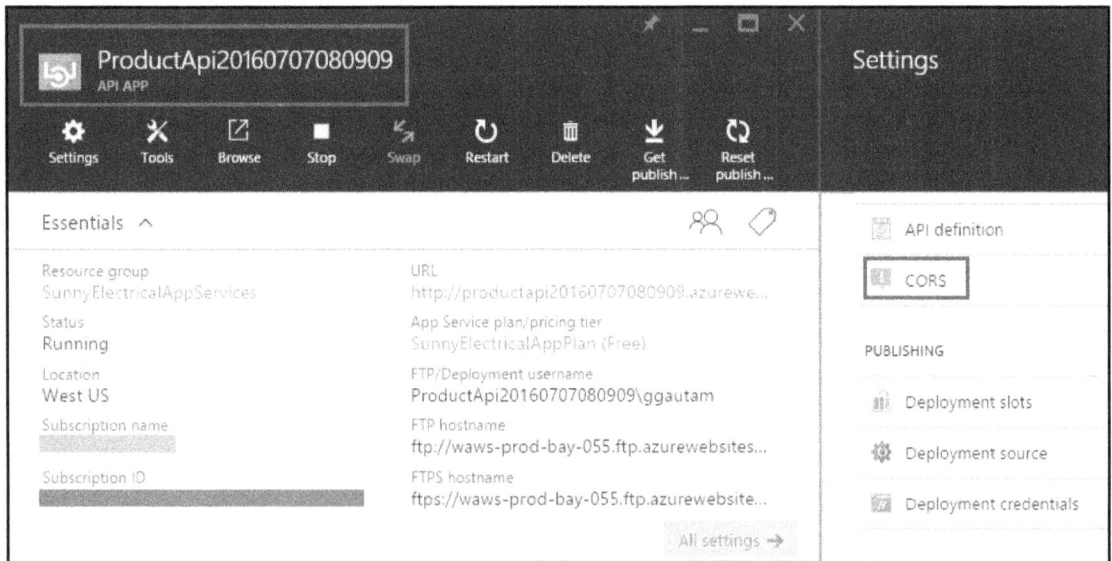

In the text box, enter the URL for the website, `http://localhost:35725`. If you have deployed your frontend app in Azure, then you need to enter `http://{frontendappname}.azurewebsites.net`.

As an alternative, you can enter an asterisk (*) to specify that all origin domains are accepted. Now click on **Save**.

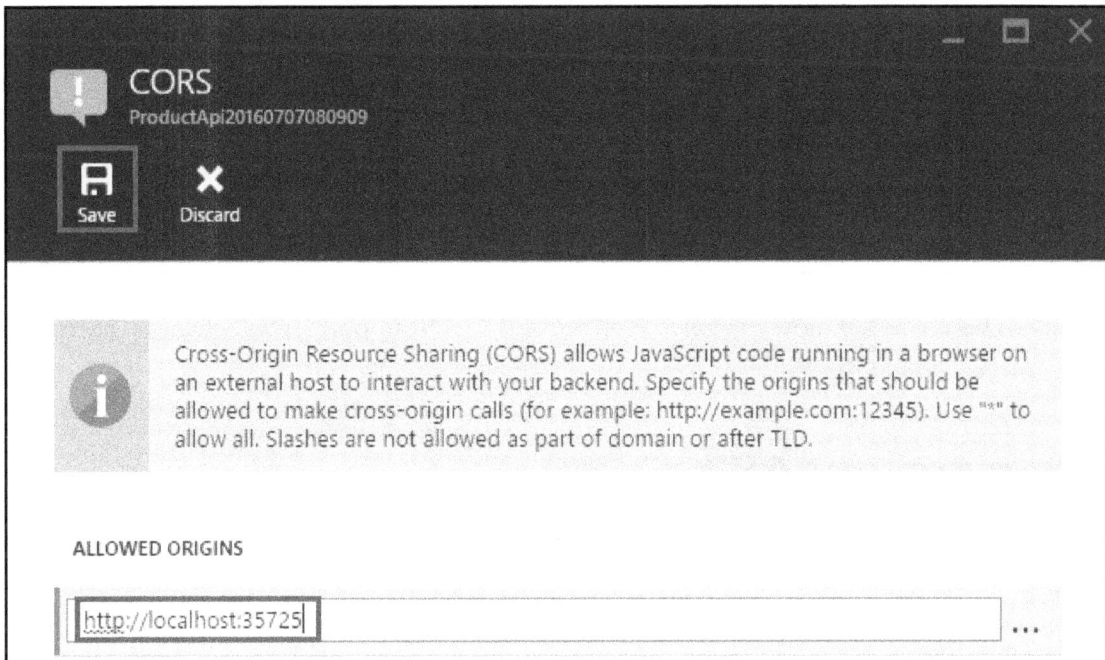

Now that we have enabled CORS, the `ProductApi` App will accept JavaScript calls from the specified URL. Now if we try running the website, it will list the products as shown here:

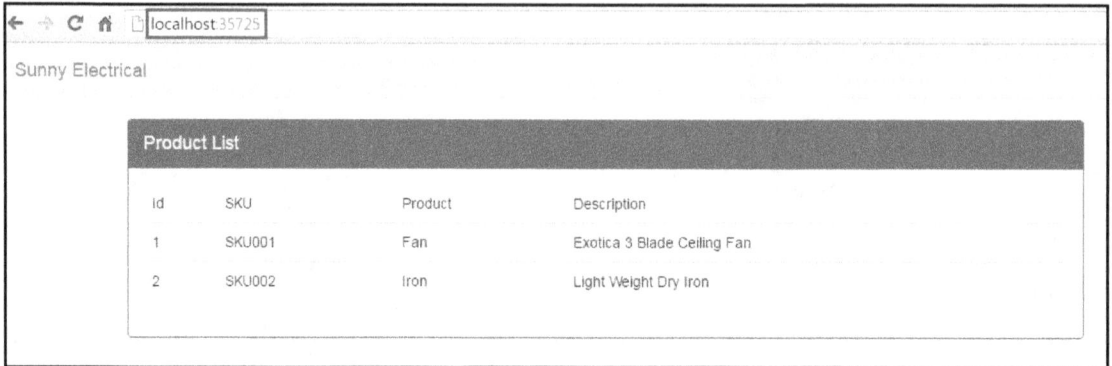

In this section, you saw how to enable App Service CORS support so that client JavaScript code can call an API in a different domain.

Bringing your APIs as-is

You can bring in your API as-is, in the language of your choice, and deploy it as API App in Azure. This would enable your existing API to take advantage of the features of the API Apps in Azure App Service—with no code changes. You can use ASP.NET, Java, PHP, Node.js, or Python for your APIs. API Apps can be used with the same SDK as Mobile Apps, so your code can easily be used on devices and the web.

To demonstrate this feature I have developed the same `ProductApi` in Node.js (`https://nodejs.org/en/`) and we will see how we can deploy it as API App in Azure App Service.

We are using the **Visual Studio Code** editor
(`https://code.visualstudio.com/docs/runtimes/nodejs`) to write the Node.js application
but you can use any editor of your choice.

```
server.js
1     //Dependencies
2     var express = require('express');
3     var mongoose   = require('mongoose');
4     var bodyParser = require('body-parser');
5
6     //MongoDB
7     mongoose.connect('mongodb://test:              .mlab.com:     /product');
8     mongoose.connection.on('connected', function() {
9         console.log("Connection established successfully");
10    });
11
12    //Express
13    var app = express();
14    app.use(bodyParser.urlencoded({ extended: true }));
15    app.use(bodyParser.json());
16
17    //Routes
18    app.use('/api',require('./routes/api'))
19
20    //Start Server
21    app.listen(process.env.PORT || 3000);
22    console.log('Api is running on port 3000');
```

Here I am using MongoDB to store the product details with the same Product model as we used before.

> MongoDB is a free and open-source cross-platform document-oriented database program. Classified as a NoSQL database program, MongoDB uses JSON-like documents with schemas. For further details please refer to: https://www.mongodb.com/.

```
product.js models

1   //Dependincies
2   var restful = require('node-restful');
3   var mongoose = restful.mongoose;
4
5   //Schema
6   var productSchema = new mongoose.Schema({
7       name:String,
8       description: String,
9       price: String
10  });
11
12  //Return Model
13  module.exports = restful.model('Products',productSchema);
```

I am using the **node-restful** (https://github.com/baugarten/node-restful) library to quickly build a REST API with express.

```
api.js routes
1    //Dependencies
2    var express = require('express');
3    var router = express.Router();
4
5    //Models
6    var Product = require('../models/product')
7
8    //Routes
9    Product.methods(['get','put','post','delete'])
10   Product.register(router,'/products')
11
12
13   //Return router
14   module.exports = router;
```

Testing an API using Postman

We can use the free tool **Postman** (`https://www.getpostman.com`) to test the `productApi` we created in Node.Js. You can use either of the Chrome extension or Chrome app to test the API. We are using the Chrome app to test the API, as shown here:

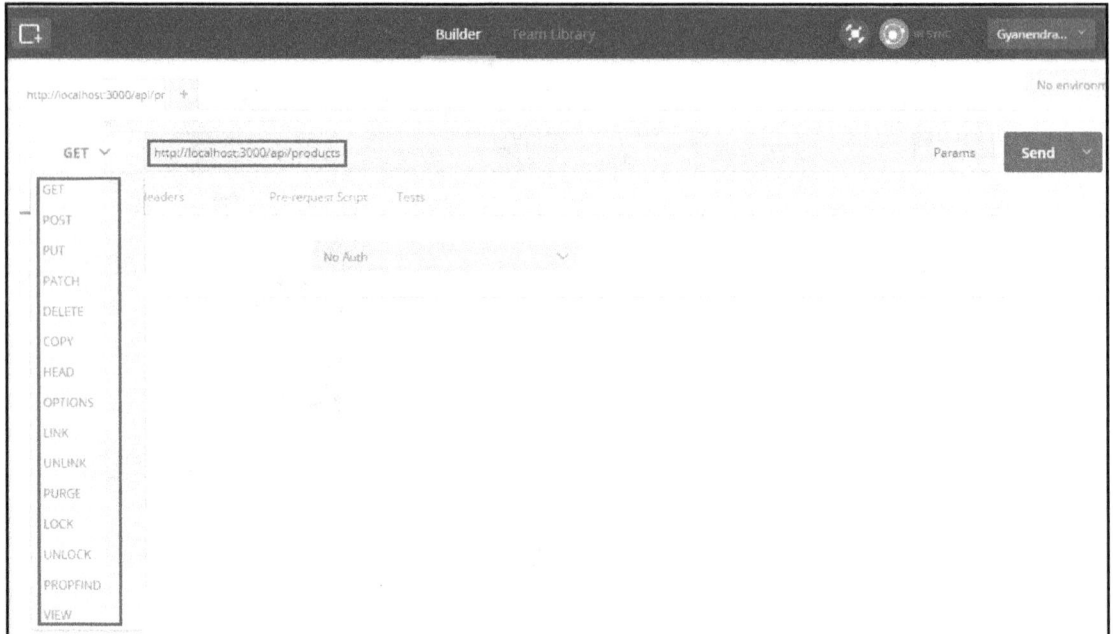

This tool is very clean and easy to use. It basically allows you to generate all the HTTP requests to your API, that is, GET, POST, PUT, and DELETE.

So first, I will create the GET request by entering the URL for the API: `http://localhost:3000/api/products`.

When we send the request, it would return nothing as we have not created any product yet.

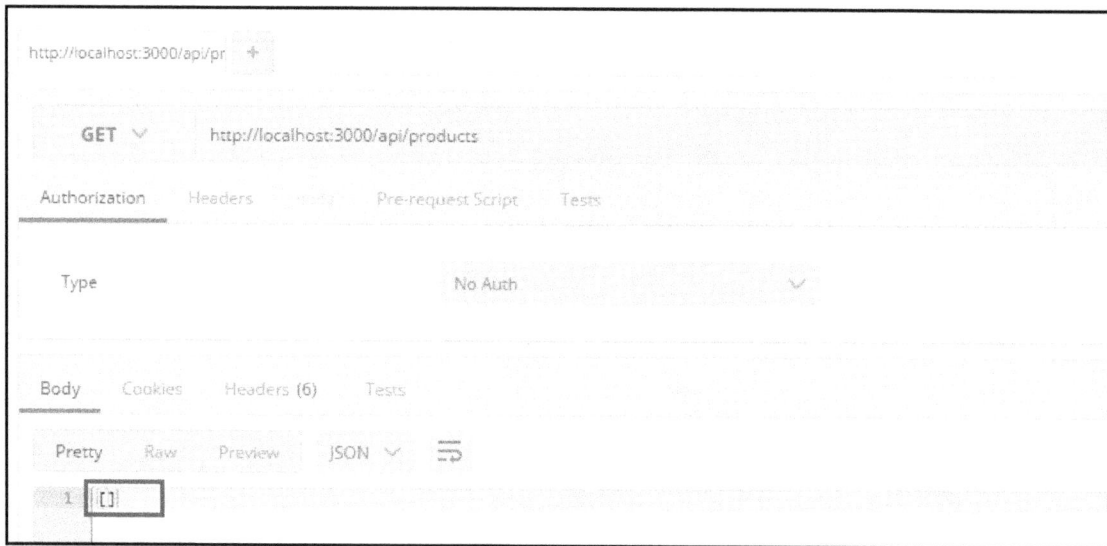

Now, let's add a couple of products, same as we have in our Product API App.

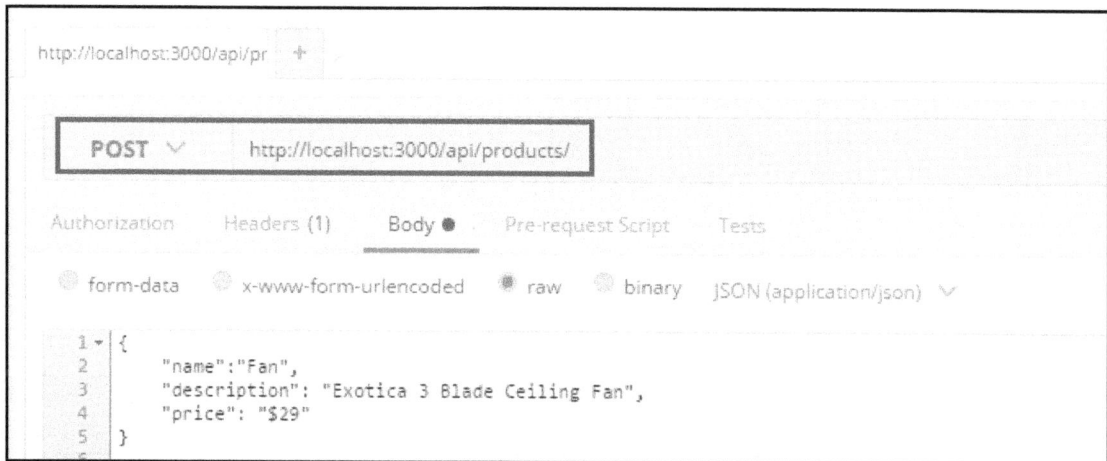

After adding the products, let's send the **GET** request again to list down the products we created.

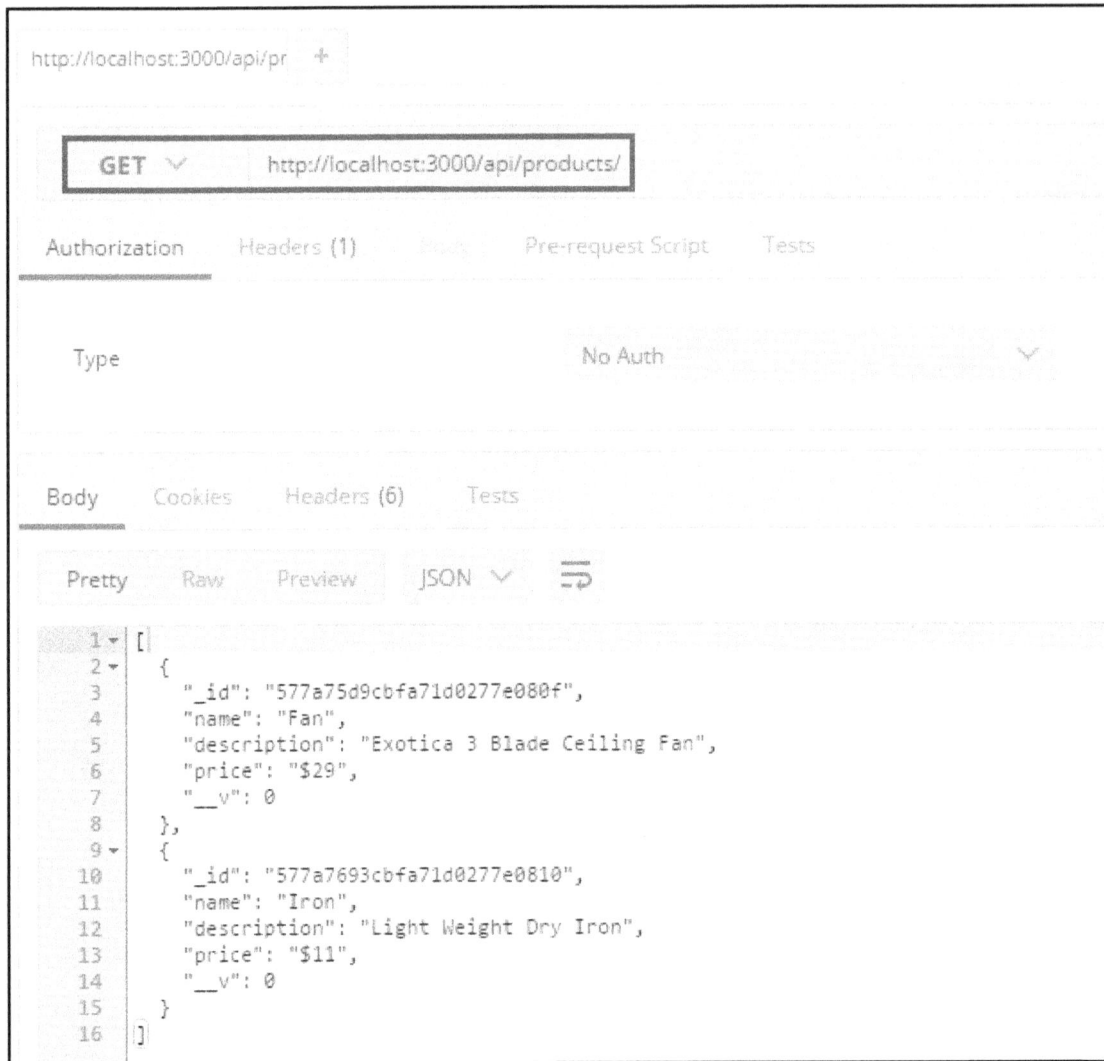

```
http://localhost:3000/api/pr    +

  GET  ∨          http://localhost:3000/api/products/

  Authorization    Headers (1)              Pre-request Script    Tests

    Type                              No Auth                        ∨


  Body    Cookies    Headers (6)    Tests

  Pretty    Raw    Preview    JSON ∨   ⇌

  1 ▾  [
  2 ▾    {
  3          "_id": "577a75d9cbfa71d0277e080f",
  4          "name": "Fan",
  5          "description": "Exotica 3 Blade Ceiling Fan",
  6          "price": "$29",
  7          "__v": 0
  8        },
  9 ▾    {
 10          "_id": "577a7693cbfa71d0277e0810",
 11          "name": "Iron",
 12          "description": "Light Weight Dry Iron",
 13          "price": "$11",
 14          "__v": 0
 15        }
 16    ]
```

Creating a new API App

Now that we have tested the API locally, we will deploy it to Azure. To deploy our node.js API first, we need to create a new API App in Azure using the Azure Portal.

Open the Azure Portal: `https://portal.azure.com`. Navigate to **New** | **Web + Mobile** | **API App**.

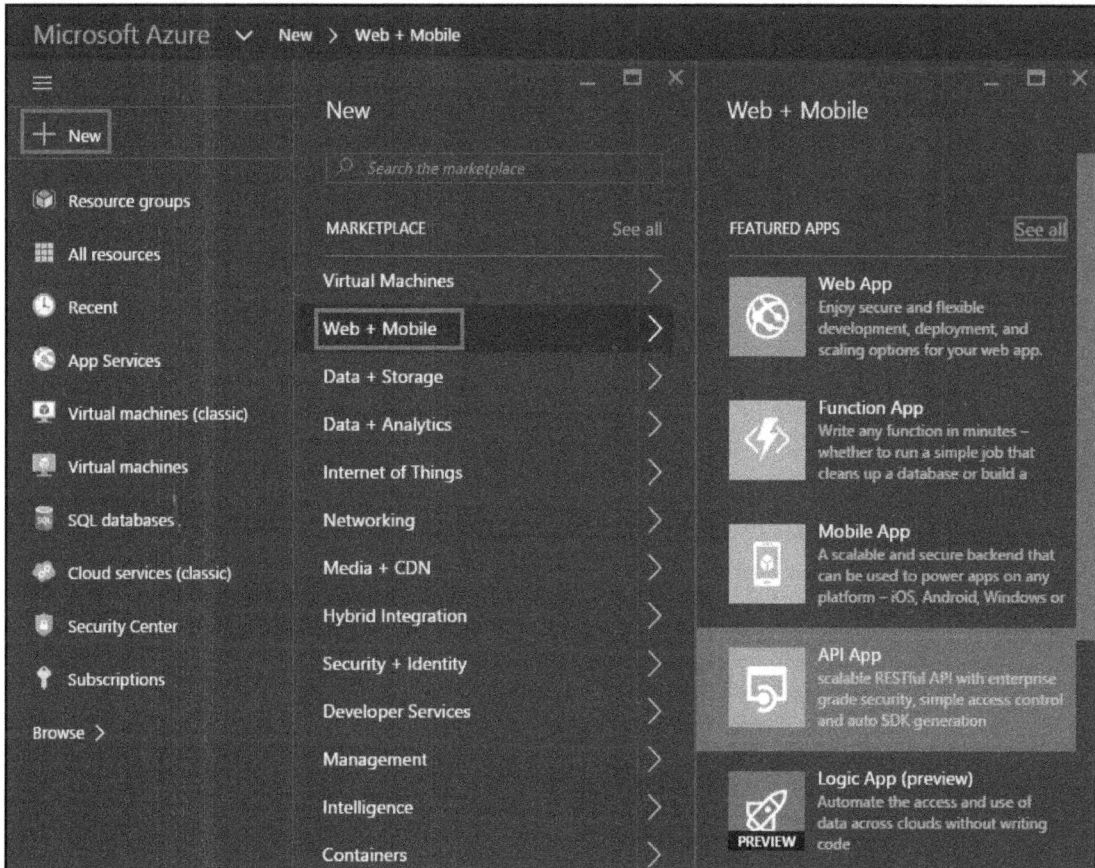

Enter a unique **App name** and then, in the **Resource Group** drop-down, click on **Create new** Then, in new Resource Group name, enter `NodejsAPIAppGroup` or another name if you prefer.

Now click on **App Service plan/Location** and then click on **Create New**.

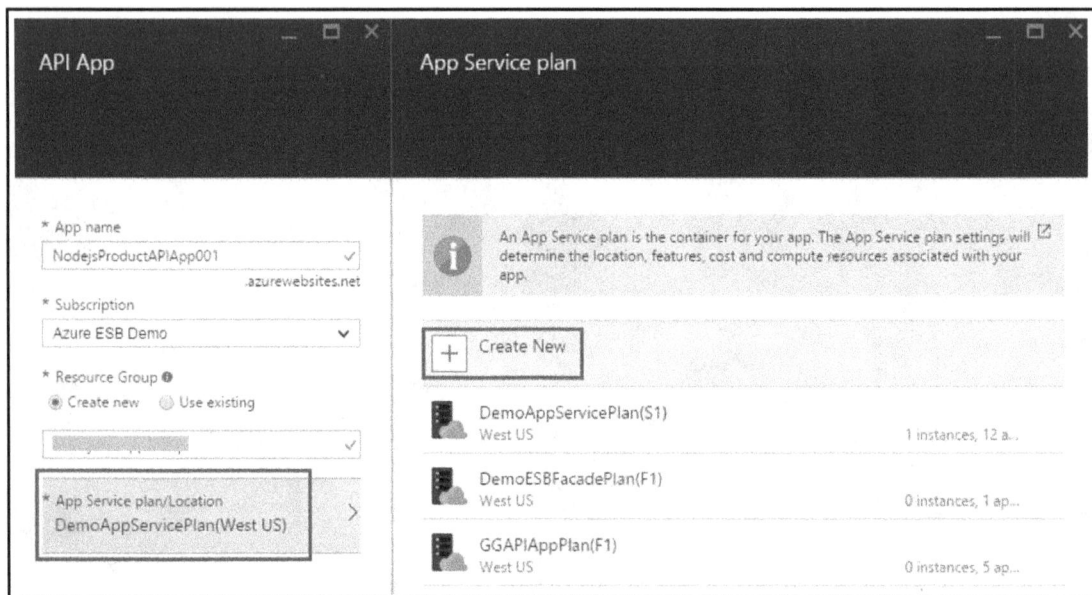

This would create a new **App Service plan** for the new Resource Group where your API App runs on. For example, if you choose the free tier, your API App runs on shared VMs, whereas for some paid tiers it runs on dedicated VMs.

In the **App Service plan** blade, enter `NodejsAPIAppPlan` or another name if you prefer, and in the **Location** drop-down list choose the location that is closest to you.

Now navigate to **Pricing tier** | **View All** | **F1 Free**. For this node API, the free pricing tier will provide sufficient performance. Refer to the following screenshot:

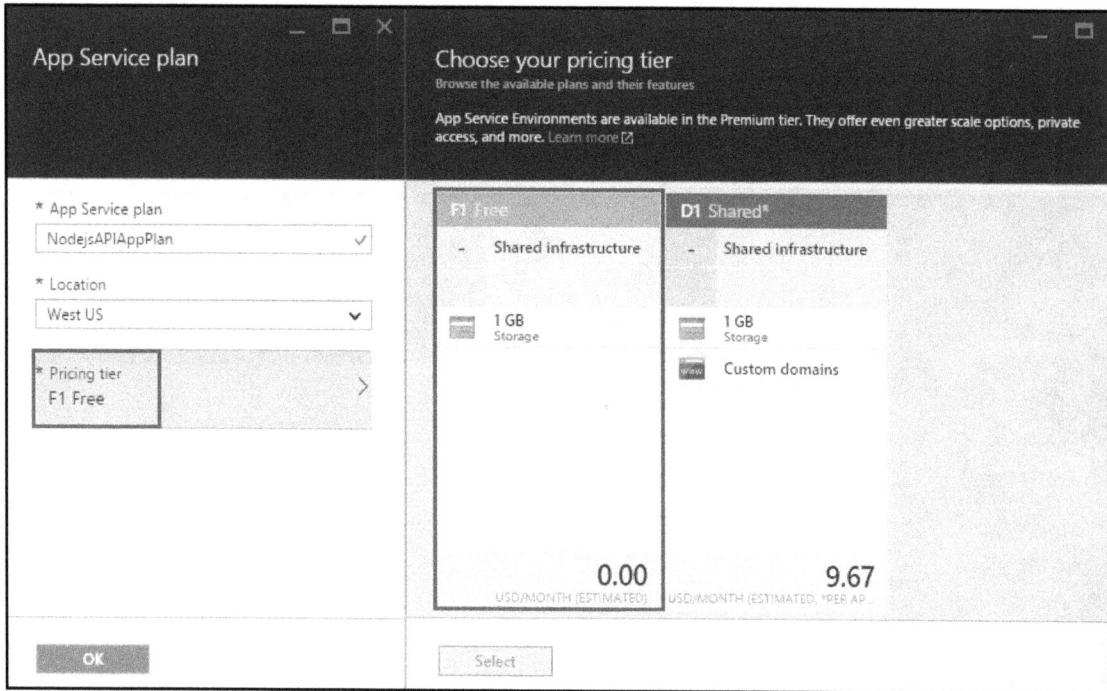

Now in the **App Service plan** blade, click on **OK** and then in the **API App** blade, click on **Create**.

Setting up the deployment source for your new API App

Now the node API App is created, we would set the Git repository in Azure App Service to deploy our node API code.

Navigate to **App Services** | {your API App} from the portal home page, which would display the **API App** and **Settings** blades. Then, in the **Settings** blade, scroll down to the **PUBLISHING** section and then click on **Deployment credentials**.

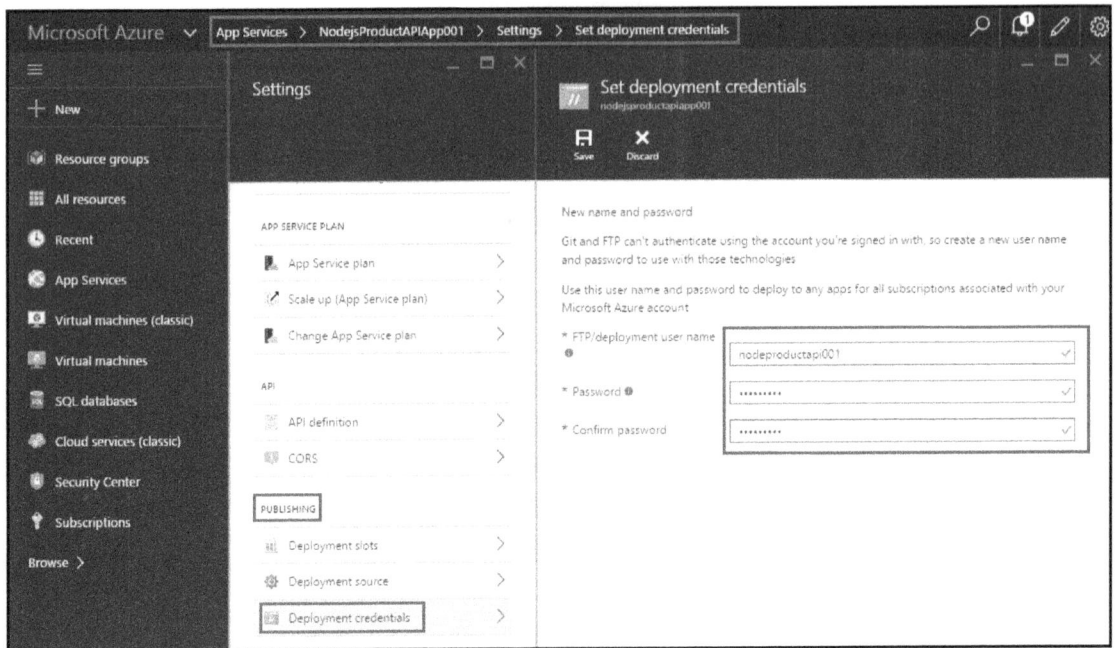

These credentials would be used in order to publish the Node.js code to the API App.

Now in the **Settings** blade, navigate to **Deployment source** | **Choose Source** | **Local Git Repository**, then click on **OK**.

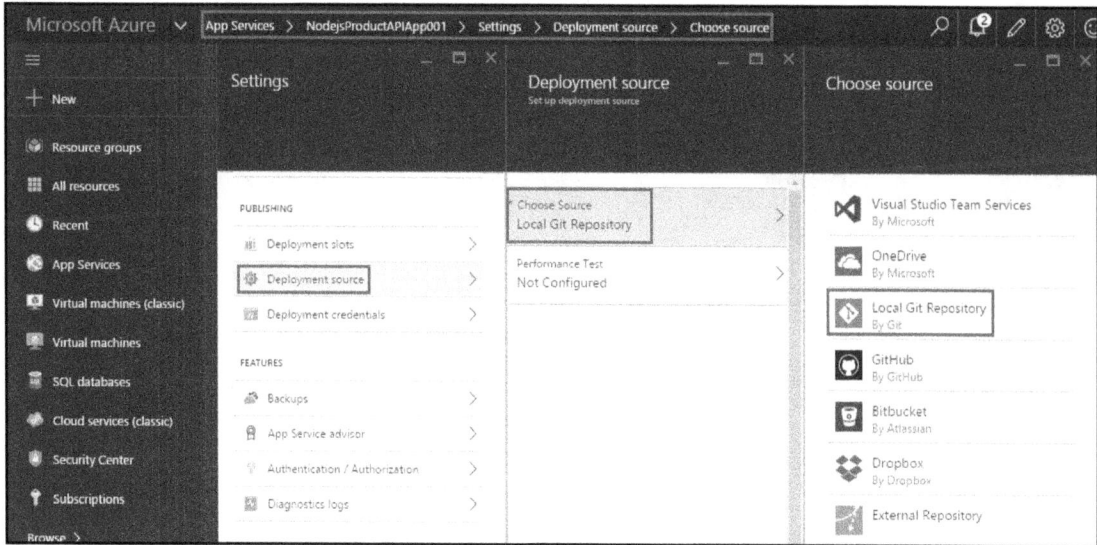

Once your Git repository has been created, you can check your active deployments, as shown later. Because the repository is new, you have no active deployments in the list.

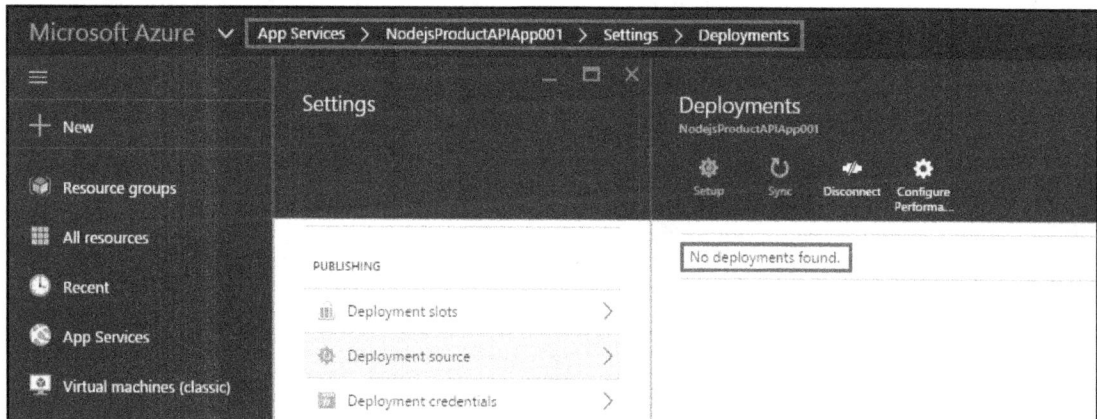

Navigate to the blade for your new API App and look at the **Essentials** section of the blade. Note the **Git clone url** in the **Essentials** section. When you hover over this URL, you see an icon on the right that will copy the URL to your clipboard. Click on this icon to copy the URL.

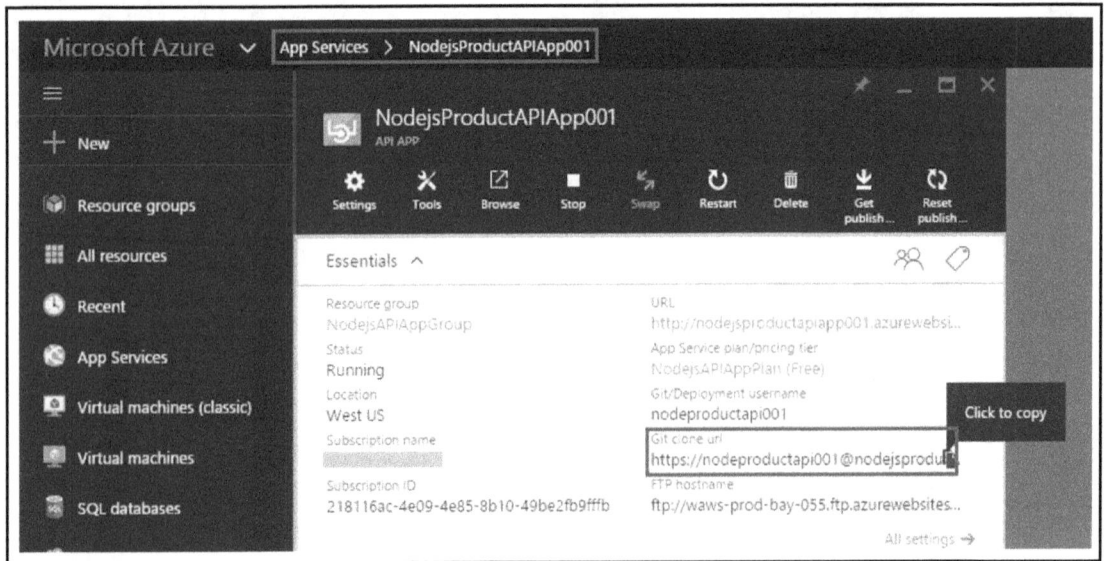

Now that you have an API App with a Git repository backing it up, you can push code into the repository to deploy the code to the API App.

Deploying Node.js API code to Azure

Now we would create a local Git repository that contains Node.js code for the API and then we will push the code from that repository to the repository in Azure that we created earlier.

Create a folder location to use it for a new local Git repository and copy your Node.js `ProductApi` code there.

Now in your command-line tool, navigate to the new folder, then execute the following command to create a new local GIT repository:

```
git init
```

Execute the following command to add a Git remote for your API App's repository:

```
git remote add azure YOUR_GIT_CLONE_URL_HERE
```

Replace the string `YOUR_GIT_CLONE_URL_HERE` with your own Git clone URL that you copied earlier.

Now execute the following commands to create a commit that contains all of your code:

```
git add
git commit -m "first version"
```

Now push the code to Azure by executing the following command:

```
git push azure master
```

When you're prompted for a password, enter the one that you created earlier in the Azure portal. This will now trigger a deployment to your API App.

Once the deployment has completed, the **Deployments** blade reflects the successful deployment of your code changes to your API App.

Now, again using the Postman, we will get the API running in Azure.

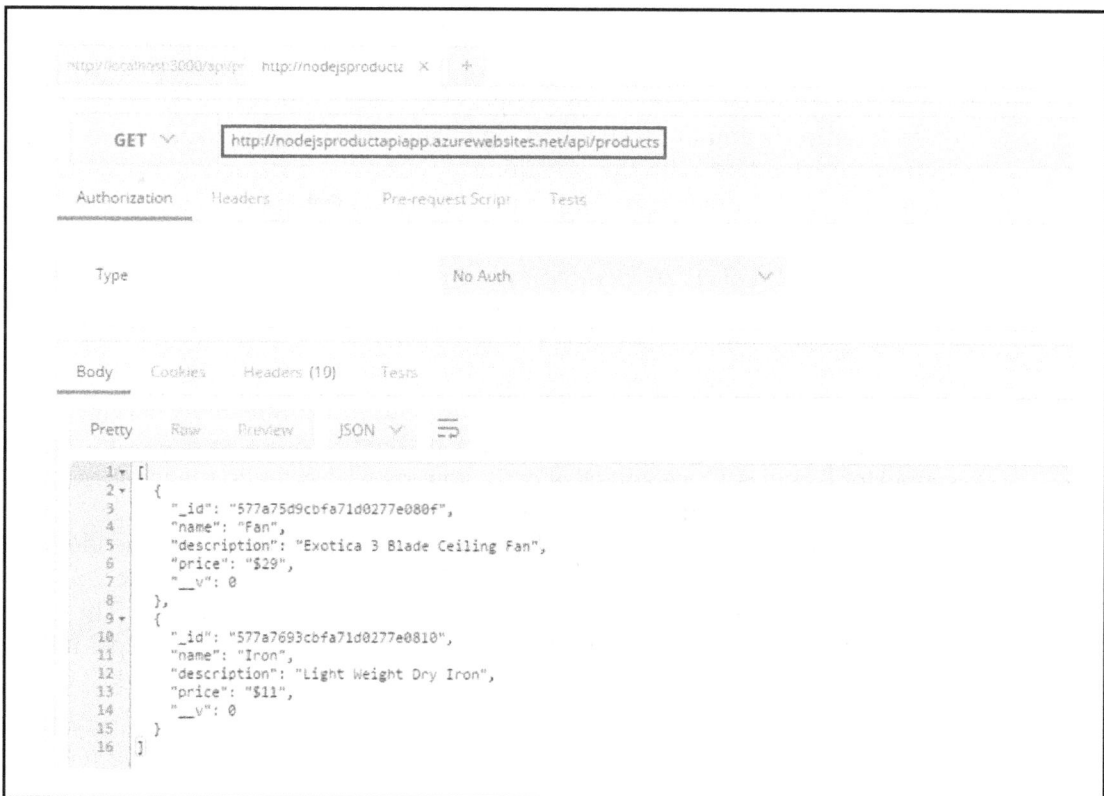

At this point, we have successfully created an API App and deployed Node.js API code to it. We also tested the API App using the Postman tool.

In the next section of this chapter, we will see the different ways to secure our API App in Azure.

Security

In this section, you will learn the various techniques used to implement security in Azure App Services. It offers services that implement the industry-renowned **OAuth 2.0** and **OpenID Connect** protocols and work with multiple identity providers. A quick definition of some of the terms used across this chapter are provided later for easier understanding.

- **Identity provider**: Services responsible for providing authentication tokens for users looking to interact with a system, for example, Facebook, Google, and Microsoft.
- **OAuth**: This is an open source protocol that allows users to share their private resources such as photos, videos, or contacts lists stored on a site to another site without having to hand out their password. For example, you sign up for a music streaming service, and it offers you an option to share your playlist with your friends. It redirects you to Facebook to log in and then you are asked if you want to share your friend list with the streaming service. You click on yes and then you are sent back to the music streaming service where you can now share your playlist with your friends.
- **OpenID Connect**: This is an identity layer on top of the OAuth 2.0 protocol. It allows clients to verify the identity of the user based on the authentication performed by an authorization server. Also, it can provide basic profile information about the end user using REST services. On the same lines as the earlier example, let's say you want to log in to your music streaming service where you are offered options to log in with an identity provider (for example, Facebook or Google). Once you click on it, you are redirected to the identity provider's site where you enter your credentials. After validating your credentials, you will be sent back to the music streaming service with the identity provider verifying your identity, and you will be able to log in to the site. OpenID is about authentication, whereas OAuth is about authorization. The difference is that OAuth is best suited for API authorization, whereas OpenID Connect is best for a single sign-on experience across multiple web Apps.

What is App Service authentication and authorization?

Azure App Service authentication and authorization is a feature that provides a way for you to restrict access to your app services. It requires no complex configuration or writing any code for implementation. Let's see how it works and manages to do this.

Authentication

For app services users to get authenticated, we can choose from a set of identity providers (Azure Active Directory, Facebook, Google, Microsoft Account, and Twitter), or we can implement our own custom authentication mechanism.

To get authenticated using one of the identity providers, you first need to configure the identity provider to know about your application. The identity provider will then provide with IDs and secrets that we provide to the App service. After this, the users can be directed to an endpoint that enables them to sign in.

In the case of service-to-service scenarios, App Service can protect your application using Azure Active Directory. The calling application needs to provide an Azure Active Directory service principal authorization token.

Authorization

You can authorize the incoming requests to allow them to reach your application only if they are authenticated. This will be enabled when you choose an identity provider from **Action to take when request is not authenticated** from the portal.

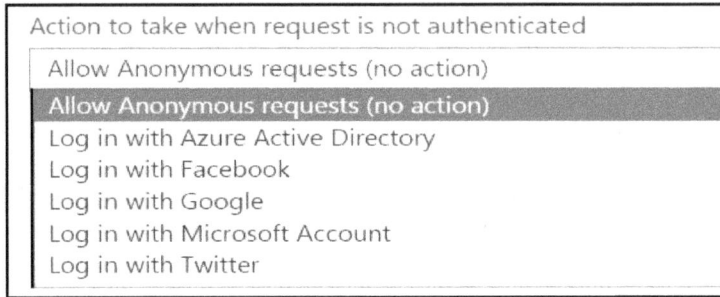

Action to take when request is not authenticated

Allow Anonymous requests (no action)
Allow Anonymous requests (no action)
Log in with Azure Active Directory
Log in with Facebook
Log in with Google
Log in with Microsoft Account
Log in with Twitter

You will choose **Allow Anonymous requests (no action)** when you want to defer the authorization decision to your code. This is done when applications have varying access restrictions for different parts of the application. In this case, the authentication information is provided in the headers of the requests.

> **TIP**
>
> A cookie will be set for the users who will interact with your application using a web browser. This will keep them authenticated as long as they browse the application. For a mobile client, the client SDK will create a JSON web token or JWT or in Azure Active Directory's case the access token is included as part of the authorization header. This is also named a bearer token.

App Service will validate any cookie or token that your application issues to authenticate users.

Scenario on Authenticating an API App and consuming the authenticated API App

In this example, we will see how to protect the Products API using AAD (Azure Active Directory).

1. Create an Azure Active Directory. Navigate to the Azure Classic Portal. Click on **Custom Create Directory:**

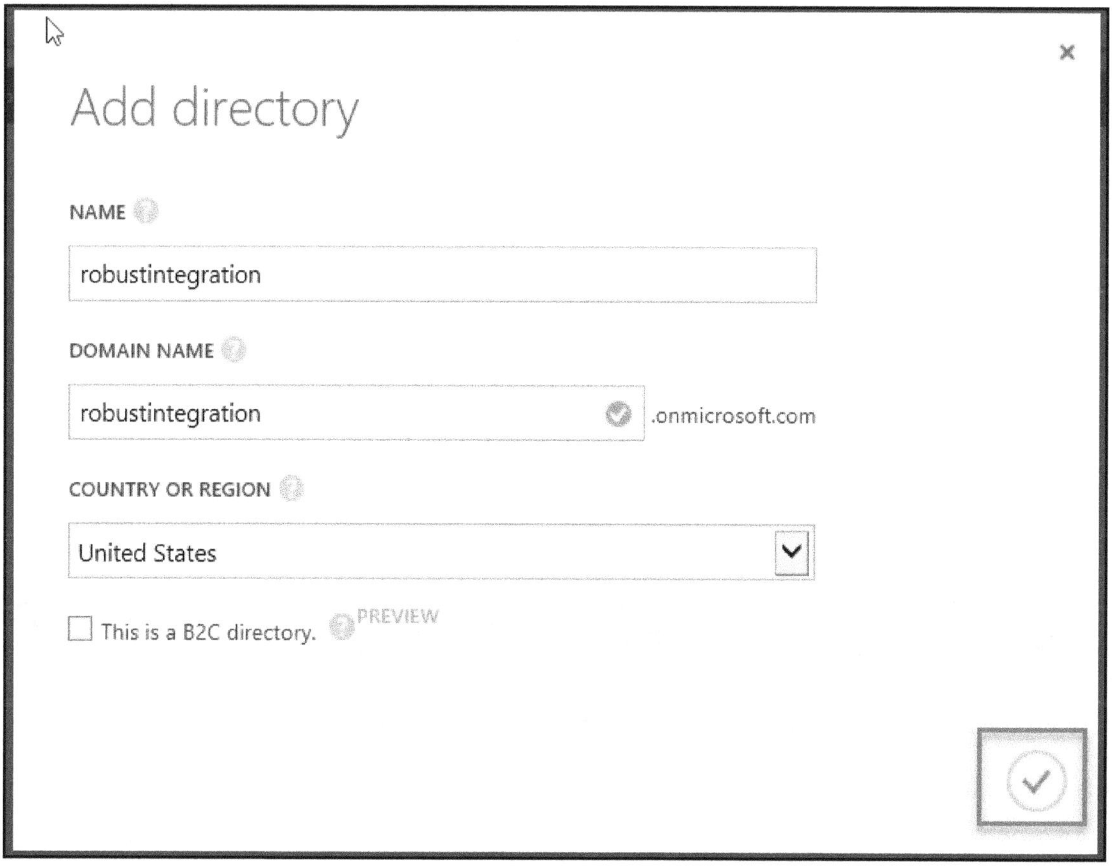

Add directory

NAME

> robustintegration

DOMAIN NAME

> robustintegration   .onmicrosoft.com

COUNTRY OR REGION

> United States

☐ This is a B2C directory. PREVIEW

2. Select your directory and then select the **APPLICATIONS** tab at the top. Click on **ADD** at the bottom to create a new app registration:

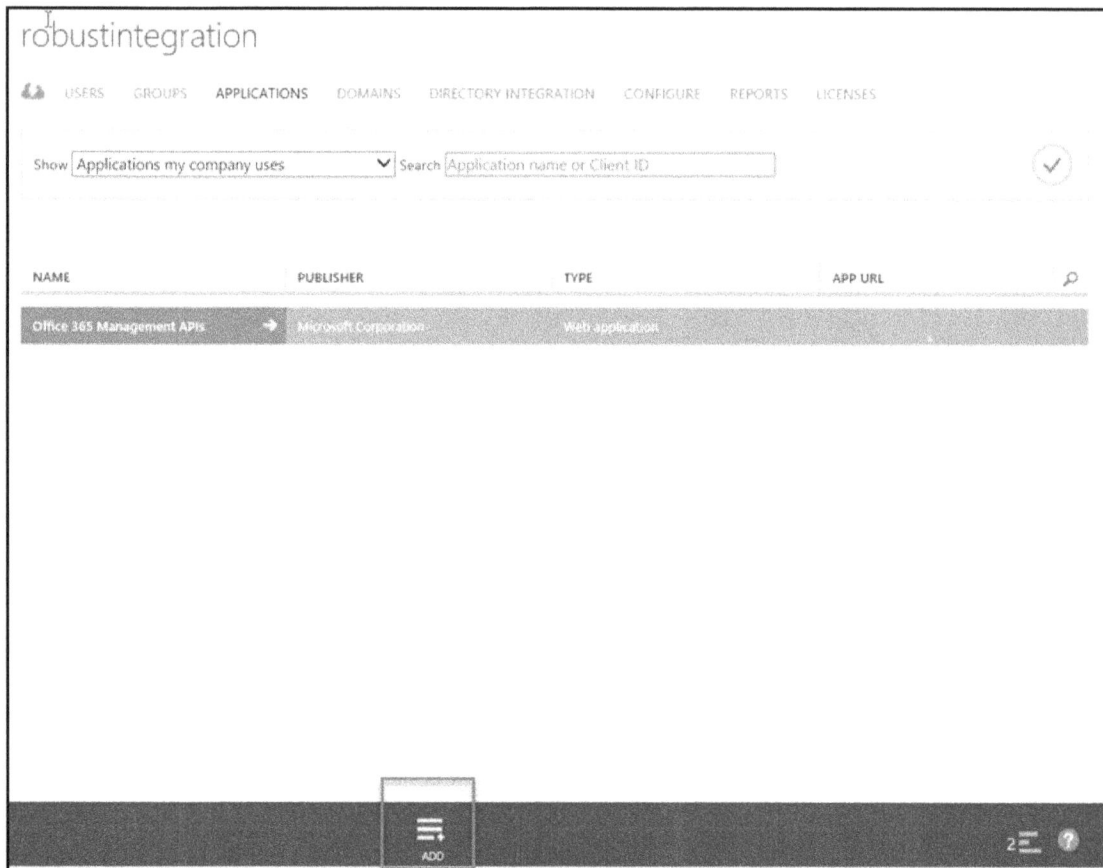

3. Click on **ADD APPLICATION** my organization is developing.

4. In the **ADD APPLICATION** Wizard, enter a **NAME** for your application, which is `ProductApi` in our case, and click on the **WEB APPLICATION AND/OR WEB API** type. Then, click to continue:

5. In the **SIGN-ON URL** box, paste the application URL you copied earlier. Enter that same URL in the**APP ID URI** box. Then, click to continue:

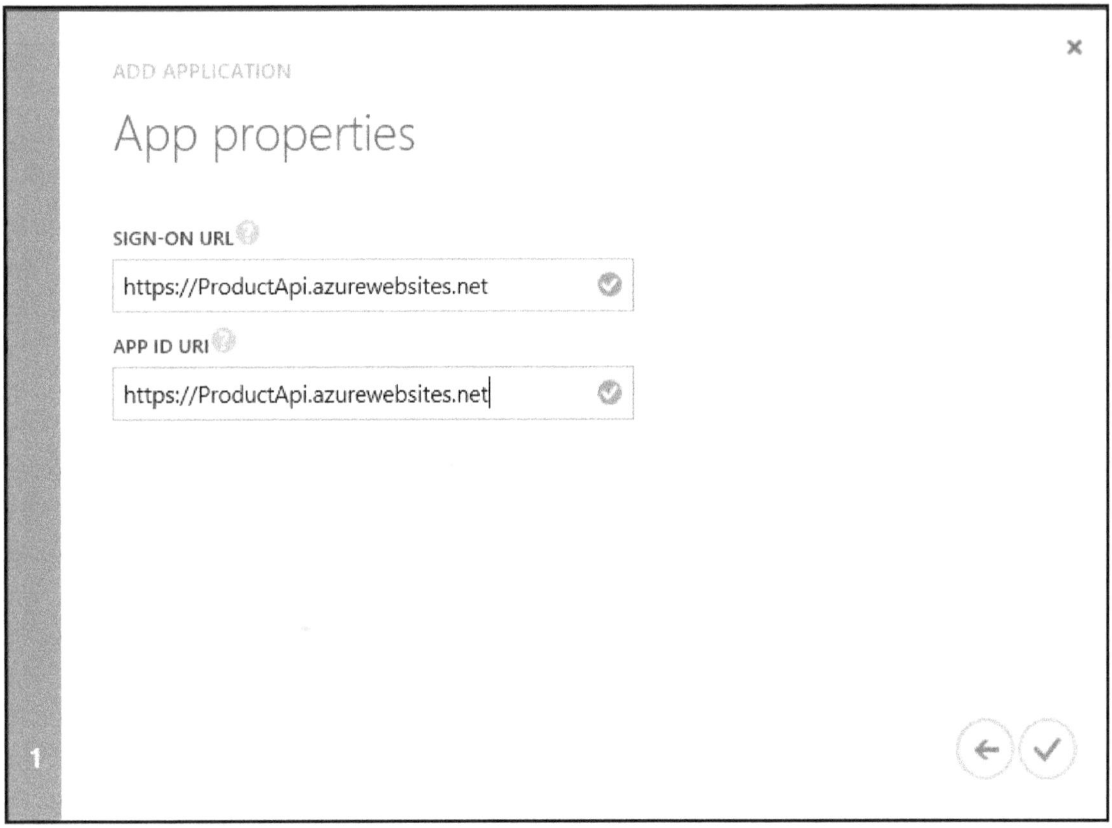

ADD APPLICATION

App properties

SIGN-ON URL

https://ProductApi.azurewebsites.net

APP ID URI

https://ProductApi.azurewebsites.net

Once the application has been added, click on the**Configure** tab. Edit the **REPLY URL** (this URL will let Azure AD return tokens to your Azure App like an API App) under **Single Sign-on** to be the URL of your application concatenated with the path, `/.auth/login/aad/callback`. For example, `https://ProductApi.azurewebsites.net/.auth/login/aad/callback`:

6. Click on **Save**. Then, copy the Client ID for the app. You will configure your application to use this later.

7. In the bottom command bar, click on **View Endpoints**, copy the Federation Metadata Document URL, and download that document or navigate to it in a browser. This document has a list of services that will be able to accept the security tokens issued by Azure Active Directory.

8. Within the root `EntityDescriptor` element, there should be an `entityID` attribute of the form `https://sts.windows.net/` followed by a GUID specific to your tenant (named `tenant ID`). Copy this value; it will serve as your **Issuer URL**. This is the URL that will uniquely identify your application. You will configure your application to use this later.

9. Add Azure Active Directory information to your application.

10. For the `ProductApi` that has been published, navigate to the settings and click on **Authentication/Authorization**.

11. If the **Authentication/Authorization** feature is not enabled, turn the switch to **On**:

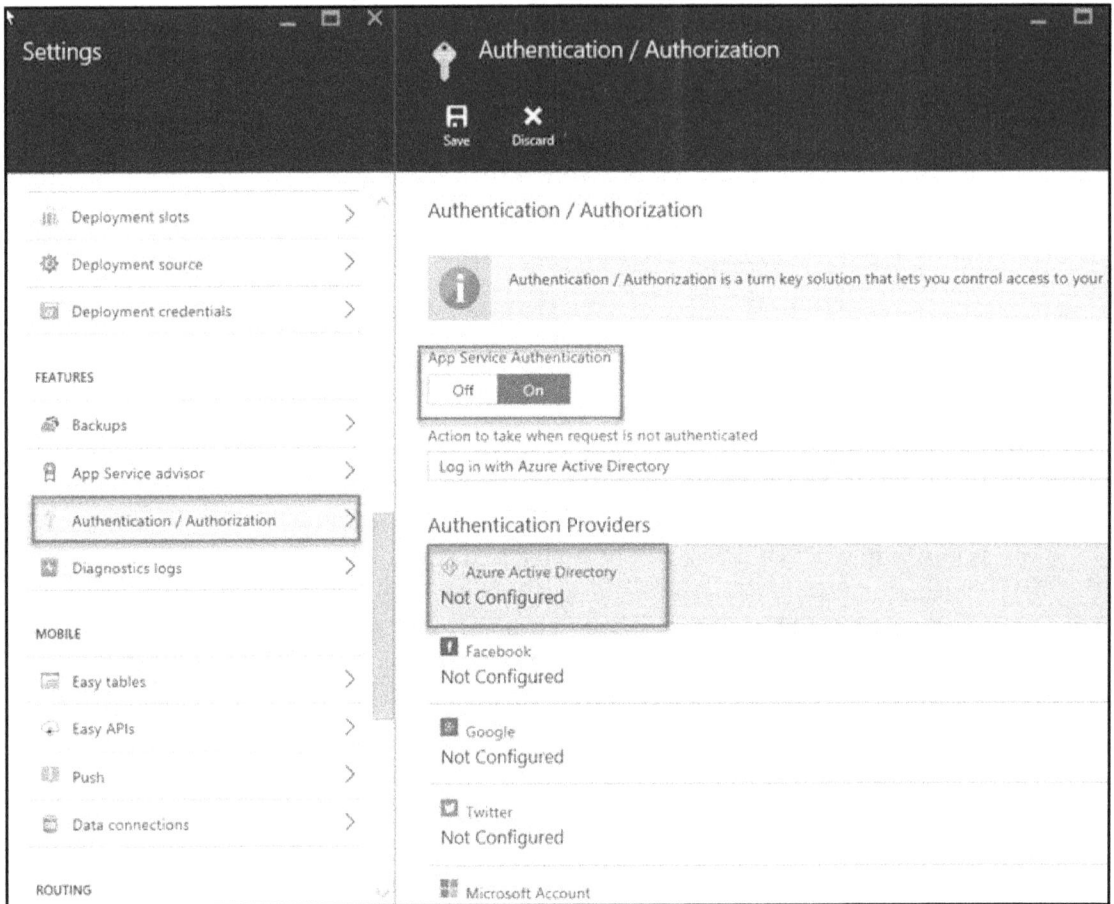

12. Click on **Azure Active Directory** and then click on **Advanced** under**Management Mode**. Paste in the **Client ID** and **Issuer URL** value, which you obtained previously. Then, click on **OK**.
    1. By default, App Service provides authentication but does not restrict authorized access to the site content and APIs. You must authorize users in your app code.

2. You should set the property **Action to take when request is not authenticated** to **Log in with Azure Active Directory** to **restrict access to only authenticated users**. This will make sure that all requests will be authenticated, and all unauthenticated requests are redirected to Azure Active Directory for authentication.

3. Click on **Save**.

13. You are now ready to use Azure Active Directory for authentication in your app.

14. After these steps, when we try to access the `ProductApi` from the browser, we are redirected to an authentication page for Azure Active Directory where we are asked to put in our credentials:

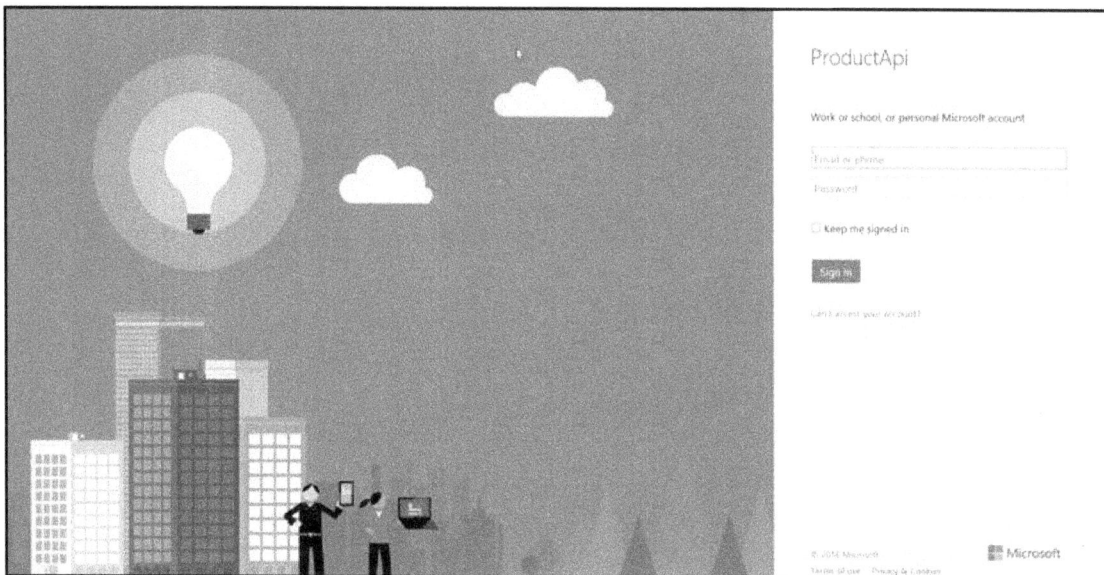

Now we will show how to consume this authenticated API. To do this, we will take the example of a native client application for Sunny Electricals, which is responsible for use by the customer service department. This application needs to access the ProductsApi to display the products.

1. In the Visual Studio solution for the app, we will add a reference to the Products API. To do so, we can select **REST API Client**:

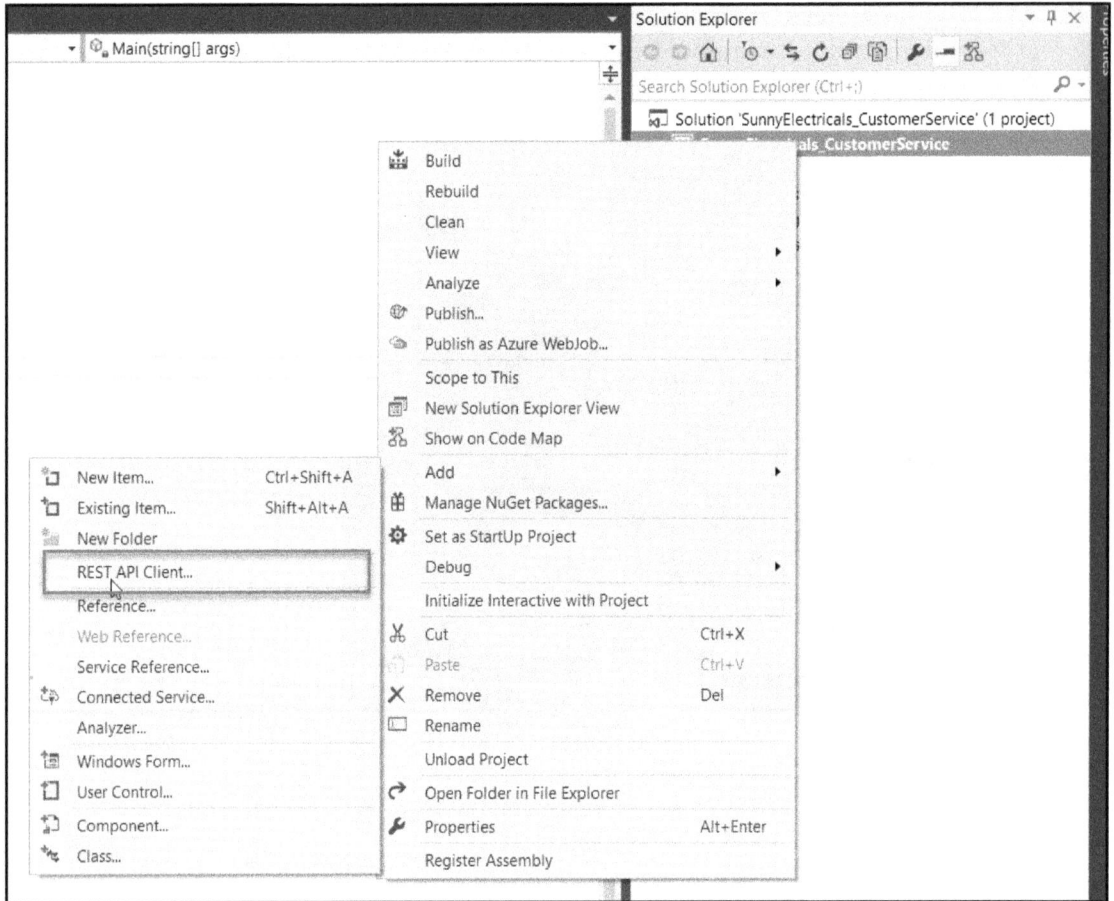

2. After this, download the Swagger metadata file for the `ProductsApi` by browsing the following URL on Internet Explorer, `https://ProductsApi.azurewebsites.net/swagger/docs/v1`, or you can provide the **Swagger Url** in the window:

3. This will install the Nuget package `Microsoft.Rest.ClientRuntime` to add Azure API App and creates the following folder:

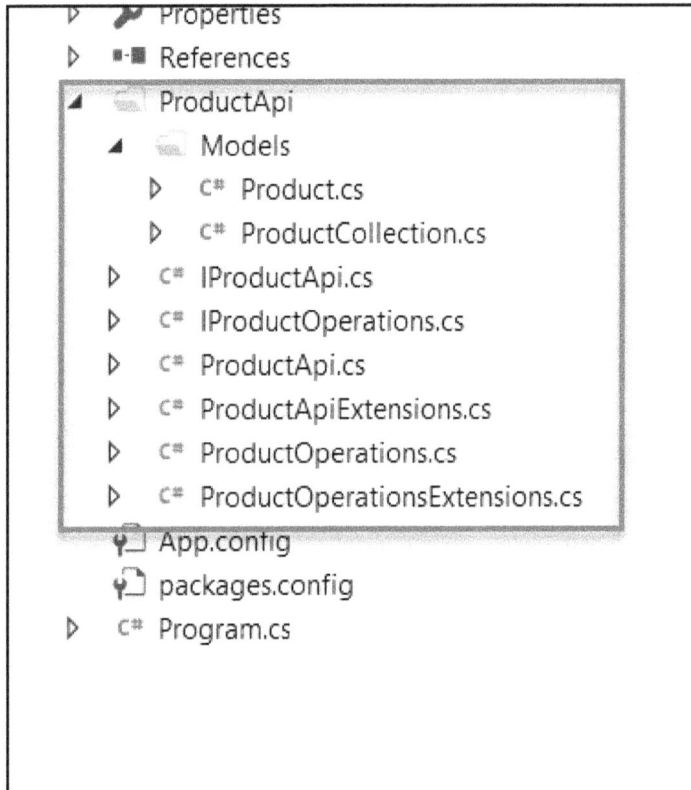

```
▷  🔧 Properties
▷  ▪-▪ References
▲  📁 ProductApi
   ▲  📁 Models
      ▷  C# Product.cs
      ▷  C# ProductCollection.cs
   ▷  C# IProductApi.cs
   ▷  C# IProductOperations.cs
   ▷  C# ProductApi.cs
   ▷  C# ProductApiExtensions.cs
   ▷  C# ProductOperations.cs
   ▷  C# ProductOperationsExtensions.cs
   📄 App.config
   📄 packages.config
▷  C# Program.cs
```

4. Now we have to log in to the Azure Classic Portal and add the new `CustomerServices` application to the Active Directoryy that we have created. Note that we are creating this app as a **NATIVE CLIENT APPLICATION**:

ADD APPLICATION

Tell us about your application

NAME

SunnyElectricals_CustomerService

Type

○ WEB APPLICATION AND/OR WEB API

◉ NATIVE CLIENT APPLICATION

→

2

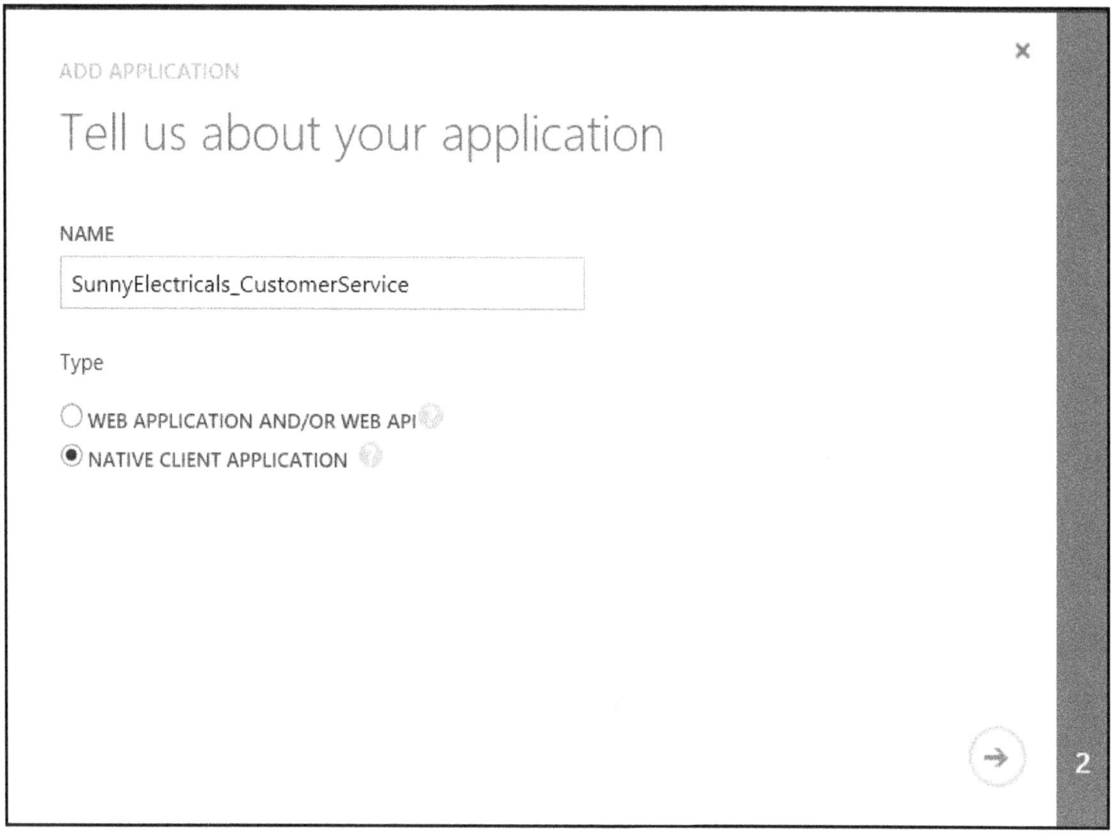

5. Then, we have to provide the **REDIRECT URI**, which can be anything related to the business objective:

6. From the Configure page, copy the Client ID and the REDIRECT URI for this application. Also, from the portal, we need to get the following parameters: Authority – From the **Active Directory Applications** tab, click on the **View Endpoints** button and copy the value for **OATH2.0 AUTHORIZATION ENDPOINT**:

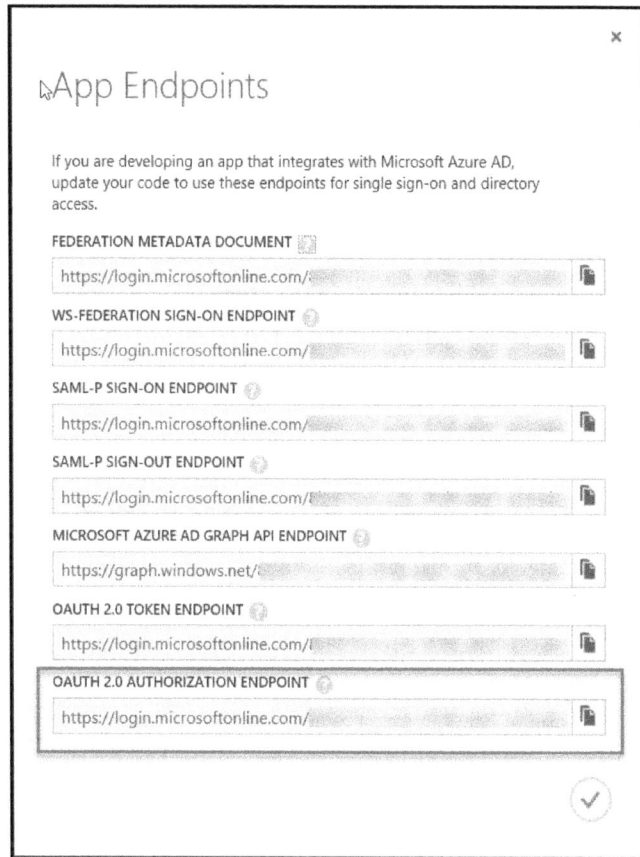

7. At this stage, you should have the following pieces of information:
   - The authority, resource, or URL of the API you are consuming
   - The Client ID of your client application
   - The secret of your client application from the Azure Portal

8. In the Visual Studio solution, add the Nuget Package: **Microsoft.IdentityModel.Clients.ActiveDirectory**. This will add the binaries for Active Directory Authentication Language, which we will be using to authenticate our request against the API:

NuGet Package Manager: SunnyElectricals_CustomerService

Package source: nuget.org ⚙

Microsoft.IdentityModel.Clients.ActiveDirectory

Version: Latest stable 3.12.0   ▼ | Install |

⌄ **Options**

Description

This package contains the binaries of the Active Directory Authentication Library (ADAL). ADAL provides a Portable Class Library with easy to use authentication functionality for your .NET client on various platforms including Windows desktop, Windows Store, Xamarin iOS and Xamarin Android by taking advantage of Windows Server Active Directory and Azure Active Directory.

Version:	3.12.0
Author(s):	Microsoft Corporation
License:	http://go.microsoft.com/fwlink/?LinkId=317295
Date published:	Monday, July 11, 2016 (7/11/2016)
Project URL:	http://go.microsoft.com/fwlink/?LinkId=258232
Report Abuse:	https://www.nuget.org/packages/Microsoft.IdentityModel.Clients.ActiveDirectory/3.12.0/ReportAbuse
Tags:	Active, Directory, Authentication, Library, ADAL, Azure, AD, AAD, Identity, .NET, Windows, Store, Xamarin, Android, iOS

Dependencies

.NETStandard,Version=v1.4
System.Runtime (> = 4.1.0)
System.Collections (> = 4.0.11)
System.Threading.Tasks (> = 4.0.11)

---

9. The following is the code where the client application passes its credentials to get a token from the Azure Active Directory. If the user is not already signed in, then the ADAL library will launch a sign-in page for the user to sign in. This can be maintained by the `PromptBehavior` property. You can have the user login every time he wants to access the API. Once authenticated successfully, a security token is issued to access the API:

```
string authority = "https://login.microsoftonline.com/8                     /oauth2/authorize";
string resource = "https://ProductAPI.azurewebsites.net";
string clientId = "                                      ";
var clientcred = new ClientCredential(clientId, "                                      ");

AuthenticationContext context = new AuthenticationContext(authority, false);
AuthenticationResult authenticationResult =
    context.AcquireTokenAsync(resource, clientId,
    new Uri("http://sunnyelectricalscustomerservice/client"), new PlatformParameters(PromptBehavior.Auto)).Result;
var client = new ProductApi();
client.HttpClient.DefaultRequestHeaders.Authorization = new
    System.Net.Http.Headers.AuthenticationHeaderValue("Bearer", authenticationResult.AccessToken);
```

Please note that the communication is happening over HTTPS to ensure that the bearer token is not visible in the HTTP header over the network.

10. After calling the API from the application, we see the same list of products from the API that we saw earlier in the chapter:

```
Fan - Exotica 3 Blade Ceiling Fan - $29
Iron - Light Weight Dry Iron - $11
```

On the similar lines, there are many other options that can be implemented to harden the API App as follows:

- **Disabling browser access**: This can be done by changing to **REPLY URL** to not point the Api App's URL
- **Restricting access to only a particular client**: This can be done by imposing restrictions to receive connections only from a particular service principal
- Using your own authentication method
- **Using the API Management Service**: This is defined in the next chapter

ADAL can also be used with iOS-, Android-, and Xamarin-based apps.

Summary

In this chapter, we discussed what an API App is, the benefits of API Apps, and how to develop API Apps using Visual Studio. We also discussed how easily we can host and secure our API in Azure. We will carry out the concept of API App throughout this book as this is a foundational exercise for the next-generation integration. In the next chapter, we will be discussing Azure API Management.

4
What is Azure API Management?

In the previous chapters, we have discussed what integration is in the new world of cloud computing and taken a look at how we can start building these integrations through the use of an Azure App Service plan and API Apps.

In order to understand how this applies more readily to an enterprise, it is important to know how to control and manage API assets that exist or are built as part of any enterprise development.

Typically, modern APIs are used to achieve one of the following two outcomes:

- To expose the on-premises line of business applications, such as **Customer Relationship Management (CRM)** or **Enterprise Resource Planning (ERP)** solutions to other applications that need to consume and interact with these enterprise assets both on-premises and in the cloud
- To provide access to the API for commercial purposes to monetize access to the assets exposed by the API

The latter use case is important as it allows organizations to extend the use of their API investment, and it has led to what has become known as the **API economy**.

The API economy provides a mechanism to gain additional value from data contained within the organizational boundary whether that data exists in the cloud or on-premises.

When providing access to information via an API, two considerations are important:

- **Compliance**: This ensures that access to the API and the use of the API meets requirements around internal or legal policies and procedures, and it provides reporting and auditing information
- **Governance**: This ensures the API is accessed and used only by those authorized to do so, and in a way that is controlled and if necessary metered, and provides reporting and auditing information, which can be used, for example, to provide usage information for billing

In order to achieve this at scale in an organization, a tool is required that can be used to apply both compliance and governance structures to an exposed endpoint. This is required to ensure that the usage of the information behind that endpoint is limited only to those who should be allowed access and only in a way that meets the requirements and policies of the organization. This is where API Management plays a significant role.

There are two main types of tools that fit within the landscape that broadly fall under the banner of API Management:

- **API Management**: These tools provide the compliance and governance control required to ensure that the exposed API is used appropriately and data presented in the correct format. For example, a message may be received in XML format, but the consuming service may need the data in JSON format. They can also provide monitoring tools and access control that allows organizations to gain insight into the use of the API, perhaps with the view to charge a fee for access.
- **API Gateway**: These tools provide the same or similar level of management as normal API Management tools, but often include other functionality that allows some message mediation and message orchestration thereby allowing more complex interactions and business processes to be modeled, exposed, and governed.

Microsoft Azure API Management falls under the first category above whilst Logic Apps, which are described in detail in subsequent chapters, when combined with Azure API Management provides the capabilities (and more) that API Gateways offer.

Another important aspect of providing management of APIs is creating documentation that can be used by consumers, so they know how to interact with, and get the best out of, the API.

For APIs, generally, it is not a case of *build it and they will come*, so some form of documentation that includes endpoint and operation information, along with sample code, can lead to greater uptake of usage of the API.

Azure API Management is currently offered in three tiers: **Developer**, **Standard**, and **Premium**. The details associated with these tiers at the time of writing are shown in the following table:

	Developer	Standard	Premium
API Calls (per unit)	32 K / day (~1 M / month)	7 M / day (~217 M / / month)	32 M / day (~1 B / month)
Data Transfer (per unit)	161 MB / day (~5 GB / month)	32 GB / day (~1 TB / / month)	161 GB / day (~5 TB / month)
Cache	10 MB	1 GB	5 GB
Scale-out	N/A	4 units	Unlimited
SLA	N/A	99.9%	99.95%
Multi-Region Deployment	N/A	N/A	Yes
Azure Active Directory Integration	Unlimited user accounts	N/A	Unlimited user accounts
VPN	Yes	N/A	Yes

Key items of note in the table are Scale-out, Multi-Region Deployment, and Azure Active Directory Integration.

- **Scale-out**: This defines how many instances, or units, of the API instance are possible; this is configured through the Azure Classic Portal
- **Multi-Region Deployment**: When using Premium tier, it is possible to deploy the API Management instance to many locations to provided geographically distributed load
- **Azure Active Directory Integration**: If an organization synchronizes an on-premises Active Directory domain to Azure, access to the API endpoints can be configured to use Azure Active Directory to provide same sign-on capabilities

The main use case for Premium tier is if an organization has many hundreds or even thousands of APIs they want to expose to developers, or in cases where scale and integration with line of business APIs is critical.

The anatomy of Azure API Management

To understand how to get the best out of an API, it is important to understand some terms that are used for APIs and within Azure API Management, and these are described here.

API and operations

An API provides an abstraction layer through an endpoint that allows interaction with entities or processes that would otherwise be difficult to consume.

Most API developers favor using a RESTful approach to API applications since this allows us easy understanding on how to work with the operations that the API exposes and provides scalability, modifiability, reliability, and performance. **Representational State Transfer (REST)** is an architectural style that was introduced by Roy Fielding in his doctoral thesis in 2000: (`http://www.ics.uci.edu/~fielding/pubs/dissertation/rest_arch_style.htm`).

Typically, modern APIs are exposed using HTTP since this makes it easier for different types of clients to interact with it, and this increased interoperability provides the greatest opportunity to offer additional value and greater adoption across different technology stacks.

When building an API, a set of methods or operations is exposed that a user can interact with in a predictable way. While RESTful services do not have to use HTTP as a transfer method, nearly all modern APIs do, since the HTTP standard is well known to most developers, and it is simple and straightforward to use. Since the operations are called via HTTP, a distinct endpoint or **Unified Resource Identifier (URI)** is required to ensure sufficient modularity of the API service.

When calling an endpoint, which may for example represent, an entity in a line of business system, HTTP verbs (GET, POST, PUT, and DELETE, for example) are used to provide a standard way of interacting with the object.

An example of how these verbs are used by a developer to interact with an entity is given in the following table:

TYPE	GET	POST	PUT	DELETE
Collection	Retrieve a list of entities and their URIs	Create a new entity in the collection	Replace (update) a collection	Delete the entire collection
Entity	Retrieve a specific entity and its information usually in a particular data format	Create a new entity in the collection, not generally used	Replace (update) an entity in the collection, or if it does not exist, create it	Delete a specific entity from a collection

When passing data to and receiving data from an API operation, the data needs to be encapsulated in a specific format. When services and entities were exposed through SOAP-based services, this data format was typically XML. For modern APIs, **JavaScript Object Notation (JSON)** has become the norm. JSON has become the format of choice since it has a smaller payload than XML and a smaller processing overhead, which suits the limited needs of mobile devices (often running on battery power). JavaScript (as the acronym JSON implies) also has good support for processing and generating JSON, and this suits developers, who can leverage existing toolsets and knowledge.

API operations should abstract small amounts of work to be efficient, and in order to provide scalability, they should be stateless, and they can be scaled independently. Furthermore, PUT and DELETE operations must be created that ensure consistent state regardless of how many times the specific operation is performed, this leads to the need of those operations being **idempotent**.

> Idempotency describes an operation that when performed multiple times produces the same result on the object that is being operated on. This is an important concept in computing, particularly, where you cannot guarantee that an operation will only be performed once, such as with interactions over the Internet.

Another outcome of using a URI to expose entities is that the operation is easily modified and versioned because any new version can simply be made available on a different URI, and because HTTP is used as a transport mechanism, endpoint calls can be cached to provide better performance and HTTP Headers can be used to provide additional information, for example security.

By default, when an instance of API Management is provisioned, it has a single API already available named **Echo API**. This has the following operations:

- Creating resource
- Modifying resource

- Removing resource
- Retrieving header only
- Retrieving resource
- Retrieving resource (cached)

In order to get some understanding of how objects are connected, this API can be used, and some information is given in the next section.

Objects within API Management

Within Azure API Management, there are a number of key objects that help define a structure and provide the governance, compliance, and security artifacts required to get the best out of a deployed API, as shown in the following diagram:

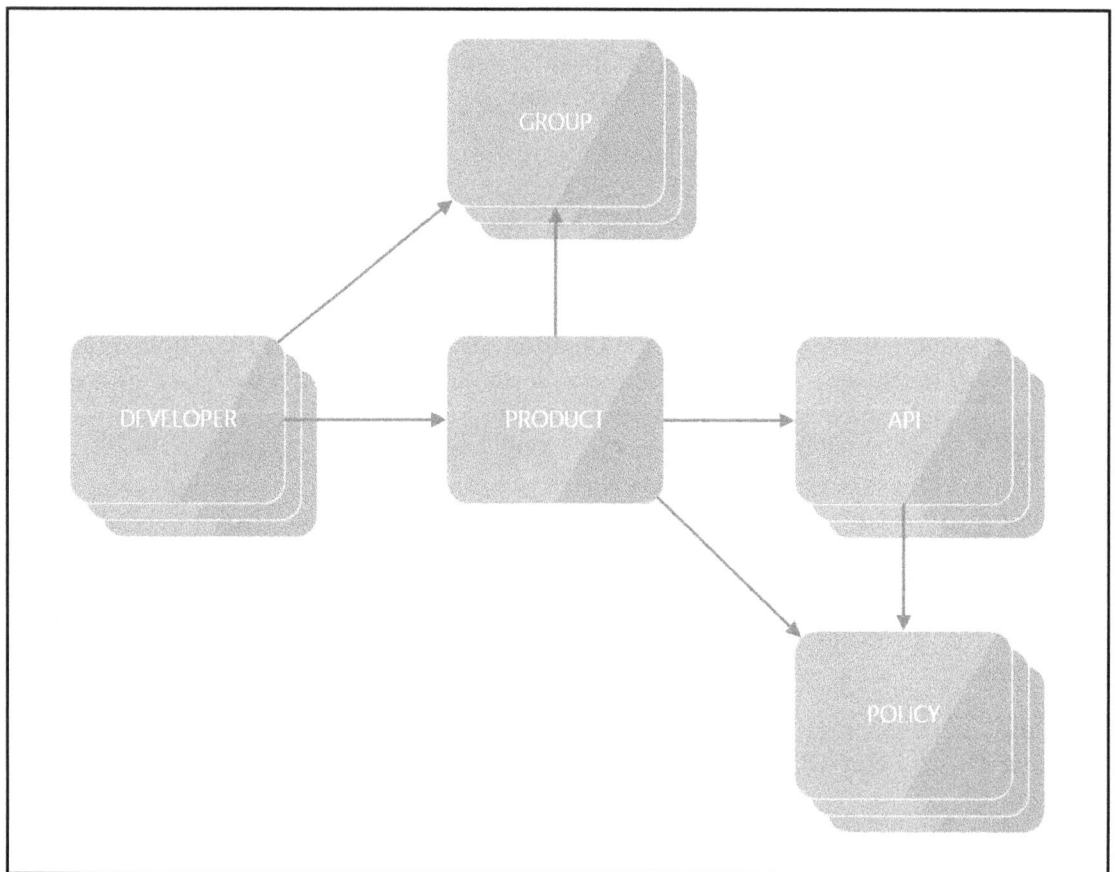

As can be seen, the most important object is a **PRODUCT**. A **PRODUCT** has a title and description and is used to define a set of **API** that are exposed to **DEVELOPER** for consumption. They can be **open** or **protected**, with an open product being publicly available and a protected product requiring a subscription once published.

GROUP provides a mechanism to organize the visibility of and access to the **API** within a **PRODUCT** to the development community wishing to consume the exposed **API**. By default, a product has three standard groups that cannot be deleted:

- **Administrators**: Subscription administrators are included by default, and the members of this group manage API service instances, API creation, API policies, operations, and products
- **Developers**: The members of this group have authenticated access to the **Developer portal**; they are the developers who have chosen to build applications that consume APIs exposed as a specific product
- **Guests**: Guests are able to browse **Products** through the **Developer portal** and examine documentation, and they have read-only access to information about the products

In addition to these built-in groups, it is possible to create new groups as required, including the use of groups within an Azure Active Directory tenant, which is discussed later in the chapter.

When a new instance of API Management is provisioned, it has the following two products already configured:

- **Starter**: This product limits subscribers to a maximum of five calls per minute up to a maximum of 100 calls per week
- **Unlimited**: This product has no limits on use, but subscribers can only use it with the administrator's approval

Both of these products are protected, meaning that they need to be subscribed to and published. They can be used to help gain some understanding of how the objects within API Management interact.

These products are configured with a number of sample policies that can be used to provide a starting point.

Azure API Management policies

API Management Policies are the mechanism used to provide governance structures around the API. They can define, for instance, the number of call requests allowed within a period, **cross-origin resource sharing (CORS)**, or certificate authentication to a service backend.

Policies are defined using XML and can be stored in source control to provide active management.

Policies are discussed in greater detail later in the chapter.

Working with Azure API Management

Azure API Management is the outcome of the acquisition by Microsoft of **Apiphany**, and as such it has its own management interfaces. Therefore, it has a slightly different *look and feel* to the standard Azure Portal content.

The **Developer portal** and **Publisher portal** are described in detail in this section, but first a new instance of API Management is required.

Once created (and the provisioning in the Azure infrastructure can take some time), most interactions take place through the **Developer portal** and **Publisher portal**.

Creating your first Azure API Management instance

Azure API Management is accessed via the Classic Portal:

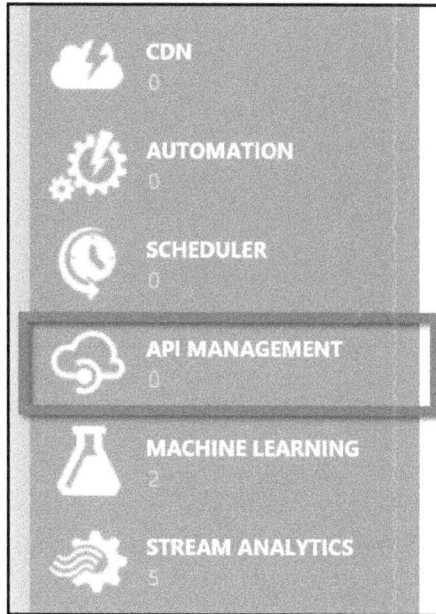

The creation of an instance is straightforward and follows three steps via a wizard:

1. Enter the **URL**, which has to be globally unique and choose the **SUBSCRIPTION** and the **REGION**.

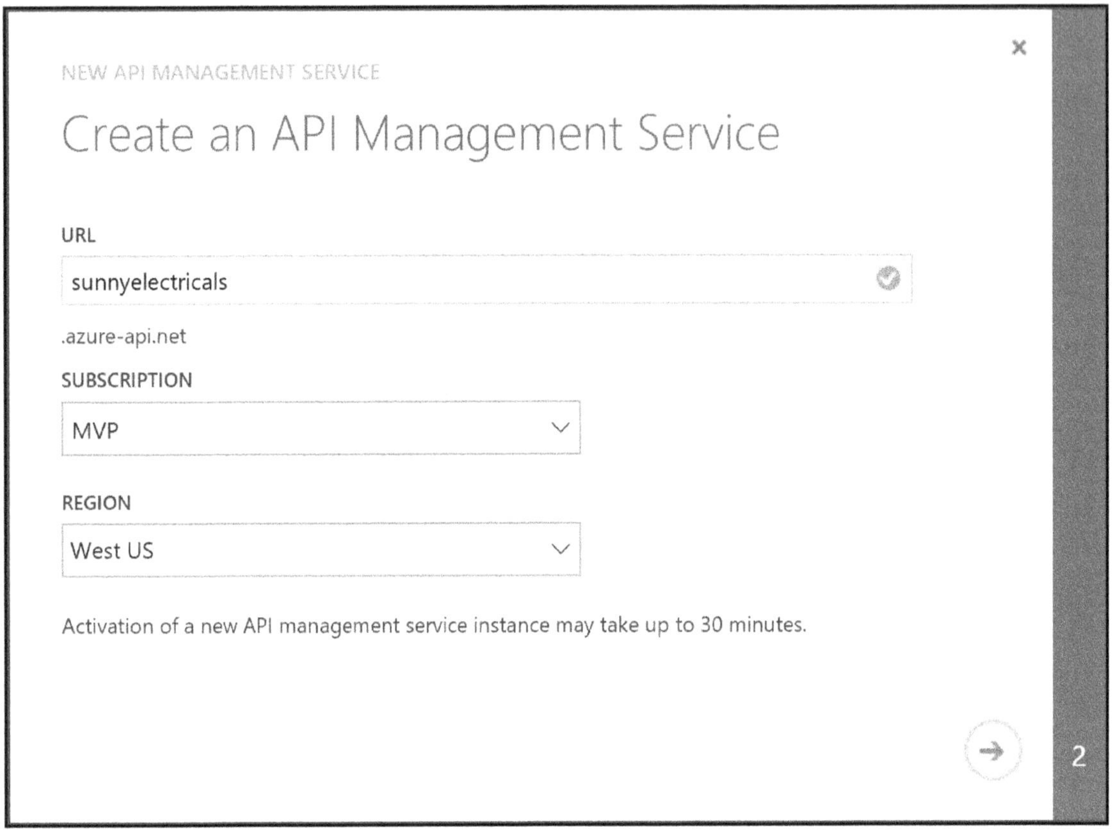

NEW API MANAGEMENT SERVICE

Create an API Management Service

URL

sunnyelectricals

.azure-api.net

SUBSCRIPTION

MVP

REGION

West US

Activation of a new API management service instance may take up to 30 minutes.

2

2. Enter an **ORGANIZATION NAME**, which appears on the portals, and an **ADMINISTRATOR E-MAIL** address to which alerts and requests for access are sent. By default, a developer instance is created, to choose either Standard or Premium, click on the **ADVANCED SETTINGS** checkbox that provides access to the third page in the wizard. At the time of writing, a developer instance is free, but has limited capabilities.

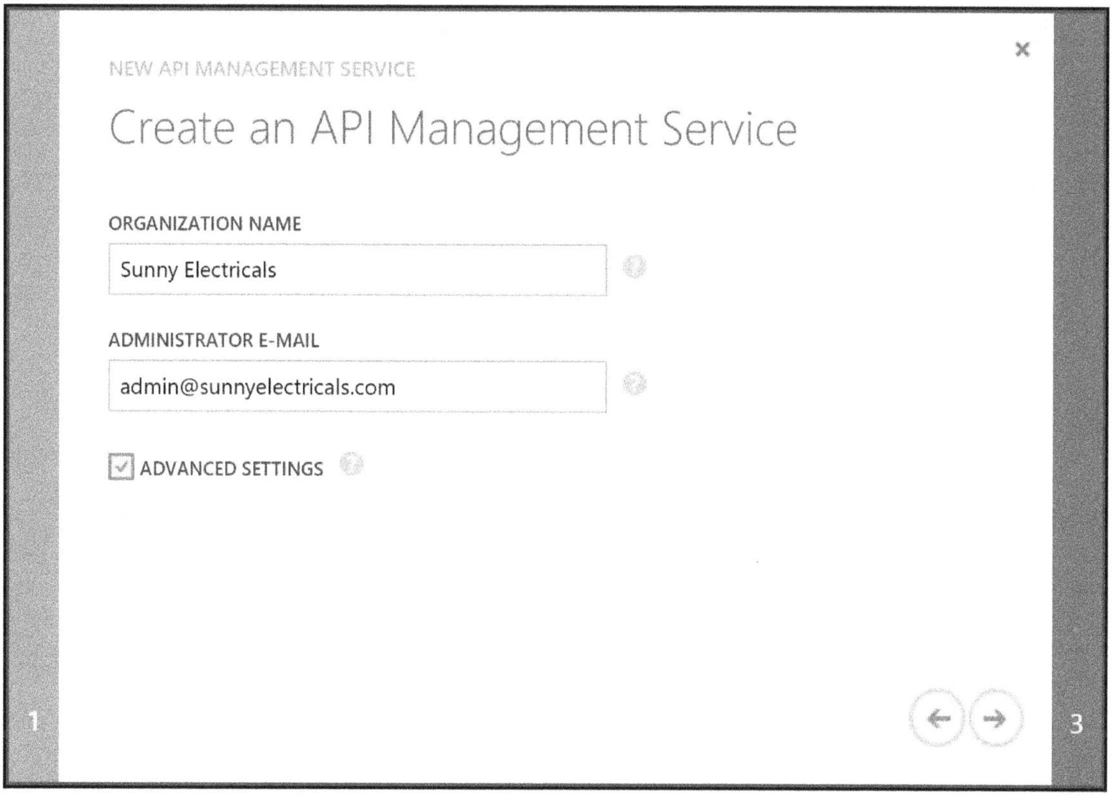

NEW API MANAGEMENT SERVICE

Create an API Management Service

ORGANIZATION NAME

Sunny Electricals

ADMINISTRATOR E-MAIL

admin@sunnyelectricals.com

☑ ADVANCED SETTINGS

1   3

3. Finally, choose the pricing tier required from **Developer**, **Standard**, or **Premium**.

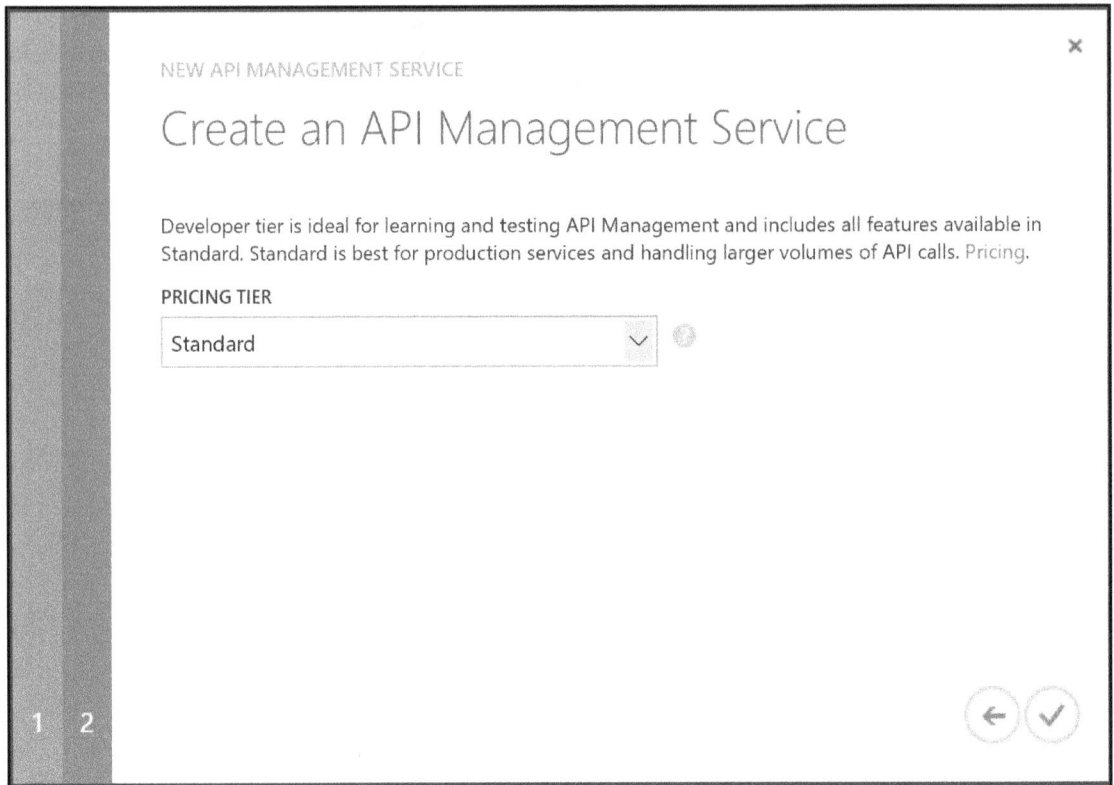

After completing the wizard, the instance is provisioned. Once complete, the instance scale and pricing tier can be configured within the Classic Portal, along with DNS names and VPN connections.

All other management tasks are handled through the **Publisher portal**, which is accessed by clicking on the **MANAGE** link, while the **Developer portal** is accessed via the **BROWSE** link.

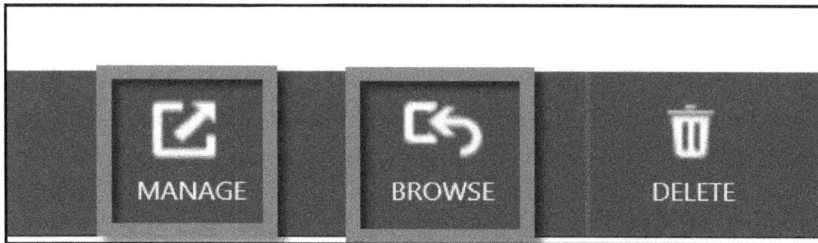

Publisher portal and Developer portal

There are two portals that allow interaction with an API Management instance, each of which has a different audience.

The **Publisher portal** is used by administrators to manage the instance and to configure and manage the **Developer portal**, including writing content such as blog entries that can be viewed by the development community. This is discussed in more detail in a later section.

The **Developer portal** is used by developers to browse the published APIs, look at documentation, and subscribe to published APIs. It can also be used to try out APIs through an interactive interface and view usage information. It is the main utility for developers and as such can be used to provide not only information about the APIs but also other information that could be of use to the development community.

Importing the API definition through the Publisher portal

It is possible to add an API definition manually, including defining endpoints and operations, but it is much simpler to import your API definition through the **Publisher portal**:

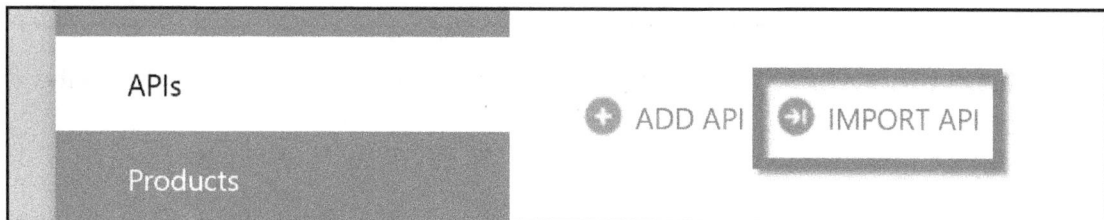

There are a number of ways to achieve this:

- **From clipboard**: This allows pasting the API definition into a text box
- **From file**: This allows browsing for the API definition from a file location
- **From URL**: This allows the entry of a web URL that contains the API definition

Azure API Management supports API definitions provided either as **WADL** or **Swagger**.

Both Swagger 1.2 and 2.0 are supported.

The **Web API URL suffix** text box is important as this defines how the API appears to the outside world.

Azure API Management does not expose the raw URL of the imported API, but instead provides a URL in the following format:

```
http(s)://<APIM Instance Name>.azure-api.net/<Web API Suffix>
```

It is this URL that developers wishing to consume the service use to access the API operations:

Once imported, the API has a number of settings that can be configured, the most important of which is how security is to be applied. Securing your backend APIs is discussed in detail later in the chapter. However, it is important to consider how developer access is controlled and maintained.

Managing user access rights for Products and APIs

User access is provided at the product level, with products being a container for APIs.

As mentioned earlier in the chapter, there are three default groups that define access to and visibility of **Products**:

- **Administrators**
- **Developers**
- **Guests**

New groups can be added that can be applied to new products to allow the customized tailoring of functionality through policies that are scoped at the product level.

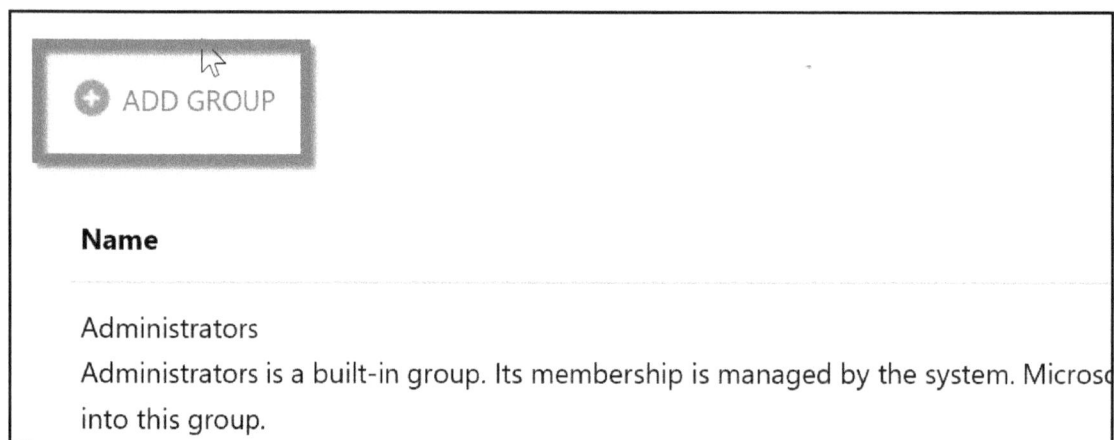

Users can be manually added or invited to products as required using the **Publisher portal**.

When developers visit the **Developer portal**, they can log in if they have previously signed up for an API Management account and can then request access if they have not already done so. If they have not signed up, they can do so by filling in a form. The sign up process uses multifactor authentication for additional security. An e-mail is sent (based on one of the e-mail templates within the **Publisher portal**) that contains a verification link to finalize sign up process:

Once logged in, developers are able to try out APIs and subscribe to products. To subscribe to a product, the developer needs to click on the **Subscribe** button under the relevant product.

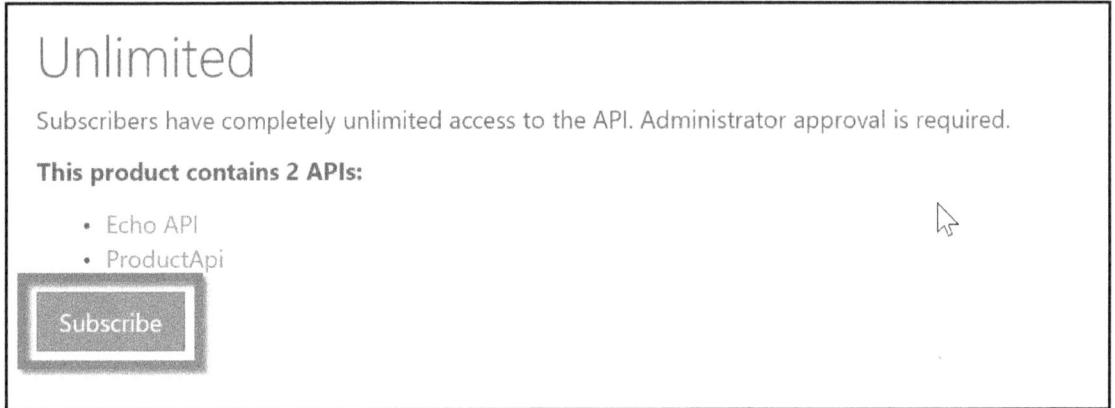

When a developer requests access through the **Developer portal**, their entry may be controlled through an approval workflow that requires an administrator to explicitly grant access, based on the setup of the product.

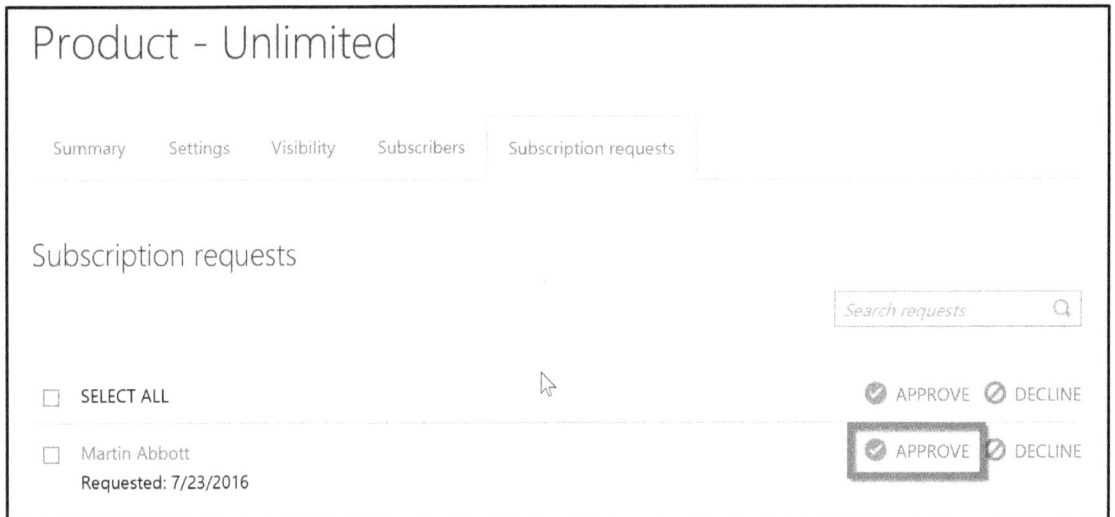

Once approved, the developer can access their subscription keys through their profile on the **Developer portal**.

This approach to security allows fine-grained control over access to products, with the product functionality being further controlled through the use of policies.

Once a developer has been granted access to the APIs managed by Azure API Management, they are able to build applications that consume them. Once built, the portal allows developers to publish and promote their applications for other developers to use.

In order to provide a good experience for developers, the **Developer portal** is highly customizable, and this is now discussed in more detail in following sections.

Customizing the developer experience

The **Developer portal** is essentially the shopfront for your organization's APIs and as such can be tailored to meet the specific needs of the target developer community.

Customizing the experience for developers is managed through both the **Publisher portal** and the **Developer portal**. The experience is familiar to anyone with the experience of content management systems.

Page layouts can be changed, including full branding of a site using different fonts and images that are accessible via a web URL. It is possible to upload media to the API Management instance for use within the **Developer portal**.

Pages can be added and removed as necessary, including full customization of how and where products are displayed to the developers.

The content management system contains a rich set of parameters that can be used as placeholders within the page structure and layout. They are replaced when a developer visits the **Developer portal**, for example, developer name and product lists.

Since the portal is just an HTML site, it is possible to include additional external controls and widgets that allow further customization.

For this example, we will change the title of the landing page, add an image, create a new menu item linking to some pages, and add a discussion and comments board.

Updating the title of the landing page and adding an image to the title bar is performed within the **Publisher portal**.

In order to add an image, it first needs to be uploaded to the **Media Library** within the instance.

First, we need to create a folder and then upload the image to that folder. Once uploaded, the link to the image can be copied by right-clicking the filename link that is part of the thumbnail information.

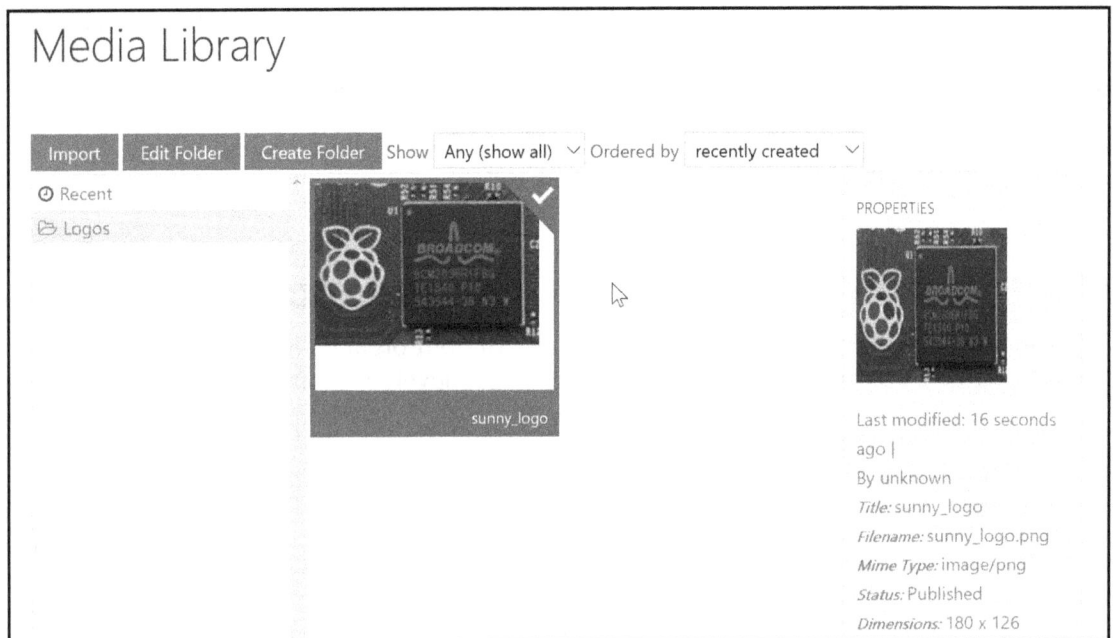

To add the image to the page and amend the title, we need to update one of the widgets on the page. Widgets are added to the areas of the screen that contain content, such as header and footer, and these can be amended as required. For instance, using an HTML widget for page content allows the content of that area to be specified using simple HTML and inline styling.

There are a number of widgets that quickly allow content to be added to a page; for example, Recent Blog Posts or Menus.

Pages within the portal are made up of a set of layers. By default, there are two layers-one for a **Regular page** that applies to each page within the **Developer portal** and one that has additional content specifically for the **Home page**.

Because we want to have the title on each page amended, we need to update the **Regular page** content; in this case, within the **Header** widget.

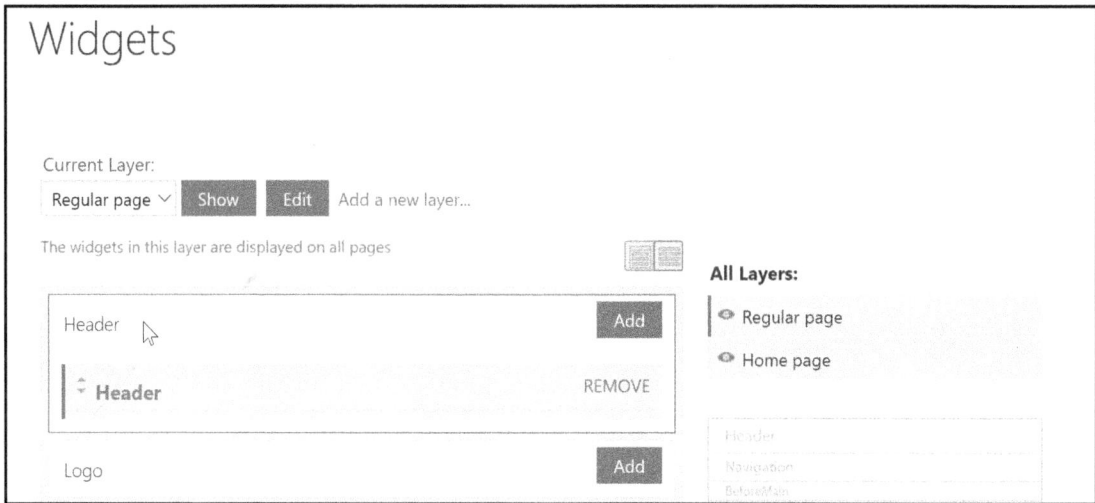

As the **Header** is an HTML widget, we can simply update the HTML with the link to the image we uploaded and update the title.

```
Body (HTML)
1   <h1>
2   <img src="https://apimgmtst0hanvkojeqwtkbq.blob.core.windows.net/content/MediaLibrary/Logos/sunny_logo.png">  
3   Sunny Electricals API Catalog
4   </h1>
```

Next, we will add a new menu to the site. In this case, the menu will contain a link to two blogs that have been created for the site. Blogs are created within the **Publisher portal** under the **Blog** link.

To create a new menu, we need to click on the Navigation side menu link and then the **Add a new menu...** link.

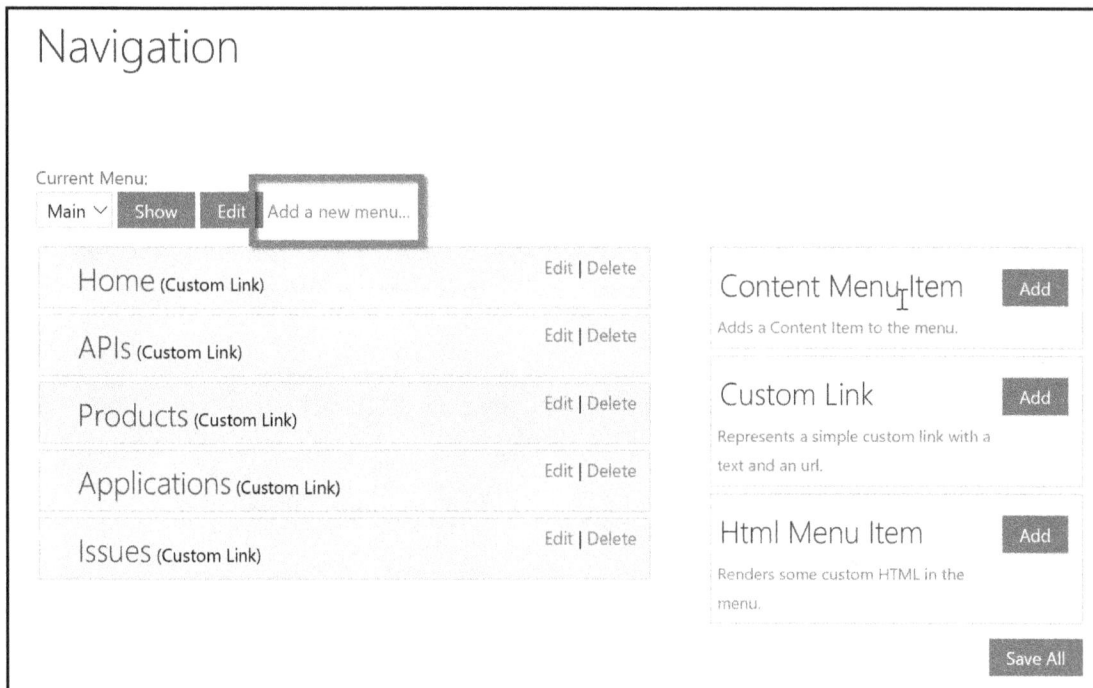

Navigation

Current Menu:

Main ∨ | Show | Edit | Add a new menu...

Home (Custom Link)	Edit | Delete
APIs (Custom Link)	Edit | Delete
Products (Custom Link)	Edit | Delete
Applications (Custom Link)	Edit | Delete
Issues (Custom Link)	Edit | Delete

Content Menu Item | Add
Adds a Content Item to the menu.

Custom Link | Add
Represents a simple custom link with a text and an url.

Html Menu Item | Add
Renders some custom HTML in the menu.

Save All

We created two blogs-one for APIs and one for Applications (not shown earlier but via the **Blog** menu item), and in order for these to appear in the menu, we need to add a custom link for each giving both the text and the URL to the blog.

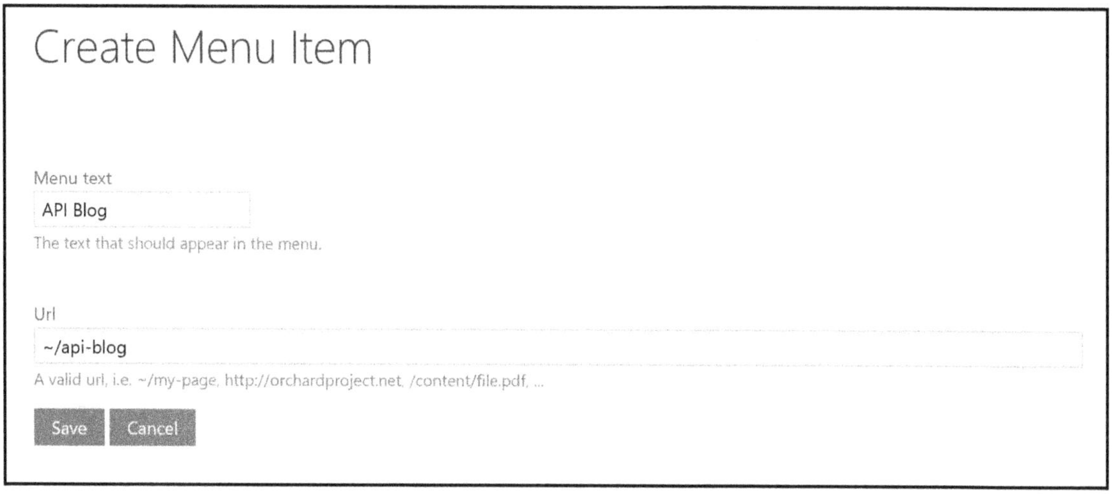

Create Menu Item

Menu text

API Blog

The text that should appear in the menu.

Url

~/api-blog

A valid url, i.e. ~/my-page, http://orchardproject.net, /content/file.pdf, ...

Save   Cancel

Once complete, we have our new menu that can now be applied to one of the layers within the pages of the **Developer portal**.

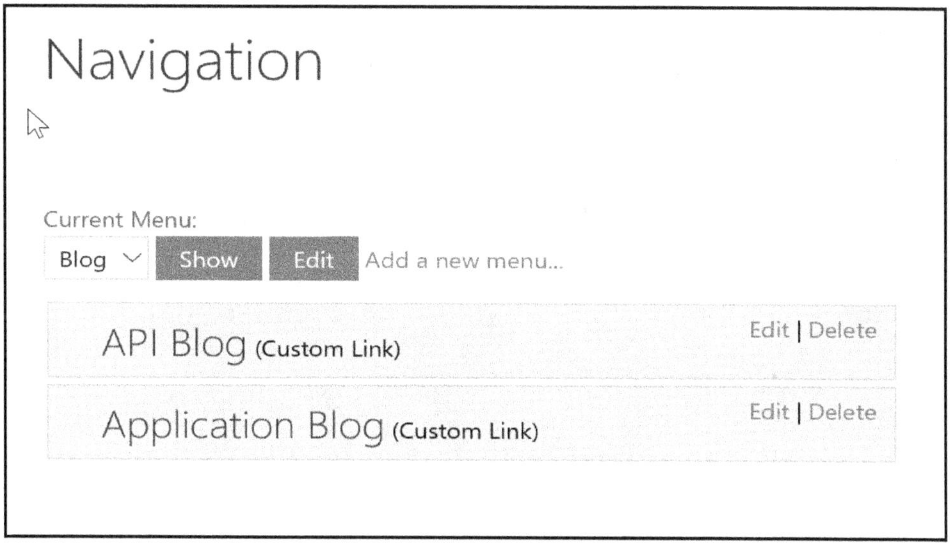

Navigation

Current Menu:

Blog ∨   Show   Edit   Add a new menu...

API Blog (Custom Link)   Edit | Delete

Application Blog (Custom Link)   Edit | Delete

We will add the menu to the **Regular page** layer so that it appears on every page. Within the **Regular page** layer, there is a **Navigation** widget containing the main site navigation. We will add the new menu widget with a position of 2, which means that it will appear after the main menu.

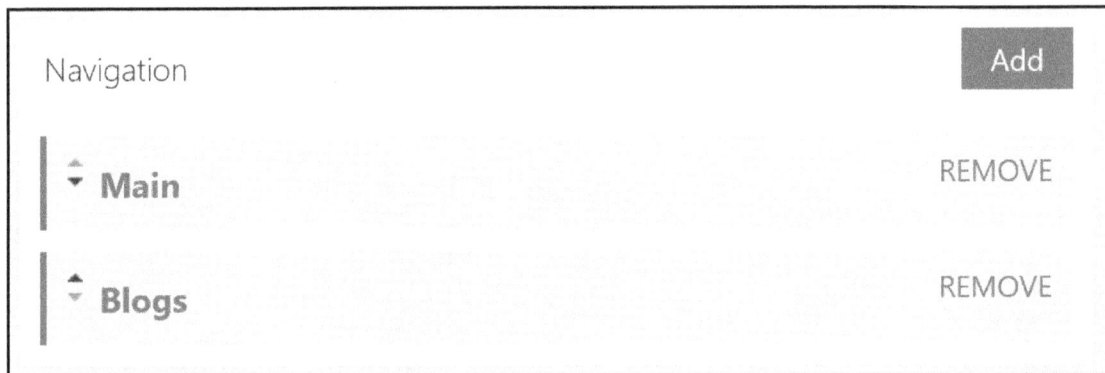

We can now view the results of these customizations by looking at any page within the **Developer portal** since all changes we made were to the **Regular page** layer.

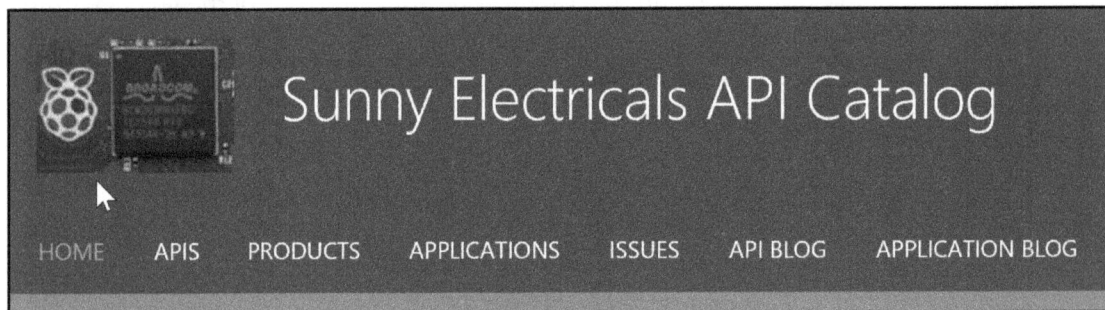

While we amend general layout and add content via the **Publisher portal**, the site can also be amended and controlled more granularly via the **Developer portal** for any user logged in as an **ADMINISTRATOR**.

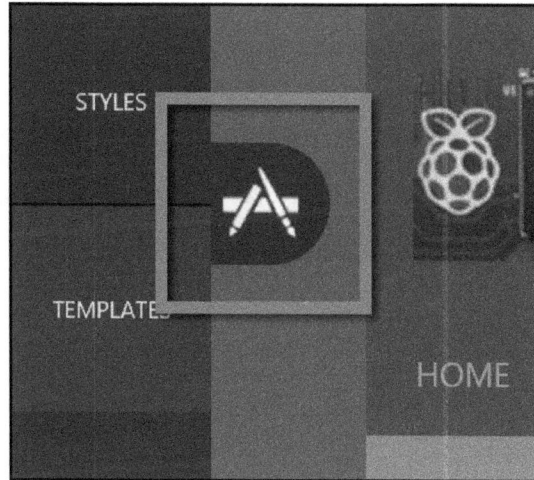

We will add a discussion board provided by the online tool **Disqus** to the operations page of all APIs. First, we need to sign up for a Disqus account and add a new page for our API Management site. We can then use a Universal Code snippet to add to the operations page.

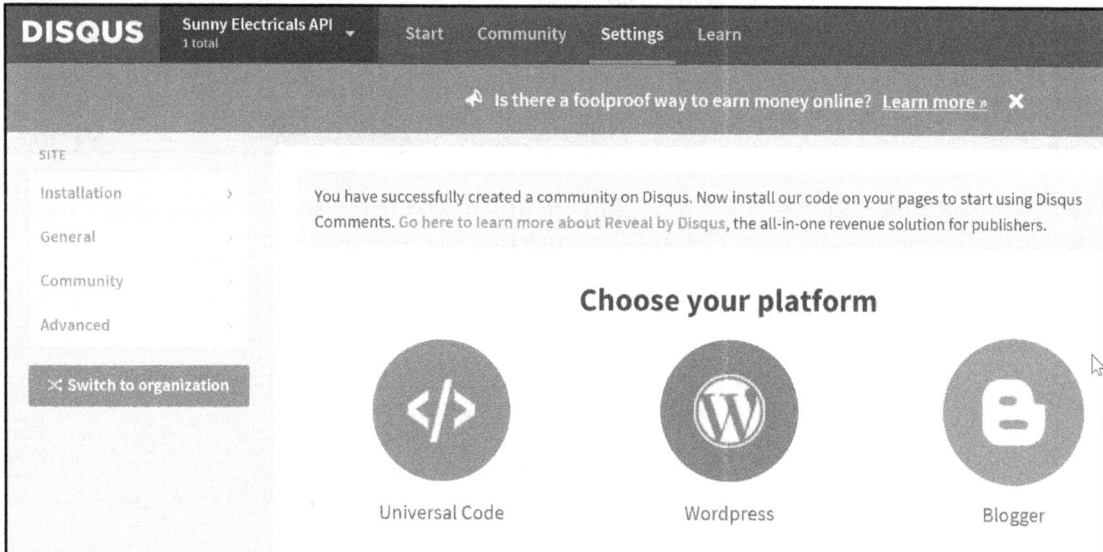

The Universal Code snippet is some HTML and JavaScript code that posts any comments back to the Disqus platform and displays the discussions and comments within the page.

To add the code to the page, we need to change the operations template within the **Developer portal**. When we chose the template we wish to change, we see the page, the HTML of the template, and a set of data that can be used within the template as placeholder information.

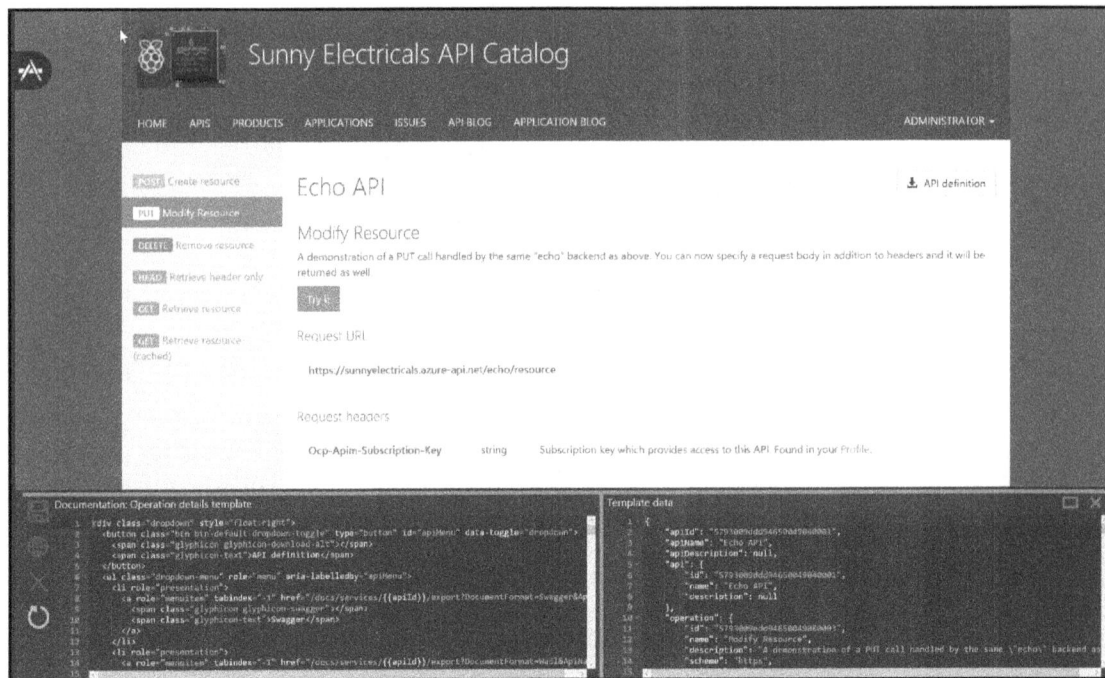

We need to add the code to the bottom of the template and make some amendments to the downloaded code snippet from Disqus to ensure that the comments are unique to the API:

```
<div id="disqus_thread"></div>
<script>
/**
 *  RECOMMENDED CONFIGURATION VARIABLES: EDIT AND UNCOMMENT THE
 *  SECTION BELOW TO INSERT DYNAMIC VALUES FROM YOUR
 *  PLATFORM OR CMS.
 *  LEARN WHY DEFINING THESE VARIABLES IS IMPORTANT:
 *  https://disqus.com/admin/universalcode/#configuration-variables
 */
var disqus_config = function () {
    this.page.url = "";  // Replace PAGE_URL with your page's
```

```
                            canonical URL variable
        this.page.identifier = "{{apiId}}"; // Replace PAGE_IDENTIFIER
                                    with your page's unique
                                        identifier variable
};
(function() { // DON'T EDIT BELOW THIS LINE
    var d = document, s = d.createElement('script');
    s.src = '//sunnyelectricalsapi.disqus.com/embed.js';
    s.setAttribute('data-timestamp', +new Date());
    (d.head || d.body).appendChild(s);
})();
</script>
<noscript>Please enable JavaScript to view the <a
href="https://disqus.com/?ref_noscript">comments powered by
Disqus.</a></noscript>
```

Once we have completed our updates, we need to save the template and then publish the changes to the site:

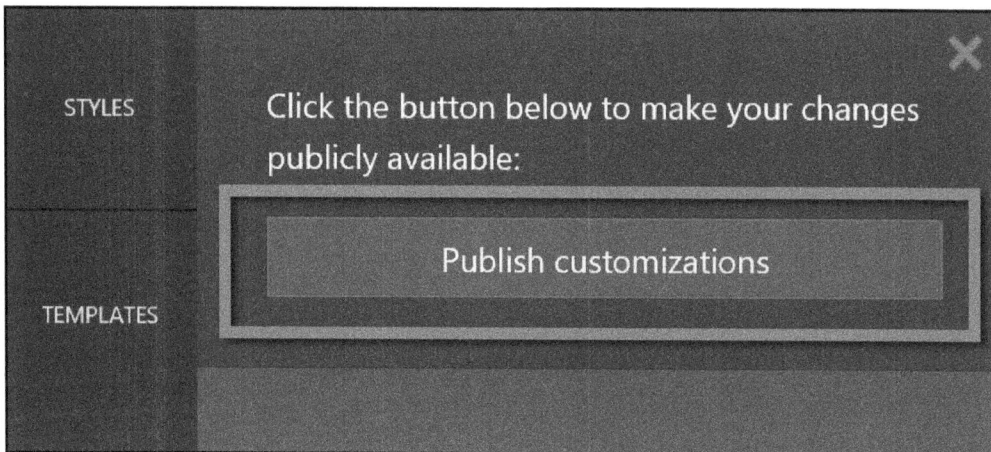

Once published, the discussion board can be seen at the bottom of the page and new comments added as normal.

```
Code samples

Curl    C#    Java    JavaScript    ObjC    PHP    Python    Ruby

@ECHO OFF

curl -v -X DELETE "https://sunnyelectricals.azure-api.net/product/api/Products/{id}"
-H "Ocp-Apim-Subscription-Key: {subscription key}"

--data-ascii "{body}"
```

1 Comment   Sunny Electricals API   ● Martin Abbott ▾

♥ Recommend   ⬆ Share   Sort by Best ▾

        Join the discussion...

        Martin Abbott **Mod** · a few seconds ago
        I love this API, it's the quickest and easiest way to get the list of Products that Sunny Electricals has to offer.
        ∧ ∨ · Edit · Reply · Share ›

We have shown how easy it is to add and update content within the **Developer portal**. This is essential to ensure that developers wishing to use your APIs are fully engaged and want to keep coming back.

By adding a discussion board to the API page or adding Blogs that showcase updates to the API catalog, it will be possible to provide closer engagement with the developer community.

Policies in Azure API Management

In order to provide control over interactions with products or APIs in Azure API Management, policies are used. Policies make it possible to change the default behavior of an API in the product, for example, to meet the governance needs of your company or product, and are a series of statements executed sequentially on each request or response of an API. Three demo scenarios will provide a *taster* of this powerful feature of Azure API Management.

How to use Policies in Azure API Management

Policies are created and managed through the **Publisher portal**.

The first step in policy creation is to determine at what scope the policy should be applied. Policies can be assigned to all products, individual products, the individual APIs associated with a product, and finally the individual operations associated with an API. This will be demonstrated further.

Click on the **Policies** option from the sidebar to specify the policy scope and to define the policy using an XSLT-like language:

In the **Policies** screen, we can find existing policies and modify them or create new policies. The drop-down menus provide a way of navigating to the desired policy level.

For example, the policy level defined later is at the operation level, where a **Product**, **API** and then **Operation** has been specified, as indicated in the scope summary section (highlighted):

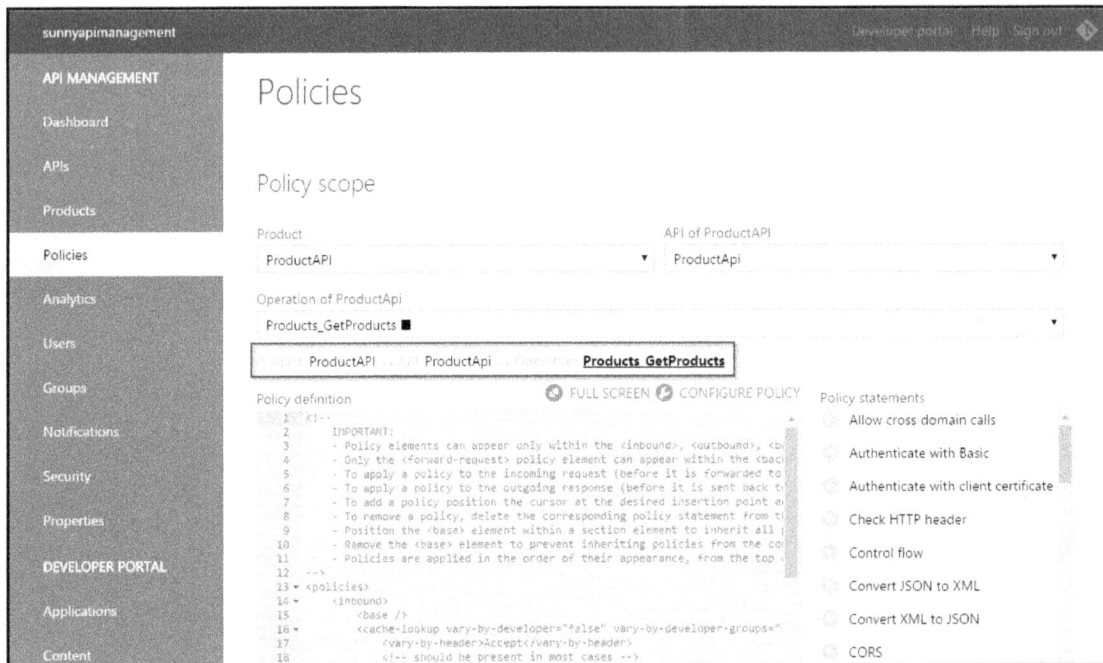

Note that operations with policies defined against them are highlighted with a ■ symbol for easier identification.

To define a policy, we click on the **Configure Policy** link, which makes the **Policy definition** editable.

If a policy hasn't yet been created at the required scope, then it will be necessary to create one by clicking on the **ADD POLICY** link, as illustrated here for the **DeleteProduct** operation:

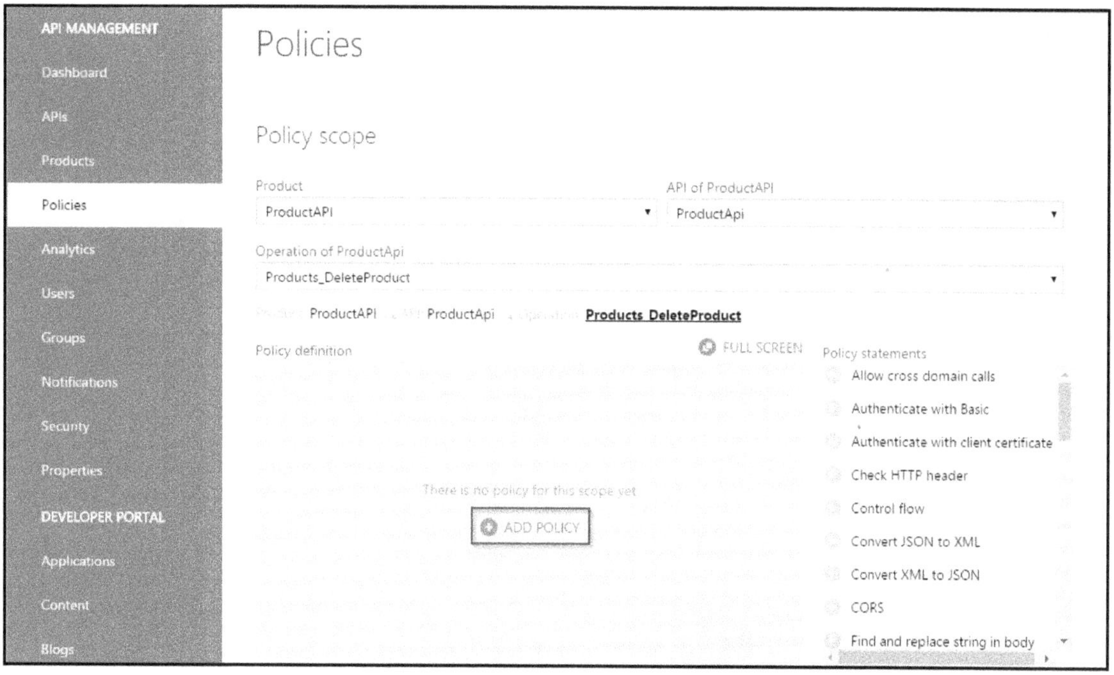

When we create a policy, we can see a definition created in an XML-like syntax. Clicking on the **FULL SCREEN** link enables easier editing of the policy where a full screen editable window then becomes available:

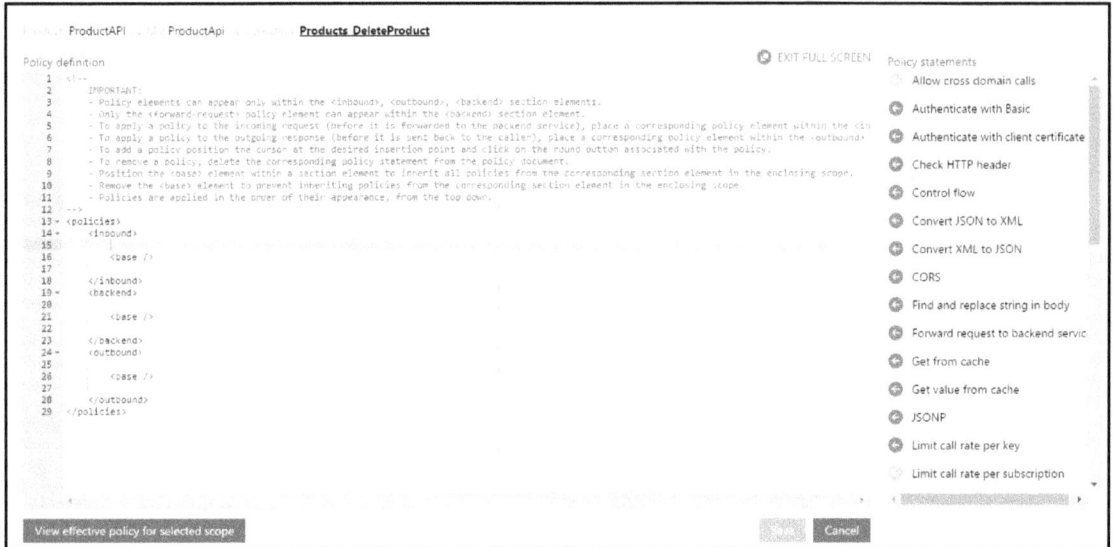

This screen enables multiple policies to be defined that control how the operation is interacted with and also how the operation behaves, perhaps beyond how the original operation was defined.

The base policy elements are applied in the following order:

- `<inbound>`: This specifies policies that should be applied to the inbound message.
- `<backend>`: This specifies policies that should be applied to the inbound message before routing to the actual backend service.
- `<outbound>`: Policies that should be applied to the outbound message, after calling the backend service, may be specified here.
- `<on-error>`: This section may actually be called at any policy stage. If there is an error at any stage processing the request, the remaining steps are skipped and processing enters this policy section for error handling the steps to be applied. Note that this policy element is not present by default when creating a new policy.

Each policy section contains the `<base />` element. This element represents the policies inherited from policies specified at a higher scope. For example, because policies may be defined at the global, product, API, and operation level, a global policy could define standard policies that should be applied to all products, APIs, and operations. This saves the chore and maintenance overhead of specifying the same policies multiple times for many products, for example. It is also a useful mechanism to ensure that consistent functionality is applied to all products as a company-wide governance decision. So, in the case of the Sunny Electricals APIs, for example, the following policy has been defined at the API level, for the **ProductAPI**:

```
Product ProductAPI    API  ProductApi    Operation

Policy definition                                            EXIT FULL SCREEN  DELETE POLICY
1   <!--
2       IMPORTANT:
3       - Policy elements can appear only within the <inbound>, <outbound>, <backend> section elements.
4       - Only the <forward-request> policy element can appear within the <backend> section element.
5       - To apply a policy to the incoming request (before it is forwarded to the backend service), place a corresponding policy element within the <in
6       - To apply a policy to the outgoing response (before it is sent back to the caller), place a corresponding policy element within the <outbound>
7       - To add a policy position the cursor at the desired insertion point and click on the round button associated with the policy.
8       - To remove a policy, delete the corresponding policy statement from the policy document.
9       - Position the <base> element within a section element to inherit all policies from the corresponding section element in the enclosing scope.
10      - Remove the <base> element to prevent inheriting policies from the corresponding section element in the enclosing scope.
11      - Policies are applied in the order of their appearance, from the top down.
12  -->
13 ▼ <policies>
14 ▼     <inbound>
15          <base />
16 ▼        <cache-lookup vary-by-developer="false" vary-by-developer-groups="false" downstream-caching-type="public" must-revalidate="false">
17              <vary-by-header>Accept</vary-by-header>
18              <!-- should be present in most cases -->
19              <vary-by-header>Accept-Charset</vary-by-header>
20              <!-- should be present in most cases -->
21          </cache-lookup>
22      </inbound>
23 ▼    <backend>
24          <base />
25      </backend>
26 ▼    <outbound>
27          <base />
28          <cache-store duration="3600" />
29      </outbound>
30  </policies>
```

Here, we can see that a caching policy has been applied at the **ProductApi** level.

This policy will be applied to all child operations of the ProductAPI via the `<base />` element, which represents all the policies defined at the higher scope. For example, the `GetProducts` operation has no policies defined except the `<base />` element. When the `GetProducts` operation is called, the response contains caching instructions for the client in the `Cache-Control` HTTP header, which would only be possible through inheriting the caching policy defined at the higher scoped API level, as shown here:

```
Response content

Vary: Accept,Accept-Charset
Ocp-Apim-Trace-Location: https://apimgmtst6rzrafdt7mapib8.blob.core.windows.net/apiinspectorcontainer/6o9bzSVLSzsvwB1H9kj6gA2-21?
sv=2014-02-14&sr=b&sig=K7nLQeOyLsWqUxGHzRQsx5VQhCRo%2BGoBZJdCD4iQ2hQ%3D&se=2016-07-25T09%3A22%3A30Z&sp=r&traceId=b097292dd18c4bc
3b5ba08fdc46829a2
Cache-Control: public, max-age=3597
Date: Sun, 24 Jul 2016 09:22:30 GMT
Set-Cookie: ARRAffinity=0d8c79d0cc614d8bfd536834da0cafd3a608ce2b18fb182b506672dfe9fcb820;Path=/;Domain=productapi20160717.azurewe
bsites.net
X-AspNet-Version: 4.0.30319
X-Powered-By: ASP.NET
Content-Length: 125
Content-Type: application/json; charset=utf-8
Expires: Sun, 24 Jul 2016 10:22:27 GMT
Last-Modified: Sun, 24 Jul 2016 09:22:27 GMT

[
    {
        "ProductId": 1,
        "SKU": "SKU023",
        "Name": "Microwave",
        "Description": "Super 1200W Microwave",
        "QtyAvailable": 100,
        "QtyBackOrder": 0
    }
]
```

It is possible to specify policies that should execute before/after higher level policies execute by positioning policies before and after the `<base />` element.

For policies that appear twice, once in a higher scope level and then at a lower level, the policy at the lower level will be applied and the higher level policy will be skipped. In such a fashion, it is possible to override higher scoped policies.

For example, if we decide that clients should be instructed not to cache calls to the
`GetProducts` operation, we can update the `GetProducts` policy definition as follows, by
redefining a caching policy after the `<base />` element, as can be seen here:

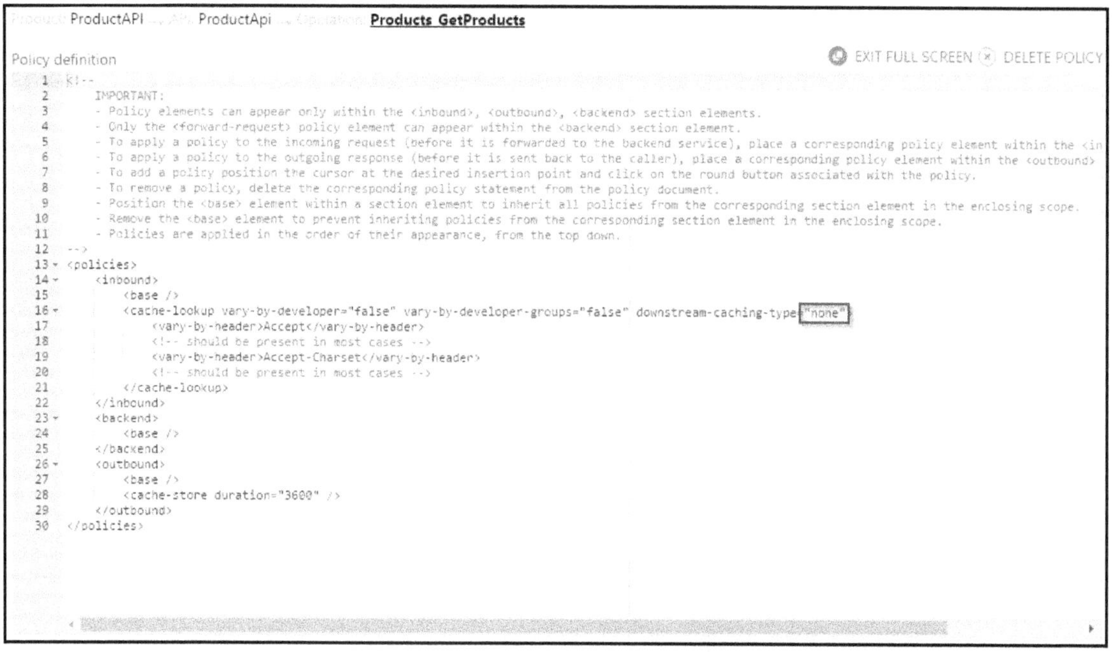

```
  Product  ProductAPI      API   ProductApi    Operation      Products  GetProducts

Policy definition                                                               ⊙  EXIT FULL SCREEN ⊗  DELETE POLICY
 1  <!--
 2      IMPORTANT:
 3      - Policy elements can appear only within the <inbound>, <outbound>, <backend> section elements.
 4      - Only the <forward-request> policy element can appear within the <backend> section element.
 5      - To apply a policy to the incoming request (before it is forwarded to the backend service), place a corresponding policy element within the <in
 6      - To apply a policy to the outgoing response (before it is sent back to the caller), place a corresponding policy element within the <outbound>
 7      - To add a policy position the cursor at the desired insertion point and click on the round button associated with the policy.
 8      - To remove a policy, delete the corresponding policy statement from the policy document.
 9      - Position the <base> element within a section element to inherit all policies from the corresponding section element in the enclosing scope.
10      - Remove the <base> element to prevent inheriting policies from the corresponding section element in the enclosing scope.
11      - Policies are applied in the order of their appearance, from the top down.
12  -->
13  <policies>
14      <inbound>
15          <base />
16          <cache-lookup vary-by-developer="false" vary-by-developer-groups="false" downstream-caching-type="none"
17              <vary-by-header>Accept</vary-by-header>
18              <!-- should be present in most cases -->
19              <vary-by-header>Accept-Charset</vary-by-header>
20              <!-- should be present in most cases -->
21          </cache-lookup>
22      </inbound>
23      <backend>
24          <base />
25      </backend>
26      <outbound>
27          <base />
28          <cache-store duration="3600" />
29      </outbound>
30  </policies>
```

When we query the `GetProducts` operation again, the response specifies different caching instructions:

```
Response content

Pragma: no-cache
Vary: Accept,Accept-Charset
Ocp-Apim-Trace-Location: https://apimgmtst6rzrafdt7mapib8.blob.core.windows.net/apiinspectorcontainer/6o9bzSVLSzsvwB1H9kj6gA2-22?
sv=2014-02-14&sr=b&sig=wpeHPMIapW50CzdnfAlTNW1U0qVr2rrIwf4Nx3spNRc%3D&se=2016-07-25T09%3A40%3A05Z&sp=r&traceId=0aac0f52647044aaa0
a09d76f5098dd0
Cache-Control: no-store, must-revalidate, no-cache
Date: Sun, 24 Jul 2016 09:40:07 GMT
Set-Cookie: ARRAffinity=0d8c79d0cc614d8bfd536834da0cafd3a608ce2b18fb182b506672dfe9fcb820;Path=/;Domain=productapi20160717.azurewe
bsites.net
X-AspNet-Version: 4.0.30319
X-Powered-By: ASP.NET
Content-Length: 125
Content-Type: application/json; charset=utf-8
Expires: Sun, 24 Jul 2016 09:40:07 GMT
Last-Modified: Sun, 24 Jul 2016 09:40:07 GMT

[
  {
    "ProductId": 1,
    "SKU": "SKU023",
    "Name": "Microwave",
    "Description": "Super 1200W Microwave",
    "QtyAvailable": 100,
    "QtyBackOrder": 0
  }
]
```

We have therefore overridden the base caching policy defined at the API level with a caching policy defined at a lower level.

Since it can be confusing (for humans anyway!) to work with such a hierarchy of abstract policies, the **View effective policy for selected scope** button can be used to help determine what policy statements will take effect for the policy we are editing.

For example, if we click on the button for the `GetProducts` operation, we are presented with a view that effectively expands the `<base />` element for each policy in the hierarchy and presents all effective policies in the order that they will be executed, in one consolidated view, as shown here:

```
Policy in effect
    <inbound>
        <cache-lookup vary-by-developer="false" vary-by-developer-groups="false" downstream-caching-type="public" must-revalida
            <vary-by-header>Accept</vary-by-header>
            <!-- should be present in most cases -->
            <vary-by-header>Accept-Charset</vary-by-header>
            <!-- should be present in most cases -->
        </cache-lookup>
        <cache-lookup vary-by-developer="false" vary-by-developer-groups="false" downstream-caching-type="none">
            <vary-by-header>Accept</vary-by-header>
            <!-- should be present in most cases -->
            <vary-by-header>Accept-Charset</vary-by-header>
            <!-- should be present in most cases -->
        </cache-lookup>
    </inbound>
    <backend>
        <forward-request />
    </backend>
    <outbound>
        <cache-store duration="3600" />
        <cache-store duration="3600" />
```

OK

We can work our way through the policies from top to bottom and determine what policies will be fired, remembering that the last policy for a particular policy statement will fire and all other policies of the same type will be skipped.

This view is also useful in that it highlights redundant/unnecessary policies, so it is useful to execute this function from time to time, to check whether redundant policies have been created that may be deleted. In such a way, fewer policies mean that it is easier to determine what policies will fire when presented with this consolidated view in the future. In the example earlier, the `<cache-store>` statement (*Store to cache*) is not required (because it is duplicated with the same value for duration), but unfortunately, this cannot be deleted from the `GetProducts` operation since the `<cache-lookup>` statement (*Get from cache*) always requires a matching `<cache-store>` element.

Working with policies in the Publisher portal

On the right-hand side of the screen, **Policy statements** provide functions that can be inserted into the policy. They are shortcuts that can be used to insert statements into the policy that can then be subsequently edited, as required. To insert a statement, position the cursor in the appropriate section of the policy and click on the arrow next to the policy.

It is possible to create complex policies to meet your needs by inserting multiple policy statements and conditional logic, for example.

What are the different policies available in the Publisher portal?

The table here summarizes the different policies available. Note that the arrow icon next to the policy statements will appear disabled, if they cannot be applied at the current scope or at the message stage (inbound or outbound).

Category	Policy	Description
Access Restriction	Check HTTP header	Enforce HTTP header existence/value.
	Limit call rate	Limit the number of calls allowed by time and frequency by subscription or key.
	Restrict caller IPs	Allow/deny connections by IP address or range.
	Set usage quota	Specify the usage by maximum allowable calls and/or data usage by subscription or key.
	Validate JWT	Enforce JWT (JSON web token) existence/validity.
Advanced	Control flow	Conditionally, apply policies based on the predicate evaluation.
	Forward request	Forward to backend service.
	Log to EventHub	Send messages to EventHub.
	Return response	Returns directly to the user, aborting execution.
	Send one way request	One way request sent to the specified URL without waiting for a response.
	Send request	Sends a request to the specified URL.

	Set request method	Specify the HTTP verb for a request.
	Set status	Set the HTTP status code to the indicated value.
	Set variable	Write a value to a variable for access later.
	Wait	Waits for enclosed Send, cache retrieval, or control flow to complete before allowing execution to proceed.
Authentication	Authenticate with Basic	Authenticate with a backend service using HTTP basic.
	Authenticate with client certificate	Authenticate with a backend service using the specified client certificate.
Caching	Get from cache	Do a cache lookup and use the valid cached response.
	Store to cache	Store the response in the cache.
	Get value from cache	Obtain an item from the cache by the specified key.
	Store value in cache	Store in the cache by the specified key.
Cross domain	Allow cross domain calls	Allows requests from other domains, enabling access for Adobe Flash and Silverlight browser-based clients.
	CORS (cross origin resource sharing)	Permits browser-based calls from other domains to an API or operation.
	JSONP (JSON with padding)	Permits browser-based calls from other domains to an API or operation, from JavaScript.
Transformation	Convert JSON to XML	Translates request or response messages from JSON to XML.
	Covert XML to JSON	Translates request or response messages from XML to JSON.
	Find and replace string in body	Replaces the specified string in the request or response body with a different string.
	Mask URLs in content	Use to modify URLs in request or response messages to or from a masked URL.
	Set backend service	Sets the backend service for an incoming message.

	Set body	Sets the body content of request or response messages.
	Set HTTP header	Specify a HTTP header value in the request or response message that will insert a new header or overwrite a pre-existing header value.
	Set query string parameter	Modifies the request query string parameter.
	Rewrite URL	Use to rewrite a URL to the format expected by the backend service.

The following sections demonstrate three scenarios where policies have been applied to the Sunny Electricals ProductAPI.

Basic Scenario #1 – Throttle Requests Using a Rate Limit Policy

In this scenario, Sunny Electricals have decided to restrict the number of requests to the ProductAPI to ensure that all developers developing against the API can have access for testing purposes. This is to prevent the API from becoming overloaded and subsequently unable to service requests to some developers.

To achieve this, the API scope is specified, the **FULL SCREEN** option is selected, and the **Configure Policy** link is clicked, enables the editing of the API level policy.

The cursor is placed on a new line in the `<inbound>` policy element and the arrow by the **Limit call rate per key** policy statement is selected, to insert a `<rate-limit-by-key />` policy element that can then be populated with real data, overriding the dummy data that is provided by default, as shown here.

```
                ProductAPI            ProductApi         Operation

Policy definition                                                      EXIT FULL SCREEN  (x)  DELETE POLICY
    1  <!--
    2      IMPORTANT:
    3      - Policy elements can appear only within the <inbound>, <outbound>, <backend> section elements.
    4      - Only the <forward-request> policy element can appear within the <backend> section element.
    5      - To apply a policy to the incoming request (before it is forwarded to the backend service), place a corresponding policy element within the <in
    6      - To apply a policy to the outgoing response (before it is sent back to the caller), place a corresponding policy element within the <outbound>
    7      - To add a policy position the cursor at the desired insertion point and click on the round button associated with the policy.
    8      - To remove a policy, delete the corresponding policy statement from the policy document.
    9      - Position the <base> element within a section element to inherit all policies from the corresponding section element in the enclosing scope.
   10      - Remove the <base> element to prevent inheriting policies from the corresponding section element in the enclosing scope.
   11      - Policies are applied in the order of their appearance, from the top down.
   12  -->
   13 ▼ <policies>
   14 ▼     <inbound>
   15            <base />
   16            <rate-limit-by-key calls="10" renewal-period="60" counter-key="@(context.Subscription.Id)" />
   17 ▼         <cache-lookup vary-by-developer="false" vary-by-developer-groups="false" downstream-caching-type="public" must-revalidate="false">
   18                <vary-by-header>Accept</vary-by-header>
   19                <!-- should be present in most cases -->
   20                <vary-by-header>Accept-Charset</vary-by-header>
   21                <!-- should be present in most cases -->
   22            </cache-lookup>
   23        </inbound>
   24 ▼     <backend>
   25            <base />
   26        </backend>
   27 ▼     <outbound>
   28            <base />
   29            <cache-store duration="3600" />
   30        </outbound>
   31  </policies>

  ◄

 View effective policy for selected scope                                                    Save      Cancel
```

Here, we can see that the rate limit policy will be applied after the product policy has been applied, indicated by the `<base />` element (so overriding any rate limit specified in it), that the number of connections will be restricted to 10, after which the service will prevent further connections for that subscription key (specified in the HTTP header) for 60 seconds.

We can test this out using the Developer Portal by repeatedly calling the `GetProducts` operation. The following response will be received when the rate limit has been reached, proving that the inbound policy is in effect:

```
Response status
429 Too Many Requests
Response latency
10 ms
Response content
Retry-After: 46
Ocp-Apim-Trace-Location: https://apimgmtst6rzrafdt7mapib8.blob.core.windows.net/apiinspectorcontainer/6o9bzSVLSzsvwB1H9kj6gA2-69?
sv=2014-02-14&sr=b&sig=nIeobL9yJ6w%2BuTdf0J5FMld5y68v5nYnqciHCtq9lrQ%3D&se=2016-07-25T11%3A02%3A17Z&sp=r&traceId=a9c0ae863609434
7b6010a85905630d3
Date: Sun, 24 Jul 2016 11:02:17 GMT
Content-Length: 84
Content-Type: application/json

{
  "statusCode": 429,
  "message": "Rate limit is exceeded. Try again in 46 seconds."
}
```

Basic Scenario #2 – Rewrite the public facing URI for the GetProducts API operation

This scenario demonstrates the `<rewrite-uri />` policy. In this simple example, a new version of the `GetProducts` operation has been written, and it is now required that all requests to look up a product are now obtained from a version 2 of the base API. This is achieved using the inbound policy specified here:

As can be observed in the screenshot earlier, the policy will rewrite the URL to include v2 (indicating Version 2). So, for example, a public request to the URL
`https://sunnyapimanagement.azure-api.net/api/Products/1` will be rewritten to
`https://sunnyapimanagement.azure-api.net/api/v2/Products/1`. This will be
transparent to the client, who need never know that their request is routed to a version 2 of the API operation.

Getting slightly more advanced – Modify default API behavior using conditional statements

Sunny Electrical has decided to implement monitoring to their ProductAPI whereby they test end-to-end connectivity to the backend API by sending a heartbeat-type message to confirm service availability.

However, they wish to retain caching for normal operation.

In order to skip the cache for heartbeat messages, cache lookup is conditionally applied depending on the value of a custom HTTP header defined as **X-MessageType**. If the value for the **X-MessageType** header is **heartbeat**, cache lookup is skipped and data is instead obtained from a direct call to the backend API. The following conditional policy is added to the policy as follows:

```
Policy definition                                                    EXIT FULL SCREEN    DELETE POLICY
13 ▾  <policies>
14 ▾      <inbound>
15            <base />
16            <rate-limit-by-key calls="10" renewal-period="60" counter-key="@(context.Subscription.Id)" />
17 ▾          <choose>
18 ▾              <when condition="@(context.Request.Headers.GetValueOrDefault("X-MessageType","")
19                    .Equals("heartbeat", StringComparison.InvariantCultureIgnoreCase))">
20                    <!-- Skip cache lookup -->
21                </when>
22 ▾              <otherwise>
23 ▾                  <cache-lookup vary-by-developer="false" vary-by-developer-groups="false" downstream-caching-type="public" must-revalidate="false"
24                        <vary-by-header>Accept</vary-by-header>
25                        <!-- should be present in most cases -->
26                        <vary-by-header>Accept-Charset</vary-by-header>
27                        <!-- should be present in most cases -->
28                    </cache-lookup>
29                </otherwise>
30            </choose>
31        </inbound>
32 ▾      <backend>
33            <base />
34        </backend>
35 ▾      <outbound>
36            <base />
37 ▾          <choose>
38 ▾              <when condition="@(context.Request.Headers.GetValueOrDefault("X-MessageType","")
39                    .Equals("heartbeat", StringComparison.InvariantCultureIgnoreCase))">
40                    <set-status code="200" reason="Heartbeat message completed" />
41                </when>
42 ▾              <otherwise>
43                    <cache-store duration="3600" />
44                </otherwise>
45            </choose>
46        </outbound>
47    </policies>

    View effective policy for selected scope                                    Save    Cancel
```

Here, we can see how conditional logic has been applied to the `<inbound>` and `<outbound>` policy elements using the XSLT syntax combined with C# 6.0 code statements. The code checks the value of the custom **X-MessageType** header, and if it matches the string literal "heartbeat", the cache lookup policy is missed and instead a direct call to the product API is made.

The `<outbound>` policy also modifies the HTTP status reason code, to indicate to the user that this was a heartbeat-type message.

We can test this policy using the **Developer portal** by specifying a header in the request message as follows, by clicking on the **Add header** link and specifying the custom header details:

Headers

Ocp-Apim-Trace   true   ✖ Remove header

Ocp-Apim-Subscription-Key   .... 👁

X-MessageType   heartbeat   ✖ Remove header

➕ Add header

Authorization

Subscription key   Primary-2abb..   ✖ ▾

Request URL

```
https://sunnyapimanagement.azure-api.net/ProductAPI/api/Products
```

HTTP request

```
GET https://sunnyapimanagement.azure-api.net/ProductAPI/api/Products HTTP/1.1
Host: sunnyapimanagement.azure-api.net
Ocp-Apim-Trace: true
Ocp-Apim-Subscription-Key: ...............................
X-MessageType: heartbeat
```

Now that the HTTP request includes our custom HTTP header, we can send the message, and the response should result from directly calling the ProductAPI, providing a mechanism to test service connectivity end-to-end, and bypassing the APIM cache.

The HTTP response message also includes the custom HTTP status reason code:

```
Response status
200 Heartbeat message completed

Response latency
109 ms

Response content
Pragma: no-cache
Ocp-Apim-Trace-Location: https://apimgmtst6rzrafdt7mapib8.blob.core.windows.net/apiinspectorcontainer/6o9bzSVLSzsvwB1H9kj6gA2-94?
sv=2014-02-14&sr=b&sig=QZUPncaU16jQ0YU%2B6DOnyTxqIC4uwhIIpJ%2FvaYkTXNo%3D&se=2016-07-26T08%3A28%3A00Z&sp=r&traceId=1635c9f3cff744
e881a1505018014cf3
Cache-Control: no-cache
Date: Mon, 25 Jul 2016 08:28:00 GMT
Set-Cookie: ARRAffinity=0d8c79d0cc614d8bfd536834da0cafd3a608ce2b18fb182b506672dfe9fcb820;Path=/;Domain=productapi20160717.azurewe
bsites.net
X-AspNet-Version: 4.0.30319
X-Powered-By: ASP.NET
Content-Length: 125
Content-Type: application/json; charset=utf-8
Expires: -1

[
   {
     "ProductId": 1,
     "SKU": "SKU023",
     "Name": "Microwave",
     "Description": "Super 1200W Microwave",
     "QtyAvailable": 100,
     "QtyBackOrder": 0
   }
]
```

We can download a trace file to also check our policy execution. The trace URL is indicated in the **Ocp-Apim-Trace-Location** HTTP header in the APIM response message, as shown earlier. Using a tool such as **Fiddler**, we can execute **HTTP GET** on the URL, and this will return a trace file in JSON format. We could also cut and paste the URL into a browser window, but Fiddler provides easier visualization of the JSON.

Trace execution is toggled via the **Ocp-Apim-Trace** HTTP header in the request message. If it is set to **true**, trace data will be available.

If we compare the trace files with and without the **X-MessageType** header set, we can see that heartbeat messages skip the cache lookup policy whilst those without the header do include execution of the cache lookup policy. The example here shows the trace for a non-heartbeat message, where the trace indicates that the inbound cache lookup policy has been hit:

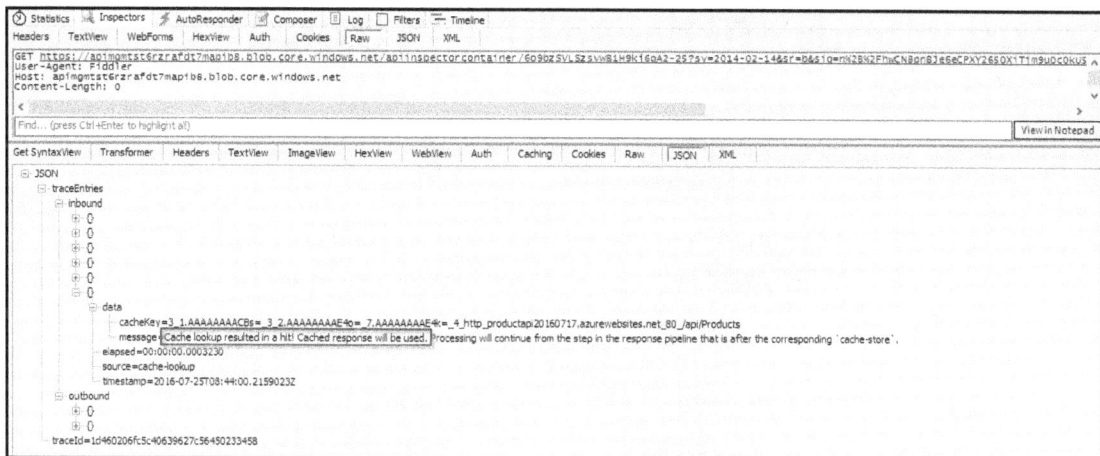

Also, it is apparent that heartbeat messages are skipping cache lookup because they take longer to execute than cached responses (cached responses are approximately 10 times faster than noncached responses).

Securing your API in Azure API Management

We have previously discussed how it is possible to organize APIs in products with those products further refined through the use of policies.

Access to and visibility of products is controlled through the use of groups and developer subscriptions for those APIs requiring subscriptions.

In most enterprise scenarios where you are providing access to some line of business system on-premises, it is necessary to provide sufficient security on the API endpoint to ensure that the solution remains compliant.

There are a number of ways to achieve this level of security using Azure API Management, such as using certificates, Azure Active Directory, or extending the corporate network into Microsoft Azure using a **Virtual Private Network** (**VPN**), and creating a hybrid cloud solution.

Securing your API backend with mutual certificates

Certificate exchange allows Azure API Management and an API to create a trust boundary based on encryption that is well understood and easy to use.

In this scenario, because Azure API Management is communicating with an API that has been provided, a self-signed certificate is allowed as the key exchange for the certificate is via a trusted party.

For an in-depth discussion on how to configure mutual certificate authentication to secure your API, please refer to the Azure API Management documentation (`https://azure.microsoft.com/en-us/documentation/articles/api-management-howto-mutual-certificates/`).

Securing your API backend with Azure Active Directory

If an enterprise already uses Azure Active Directory to provide single or same sign-on to cloud-based services, for instance, on-premises Active Directory synchronization via **ADConnect**, then this provides a good opportunity to leverage Azure Active Directory to provide a security and trust boundary to on-premises API solutions.

For an in-depth discussion on how to add Azure Active Directory to an API Management instance, please see the Azure API Management documentation (`https://azure.microsoft.com/en-us/documentation/articles/api-management-howto-protect-backend-with-aad/`).

VPN connection in Azure API Management

Another way of providing a security boundary between Azure API Management and the API is managing the creation of a VPN.

A VPN creates a tunnel between the corporate network edge and Azure, essentially creating a hybrid cloud solution. Azure API Management supports site-to-site VPNs, and these are created using the Azure Classic Portal.

If an organization already has an **ExpressRoute** circuit provisioned, this can also be used to provide connectivity via private peering.

Because a VPN needs to communicate to on-premises assets, a number of firewall port exclusions need to be created to ensure the traffic can flow between the Azure API Management instance and the API endpoint. These are shown in the following table: only those ports relating to APIs on-premises need to be opened, not all the ports in the table.

Port(s)	Direction	Transport Protocol	Purpose	Source / Destination
80, 443	Inbound	TCP	Client communication to API Management	INTERNET / VIRTUAL_NETWORK
80,443	Outbound	TCP	API Management Dependency on Azure Storage and Azure Service Bus	VIRTUAL_NETWORK / INTERNET
1433	Outbound	TCP	API Management dependencies on SQL	VIRTUAL_NETWORK / INTERNET
9350, 9351, 9352, 9353, 9354	Outbound	TCP	API Management dependencies on Service Bus	VIRTUAL_NETWORK / INTERNET
5671	Outbound	AMQP	API Management dependency for Log to EventHub policy	VIRTUAL_NETWORK / INTERNET
6381, 6382, 6383	Inbound/Outbound	UDP	API Management dependencies on Redis Cache	VIRTUAL_NETWORK / VIRTUAL_NETWORK

445	Outbound	TCP	API Management Dependency on Azure File Share for GIT	VIRTUAL_NETWORK / INTERNET

Monitoring your API

Any application tool is only as good as the insight you can gain from the operation of the tool.

Azure API Management is no exception and provides a number of ways of getting information about how the APIs are being used and are performing.

Analytics in the Publisher portal

Developers are provided access to analytics information regarding their own usage of APIs through the **Developer portal** on their profile page by clicking on the **Analytics** button.

This is a subset of the full data provided by the **Publisher portal**. In the **Publisher portal**, access to the organization's API usage information is via the **Analytics** link on the side menu.

When opened, a summary page is shown containing a roll-up of information in other sections including API by API usage.

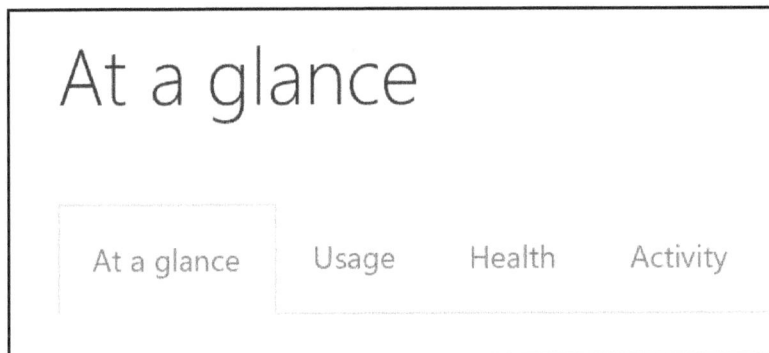

Clicking on **Usage** in the navigation tab shows the overall usage and bandwidth information for the API instance along with an indication on where calls originated. The information is further broken down by API.

Usage information can be used to show where and how often certain APIs are called. This can be helpful when considering scale out of services that an organization provides.

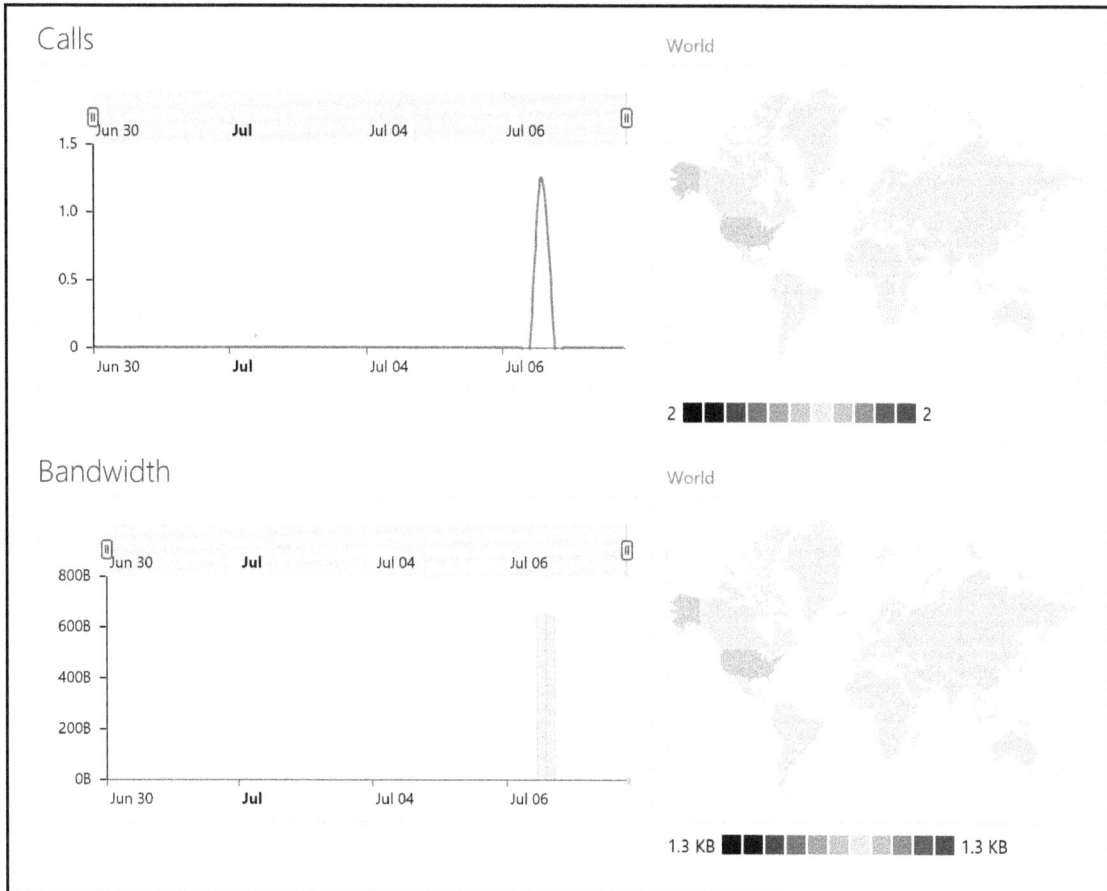

The **Health** tab provides information around items such as **Status codes** and **Cache** usage. **Status codes** can give an indication on whether a lot of requests are coming through as *unauthenticated (401)* or if there are any *server errors (500)*.

Looking for codes that are an exception can help understand when things are going wrong.

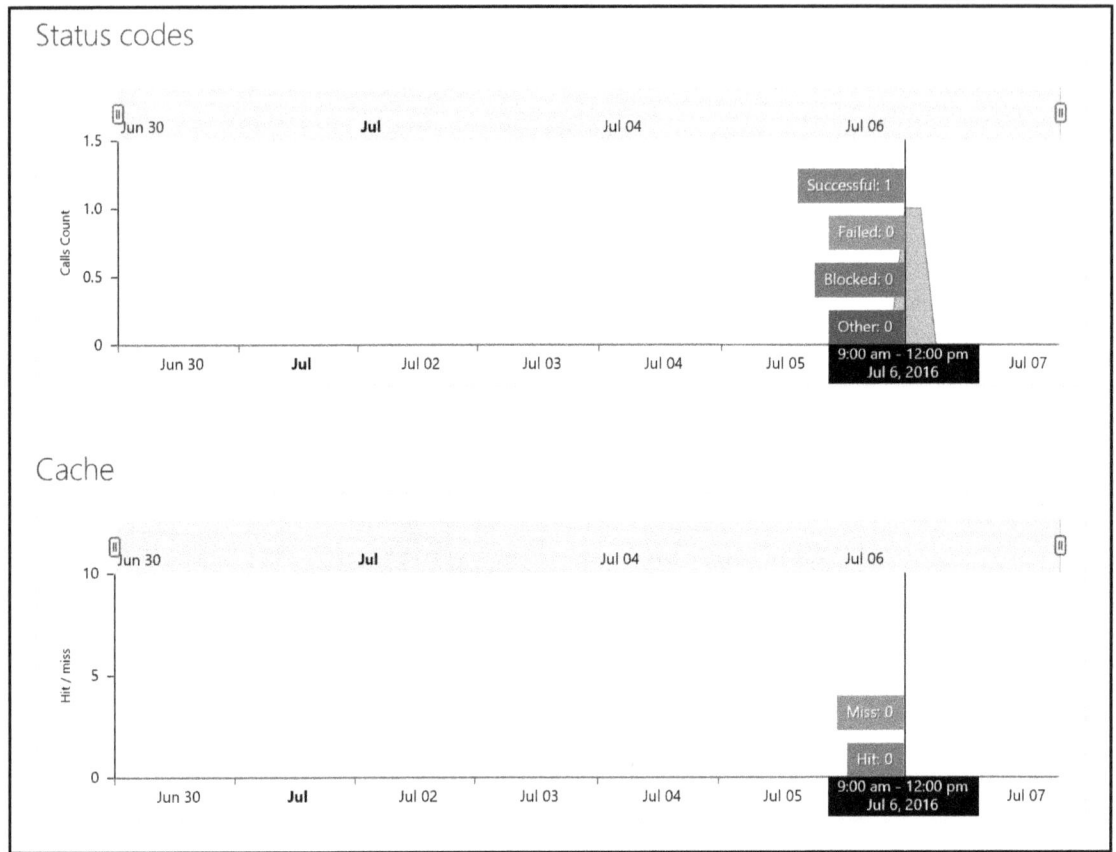

Logging to EventHub

Another way of monitoring your API is to log information about calls received to EventHub.

EventHub is part of Azure Service Bus and allows massive ingestion of data, and it is discussed later in the book. Once data has been ingested into EventHub, it can be processed by a number of services, for instance, **Azure Stream Analytics** or **Azure Functions**, or can be processed by an **Event Processor Host** running within an **Azure Web Job**.

In order to log to EventHub, the API Management instance needs to have a logger added pointing to the EventHub and a policy added to those products or APIs that need to be logged. There is not a way to do this through the **Publisher portal**, so this needs to be performed through the API Management REST API. To use the REST API, it must first be enabled within the **Publisher portal** because it is disabled by default. This is performed via the **Security** page.

Security

| API | Configuration repository | Identities | Client certificates | Delegation | OAuth 2.0 | OpenID Connect |

The API Management REST API allows you to programmatically perform any operation you can manually perform on the developer and publisher portals (e.g. configure your APIs, access analytics data, etc.).

☐ Enable API Management REST API

Like many other Azure services, access via the REST API is secured by shared access signatures. These can be generated programmatically, but for convenience, the token can also be manually created using the **Access Token** information within the **Security** | **API** page, setting a future date and time so the signature expires.

Access Token

Review documentation to learn how to use the credentials to create an API access token programmatically or press the button below to generate it manually.

Management API URL

https://sunnyelectricals.management.azure-api.net/

Expiry	Secret Key	
07/24/2016 5:14 PM	Primary Key	Generate Token

Provide this token in its entirety in the request Authorization header.

SharedAccessSignature uid=5793009ddd94650049030003&ex=2016-07-24T09:14:00.0000000Z&sn=9yYRCcg7gmQhLeGyv1q+1533c

Once generated, the token can be used with API tools to call the API Management REST API, the URL of which is displayed in the **Access Token** information. For the purpose of this discussion, we will use Postman (`https://www.getpostman.com/`), which is a Google Chrome application.

In this case, we will create a logger named `eventhublogger`, so we need to set the correct URL for the REST API and configure a number of headers. We set the URL to the following:

```
https://<APIM Instance Name>.management.azure-
api.net/loggers/<LoggerName>?api-version=2014-02-14-preview
```

We need to set an **Authorization** header to the value created when we manually generated the access token and the **Content-Type** to `application/json`.

To create the logger, we need to call PUT against the URL passing in a body that contains the configuration information for the EventHub we have created to receive the inbound API request information.

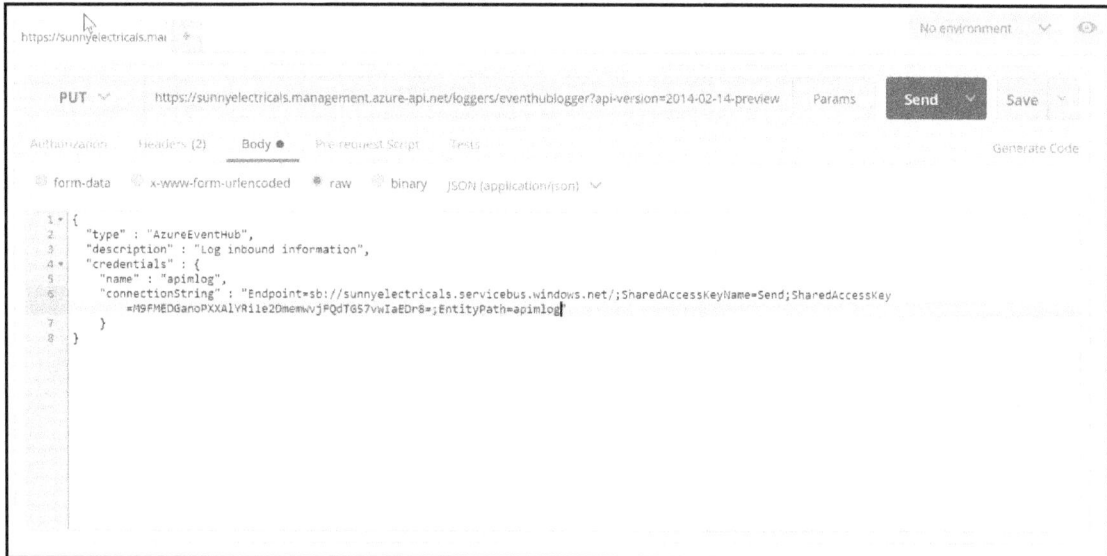

The format of the body that needs to be posted is:

```
{
  "type" : "AzureEventHub",
  "description" : "<LOGGER DESCRIPTION>",
  "credentials" : {
    "name" : "<EVENT HUB NAME>",
    "connectionString" : "<EVENT HUB CONNECTION STRING>"
    }
}
```

When executed, an HTTP response of 201 indicates that the logger was successfully created.

Lastly, we ensure the data is logged to EventHub by configuring a policy that applies to either a product or an API. Policies were discussed in depth earlier in the chapter, so in this case, we will show only the policy that needs to be applied.

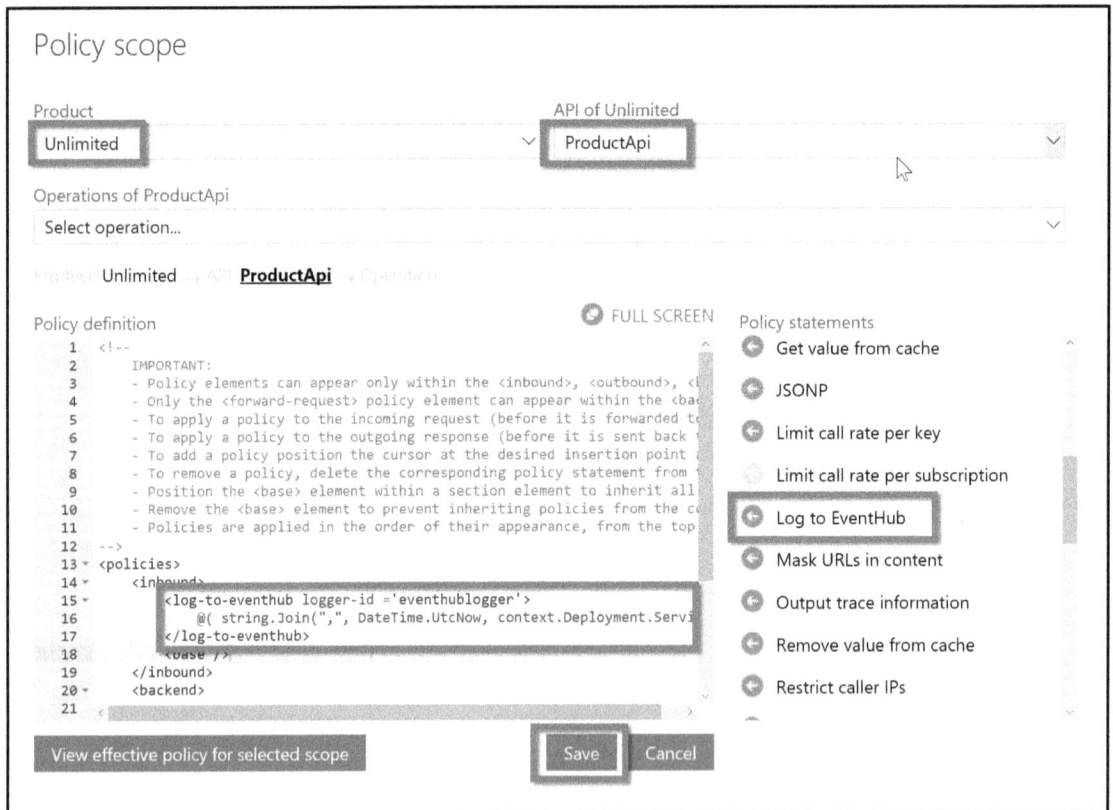

In this case, we are applying the policy to the **Unlimited** product and to the **ProductApi** API across all operations. The policy needs to be configured by setting `logger-id` to the name of the logger created through the REST API; in our case, this was `eventhublogger`.

Once saved, information about calls to the API will be logged directly to EventHub and can be processed as required. For instance, we can create an Azure Function that is triggered when a message is received on the EventHub. Azure Functions are described in detail in a later chapter, but it is useful to test that the logger is working correctly.

For details on creating an Azure Function, refer to `Chapter 7`, *Azure Functions in Logic Apps*. In this case, we just create a very basic function that reads messages and outputs the information to the function **Logs** window.

As can be seen within the **Logs** window, when a message is received on the EventHub, the Azure Function picks up the message for further processing if required. In the earlier example, the following information can be seen:

```
Date:           7/23/2016 9:10:37 AM
Service Name:   sunnyelectricals.azure-api.net
RequestId:      fec00577-9b17-4390-a85a-42eb913f36bd
IP Address:     <Client IP Address>
Operation:      Products_GetProducts
```

Summary

API Management can be used to provide developer access to key information in your organization, information that could be sensitive, or that needs to be limited in use.

Through the use of products, policies, and security, it is possible to ensure that firm control is maintained over the API estate.

The developer experience can be tailored to provide a virtual storefront to any APIs along with information and blogs to help drive deeper developer engagement.

Although not discussed in this chapter, it is also possible for developers to publish their own applications to the API Management instance for other developers to use.

API Management is an important tool in the management, governance, and monitoring of your organization's API assets.

5
Trigger Your First Logic App in Azure

Logic is the beginning of wisdom; not the end
– Mr. Spock, Star Trek

Logic Apps are **Platform as a Service** (**PaaS**) offering from Microsoft that allows any technical user or developer to automate business process execution and workflow. With Logic Apps, you can connect devices, applications, and data residing on cloud or on premises.

This chapter introduces the following topics:

- Logic Apps help us understand why and when to use them
- We will be going over the key components and concepts of building a Logic App
- We will also understand the Logic App templates and how they help us quickly get started building our integration applications

An introduction to Logic App

Logic Apps are PaaS, which comes under Azure App Services, that provides the framework for developers to design simple or a complex business workflows without writing any code. The introduction of this service by Microsoft fills the void in Microsoft's enterprise cloud integration roadmap. As with the other App Services, it can dynamically scale up to meet your demand or scaled back when the demand eases off.

The main benefits of using this service is the simplicity of designing complex workflows using easy-to-understand design templates and implementing business process scenarios that would be difficult to develop using code and are time consuming. Connecting to disparate systems is more easily accomplished using the rich set of enterprise connectors and APIs. If you have constructed a generic Logic App connector, you also have the ability to monetize your Logic App in the Azure Marketplace.

> Here is the URL: `https://github.com/logicappsio` for the community repository for Logic Apps.

Logic Apps may be designed using the web-based visual designer available in the Azure portal, as shown here:

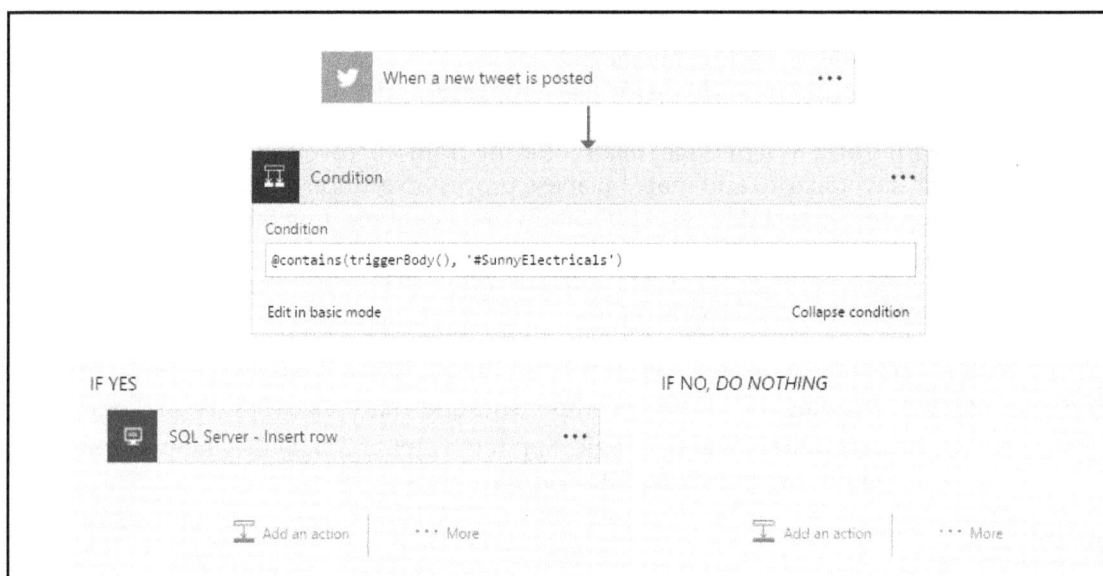

From Visual Studio 2015 by installing the Visual Studio tools for Logic Apps. The link to the tool kit is: `https://visualstudiogallery.msdn.microsoft.com/e25ad307-46cf-412e-8ba5-5b555d53d2d9`.

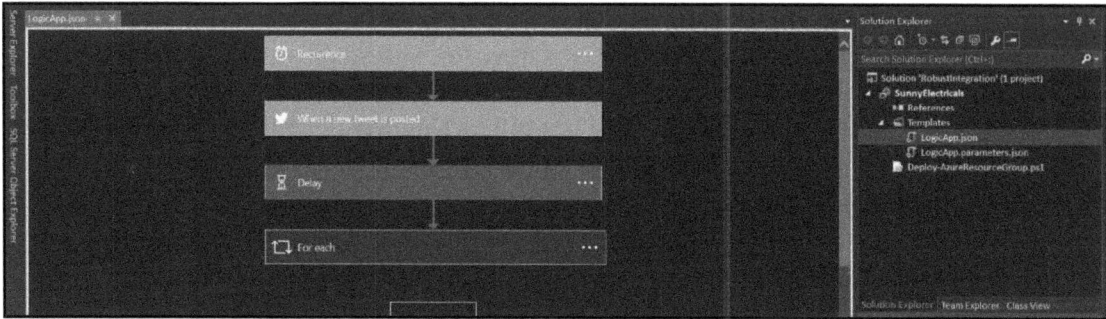

Using the designer, you start orchestrating your process workflow by either adding templates from the Azure Marketplace or by creating your own APIs.

There is a support for many popular SaaS and on-premise apps available in the Azure Marketplace. These templates have input and output connectors to link them together. Think of the templates as building blocks, where you can link the templates to construct workflows. You also have the option to start or nest other Logic Apps from within your own Logic App.

There are three core concepts that you should be familiar with:

- **Triggers**: A trigger is an event that initiates a new instance of the workflow process. There are two types available:
    - **Polling**: This is where the client (Logic App) polls a service for any new notifications. The service itself is stateless; however, the client may maintain state to compare the last notification message.
    - **Push**: This is where a client (Logic App) is notified either by a callback mechanism from the service or the service directly calling the client. Normally for the callback mechanism, the service would have a list of registered subscribers that would be called when an event is to be published.

There are six types of trigger mechanisms available. More information on these triggering types are discussed in the following Chapter 6, *Working with connectors in Logic Apps.*

- **Manual**: This is a manually initiated event.
- **Recurrence**: This is based on a recurring schedule
- **HTTP**: This is by polling an HTTP endpoint

- **API connection**: This managed APIs created by Microsoft for standard (Facebook, Dropbox FTP, Office365, and so on) and Enterprise (AS2 encode/decode, XML, flat file, and so on) services
- **HTTP WebHook**: This is a callback endpoint; it allows the workflow to wait until a message is received on the WebHook
- **API connectionWebHook**: As above but for WebHooks created by Microsoft
- **Actions**: These are the result of a trigger being fired and requiring some operation to be performed; it can also depend on other actions that will determine the execution order.
- **Connectors**: These are special types of APIs that expose an interface that abstracts the underlying connectivity to a resource, and they can either act as triggers or actions.

Logic Apps include the following flow controls:

- **Condition**: This is equivalent to *If and Else-If* decision trees, where an expression must evaluate to true before an action is executed
- **Scope**: This is used to group a set of activities
- **For Each**: This iterates over an array and will execute an action for each item found
- **Do Until**: This will iterate over an array while a condition is true
- **Switch**: Executes different branches of code depending upon a value

The comparison between BizTalk server and Logic Apps

BizTalk Server has been around since 2000, and there has been a number of new product releases since then. It is a very mature platform with excellent enterprise integration capabilities. On the other hand, Logic Apps is a fairly recent edition to the Azure PaaS list.

Logic apps can be likened to a BizTalk orchestration but has a much easier learning curve, and you don't have the deployment hassle of a full BizTalk solution. Although Logic Apps and BizTalk Server are not functionally equivalent, they do have some similarities.

Most of the enterprise features available in BizTalk are now available in Logic Apps using the Logic Apps **Enterprise Integration Pack**. This provides the following features and capabilities:

- XSLT-based maps
- XML schemas
- Trading Partners
- Trading Partner Agreements
- Certificates

The Enterprise Integration Pack is covered in more detail in Chapter 12, *EAI / B2B Integration using Logic Apps*.

Below is a comparison matrix between BizTalk and Logic Apps:

Feature	BizTalk	Logic Apps
Long running transactions	Out of the box support.	Required to be architectured at design time into the solution.
Exception handling	Built in exceptions scopes and compensation transactions.	Need to check the inputs and outputs for error conditions after each action. You can have a scope action to capture the exception.
Scalability	Requires the **Enterprise Edition** of BizTalk.	Can scale up and out by simply selecting the required tier.
Transactional support	Fully supported	Stateless, unless architected into solution.
Development experience	Full Visual Studio debugging experience is available during development and at runtime by attaching to a process.	Use Azure portal and Visual Studio for creating the workflows.
Deployment process	Can be complex if there are a lot of dependencies on 3rd party components.	Relativity easy and quick.

Process monitoring	The **Business Activity Monitoring** (**BAM**) is the built-in tool for monitoring KPI's and generating alerts. Built in message tracking capability on nearly all artefacts.	Azure Diagnostics for tracking workflow events. Has built in properties for tracking. Has native support to OMS in Azure.
High availability	Requires a windows clustering environment to be setup.	Built on top of Azure geo replication fabric.
Enterprise message type support.	Supports multiple messaging formats, for example, EDI, SWIFT, EDIFACT, HL7.	With Enterprise Integration Pack Logic Apps supports equal amount of message format as BizTalk.
Adaptors	Large number of adaptors available for B2B integration scenarios. Can develop custom adaptors with a steep learning curve.	Both enterprise and social media adaptors available. List is still growing. Can easily build custom API type adaptors.
ROI	Large initial investment on infrastructure and licensing. Dependency on MS SQL Server.	Very cost effective. Short ROI time period.
BAU management	Has a very comprehensive management console. Built in message tracking.	Basic management views.

Why and when to use

Many enterprises now use a multitude of cloud-based SaaS services, and being able to integrate these services and resources can become complex. This is where the native capability of Logic Apps can help by providing connectors for most enterprise and social services and to orchestrate the business process flows graphically.

If your resources are all based in the cloud, then Logic Apps is a definite candidate to use as an integration engine.

When you have resources scattered in the cloud and on premise, then you may want to consider BizTalk as a choice for this type of hybrid integration along with Logic Apps. BizTalk 2016 include an adapter for Logic Apps. This Logic App adapter will be used to integrate Logic Apps and BizTalk sitting on premise. Using the BizTalk 2016 Logic App adapter on-premise, resources can directly talk to a multitude of SaaS platforms available on cloud. We will explain this in more details in the following chapters.

You can think of Logic Apps as a coordinator of services and integrations across a range of solutions and services. The design of Logic App workflows should be modular in nature and promote reusability of the components. This can be made possible by chaining and nesting other Logic Apps together to form a composite service.

> A composite service is a service whose implementation calls other services. Refer to:
> `https://www.ibm.com/developerworks/community/blogs/woolf/entry/composite_services?lang=en`.

Natively, Logic Apps provides the following key features:

- **Rapid development**: Using the visual designer with drag and drop connectors, you design your workflows without any coding using a top-down design flow. To get started, Microsoft has a large number of templates available in the marketplace that can be used as is, or modified to suit your requirements. There are templates available for Enterprise SaaS services, common integration patterns, Message routing, DevOps, and social media services.
- **Auditing**: Logic Apps have built-in auditing of all management operations. Date and time when workflow process was triggered and the duration of the process. Use the trigger history of a Logic App to determine the activity status:
    - **Skipped**: Nothing new was found to initiate the process
    - **Succeeded**: The workflow process was initiated in response to data being available
    - **Failed**: An error occurred due to misconfiguration of the connector

A run history is also available for every trigger event. From this information, you can determine if the workflow process succeeded, failed, cancelled, or is still running.

- **Role-based access control** (**RBAC**): Using RBAC in the Azure portal, specific components of the workflow can be locked down to specific users. Custom RBAC roles are also possible if none of the built-in roles fulfills your requirements. Refer to:
  `https://github.com/Azure/azure-content/blob/master/articles/active-dir`
  `ectory/role-based-access-control-custom-roles.md`.

- **Microsoft managed connectors**: There are a number of connectors available from the Azure Marketplace for both enterprise and social services, and the list is continuously growing. The development community also contributes to this growing list of available connectors as well.

- **Serverless scaling**: Automatic and built in on any tier.

- **Resiliency**: Logic Apps are built on top of Azure's infrastructure, which provides a high degree of resiliency and disaster recovery.

- **Security**: This supports OAuth2, Azure Active Directory, Cert auth and Basic auth, and IP restriction.

The days of building monolithic applications are slowly diminishing as more enterprises see the value of consuming SaaS as an alternative to investing large amounts of capex to buy **Commercial Off The Self** (**COTS**) applications. This is where Logic Apps can play a large part by integrating multiple SaaS solutions together to form a complete solution. One scenario is when you have an online CRM, inventory, and financial management systems and you use Logic Apps to orchestrate messages between these applications.

For our hypothetical organization Sunny Electricals, we have used Logic Apps in several scenarios. The Logics Apps are used to orchestrate the requests from the website, to enrich messages, and to publish the same message to several subscribers.

When building applications based on Logic Apps, one area that should not be overlooked is the request/response times when chaining several workflows or API Apps together to return the final response message. If the downstream services are deterministic, then you may want to consider implementing caching. Another option is to use WebHooks if you have no control over the response times from the downstream services and they are nondeterministic.

To know more about WebHooks and caching, you can refer to the MSDN links here:

- `https://msdn.microsoft.com/en-us/library/azure/gg278356.aspx`
- `https://azure.microsoft.com/en-us/updates/webhooks-available-for-logic-apps/`

Diagnosing Logic Apps

Logic App Diagnostics provides the capability to export the logs to either Event Hubs and to storage. Using Event Hubs, you can set up **Streaming Analytics** to gather any trends.

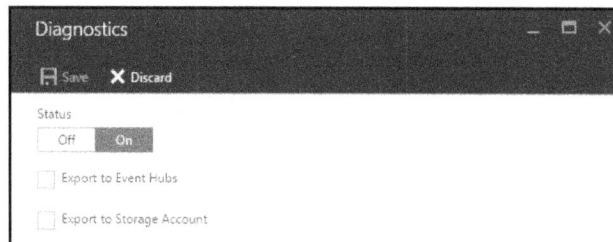

Another feature to help tracking messages through a workflow is the **Client Tracking ID**. This will allow you to correlate messages between actions and any nested workflows. The client can set the header property `x-ms-client-tracking-id` to a unique value that can be tracked. If no ID is provided by the client, the value is `autopopulated`.

Also, under the **Logic app action** blade as shown later, you have access to the input and output message links. From this, you can view the contents of the messages.

The two tools that should be part of your tool belt when performing end-to-end testing:

- **Postman**: `http://www.getpostman.com/` to construct HTTP request messages to your Logic Apps
- **RequestBin**: `http://requestb.in/` to capture the HTTP requests that will be sent to an API App from the Logic App by replacing the URL of the API App with the temporary URL provided by RequestBin

Another useful tool is JSONSchema: `http://jsonschema.net`. This automatically generates JSON schema from a sample JSON message according to the **IETF JSON Schema Internet Draft** Version 4. This is useful to validate the schema definition in a Logic App HTTP trigger, for example.

Building your first Logic App

As this chapter is an introduction to Logic Apps, the sample solution will consist of a very basic workflow to get you familiar with creating a Logic App. Sunny Electricals wishes to store messages whenever one of their customers tweet about a product they have purchased from a store. The tweet message inserted into Azure SQL Database table will be used for organization internal product and service analysis purposes.

The First step is to create Azure SQL server and database and a table to hold tweet messages.

Create Azure SQL server, database, and table

Open the browser and log in to Azure portal: `https://portal.azure.com`.

On Azure portal dashboard, click on the **SQL databases** option and click on **Add** to create new SQL database instance.

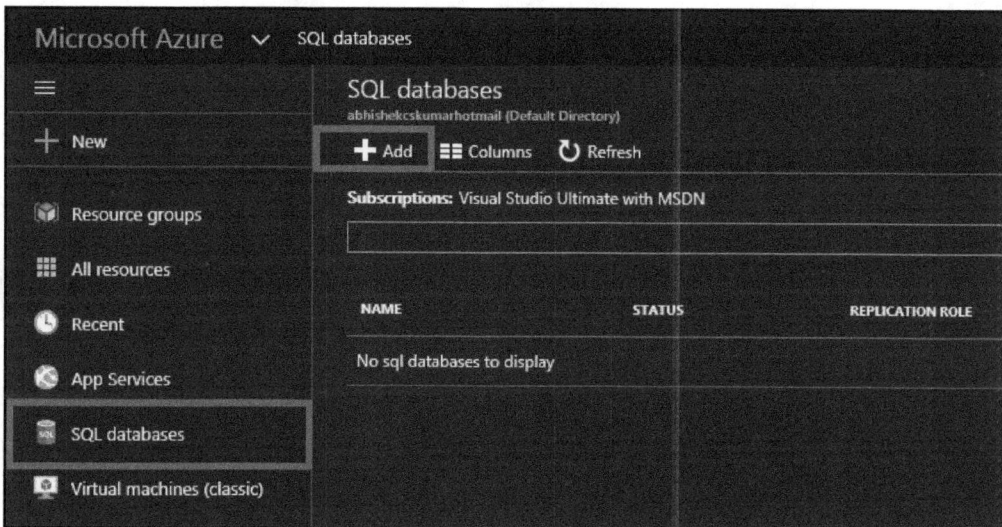

If the **SQL databases** option is not present on the Azure portal dashboard, you can find it by clicking to **New,** then click on **Databases**, and click on **SQL Database**.

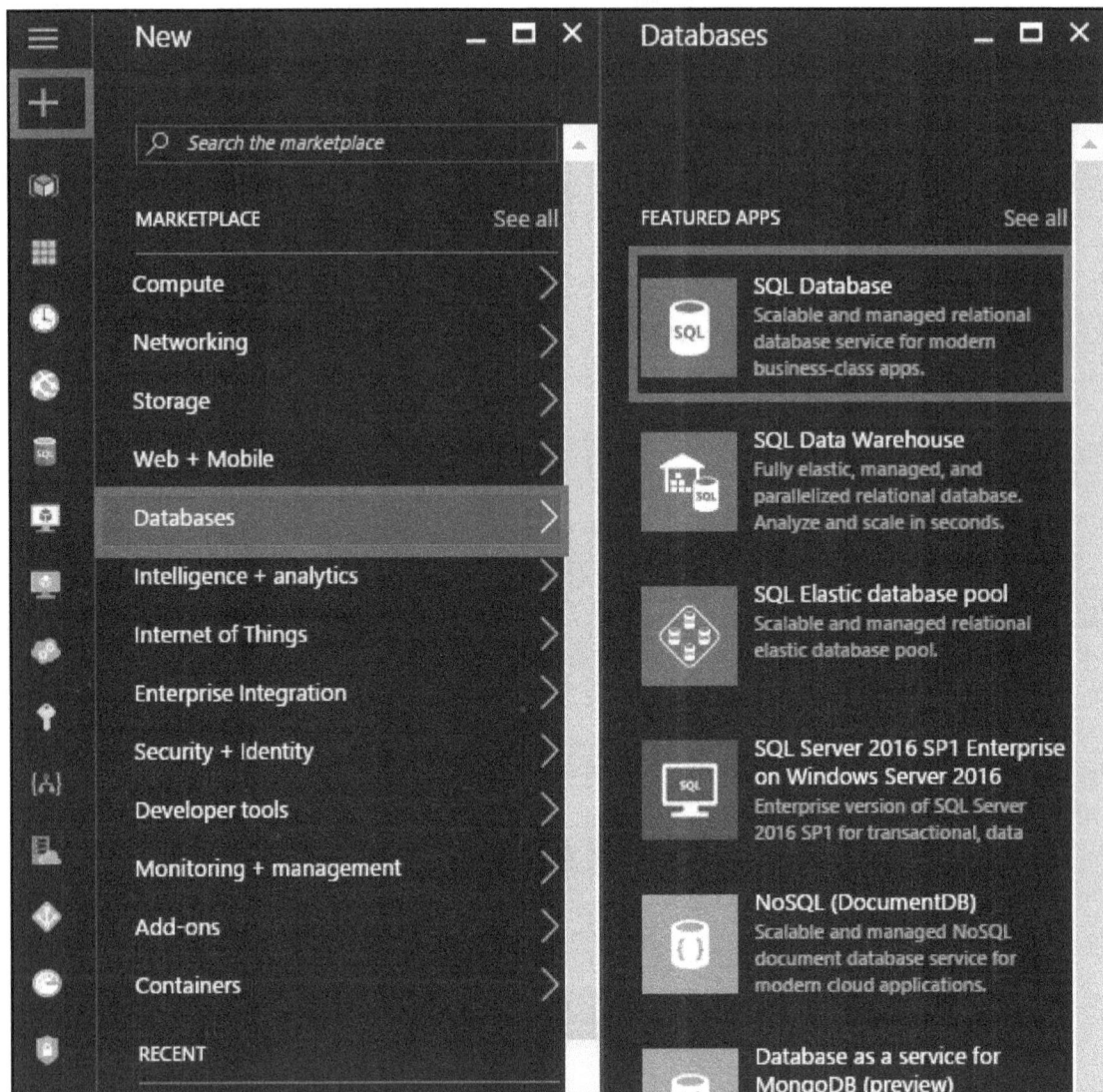

Enter name in the **Database name** field followed by selecting valid Azure subscription, **Resource group**, and source.Click on **Server** (Configure required settings) and click on **Create a new server**. Enter the following details in the **New server** configuration page:

- **Server name**

- **Server Admin login**
- **Password**
- **Confirm Password**
- **Location**

Once done, clickon **Select** toget a new Server and click on **Create** to have a new instance of Sunny Electricals database created in Azure.

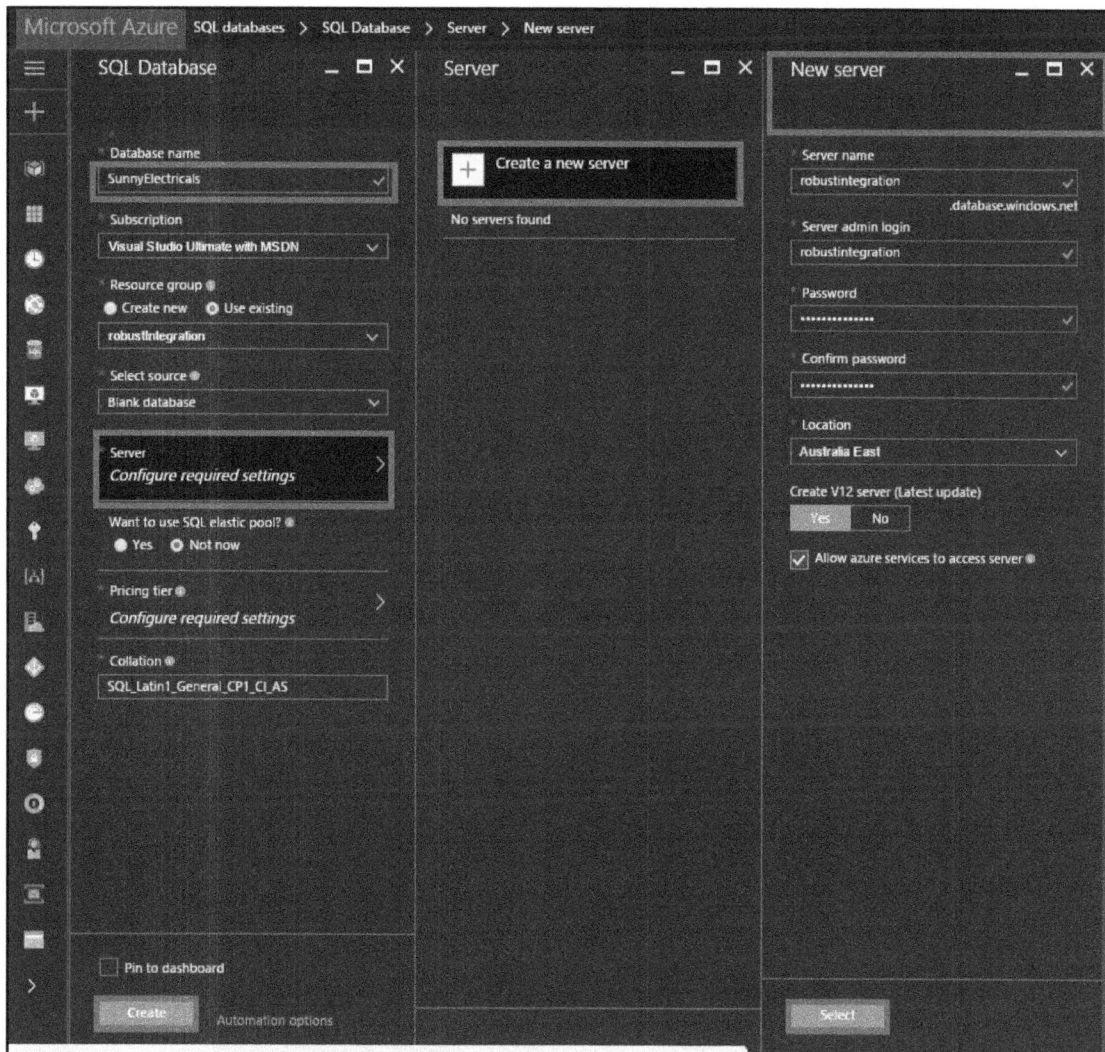

You may need to add firewall rule to access Azure SQL Database from your machine. Read MSDN article to set up firewall rule at: `https://azure.microsoft.com/en-us/documentation/articles/sql-database-get-started/`.

To create table under the SunnyElectricals database, open **SQL Management Studio**, enter the Azure SQL Database information, and click on **Connect**.

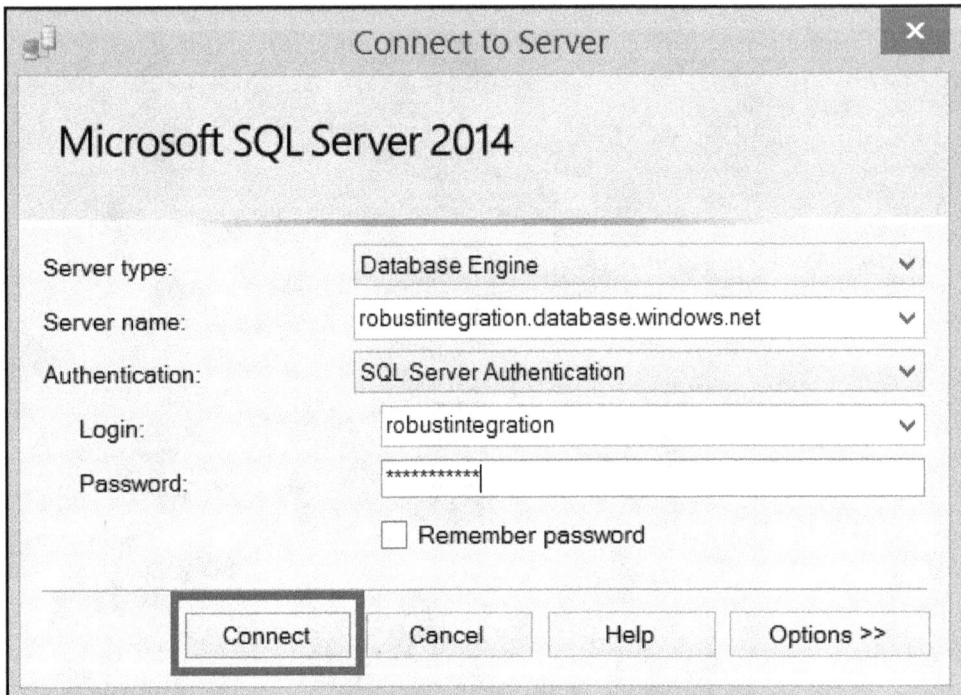

On SQL Management Studio home page, click on **New Query** and create a new table by executing the following SQL statement:

```
CREATE TABLE [dbo].[TweeterTble]
(
  [Id] [int] IDENTITY(1,1) NOT NULL,
  [tweetBy] [varchar](max) NULL,
  [tweetText] [varchar](max) NULL

)
```

Let's go ahead and build a Logic App to poll tweet messages from Twitter. By the end of this exercise, you will find how easy it is to run a Logic App and store the information in few minutes.

Create Logic App and workflow

Log in to Azure portal: `https://portal.azure.com` using your Azure subscription.

On the Azure portal dashboard, click on the **Logic Apps** option and click on **Add** to create new Logic App instance.

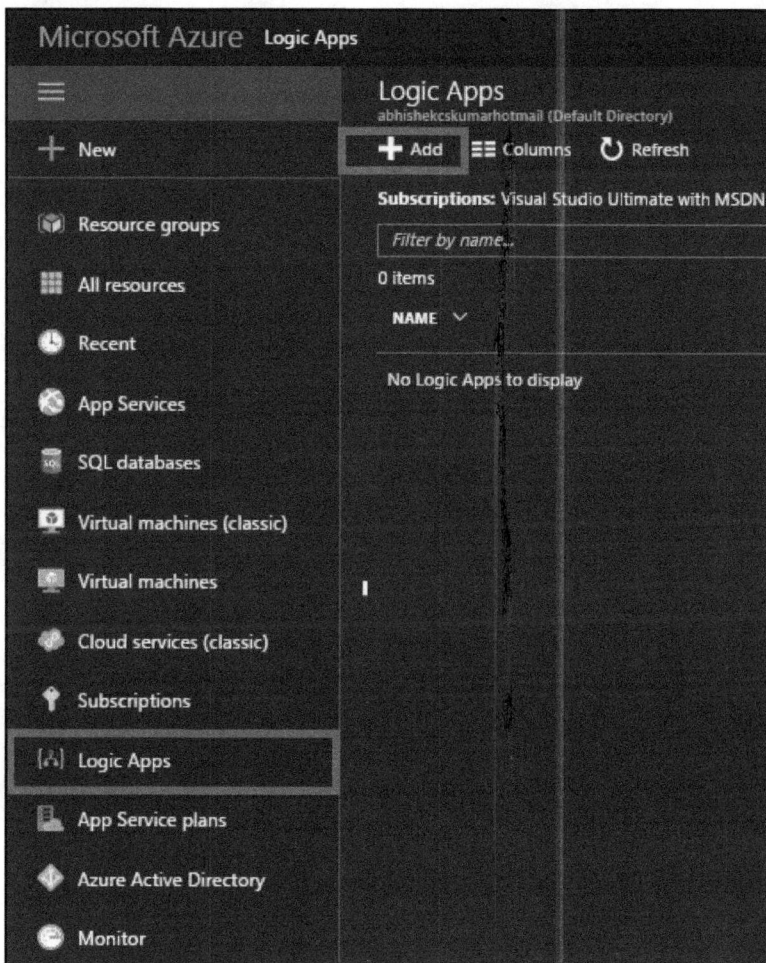

If you are unable to see the **Logic Apps** option on the Azure portal dashboard, you can find it by clicking on **New**, then selecting **Web+Mobile**, and clicking on **Logic App**.

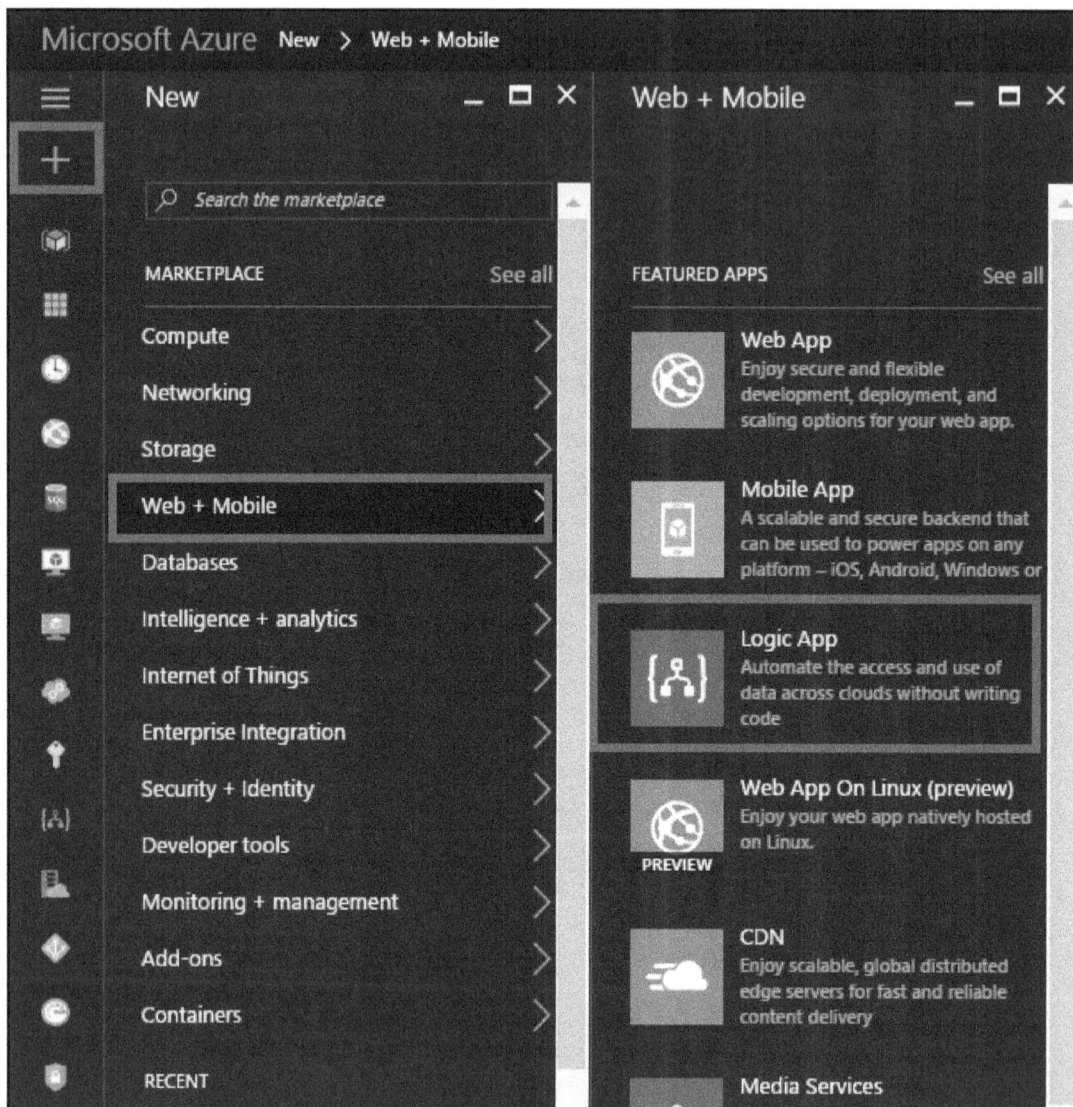

This will pop up the **Create logic app** window. You need to provide an appropriate Logic App name, select the Azure subscription, and select **Resource** group within which you wish to run your Logic App and click on **Create**.

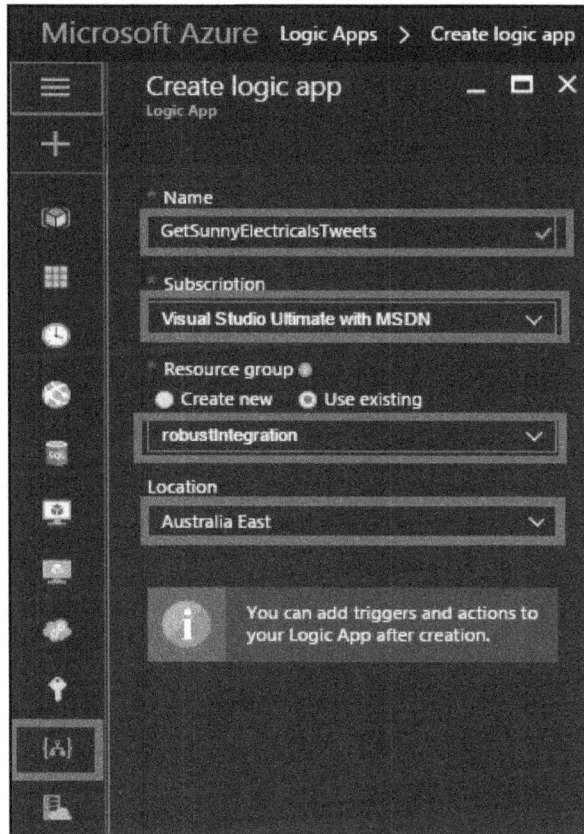

Note that we have selected an existing resource group; you can also create a new resource group and App plan of your choice. The process of creating resource group and App plan through Azure portal is been discussed in `Chapter 2`, *What is an Azure App Service?*

You will need to wait a few seconds for the Logic App deployment process to finish. Once deployment is done, you will be notified in the Azure portal notification area.

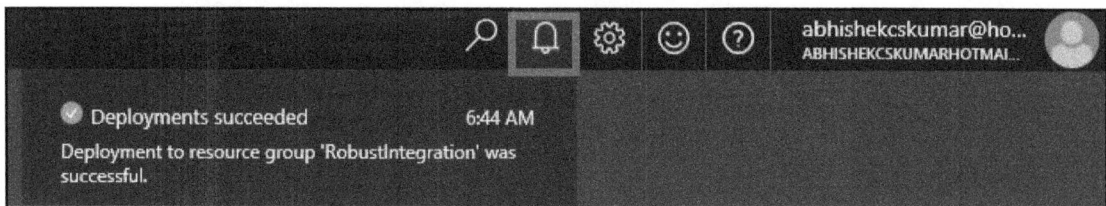

Now if you refresh and navigate to the **Logic Apps** page, you can see new Logic App being created with the **GetSunnyElectricalsTweets** name.

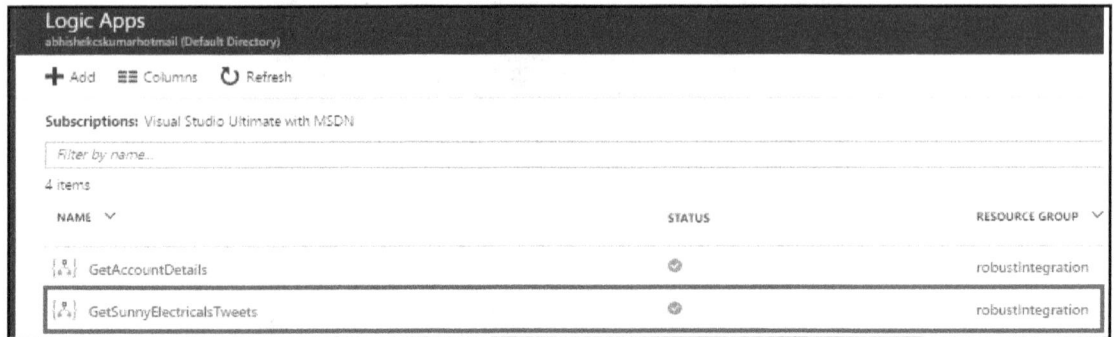

To edit Logic App workflow, click on the **GetSunnyElectricalsTweets**Logic App .This will open the Logic App window, Click on **Logic Apps Designer** to open up the Logic Apps **Templates** window, select **Blank LogicApp** to create new workflowfrom scratch.

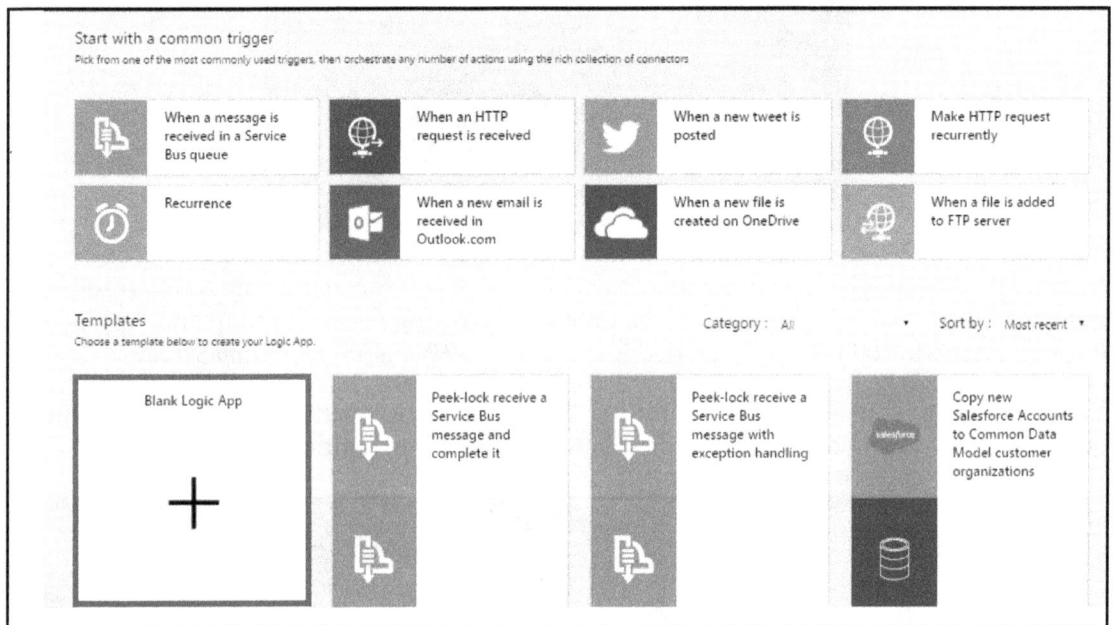

On **Logic Apps Designer**, a search box is available where you can look for the available Microsoft managed connectors and APIs available within your subscription. From the Microsoft managed APIs' list, click on **Twitter – When a new tweet is posted**.

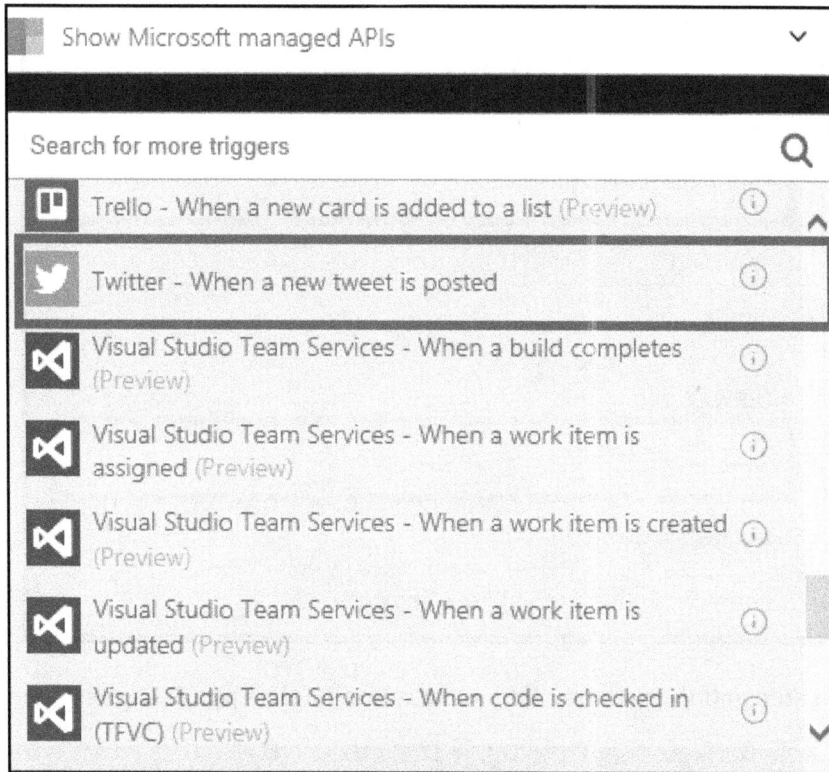

You need to provide authorization details to validate your twitter account, click on **Sign in** to enter your twitter details.

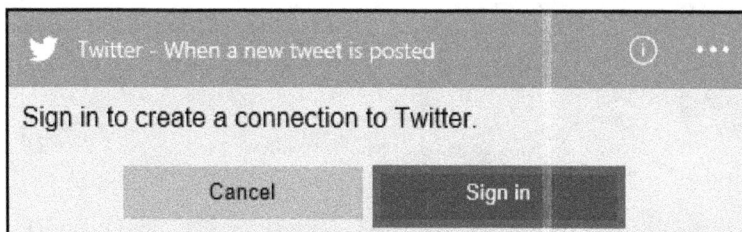

To enable Logic App poll for tweets containing Sunny Electricals, you have populated the Twitter connector. In this solution, we will be polling Twitter for messages containing the hashtag **#SunnyElectricals** at an interval of 15 minutes.

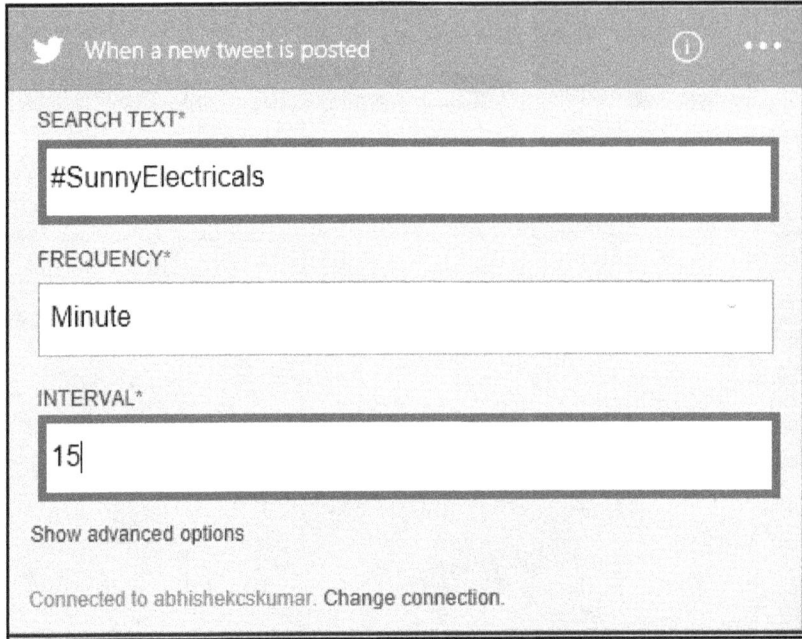

Click on **Next step** and then choose **Add an action** on **Logic Apps Designer** window.

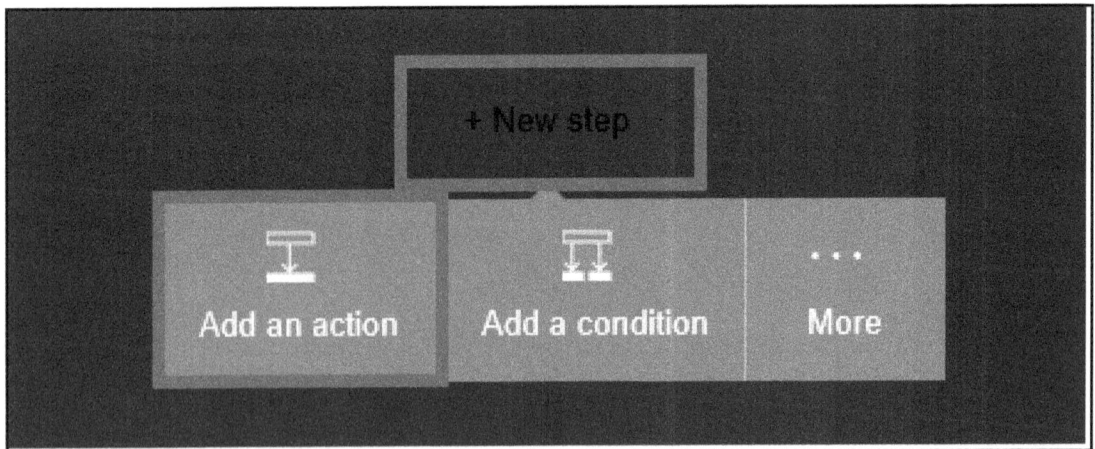

When you select **Add an Action**, again Microsoft managed APIs will be available; in the search box, type `insert`. This will pop up with **SQL Server – Insert row**.

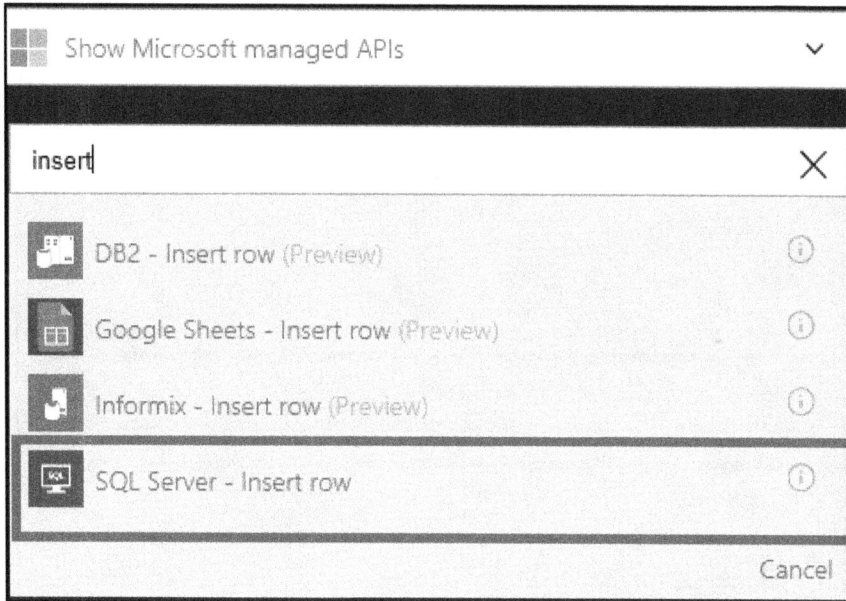

Provide connection information to connect to your Azure SQL Database. Enter the connection information for the SQL instance created as part of this exercise:

- **CONNECTION NAME**
- **SQL SERVER NAME**
- **SQL DATABASE NAME**

- **USERNAME**
- **PASSWORD**

Once the SQL connection has been made, you can perform insert operations for each polled message containing the #**SunnyElectricals** hashtag.

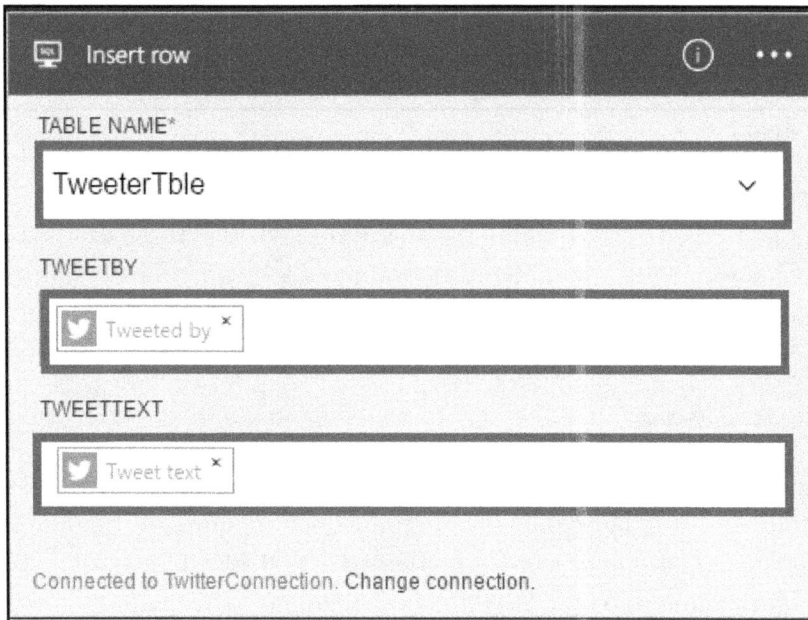

Once the Logic App design is completed, click on **Save** to start the Logic App. In this solution, we are using two Microsoft managed APIs: one for polling Twitter and another for the SQL insert operation.

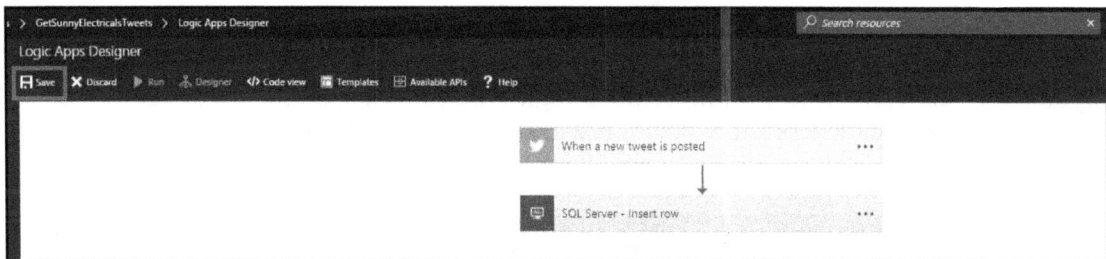

You can look at the traffic going through your Logic App by clicking on the **Overview** section of the newly created Logic App.

If you are wish to see the flow of individual Logic App call, click on the particular Logic App run, and verify the workflow detail. It will show you the sequence of steps within your Logic App, and you can easily track if any exception raised during Logic App run.

Logic Apps using Visual Studio

In the earlier section, you have built a Logic App using the Azure portal. Now we will walk through developing Logic Apps using Visual Studio 2015. Logic Apps support a rich visual designer, and you can leverage the Visual Studio capability to build Logic App workflows. You can use Azure resource PowerShell scripts that ship with Logic Apps for automated deployment.

Visual Studio 2015 configuration steps for Logic App

To start working with Logic App using Visual Studio 2015, there are certain prerequisites that need to be installed and configured properly:

- **Visual Studio 2015**
- **Latest Azure SDK (2.9.1 or greater)**
- **Access to Internet and valid Azure subscription**

Once you have Visual Studio 2015 and Azure SDK 2.9.1 or higher, you can follow the steps later to configure your Logic App template within Visual Studio.

Run Visual Studio 2015 as administrator

On the Visual Studio designer surface, navigate to **Tools** | **Extensions and Updates** | **Azure Logic Apps Tools for Visual Studio**, and Click on the **Download** button to install the Logic App extension.

You can also use direct link:
`https://visualstudiogallery.msdn.microsoft.com/e25ad307-46cf-412e-8ba5-5b555d53 d2d9` for Logic App extension download.

Create Resource group template for Logic App

On Visual Studio, navigate to **File | New Project | Cloud | Azure Resource Group**. Type a name for the resource group and then click on **OK**.

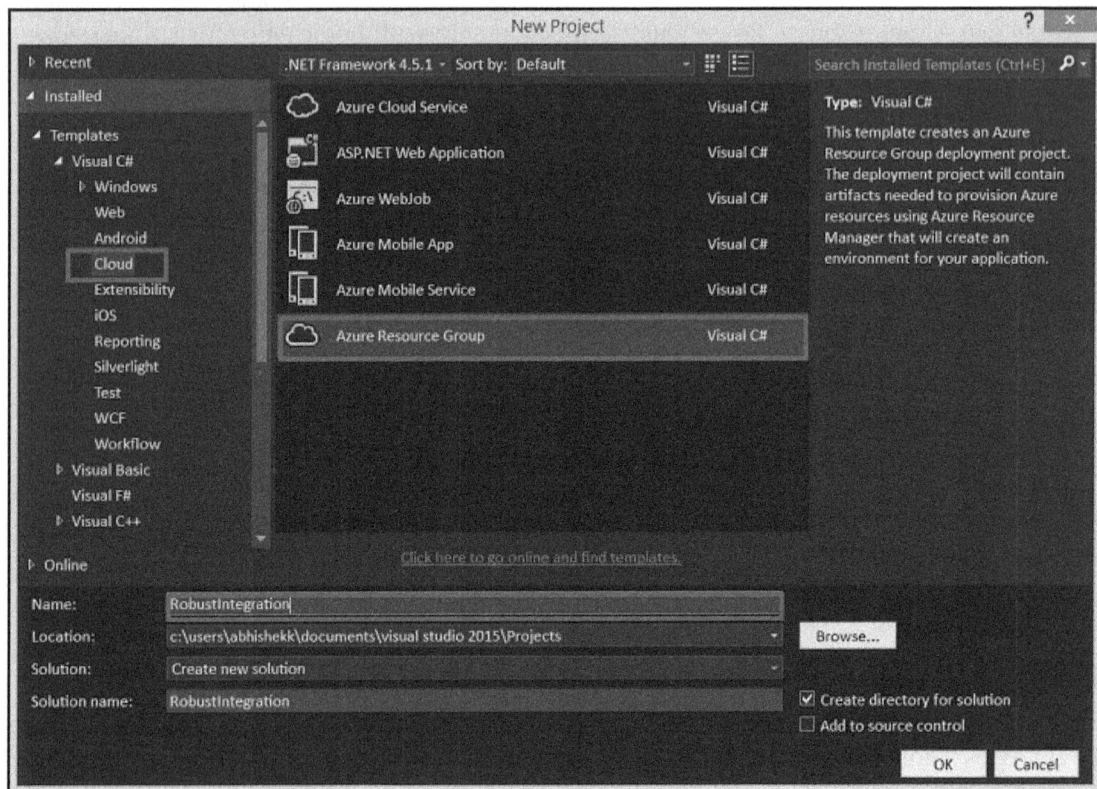

From the list of templates, select **Logic App**, and this will create an empty Logic App project.

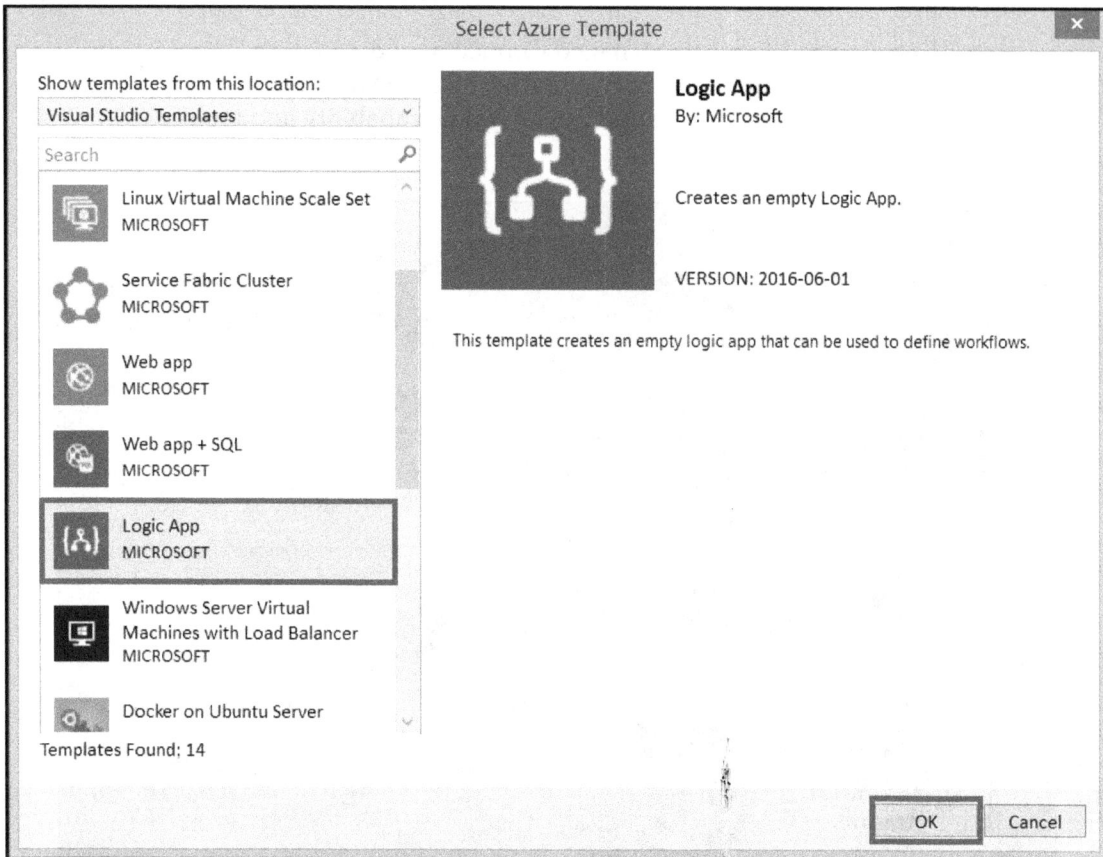

This will create an empty Logic App project in Visual Studio 2015; you will be able to see that the LogicApp.json and Deploy-AzureResourceGroup.ps1 files have been added to the solution. The LogicApp.json file will be using for workflow design, and Deploy-AzureResourceGroup.ps1 will be for the purposes of deployment.

Polling Twitter for #SunnyElectricals

The Logic App will poll twitter for new tweets with **#SunnyElectricals** and store all tweet information in the Azure SQL table. Here, twitter is acting as polling trigger and instantiates a runtime workflow with each single tweet message posted over tweeter. This is similar to what we have developed through Azure portal.

To open the Visual Studio designer for Logic App, right-click on the `<template>.json` file, and click on **Open With Logic App Designer**. You need to select the correct Azure subscription, resource group, and location for the deployment template.

> To populate Microsoft Managed Connector and API with Visual Studio, it is necessary to have Internet connectivity at the time of writing this book. You will be seeing more updates on Visual capability and tooling in coming time.

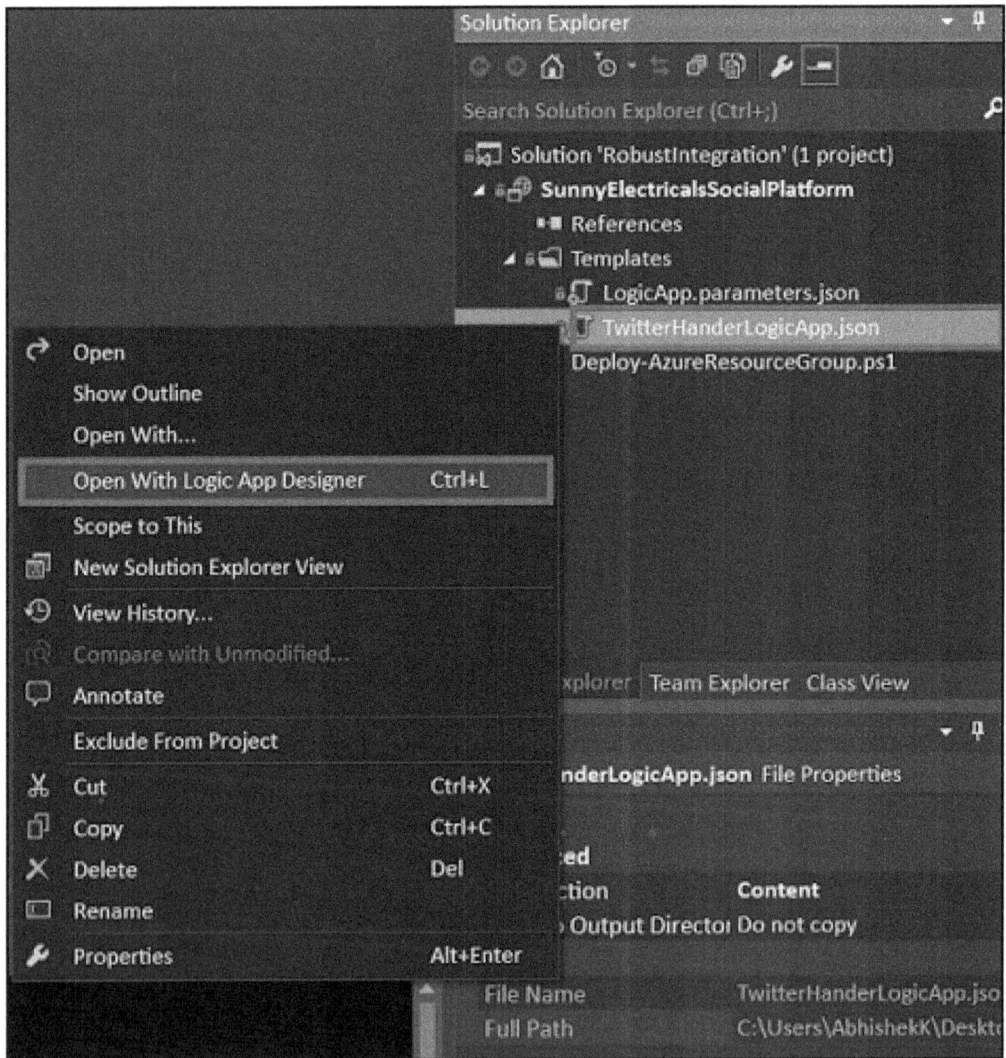

- Use the Visual Studio designer to build the Logic App workflow. Here, we have created a similar Logic App that will be triggered whenever there is specific tweet for Sunny Electricals with the **#SunnyElectricals** hashtag.

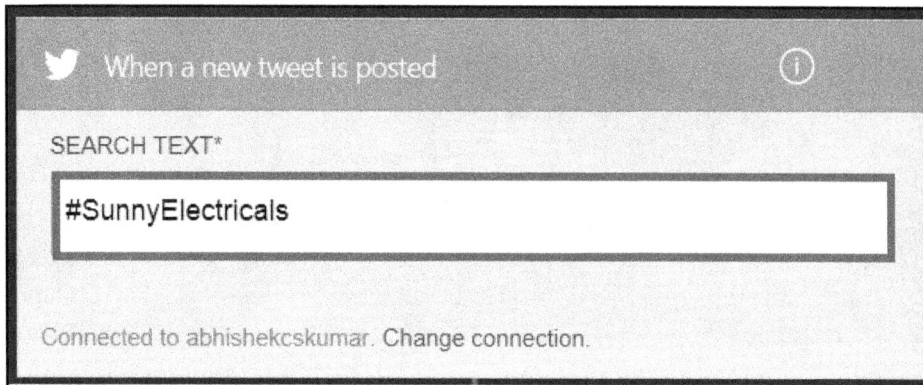

We then store all the tweet information in an Azure SQL table for further analysis purposes:

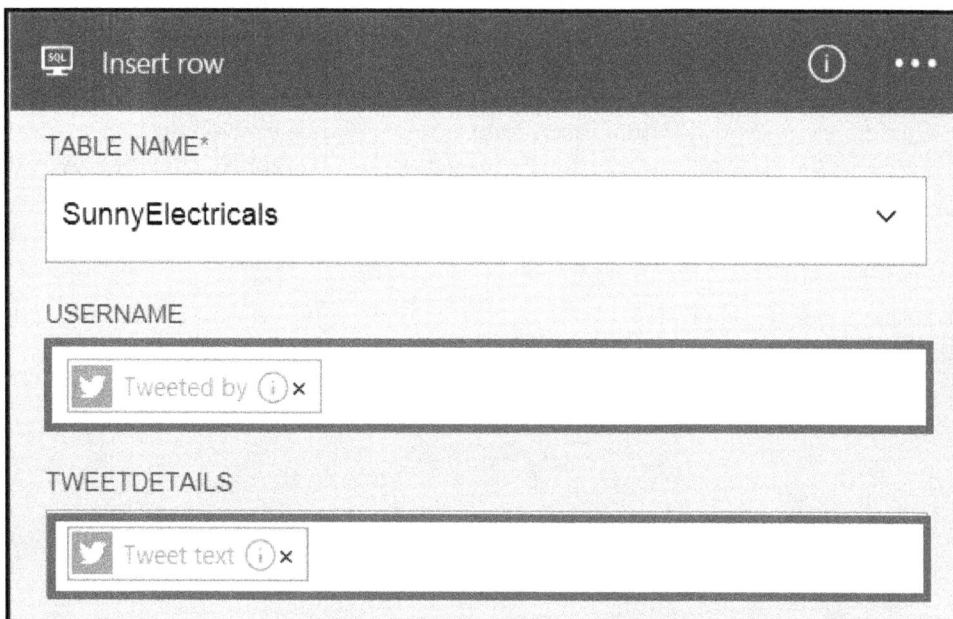

The overall solution structure will look like the figure mentioned later. You can download the solution from a GitHub repository and source code attached with the book.

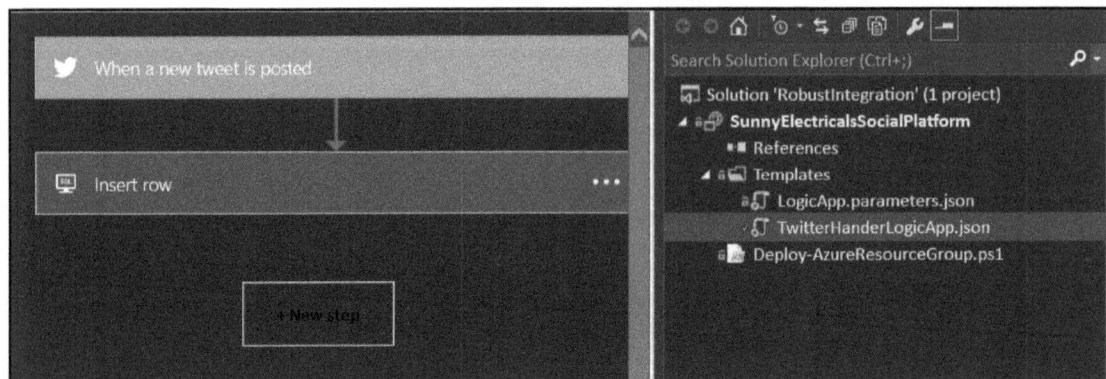

Code view

You can go through code behind by navigating code view tab at the bottom of Visual Studio designer. This way, you can see trigger and action code associated with Logic App. If you look at the code behind for the earlier solution, you can find a trigger and associated action within Logic App code behind:

- Trigger is a condition that instantiate a new instance of workflow. Here, if we look at the code behind twitter API is acting as a trigger for the Logic App and is polling on condition `"When_a_new_tweet_is_posted"`. You can also verify the method type and recurrence polling interval for the Microsoft managed twitter API.

```
"triggers": {
  "When_a_new_tweet_is_posted": {
    "type": "ApiConnection",
    "inputs": {
      "host": {
        "api": {
          "runtimeUrl": "https://logic-apis-centralus.azure-apim.net/apim/twitter"
        },
        "connection": {
          "name": "@parameters('$connections')['twitter']['connectionId']"
        }
      },
      "method": "get",
      "queries": {
        "searchQuery": "#SunnyElectricals"
      },
      "path": "/onnewtweet"
    },
    "recurrence": {
      "interval": 15,
      "frequency": "Minute"
    },
    "splitOn": "@triggerBody()?.value"
  }
}
```

- The action is the operation performed after a trigger. In current solution, we are using Insert operation against SQL. The code behind will show the actual workflow logic for your logic App:
  - Action Type = Insert_row
  - Method =post

- "tweetBy": "@{triggerBody()['TweetedBy']}"
- "tweetText": "@{triggerBody()['TweetText']}"

```
"actions": {
    "Insert row": {
        "type": "ApiConnection",
        "inputs": {
            "host": {
                "api": {
                    "runtimeUrl": "https://logic-apis-centralus.azure-apim.net/apim/sql"
                },
                "connection": {
                    "name": "@parameters('$connections')['sql_2']['connectionId']"
                }
            },
            "method": "post",
            "path": "/datasets/default/tables/@{encodeURIComponent(encodeURIComponent('[dbo].[TweeterTble]'))}/items",
            "body": {
                "tweetBy": "@{triggerBody()['TweetedBy']}",
                "tweetText": "@{triggerBody()['TweetText']}"
            }
        },
        "runAfter": {}
    }
}
```

Deployment

After creating Visual workflow associated with Logic App, you can right-click the solution and click on **Deploy**. This will prompt you to select proper Azure Resource Group and the plan.

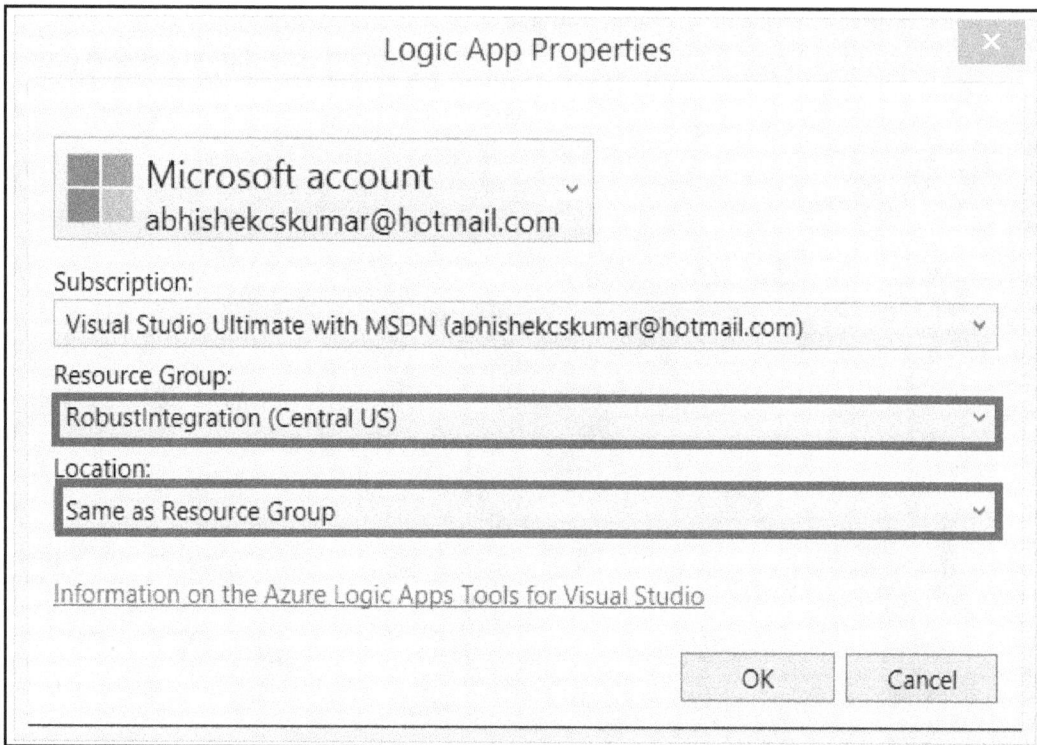

Once deployment of Logic App is succeeded, log in to the Azure portal and verify the Logic app activity log and summary by clicking on the **Overview** section and **Activity log** section. Logic App activity log gives you better insight into resource group monitoring.

Logic App diagnostics will give overall analysis of workflow run. You can click on the **Diagnostics** section of **Logic App** blade to see the graphical representation of all the runs.

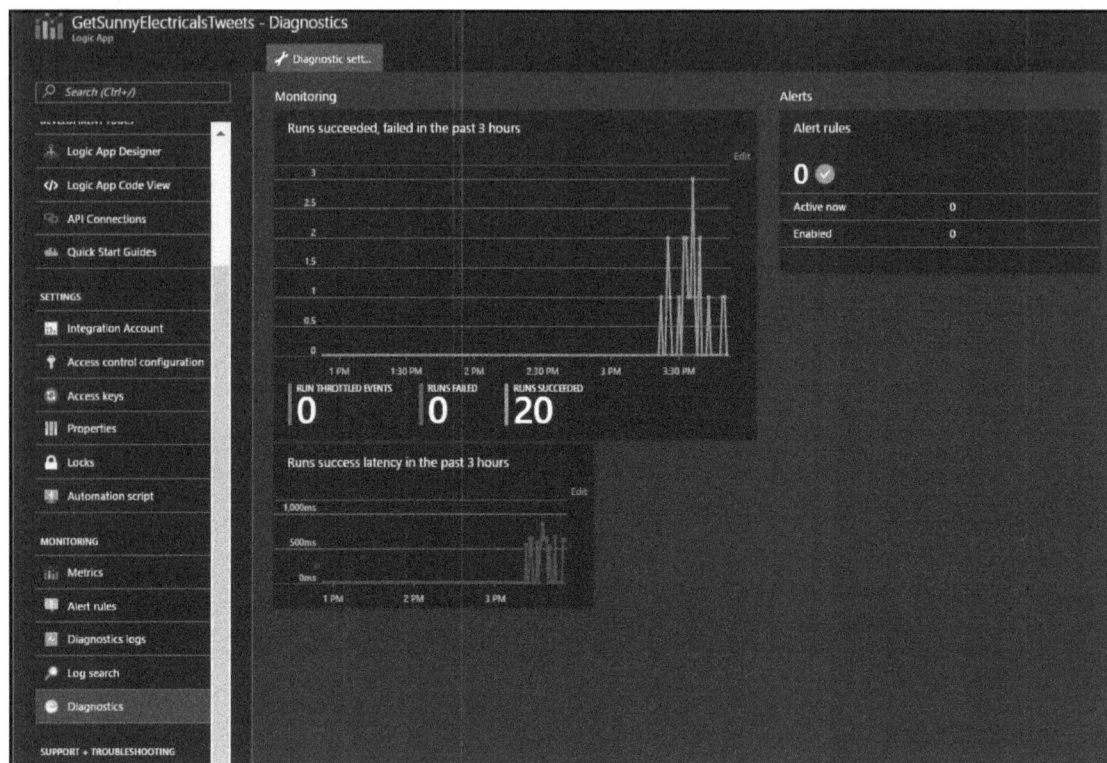

Summary

In this chapter, we discussed how Logic Apps came about and their intentional uses in the world of integration. You learnt about the three main concepts of triggers, actions, and connectors when using Logic Apps. We compared development and integration features between Logic Apps and BizTalk server and discussed different integration scenarios. We looked at some tools to help test and diagnose Logic Apps and built our very first Logic App using both the Azure portal and Visual Studio 2015.

In the next chapter, we will take a deep dive into Logic App connectors and develop our very own adaptor.

6

Working with Connectors in Logic Apps

Insufficient facts always invite danger.
— Mr. Spock, Star Trek

Azure Logic Apps is a cloud-based service that you can use to create workflows that run in the cloud. It provides a way to connect your applications, data, and SaaS application using a rich set of connectors. Connectors get data in and out of a Logic App. It is created specifically to help you when you are connecting to different data source or applications and working with your data.

In this chapter, you will learn the following topics:

- What are the different types of connector available in Logic Apps?
- What are Workflow Triggers and Actions?
- How can we create our own custom connector?

Traditionally, the two of mainstream integration scenarios are as follows:

- **EAI (Enterprise Application Integration)**
- **B2B (Business-to-Business)** integration using EDI protocols, such as **EDIFACT** or **ANSI X12**

However, in today's world, many systems and users need to integrate with SaaS-based systems and API-centric providers that handle everything from sales lead to invoicing, e-mail communication, and social media. Also, these systems or services can be well beyond corporate firewall.

As discussed in `Chapter 5`, *Trigger Your First Logic App in Azure*, Logic Apps provides a new way to build a business process that orchestrate data and services across cloud and on-premise data center. It is a browser-based workflow engine that makes integrating disparate applications and data sources from cloud to on-premises easy.

Also, modern integration is often not about enterprise systems and services only, but it has expanded to various mobile devices that drives the need of lightweight, modern API (connectors) primarily HTTP/REST-based protocols using JSON.

A connector is basically a type of API app that focuses on connectivity. Connectors get data in and out of a Logic App. It is created specifically to help you when you are connecting to different data source or applications and working with your data. It also aids you to extract and transform data from different enterprise applications or run complex business rules. Often in complex and advanced integration scenarios, these applications and data stores can span across cloud and on-premises resources.

Connectors can help to connect cloud and on-premises applications that are located behind a firewall using **On-premises data gateway** at: `https://azure.microsoft.com/en-us/doc umentation/articles/app-service-logic-gateway-connection/`.

Connectors make it easy to integrate systems and services and can also be used in order to manage authentication, monitoring, analytics, and more.

Essentially, all connectors are technically API Apps that uses a metadata format named **Swagger** (`http://swagger.io/`), **REST** as pluggable interfaces, and **JSON** as the data interchange format, which is easy for humans to read and write, and it's also easy for the systems to generate and parse data.

Connectors can act as a trigger or an action. A trigger starts a new instance of a workflow based on a specific event, such as the arrival of an e-mail or an insert of a new record in the table of a database or a change in your Azure storage account. Connector exposes some capability that after being triggered will be piped into other connectors (actions). By chaining these triggers and connectors, you can create potentially complex and powerful integrations between applications. We will discuss trigger and action in detail later in this chapter.

So, in a nutshell, Logic Apps are a collection of connectors that are primarily API Apps. These connectors can also be used to build **PowerApps** (`https://powerapps.microsoft.com`) and **Flow** (`https://flow.microsoft.com`). We will discuss about PowerApps and Flow later in the book. In this chapter, we will dig into the types of connector available from Microsoft, how can we use them in Logic Apps, and how can we create our own custom connector.

Categorizing Microsoft connectors

Connectors can be categorized into several groups based on the kind of operation they perform. These groups primarily include standard connectors and enterprise integration connectors.

Standard connectors

Standard connectors are the connectors created by Microsoft to work with SaaS applications or network services, and they include Office 365, SharePoint, Service Bus, Salesforce, SFTP, FTP/FTPS, and many more.

The following are the current list of available connectors created by Microsoft that are available as standard connectors.

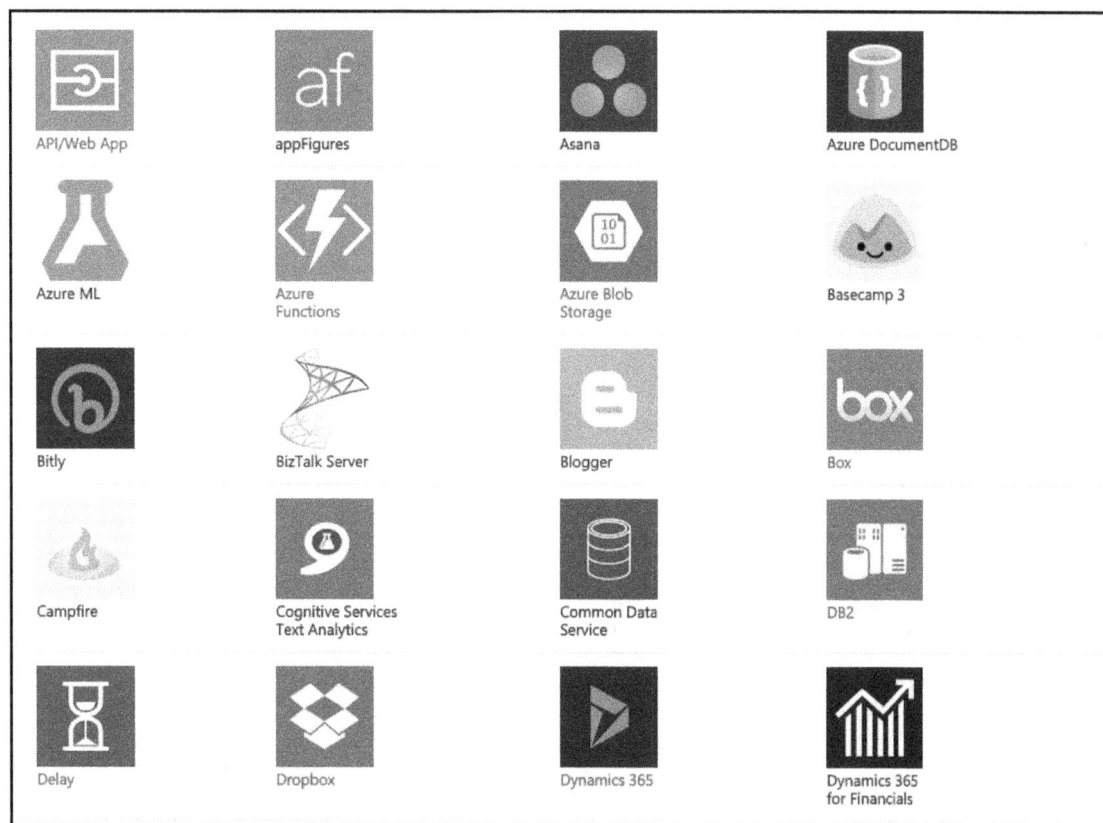

This list will keep growing. Please refer to the link: `https://azure.microsoft.com/en-us/documentation/articles/apis-list/` for the latest list of standard connectors.

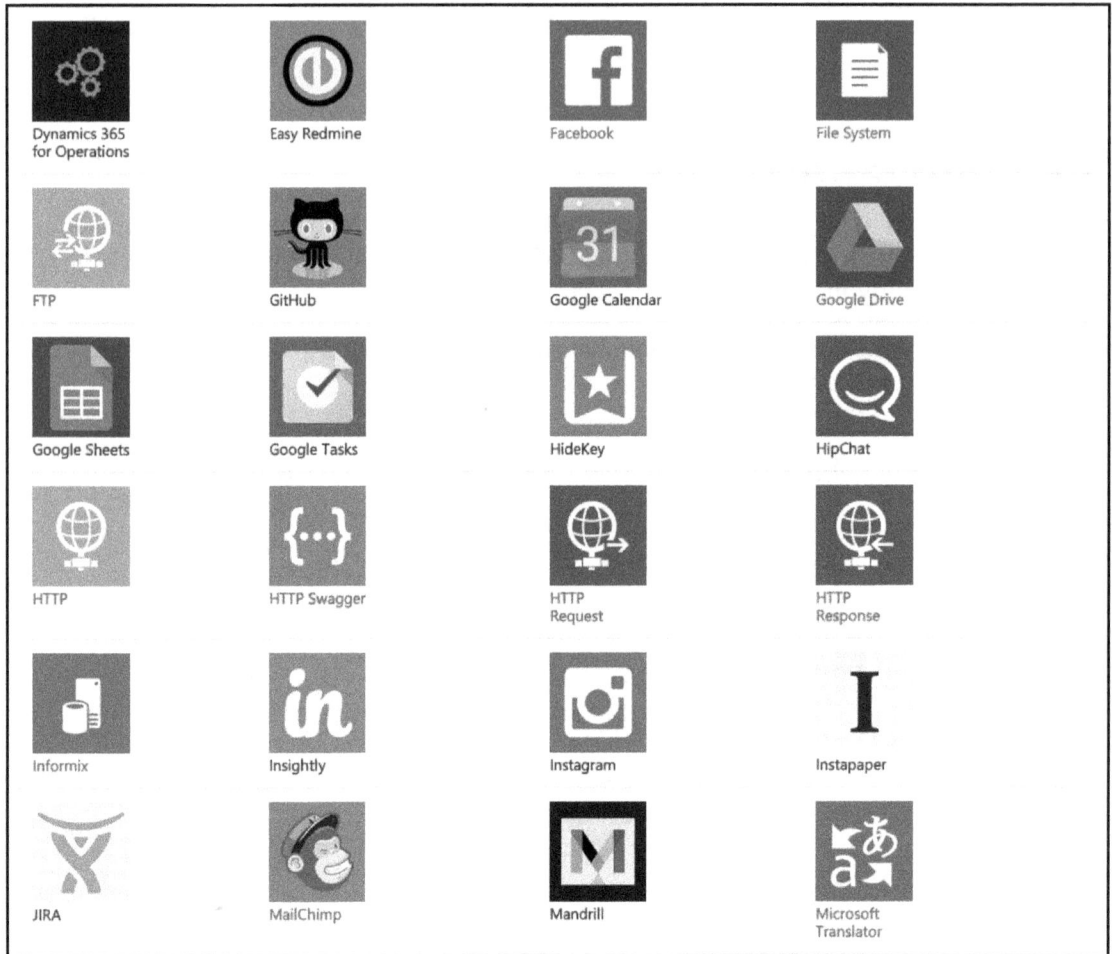

Dynamics 365 for Operations	Easy Redmine	Facebook	File System
FTP	GitHub	Google Calendar	Google Drive
Google Sheets	Google Tasks	HideKey	HipChat
HTTP	HTTP Swagger	HTTP Request	HTTP Response
Informix	Insightly	Instagram	Instapaper
JIRA	MailChimp	Mandrill	Microsoft Translator

Some of these managed APIs can be used as is, such as Bing Translator, whereas others require configuration. This configuration is named a **connection**.

For example, when you use Office 365 connector, you need to create a connection that contains your sign-in token. This token will be securely stored and refreshed so that your Logic app can always call the Office 365 API. Alternatively, if you want to connect to your SQL or FTP server, you need to create a connection that has the connection string.

These actions are named as `"ApiConnection"` in the workflow definition language. The example here shows a connection that calls Office 365 to send an e-mail.

```
{
  "actions": {
    "Send_Email": {
      "type": "ApiConnection",
      "inputs": {

        "host": {
          "api": {
            "runtimeUrl": "https://msmanaged-na.azure-apim.net/apim/office365"
          },
          "connection": {
            "name": "@parameters('$connections')['shared_office365']['connectionId']"
          }
        },

        "method": "post",
        "body": {
          "Subject": "Reminder",
          "Body": "Don't forget!",
          "To": "hi.gyan@outlook.com"
        },
        "path": "/Mail"
      }
    }
  }
}
```

The portion of the inputs that is unique to API connections is the `"host"` object. This contains two parts: `"api"` and `"connection"`. The `"api"` has the runtime URL of where that managed API is hosted.

When you use an API, it may or may not have any connection parameters defined. If it doesn't, then no connection is required. If it does, then you will have to create a connection. When you create that connection, it'll have the name you choose and then you reference that in the connection object inside the host object. To create a connection in a resource group, call:

```
PUT
https://management.azure.com/subscriptions/{subid}/resourceGroups/{rgname}/
providers
```

With the following body:

```
{
  "properties": {
    "api": {
      "id": "/subscriptions/{subid}/providers/Microsoft.Web/managedApis/azureblob"
    },
    "parameterValues": {
      "accountName": "{The name of the storage account -- the set of parameters is different for each API}"
    }
  },
  "location": "{Logic app's location}"
}
```

Enterprise Integration connectors

These are primarily **EAI and EDI connectors** used for **B2B scenarios** with Logic Apps . As of Now we are having SAP and MQ connector available to connect the Logic Apps to enterprise system. This list is also growing and you can see lot of enterprise connector getting shipped with Logic Apps.

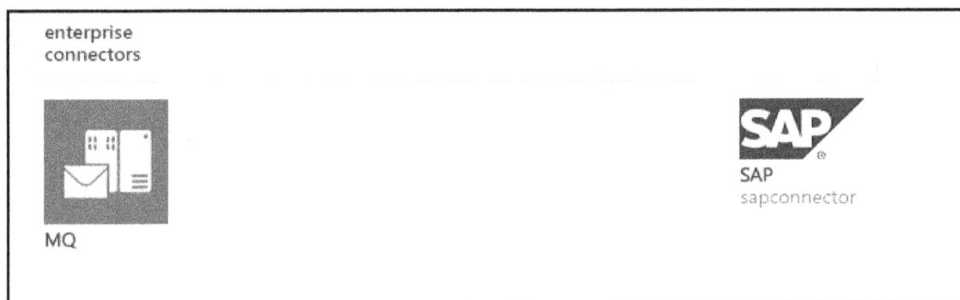

Connectors as triggers

A trigger specifies the calls that can initiate a run of your Logic App workflow. It's a common scenario where based on an event such as an arrival of an e-mail or new tweets that contain specific words, your workflow kicks off and take the appropriate action in response to the event.

Let's refer the example from the previous chapter, where the Logic App is using the Twitter API app and your workflow needs to perform an action based on new tweets that contain specific words. In this case, your Twitter connector can be used as trigger so that a new instance Logic App workflow instantiate.

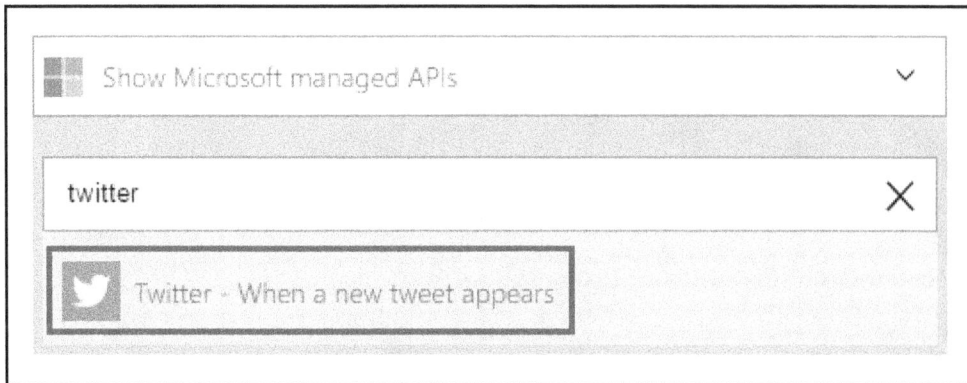

Here is the code view for the Twitter Connector as a trigger:

```json
{
  "triggers": {
    "When_a_new_tweet_appears": {
      "type": "ApiConnection",
      "inputs": {
        "host": {
          "api": {
            "runtimeUrl": "https://logic-apis-westus.azure-apim.net/apim/twitter"
          },
          "connection": {
            "name": "@parameters('$connections')['twitter']['connectionId']"
          }
        },
        "method": "get",
        "path": "/onnewtweet",
        "queries": {
          "searchQuery": "#LogicApps"
        }
      },
      "recurrence": {
        "frequency": "Hour",
        "interval": 1
      },
      "splitOn": "@triggerBody()?.value"

    }
  }
}
```

All triggers can contain these top-level elements:

```
"<name-of-the-trigger>": {
  "type": "<type-of-trigger>",
  "inputs": { "<settings-for-the-call>" },
  "recurrence": {
    "frequency": "Second|Minute|Hour|Week|Month|Year",
    "interval": "<recurrence interval in units of frequency>"
  },
  "conditions": [ "<array-of-required-conditions", ">" ],
  "splitOn": "<property to create runs for>"
  "operationOptions": "<operation options on the trigger>"
}
```

There are the following two ways to initiate your Logic App workflow:

- **Poll triggers**: Logic Apps polls your service (API App) endpoint at a specified interval to check for the new event. When new event data is available, a new instance of workflow runs with the event response data as input.

- **Push triggers**: In this case, Logic Apps are notified by the API App when an event occurs. A push trigger is implemented as a regular REST API that pushes notifications to Logic Apps by calling Workflow Service REST API (`https://doc s.microsoft.com/en-us/rest/api/logic/?redirectedfrom=MSDN`), which is a Logic App as callable endpoint.

There is also native support for triggering Logic Apps via WebHooks, including the ability to define a synchronous response to the trigger. To create something that can be used as a push trigger, you need to expose an API endpoint to subscribe to your WebHook.

> A WebHook is an HTTP callback: an HTTP POST that occurs when something happens, a simple event-notification via HTTP POST.

Types of triggers

The following six types of triggers are supported in Logic Apps as of now:

- **Recurrence trigger**: This fires based on a defined recurring schedule—"every X second/minutes/hour/day".

- **HTTP trigger**: This polls an HTTP web endpoint for a response. Here, the connector as a trigger will either return 200 or 202 response.
    - A 200 response means "**Run**"—workflow will be executed
    - A 202 response means "**Wait**"—do not start the workflow as the connector does not have any response data to pass over to workflow

- **ApiConnection trigger**: These are polls such as the HTTP trigger. However, it takes advantage of the Microsoft managed APIs (For more information refer to: h ttps://azure.microsoft.com/documentation/articles/apis-list/). The basic functionality of API connection trigger is similar to the HTTP trigger.Here is an example of the Dropbox connector that polls a defined folder for a new file.

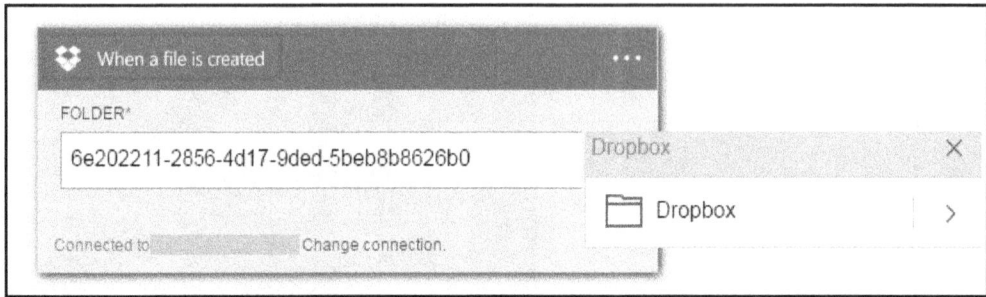

```
"triggers": {
  "When a file is created": {
    "type": "ApiConnection",
    "inputs": {
      "host": {
        "api": {
          "runtimeUrl": "https://logic-apis-westus.azure-apim.net/apim/dropbox"
        },
        "connection": {
          "name": "@parameters('$connections')['dropbox']['connectionId']"
        }
      },
      "method": "get",
      "path": "/datasets/default/triggers/onnewfile",
      "queries": {
        "folderId": "6e202211-2856-4d17-9ded-5beb8b8626b0"
      }
    },
    "recurrence": {
      "frequency": "Hour",
      "interval": 1
    }
  }
}
```

- **Manual trigger**: This trigger serves as an endpoint that you call manually to invoke your Logic App. This is one of the three types of Push triggers that can receive request. The other two are HTTPWebhook and ApiConnectionWebhook, which are discussed next.

You can use the "HTTP Request" trigger as a manual trigger.

Once you add the trigger in your designer, you need to define a request body JSON schema and the designer will generate tokens to help you parse and pass data from the manual trigger through the workflow. You can use a tool such as `jsonschema.net` to generate a JSON schema from a sample body payload.

```json
"triggers": {
  "manual": {
    "type": "Manual",
    "inputs": {
      "schema": {

        "$schema": "http://json-schema.org/draft-04/schema#",
        "properties": {
          "address": {
            "properties": {
              "street": {
                "type": "string"
              },
              "zip": {
                "type": "string"
              }
            },
            "required": [
              "street",
              "zip"
            ],
            "type": "object"
          },
          "name": {
            "type": "string"
          },
          "phone": {
            "type": "string"
          }
        },
        "required": [
          "name",
          "phone",
          "address"
        ],
        "type": "object"

      }
    }
  }
}
```

After you save your Logic App definition, a callback URL will be generated similar to:

```
https://prod-13.australiaeast.logic.azure.com:443/workflows/3g4
f50a60a3560938581f70d8c47hf45/triggers/manual/paths/invoke?api-
version=2016-06-01&sp=%2Ftriggers%2Fmanual%2Frun&sv=1.0&sig=RRv
N4GwgKta-cqH940wxqO2o6BuAUxonuy3sgsgmSg.
```

You can also get this endpoint in the Azure portal:

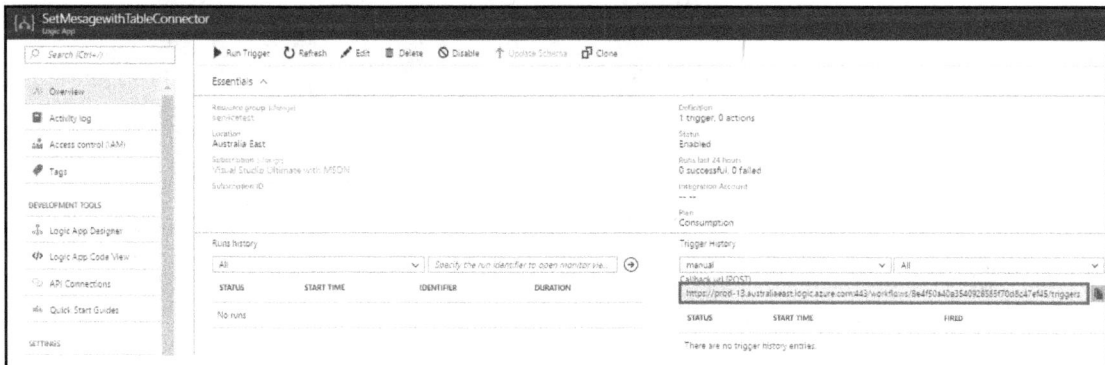

Once you have created the endpoint for your trigger, you can save it in your callback store in your system and call it via a POST to the full URL.

- **HTTPWebhook trigger**: This opens an endpoint, similar to the manual trigger. However, it also calls out to a specified URL to register and unregister.

Logic Apps now allow you to subscribe to external events via Webhooks. Webhooks can be used as a trigger that will instantiate a workflow. The Logic App engine will call the **subscribe** endpoint whenever a Webhook trigger is added and saved. Your API can register the webhook URL and call it via **HTTP POST** whenever data is available. The content payload and headers will be passed into the Logic App run.

If a Webhook trigger is ever deleted (either the Logic App entirely, or just the webhook trigger), the engine will make a call to the unsubscribe URL where your API can unregister the callback URL and stop any processes as needed.

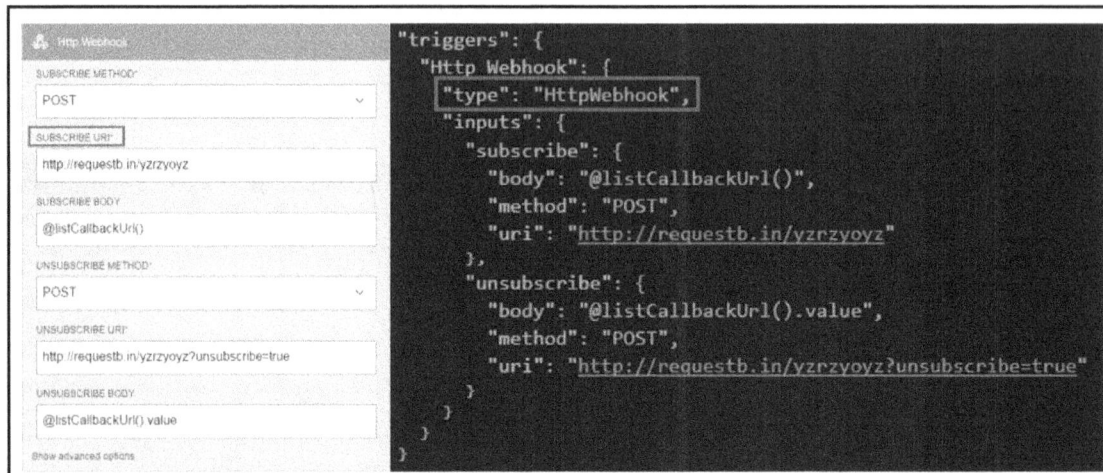

Subscribe is the outgoing call that makes Logic App to start listening to events. The function `@listCallbackUrl()` returns a unique URL for this specific trigger in this workflow.

Unsubscribe is called when the user performs an operation that renders this trigger invalid including the following:

- Deleting/disabling the trigger
- Deleting/disabling the workflow
- Deleting/disabling the subscription

The Logic app automatically calls the unsubscribe action. The parameters to this function are the same as the HTTP trigger. The outputs of the HTTPWebhook trigger are the contents of the incoming request.

- **ApiConnectionWebhook**: This operates like the HTTPWebhook trigger by taking advantage of the Microsoft-managed APIs.

Connector as an action

Each step after the trigger in a workflow is an action. Connectors can also be used as actions within your Logic Apps. Each action typically maps to an operation on your connector or custom API Apps that are defined in the Swagger metadata. Actions can have dependency, and they can be executed based on the condition such as success or failure of the previous action.

You can use the action for variety of operations such as to look up customer data from a SQL database when processing an order or may be to write, update, or delete data in a destination table.

Actions can be categorized as Standard Action and Collection Action.

Standard Actions:

There are six valid types of standard actions, each with unique behavior.

- **HTTP**: This action calls an HTTP web endpoint.

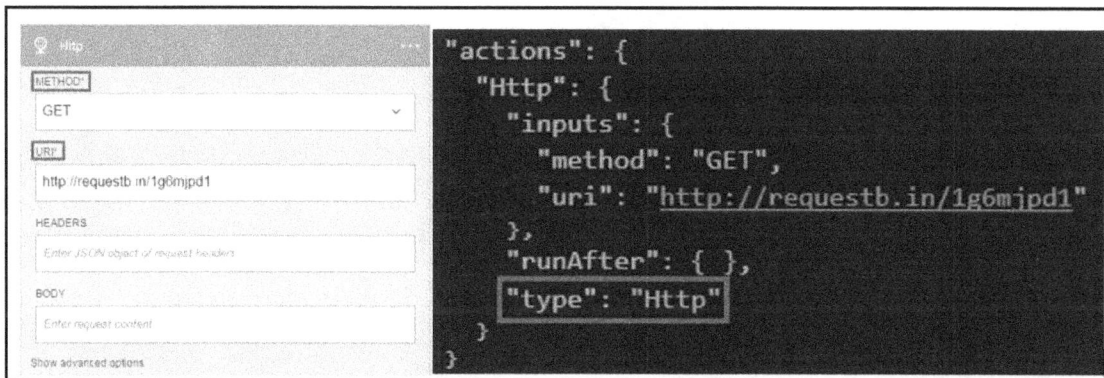

- **ApiConnection**: This action has behavior similar to the HTTP action; however, it takes advantage of the Microsoft-managed APIs. Here is a Dropbox action to create a file in the specified folder.

```
"actions": {
  "Create_file": {
    "inputs": {
      "body": "This is a test text.",
      "host": {
        "api": {
          "runtimeUrl": "https://logic-apis-westus.azure-apim.net/apim/dropbox"
        },
        "connection": {
          "name": "@parameters('$connections')['dropbox']['connectionId']"
        }
      },
      "method": "post",
      "path": "/datasets/default/files",
      "queries": {
        "folderPath": "/logicapps",
        "name": "TestFile"
      }
    },
    "runAfter": {
      "Http": [
        "Succeeded"
      ]
    },
    "type": "ApiConnection"
  }
}
```

- **ApiConnectionWebhook**: Webhook action act much like Webhook trigger is discussed earlier. You can have the Logic App pause and wait for a *callback* to continue. This callback comes in the form of an HTTP POST. To implement this pattern, you need to provide two endpoints on your controller: subscribe and unsubscribe.

  On *subscribe*, the Logic App will create and register a callback URL that your API App can store and call back when ready as an HTTP POST. The content payload and headers will be passed into the Logic App and can be used within the remainder of the workflow. The Logic App engine will call the subscribe point on execution as soon as it hits that step.

  If the run was canceled, the Logic App engine will make a call to the *unsubscribe* endpoint. Your API can then unregister the callback URL as needed.

- **Response**: This action type contains the entire response payload from an HTTP request. This includes a **STATUS CODE**, **BODY**, and **HEADERS**.

- **Wait**: This simple action will suspend the execution of the workflow for the specified interval. For example, to wait for 15 minutes, you can use the following code:

- **Workflow**: This action represents a nested workflow and can be used for chaining different child workflows. You can see the option of adding a Logic App workflow in the **Add an action** drop-down menu.

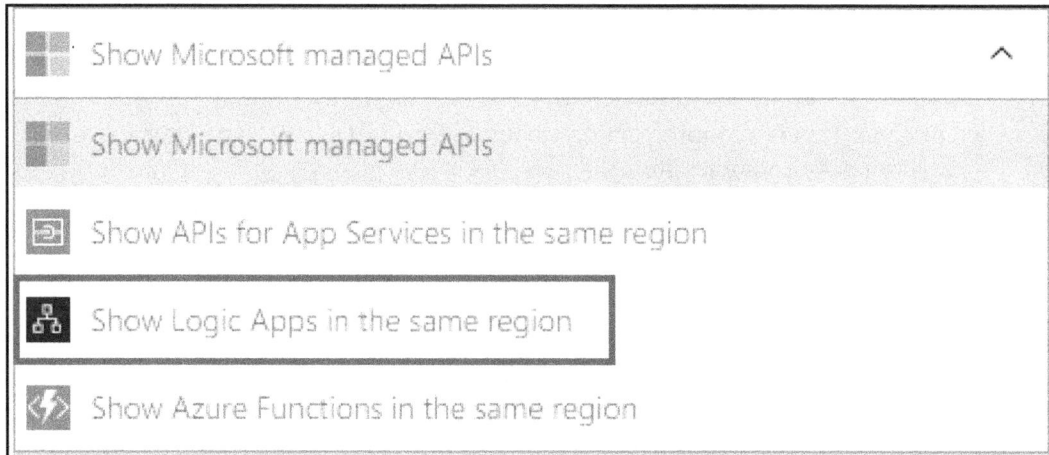

The output of the workflow action are based on what you defined in the response action in the child workflow. If you have not defined any response, then the outputs will be empty.

Collection Actions

These actions can contain many other actions within itself.

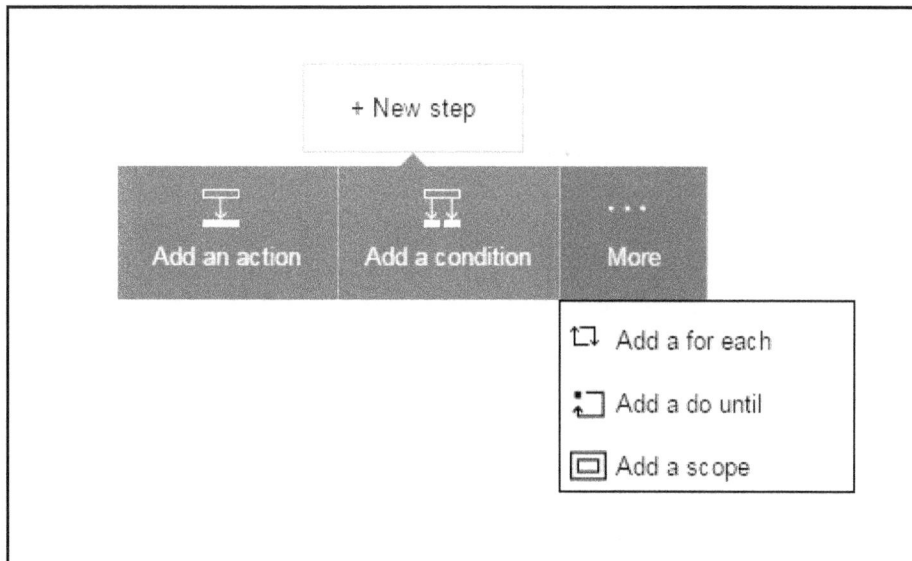

- **Scope:** This is used for logical grouping of actions within a Logic App workflow
- **Condition:** It allows you to evaluate a condition to execute a branch based on the true output of the conditional logic
- **For each:** This is a looping action to iterate through a list or an array and execute an inner action for each item
- **Until:** This is a looping action that will execute inner actions until a condition results to true

Building your first connector

As discussed in the beginning of this chapter, a connector is basically an API app that focuses on connectivity and gets data in and out of Logic Apps. In this section, we will try to build an **Azure Storage Table** connector. At the time of writing this chapter, **Azure Storage Table** connector was not available in the marketplace.

Azure Storage Table connector

We are building this connector to pull author or chapter details for this book from a Book Entity in the storage table.

PartitionKey	RowKey	AuthorName	Twitter	ChapterTitle
author	1	Gyanendra Gautam	@ggauta	
author	2	Ashish Bhambhani	@ashbham	
author	3	Abhishek Kumar	@abhishekcskumar	
author	4	Mahindra Morar	@mmorarnz	
author	5	James Corbould	@jamescorbould	
author	6	Martin Abbott	@martinabbott	
chapter	1			Chapter1: Introduction to Systems Integration in the Cloud
chapter	10			Chapter 10: Advanced Integration with Powerful, Scalable, Service Bus in the Cloud
chapter	11			Chapter 11: Connecting to Event Hubs and an Introduction IoT Hubs
chapter	12			Chapter 12: EAI/B2B Integration using Logic Apps
chapter	13			Chapter 13: Hybrid Integration using BizTalk Server 2016 and Logic Apps
chapter	15			Chapter 15: What's next?
chapter	2			Chapter2: What is an Azure App Service.
chapter	3			Chapter 3: Getting Started with API Apps
chapter	4			Chapter 4: Azure API Management
chapter	5			Chapter 5: Trigger your first Logic App in Azure
chapter	6			Chapter 6: Working with Connectors in Logic App
chapter	7			Chapter 7: Azure Functions in Logic Apps
chapter	8			Chapter 8: Deep Dive into Logic Apps
chapter	9			Chapter 9: Powerful Integration with SaaS using Logic Apps

First of all, we will create the API App project for storage table connector. Please follow the steps described to create an API App in `Chapter 3`, *Getting Started with API Apps.*

API App project will have a `BookEntity` model and a controller `BookController` as shown here:

```csharp
namespace AzureStorageTableConnector.Models
{
    /// <summary> Book Entity
    14 references
    public class BookEntity: TableEntity
    {
        /// <summary>
        /// Initializes a new instance of the <see cref="BookEntity"/> class.
        /// </summary>
        0 references
        public BookEntity()...

        /// <summary> Initializes a new instance of the BookEntity class. Defines the PK and RK.
        1 reference
        public BookEntity(string authorOrChapter, string sequenceNumber)
        {
            PartitionKey = authorOrChapter;
            RowKey = sequenceNumber;
        }

        /// <summary> Author Name
        2 references
        public string AuthorName { get; set; }

        /// <summary> Twitter handle
        2 references
        public string Twitter { get; set; }

        /// <summary> Chapter Title
        2 references
        public string ChapterTitle { get; set; }

    }
}
```

BookController will have an operation `GetBookEntity`. This operation primarily takes the `PartitionKey` and the `RowKey` to fetch the record from the storage table. If you see the model, the author or the chapter is the partition key and the sequence number is the row key. BookEntity contains 6 authors and 15 chapters. So, to get any author or chapter details, query should have the partition key and the row key. Please refer to the link for how to retrieve an entity from the storage table: `https://docs.microsoft.com/en-us/azure/storage/storage-dotnet-how-to-use-tables`.

```
namespace AzureStorageTableConnector.Controllers
{
    /// <summary> Controller to handle Book Entities
    1 reference
    public class BookController : ApiController
    {
        private CloudTableClient tableClient;
        private CloudTable table;
        internal const string TableName = "BookEntity";
        /// <summary> Constructor

        0 references
        public BookController()
        {
            // Retrieve storage account information from connection string.
            string connectionString = System.Configuration.ConfigurationManager.AppSettings["StorageConnectionString"];
            CloudStorageAccount storageAccount = CloudStorageAccount.Parse(connectionString);

            // Create a table client for interacting with the table service
            this.tableClient = storageAccount.CreateCloudTableClient();

            // Retrieve a reference to the table.
            this.table = tableClient.GetTableReference(TableName);

            // Create the table if it doesn't exist.
            table.CreateIfNotExists();

        }

        #region Actions
        /// <summary> Get Book Entity
        0 references
        public BookEntity GetBookEntity(string authorOrChapter, string sequenceNumber)
        {
            // Create a retrieve operation that takes a BookEntity entity.
            TableOperation retrieveOperation = TableOperation.Retrieve<BookEntity>(authorOrChapter, sequenceNumber);

            // Execute the retrieve operation.
            TableResult retrievedResult = table.Execute(retrieveOperation);

            //Return BookEntity entity
            return (BookEntity)retrievedResult.Result;

        }
        #endregion
```

Once you have created the project, you can test it locally using Swagger UI.

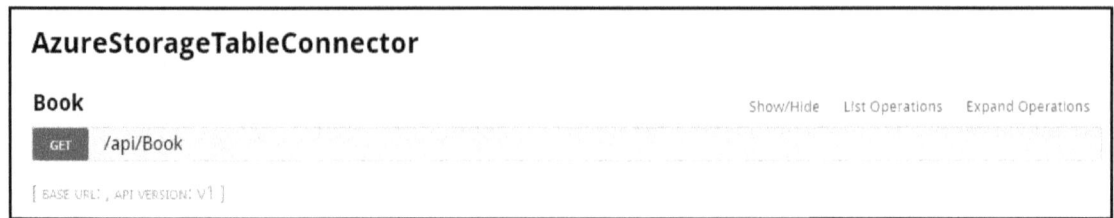

AzureStorageTableConnector

Book   Show/Hide   List Operations   Expand Operations

GET   /api/Book

[BASE URL: , API VERSION: V1]

You need to provide the value of the **authorOrChapter** and **sequenceNumber** parameters. So, here is the query to get the first author from the storage table.

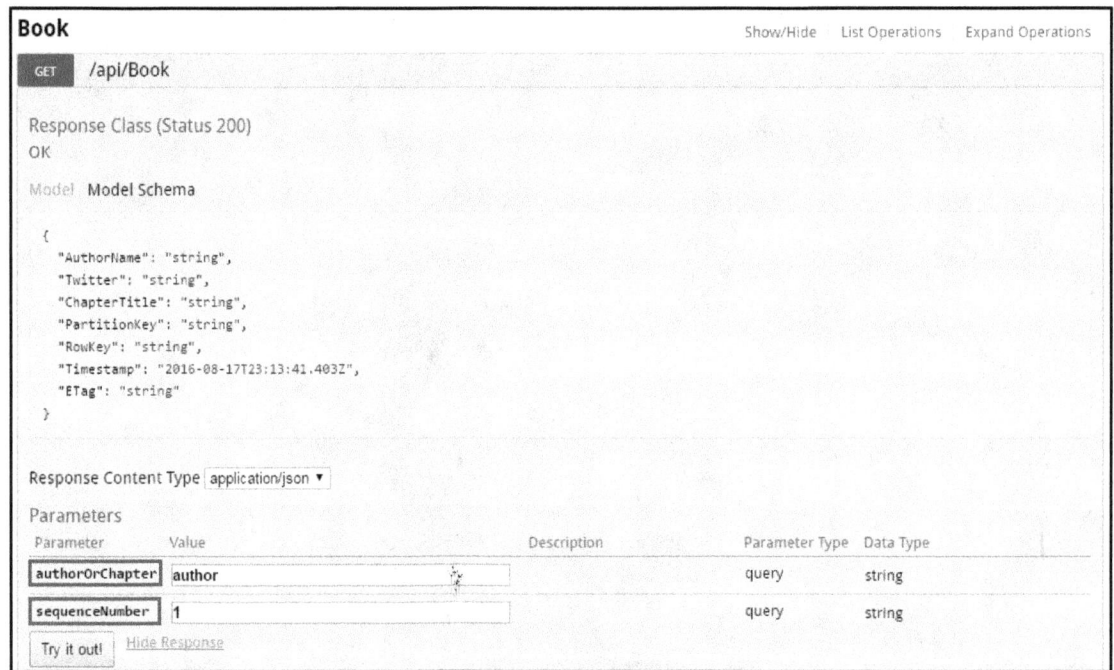

Book   Show/Hide   List Operations   Expand Operations

GET   /api/Book

Response Class (Status 200)
OK

Model   Model Schema

```
{
    "AuthorName": "string",
    "Twitter": "string",
    "ChapterTitle": "string",
    "PartitionKey": "string",
    "RowKey": "string",
    "Timestamp": "2016-08-17T23:13:41.403Z",
    "ETag": "string"
}
```

Response Content Type application/json ▼

Parameters

Parameter	Value	Description	Parameter Type	Data Type
authorOrChapter	author		query	string
sequenceNumber	1		query	string

Try it out!   Hide Response

Here is the response with the first author as Gyanendra Gautam.

Response Body

```
{
    "AuthorName": "Gyanendra Gautam",
    "Twitter": "@ggauta",
    "ChapterTitle": "",
    "PartitionKey": "author",
    "RowKey": "1",
    "Timestamp": "2016-08-17T17:33:40.7940523+00:00",
    "ETag": "W/\"datetime'2016-08-17T17%3A33%3A40.7940523Z'\""
}
```

Response Code

```
200
```

Once it is locally tested, we can publish it in Azure. So, this is what we have done so far:

- Created an API App in Visual Studio
- Enabled Swagger UI and tested API App locally
- Published your API App in Azure

Make your connector work for Logic Apps

Now when we try to use this API App as a custom connector in Logic Apps, there are certain gaps that we will cover now. First of all, we need to enable the CORS setting for the API App (**AzureStorageTableConnector**) we have created. Add a CORS policy for * to allow the requests from the **Logic Apps Designer**. Please refer to `Chapter 3`, *Getting Started with API Apps*, for understanding CORS.

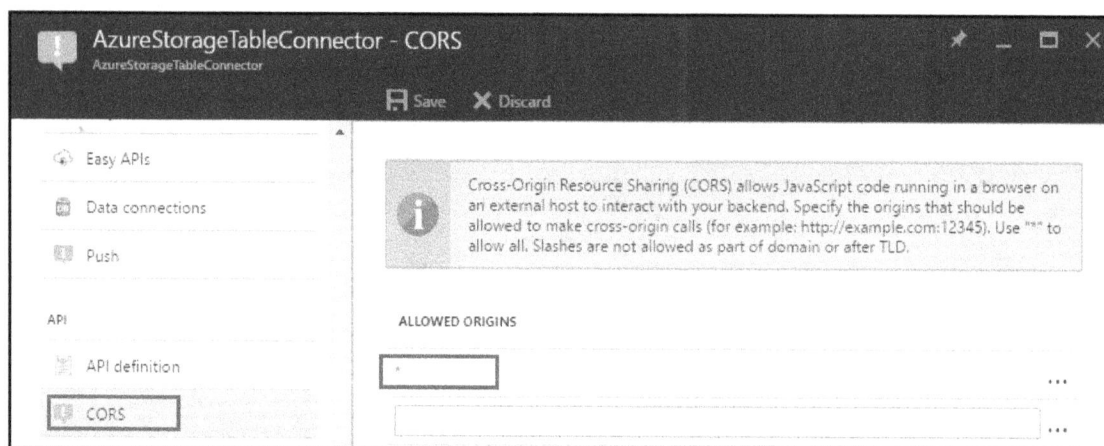

We have created an empty Logic App in the portal where we select the custom connector – **AzureStorageTableConnector**. Once you have enabled the CORS, you would be able to see the **AzureStorageTableConnector** in custom connector list in Logics App.

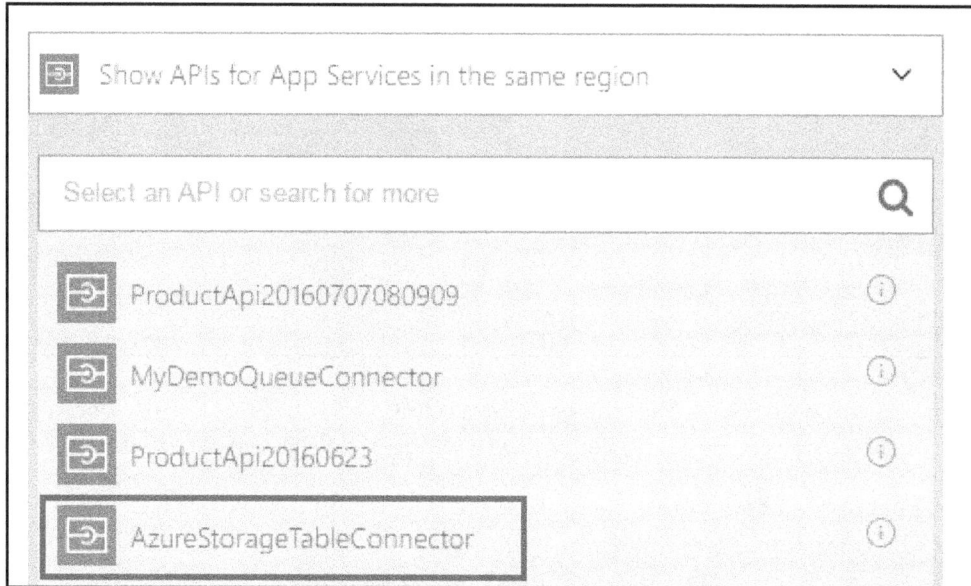

Once you select the **AzureStorageTableConnector** in the Logic App, you can see the get operation with input parameters **AUTHORORCHAPTER** and **SEQUENCENUMBER** as shown later. And if you select the next connector in the Logic App (for example, I have selected the Dropbox connector), it shows all the outputs from the GetBookEntity operation of the custom connector.

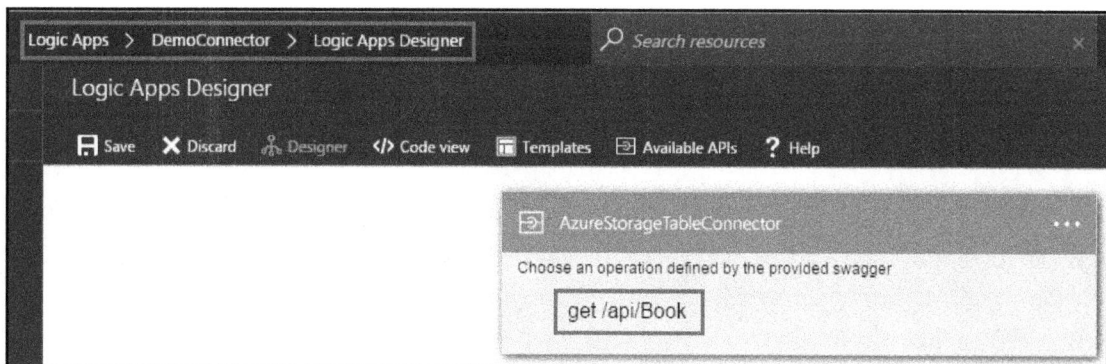

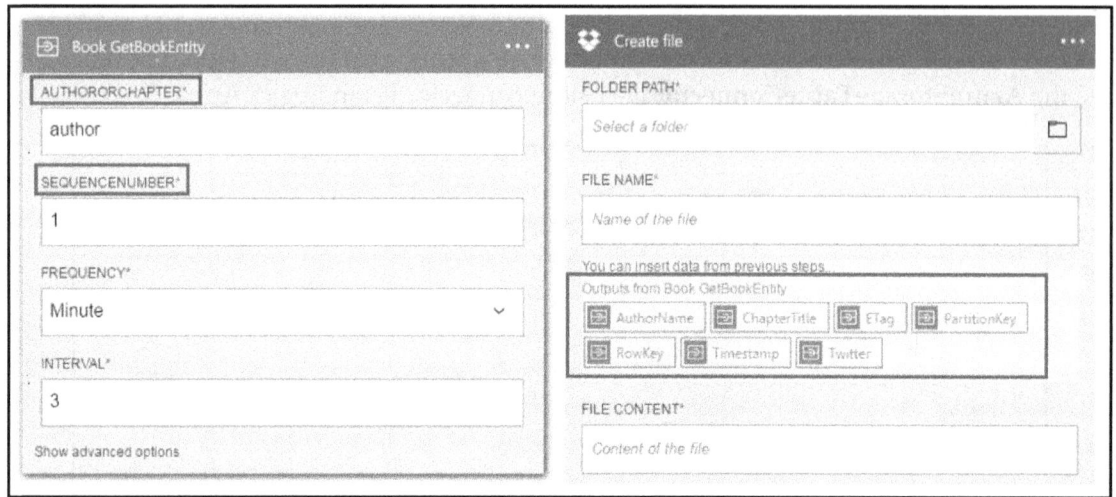

One thing you can note here is that the operation name `get/api/Book` is not very user friendly. To customize the Swagger generation `Swagger.cs` file, we can do the following:

- Enable XML comments
- Use operation filter

An operation filter is a piece of code that Swasbuckle will call before the Swagger of a particular operation is generated. We will now customize or Swagger for couple of things:

- To put the summary for our operation by enabling XML comments
- Discover partition keys from the storage table

Adding summary and XML Documentation

First, we need to turn on the generation of XML documentation in the **Build** properties page of API App project.

Now uncomment the line that tells Swasbuckle to include XML comments in the `Swagger.cs` file.

```
//c.IncludeXmlComments(GetXmlCommentsPath());
```

You now need to implement the function `GetXMLCommentsPath()` that would return the XMLComment file for the API.

```
0 references
private static string GetXmlCommentsPath()
{
        return System.String.Format(CultureInfo.InvariantCulture,
                        @"{0}\bin\AzureStorageTableConnector.xml",
                        System.AppDomain.CurrentDomain.BaseDirectory);
}
```

Now if you run the project, you can see the following in the Swagger UI. Now you can see the summary for API and description for parameters as shown here:

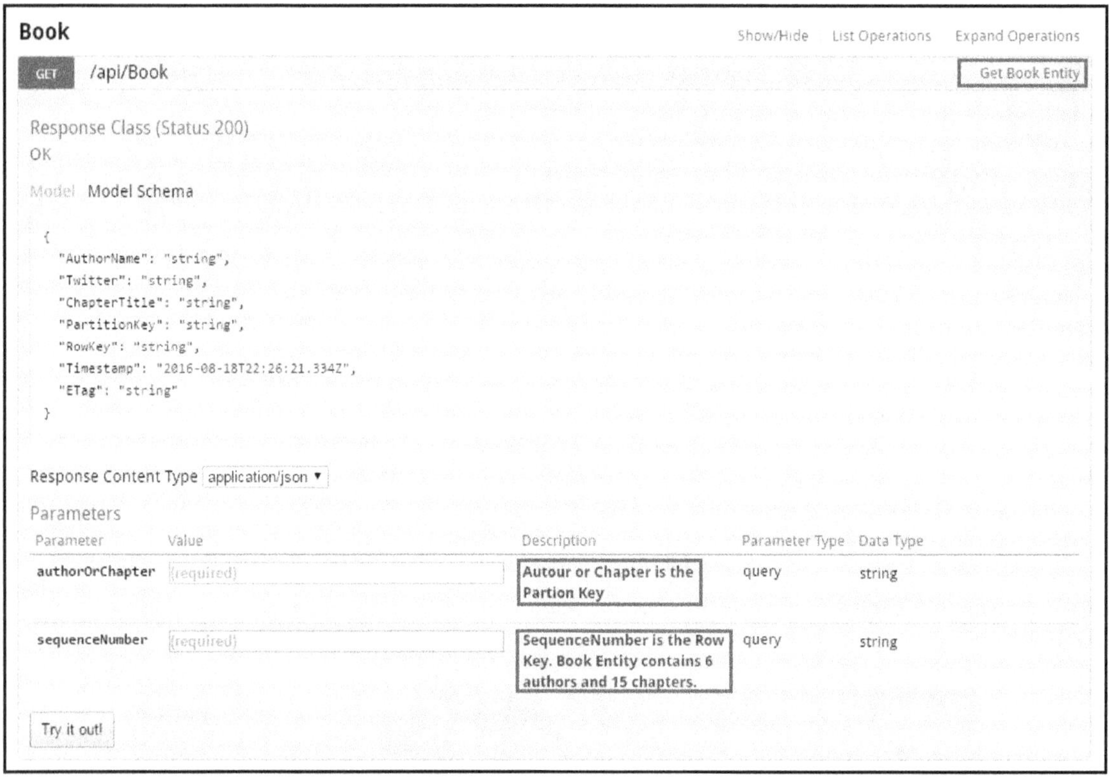

Book   Show/Hide   List Operations   Expand Operations

`GET` /api/Book   Get Book Entity

Response Class (Status 200)
OK

Model   Model Schema

```
{
    "AuthorName": "string",
    "Twitter": "string",
    "ChapterTitle": "string",
    "PartitionKey": "string",
    "RowKey": "string",
    "Timestamp": "2016-08-18T22:26:21.334Z",
    "ETag": "string"
}
```

Response Content Type application/json ▼

Parameters

Parameter	Value	Description	Parameter Type	Data Type
authorOrChapter	(required)	Autour or Chapter is the Partion Key	query	string
sequenceNumber	(required)	SequenceNumber is the Row Key. Book Entity contains 6 authors and 15 chapters.	query	string

Try it out!

Discovering partion keys in the storage table

One more thing if you note here is that when we use the **AzureStorageTableConnector**, it asks us for the partion key that can have only two values in our scenario, either author or chapter. It would be nice if our custom connector can go to storage table and find all the partion keys available and then may be provide it as a drop-down so that we can select the partion key instead of entering the value. This can be done using dynamic Swagger to enhance user experience. Swagger dynamically generates metadata depending on API App configuration.

To do this, you need to add a filter, as follows:

```
c.OperationFilter<DiscoverPartitionKeyFilter>();
```

```
public class DiscoverPartitionKeyFilter : IOperationFilter
{
    /// <summary> Add a dynamic enumeration of the Queues
    2 references
    public void Apply(Operation operation, SchemaRegistry schemaRegistry,
                    System.Web.Http.Description.ApiDescription apiDescription)
    {
        // Add a dynamic enumeration of the Queues
        var param = operation.parameters.FirstOrDefault(x => x.name.Equals("authorOrChapter"));
        if (param != null)
        {
            if (param.@enum == null)
            {
                param.@enum = new System.Collections.Generic.List<object>();
            }

            foreach (string authorOrChapter in this.GetPartionKeys())
            {
                param.@enum.Add(authorOrChapter);
            }
        }
    }
}
```

In the filter implementation, it looks for the parameter `authorOrChapter`, and if it finds the parameter, it will add it as an enumeration, which means the `authorOrChapter` parameter can take all the partition keys (author and chapter) as the enumeration value. To add the partition keys to `enum`, we have the method `GetPartionKeys` that abstracts how you get all the partition key from the storage table. In our scenario, we know that we have only two partition keys — `author` and `chapter`; so, we have added them in a list and returned it as a string collection.

```
private System.Collections.Generic.IEnumerable<string> GetPartionKeys()
{
    List<string> partionKeyList = new List<string>();
    partionKeyList.Add("author");
    partionKeyList.Add("chapter");

    foreach (string partionKey in partionKeyList)
    {
        yield return partionKey;
    }
}
```

Now if you test the connector locally using Swagger UI, you can see the drop-down for the **authorOrChapter** parameter with values, **author** and **chapter**.

Parameters					
Parameter	Value		Description	Parameter Type	Data Type
authorOrChapter	author ▾ author chapter		Autour or Chapter is the Partion Key	query	string
sequenceNumber	(required)		SequenceNumber is the Row Key. Book Entity contains 6 authors and 15 chapters.	query	string

If you again publish the API App project in Azure, you can see the changes in the custom connector as shown here:

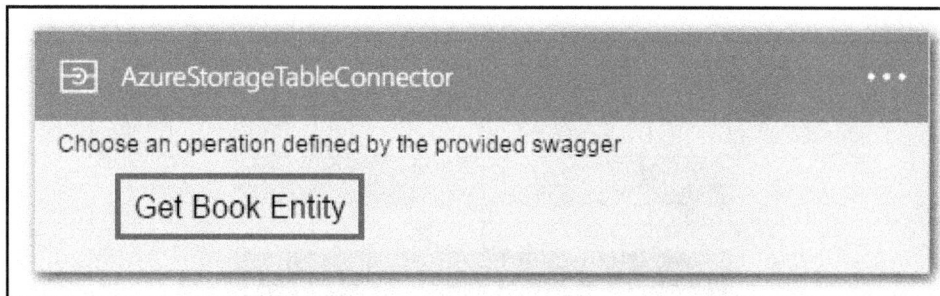

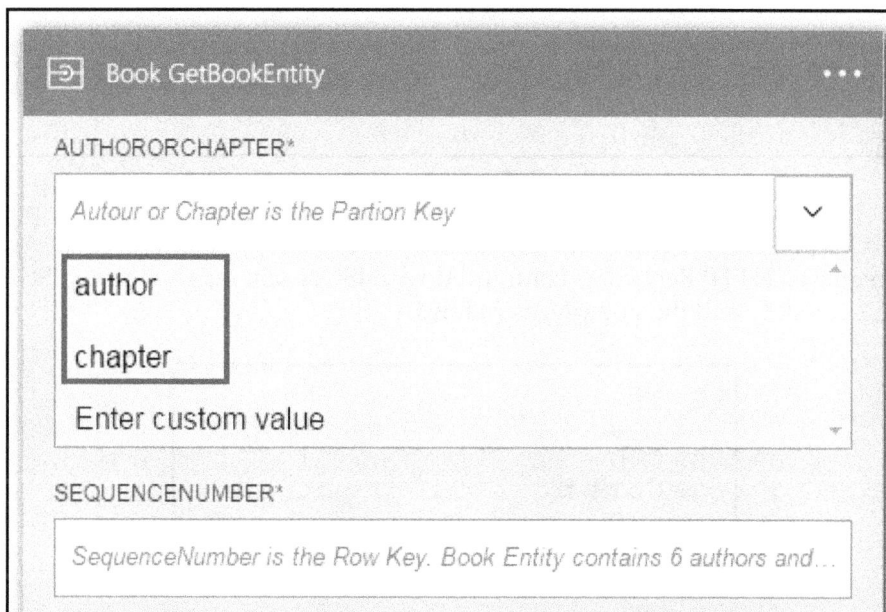

Now you can create Logic App workflow using our customer connector. In our case, we are using the HTTP request connector that serves as an endpoint and makes this Logic App a callable endpoint. This HTTP endpoint will act as a trigger for the workflow.

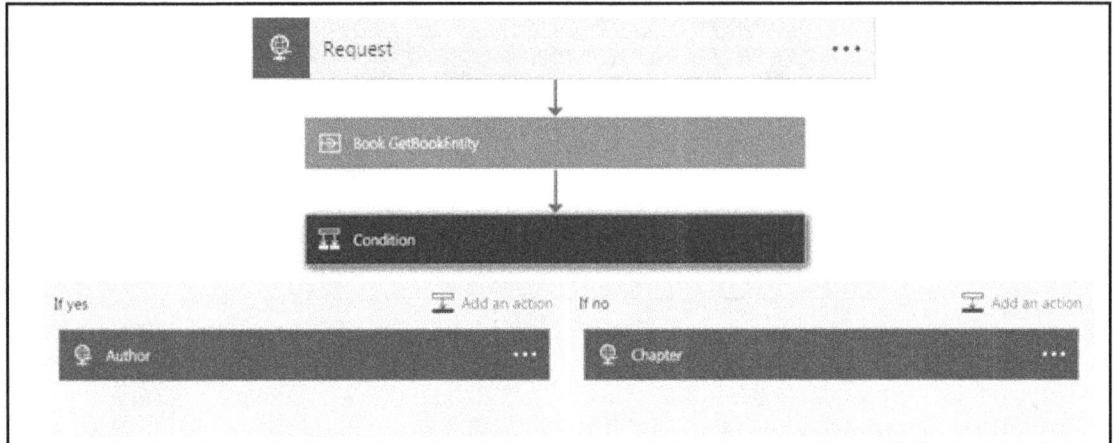

Please refer to manual trigger explained in the *Types of triggers* section of this chapter. The first step is to add a *HTTP Request* as a trigger to your Logic App definition that can receive incoming requests. HTTP Request is configured with JSON schema to accept a JSON input with the partionKey and the rowKey, as follows:

```
{
    "partionKey": "author",
    "rowKey": "1"
}
```

You can define a request body JSON Schema by using sample json payload on the request trigger or by using a tool such as: `http://jsonschema.net`, and the designer will generate tokens to help you parse and pass data from the manual trigger through the workflow. After you save your Logic App definition, a callback URL will be generated, which can be used to trigger the Logic App workflow.

After you save your Logic App definition, a callback URL will be generated, which can be used to trigger the Logic App workflow.

```
"triggers": {
    "manual": {
        "inputs": {
            "schema": {
                "$schema": "http://json-schema.org/draft-04/schema#",
                "properties": {
                    "partionKey": {
                        "type": "string"
                    },
                    "rowKey": {
                        "type": "string"
                    }
                },
                "required": [
                    "partionKey",
                    "rowKey"
                ],
                "type": "object"
            }
        },
        "type": "Manual"
```

Now the `partionKey` and `rowKey` values from the trigger output would be passed as an input to custom connector, and it would be used to fetch the book entity from the storage table.

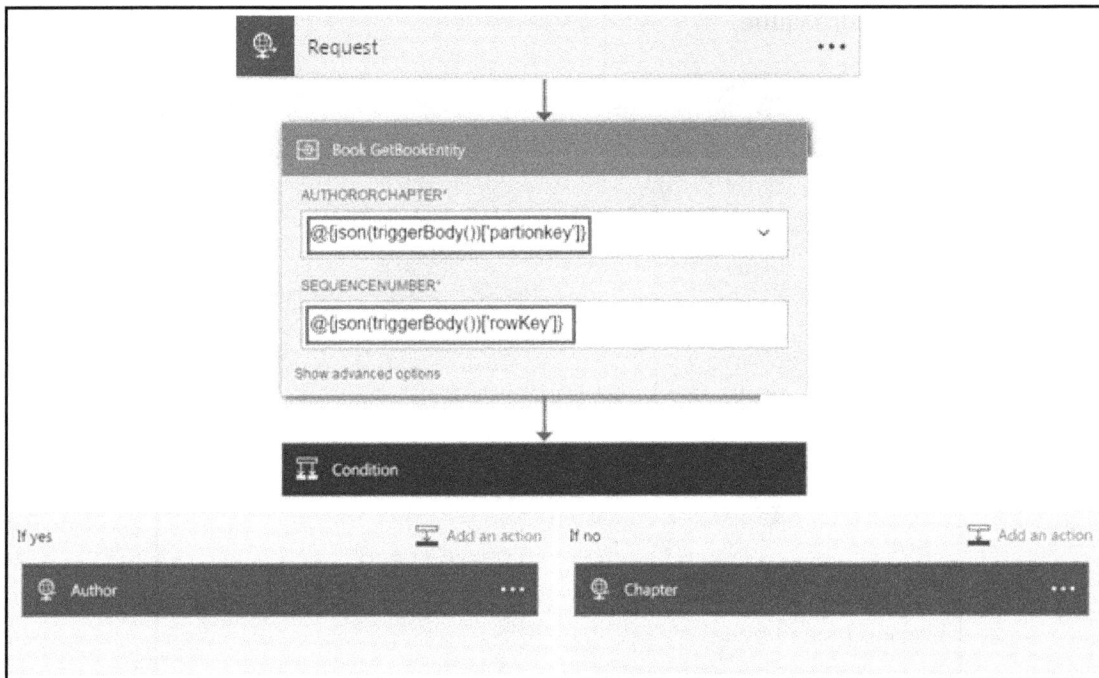

Before we send the book entity result as a response from workflow, we will check the partition key by adding a conditional logic shown later. More about **Condition** is explained in Chapter 8, *A Deep Dive into Logic Apps*. Conditional logic executes an action only when a certain condition is met, and in our case, the condition is to check whether the partition key value is equal to author's value.

If a partition key is equal to the author, **Author** action would be executed, else **Chapter** action. Depending on the partition key, either author or chapter details will be sent out as the response from the Logic App workflow.

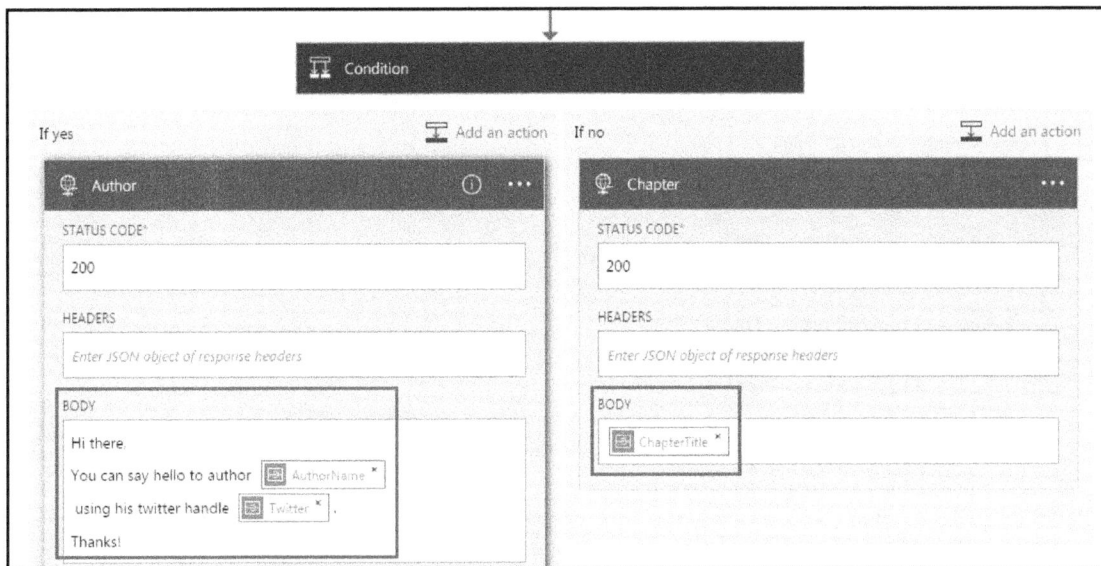

Here are the sample request and response using Postman.

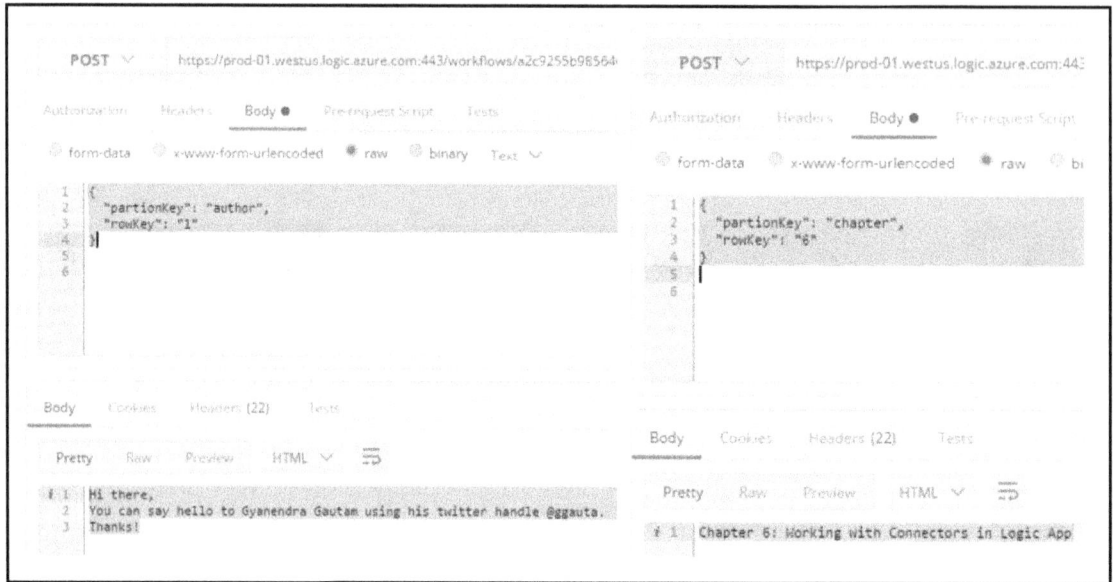

Summary

In this chapter, we discussed about the Logic App Connectors, which are basically API Apps that focus on connectivity. We looked into different types of connector currently available in Logic Apps to build your business process workflows.

We also discussed about triggers and actions and their different types. Finally, we created custom connector to pull records from the Azure Storage Table. We used the custom connector to create a Logic App workflow, which can be invoked using an endpoint. We tested the Logic App using the tool Postman.

In the next chapter, we will understand Azure function and how it can be used in Logic Apps.

7
Azure Functions in Logic Apps

Azure Functions were introduced during Microsoft Build 2016 as a means to provide a serverless computing environment that could scale as needed and provide a pay-as-you-go service. Serverless computing is a means of providing computing power and resources for solutions without the need to be concerned about the underlying infrastructure.

They provide a mechanism that allows developers and solution architects to react to events and process usually small amounts of functionality before either passing back a response or creating another event.

Given this, **Azure Functions** provide a mechanism to deliver a truly event-driven architecture, including the ability to chain and fan out events to multiple sources.

In the previous chapters, we have spoken about how Logic Apps and the App Service model within Microsoft Azure provide a good basis to build solutions that follow microservices architectural principles.

One of the key requirements for a microservices architecture is that each service should have responsibility for its own work and data. This leads to added complexity when data needs to be shared or updated across different services because it is essential to maintain this single responsibility principle.

One solution to the problem is to use an event-driven architecture and principles around eventual consistency to provide a highly decoupled and highly scalable solution architecture
(https://www.nginx.com/blog/event-driven-data-management-microservices/).

Azure Functions provide this event-driven solution, but they can be used across a range of other workloads.

In this chapter, we will discuss these workloads, provide an overview of Azure Functions, and pay particular attention on how they can be used from within Logic Apps.

We will continue to build out our Sunny Electricals solution and use an Azure Function to provide some basic checking of data as it flows through.

The basics of Azure Functions

Azure Functions are essentially a managed service for WebJobs SDK that provide similar functionality but in a fully serverless environment.

WebJobs provide a means to run background tasks in the context of a Web App, Mobile App, or API App. With them, you can upload a script such as PowerShell or a command file and have them run on a schedule
(https://azure.microsoft.com/en-us/documentation/articles/websites-webjobs-resources/).

At the very basic level, Azure Functions can be thought to be defined by:

```
Events + Code + Data = Function App
```

The key part of a Function App is the initial trigger that starts the process of running the code contained within a function. This trigger can be in the form of an input event, such as a message being written to a queue, or a timed event. A function can have a number of outputs that send data and information to a range of endpoints.

A Function App represents a unit of computing, and it can contain a number of functions, each of which can be triggered separately by different trigger mechanisms with different outputs and can be written in any of the supported languages. This allows functions to be grouped together; care needs to be taken to ensure that the memory of the Function App is not exhausted.

Runtime environment

Function Apps are part of App Services that we have discussed in detail in previous chapters, and they sit in the same model as Web Apps, API Apps, Mobile Apps, and Logic Apps.

An App Service can be scaled as necessary, either up to a larger virtual machine size or out to a greater number of virtual machines, either manually or automatically, or an App Service Environment can be used that provides isolated computing resources that can also run within a virtual network.

Azure Functions can be hosted and executed in an App Service Plan that already exists, a new App Service, a fully isolated App Service Environment, or they can be hosted in a Consumption Service Plan and executed purely on demand and charged based on consumption. This *pay-as-you-go* execution model makes Azure Functions an attractive solution when there is a need for large-scale deployment because you are only required to pay when the code is triggered and executed.

The concept of a Consumption Service Plan was introduced with Azure Functions, and it has since been extended to include Logic Apps, which also support a consumption-based model.

When using a Consumption Service Plan, it is important to understand how functions scale. The unit of scale is the Function App and not the individual functions within it. When creating a Function App, which is described later, 1.5 GB of memory is allocated to it. This memory is provided to the Function App and not the functions within it.

The function runtime is single-threaded, so in the instance of event triggers arriving more quickly than a function can process them, multiple instances of the function may be invoked in parallel.

The Functions runtime is open source and available on GitHub (`https://github.com/azure/azure-webjobs-sdk-script`).

Bindings, languages, and function types

In order for a function within a Function App to execute, an event trigger needs to occur. A function can be triggered by a number of bindings, and triggers can either provide input as required for the function or as a result of event an input can be read as appropriate.

The following table provides a list of supported triggers and bindings. Bindings can provide input to the function and output that can be used by other services, including other Azure Functions. In this latter case, it is possible to create a chain of events that can effectively fan out and scale as necessary.

Type	Service	Trigger	Input	Output
Schedule	Azure Functions	Yes		
HTTP (REST or WebHook)	Azure Functions	Yes		Yes
Blob Storage	Azure Storage	Yes	Yes	Yes
Events	Azure Event Hubs	Yes		Yes
Queues	Azure Storage	Yes		Yes
Queues and topics	Azure Service Bus	Yes		Yes
Tables	Azure Storage		Yes	Yes
Tables	Azure Mobile Apps		Yes	Yes
No-SQL DB	Azure DocumentDB		Yes	Yes
Push Notifications	Azure Notification Hubs			Yes
Twilio SMS Text	Twilio			Yes

- WebHooks (https://en.wikipedia.org/wiki/Webhook)

- DocumentDB
  (https://azure.microsoft.com/en-us/documentation/servic
  es/documentdb/)

- Push Notifications (https://azure.microsoft.com/en-us/doc
  umentation/services/notification-hubs/)

It can be seen from the table that some bindings can be used to only provide input to a function rather than as a trigger.

In the case of HTTP, the output can only be provided when the input is also HTTP, which provides a mechanism to provide the Function as a REST endpoint or WebHook that can be called by another function. We will use this later in the chapter to provide the processing of information as part of a Logic App.

Another binding of particular interest is the schedule; this allows a Function to be executed on a specific timed schedule with that schedule based on a **Cron** expression.

Azure Functions have been created to provide the broadest level of support for both modern and more traditional programming languages and scripts.

Along with support for multiple bindings and triggers, Azure Functions also supports a range of common programming languages to allow developers to easily and comfortably create functions using existing knowledge.

At the time of writing, the following languages are supported:

- **First class support**: C# and JavaScript
- **Experimental support**: Batch, Bash, F#, PHP, PowerShell, and Python

When creating a template, choices can be limited by choosing from a list of specific types:

- Core
- API and WebHooks
- Data processing
- Samples
- Experimental

The process for creating a function within a Function App is described in the next section

Building Azure Functions

Azure Functions are created in the main Azure portal in a Resource Group in the same way as other resources.

When creating a Function App, the App Service plan needs to be selected. This can be either Classic, which allows the creation of a new App Service Plan or reuse of an old one, or Consumption based to use pay-as-you-go and on demand processing.

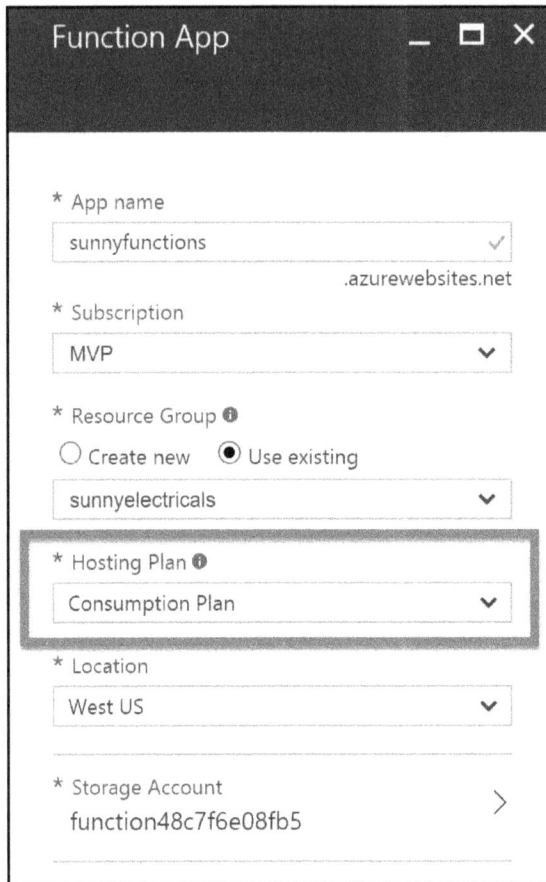

The Function App takes a few minutes to be created, but once created, functions can be added to perform the tasks required.

The Function App has a number of settings that can be used to configure it once it has been created.

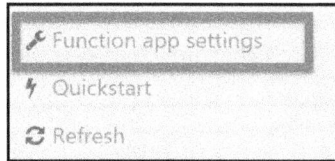

The settings page provides options for setting a daily usage quota for the Function App, accessing development resources including app settings such as connection strings, setting up **Continuous Integration**, configuring **Authentication/Authorization** and cross-origin resource sharing and providing a link to a URL that contains the Swagger API definition for a Function App that contains HTTP triggers.

The final important option on the settings page provides access to the **App Service settings**, which allows further configuration of other application configuration settings.

Manage

App Service Settings
Advanced Features. Access all the underlying features of Azure App Service

Go to App Service Settings

The **App Service Settings** page is consistent with the normal App Service settings that are part of any App Service Plan used by Web Apps, API Apps, Mobile Apps, or Logic Apps.

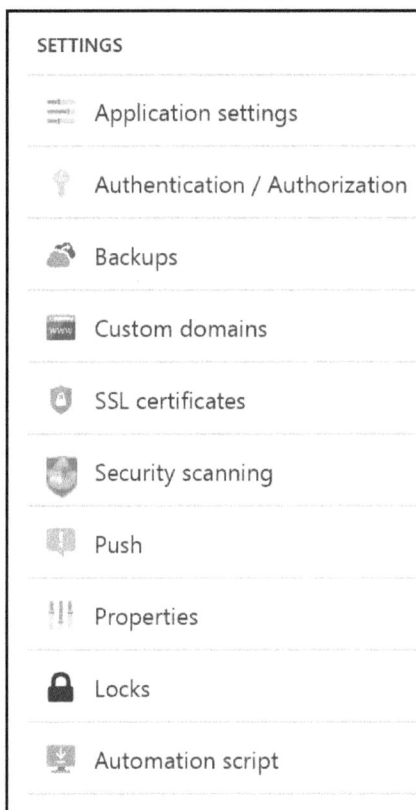

SETTINGS

Application settings

Authentication / Authorization

Backups

Custom domains

SSL certificates

Security scanning

Push

Properties

Locks

Automation script

The Function App can be configured at any time after creation.

Creating a function

The first step to create a new function within the Function App is to click **New Function**.

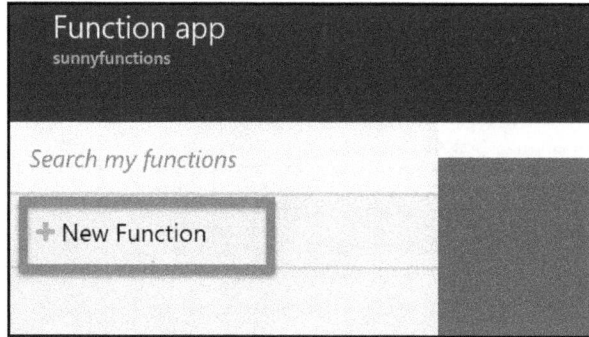

Clicking on **New Function** displays a set of templates that can be filtered to provide guidance on the best function for your needs. In types, it is possible to select samples that can be used to create a fully coded sample to help with getting started. For our Sunny Electricals scenario later in the chapter, we will use a C# function that is called from a Logic App.

To get a better understanding of Azure Functions, it is useful to start with simple example. A **Timer Trigger** function runs on a schedule defined by a **Cron** expression and is a good way to look at the overall functionality of an individual function.

> For more information on Cron expressions, refer to: https://en.wikipedia.org/wiki/Cron.

First, we need to give the function a name, and this has to be unique within the Function App due to the way a Function App is structured. This will be discussed later in the chapter.

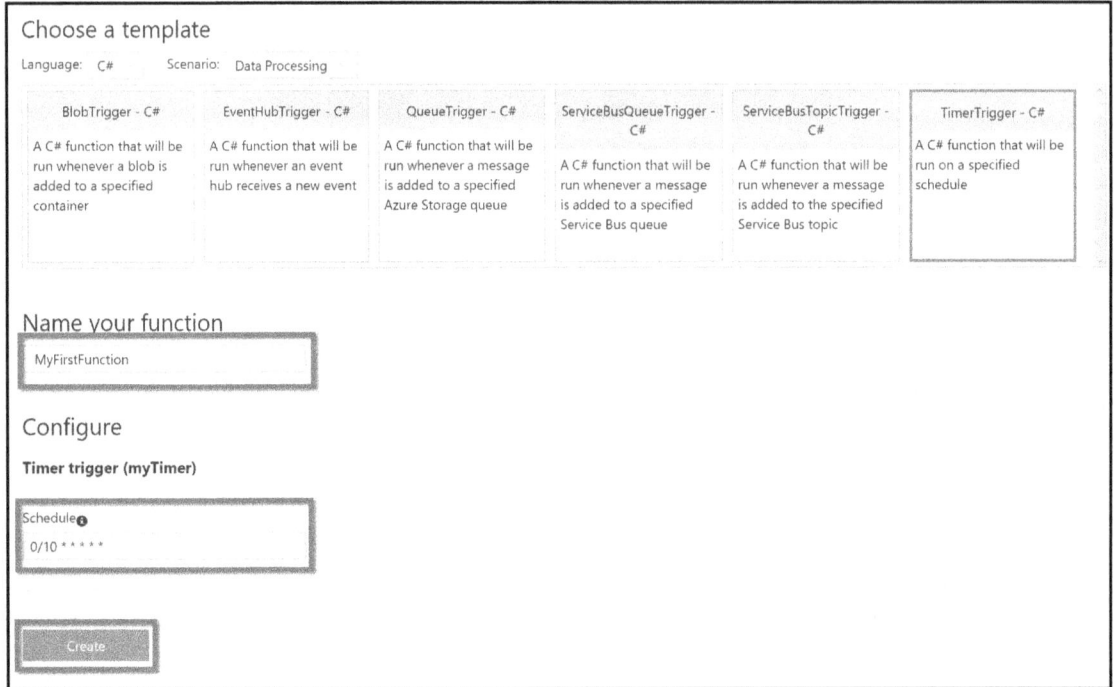

The Cron expression mentioned earlier (`0/10 * * * * *`) triggers the function to run every 10 seconds. Clicking on **Create** creates the function.

The function code is displayed after creation and can be edited and saved directly in the browser. For certain function types, it is possible to test the function by passing in a sample message and clicking the **Run** button.

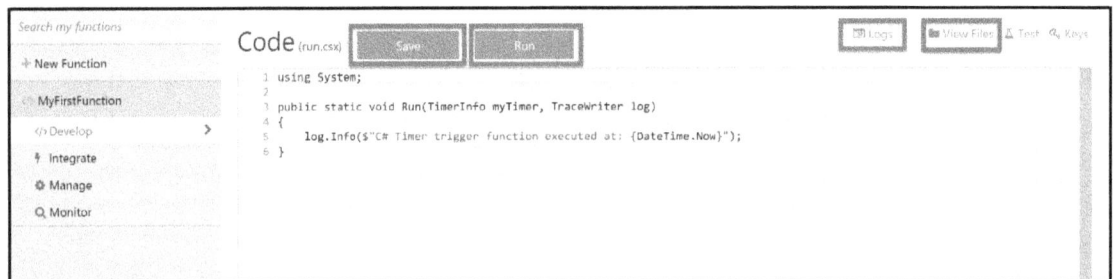

A log stream that shows function invocations and provides immediate feedback on the state of the function is displayed by clicking on the **Logs** link. This can be useful when testing the function and making code changes. After a function is saved, there is immediate feedback in the log stream to show any compilation errors.

```
Logs                                              ❚❚ Pause    ▦ Clear    ▢ Copy Logs    ⤢ Expand    ✖ Close

2017-01-28T04:33:10.008 Function started (Id=230e53ae-dc68-4bb2-bd4b-9736b6873b88)
2017-01-28T04:33:10.008 C# Timer trigger function executed at: 1/28/2017 4:33:10 AM
2017-01-28T04:33:10.008 Function completed (Success, Id=230e53ae-dc68-4bb2-bd4b-9736b6873b88)
```

The files related to a specific function can be viewed and edited directly from the function by clicking on the **View Files** link.

It is possible to upload files or create new files as well as delete as required.

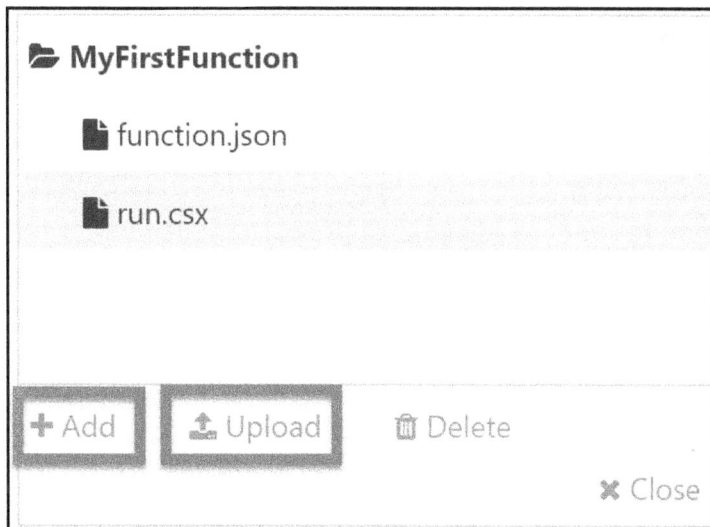

In order to understand why a function needs to have a unique name and what files make up a function, it is useful to look at the structure of a Function App and the files associated with them.

In this chapter, we will concentrate on C# functions and point out where there are differences for functions written that target Node.js.

The structure of a Function App

Since a Function App is just another part of an App Service, you are able to use the same and familiar tools to interact with it, either for development or management.

This includes, but is not limited to the following:

- **Advanced Tools**: This is web-based interface that is accessed via an amended URL for the App Service
- **App Service Editor**: This uses a browser implementation of Visual Studio that allows the user to both manage and develop function code

To access either of the tools, you need to first go to the **App Service Settings** from the Function App settings page.

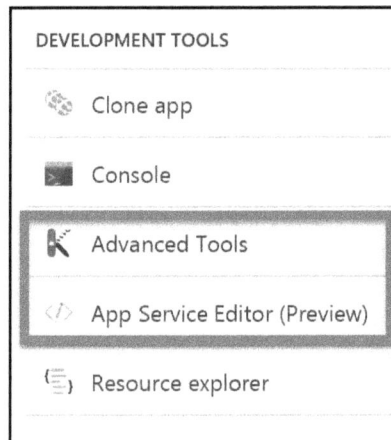

Because the experience is richer using the **App Service Editor**, we will concentrate on showing the functionality that contains. However, using Kudu also supports the same functionality but from a more console-driven perspective. Kudu is the engine that powers git deployments in Azure App Service (`https://github.com/projectkudu/kudu/wiki`).

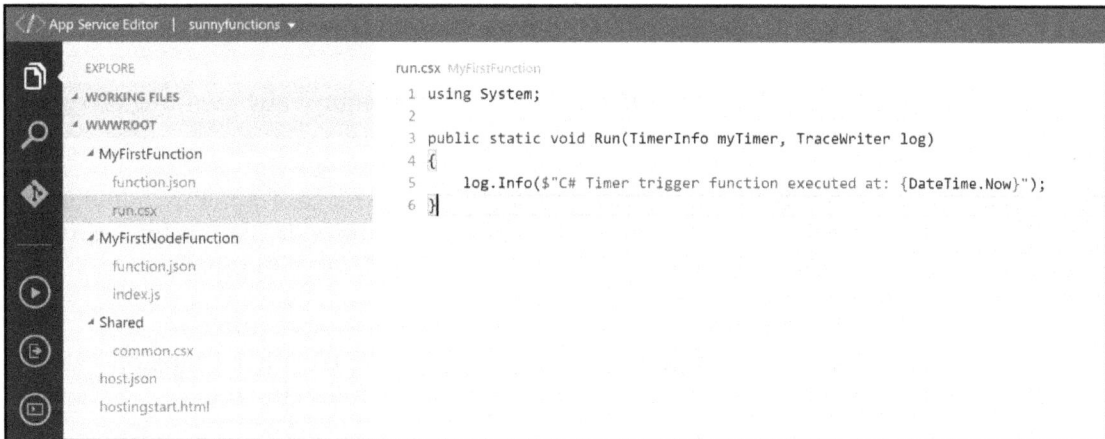

When functions are created within a Function App, an individual folder is created under the website within the App Service. This is the reason why a function name has to be unique within a Function App instance, but it is possible to reuse function names in different instances.

Code can be edited directly in the browser using the **App Service Editor**, new files can be uploaded or created, and it is possible to download the entire workspace.

A C# function contains the following files:

- `run.csx`: This contains the code for the function and closely follows the rules of C# coding with a few exceptions that are described in detail later when we add some complexity to our function
- `function.json`: This contains the definition for the function, including any integrations
- `project.json`: This contains the NuGet packages that need to be restored for the function and is optional

A Node.js function contains the following files:

- `index.js`: This contains the code for the function
- `function.json`: This contains the definition for the function, including any integrations
- `package.json`: This contains the npm packages that need to be restored for the function and is optional
- `node_modules`: This folder contains the modules required by the function code and is optional

It is possible to share code between functions to help promote reuse. To do this, a folder should be created off of the root of the Function App to store the code files, so they can be loaded in to individual functions. We will discuss this briefly later in the chapter.

The `function.json` file contains all the configuration information required for an individual function. It can be accessed by going to the **Integrate** tab and clicking on **Advanced editor**. In our simple example, the file contains the following code:

```
{
  "bindings": [
    {
      "name": "myTimer",
      "type": "timerTrigger",
      "direction": "in",
      "schedule": "0/10 * * * * *"
    }
  ],
  "disabled": false
}
```

The information this contains is related only to the configuration, integration, and operation of the function, it does not contain any code. We will look at a more complex example when we look at how we extend the function to integrate with other sources.

Adding complexity

Any real-world scenario will contain more complex code and will need to include referenced libraries, package restores, and shared code.

A Function App supports a number of .NET assemblies out-of-the-box both directly and indirectly. For directly addressable assemblies, there is no need to add a reference to the assembly within the code of the function although as usual providing using statements reduces coding effort.

The following is a list of assemblies that are automatically imported:

- `System`
- `System.Collections.Generic`
- `System.IO`
- `System.Linq`
- `System.Net.Http`
- `System.Threading.Tasks`
- `Microsoft.Azure.WebJobs`
- `Microsoft.Azure.WebJobs.Host`

There are a number of external assemblies that are automatically added by the Azure Functions runtime:

- `mscorlib`
- `System`
- `System.Core`
- `System.Xml`
- `System.Net.Http`
- `Microsoft.Azure.WebJobs`
- `Microsoft.Azure.WebJobs.Host`
- `Microsoft.Azure.WebJobs.Extensions`
- `System.Web.Http`
- `System.Net.Http.Formatting`

There are a number of assemblies that are special cases and do not require the full filename:

- `Newtonsoft.Json`
- `Microsoft.WindowsAzure.Storage`
- `Microsoft.ServiceBus`
- `Microsoft.AspNet.WebHooks.Receivers`
- `Microsoft.AspNet.WebHooks.Common`

External assemblies are loaded differently to the way we would normally reference them in an environment such as Visual Studio. In order to add a reference to an external assembly you need to use `#r "[Assembly Name]"`, for example, `#r "Newtonsoft.Json"`.

To promote reuse and to provide opportunities for source control and proper application life cycle management, it is possible to add user-created assemblies. A user-created assembly should be uploaded to the `bin` folder relative to the `root` folder of the function, and it can then be referenced using the filename, for example, `#r "MyCompany.Model.Objects.dll"`.

An external file is used to satisfy the need of performing a package restore. For C# functions using NuGet as the package manager, a `project.json` file is placed in the `root` folder of the function. For Node.js functions using npm as their package manager, this is replaced by the `packages.json` file.

For example, to restore the Emotion API code from Cognitive Services, the following `project.json` file would be used, note the dependency of .NET 4.6:

```
{
  "frameworks": {
    "net46":{
      "dependencies": {
        "Microsoft.ProjectOxford.Emotion": "1.0.251"
      }
    }
  }
}
```

Assemblies that are provided by package restore do not need to be separately referenced using `#r` as they are included by default.

The final technique to show is how to share code between functions. Code can be written in the `.csx` files as normal and stored in a folder within the Function App that is easily referenceable from individual functions, for instance, in the same folder or subfolder of the function, or a separate folder under the Function App.

Once the code is complete, the `#load "[File name]"` command is used to include the file and code within the current function. To reference a file, you need to specify the relative path to the file within the folder structure of the Function App, for example, `#load "..\Shared\ommon.csx"`.

Adding integration

Now that we know how to add references and reuse code, we can create a more realistic solution using these techniques and external integration.

Integration is added by clicking on the **Integrate** tab in the function designer.

Search my functions	Code (run.csx)	Save	Run

```
1  using System;
2
3  public static void Run(TimerInfo myTimer, TraceWrite
4  {
5      log.Info($"C# Timer trigger function executed at
6  }
```

- **+** New Function
- **</>** MyFirstFunction
  - **</>** Develop **>**
  - **⚡** Integrate
  - **⚙** Manage
  - **Q** Monitor

For our example, we will add a storage queue and send a message. We will use references and external code to show how to bring together some of the ideas detailed so far through the chapter. First, we need to add a **New Output**.

Triggers ❶	Inputs ❶	Outputs ❶	✏ Advanced editor
Timer (myTimer)	**+** New Input	**+** New Output	

Timer trigger (myTimer) delete

Timestamp parameter name ❶	Schedule ❶
myTimer	0/10 * * * *

Cancel

We then need to choose the type of external integration we would like to use, so we select **Azure Storage Queue**.

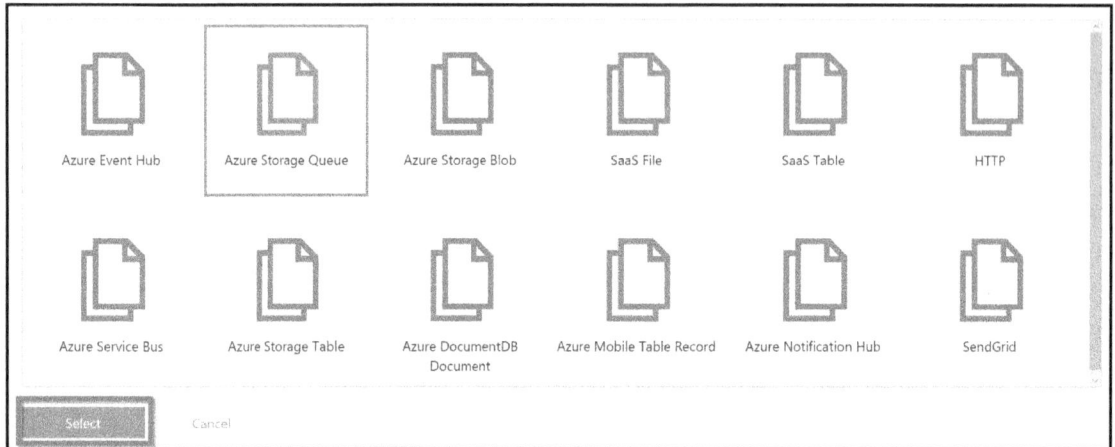

The designer provides the opportunity to update the default information for a queue and to select the storage account, in this case, that the integration will use.

If a queue does not exist with the chosen name, one will be created when the function first writes a message.

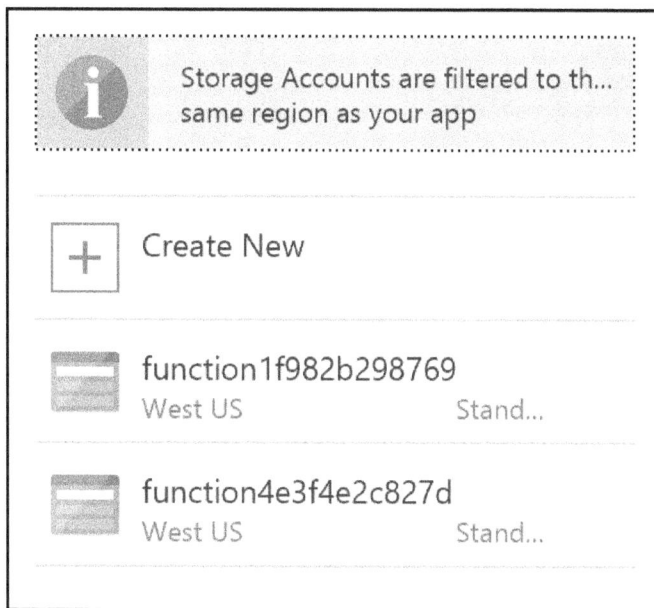

The process automatically creates a connection string to the storage account or any other integration, in the application settings of the Function App instance.

Finally, clicking on **Save** finishes the task of adding the integration.

We need to update our code. First, we create a file, `common.csx`, in the shared folder of our Function App that will contain reusable code. We will only use this code once, but we will show how easy it is to share code between functions.

```
public class Message
{
    public string msg;
    public DateTime msgtime;
}
```

This file needs to be included in our `Timer Trigger` function using the `#load` directive described previously. We will serialize our message to JSON before sending to the queue using the `Newtonsoft.Json` assembly referenced using the `#r` directive.

```
#r "Newtonsoft.Json"
#load "..\Shared\common.csx"

using System;

public static void Run(TimerInfo myTimer, out string outputQueueItem,
TraceWriter log)
{
    log.Info($"C# Timer trigger function executed at:
    {DateTime.Now}");
    var msg = new Message
    {
      msg = "From trigger",
      msgtime = DateTime.UtcNow
    };
    outputQueueItem =
    Newtonsoft.Json.JsonConvert.SerializeObject(msg);
}
```

Note that we have referenced the `Newtonsoft.Json` assembly using the simple name without the extension. We can do this as it is one the special cases as mentioned previously in the chapter.

Also, note that the method signature has been changed to include an out parameter. The parameter name is the name we chose as the message parameter name when we created the integration to the storage queue.

We create the new Message object based on the class that is defined in our external file that is loaded into the function with the use of the #load directive.

When we click on the **Save** button, the code is checked and compiled ready for execution. Any errors found are displayed in the log stream window:

```
Logs                                                          ▌▌ Pause  ▤

2016-08-14T11:53:05  Welcome, you are now connected to log-streaming service.
2016-08-14T11:53:10.016 Function started (Id=e259aaf4-0c12-4aa4-9e27-77d95d8a4b0d)
2016-08-14T11:53:10.016 C# Timer trigger function executed at: 8/14/2016 11:53:10 AM
2016-08-14T11:53:10.016 Function completed (Success, Id=e259aaf4-0c12-4aa4-9e27-77d95d8a4b0d)
2016-08-14T11:53:10.269 Script for function 'MyFirstFunction' changed. Reloading.
2016-08-14T11:53:10.269 Compiling function script.
2016-08-14T11:53:10.331 Compilation succeeded.
```

Once the code is saved, the next invocation of the function picks up changes immediately and we are able to see the effects of the changes. In this case, the effect is that we should see messages being written to our queue, which should have been created as it did not previously exist.

To look at our queue, we can use **Microsoft Azure Storage Explorer** (`http://storageexplo rer.com/`), which is a free tool that can be downloaded for most operating systems.

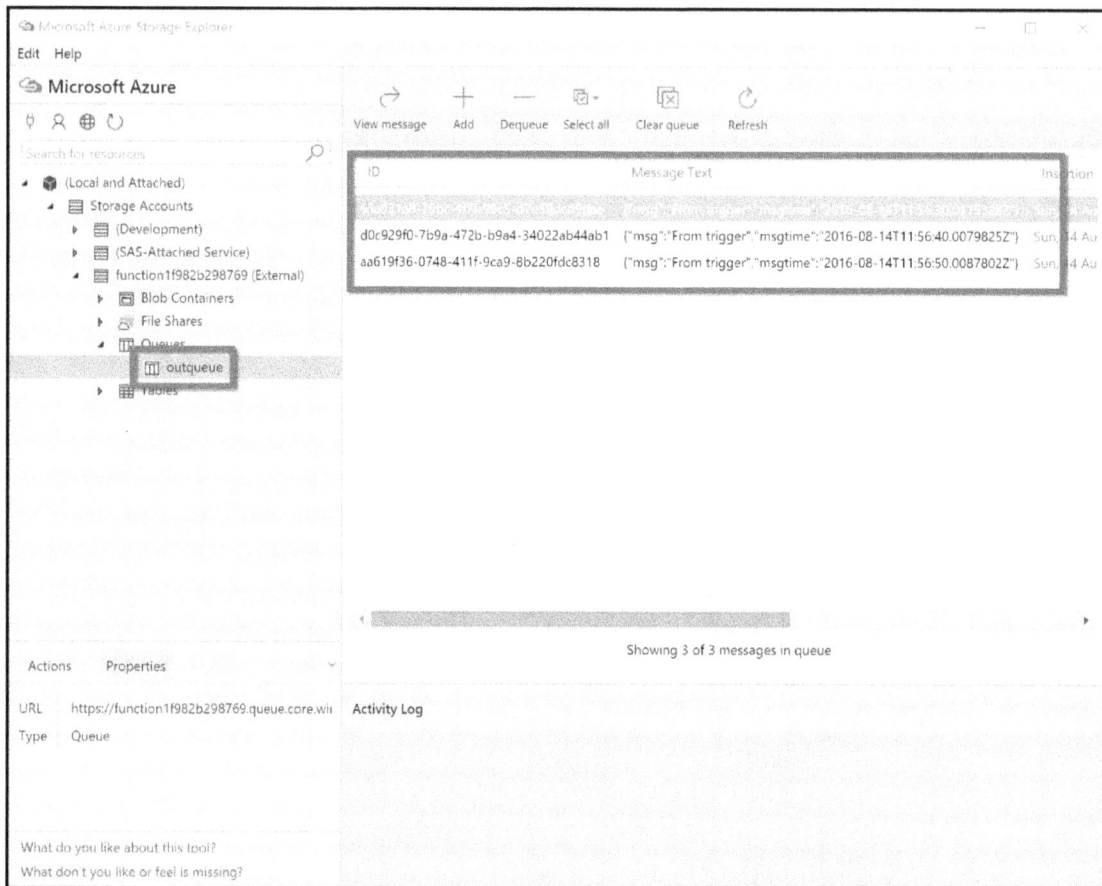

Previously, we looked at the function.json file that is created for a very basic function. Once we have added integration, the file contains more information that defines the structure, integration, and configuration of the function:

```
{
    "bindings": [
        {
            "name": "myTimer",
            "type": "timerTrigger",
            "direction": "in",
            "schedule": "0/10 * * * * *"
        },
        {
            "type": "queue",
            "name": "outputQueueItem",
            "queueName": "outqueue",
            "connection": "function1f982b298769_STORAGE",
            "direction": "out"
        }
    ],
    "disabled": false
}
```

We can see that our integration point is defined by type, name, the name of the connection string, and a direction. In cases where more configuration is required, for example, output to DocumentDB, the information contained is more extensive.

Because we now have a trigger that is placing messages on to a queue, it would be useful to create a function that reads these messages. This would be similar to a real-world example where some form of asynchronous process uses a secondary store to offload processing and provide better scalability.

For this, we need to create a function that uses a queue trigger because this will then process the messages.

Again, we click on **New Function** in the Function App—this time by choosing a **Queue Trigger**. We give the function a name and need to provide the storage queue and the storage connection string, which has been saved in the App Service application settings.

Name your function

MyQueueFunction

Configure

Azure Storage Queue trigger (myQueueItem)

Queue name🛈

outqueue

Storage account connection🛈

function1f982b298769_STORAGE   *select*

Create

Once created, the function will read messages off the queue and just log the output to the log stream as the function at creation time is very simple. If we examine Microsoft Azure Storage Explorer, we would expect to see an empty queue because when the Timer Trigger function puts a message into the queue, the Queue Trigger picks it up.

If we look at the log stream, we can see that the function is working successfully.

Logs   ❚❚ Pause   ▨ Clear

```
2016-08-14T12:08:21  Welcome, you are now connected to log-streaming service.
2016-08-14T12:08:30.029 Function started (Id=9df2a82e-c8c5-4124-a077-39dc9ed5ca97)
2016-08-14T12:08:30.029 C# Queue trigger function processed: {"msg":"From trigger","msgtime":"2016-08-14T12:08:30.0118695Z"}
2016-08-14T12:08:30.029 Function completed (Success, Id=9df2a82e-c8c5-4124-a077-39dc9ed5ca97)
2016-08-14T12:08:40.023 Function started (Id=45f95cbf-a976-4fe0-83af-602a0a4a685e)
2016-08-14T12:08:40.023 C# Queue trigger function processed: {"msg":"From trigger","msgtime":"2016-08-14T12:08:40.0082797Z"}
2016-08-14T12:08:40.023 Function completed (Success, Id=45f95cbf-a976-4fe0-83af-602a0a4a685e)
```

Using this simple example, we have been able to show how easy it is to use referenced assemblies, bring in external code, and chain two functions together to create an event-driven pipeline.

Most examples of functions will follow this process. It is possible to mark function signatures as `async` when needing to call external code that is `awaitable`, see the **Developer Reference** for more details (https://azure.microsoft.com/en-us/documentation/articles/functions-reference-c sharp/#async).

Using functions with Logic Apps

Up to this point, we have been discussing how to create and use functions within a Function App for general use cases when serverless computation is required or when we wish to create an event-driven solution.

Functions can also be called directly from a Logic App. While it is possible to use the event-driven nature of functions to create a highly decoupled and scalable solution, using functions directly called within a Logic App provides a mechanism to add simple business logic that cannot be achieved through the standard functionality available within Logic Apps.

This introduces the Logic Apps equivalent of lambda expressions, which are essentially anonymous functions that are invoked only when required (https://msdn.microsoft.com/en-us/library/bb397687.aspx).

Calling functions directly

How to create a Logic App has been discussed previously, so for the purpose of this scenario, we will assume that one has already been created using the **Blank Logic App** template.

A call to a function is an action within a Logic App. Therefore, in order for the function to be called, we need a trigger that starts a new instance of the Logic App.

For the purpose of testing and building, we will use a simple request/response pattern for the Logic App. Using a request/response allows us to use a simple tool, such as Postman (https://www.getpostman.com/), to POST a message to the API endpoint and wait for the response.

Once we have added the initial request to the Logic App and configured it appropriately, we choose **+New step** followed by **Add an action**.

We expand the dropdown at the top of the action and choose **Azure Functions**.

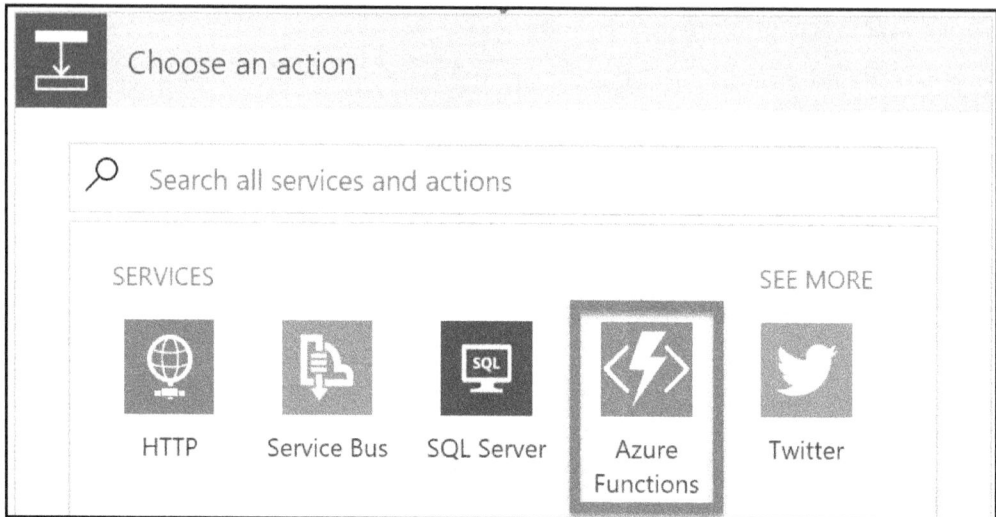

You can then click through and select the Function App that will contain or already contains the required function.

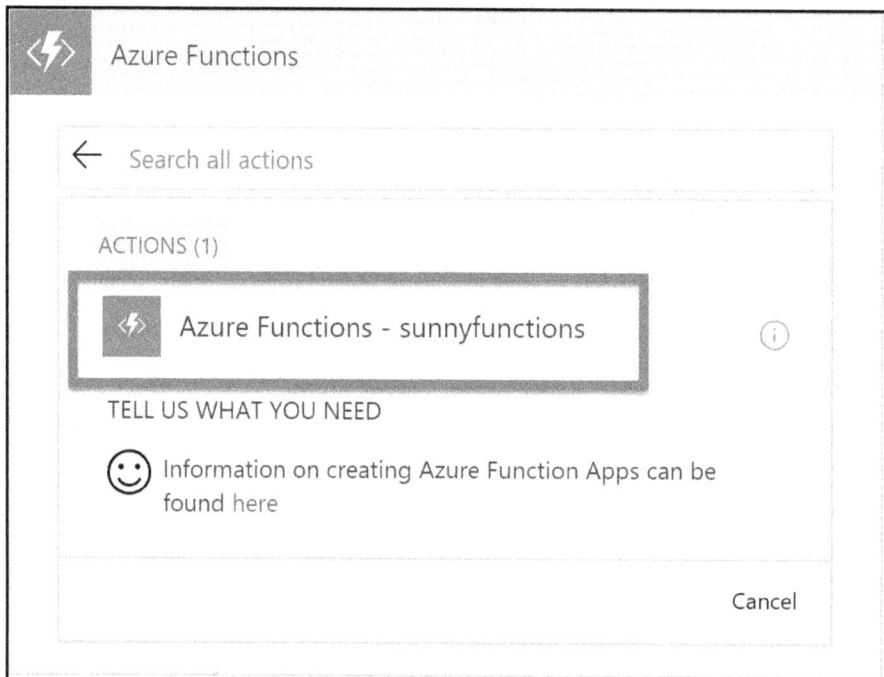

After selection, only functions within the Function App that are generic WebHooks are displayed and can be selected. Generic WebHooks are the only supported functions that can be used within a Logic App. Alternatively, a new generic WebHooks function can be created directly from the Logic Apps designer, including code.

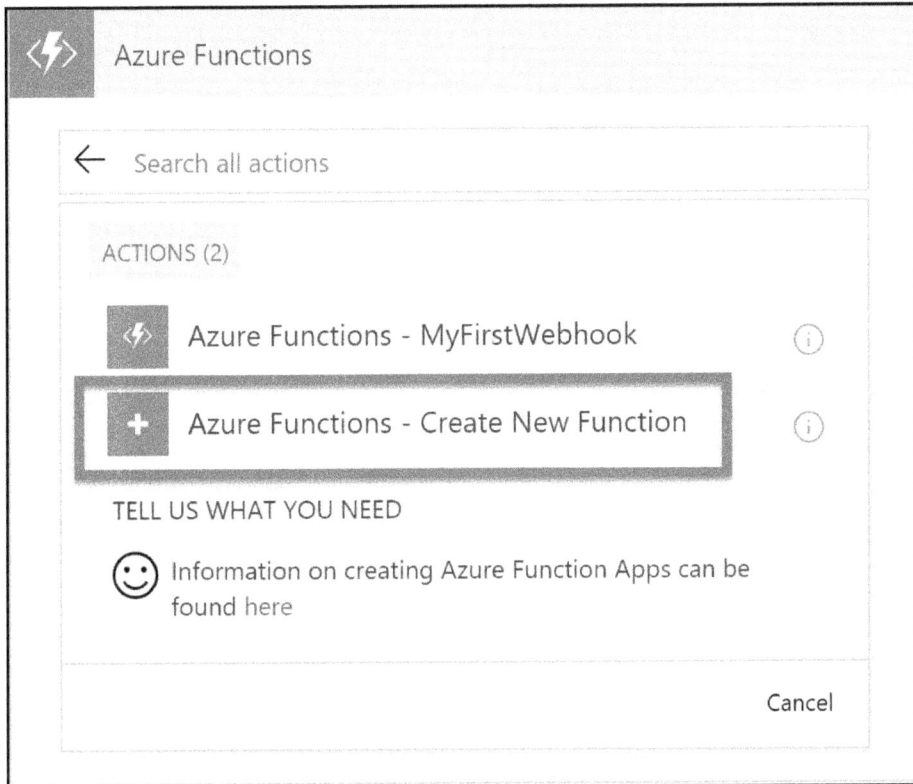

Azure Functions

← Search all actions

ACTIONS (2)

Azure Functions - MyFirstWebhook ⓘ

Azure Functions - Create New Function ⓘ

TELL US WHAT YOU NEED

☺ Information on creating Azure Function Apps can be found here

Cancel

It is possible to use data from the previous trigger within the Logic App or pass a blank payload by specifying { }.

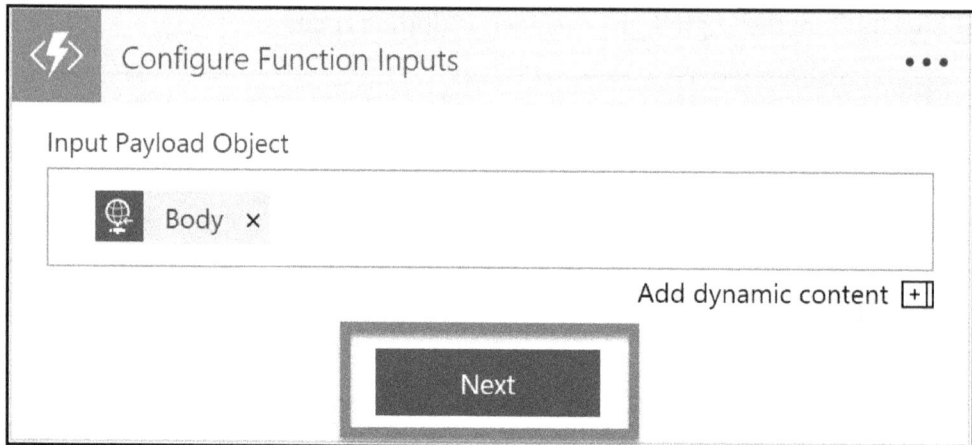

Clicking on **Next** allows you to then choose a name for the function and provide code inline.

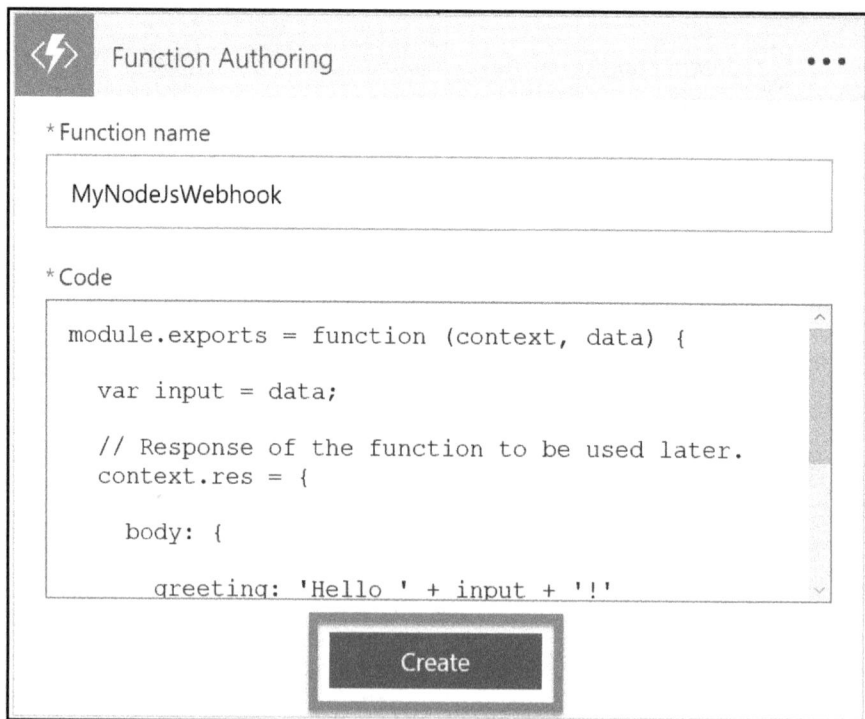

Clicking on **Create** finishes the process and creates the function in the chosen Function App directly.

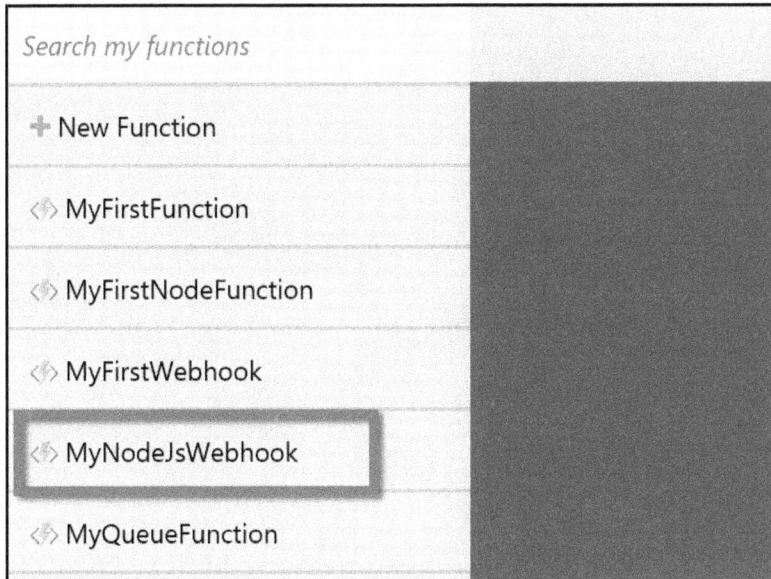

To provide a more concrete walkthrough of the process, it is useful to consider a scenario that is specific to our reference implementation used throughout this book.

Scenario – Invoice checker

When an invoice is received by Sunny Electricals, it needs to be checked to make sure the invoice value contained in the inbound message is equal to the total provided by the items that are selected by the customer.

We define a JSON message that will be received by the Logic App request trigger and processed by the function:

```json
{
   "Invoice": {
      "Number": "123",
      "CustomerID": "10",
      "CustomerName": "John Smith",
      "Items": {
         "Item": [
            {
               "ProductCode": "SCW01",
               "ProductDescription": "50mm Screws",
               "Quantity": "100",
               "Price": "5.99",
               "Total": "599.00"
            },
            {
               "ProductCode": "SCW02",
               "ProductDescription": "75mm Screws",
               "Quantity": "100",
               "Price": "7.99",
               "Total": "799.00"
            }
         ]
      },
      "TotalCost": "1398.00"
   }
}
```

We can see that we have an `Invoice`, `Number`, `CustomerID`, and `CustomerName`, and a list of items that have been ordered. The final element is the calculated cost as created by our store frontend. We want to check that the value of `TotalCost` is equal to the sum of totals for the items based on the item `Total`.

We start by creating a new function, `CheckInvoiceTotal`, remembering that in order for it to be called from a Logic App it needs to be a generic WebHook.

Choose a template

Language C# ⌄   Scenario API & Webhooks ⌄

Generic Webhook - C#	GitHub WebHook - C#	HttpTrigger - C#
A C# function that will be run whenever it receives a webhook request	A C# function that will be run whenever it receives a GitHub webhook request	A C# function that will be run whenever it receives an HTTP request

Name your function

CheckInvoiceTotal

Create

For our function, we need a C# class that represents our JSON payload. We can create this by hand or use a tool to do the work for us. In this case, we use an online resource for this (`http://json2csharp.com/`), which produces the following code:

```
public class Item
{
    public string ProductCode { get; set; }
    public string ProductDescription { get; set; }
    public string Quantity { get; set; }
    public string Price { get; set; }
    public string Total { get; set; }
}
```

```
public class Items
{
    public List<Item> Item { get; set; }
}

public class Invoice
{
    public string Number { get; set; }
    public string CustomerID { get; set; }
    public string CustomerName { get; set; }
    public Items Items { get; set; }
    public string TotalCost { get; set; }
}

public class RootObject
{
    public Invoice Invoice { get; set; }
}
```

We could place this code in an external assembly or a shared `.csx` file for inclusion across many functions or simply include inline with the function itself, as shown previously in the chapter.

To perform the calculation for the function, we need to read the incoming request, deserialize to our invoice object and then check values:

```
#r "Newtonsoft.Json"

using System.Net;
using Newtonsoft.Json;

public static async Task<HttpResponseMessage> Run(HttpRequestMessage req,
TraceWriter log)
{
    log.Info($"C# HTTP trigger function processed a request.
    RequestUri={req.RequestUri}");

    // Get request body.
    dynamic data = await req.Content.ReadAsAsync<object>();

    // Validate the invoice.
    RootObject r =
    JsonConvert.DeserializeObject<RootObject>(data.ToString());
    decimal totalCost = 0M;
    decimal itemTotal = 0M;
    decimal runningTotal = 0M;

    log.Info(data.ToString());
```

```
    log.Info(String.Format("Total cost = {0}", r.Invoice.TotalCost));

    if (!Decimal.TryParse(r.Invoice.TotalCost, out totalCost))
    {
        return req.CreateResponse(HttpStatusCode.InternalServerError,
    "Failed to process Invoice - cannot parse value for TotalCost.");
    }

    // Loop through the invoice items and check that the calculated
       cost equals the specified total cost.
    foreach (var item in r.Invoice.Items.Item)
    {
            itemTotal = 0M;
            if (!Decimal.TryParse(item.Total, out itemTotal))
            {
                return
req.CreateResponse(HttpStatusCode.InternalServerError, "Failed to process
invoice item - cannot parse value for Total.");
            }
            runningTotal += itemTotal;
    }

    log.Info(String.Format("Running total = {0}", runningTotal));

    if (totalCost != runningTotal)
    {
        return req.CreateResponse(HttpStatusCode.BadRequest,
            String.Format("Invoice total cost = ${0}.  Calculated total
        cost = ${1}", totalCost, runningTotal));
    }

    return req.CreateResponse(HttpStatusCode.OK,
            String.Format("Invoice total cost = ${0}.
    Calculated total cost = ${1}", totalCost, runningTotal));
}
```

Finally, we need to return a response with an appropriate HTTP status code—either `HttpStatusCode.OK` if we have equality or `HttpStatusCode.BadRequest` if we do not.

Once we have created the function, we need to save it and ensure that it compiles correctly. We can use the test harness within the function itself to test the function behaves as expected for all our conditions.

We can now create the Logic App that will call the function. As before, we create a Logic App that starts with a request trigger. Within the request trigger, we can define the schema that represents the request body. This is a great way to make the inbound request strongly typed. To create the schema, we can use the sample message and a tool to generate the schema (`http://jsonschema.net/`) and then paste the result into the Logic App `REQUEST BODY JSON SCHEMA` configuration.

When we add an Azure Function from the same region and select the Function App in which we created our function, we can select it from the list.

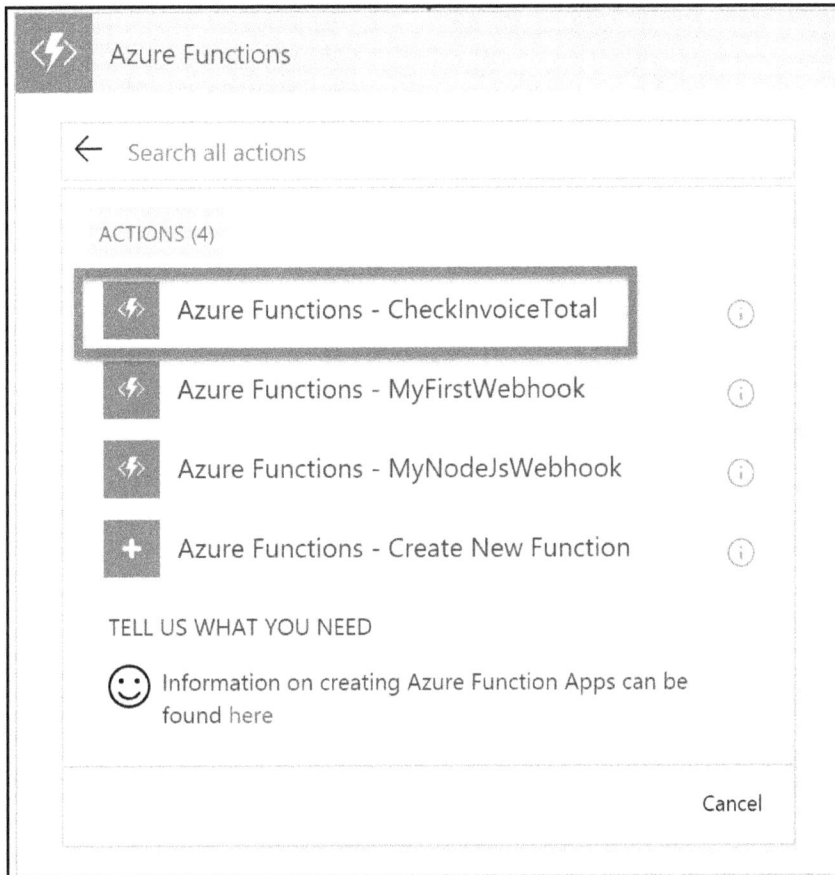

We need to define the payload object that will be passed in to the function, which for this scenario, will simply be the body of the request.

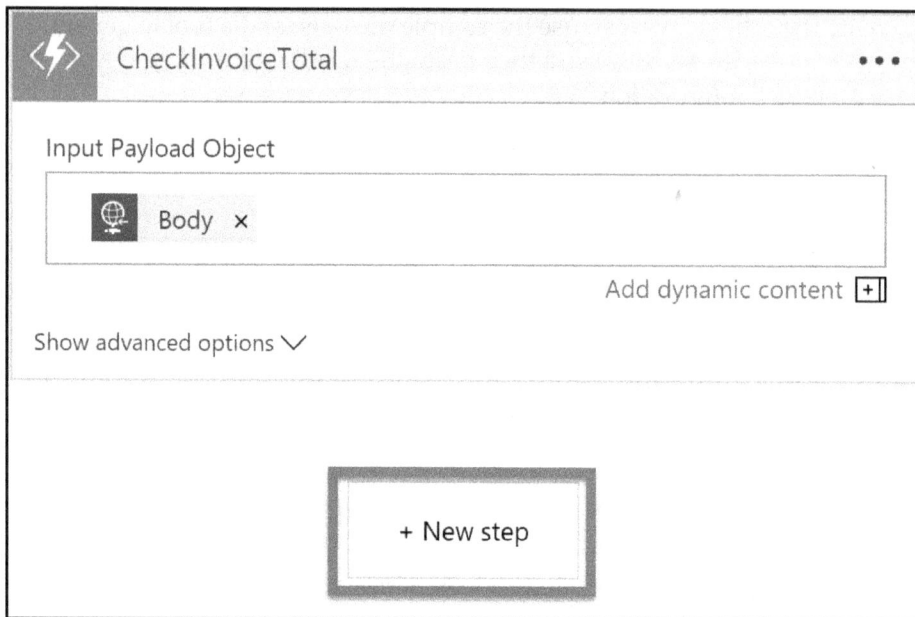

Finally, we click on **+ New step** and add a response that uses the status code and body of the response from the function.

This completes the Logic App that we can build from within the designer. When our function returns an HTTP response, a status code of 200 indicates success, whereas a status code of 400 or 500 indicates failure.

We need to amend the Logic App to ensure that both conditions return a response as, by default, only a Succeeded message is returned. For this, we switch to **Code View** and add Failed to the runAfter entry in the Response action.

```
"Response": {
    "inputs": {
        "body": "@body('CheckInvoiceTotal')",
        "statusCode": "@outputs('CheckInvoiceTotal')['statusCode']"
    },
    "runAfter": {
        "CheckInvoiceTotal": [
            "Succeeded",
            "Failed"
        ]
    },
    "type": "Response"
}
```

We need to test that we have a functioning Logic App, and we can do this using Postman. First, we need the URL to which we need to post our payload.

Once the Logic App has been saved, we obtain the URL from the URL box in the **Request** object within the Logic App.

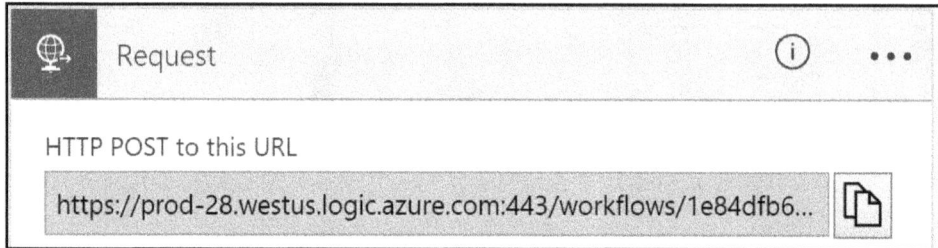

Within Postman, we set the method to POST, paste in the URL for the Logic App, paste in our message, and set the content type to `application/json` and then click on **Send**. If we have configured the Logic App correctly, we expect to see a status code of **200 OK** if we have sent a valid message that contains totals that match.

We can test our other scenarios to ensure that we get the correct responses.

Once we have completed our testing, the Logic App can now be used elsewhere by simply calling the URL and passing the correct payload as shown.

Other considerations

Deploying your Function App

Function Apps are stored using a basic file structure, as shown previously. Given this, they can be deployed through mechanisms that support a file structure in a similar way to Web Apps, including the use of continuous integration and continuous deployment.

Deployment options are available in the App Service settings.

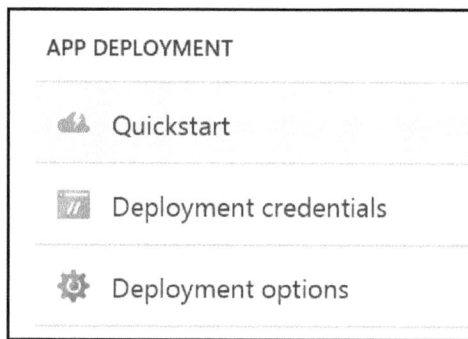

Deployment credentials allows the setting of the username and password for deployment via FTP or Git. The FTP endpoint for the Function App can be found in **Properties** of the App Service.

Deployment options provides access in order to set up deployment from a number of sources.

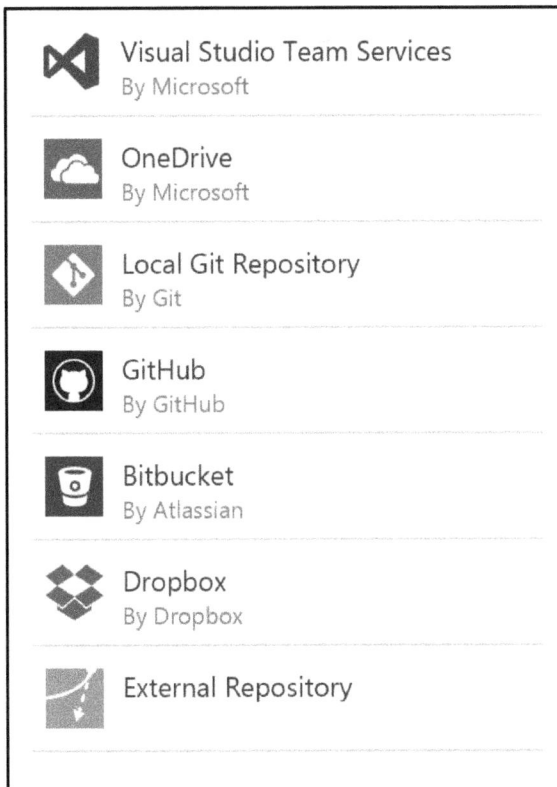

For example, to set up Github as the deployment source, we would choose GitHub from the list. For most of the sources, we need to authorize access to the specific account. Once this has been provided, the source can be configured.

* Choose Source GitHub	>
* Authorization	>
* Choose your organization	>
* Choose project sunnyelectricals	>
* Choose branch master	>
Performance Test Not Configured	>

If Visual Studio Team Services is chosen as the deployment, it is not necessary to authorize access if the instance of Visual Studio Team Services has already been configured within the Azure subscription.

Testing your Function App

When developing functions, as with all development, it is important to ensure that it can be easily tested and that it is then fully tested before production deployment.

There are many ways to test a function, some of which have been shown previously through the chapter, but it is worth reviewing them here:

- Use the log stream to check the status of incoming messages, compilation warnings, and errors.
- A **Timer** trigger can be used to trigger other functions by integrating outputs that form the input for the trigger to be tested. For example, a Timer trigger could place a message on a Service Bus queue that has another trigger using the queue as input. This technique works for any functions that can act as a triggered event, and for other functions that need to read input from sources that require a triggered event such as reading documents out of DocumentDB.
- For HTTP triggers and WebHooks, Postman (`https://www.getpostman.com/`) can be used to perform any HTTP operation, such as GET, POST, or DELETE, against the function.
- For HTTP triggers, a browser can be used against the function endpoint to perform a GET operation. The function endpoint is available on the code page under **Function Url**.
- A storage-based trigger function can be tested using any tool that supports interacting with Azure storage such as Visual Studio or Microsoft Azure Storage Explorer.
- For the majority of triggers, the **Run** dialog on the function development page can be used to provide input in any text-based format.

Using these approaches either individually or together there can be confidence that the function will operate as expected.

Scaling your Function App

Function Apps can exist in the context of a current **App Service Plan** or **App Service Environment**, or it can be serverless and used via a **Consumption Service Plan** where the user needs to have no knowledge of or responsibility for the underlying infrastructure.

When used in an App Service Plan, the Function App can be scaled in the same way as any other service within an App Service plan by changing the plan settings.

- **Scale up**: The plan can be moved to a different pricing tier that provides machines with greater capability
- **Scale out**: The plan can have the number of instances of machines increased either manually, due to CPU percentage load or based on a schedule

When the Function App is in a Consumption Service Plan, it is scaled based on need. The unit of scale is the Function App itself, and scaling is automatic and adds new instances as required. When the instances are no longer required based on the demand, they are removed automatically.

Monitoring your Function App

Another important feature of Function Apps is the ability to monitor the executions of each function. Monitoring is available in each function via the **Monitor** tab.

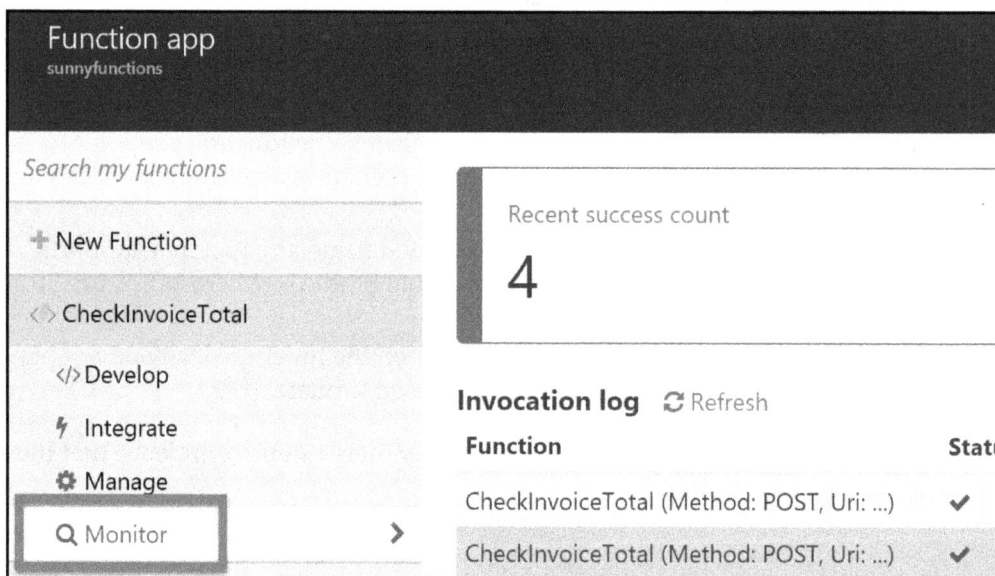

You can look at the invocation logs to see the specific messages and the number of successful or failed messages, and drill in to the message content.

The live event stream displays a graphical representation of the performance of the specific function including number of executions started and completed each second, number of failed executions per second, and the average execution time.

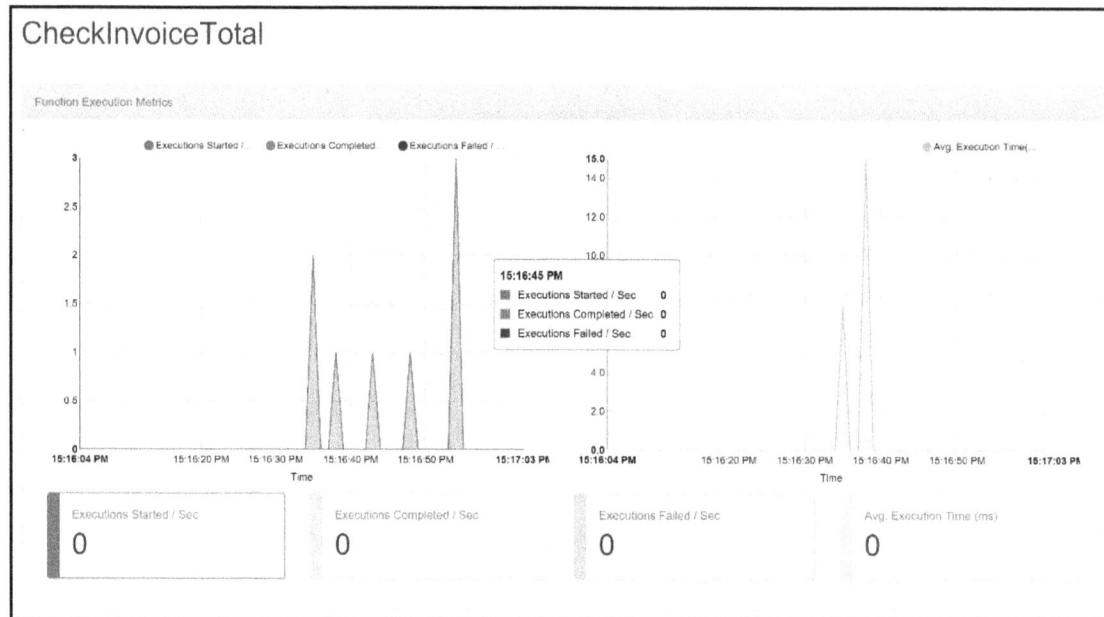

Using the monitoring is not only a way of getting an understanding of how exactly a function is performing, but also a good way of checking on invocations of functions and if errors are detected across your application.

Managing your Function App

The final tab within a function provides some options to manage the function.

The tab can be used to enable or disable the function, delete the function, or provide application and webhook-specific keys that can be provided to developers.

Summary

In this chapter, we showed the capabilities of Azure Functions. We discussed the basics and structure of Function Apps.

We gave some examples of functions, how they can be used to trigger events, and how they can be integrated with each other to create a chain of events that can also fan out.

Azure Functions can be used directly within Logic Apps and can act as anonymous units of code in a similar way to lambda expressions. Functions within Logic Apps can be used to provide business logic and can additionally be used to trigger other events during the execution of the Logic App.

We created a sample scenario to check the information in an invoice as an example of how to call a function within a Logic App.

Finally, we showed other important parts of Azure Functions that can be used to deploy, monitor, and scale them, and how to disable and delete them.

Azure Functions are a good platform service to use if you need scale on demand and serverless computing power. They are a good solution for microservices, and they can be used to provide eventual consistency via an event-driven architecture.

In the next chapter, we will start taking a deeper look into the capabilities of Logic Apps, the language that defines them and present the flow structures that you can use to build robust integration scenarios.

8
A Deep Dive into Logic Apps

Logic is the beginning of wisdom; not the end
– Spock Star Trek

In previous chapters, we discussed how to automate business process with Azure Logic Apps and its different concepts such as workflow, connectors, trigger, and actions. In this chapter, we will dive deep into Azure Logic Apps by creating a complex business workflow using features such as control flow, looping, and exception handling. We will look at the Logic Apps code view and play around with the workflow definition language. We will explore the ability to call nested Logic Apps directly from Logic Apps designer.

This chapter introduces the following topics:

- Workflow definition language
- Content type in Logic Apps
- Logic Apps loops, scopes, and SplitOn
- Exception handling in Logic Apps
- How to build a complex workflow using on-premise data gateway for Logic Apps

Azure Logic Apps provide a new way to automate business processes and running them in reliable way in cloud. Anyone who can use Azure should be able to start building business process that orchestrate data, connect systems, and services across cloud and on-premise resources.

Any workflow that is created in Logic Apps has an associated workflow definition that contains the actual logic that gets executed within the Logic App engine. The workflow definition is a JSON definition file that contains one or more triggers that initiate the Logic app and associated single or multiple actions.

Workflow definition language

The workflow definition contains the actual business logic that is defined as part of the Logic Apps built. Workflow definition language is described thoroughly over Microsoft documentation: `https://docs.microsoft.com/en-us/rest/api/logic/definition-language`.

The basic structure of workflow definition Language is as follows:

```
{
        "$schema": "<schema-of the-definition>",
        "contentVersion": "<version-number-of-definition>",
        "parameters": { <parameter-definitions-of-definition> },
        "triggers": [ { <definition-of-flow-triggers> } ],
        "actions": [ { <definition-of-flow-actions> } ],
        "outputs": { <output-of-definition> }
}
```

Element name	Description
$schema	This specifies the location of the JSON schema file that is used for workflow definition language. This is required when you reference a definition externally.
contentVersion	This specifies the version of the definition.
parameters	This is the list of parameters that are used to input data into the definition. A maximum of 50 parameters can be defined.
triggers	Data that can start a Logic App workflow. A maximum of 250 triggers can be defined.
actions	This specifies actions that are taken as the flow executes. A maximum of 250 actions can be defined.
outputs	Any information that is returned from a workflow run. Maximum of 10 outputs can be defined.

In the previous chapter, we looked into details about trigger and action and how it works within the Logic Apps to build a reliable workflow in cloud. In this chapter, we will cover the rest of workflow definition sections to make a deep understating on the underlying concept.

Parameters

Parameters are place holders to keep the values that are subject to change. For example, if you have a different URL property for an API App hosted for development, test, and production, then it is viable to have a parameter defined that we can change at deployment time.

The basic structure for parameters is shown here:

```
"parameters": {
 "<parameter-name>" : {
    "type" : "<type-of-parameter-value>",
    "defaultValue": <default-value-of-parameter>,
    "allowedValues": [ <array-of-allowed-values> ],
    "metadata" : { "key": { "name": "value"} }
  }
}
```

Here is the code view where we have a parameter named `useremail` within the `parameters` section:

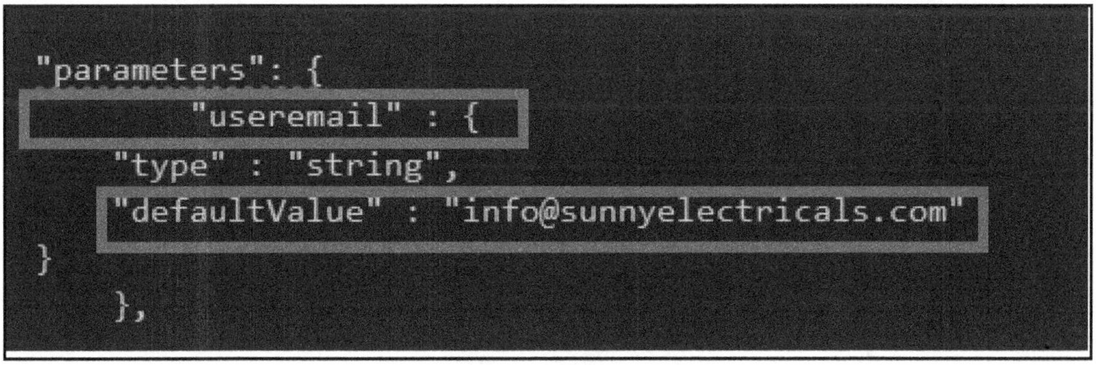

```
"parameters": {
        "useremail" : {
    "type" : "string",
    "defaultValue" : "info@sunnyelectricals.com"
}
    },
```

Once the parameters are defined, we can use them within Logic App workflow repetitively using workflow expression language.

```
"actions": {
    "Send_an_email": {
        "inputs": {
            "body": {
                "Body": "Invoce Message",
                "Subject": "New Invocie Created",
                "To": "@{parameters('useremail')}"
            },
            "host": {
                "api": {
                    "runtimeUrl": "https://logic-apis-centralus.azure-apim.net/apim/outlook"
                },
                "connection": {
                    "name": "@parameters('$connections')['outlook']['connectionId']"
                }
            },
            "method": "post",
            "path": "/Mail"
        },
        "runAfter": {},
        "type": "ApiConnection"
    },
},
```

Output

In Azure Logic Apps, if you have a particular status or value in your Logic App workflow that you want to track for each run, you can define that within run output section and it will appear in the **Management REST API** for that run, and in the management UI for that run in the Azure Portal.

Outputs are not used to respond the caller service. To respond to an incoming request response, action type should be used.

The basic structure for parameters is shown here:

```
"outputs": {
  "key1": {
    "value": "value1",
    "type" : "<type-of-value>"
  }
}
```

- key1: Specifies the key identifier for the output. Replace key1 with a name that you want to use to identify the output.

- `value1`: Specifies the value of the output.
- `<type-of-value>`: Specifies the type for the value that was specified. The possible types of values are:
  - string
  - secure string
  - int
  - bool
  - array
  - object
  - Expression, operators and functions

You can execute expressions including operators and functions within Logic Apps workflow definition language and designer view as well.

Expression

Logic Apps expression is used to evaluate a value of a specific JSON field. In Logic Apps, JSON values can either be fixed string or can be derived from the expression language. Expression can be applied anywhere within value and always evaluates a JSON field. To read more about expression, refer to the Microsoft documentation available at: https://docs.microsoft.com/en-us/rest/api/logic/definition-language.

```
"name": "value"
Or
"Email": "@parameters('Emailaddress')"
```

Expressions can also appear within strings, using the **string interpolation** feature where expressions are wrapped within @{ ... }. See the following example:

```
"name" : "First Name: @{parameters('firstName')} Last Name:
@{parameters('lastName'}"
```

String interpolation is the process of evaluating a string literal containing one or more placeholders. These placeholders are replaced by their corresponding values.

When a JSON value has been determined to be an expression, the body of the expression is extracted by removing the at sign (@). If a literal string is needed that starts with @, it must be escaped using @@.

Let's say I have defined `myString` as `LogicApps` and `myNumber` as 11.

JSON value	Result
`"@parameters('myString')"`	Returns `LogicApps` as a string.
`"@{parameters('myString')}"`	Returns `LogicApps` as a string.
`"@parameters('myNumber')"`	Returns 11 as a number.
`"@{parameters('myNumber')}"`	Returns 11 as a string.
`"Count is: @{parameters('myNumber')}"`	Returns the string `Count is: 11`.
`"Count is: @@{parameters('myNumber')}"`	Returns the string `Count is: @{parameters('myNumber')}`.

Operators

There are four operators that are the characters that you can use inside expressions/functions.

Operator	Description
. (dot Operator)	The dot operator allows you to iterate over object properties
? (question mark)	The question mark operator allows to reference null properties of an object
' (single quotation mark)	Single quotation mark is used to wrap literal values
[ ] (Square bracket)	The square bracket is used to get a value from an array with a specific index

Functions

You can also call function within expressions in Logic Apps. Here is the list of few frequently used functions.

Functions	Description
`@guid()`	Generate a GUID
`@replace(string, old, new)`	Replace old with new in string

`@equals(left, right)`	Returns true if left equals right
`@utcnow('yyyy-mm-dd')`	Generate a date/time
`@string()`	Convert to plain/text
`@json()`	Convert to application/json – can parse like JSON
`@xml()`	Convert to application/xml
`@xpath(<xml>,<expression>)`	Execute Xpath expression
`@if(<condition>,<true>,<false>)`	Set a value based on condition
`@result(<scope>)`	Return the run result for a scope of actions

> For the detailed list of functions, please refer to the following MSDN link: `https://docs.microsoft.com/en-us/rest/api/logic/definition-language#Anchor_6`.

Content type in Logic Apps

Content type defines the actual format of the data that flows through system. Logic Apps engine can process multiple content types, such as JSON, XML, Flat Files, and binary data. There are some natively supported content type for Logic App workflow engines such as JSON, Text, and XML, and other requires casting from one format to another.

Content-Type header

The **Content-Type** header is used to specify the nature of the data in the body of an entity, by giving type and subtype identifiers, and by providing auxiliary information that may be required for certain types. When a client posts a request to the server and specifies the content type, it makes easy for the server to understand the data and parse it.

These are the basic Content-Type, we use within a Logic App.

- text/plain
- application/json
- application/xml

Text/plain

The text Content-Type is intended to send data that is principally textual in form. The primary subtype of text is *plain*. This indicates the plain (unformatted) text. A critical parameter that may be specified in the Content-Type field for text data is the character set. This is specified with a *charset* parameter, as in: `Content-type: text/plain; charset=us-ascii.`

If calling application have not set the content header, in Logic Apps, you can manually cast it to text using the `@string()` function .

```
"actions": {
        "HTTP": {
            "inputs": {
                "body": "@string(triggerBody())",
                "method": "POST",
                "uri": "http://requestb.in/15iusss1"
            },
            "runAfter": {},
            "type": "Http"
        }
    },
```

Application/json

Application/json are natively supported by the Logic Apps workflow engine, and we do not require any conversion or casting within Logic Apps. Any request with the content type application/json will be processed as a JSON object, and iteration through object parameter is easy with workflow expression language.

To explain the earlier concept, we will create a simple Logic App that gets triggered with JSON-formatted data with the content type header as application/json. We have used **Request/Response** pattern within **Compose** operation within Logic Apps.

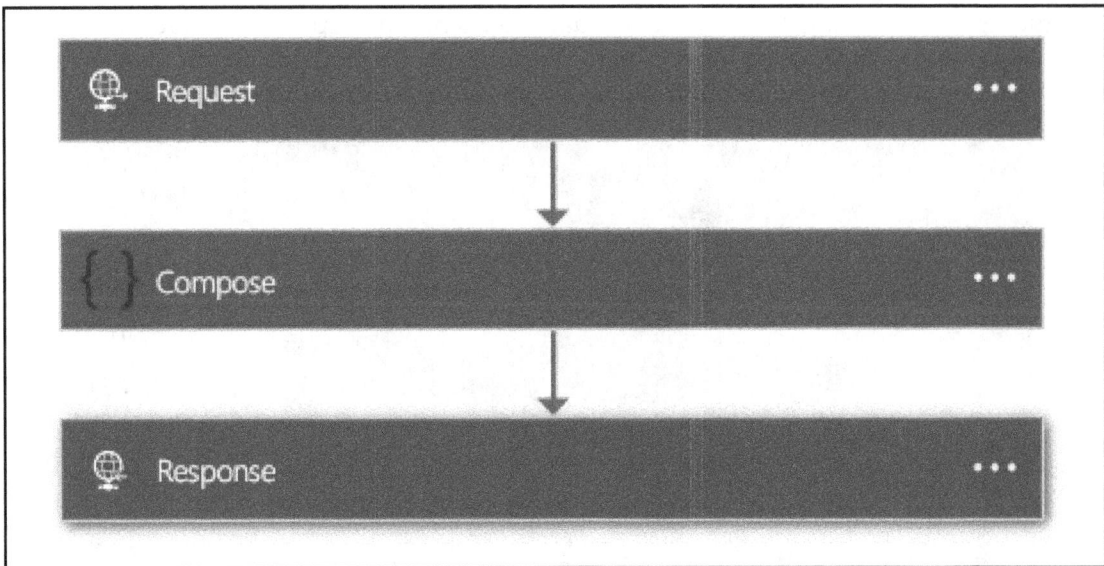

If you look at the **Compose** action in Logic App **Code View** page. You can see how easily we have iterated through the JSON request body and created a response for calling application.

```
"actions": {
        "Compose": {
            "inputs": {
                "Customer": {
                    "AccountNo": "004SE221",
                    "Address": "@{triggerBody()['Invocie']['Address']}",
                    "Amount": "@triggerBody()['Invocie']['Amount']",
                    "Comments": "@{triggerBody()['Invocie']['Comments']}",
                    "Date": "@{triggerBody()['Invocie']['Date']}",
                    "InvoiceId": "@{triggerBody()['Invocie']['InvoiceId']}",
                    "Status": "@{triggerBody()['Invocie']['Status']}",
                    "UserEmail": "@{triggerBody()['Invocie']['UserEmail']}",
                    "UserName": "@{triggerBody()['Invocie']['UserName']} "
                }
            },
            "runAfter": {},
            "type": "Compose"
        },
```

If Logic Apps is receiving data in JSON format and client didn't specified header, you can manually cast it to JSON using the `@json()`. You can use `@json()` to convert the content type from one format to another (for example, application/xml to application/json).

```
"actions": {
        "Response": {
            "inputs": {
                "body": "@json(triggerBody())",
                "statusCode": 200
            },
            "runAfter": {},
            "type": "Response"
        }
    },
```

Application/XML

Application/xml is intended to send data in XML form. Logic Apps has predefined function `@xml`, which can convert content to XML representation.

```
"actions": {
        "Response": {
            "inputs": {
                "body": "@xml(triggerBody())",
                "statusCode": 200
            },
            "runAfter": {},
            "type": "Response"
        }
    },
```

There are other built-in functions that will be used in content type conversion. The list is shown in table here:

Function	Description
@json()	Casts data to application/json
@xml()	Casts data to application/xml
@binary()	Casts data to application/octet-stream
@string()	Casts data to text/plain
@base64()	Converts content to a base64 string
@base64toString()	Converts a base64-encoded string to text/plain
@base64toBinary()	Converts a base64-encoded string to application/octet-stream
@encodeDataUri()	Encodes a string as a data URI byte array
@decodeDataUri()	Decodes a data URI into a byte array

Flow controls, SplitOn, and scope in Logic Apps

Integration solutions are complex to build where we need to communicate with multiple systems and devices and follow different design patterns based on application requirement. When we develop integration solution, we are not confined to the same architecture design, but we use combination of multiples patterns for our solutions.

For each loop

In Logic Apps, you can use the add a **For each** action to iterate over an array item and perform the action or set of actions on each item.

To demonstrate the use case of the add a **For each** action, here is a simple Logic App that gets a list of new products from HTTP request and Logic App iterate through individual product in the array and send a notification mail to inventory.

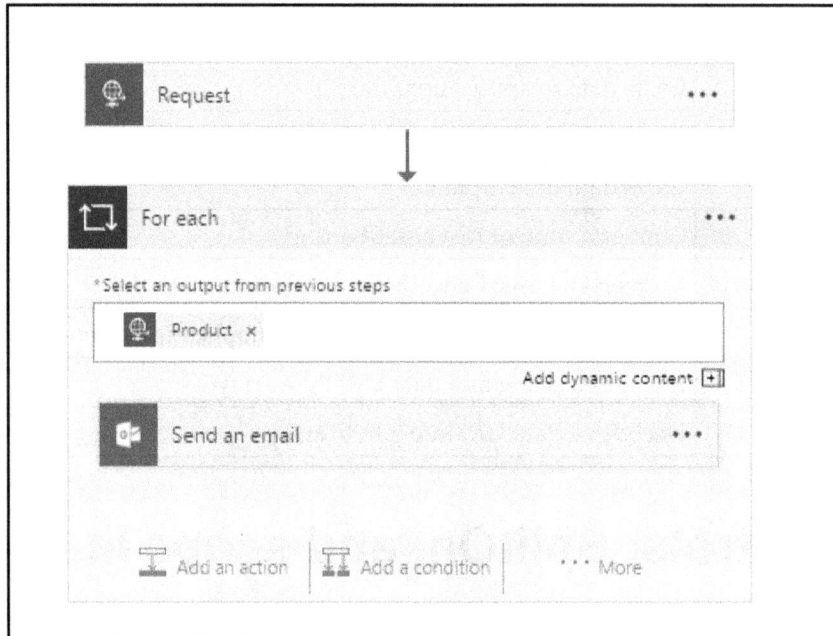

We have used a single trigger and an action that is send the email. You can have multiple actions associated with your add a **For each** action, which can perform a necessary action based on your workflow design. To get deep understanding, we would advise to look at the code behind the file of Logic App workflow.

```
    "For_each": {
        "actions": {
            "Send_an_email": {
                "inputs": {
                    "body": {
                        "Body": "Item Name in Inventory is @{item()?['name']}",
                        "Subject": "New Item arrived with SerialNumber @{item()?['serialNo']}",
                        "To": "████████████@hotmail.com"
                    },
                    "host": {
                        "api": {
                            "runtimeUrl": "https://logic-apis-australiaeast.azure-apim.net/apim/outlook"
                        },
                        "connection": {
                            "name": "@parameters('$connections')['outlook']['connectionId']"
                        }
                    },
                    "method": "post",
                    "path": "/Mail"
                },
                "runAfter": {},
                "type": "ApiConnection"
            }
        },
        "foreach": "@triggerBody()?['Products']?['Product']",
        "runAfter": {},
        "type": "Foreach"
    }
},
```

A foreachaction can iterate up to 5000 rows, and each of the iteration will be executed in parallel to the running instances.

> You can run the foreach action in Logic Apps as single threaded by using operationsOptions within the Logic Apps workflow.

```
"For_each": {
    "actions": {
        "HTTP": {
            "inputs": {
                "body": "@item()",
                "method": "POST",
                "uri": "http://requestb.in/148ogof1"
            },
            "runAfter": {},
            "type": "Http"
        }
    },
    "foreach": "@triggerBody()?['Products']?['Product']",
    "operationOptions": "Sequential",
    "runAfter": {},
    "type": "Foreach"
}
```

The Do Until loop

This indicates looping until a condition is met. Once you add Do Until within your Logic app designer, you need to define the entry and exit conditions.

Exit criteria includes the following:

- Time
- Count of iterations

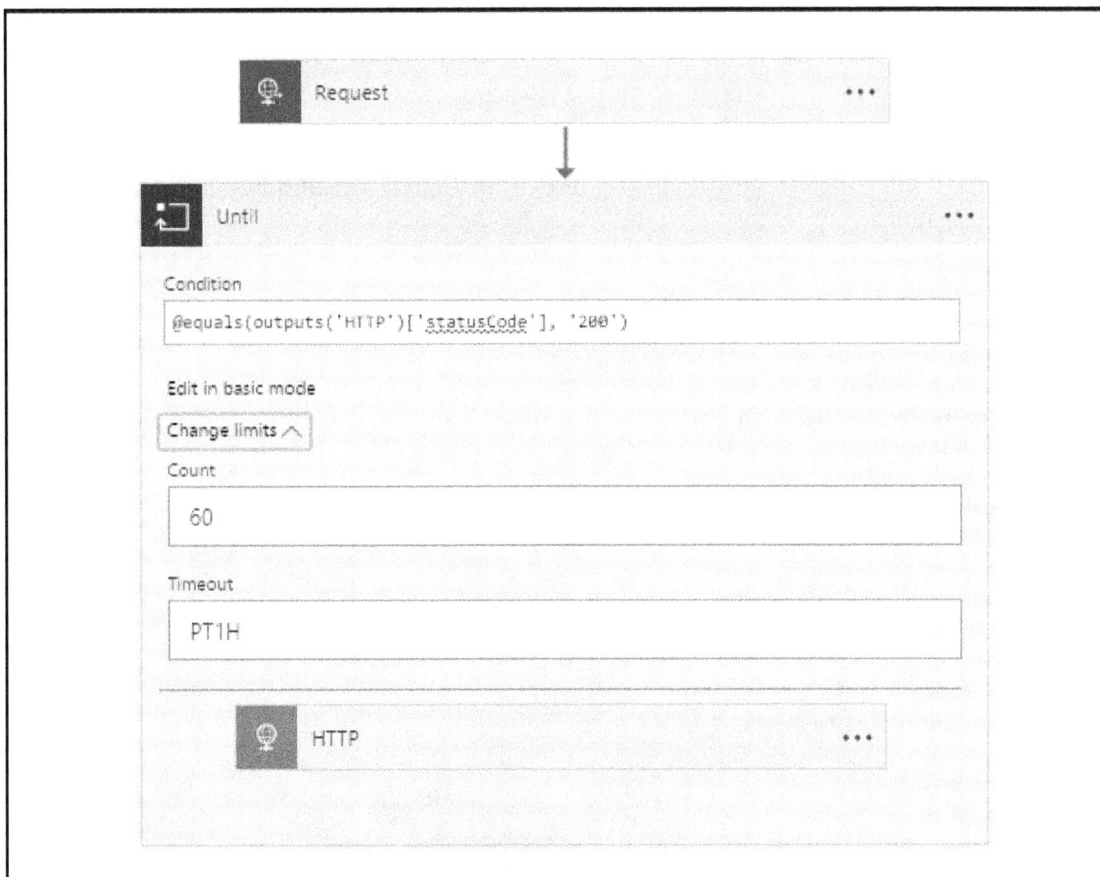

To demonstrate the use case with Do Until, here is a Logic App that will be triggered from an HTTP endpoint; once the request is received through trigger, Logic App posts the request message to another external endpoint and checks for the HTTP status code – success or failure. In case of failure, Logic App retries to service call.

This logic App will complete its processing or exit the loop if any of the following conditions are met:

- HTTP status code is 200
- Loop until 60
- Timeout 1 hour

Exit conditions mentioned earlier are default values. You can modify `timeout` and retry `count` properties directly from Logic Apps code behind file.

```
"Until": {
    "actions": {
        "HTTP": {
            "inputs": {
                "headers": "@triggerBody()",
                "method": "POST",
                "uri": "http://requestb.in/p9914dp9"
            },
            "runAfter": {},
            "type": "Http"
        }
    },
    "expression": "@equals(outputs('HTTP')['statusCode'], '200')",
    "limit": {
        "count": 60,
        "timeout": "PT1H"
    },
    "runAfter": {},
    "type": "Until"
}
},
```

Similar to the for each loop, you can have multiple actions associated with the Do Until loop. You can also associate variety of conditional expression within the Do Until loop.

SplitOn

Let's say you have a trigger in your Logic App that receives an array items. Now you want to debatch array items and start a new workflow per item. You can accomplish that using SplitOn. This is very useful when you want to poll an endpoint that can have multiple new items between polling intervals.

For example, consider the following message you receive in your Logic App workflow. Now here I may only need the item detail to pass to my database table or to other API for further processing.

```
{
    "Status": "success",
    "Items": [
        {
            "id": 1,
            "item": "book"
        },
        {
            "id": 2,
            "item": "pen"
        }
    ]
}
```

You can use the following SplitOn command in the workflow definition:

```
"splitOn": "@triggerBody()?.Items"
```

```
"inputs": {
    "schema": {
        "$schema": "http://json-schema.org/draft-04/schema#",
        "properties": {
            "Items": {
                "items": {
                    "properties": {
                        "id": {
                            "type": "integer"
                        },
                        "name": {
                            "type": "string"
                        }
                    },
                    "required": [
                        "id",
                        "name"
                    ],
                    "type": "object"
                },
                "type": "array"
            },
            "Status": {
                "type": "string"
            }
        },
        "required": [
            "Status",
            "Items"
        ],
        "type": "object"
    }
},
"kind": "Http",
"splitOn": "@triggerBody()?.Items",
"type": "Request"
}
```

This will return each item detail as shown here and can be used to start a new event or other next action:

```
{"id":1,"name":"book"}
{"id":2,"name":"pen"}
```

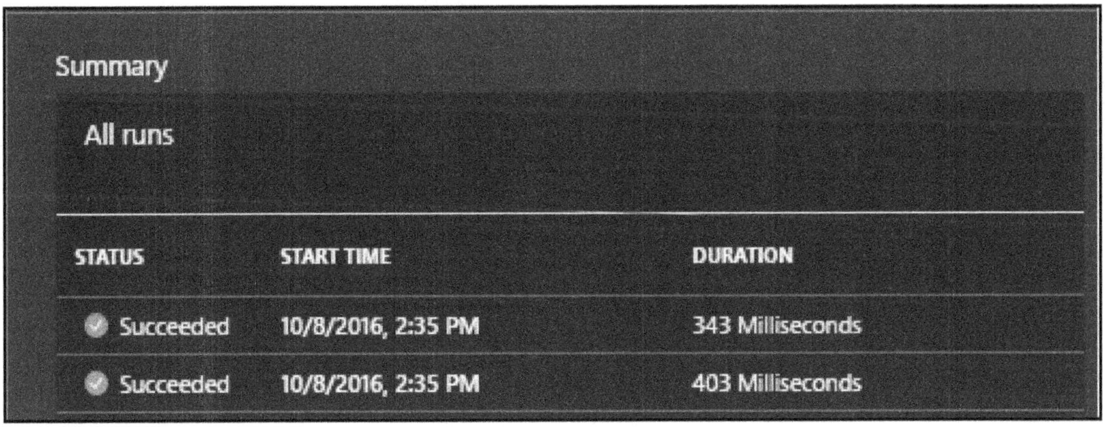

Summary		
All runs		
STATUS	**START TIME**	**DURATION**
Succeeded	10/8/2016, 2:35 PM	343 Milliseconds
Succeeded	10/8/2016, 2:35 PM	403 Milliseconds

Currently, SplitOn arrays are limited to 1000 items.

Switch statement

While creating workflow for your enterprise you are often required to take different actions based on the content of the message. For example in case of polling your outlook for new messages you might need to take different actions based on the subject of the email.

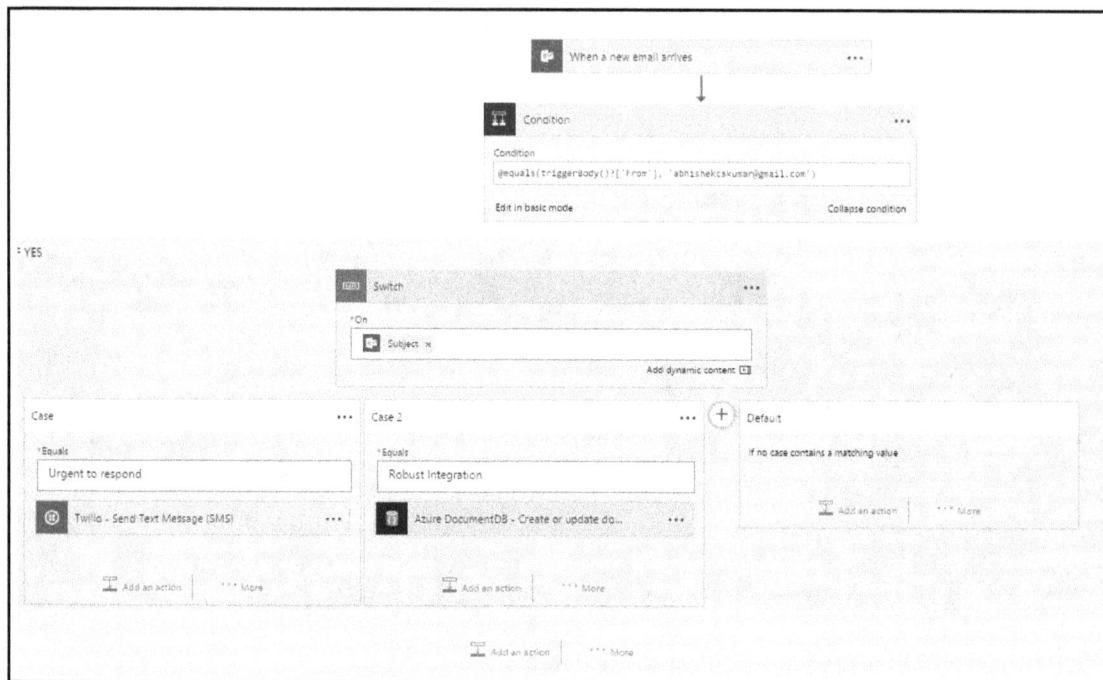

Single run instance

There will be multiple instances where you want to process the incoming request in sequential basis. In Logic Apps sequential workflow can be easily done by using `operationOptions` to `singleInstance` on the trigger definition.

```
"triggers": {
    "mytrigger": {
        "type": "http",
        "inputs": { ... },
        "recurrence": { ... },
        "operationOptions": "singleInstance"
    }
}
```

Scope

Scope is defined as grouping of executable actions within the Logic App. The group of actions include workflow actions and exception handling. You can use a Logic App designer to add a scope and its associated actions.

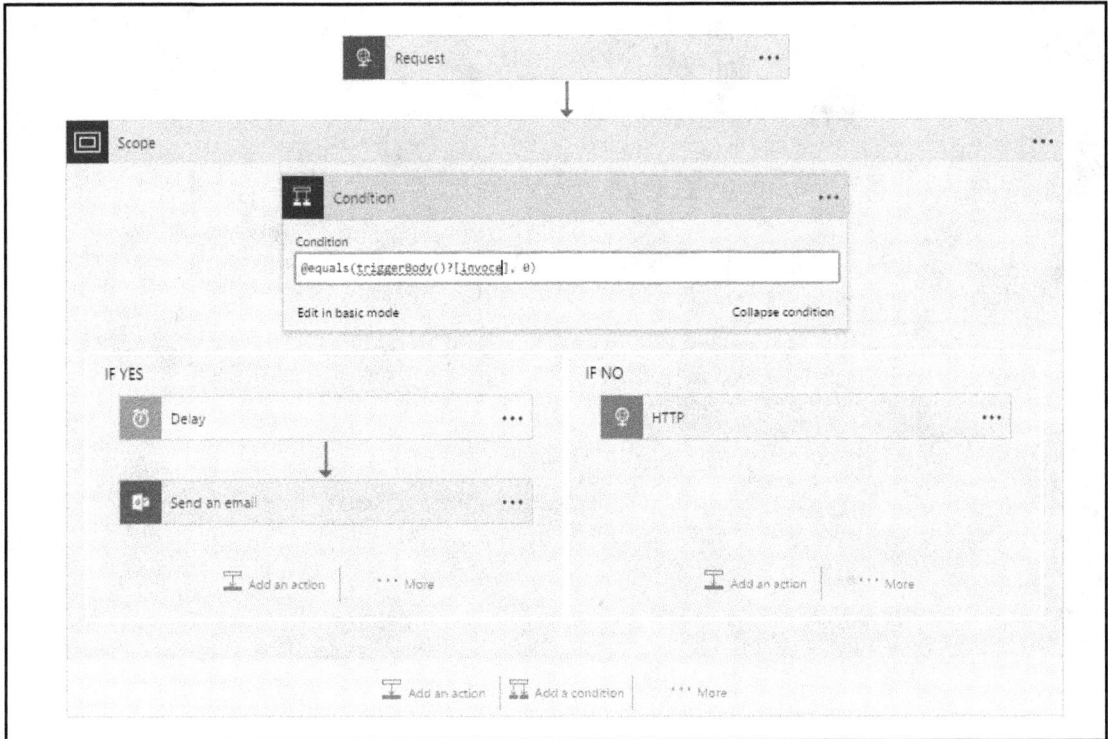

Here, we have a Logic App that is being invoked by manual http trigger. In scope, we have two actions – one is to post every request to the HTTP endpoint and other if an amount is greater than a fixed value, then send a mail for the workflow approval.

```
"Scope": {
  "actions": {
    "Condition": {
      "actions": {
        "Delay": {
          "inputs": {
            "interval": {
              "count": 12,
              "unit": "Minute"
            }
          },
          "runAfter": {},
          "type": "Wait"
        }
      },
      "else": {
        "actions": {
          "HTTP": {
            "inputs": {
              "body": "@triggerBody()",
              "method": "POST",
              "uri": "http://requestb.in/p9914dp9"
            },
            "runAfter": {},
            "type": "Http"
          }
        }
      },
      "expression": "@equals(triggerBody()?['Invoice']?['Price'], 0)",
      "runAfter": {},
      "type": "If"
    }
  },
  "runAfter": {},
  "type": "Scope"
},
```

Exception handling in Logic Apps

It is always advisable to have good exception handling mechanism in place before you start implementing any business flow using Logic Apps. Logic Apps provide a robust way to handle exception within the workflow, and later sections are dedicated with some common ways to do exception handling if the workflow do not go with happy design flow.

You can get more information on Microsoft documentation shared in the following links:

- https://docs.microsoft.com/en-us/azure/app-service-logic/app-service-logic-exception-handling
- https://docs.microsoft.com/en-us/azure/app-service-logic/app-service-logic-scenario-error-and-exception-handling

Scopes to catch failures

As discussed in the previous section, the scope allows you to group actions together. So, it primarily acts as a logical grouping of actions, which is useful for organizing your logic app actions and for performing aggregate evaluations on the status of a scope.

The scope itself has its own status, which it receives after all the actions within a scope have completed. The scope status is determined with the same criteria as a run and, if the final action in an execution branch is Failed or Aborted, the status is failed.

We can refer to the earlier figure where we can use runAfter, if the scope has been marked as Failed. In this scenario, runAfter can help us create a single action to catch failures if any actions within the scope fail.

We can also get the context of failure to understand exactly which actions failed using @result() workflow function. @result() takes a single parameter, scope name, and returns an array of all the action results from within that scope.

```
"Exception_array": {
    "inputs": {
        "from": "@result('My_Scope')",
        "where": "@equals(item()['status'], 'Failed')"
    },
    "runAfter": {
        "My_Scope": [
            "Failed"
        ]
    },
    "type": "Query"
}
```

The `Exception_array` is a **Filter array** action to filter `@result('My_Scope')` to get the result of all actions within `My_Scope`.

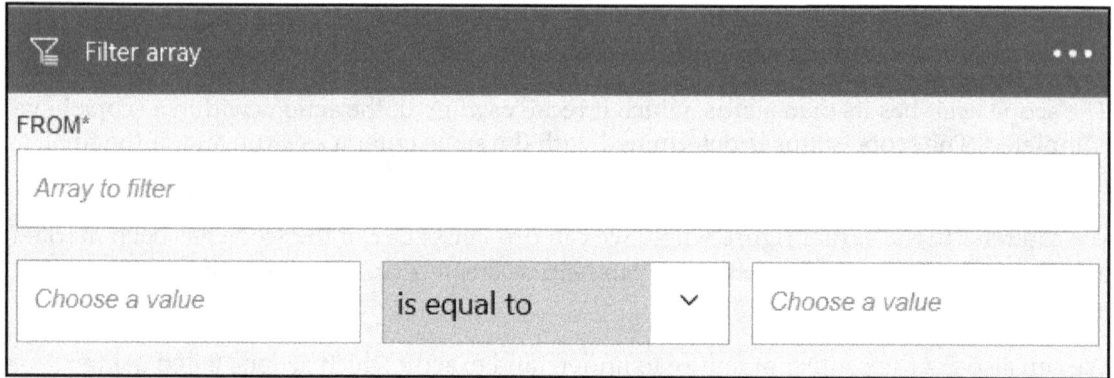

The condition of the **Filter array** is any `@result()` item with the status equal to `Failed`. This will filter the array of all action results from `My_Scope` to only an array of failed action results.

These action objects include the same attributes as the `@result()` object, including action start time, action end time, action status, action inputs, action correlation IDs, and action outputs. We can combine the `@result()` function with a `runAfter` to send context of any actions that failed within a scope, as shown in the earlier example.

Once you have the **Filter array** of exceptions, you can perform an action for each failed action. For example, send an HTTP POST request with the response body of any actions that failed within the scope `My_Scope`.

```
"Foreach_exception": {
{
"actions": {
        "Log_Exception": {
            "inputs": {
                "body": "@item()['outputs']['body']",
                "method": "POST",
                "headers": {
                    "x-failed-action-name": "@item()['name']",
                    "x-failed-tracking-id": "@item()['clientTrackingId']"
                },
                "uri": "http://requestb.in/"
            },
            "runAfter": {},
            "type": "Http"
        }
```

```
    },
    "foreach": "@body('Exception_array')",
    "runAfter": {
        "Exception_array": [
            "Succeeded"
        ]
    },
    "type": "Foreach"
}
```

As shown in the earlier example code, you can send an HTTP POST on the `foreach` item response body, or `@item()['outputs']['body']`. The `@result()` item shape is the same as the `@actions()` shape, and it can be parsed the same way.

Also, include two custom headers with the failed action name `@item()['name']` and the failed run client tracking ID `@item()['clientTrackingId']`. You can also include other useful properties from the `@result()` such as `startTime`, `endTime`, and `status`.

We also have option to just terminate the workflow using the **Terminate** action, if the status of the scope is failed.

Retry Policies

These allow you to customize the retry behavior for **4xx** or **5xx** errors. If a request in a Logic App workflow is timed out or failed (Error code 4xx or 5XX), Retry Policy can be defined for an action to retry.

```
"retryPolicy" : {
    "type": "<type-of-retry-policy>",
    "interval": <retry-interval>,
    "count": <number-of-retry-attempts>
}
```

The retry interval is specified in the **ISO 8601** format, which is representation of dates and times is an international standard covering the exchange of date and time-related data. By default, all actions retry three additional times over 20-second intervals. To disable the retry policy, set its `type` to `None`.

So, for example, if the first request received a `500 Internal Server Error` response, the workflow engine pauses for 20 seconds and attempts the request again. If after all retries the response is still an exception or a failure, the workflow will continue and mark the action status as `Failed`.

The following action will retry fetching the latest stock news two times in case of intermittent failures, for a total of three executions, with a 30 second delay between each attempt.

The runAfter property to catch failures

As used in our earlier example, the `runAfter` property is used to set to fire a specific task if the previous step/action has failed in the Logic app workflow.

By default, all actions added through the designer are set to `runAfter` the previous step if the previous step was `Succeeded`, as shown in the earlier figure. However, you can customize this value to fire actions when previous actions are `Failed`, `Skipped`, or a possible set of these values.

If a specific action fails, for example, `Insert_Row` fails for any record in a SQL table, you can use the following `runAfter` configuration:

```
"runAfter": {
        "Insert_Row": [
            "Failed"
        ]
```

Logic App to update on-premise warehouse with data gateway

Consider the scenario where Sunny Electricals (Fictitious company for this book) has a website that is inserting purchase orders (PO's) into an Azure SQL database. There is a need to send the PO to the warehouse for further processing. We are going to do this using two Logic Apps in a parent child relationship. The parent Logic App is going to get the records from the PO database and call child Logic App to insert them into the on-premise warehouse. The warehouse is on-premise SQL server database, whereas the PO database is in Azure SQL.

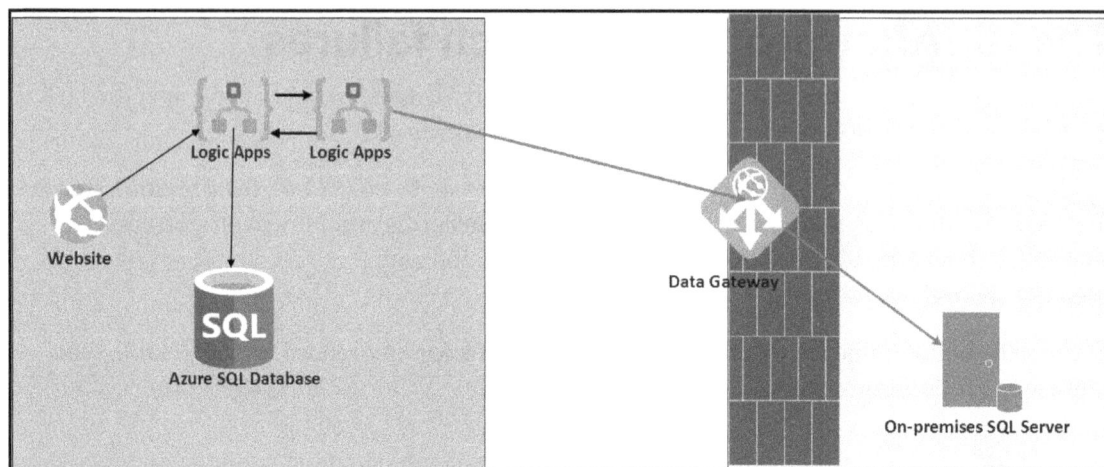

On-premise data gateway for Logic Apps

The on-premise data gateway acts as a bridge, providing quick and secure data transfer between on-premise data and the Azure cloud services, such as Logic Apps, Microsoft Flow, and Microsoft Power BI.

On-premise data gateway is very important in Logic App to do hybrid integration (Integration with Azure resources and on-premise data). There are multiple Logic Apps connectors that uses on-premise data gateway to make connection with on-premise resources, such as SQL connector, BizTalk connector, and MSMQ connector.

We will go through step by step to install and configure on-premise data gateway.

Microsoft account prerequisites for installing on-premise data gateway for Logic Apps

You should use work or school e-mail address that is being associated with Azure subscription to install on-premise data gateway.

Installation and configuration on-premise data gateway

There are certain hardware and software prerequisites to install on-premise data gateway:

- NET 4.5 Framework
- 64-bit version of Windows 7 or Windows Server 2008 R2 (or later)

You can refer to MSDN-shared link here to find recommended configuration settings: `https://docs.microsoft.com/en-us/azure/app-service-logic/app-service-logic-gateway-install`.

Installing on-premise data gateway:

On your server, download the on-premise data gateway from the following Microsoft link: `https://docs.microsoft.com/en-us/azure/app-service-logic/app-service-logic-gateway-install`.

Once you have downloaded the setup file, you can run the setup file that will prompt with **On-premise data gateway installation** screen.

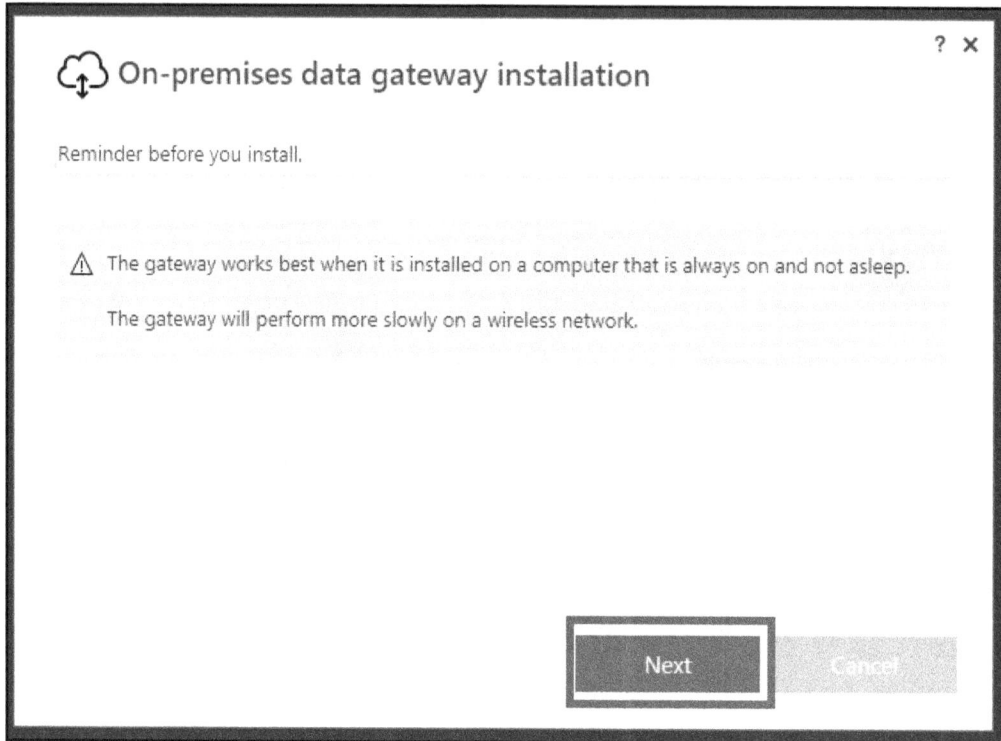

Click on **Next** and set installation path and click on **I accept the terms of use and privacy statement** and then click on **Install** to install the on-premise data gateway.

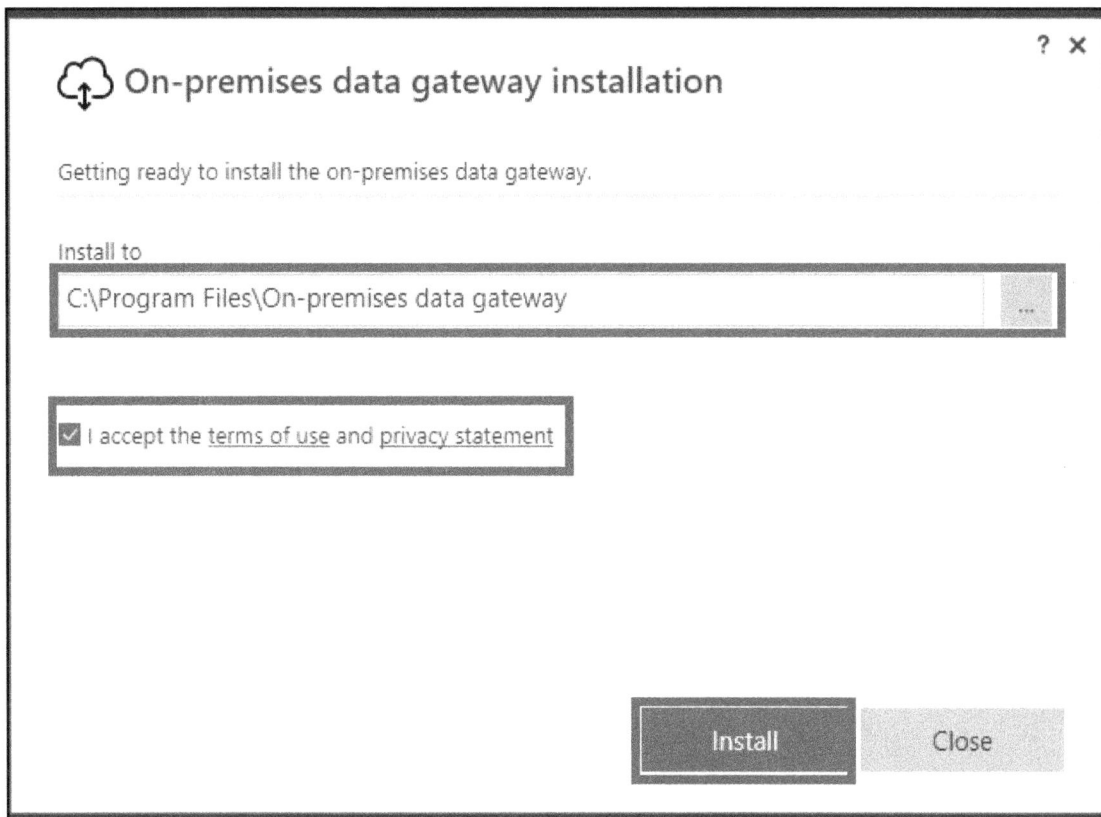

This will prompt you with installation complete screen as shown here. You need to sign in with your work e-mail or school e-mail ID that has associated Azure subscription.

On the **Sign in** Screen, enter the valid e-mail address and password for your work or school account.

If you are using Hotmail, Live or Outlook Microsoft account, then you need to create a work e-mail through the Azure Active Directory. We will show how you can use your personal account and subscription in the coming section.

Once you have successfully logged in with your credentials, select **Register a New Gateway on this computer** and click on **Next**.

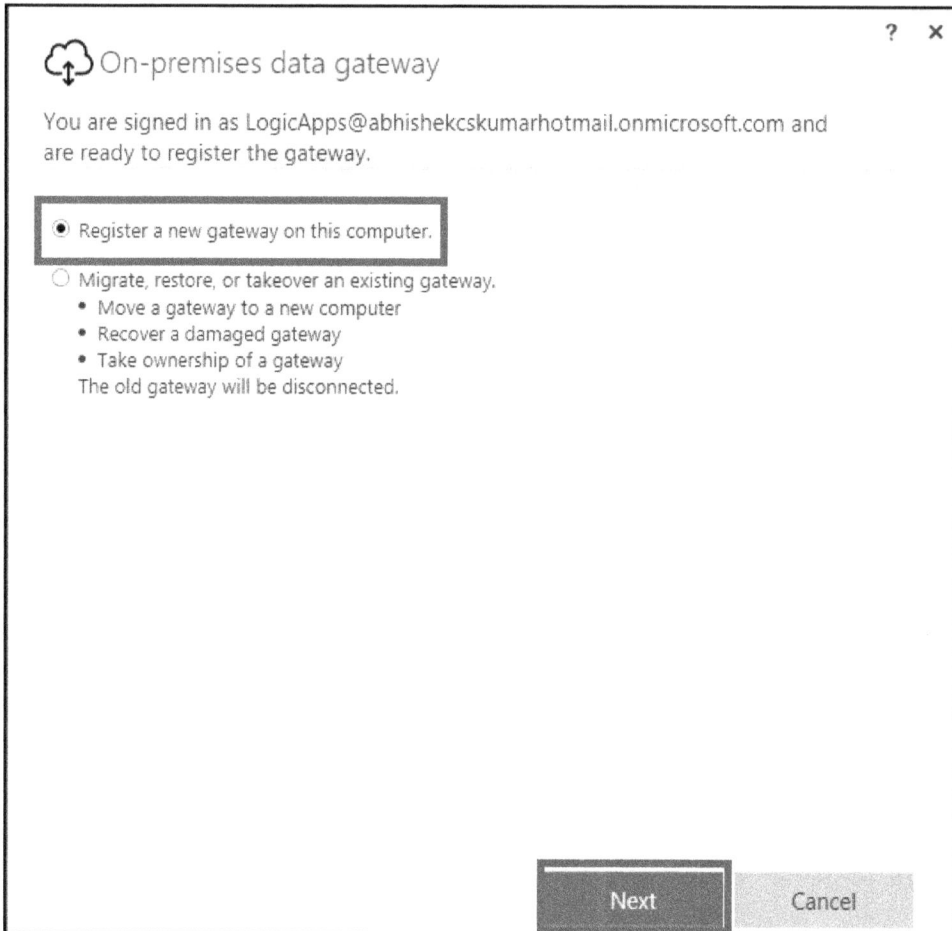

On the next screen, populate **New on-premise data gateway name** and **Recovery key** and click on **Configure**. A recovery key that contains at least eight characters is useful when you want to migrate, restore, or take over the gateway.

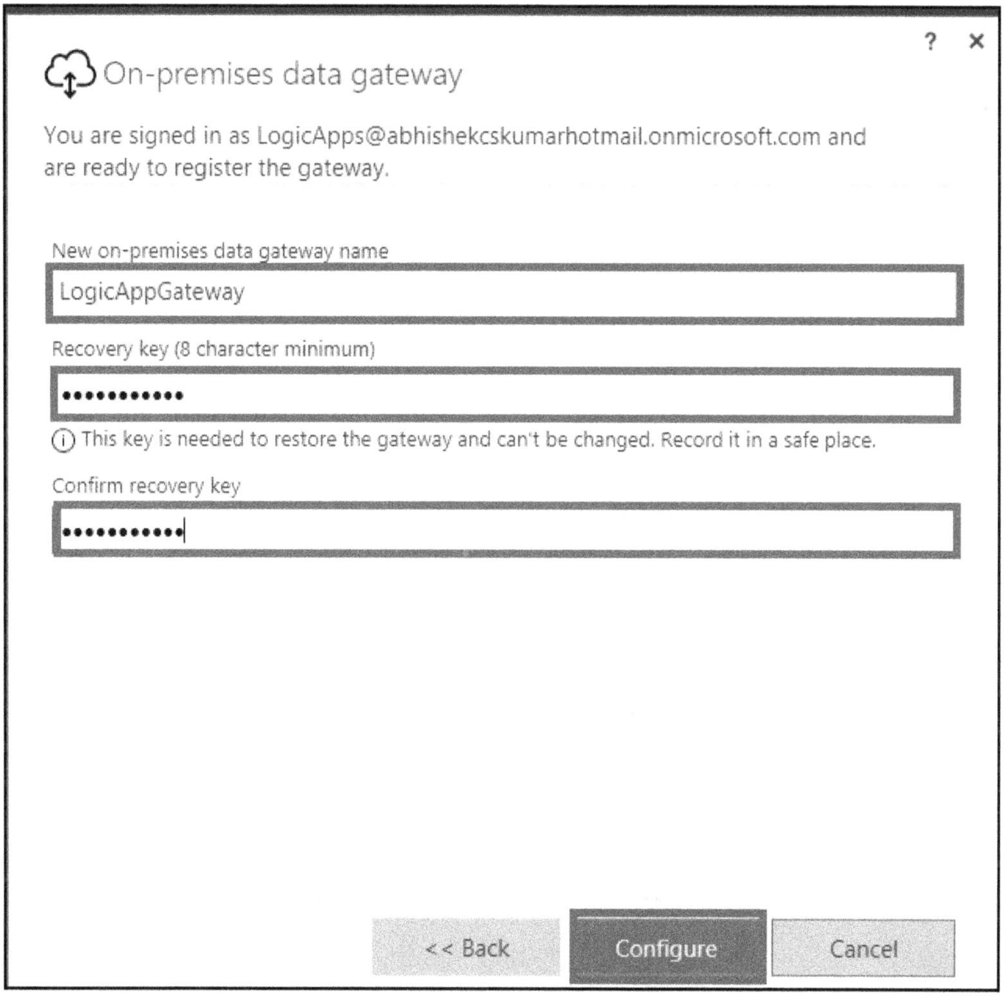

On configuring successfully, a new screen will pop up. If you want to see logs for the configuration you can export the logs or you can **Close** the window.

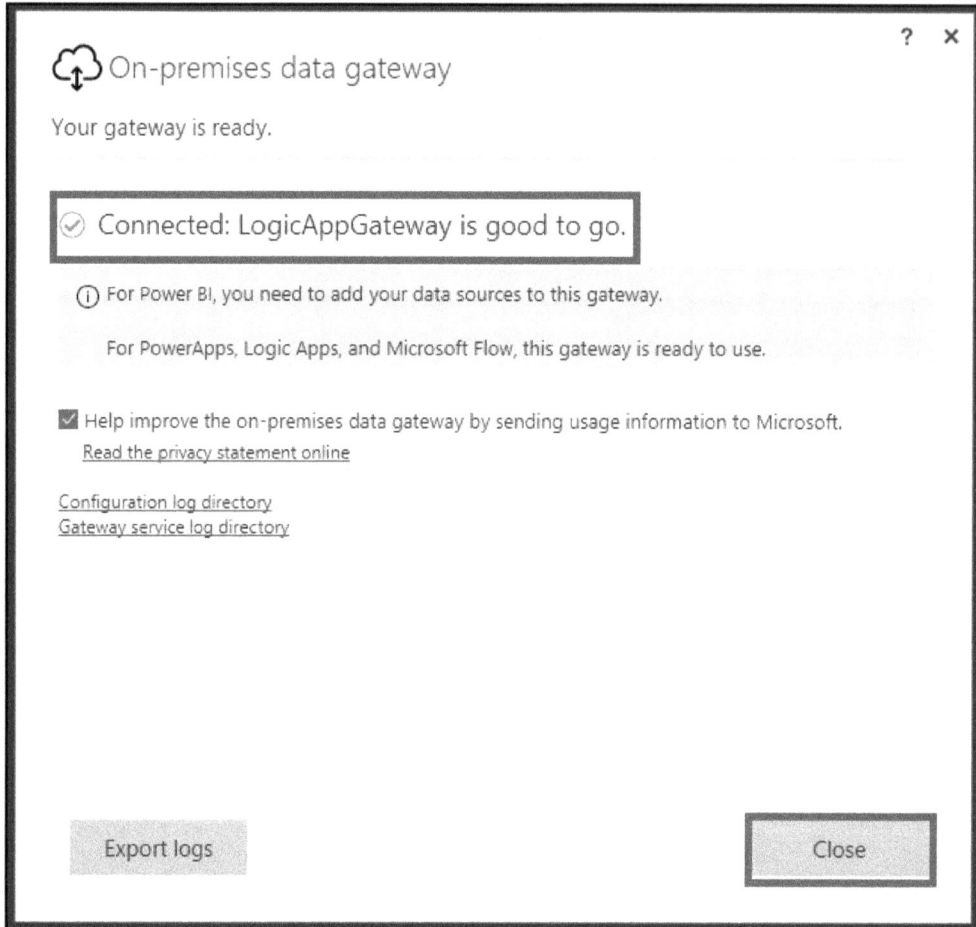

You can verify the run status of on-premise data gateway by looking into windows services running on machine. Go to **Run** and type `services.msc` and check for the status of on-premise data gateway service:

On-premises data gateway ...	The on-pre...	Running	Automatic	NT SERVICE\PBIEgwService

> If you are working with a corporate network, you might need to set firewall rules to work with on-premise data gateway. For further information, about setting up on-premise data gateway, please refer to the following MSDN: `https://docs.microsoft.com/en-us/azure/app-service-logic/app-service-logic-gateway-install`.

Creating a work or school identity in Azure Active Directory

It is always a case that your Azure subscription is associated with your personal Microsoft account such as Hotmail, Live, or Outlook. If this is the condition you will require to create a tenant user within your Azure Active directory to get a school or work e-mail, which can be used to install the on-premise gateway. Steps to create tenant user is well explained in the following Microsoft shared
resource: `https://docs.microsoft.com/en-us/azure/virtual-machines/virtual-machines-windows-create-aad-work-id?toc=%2fazure%2fvirtual-machines%2fwindows%2ftoc.json#locate-your-default-directory-in-the-azure-classic-portal`.

Once the **On-premise data gateway** is installed and configured on the On-premise server, go to the Azure portal to create an **Azure on-premise data gateway resource**.

- Log in to Azure using the same work or school e-mail address that was used during the installation of the gateway.
- Click on the **New** resource button.
- Search and select the on-premise data gateway.

- Complete the information to associate the gateway with your account, including selecting the appropriate installation name. An important thing to note here is that `LogicAppGateway` is the name of the gateway that we installed on the on-premise server. This gets autopopulated, the portal will show all the available gateways that are installed and display them.
- Click on the **Create** button to create the resource.

We will be using Visual Studio to create the Logic Apps solution.

In Visual Studio, navigate to **File** | **New Project** | **Visual C#** | **Cloud** | **Azure Resource Group**. Enter the project **Name**, **Location**, and **Solution name**, as shown in the following screenshot:

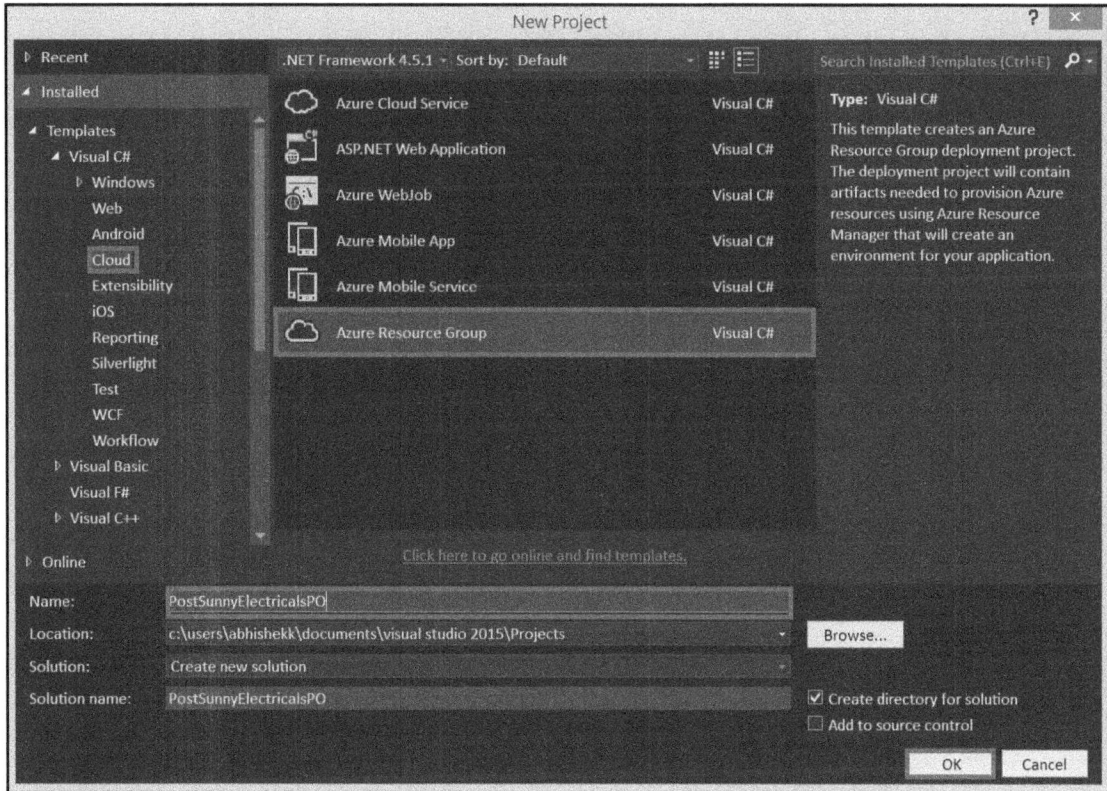

From the drop-down menu of **Select Azure Template** window, select **Logic App** and click on **OK**.

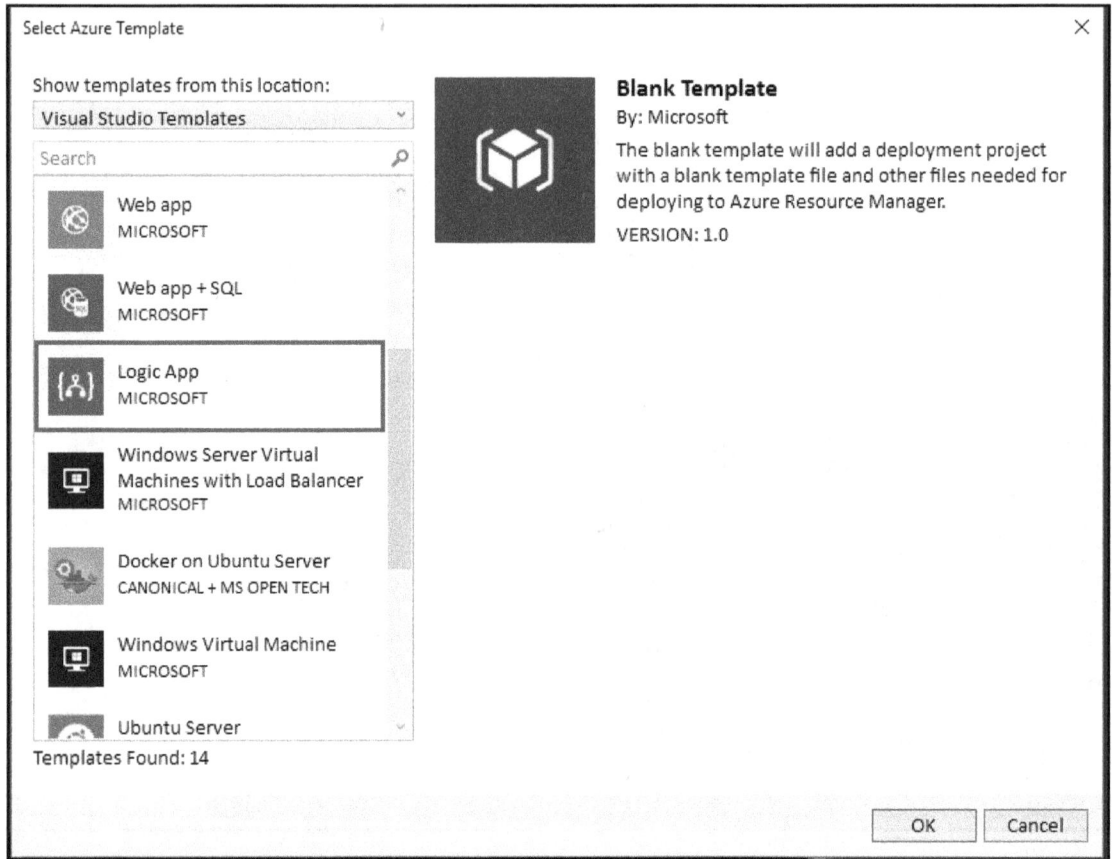

We will see the following files created in **Solution Explorer**. The `LogicApp.json` file is the code for the logic app, and the `LogicApp.parameters.json` file has the configurable parameters that the Logic App needs, such as username and password for SQL database servers. Both these files keep building and growing as and when you add shapes from the designer view.

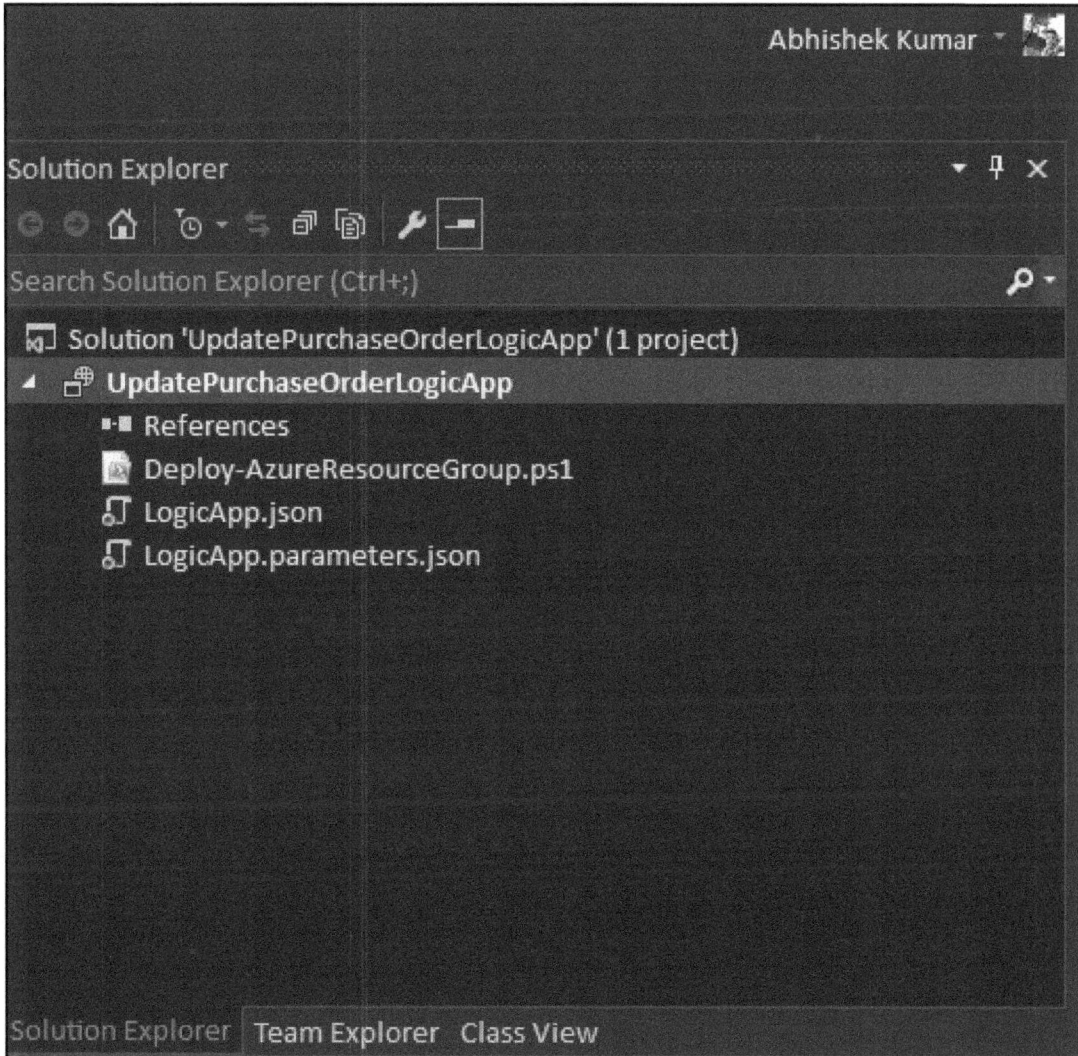

We can take a look at the designer view by right-clicking on the `LogicApp.json` file. As discussed, we have two logic apps chaining together to create the following solution:

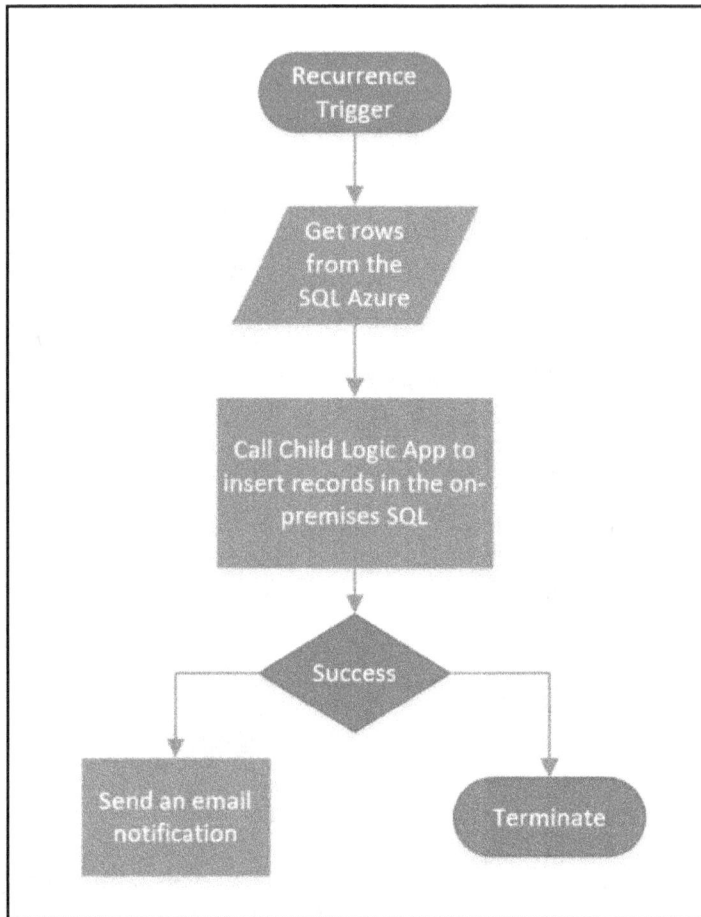

Logic Apps and API Apps can also be used as a microservices pattern-discrete reusable single-purpose service/component with HTTP/Rest endpoint, which can be fabricated together to form composite service. So, we can have multiple Logic Apps with distinct functionality/purpose and then by chaining them together a composite business processes can be accomplished. In our scenario, there are two Logic Apps with the following purposes:

- **Parent Logic App**: This polls PO records from Azure SQL database in particular intervals
- **Child Logic App**: This inserts PO records to on-premise SQL database and returns the status

The Logic App (parent) is having recurrence trigger that will run every 3 minutes to poll data from the Azure SQL database and pass on the data to the child Logic App `UpdateWarehouse`.

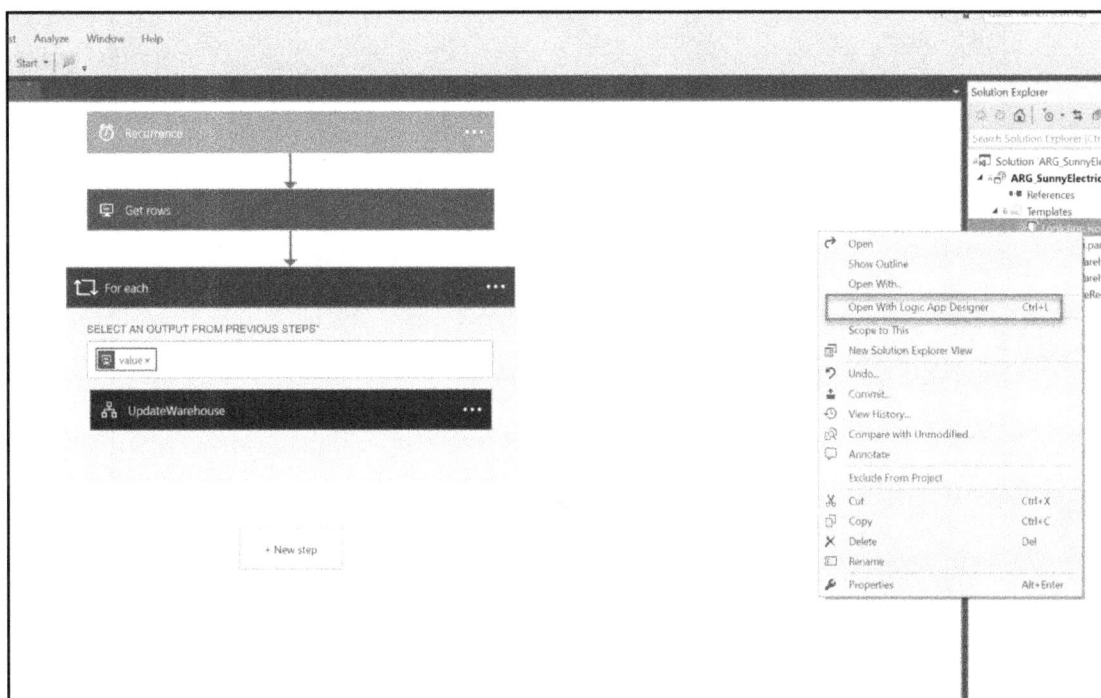

In Logic App designer after making successful connection with Azure SQL database by providing correct connection information, you need to populate Azure SQL **Get rows 2** properties.

Properties	Description
TABLE NAME	The name of the table from which data is retrieved
FILTER QUERY	Filter expressions in OData URIs to limit the results that are returned
ORDER BY	ODATA orderBy query to specify order by entries
SKIP COUNT	The number of elements that need to be skipped from the result set.
MAXIMUM GET COUNT	Maximum number of rows to retrieve

If we look at the PurchaseOrder table that is hosted over Azure for Sunny Electricals, we have certain records with column Id, PO number, and IsNew items, which specify whether the order is new or old one. The snap of the existing data in Azure SQL database is as follows:

Now we go back to our child Logic App and show how we are inserting the purchase order into our warehouse.

The child logic app is simple, and it is invoked by the HTTP trigger from the parent logic app. Once it receives the purchase order request from parent Logic App, it inserts the records in the on-premise SQL Server database and gives the response back to the parent app based on response code received from on-premise SQL insert operation.

To make connection with on-premise SQL database, Logic App is using on-premise data gateway. In this solution, child Logic App is receiving request message from the parent Logic App and inserting rows into on-premise SQL Server. The child Logic App also responds with the status code that can be either success or failed.

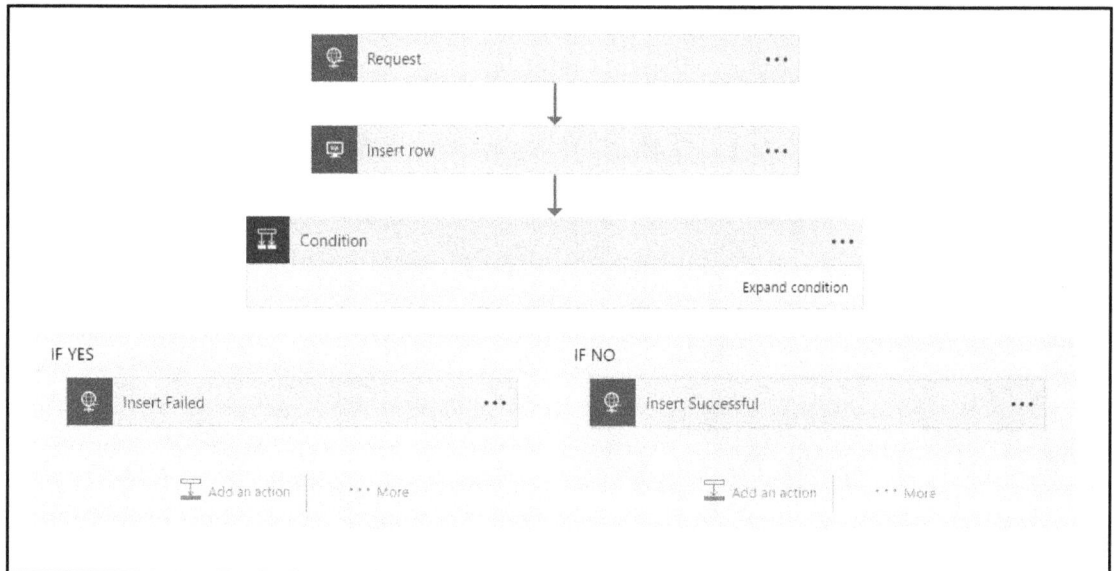

Now coming back to the solution, we have followed the steps mentioned earlier to install on-premise data gateway to the on-premise SQL server. We need to select the checkbox for **Connect via On-premise data gateway**, then select the **GATEWAY** to connect to, and complete any other connection information required as shown here:

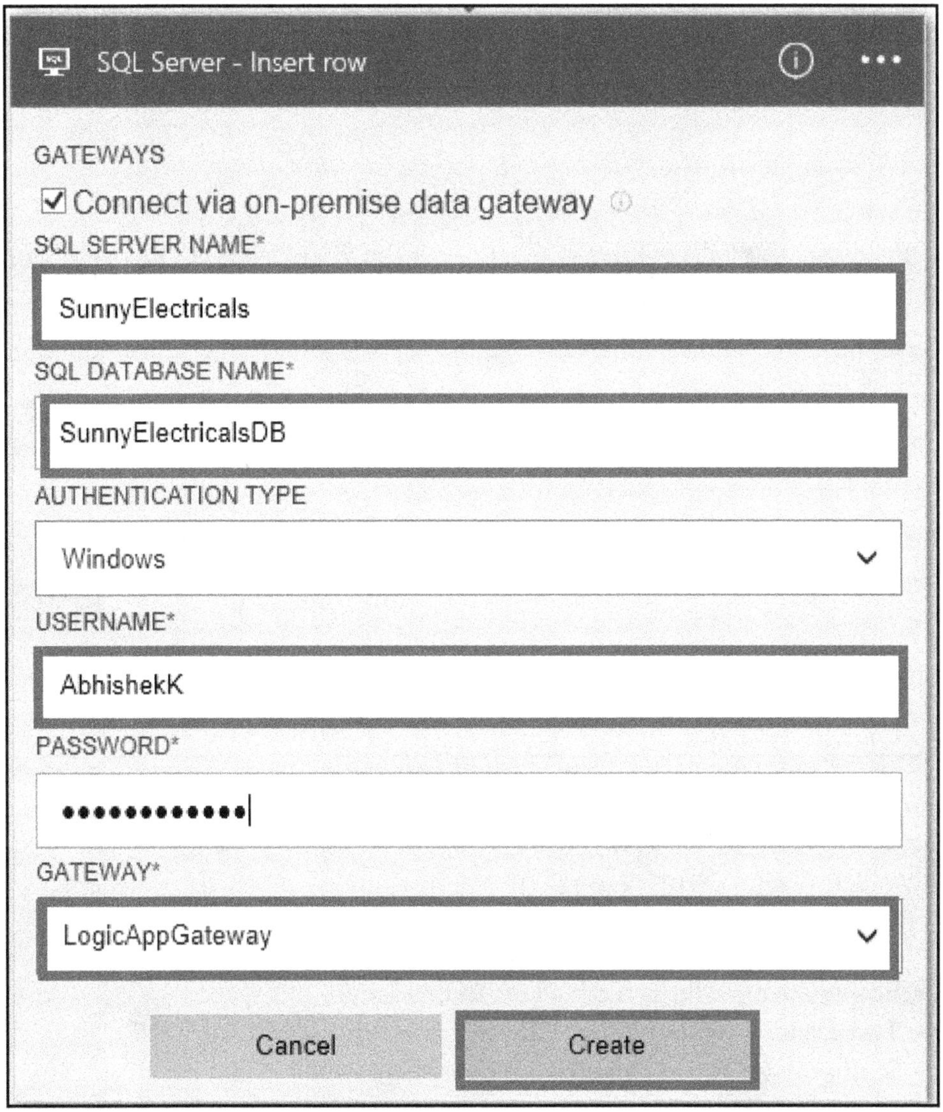

Now we will check whether the insert operation result status by checking the `Insert_row` status value as follows:

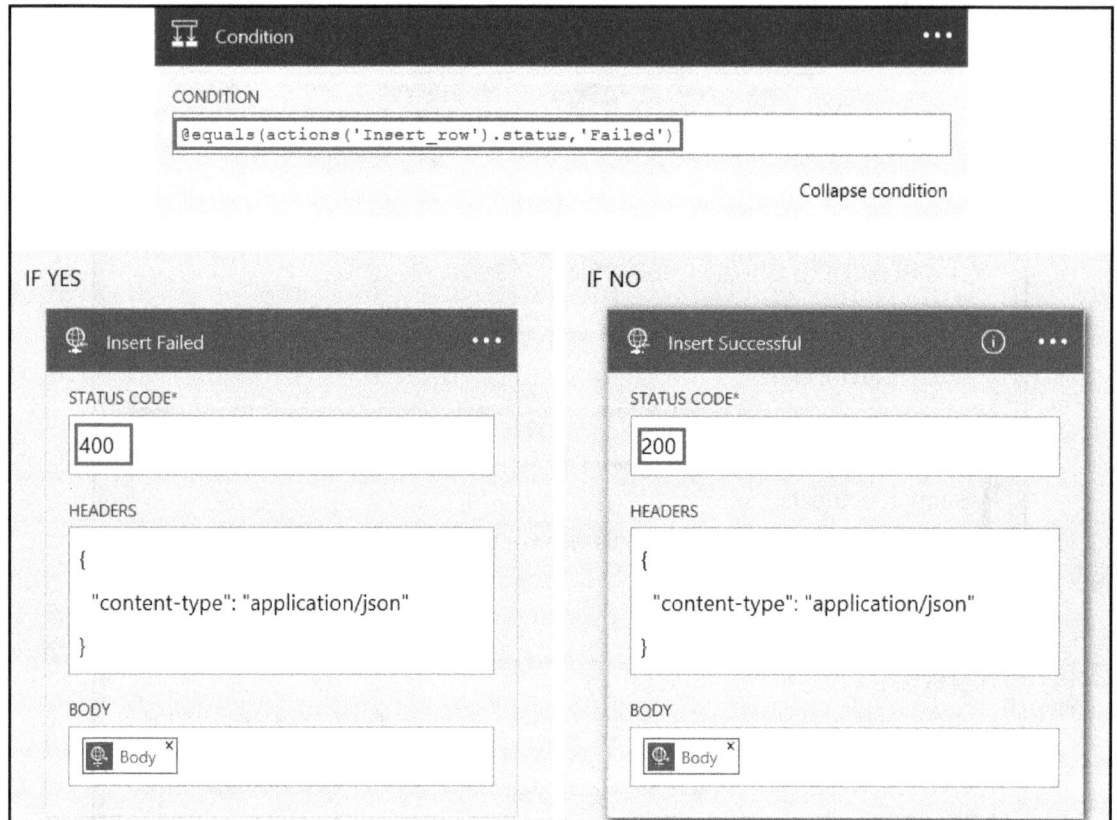

Depending on the status value, success (status code = 200) or failure (status code = 400), Response shape would return a response to the parent Logic App. Any response code / status more than 399 is an error in Logic Apps.

Now for exception handling, we have added the following three actions:

- **Scope**: To move the foreach action in this action
- **Terminate**: To stop the flow if there is an error
- Send an e-mail action when the flow is successful

To do this, we make a few changes in the code view of the parent Logic App.

On the **Terminate** action in the `runAfter` segment, we change from `"Succeeded"` to `"Failed"`. Basically, we are mentioning that Terminate action runs if the Scope action above it fails:

```
"Terminate": {
    "inputs": {
        "runError": {
            "code": "@{outputs(
        },
        "runStatus": "Failed"
    },
    "runAfter": {
        "Scope": [
            "Failed"
```

On the `Send_an_email` action in the `runAfter` segment, we leave it as `"Succeeded"`. This means that that `Send_an_email` action runs if the `Scope` action above it succeeds:

```
"Send_an_email_-_PO_successfully_created": {
    "inputs": {
        "body": {
            "Body": "PO created!",
            "Subject": "Success",
            "To": "asbhambh@microsoft.com"
        },
        "host": {
            "api": {
                "runtimeUrl": "https://logic-apis-westus.azure-apim.net/apim/office365"
            },
            "connection": {
                "name": "@parameters('$connections')['office365']['connectionId']"
            }
        },
        "method": "post",
        "path": "/Mail"
    },
    "runAfter": {
        "Scope": [
            "Succeeded"
        ]
    },
    "type": "ApiConnection"
},
```

The overall Logic App workflow will be triggered through recurrence trigger and do have multiple associated action to constitute the Logic App workflow.

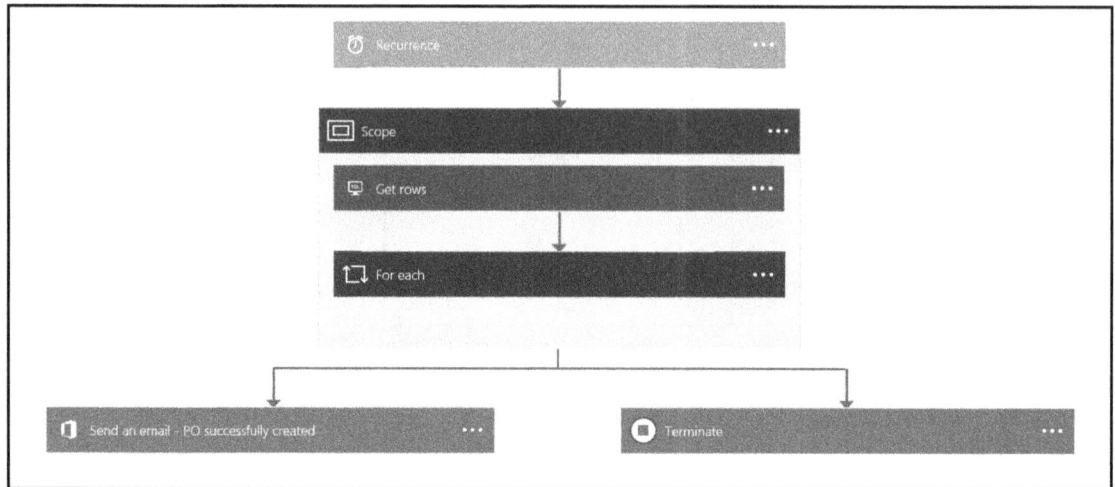

The following picture shows a run instance of the Logic App. As we can see that since the child Logic App is responding in a 400 status code, the flow goes to execute the **Terminate** shape and the **Send an email** shape is skipped.

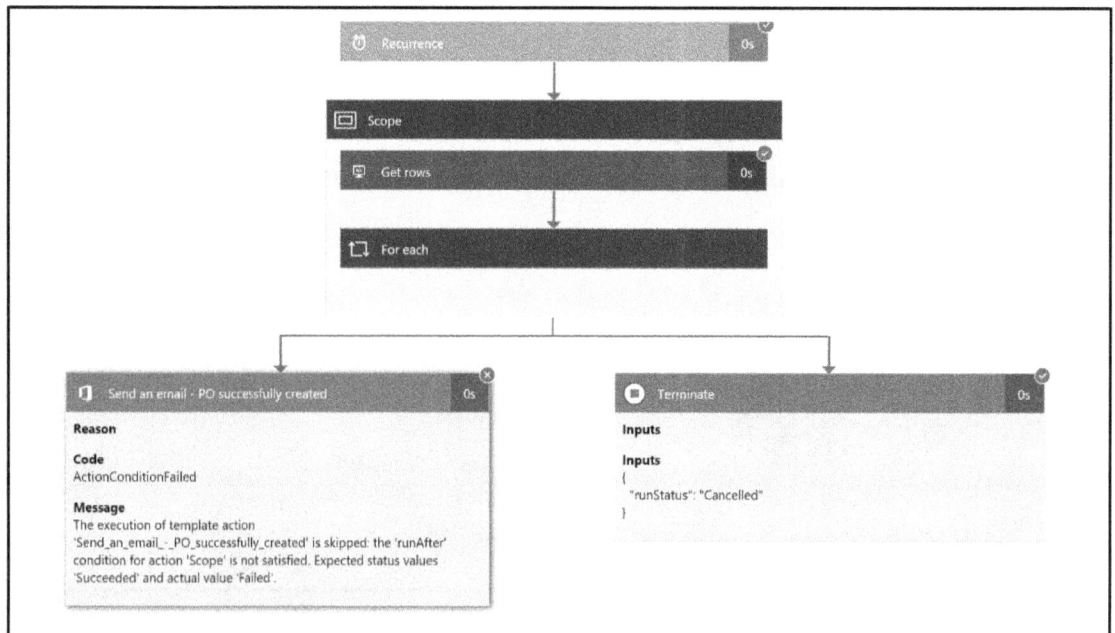

Summary

In this chapter, we started with workflow definition language for Logic Apps including expressions, operators, and functions. The workflow definition contains the actual logic that gets executed within the Logic App engine. The workflow definition is a JSON file that contains a one or more triggers that initiate the Logic App and associated single or multiple actions within the Logic App. We also looked into the types of header content supported in Logic Apps and how can we loop through the array items in the message using flow control - **foreach**, **until**, and **Terminate**. We also discussed how to implement exception handling using **scope** in Logic Apps.

Finally, we covered the hybrid integration scenario using **On-premise data gateway**, where Logic App connects securely to on-premise SQL server to insert records in database tables. We also created a nested workflow where once Logic App calls another to achieve a composite service-type workflow.

In the next chapter, we will introduce SaaS connectivity and how SaaS application can be used in Logic Apps workflow.

9
Powerful Integration with SaaS Using Logic Apps

Mix-and-match – verb (used with or without object)
To combine in a harmonious or interesting way, as articles of clothing in an ensemble.
    - http://www.dictionary.com/browse/mix-and-match

Software as a Service (SaaS) is taking the world by storm, epitomized by software that runs in your web browser, such as Salesforce, Microsoft Dynamics 365, and Office 365.

As discussed in Chapter 1, *An Introduction to Systems Integration in the Cloud*, powerful, fully featured business software that is easily accessible via the Internet and requires no underlying investment in IT infrastructure could be viewed by some as the *pinnacle* of achievement in business software. The big drawcard for firms is that the headache of building and supporting IT infrastructure and maintaining complex software disappears: instead, it is possible to subscribe in a *pay as you go* model to use the software, and the software vendor manages the underlying platform.

However, one of the downsides of SaaS is that important data is siloed in the system. This data is an enabler and the fuel that drives business revenue. As such, it is valuable, but the SaaS model, while allowing some customizations, could not possibly support the unique demands of every customer who wishes to drive their business through smart process automation; this is where Logic Apps come in, with the supporting range of easy-to-use SaaS connectors that leverage the ubiquitous API.

With Logic Apps, firms can blend the convenience and cost savings of a shared feature software platform with unique business process automation.

In this chapter, we demonstrate how it is possible, with the use of Logic Apps, to get the maximum out of SaaS by mixing and matching the different capabilities of SaaS applications in new and special ways that will provide a business with a competitive edge. Particularly, instead of concentrating on one automation at a time, we touch on how it is possible to build a platform that integrates many SaaS applications and on-premises solutions, by getting data out of the silos and really putting it to work to create smart business process flows.

A challenge that many businesses come across as they grow and leverage various SaaS and on-premises applications is the thorny issue of syncing data across the various systems in an efficient and timely manner. In this chapter, we show how Logic Apps can help with this scenario.

In summary, the following topics will be discussed and demonstrated by building *real world* applications for our fictitious Sunny Electricals company:

- Building connectivity to Office 365 to manage e-mails, calendars, and contacts; managing staff efficiently and keeping them updated by linking customer leads with available staff in an automated way
- Utilizing Logic Apps to increase the efficiency of the sales pipeline and reduce administrative burden by hooking up to Salesforce and automating the process of converting a customer from a *prospect* to having an actual account
- Keeping disparate SaaS systems in sync using the Dynamics 365 connector and the SQL connector to extend the reach of Sunny Electricals on-premises ERP system to the cloud and blending on-premises functionality with cloud functionality.

While exploring these topics, it should reinforce how powerful the concept of a Logic App connector is, as explored previously in `Chapter 6`, *Working with Connectors in Logic Apps*. We can see that connectors enable a *code free* experience, and instead we shield ourselves from having to have intimate knowledge of the SaaS provider's API, relying on the connector to manage this for us. In this way, a connector acts as a layer of abstraction and shields its users from changes to the underlying SaaS vendor's API. Connectors also provide an opportunity to build a consistent experience, no matter what SaaS API is being leveraged.

Exploring the Logic App SaaS connectors

`Chapter 6`, *Working with Connectors in Logic Apps*, describes in detail what a Logic App connector is. In this section, we delve deeper into the SaaS connectors, highlighting what is common between them, key features and things to know, in order to get a head start using these connectors in your workflows.

The SaaS connectors are fundamentally API apps that have been written and are managed by Microsoft, hosted in Azure. They wrap the SaaS vendor's APIs, providing a consistent interface and user experience that reduces the learning curve required to start using a new API. As new SaaS products come online, it is relatively easy for a developer to pick up the new connector and based on previous experience using other connectors, get to grips quickly with hooking up to the SaaS vendor's API.

It is true that any SaaS provider wanting to extend its reach will have an API, and certainly, it is possible to use the vendor's API directly (using the HTTP connector for instance). It is also possible to build a custom connector if one doesn't exist yet (as detailed in `Chapter 6`, *Working with Connectors in Logic Apps*). However, using the out-of-the-box SaaS connectors takes away much of the complexity of working with a vendor's API.

Some of the key features of the SaaS connectors are listed here:

- **Authentication and authorization is managed for you**: There is no need to write and maintain complex custom code to do this, such as would be required if writing code to obtain and manage OAuth 2.0 tokens, for example.
- **Event triggering**: When an event occurs in the SaaS application, it is possible to trigger a Logic App to run that can automate a business process. In this way, it is possible to extend the reach of a SaaS solution and complement it with a custom workflow.
- **Actions**: It is possible to augment and drive a workflow through the looking up of data in the SaaS application, such as customer data. Again, no coding is required to do this.

- **Sharing of SaaS data**: Obtain data from one SaaS application and insert it or update existing data in another SaaS solution, by passing the output of a trigger or action into another SaaS connector.

The key features mentioned earlier are fleshed out in the following sections, with reference to how Sunny Electricals have leveraged the connectors to automate their business processes.

> To follow along with the examples, you will need subscriptions to Salesforce, Microsoft Dynamics 365, and Office 365. It is possible to sign up for a free trial for Salesforce via the company website at: https://www.salesforce.com and for Dynamics 365, via the Microsoft website at: https://www.microsoft.com/en-us/dynamics365/home.

Hooking up to SaaS solutions using the SaaS connectors

Connecting to a SaaS solution is greatly simplified and it is a key feature of the SaaS connectors.

Consider what would be required to connect to a cloud-based solution without an accelerator such as a Logic App SaaS connector. With Dynamics 365 in the cloud, for example, custom code would be required to manage the process of obtaining an OAuth 2.0 token, caching the token for maximum performance, and managing the steps of obtaining a new token when it expires. This is summarized in the following sequence diagram:

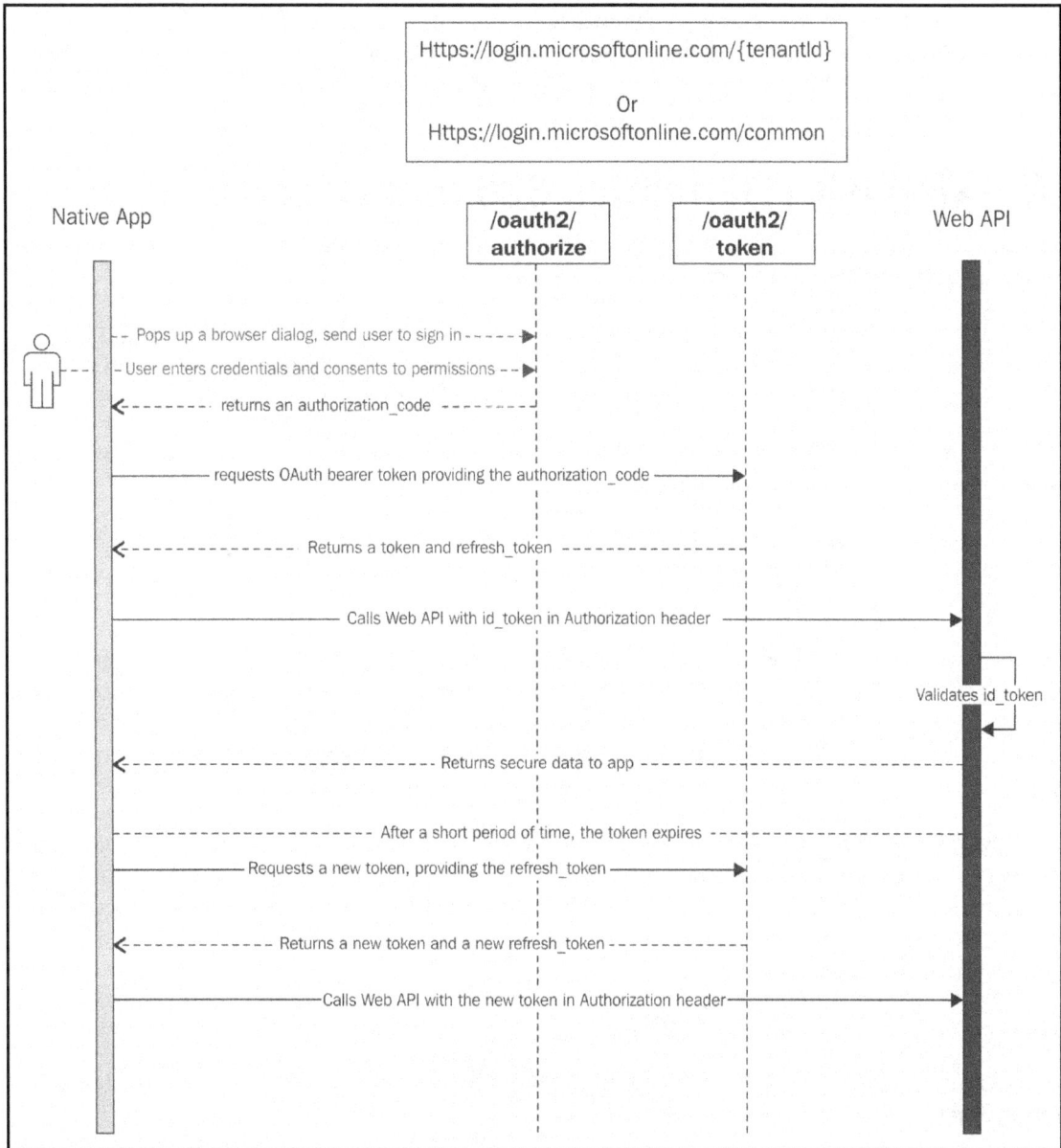

An alternative option to writing custom code to support the interactions mentioned earlier is to let Microsoft do the *heavy lifting* and manage this process instead.

Office 365 follows the same approach, and once authenticated with both, it is possible to start building a solution that allows Sunny Electricals to create a process that ties together these two popular Microsoft SaaS solutions. This will form the basis for our first scenario.

Working with Dynamics 365 and Office 365

In our scenario, we will create a contact, send an e-mail, and create a calendar reminder for when a Lead is added to Dynamics 365.

The purpose of this process is to give some insight into how quickly a workflow can be created with SaaS solutions, along with providing at least a good overview of a potential sales workflow whereby any new leads would be followed up by a sales team.

When working with Dynamics 365 and Office 365, it is important to understand how and where user authentication takes place.

When a new Dynamics 365 and Office 365 instance is created, a new instance of an Azure Active Directory is also created. This directory and the instances that use it are part of the appeal of using a SaaS solution.

With a traditional application, each instance of a directory would be provisioned with an instance of the application. This makes maintenance and updates more onerous since they have to be applied to many instances of the application to ensure that every instance is on the same version. If this rolling update is not performed, the vendor is left supporting many versions of a running application that can be expensive and difficult to control.

However, each instance of the SaaS solution has its own Azure Active Directory tenant for security and content while leveraging a common infrastructure and application solution in Dynamics 365 and Office 365. In this way, it is possible to update and improve the common infrastructure and applications for all customers, while ensuring that their security and content remains their responsibility.

This is one of the key use cases for Software as a Service (SaaS).

After creating a new Logic App, we need to create the workflow that is going to follow the requirements of our process.

In our scenario, first, we create a connection using the Microsoft-managed connector for Dynamics 365:

1. We choose the Microsoft-managed connector for **Dynamics 365 – when a record is created**.

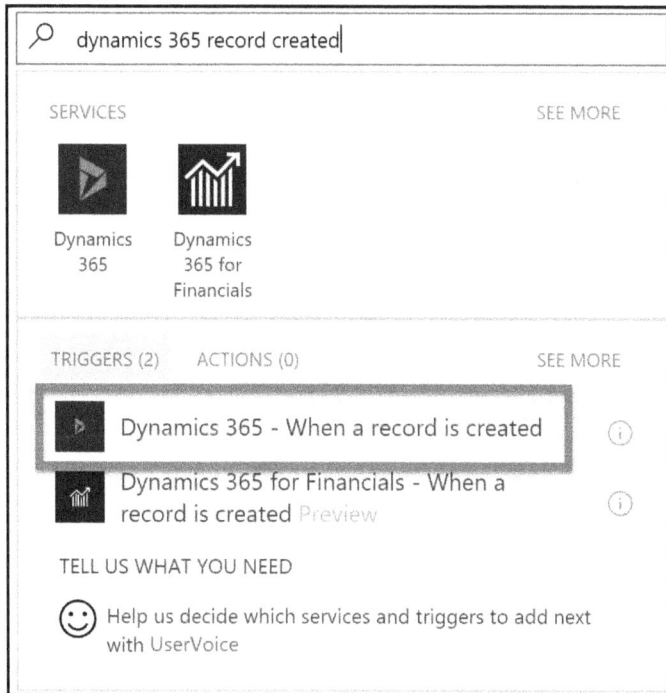

2. We need to authenticate to our Dynamics 365 Active Directory tenant by providing a user and password that has the necessary access rights to create and maintain Leads.

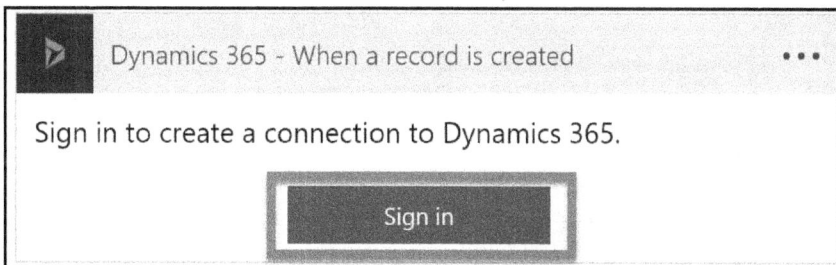

3. Once authenticated, we chose the Organization we want to monitor, the Entity Name we wish to monitor, in our case, Leads, and the frequency we want to use to check for new leads.

> Dynamics 365 is polled by the connector and any new leads found initiate a new instance of the Logic App.

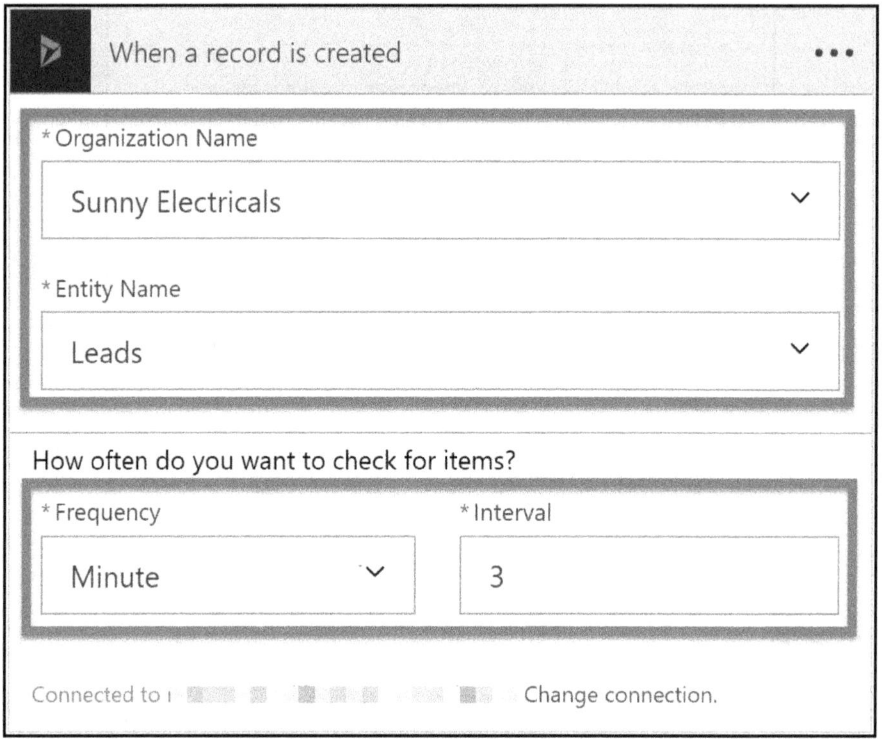

▷ When a record is created   **• • •**

* Organization Name

| Sunny Electricals ⌄ |

* Entity Name

| Leads ⌄ |

How often do you want to check for items?

| * Frequency | * Interval |
| Minute ⌄ | 3 |

Connected to ▮ ▮▮▮ ▮ ▮ ▮▮ ▮ ▮▮ ▮▮   Change connection.

Once we have created our connection to Dynamics 365, we can continue to create the workflow process by adding steps for each of the Office 365 Outlook tasks we need to be complete when a new lead is added.

1. First, we choose the Microsoft-managed connector for Office 365 Outlook to create a new contact .

If the connector does not appear in the list, click on **Load More** at the bottom.

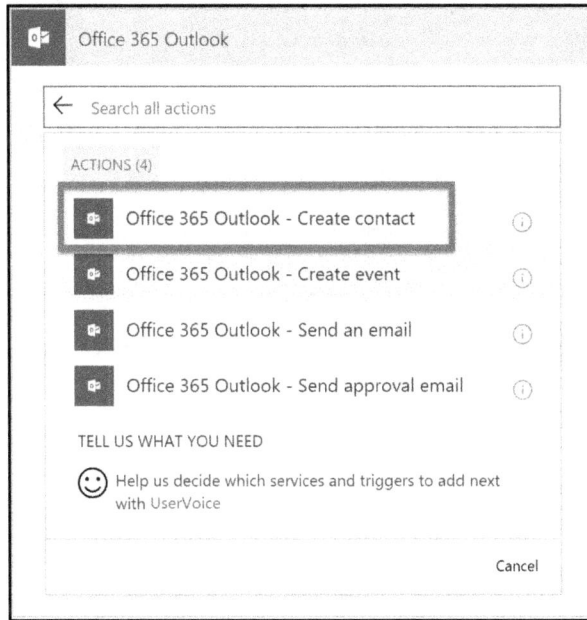

2. We need to authenticate to our Office 365 Outlook account; because this is the first time we have connected to Office 365 Outlook, we need to sign in, the authenticated user is the user account in which the contact needs to be created.

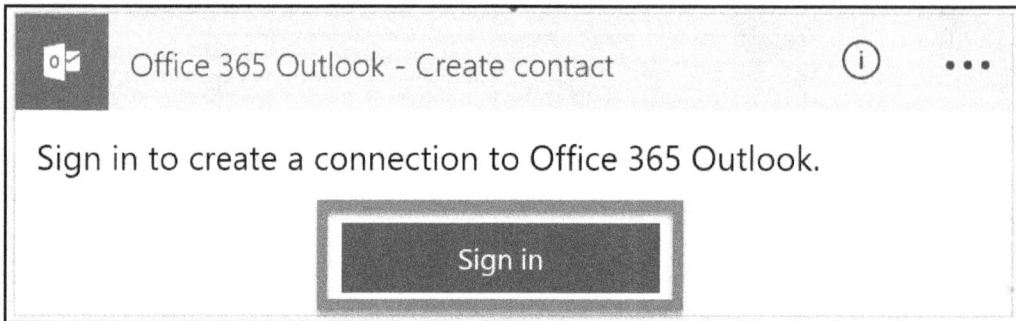

3. Once authenticated, we need to set the information we want to capture to ensure that the contact is created appropriately with the information brought in by the Dynamics 365 connector, for instance:

- Folder ID
- Given Name
- Display Name
- E-mail Addresses Address
- Company Name
- Mobile Phone

4. Next, we choose the Microsoft-managed connector for Office 365 Outlook to send an e-mail.

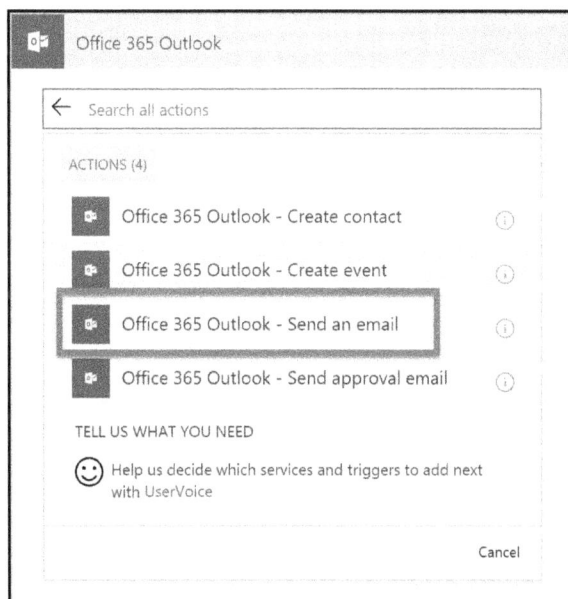

5. We are already authenticated from the previous Office 365 Outlook step, so we can either connect as the same user or create a new connection; the uthenticated user is the user from which is the e-mail is sent.

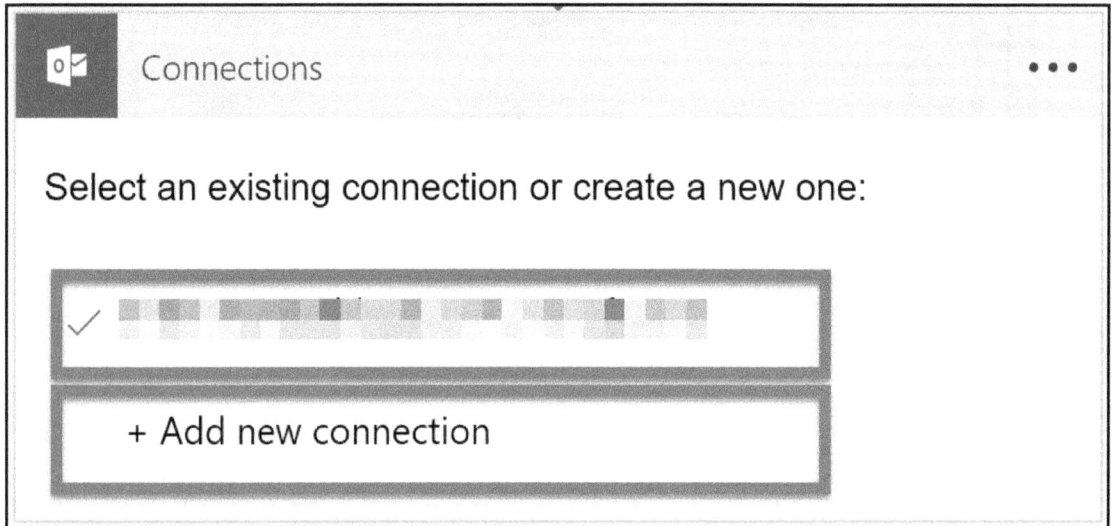

6. Once authenticated, we set the necessary information to send an e-mail based on the information brought in by the Dynamics 365 or Office 365 Outlook connectors from the previous steps, for instance:

- **To** – which could in this case be a distribution list
- **Subject**
- **Body**
- **Importance**

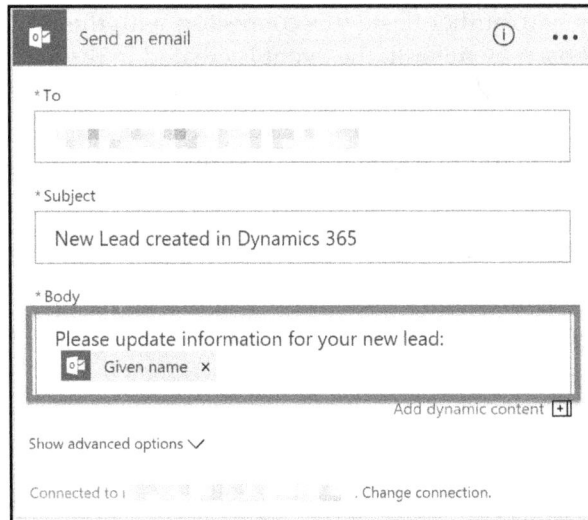

7. Finally, we choose the Microsoft-managed connector for Office 365 Outlook to create a new event.

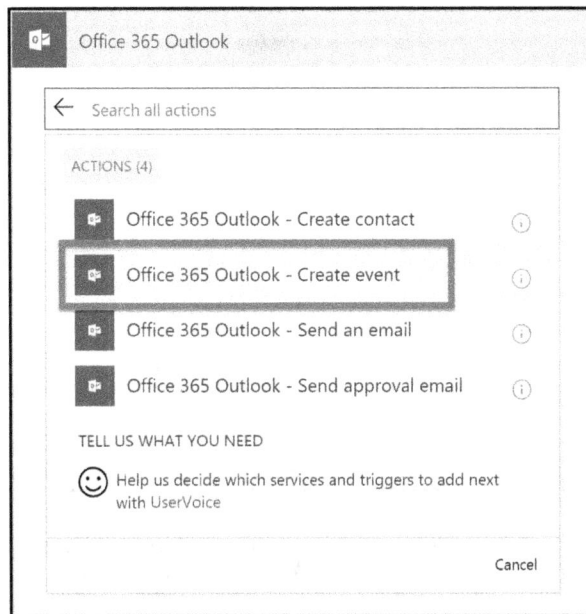

8. We choose how to authenticate this connector, with the previously authenticated user being chosen by default; the event is created in the account used to authenticate for the connector.

9. Once authenticated, we need to set the correct information to ensure that the event is created with the information brought in by the Dynamics 365 or Office 365 Outlook connectors from the previous steps:

- **Calendar id**
- **Start time**
- **Subject**
- **Content**
- **End time**

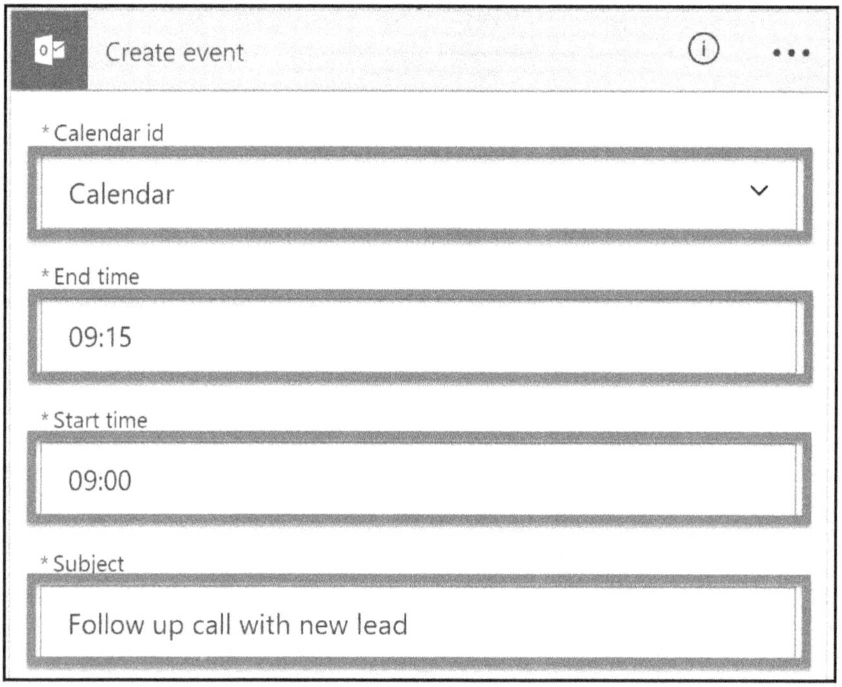

We have now completed our simple workflow, and we can save the Logic App. Once saved, it will poll Dynamics 365 based on the interval specified in the Dynamics 365 connector to check for any new Leads.

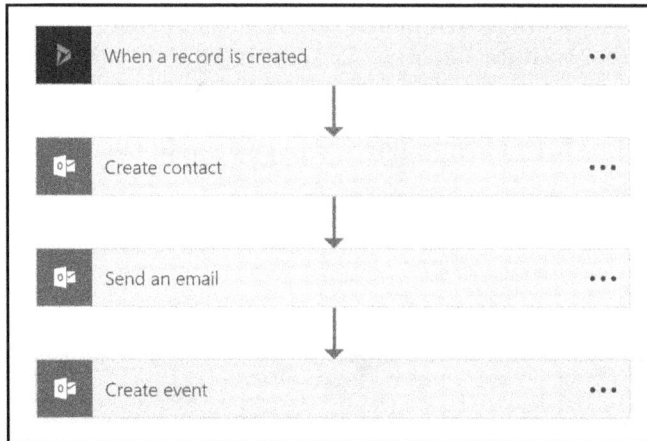

To ensure that the workflow described by the Logic App executes correctly, we need to test it. First, we need to create a new lead in Dynamics 365.

Since the Logic App is controlled by the interval set when we created the Dynamics 365 connection, we can either wait for the interval to expire or manually start the trigger.

Once the Logic App has triggered and executed, we can examine the details of the run to ensure that it has met our requirements and completed successfully.

> More information on monitoring and logging information in Logic Apps is provided in a future chapter.

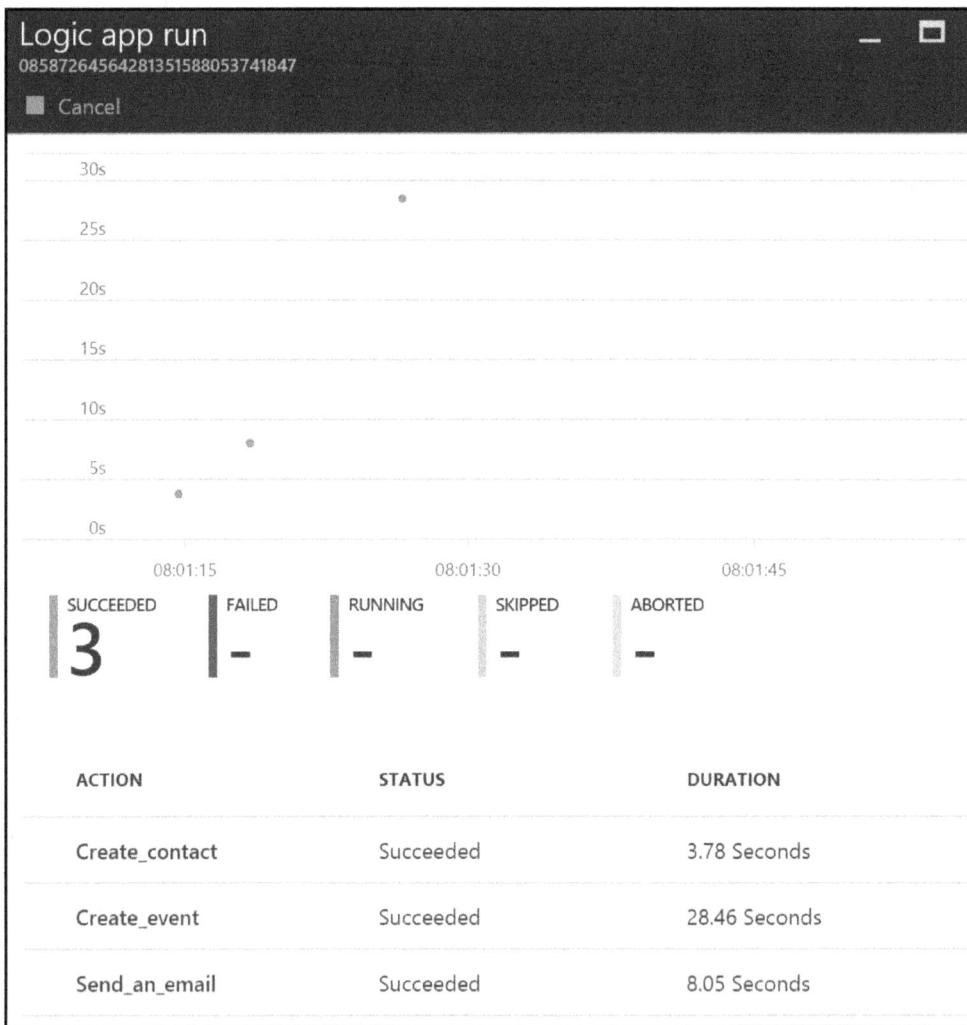

We can see that the three Office 365 Outlook actions have completed successfully, so we can check in the chosen Office 365 accounts to ensure that the results satisfy our expectations.

First, we can check to see whether a new contact has been created in the account chosen when we authenticated in the Office 365 Outlook connector from creating a contact.

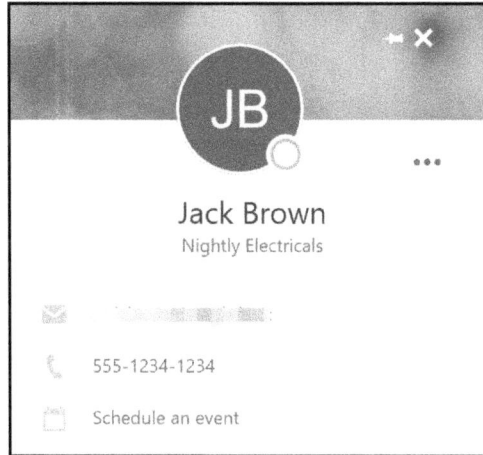

Next, we can check to see whether an e-mail has been received by the account chosen when the Office 365 Outlook connector to send an e-mail was created.

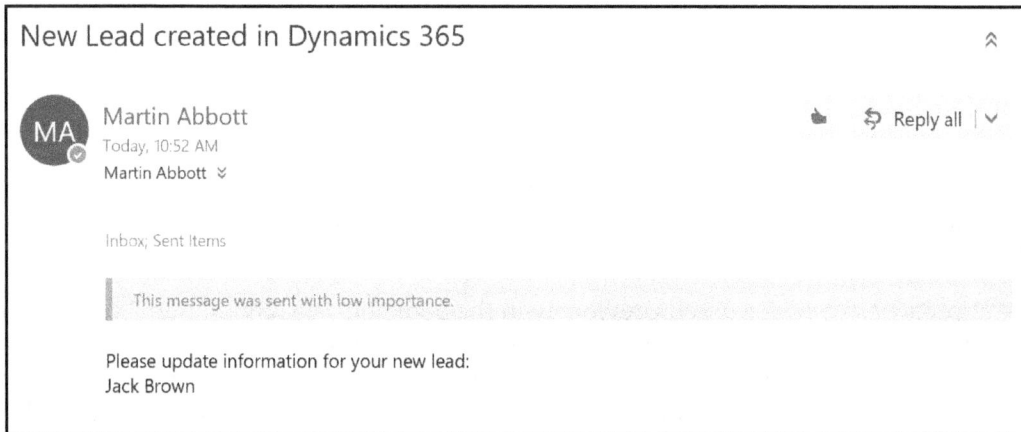

Finally, we are expecting a new event to have been created to remind us to follow up with a telephone call to the lead created in Dynamics 365.

Details		People	Scheduling assistant
Follow up call with new lead		Add people	+
Add a location or a room		**MA** Martin Abbott Busy - Follow up call with new lead	

Start

| Sun 29/01/2017 | ▼ | 9:00 AM | ▼ |

End

| Sun 29/01/2017 | ▼ | 9:15 AM | ▼ |

☐ All day   ☐ Private

| Repeat | | Save to calendar | |
| Never | ▼ | Calendar | ▼ |

| Reminder | | Show as | |
| 15 minutes | ▼ | Busy | ▼ |

Add an email reminder

🖼 😊 | B *I* U A̳A A˙ A̰ A̲ ☰ ☷ ☰ ☰ ⌄

Call Jack Brown on 555-1234-1234

We can see that the Logic App has completed successfully, and all tasks have executed and performed the actions required.

At this point, we do not have a production-ready solution, and in a full scenario, we would add in handling for when issues are encountered or have other flows that may branch and perform other actions.

These approaches were discussed previously in the book, but we have shown how we can create a workflow that it is simple and codeless to set up a basic integration between two different SaaS applications. We have shown that we can chain events together to build a flow that can articulate what would be separate processes typically, thereby reducing the effort required for our sales team.

It is now time to consider a more complex workflow that uses other SaaS products.

User authorization using the Salesforce connector

In the case of the Salesforce connector, we can select it in the Logic App designer (from the list of Microsoft-managed APIs), and from there, it is the possible to authorize the connector to connect to Salesforce on behalf of the user, obtaining and managing the OAuth tokens required.

The first step is to select the Salesforce connector, as shown in the following screenshot:

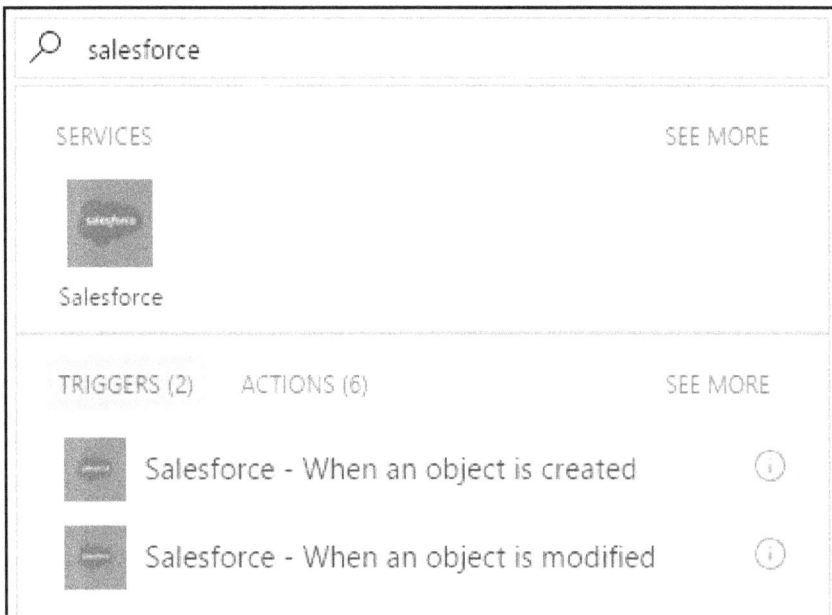

Here, we can specify what should trigger the connector, based on the addition or modification of data in Salesforce.

Before the connector can be used, a username and a password must be entered into the connector. This allows the connector to act on the user's behalf, connecting to the Salesforce API under the hood. The connector will store credential information in blob storage in Azure.

Note that the connector will fail to connect to Salesforce if the password changes or expires. If this occurs, it will be necessary to re-enter credentials into the connector, for the connection to be restored.

As shown in the screenshots here, the connector redirects to a Salesforce login page where the Salesforce username and password should be entered. After clicking on the **Allow** button, the Logic App connector will now have the required information to connect to Salesforce on behalf of the user, issuing a token received from Salesforce as a result of this login process. The connector will neither store the username and password and nor will the connector know what the username and password is: it will just store the authorization code and token issued by Salesforce instead.

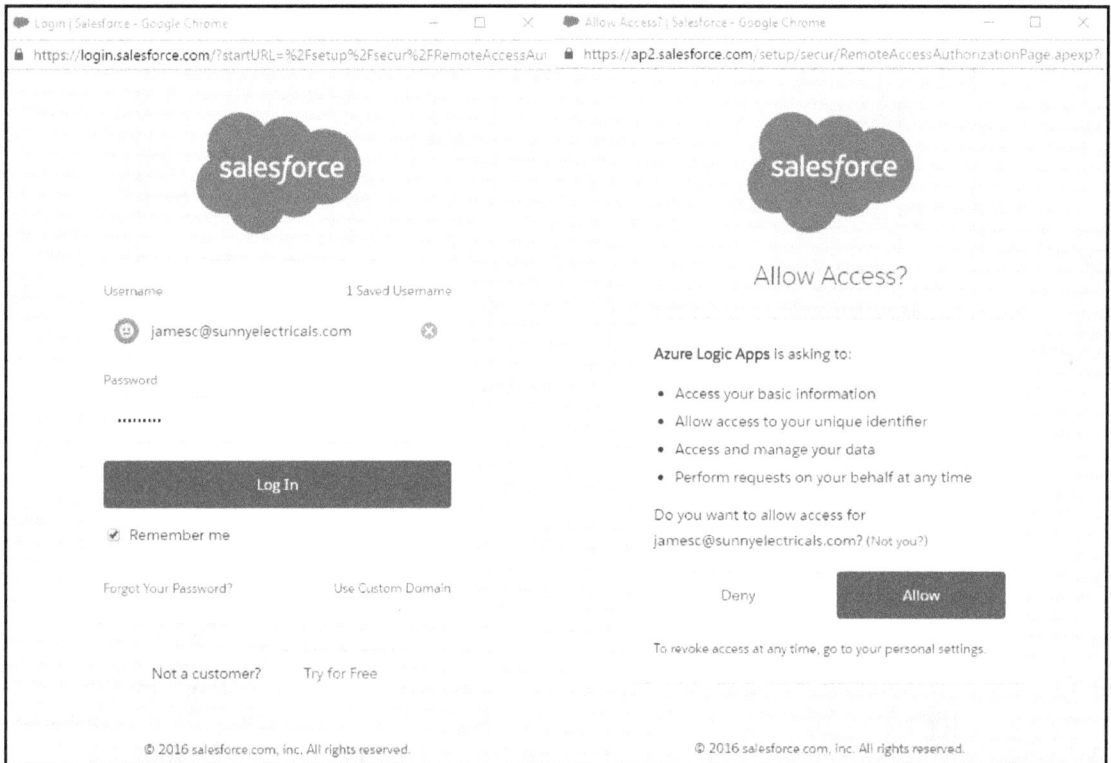

Once authentication and authorization has been set up, it is possible to modify the connection details in the connector by clicking on the **Change connection** link at the bottom of the Salesforce card, as highlighted here:

Show advanced options ∨

Connected to jamesc@datacom.co.nz. Change connection.

Salesforce connector – Under the hood

It is interesting to examine the Logic App code view, after adding the connector. If we look at the JSON, we can see that the connector is actually a pointer to an endpoint hosted in Azure API Management. The URL represents the Microsoft-managed API, which in turn wraps the Salesforce API. In this way, we have a layer of abstraction that permits a common mechanism to connect to different SaaS applications (that is, via the standard Microsoft API pattern) and also we can enjoy increased stability, where it is the responsibility of Microsoft to manage changes to the Salesforce API in the internal workings of the Microsoft wrapper API. Of course, the addition of a management layer must be weighed up against the inevitable increased latency in response times that will be incurred.

Logic Apps Designer

🖫 Save   ✕ Discard   ⚒ Designer   </> Code view   ▣ Templates   ▣ Available APIs   ? Help

```
25              }
26          },
27          "triggers": {
28              "When_an_object_is_modified": {
29                  "inputs": {
30                      "host": {
31                          "api": {
32                              "runtimeUrl": "https://logic-apis-australiasoutheast.azure-apim.net/apim/salesforce"
33                          },
34                          "connection": {
35                              "name": "@parameters('$connections')['salesforce']['connectionId']"
36                          }
37                      },
```

Leveraging the Salesforce connector: Sunny Electricals automated credit check solution

In the case of our fictitious electrical retail company, Sunny Electricals, the management team decides to sign off allowing the sales team to manage the sales pipeline using Salesforce. The management team expects the investment in Salesforce subscriptions to be outweighed by the increased revenue the software will bring in, by better matching products to customers.

However, one aspect that remains a cause of frustration after purchasing the subscriptions is the customer onboarding process. This is relevant for the larger customers, who typically purchase items in bulk and wish to have an account with Sunny Electricals; such customers are entered into the Sunny Electricals debtor ledger, and the payment is expected on the agreed date and not necessarily on the date of purchase.

In order to have confidence that these customers are good customers (that is, they pay their invoices and pay on time!); Sunny Electricals have a credit check process to ensure that prospective customers have a good credit rating and are likely to pay their account. The credit check process occurs when a new customer is converted from a *sales lead* to a customer requiring an account (since they wish to make a purchase). Currently, this process is a manual one: the sales consultant completes a form, which is then couriered to a third-party company that then carries out the credit check and informs Sunny Electricals of the credit risk. If the decision is a positive one, the sales consultant may then create an account for the customer and the customer may then make purchases against the account.

This manual process is time consuming and demanding of the sales consultant's time, so the Sunny Electricals IT team is requested to build an automated credit check solution. The credit check company, **Credit Checkers Limited** (**CCL**), have an API that can be queried that will return a report for the indicated customer; the IT team decides to leverage this API in the Logic App solution, to determine if an account should be created in Salesforce for the customer (this step will also be automated using the Salesforce connector).

The first step in building the credit check solution is to create a new Logic App (using a blank template) and configure the Salesforce connector as follows:

The connector is a trigger that will fire when all the conditions specified in each field are met, at the configured polling interval. Each field is summarized as follows:

- **Object type**: This is a mandatory field and is a drop-down list of all the available entities in Salesforce that can be queried and a Logic App instance triggered on. In the case of Sunny Electricals, the **Leads** object is selected.

- **Filter Query**: As it is now becoming increasingly commonplace in APIs from the major vendors, the **OData** (**Open Data Protocol**) standard is available in the connector for sorting and filtering the results from Salesforce. The filter specified will ensure that only those leads with the status `Closed - Converted` will be returned, to trigger

> an instance of the Logic App.
> Further information about the OData OASIS standard to build RESTful APIs may be found here on the OData website: `http://www.odata.org/`.

- **Order By**: It is possible to provide a sort order to the data returned by specifying an OData orderBy query here. This is applicable only if multiple records will be returned.
- **Skip Count**: If multiple records are returned, this value indicates the number of records that should be skipped/ignored. The default value is `0`.
- **Maximum Get Count**: This specifies the maximum number of records that will be returned for those records matching the trigger criteria. The maximum number of records that may be returned is 256.
- **Frequency**: This indicates the time parameter at which the connector will query the Salesforce API. The values that may be selected are as follows: **Day**, **Hour**, **Minute**, or **Second**. It is also possible to specify a custom value that must match an allowable value as specified in the Logic Apps trigger definition; this defines the following additional values that may be manually typed in: Week, Month, or Year.
- **Interval**: This is an integer to specify the polling interval of the trigger.

If we take a look *under the hood* and view the underlying JSON Logic App workflow definition, we can see our trigger definition with all the parameters specified, as shown here:

```
Logic Apps Designer

🖫 Save    ✕ Discard    ⚖ Designer    </> Code view    ▦ Templates    ⊞ Available APIs    ? Help

27          "triggers": {
28              "When_a_lead_is_converted": {
29                  "inputs": {
30                      "host": {
31                          "api": {
32                              "runtimeUrl": "https://logic-apis-australiasoutheast.azure-apim.net/apim/salesforce"
33                          },
34                          "connection": {
35                              "name": "@parameters('$connections')['salesforce']['connectionId']"
36                          }
37                      },
38                      "method": "get",
39                      "path": "/datasets/default/tables/@{encodeURIComponent(encodeURIComponent('Lead'))}/onupdateditems",
40                      "queries": {
41                          "$filter": "Status eq 'Closed - Converted'"
42                      }
43                  },
44                  "recurrence": {
45                      "frequency": "Minute",
46                      "interval": 3
47                  },
48                  "splitOn": "@triggerBody()?.value",
49                  "type": "ApiConnection"
50              }
51          }
```

Note that it is possible to overwrite the default trigger name with our own meaningful name, as highlighted in the screenshot, with underscores between each word; the underscores are replaced by spaces in the Logic Apps designer.

Reaching out to the credit check API

At this point, we have quite easily configured secure access to Salesforce through the Microsoft-managed API. Next, the Sunny Electricals IT team builds the next step in the workflow, which is requesting a credit check report on the prospective customer; this should be initiated after the Salesforce connector has triggered the Logic App to execute.

CCL have a credit check API configured in **Azure API Management** (**APIM**), and Sunny Electricals signs up to use the API through the APIM Developer portal, where the Sunny Electricals developers are issued with subscription keys to access the credit check API.

For a walkthrough of APIM, please see Chapter 4, What is Azure API Management?

The screenshot here shows the APIM Developer portal view:

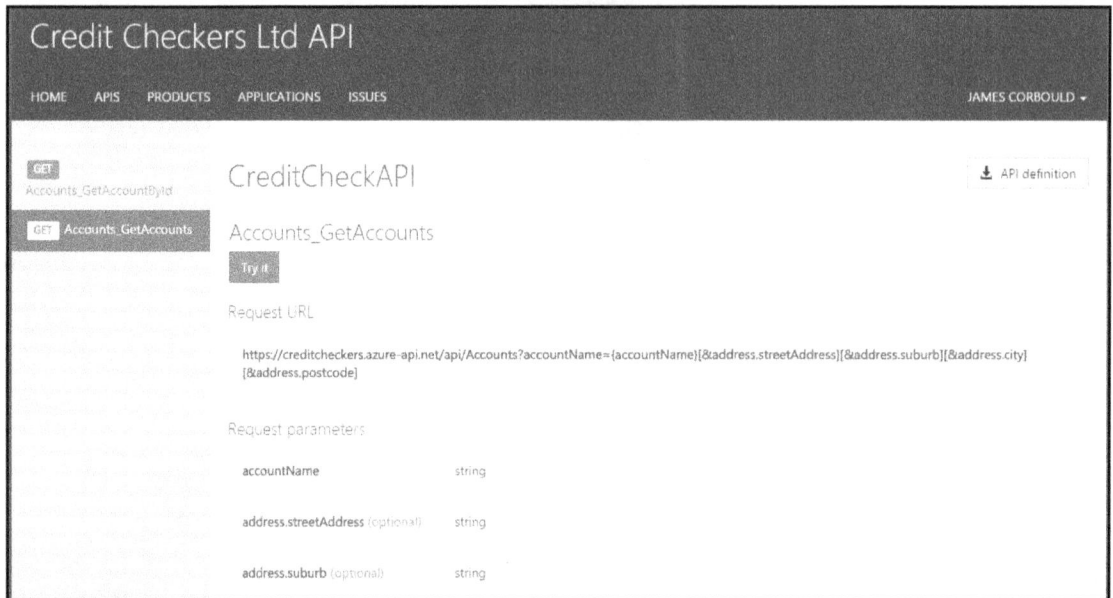

The **Accounts_GetAccounts** operation enables CCL customers to search for accounts and their history, using the endpoint query parameters to specify the search filter.

In order to invoke the custom API from our credit check Logic App, a new step is selected in the designer and an HTTP call endpoint card is added and configured in the workflow as follows:

The HTTP connector allows us to call any custom API, and we don't have to write any code to do this. A summary of each field is explained here:

- **Method**: This corresponds to the HTTP verb that is required when calling the URI. This is a mandatory field.
- **Uri**: This specifies the URI endpoint that will be called. In this example, the APIM endpoint has been configured, when the accountName query parameter dynamically created by passing in parameters from the Salesforce connector trigger, for the customer we wish to create an account for.

- **Headers**: HTTP headers may be specified here. In this case, the APIM subscription key has been entered to enable authentication against the API endpoint.
- **Body**: A content body may be entered here. In this example, there is no body because this is an HTTP GET request. However, this would be required for a HTTP POST request, for example.

It is also possible to use the **HTTP + Swagger** connector to invoke an API that has a Swagger endpoint defined. This is convenient because URL creation is handled on our behalf and URL query parameters are called out for us in the connector, with a requirement only to input data into the provided fields.

However, there is currently a limitation with the designer where it is not possible to download Swagger documents for authenticated endpoints. The following error will be returned:

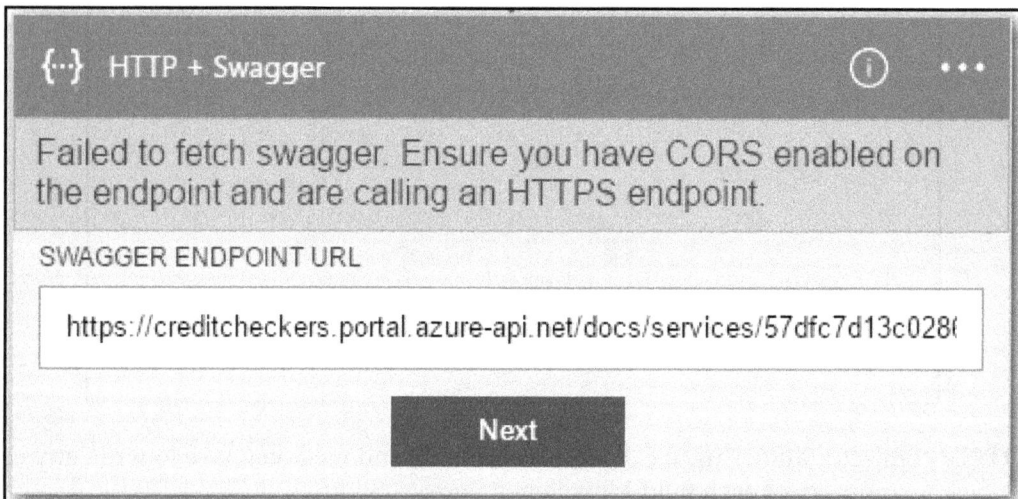

In our case, CORS has been enabled, and the endpoint is secured over HTTP.

What has happened is that since authentication has been configured on the APIM endpoint and there is no facility to configure the authentication required, the Logic Apps designer cannot download the Swagger API definition.

The API definition may be downloaded from the APIM Developer portal directly however, as shown here:

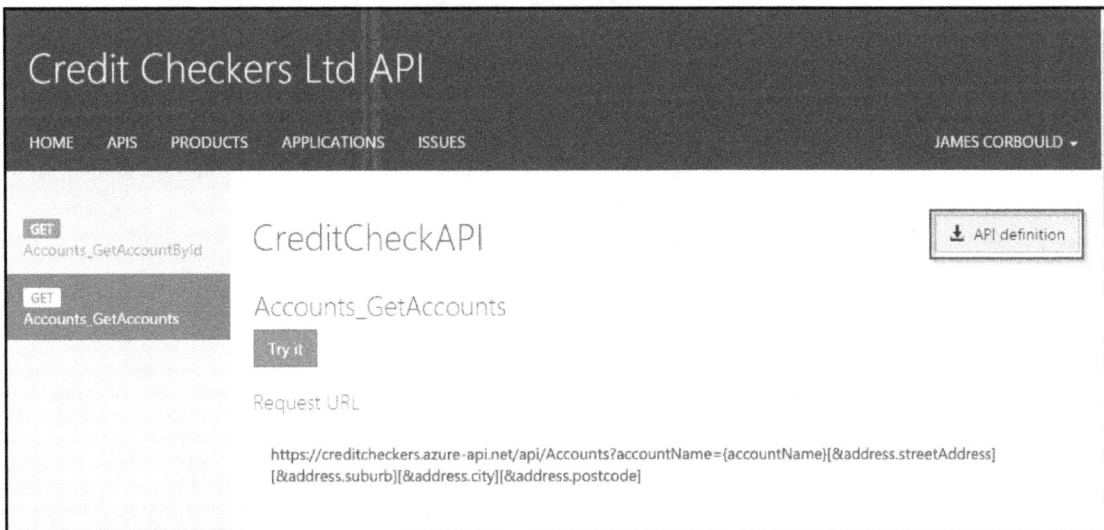

A simple workaround for this issue is to download the API definition and expose it via an unauthenticated endpoint in blob storage. The URL for the unauthenticated endpoint can be entered instead and then it is possible to specify the API operation required.

Note that it is also necessary to enable CORS on the Swagger endpoint to allow the Logic Apps designer running in the web browser to access the Swagger document. If this is not implemented, the error in the screenshot earlier will also be returned.

A tool such as **Microsoft Azure Storage Explorer** can be used to enable CORS on the blob container containing the Swagger file, as shown here:

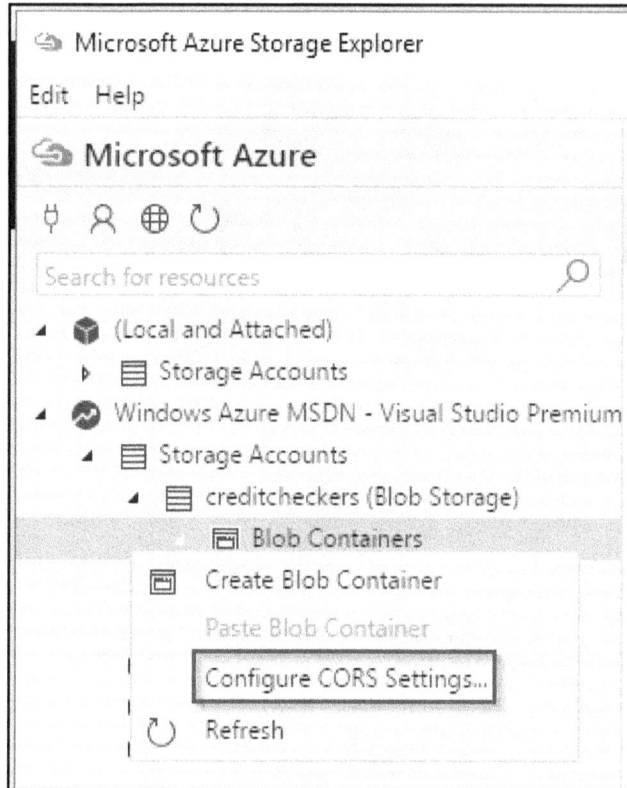

The Microsoft Azure Storage Explorer tool may be downloaded from `http://storageexplorer.com/`.

In the screenshot later, we can see that we have worked around the limitation of the HTTP + Swagger connector and have successfully loaded the Swagger JSON definition file from the public-facing blob storage endpoint. It is possible now to select the API operation required, as specified in the Swagger file.

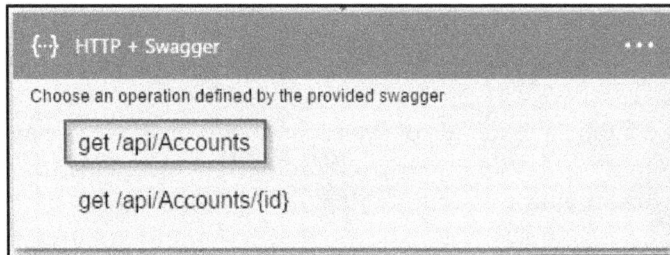

Processing the credit check report using an Azure Function

On successfully calling the custom credit check API, CCL customers will receive back a report that contains account(s) on record for the person that they are interested in doing business with. We can see a sample JSON report later that is an array of account records containing the details of payment histories; customers may examine the report and determine if they wish to do business with the person:

```
[
  {
    "PaymentHistoryCollection": [
      "OK",
      "PD30",
      "PD30",
      "PD30",
      "PD30",
      "PD30",
      "PD30",
      "PD30",
      "COLL"
    ],
    "AccountName": "Bob Smith",
    "Balance": 4000,
    "OpenDateTime": "2016-03-19T16:30:51.9189083+00:00",
    "Terms": "4 month(s)",
    "OriginalAmount": 40000,
    "MonthlyPaymentAmount": 265,
    "LastPaymentDate": "2016-06-21T08:30:14.1958915+00:00",
    "AccountStatus": "Active",
    "CurrentAddress": {
      "StreetAddress": "3 Emerald Way",
      "Suburb": "Rosefield",
      "City": "Townsville",
      "Postcode": "2344"
```

```
                }
            }
        ]
```

Briefly, each record contains the details of the account and an array of payment history codes where, for example, the code PD30 specifies that payment was *past due by 30 days* and COLL indicates that the account was referred to a debt collection agency.

Sunny Electricals decide that any customer with payments past due by greater than 30 days will not be promoted to have an account and also those customers with accounts that have been referred to a debt collection agency. These rules are captured in an Azure Function. It is the job of the Logic App to pass the credit report into the function, where it is determined if the customer has a *good* credit history.

We can see here how Logic Apps may be used to automate entire business processes and stich varied disparate systems together to reduce the operational expenditure of a business. Human intervention, for example, is not needed to process the report.

The following C# code is the business logic in the Azure Function:

```csharp
#r "Newtonsoft.Json"
#r "SunnyElectricalEntities.dll"
using System.Net;
using Newtonsoft.Json;
using SunnyElectricalEntities;

public static async Task<HttpResponseMessage> Run(HttpRequestMessage req,
TraceWriter log)
{
    // Get request body.
    dynamic data = await req.Content.ReadAsAsync<object>();

    List<RootObject> c =
JsonConvert.DeserializeObject<List<RootObject>>(data.ToString());
    log.Info(data.ToString());
    // Check the payment history for each account to determine if too late
payments disqualifies the customer.
    // Where "PDnn" == "Past Due nn days" and "COLL" == "Assigned to
collection agency".
    string[] pastDueExclusion = new string[] {"PD60", "PD90", "PD120",
"PD150", "PD180", "COLL"};

    var results = from account in c
                  from ph in account.PaymentHistoryCollection
                  where pastDueExclusion.Contains(ph)
                  select ph;
    return req.CreateResponse(results.Count() > 0 ?
```

```
HttpStatusCode.Forbidden : HttpStatusCode.OK,
          results.Count() > 0 ? String.Format("Credit check failed due to
bad payment history.") : String.Format("OK"));
  }
```

Chapter 7, *Azure Functions in Logic Apps,* of this book covers Azure Functions in more depth.

Triggering automatic account creation using the Salesforce connector

Depending on the results of the credit check, encapsulated in the Azure Function, we optionally trigger the Salesforce connector to create an account in Salesforce on behalf of the sales consultant. (If the credit check fails, an e-mail containing the error information will be sent to an administrator for processing).

A setup is similar to that of the Salesforce trigger connector; however, authentication details do not need to be re-entered.

In the Logic App designer, the **Salesforce – Create object** connector is selected from the list of Microsoft-managed APIs, as shown here:

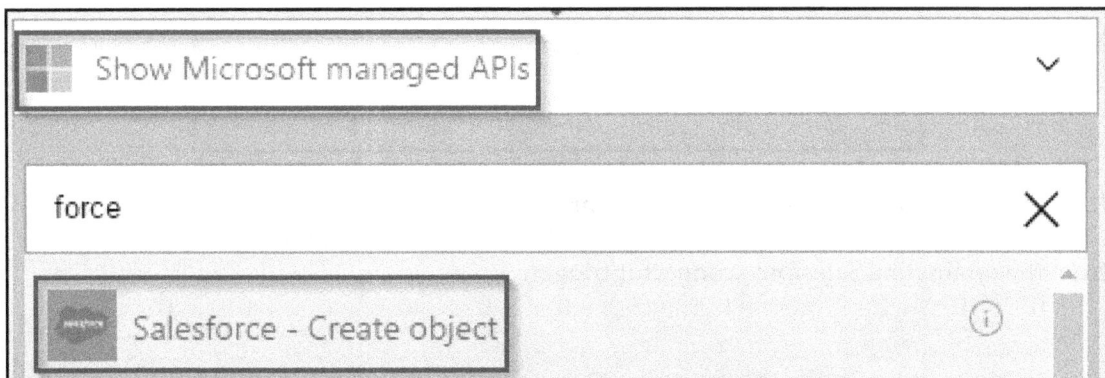

Once the connector has been added to the designer, it is possible to choose the type of object that should be created, along with any associated properties. This is demonstrated here (where the connector has also been renamed to something more meaningful for this workflow).

In this use case, we need to create an account, and here, we can see the account will be created with the account name matching the title and full name of the lead, as passed in from the originating Salesforce connector trigger.

Testing the credit check solution

At this point, we have a complete solution, as can be seen from the following screenshot:

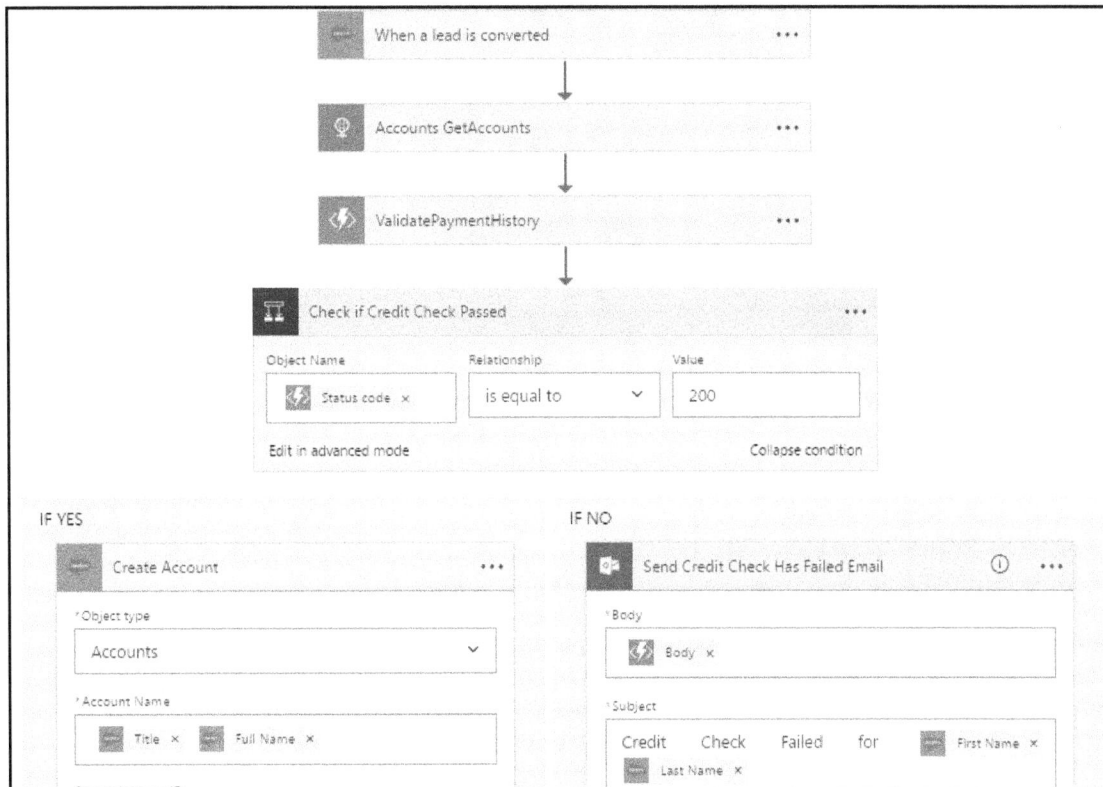

In order to test it, a lead can be changed to the triggering status via the Salesforce website, as can be seen in the following screenshot. This simulates the action that the sales consultant would carry out:

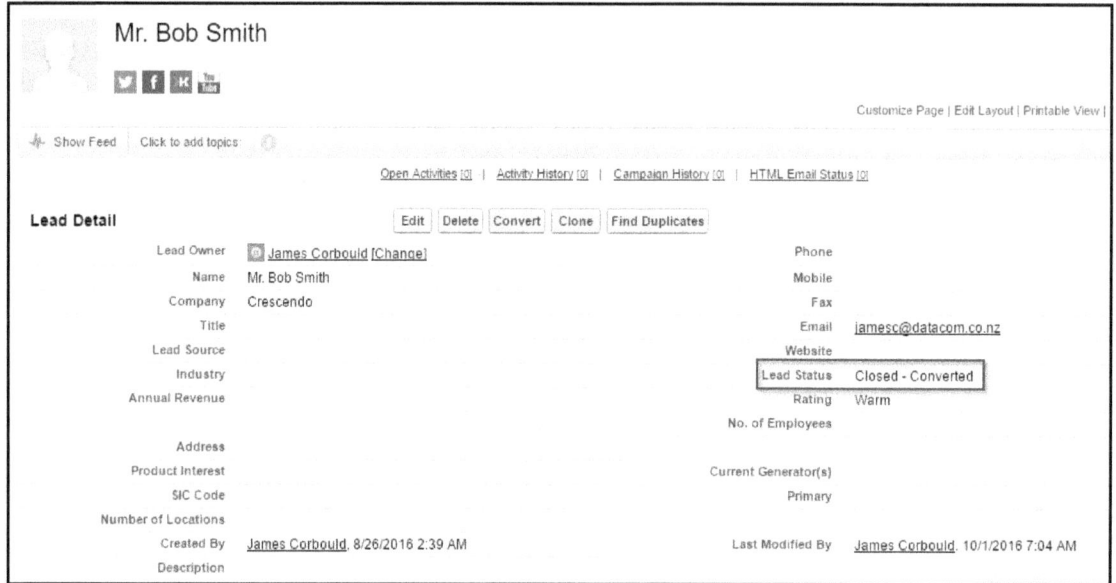

As mentioned in the previous scenario, it is possible to manually trigger the Logic App to run via the Azure portal or wait for the Salesforce trigger to do its next poll against the Microsoft-managed API. The Salesforce connector should successfully detect the change of status and cause the Logic App workflow to activate.

In this case, the credit check is favorable, and an account is created for our test lead, as can be seen here:

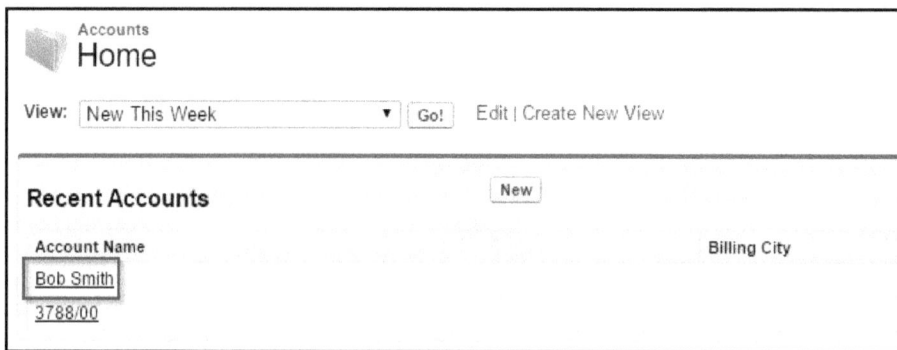

In this more complex scenario, we can see how Logic Apps can orchestrate a flow across multiple SaaS solutions, from the mainstream Salesforce connector to the custom API of the credit check company. In this way, data is being extracted out of the silos of each SaaS provider and utilized to drive the automation of business processes.

Hybrid scenarios

The two scenarios earlier show how easy it is to create simple and more complex workflows between SaaS products to deliver real-world operational efficiencies.

However, in many situations, it is necessary to provide workflows that connect cloud-based SaaS solutions with key on-premises line of business applications such as an ERP system.

There are many ways to achieve connectivity between the cloud and on-premises infrastructure including establishing a Virtual Private Network (`https://azure.microsoft.com/en-us/services/virtual-network/`) or using a technology solution such as ExpressRoute (`https://azure.microsoft.com/en-us/services/expressroute/`) for more guaranteed connection and bandwidth.

Whatever the networking infrastructure solution chosen, Logic Apps provide a number of ways to connect together on-premises and cloud-based assets to provide ongoing business benefit.

In scenarios where an on-premises application has the capability to call out to an Internet-hosted service, Logic Apps can expose an HTTP endpoint that can be used to initiate an instance of a workflow.

When real-time messaging is not required, an Azure Service Bus queue or topic can be used as a store and forward mechanism to a Logic App via a provided connector.

In more complex on-premises workflow scenarios, where message transformation and orchestration is required before invoking any cloud-based workflow service, an on-premises messaging and orchestration broker, such as BizTalk Server, can be used since with BizTalk Server 2016 it is possible to create a connection between BizTalk Server and a Logic App.

The discussion of BizTalk Server connectivity and Logic Apps is beyond the scope of this chapter, but it is discussed later in the book.

Summary

In this chapter, we explored the capabilities of Logic Apps and how they can be applied to typical SaaS application scenarios.

SaaS applications provide many benefits over more traditional custom-built commercial off-the-shelf products, including pay as you price options, and evergreen software updates.

Given these benefits, it is important to ensure that our working practices and processes can be automated and delivered in a scalable way.

Logic Apps provide connectivity to many SaaS applications. We have shown how we can connect together Dynamics 365, Office 365, and Salesforce, all of which have a key role to play in major enterprises, to build processes that reduce the effort and workload required to achieve typical tasks in an organization.

We further discussed hybrid scenarios that allow an organization to build on key line of business software assets and make use of the new paradigm of SaaS solutions.

In this way, Logic Apps are an excellent complement to an organization's SaaS story.

10
Advanced Integration with Powerful, Scalable Service Bus in the Cloud

Azure Service Bus is an asynchronous messaging service based on **Platform as a Service (PaaS)** architecture. It is designed as a highly scalable and reliable messaging system used to connect applications, services, and devices. Being a lightweight, messaging-only architecture, it is also used as the backbone communications channel between many cloud-based solutions.

Service Bus supports two types of message exchange patterns, relayed messaging, and brokered messaging. The main distinction between the two exchange patterns is that relayed service requires both the service consumer and provider to be online simultaneously, whereas with the brokered service, either the consumer or provider may be taken offline at any time without affecting the communication channel.

In this chapter, you will learn the following topics:

- What is Azure Service Bus and where it sits in the integration use cases
- Publishing and subscribing messages to/from Azure Service Bus
- Connecting your Logic App to Azure Service Bus
- How to scale your solution using Service Bus connectors in Logic Apps

Service Bus types

Azure Service Bus offers a collection of four different types of messaging technologies:

- **Queues**: This type provides asynchronous one-way messaging
- **Topics/Subscriptions**: This type provides a publish/subscribe architecture style of integration
- **Event Hubs**: This type is used to ingest event-type messages on a massive scale
- **Relays**: This type allows the relaying of messages through a common channel

Each type has distinctive characteristics that make it suitable for different messaging scenarios. In the following sections, we will discuss queues, topic/subscriptions, and in `Chapter 11`, *Connecting to Event Hubs and an Introduction to IoT Hubs*, we will cover event hubs.

Service Bus tiers

Azure Service Bus is available in three tiers - **Basic**, **Standard**, and **Premium**. The Basic tier provides only very basic queuing, whereas the Standard tier provides many more features such as topics, transactions, de-duplication, sessions and forwardTo/SendVia. The Premium tier is based on the existing Standard tier but with the added enhancements consisting of isolated CPU and memory resources. This isolation from other tenants provides scalability, greater predictability, performance, and a larger message payload.

Normally, you would use the Premium tier for systems that are latency sensitive; if you are receiving server busy errors from Azure, you need to scale your systems on a massive scale and you will send more than 3000 messages to a topic per second.

Pricing for the Premium tier is priced at a daily flat rate per the messaging unit purchased. There are no other charges included.

> A Messaging Unit is a set of dedicated resources exclusively reserved for the Premium namespace.

Service Bus Queue characteristics

Service Bus Queues provide a one-way message exchange pattern to pass messages between distributed and loosely coupled applications using the Azure SDK, WCF, AMQP, or HTTPS endpoints. These queues provide load leveling, by default, where the receiver processes messages off the queue at its own pace.

Load leveling can also be easily implemented by reading the queue length property and spinning up more processes to read the queue concurrently. As the queue length diminishes, the extra processors can be taken offline. When using multiple processors to read messages from the same queue concurrently, careful consideration must be given to the type of read lock you wish to perform. More about this is explained in the section *Retrieving messages off a Queue*.

There are many uses for this type of coupling pattern:

- Hybrid applications, which allow you to connect an on-premises application to a cloud-hosted service or application
- Loosely coupled applications, where Service Bus acts as a message broker between different systems
- Mobile applications, where clients are occasionally connected to a network
- Offline/batch processing, where the queue consumer is only available for a limited time span

Message size

While designing a queuing mechanism, consideration should be given to the size of each message. The current maximum content message size for Azure Queue Storage is restricted to 64 KB, whereas for Service Bus Queues, the restriction is 256 KB for the Basic and Standard tier whereas 1 Mb for the Premium tier.

To deal with the message size restriction, there are several options available. One option would be to use blob storage to store the message content and use the queues to hold metadata about the message and URI path.

Another option is to use sessions and break up the messages into smaller sizes (known as **chunking**). Each message chunk is placed on the queue with the same session identifier key. This instructs Service Bus to place all the received message chunks onto the same partition and in the correct sequence. The consumer would then read all the message chunks from the queue with the matching session identifier to reconstruct the entire message.

Time to live

Each message has a **time to live** (**TTL**) property, which specifies how long a message will be available in the queue. If the message does not get consumed within the specified TTL value, it will be moved to dead letter queue. The maximum TTL for Azure Queues is seven days, whereas it is unlimited for Service Bus Queues.

Dead-lettering

Dead-lettering normally occurs when a message cannot be processed, either because the message is formatted incorrectly or because the TTL period has been exceeded.

In Azure Service Bus, the message will be placed on the `$DeadLetterQueue` subqueue for the following reasons:

- If the read message fails to get processed and reappears on the queue more than 10 times. This is the default maximum delivery count.
- When the message reaches the TTL threshold and the dead-lettering flag has been set in the queue or subscription.
- When a subscription filter evaluation exception occurs and dead-lettering is enabled on the filter.

Automatic dead-lettering does not occur for the `ReceiveAndDelete` read mode. This is because the message is automatically deleted from the queue once it has been read.

> Messages in a dead letter queue do not expire and must be removed manually.

If using topics with multiple subscriptions, each subscription will have its own
`$DeadLetterQueue` subqueue.

Sessions

Sessions allow grouping of related messages to be processed in a single batch by the
consumer. This guarantees FIFO delivery of the related messages.

Typically, the `SessionId` property on the `BrokeredMessage` class is used as the partition
key. This allows all messages that have the same `SessionId` key to be handled by the same
message broker.

Sessions are ideal when sending a large message (that must be broken up into smaller sizes)
to a queue. The deconstructed message parts are then reconstructed into one message at the
consumer end.

Retrieving messages off a queue

Reading a message off the queue may be requested using one of two modes. `PeekLock`,
which is the default mode, reads the message of the queue and places a lock on the read
message. This makes the message invisible to other consumers of the queue. The message
will reappear on the queue if the consumer does not issue a `Complete` command within the
specified `VisibilityTimeout` period. The message can also reappear if the consumer calls
the `Abandon` method. This type of processing is ideal for when guaranteed processing of a
message is mandatory.

The following process flow describes reading a message from the queue using the `PeekLock` method. Note the two scenarios when a message is placed on the dead-letter queue. First one is when the message is not read within the specified TTL period, and the second scenario is when the de-queuing count equals zero.

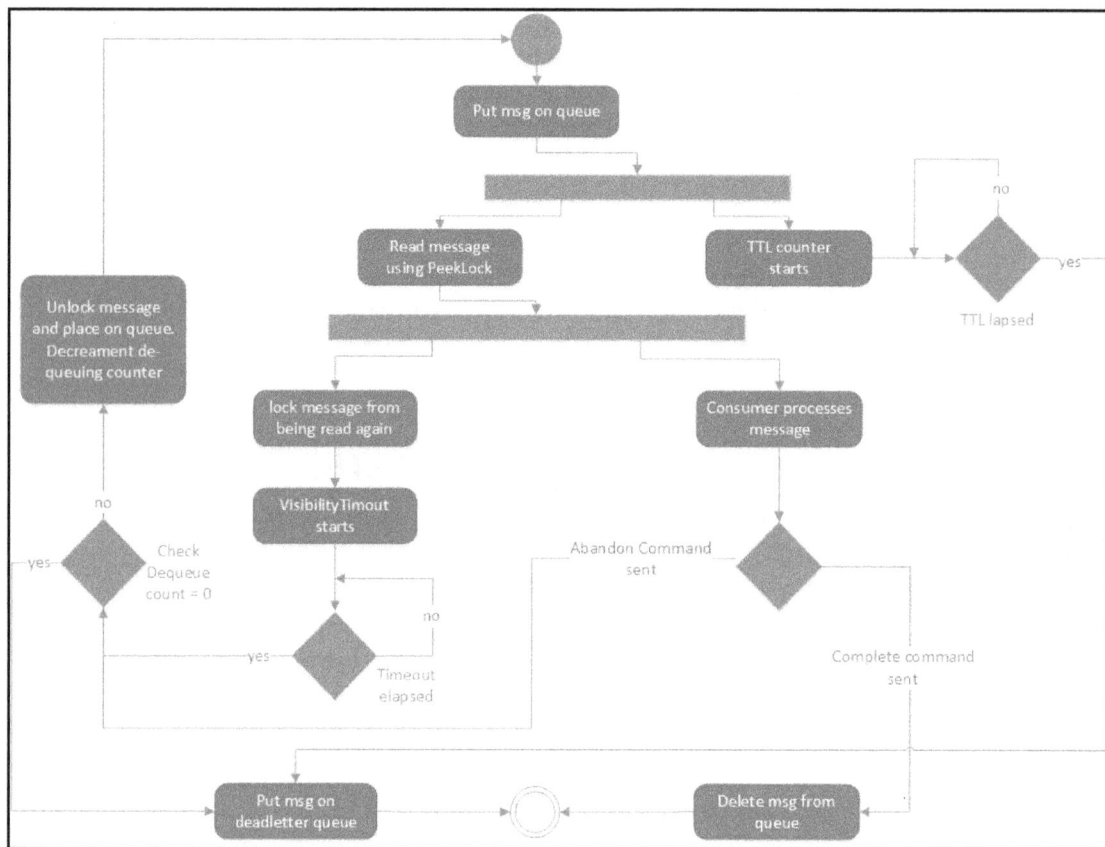

The second option is the `ReceiveAndDelete` mode. This is when once the message is read, it will immediately be deleted from the Queue. This ensures that the message will get processed once only and is processed in the FIFO order. However, there is a risk of the message getting lost if the process that consumed the message hangs.

To help your downstream systems, ensure that your message is idempotent, and there are several strategies that may be adopted:

- Setting the `VisibilityTimeout` parameter to a suitable period that will allow enough time for the message to be processed and to issue a complete command.
- Using `DequeueCount` to check how many times the message has been read from the queue.
- Using a unique transaction identifier for each message. The identifier is persisted in Azure storage and matched when each message is de-queued in order to ensure that it has not been processed again.

Service Bus also offers the ability to detect duplicate messages by tracking the value of the system `MessageId` property, which can be set to any unique string value. This is enabled by setting the **Duplicate Message Detection** and the **Duplication Detection History Time Window** properties. If a message arrives with the same `MessageId` value within the duplicate detection history window, it will simply be ignored.

Deferring message processing

Deferring messages allows the processing of higher priority messages first and then servicing the lower priority messages at a later time.

To use this feature, the receive mode must set to `PeekLock`. The client receiving the message then has the option to mark the message as being deferred. When the client marks the message to be deferred, they must keep track of the message sequence number in a durable store to be retrieved later.

When a message has been deferred, it will stay in the queue until it is retrieved and the `Complete()` method has been called. The message will also be removed from the Queue if a message TTL expiry timeout occurs.

The message is read from the queue using the `QueueClient` class available in the Azure Service Bus SDK and passing the message sequence number that was persisted previously.

Security

Clients access Service Bus resources by presenting an access token. The token specifies the URI to be accessed and an expiry time of the token.

> The Service Bus Namespace owner account
> (`RootManageSharedAccessKey`) should not be shared or embedded in
> code. This is a highly privileged account that gives rights to delete and
> create Azure artifacts and should only be used for administrative tasks.

There are two options available for clients to be authenticated to allow access to the Service Bus:

- **Shared Access Signature** (**SAS**): This provides authentication using a shared key configured on the namespace or on a Service Bus entity (Queues, Topics, and Subscriptions) with specific rights for listening, sending, or managing. The key is then used to generate a SAS token, which the client uses to authenticate with the Service Bus.
- **Access Control Service** (**ACS**): This provides identity federation with various providers. To access the Service Bus entities, the client requests a **Simple Web Token** (**SWT**) from the ACS. The token is then sent with every request to the Service Bus.

> The Azure Service Bus product team has recommended to use SAS tokens
> whenever possible as it provides more granular level of control to
> resources.

While creating a Service Bus Queue using the Azure portal, the only available authentication option is SAS. To use ACS, you will need to use the following Azure PowerShell command to create the namespace and associated ACS artifacts:

```
New-AzureSBNamespace <namespaceName> "<Region>" -CreateACSNamespace $true
```

More information on this can be found at: https://msdn.microsoft.com/en-us/library/azure/dn170478.aspx.

Service Bus provides the following three types of access rights that can be assigned to shared access policies:

- **Listen**: This is receiving messages from the queue
- **Send**: This is sending messages to the queue
- **Manage**: This allows creating, changing, or deleting entities

Handling service bus subscription security

When setting up subscriptions (which will be explained in the upcoming sections), you cannot implement authorization policies on the subscription queue, only on the topic itself. To work around this scenario, you can provision a service bus queue for each subscription and then set authorization policies on these queues.

Using the auto-forwarding feature on a queue or subscription, you set the `ForwardTo` property to the other queue that has the authorization polices applied. When a message arrives in the subscription queue, it will be automatically forwarded to the queue defined in the `ForwardTo` property. Only consumers with the Listen policy will then be allowed to read the messages.

> Auto-forwarding a message from one queue to another will be billed as another billable operation.

Managing Service Bus outages and disasters

One of the items that is overlooked when using cloud services in general is disaster recovery. Many IT professionals overlook the fact that most services are not geo replicated by default to other data centers unless you specifically configure it. Azure Service Bus does not provide any configuration settings for geo replication; therefore, you must implement your own DR strategy.

There are two types of outages that can occur-message store failures and data center outages. Message store failures occur when the underlying storage subsystem fails due to hardware faults. Data center outages may occur due to a failed update deployment to the subsystem services, power outages due to a power supply failure or backup generators and network connectivity failures.

To mitigate against message store failures, you will need to create a queue with multiple partitions. These partitions are guaranteed to be created on different storage systems within the same data center by the underlying Azure framework. If the message store fails for that partition while writing the message, it will be rewritten to another healthy partition.

Partitions must be set at the time the queue or topic is created.

In scenarios where a whole data center may not be available, you will need to create a service bus namespace in two data centers to replicate the message using custom code in your application. For example, you would create a namespace named `sunnyelectrical-primary.servicebus.windows.net` in **South East-Australia** and another namespace named `sunnyelectrical-secondary.servicebus.windows.net` in **South East Asia-Singapore**.

In an active/active replication mode, the application would send the message to both Service Bus Queues located in the different regions. The consumer would read messages from the queues in both regions and decide how to handle the duplicated message. With this option, you are doubling the number of operations and hence the costs.

In an active/passive replication mode, the application would send the message to target the primary namespace service bus first and only send to the secondary namespace if connectivity errors were occurring. The consumer would still be required to read from both the primary and secondary service bus, but the number of operations would be far less than the active/active replication option.

To cope with the consumer receiving duplicate messages from both queues, the message will need to be tagged with a unique identifier before being placed onto the queues by setting either the `BrokeredMessage.MessageId`, `BrokeredMessage.Label`, or a custom property (for more information refer to: `https://docs.microsoft.com/en-us/dotnet/api/microsoft.servicebus.messaging.brokeredmessage?redirectedfrom=MSDN#Microsoft_ServiceBus_Messaging_BrokeredMessage_MessageId`). The consumer would then disregard a message if it has been received before with the same identifier. The consumer will need to keep track of the message identifiers in persistence storage.

Service Bus topics

Topics are another communication model that provides a publish/subscribe architecture pattern. This allows a message to be consumed by many subscribers, and each subscriber is able to process the message independently.

The following image shows a component publishing a message to a topic with two subscribers. Each subscriber setting up a **Subscription** filter on the **purchase amount**.

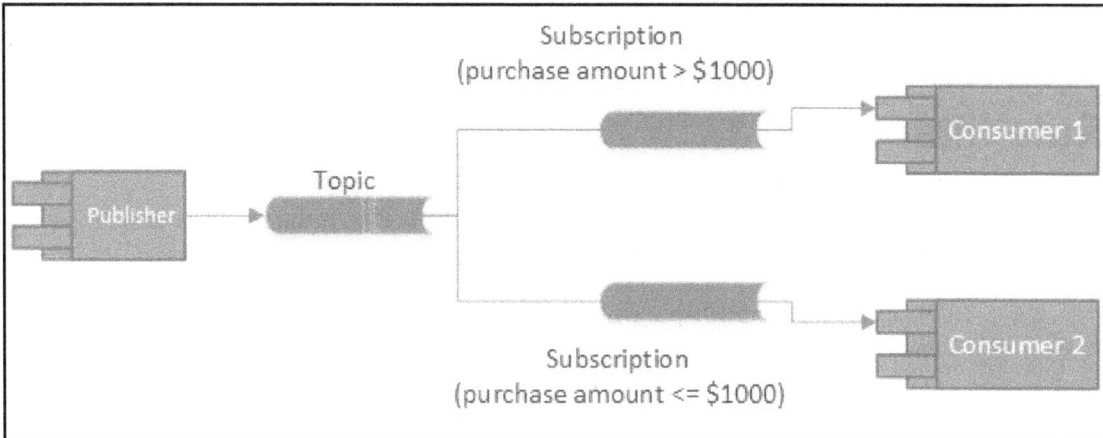

Subscriptions

To receive messages from a topic queue, you would create a subscription. A subscription resembles a virtual queue that receives a copy of the message sent to a topic queue.

> Note that a single subscription cannot be used for multiple topics. Instead, you need to create multiple subscriptions.

Subscription rules

In some scenarios, it would be helpful to filter message properties and only receive messages that satisfy the filter condition. Currently, if a subscriber creates a subscription to a topic, all messages arriving at that topic are made available to the subscriber. This is because the default filter MatchAll is applied when no filters are specified on the creation of a subscription.

Azure Service Bus has the concept of subscription rules, which allows you to define filters and actions that are applied to a Topic.

> More information on creating subscriptions from Microsoft can be found at: `http://msdn.microsoft.com/en-us/library/microsoft.servicebus.namespacemanager.createsubscription.aspx`.

Rule filter

A filter is an expression in the form of a SQL 92 style predicate, for example, `"StoreLocation = 'Auckland'"`. These filters are applied to either system or user-defined application properties that are available in the `BrokeredMessage` class.

> You may apply multiple rules for a subscription, but bear in mind that each rule evaluating to true will result in a copy of the message being placed in the subscriber's virtual queue.

The actual code to create a filter and subscription will look like the following example:

```
//create the filter
SqlFilter cityFilter = new SqlFilter("StoreLocation = 'Wellington'");
```

This will forward all messages to the subscription named `SouthernRegion` if the `StoreLocation` name equals `Wellington`.

Remember that the filter expression is based on the SQL 92 syntax, which will allow you to add more filtering options in the syntax. Here is an example:

```
SqlFilter highValuecityFilter = new SqlFilter("StoreLocation = 'Wellington'
OR StoreLocation = 'Levin' AND SalesValue > 5000");
```

The filter is then added to the namespace instance and topic, using the `CreateSubscription` method, as shown here:

```
//create a filtered subscription
nsManager.CreateSubscription("SalesTopicQueue", "SouthernRegion",
cityFilter);
```

Rule action

A rule can also define an action using the `RuleDescription` object. With actions, you can modify the value of an existing property when the filter condition evaluates to `true`. The following code demonstrates how to set the value of a user-defined application property named `Priority` when the filtered condition evaluates to `true`, using the SQL 92 syntax:

```
var ruleLowPrice = new RuleDescription()
{
    Filter = new SqlFilter("SalesValue < 1000")
Action = new SqlRuleAction("set Priority='Low'"),
    };

var ruleHighPrice = new RuleDescription()
{
    Filter = new SqlFilter("SalesValue >= 1000")
Action = new SqlRuleAction("set Priority ='High'"),
};
```

Once the filter and actions have been defined, they can be added to the namespace manager, as before:

```
nsManager.CreateSubscription("SalesTopicQueue","AccountsLow",
ruleLowPrice);
nsManager.CreateSubscription("SalesTopicQueue","AccountsHigh",
ruleHighPrice);
```

> Note that the rules will be executed in the order in which they are registered.

Partitioned queues/topics

Without partitions, a queue or topic is handled by a single message broker and stored in a single messaging store, which can constrain performance. Using partitions, a queue or topic can be spread across multiple brokers and stores, thereby providing a higher throughput rate than a single message broker and store. These partitions contain all the features of a no partitioned queue or topic, such as transactions and sessions.

When messages arrive at the queue or topic, they are distributed in a round-robin fashion to all the fragments of a partitioned queue or topic if no partition key has been defined.

To control which fragment receives what message, the properties `SessionId`, `PartitionKey`, and `MessageId` may be used as partition keys. All messages received using the same partition key will be processed by that specific fragment. If that fragment is temporarily unavailable, an error will be returned.

When a client reads a message from a partitioned queue or topic, the Service Bus queries all fragments for the next message. Note that the client is unaware of the fragmentation while reading the queue.

Administration tools

Being able to view and administer messages in a production environment is mandatory, especially when things go wrong. Fortunately, there is a tool available named Service Bus Explorer, which allows you to connect to a Service Bus namespace and administer the message entities. It can be downloaded at
`https://code.msdn.microsoft.com/windowsazure/Service-Bus-Explorer-f2abca5a`.

Scenario

In this code sample, we will use our fictitious company Sunny Electricals to add purchase orders received from our website to a Service Bus via a Logic App.

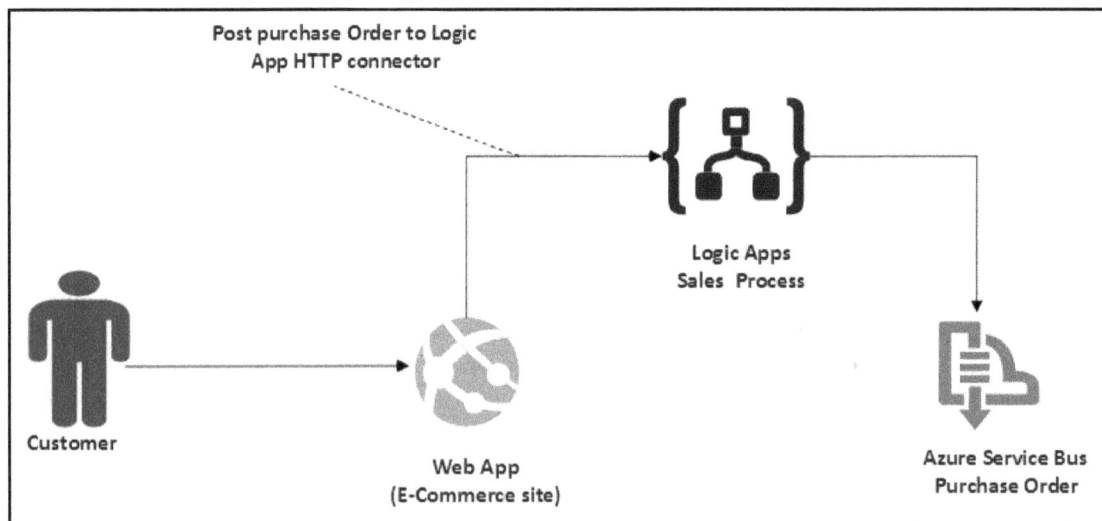

The Service Bus will be configured with two topics-one for purchase orders over $5000 and another topic for orders under $5000 to receive message from the Logic Apps.

Let's go ahead, step by step, to create the necessary artifacts for the Sunny Electricals purchase order solution. We will start with creating a new instance of Azure Service Bus namespace in the Azure Portal.

Log in to Azure portal using your official or personal Azure subscription at `https://porta l.azure.com/`. On the Azure portal dashboard, click on **More services** and use the dropdown to navigate to **Enterprise Integration** and click on **Service Bus**.

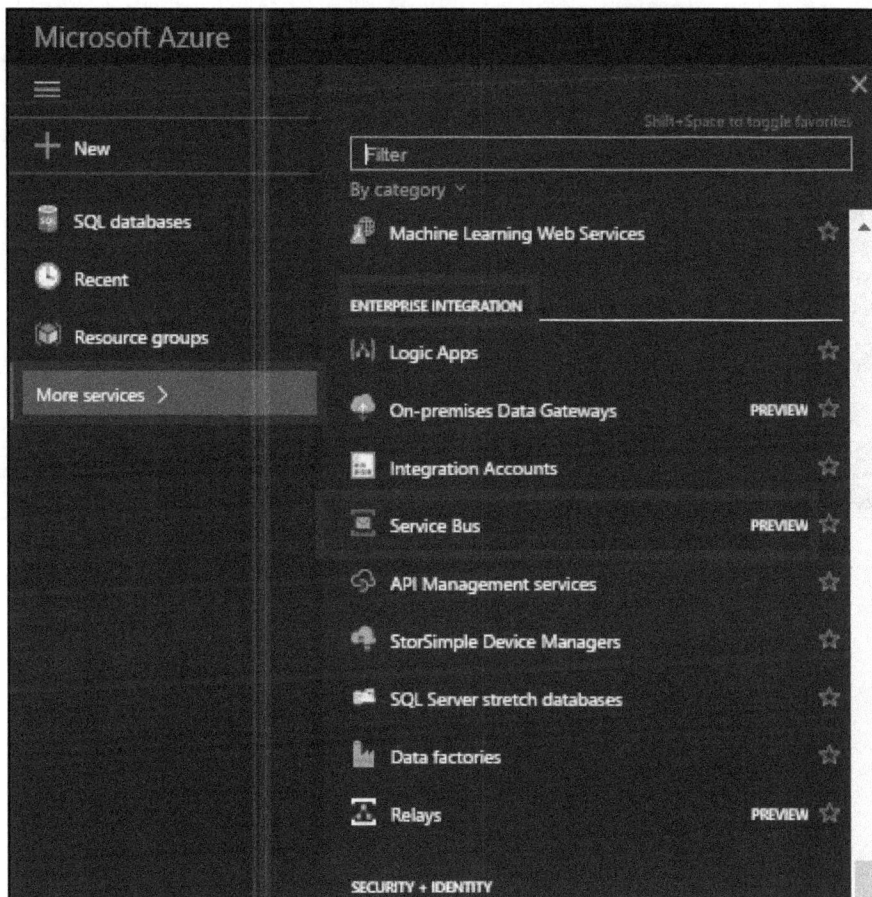

It will open a Service Bus window on the Azure portal dashboard. Click on **Add** to make a new instance of Azure Service Bus.

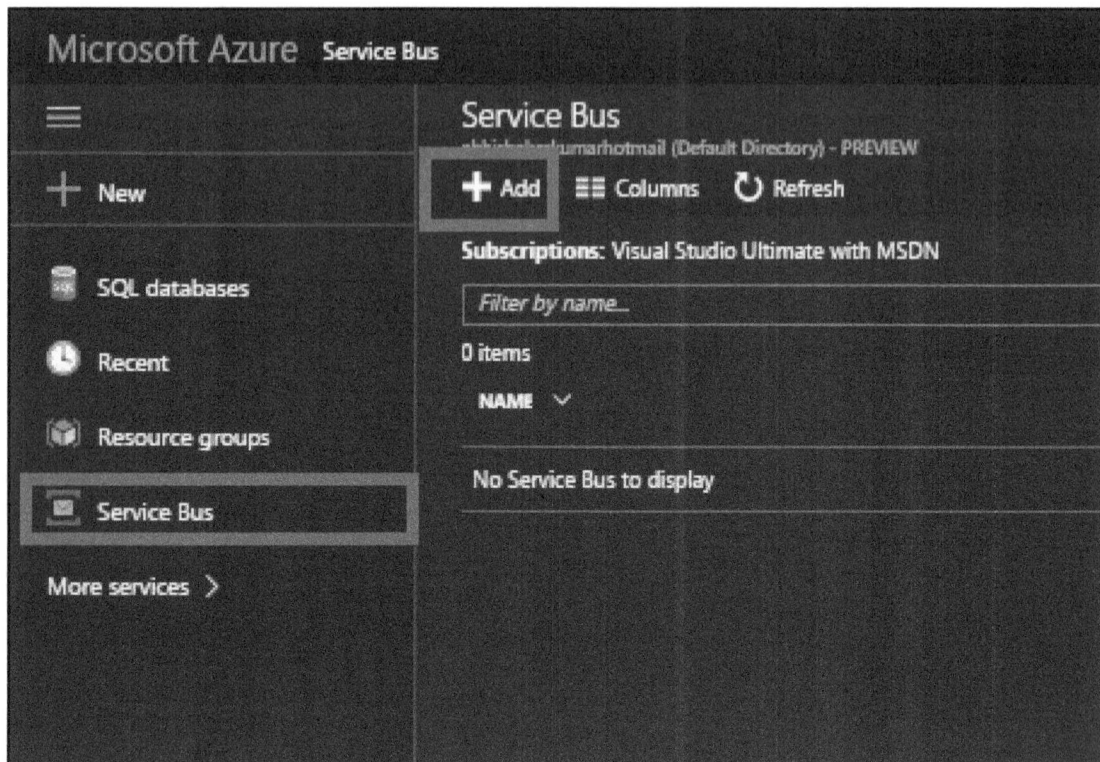

Populate Service Bus details at the **Create namespace** blade. Give a proper name to your Service Bus, select pricing tier based on your usages and then the resource group in which you want to run your service. If you do not have existing resource group or you require to create separate resource group, then select **Create new** resource group. Click on **Create** at the bottom of the blade to get a new instance of Service Bus.

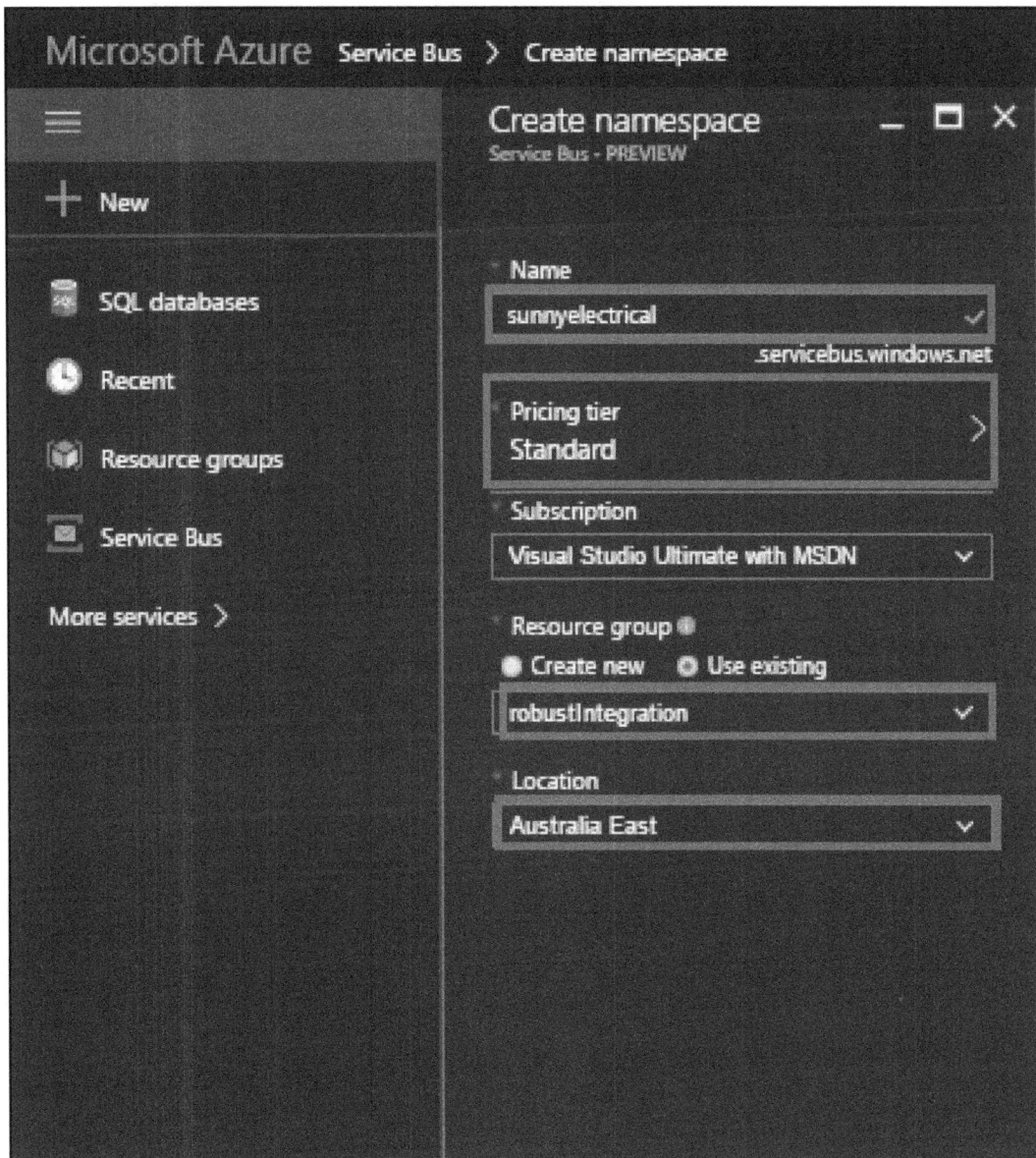

This will create a new instance of Service Bus in the Azure. Click on the newly created Service Bus to open the Service Bus overview window.

To create Azure Service Bus, you can also use Microsoft Azure PowerShell scripting. The use of PowerShell will automate your deployment process, and you do not need to go through Azure portal to create a Service Bus namespace manually for each different environment. To install and configure Azure PowerShell, you can follow the instructions available at the MSDN link shared here: `https://docs.microsoft.com/en-us/powershell/azureps-cmdlets-docs/`.

To create a new Azure Service Bus namespace in Azure using PowerShell, you can use the `New-AzureSBNamespace` PowerShell cmdlet command.

```
Parameter Set: Default
New-AzureSBNamespace [-Name] <String> [[-Location] <String> ] [[-CreateACSNamespace] <Boolean> ] [-NamespaceType] <NamespaceType> {Messaging | NotificationHub} [ <CommonParameters>]
```

> For more description of each of the parameters, you can refer to the MSDN link at: `https://docs.microsoft.com/en-us/powershell/servicemanagement/azure.compute/v1.6.1/New-AzureSBNamespace?redirectedfrom=msdn`.

For this solution, create two topics within Azure Service Bus to hold invoice details. Here, we have created `PremiumInvoice` topic and `Invoice` topic within the Sunny Electricals Service Bus namespace.

The following steps demonstrate how to create the `PremiumInvoice` topic; you can follow the same instructions to create the `Invoice` topic.

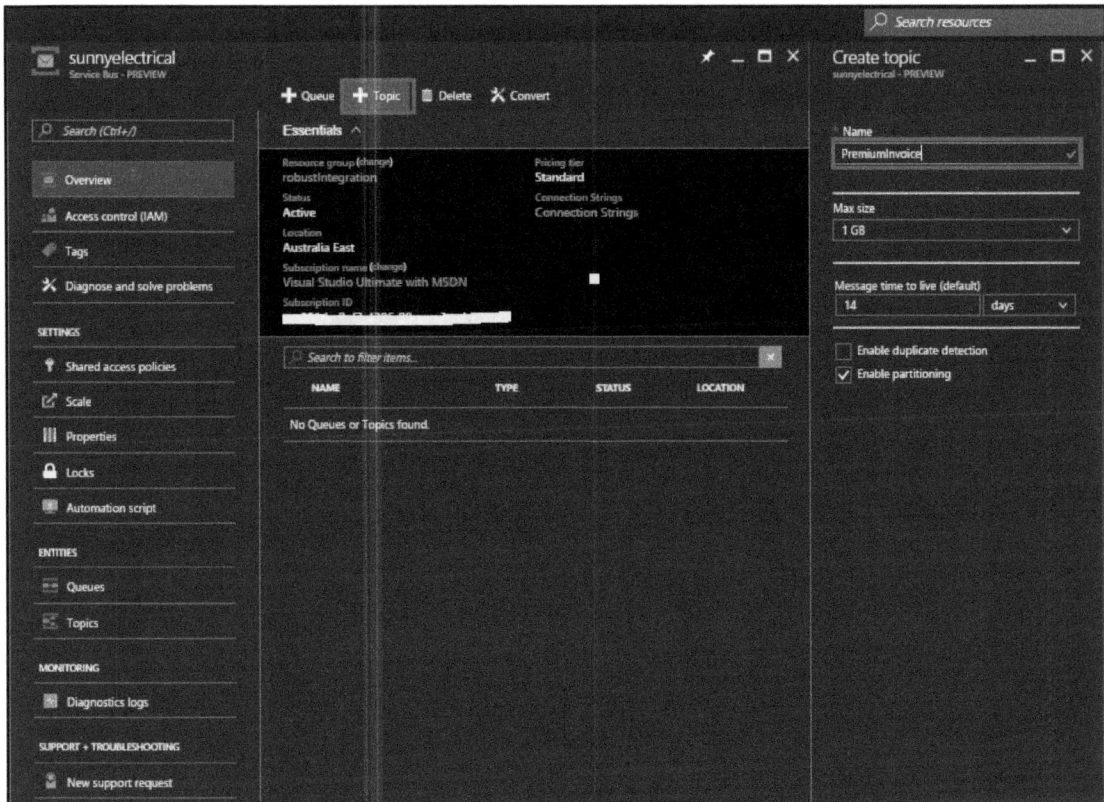

While creating topics, there are certain properties that need to be populated based on your requirement and usage. The list is shown in the following table:

Properties	Description
Name	The name of the topic
Max size	The total size of the message in the topic/queue
Message time to live	This is the duration of time after which the message in Service Bus expires, Messages older than their TimeToLive value will expire and no longer be retained and moved to dead-letter subqueue.
Enable duplicate detection	By enabling duplicate detection, if any duplicate message is posted to the Service Bus topic, the service will automatically ignore the message

Enable partitioning	Enabling partitioning will give you multiple message broker capability, and incoming messages can be stored in multiple message stores.

Once you have created both the topics, verify the topics/queues by clicking the **Topics** or **Queues** section within the Service Bus **Overview** blade.

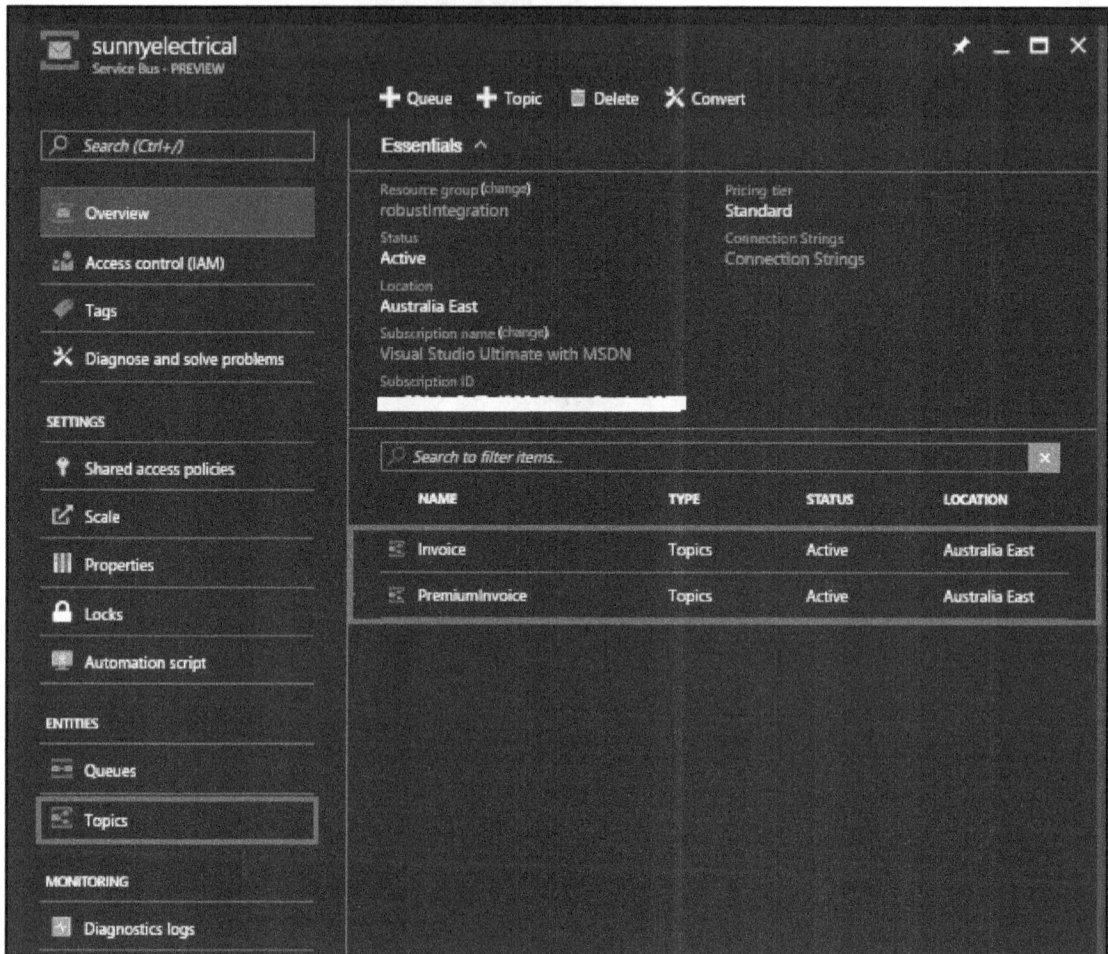

This is not completed yet; for Logic Apps to push or pull messages in or out of the Service Bus topic, you need to define a topic subscription. The creation of a subscription is necessary to facilitate the publish/subscribe mechanism that is supported by Azure Service Bus.

For this solution, you need to create two subscriptions: one is for `Premiuminvoice` andother for `Invoice` topic.

The following table hold the list of properties which you require to populate in order to create subscription for the topic.

Properties	Description
Name	The name of the subscription for the topic
Message time to live	Time duration after which the message in Service Bus topic expires.
Lock duration	Sets the duration of a peek lock; that is, the amount of time that the message is locked from other receivers.
Move expired message to dead-letter sub queue	By enabling dead-letter subqueue, you explicitly move expired message to dead-letter queue and expired message is not lost
Move message that cause filter evaluation exception to the dead-letter subqueue	Determines how Service Bus handles a message that causes an exception during a subscription filter evaluation. If true, the message that caused the exception is moved to the subscription's dead-letter queue. Otherwise, it is discarded.
Enable Session	If set to true, the topic is session aware and only session receiver is supported. Session-aware topics are not supported through REST. The default value is false

PremiumInvoice and Invoice topic subscription creation

PowerShell can automate these manual tasks to create topics and associated subscriptions.

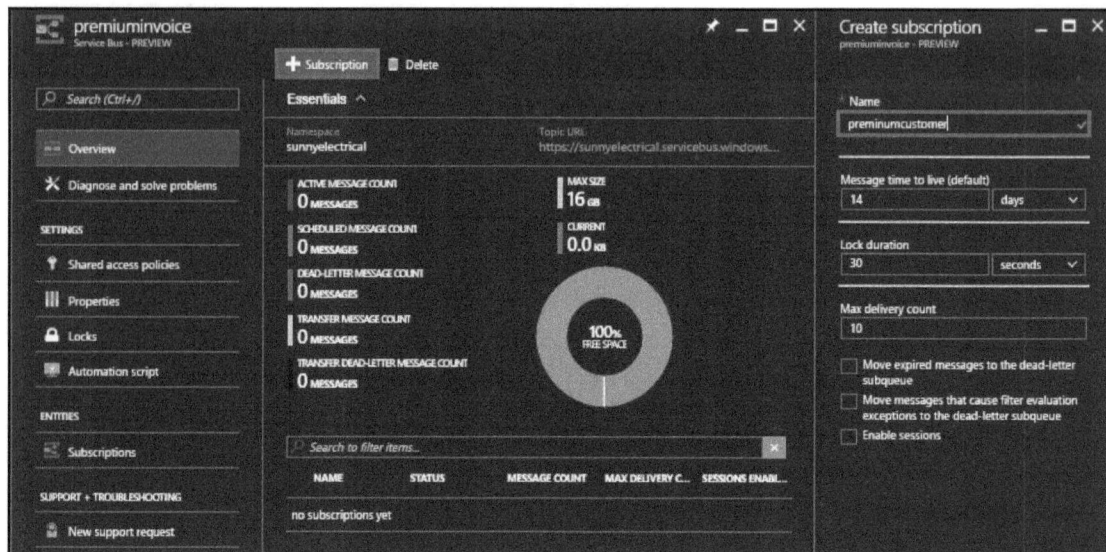

You can follow the steps and scripts available at the following Microsoft blog post : `https://blogs.msdn.microsoft.com/paolos/2014/12/02/how-to-create-service-bus-queues-topics-and-subscriptions-using-a-powershell-script/`.

Up to now, we have done all the setup steps required for the Service Bus setup. We will move a step ahead and create a new Logic App in Azure portal, which will use the HTTP trigger to get the invoice message from the web App. We will use similar steps as described in previous chapters to create a new `sunnyElectricalsGetInvoice` Logic App through Azure portal or with Visual Studio 2015.

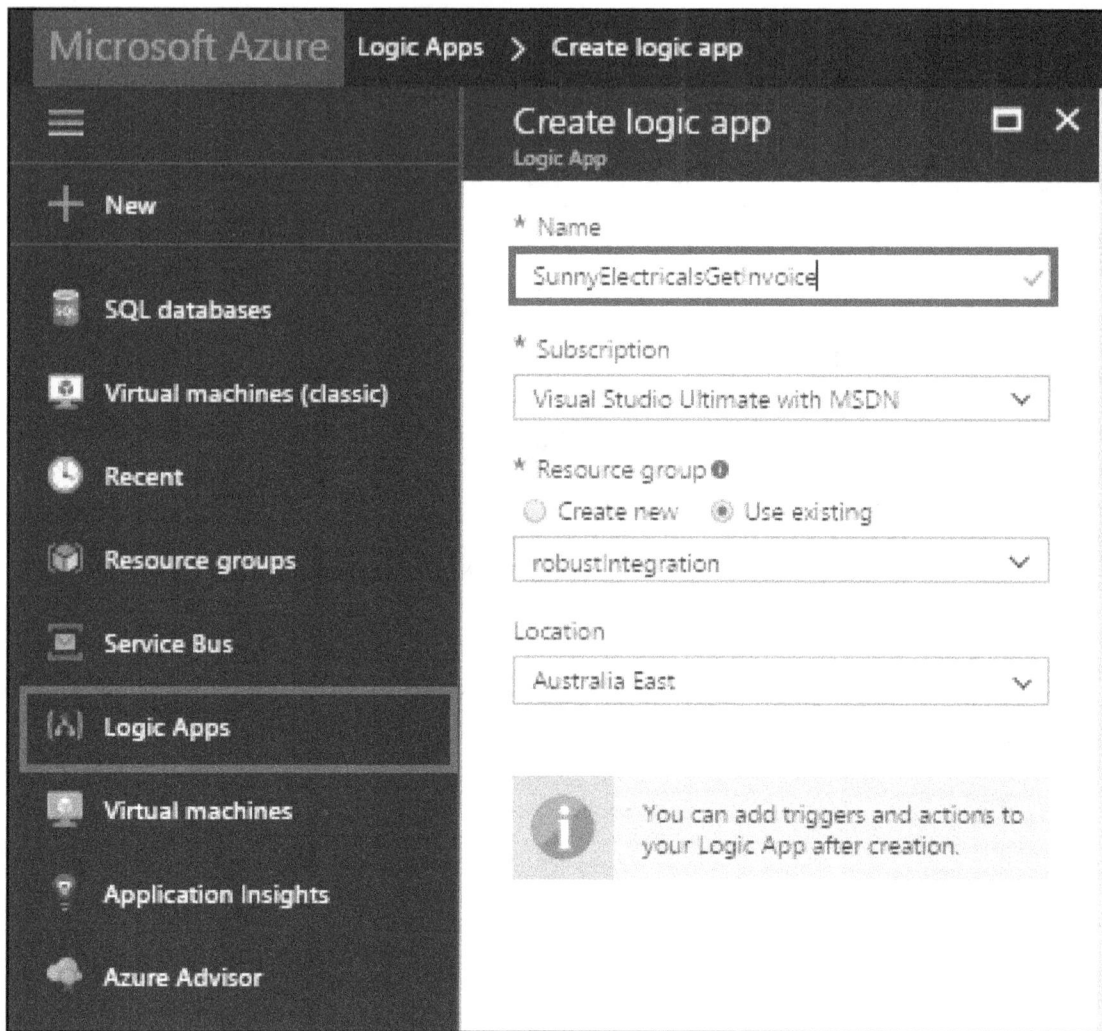

The Logic App workflow is quite simple and easy to implement. We are receiving an HTTP request for an invoice in the application/JSON format. If you pass content type in another format, such as application/text or xml, then convert the content type to application/JSON within logic workflow using expression language to get the desired JSON string.

> By setting the content type to application/JSON in the request HTTP header, Logic App will convert the JSON to a typed object using the provided JSON schema.

Copy the JSON request schema in the body section of **Request** Http trigger.

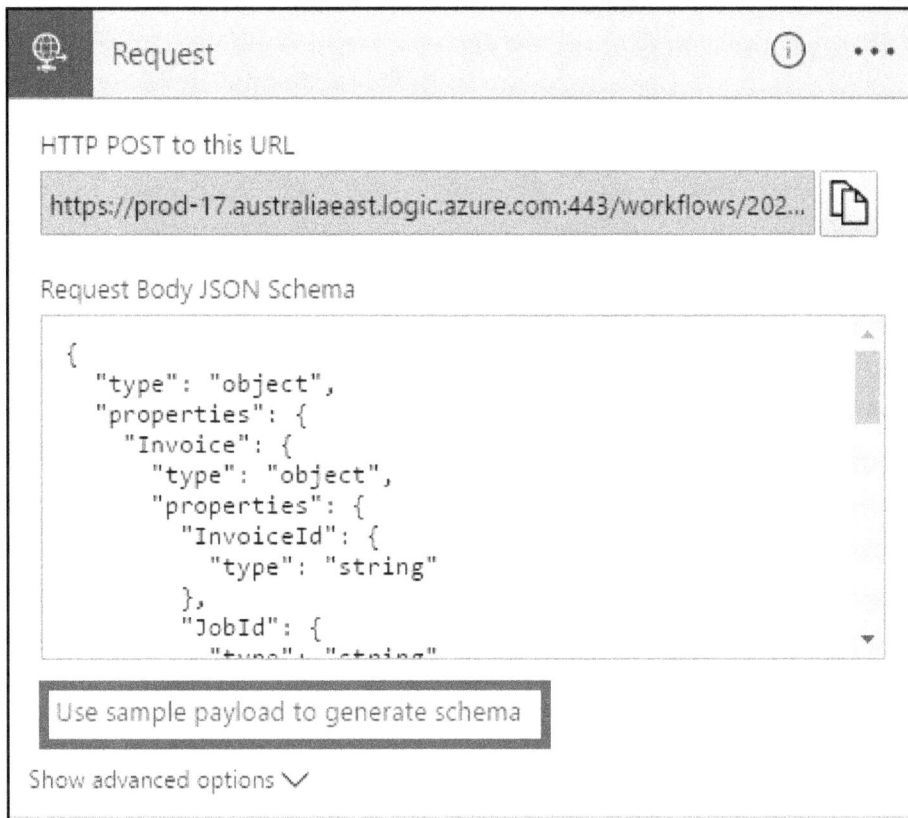

Save the Logic App by clicking on the **Save** button on the top. This will generate the HTTP endpoint, which will be used for application integration and test.

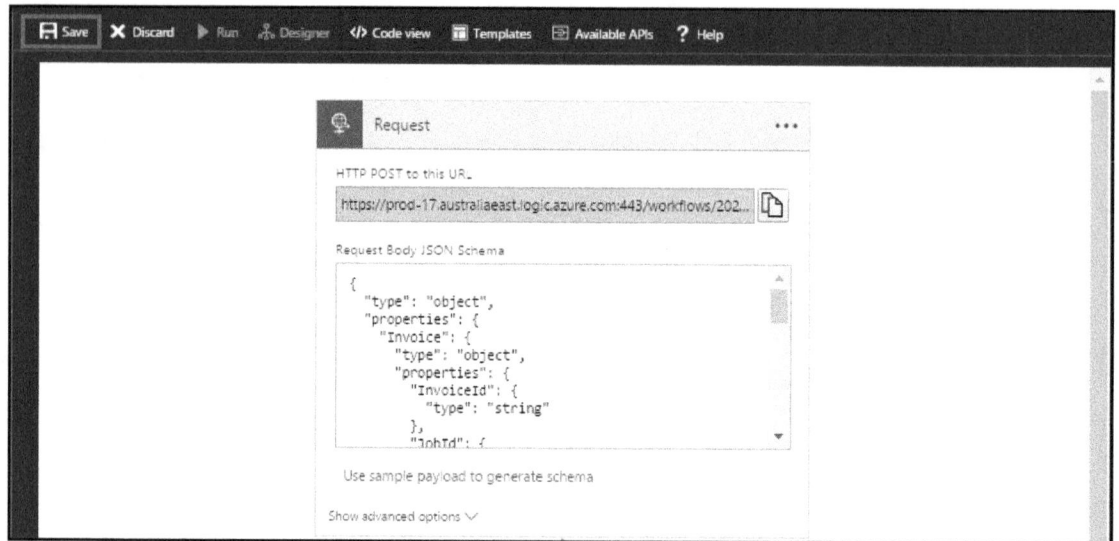

If you do not have the JSON Schema, you can use sample request JSON payload to generate the JSON Schema. It is quite simple as demonstrated here. For this sample, we have used JSON message shown in the following table:

```
{
"Invoice": {
"InvoiceId": "SE0034BD001",
"JobId": "SE005",
"Status": "PENDING",
"UserId": "BD001",
"UserName": "JOHN MAC",
"UserEmail":"infor@sunnyelectricals.com",
"Date": "04/01/1986",
"Amount": 8000,
"Comments": "PENDING INVOICE",
"Address": "NZ"
}
}
```

Once you populated the trigger section with the correct JSON schema, you can construct the workflow with decision shape (the Condition Amount is greater than 5000).

> For more information refer to: https://docs.microsoft.com/en-us/azu re/app-service-logic/app-service-logic-content-type.

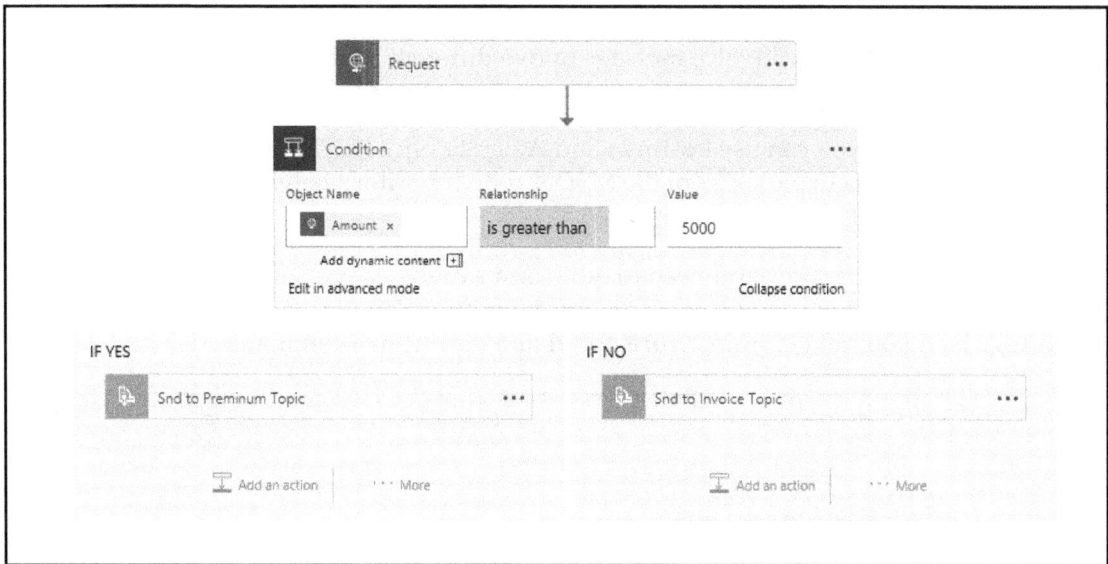

While configuring send to topic action, there are some mandatory fields that need to be populated with correct values, which include **Queue/Topic name**, **Content**, and proper connection information for the Service Bus.

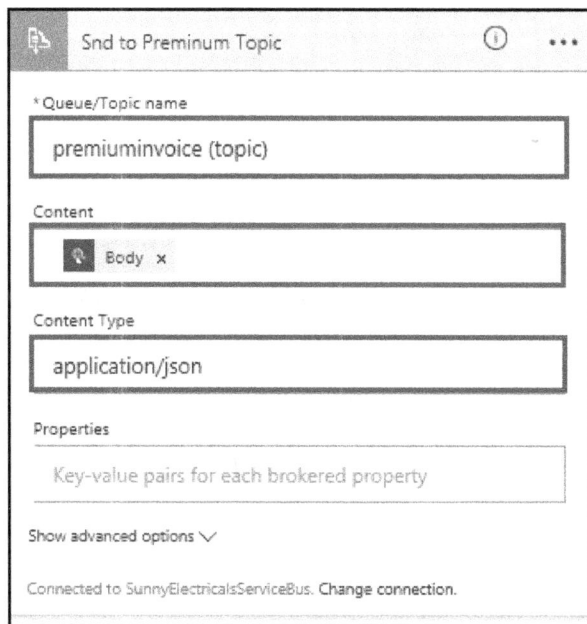

So, we are done with solution design for our first logic App, which is invoked by the HTTP request and by sending the invoice message to two different Service Bus Topics based on the amount.

To test this solution, you can use Postman and Azure Service Bus Explorer. You can download Service Bus Explorer from the MSDN code repository here: `https://github.com /paolosalvatori/ServiceBusExplorer`.

After downloading the code, you need to build and run the Azure Service Bus Explorer project. You also need to provide correct connection information in Azure Service Bus Explorer, which you can get from Azure portal or a PowerShell command.

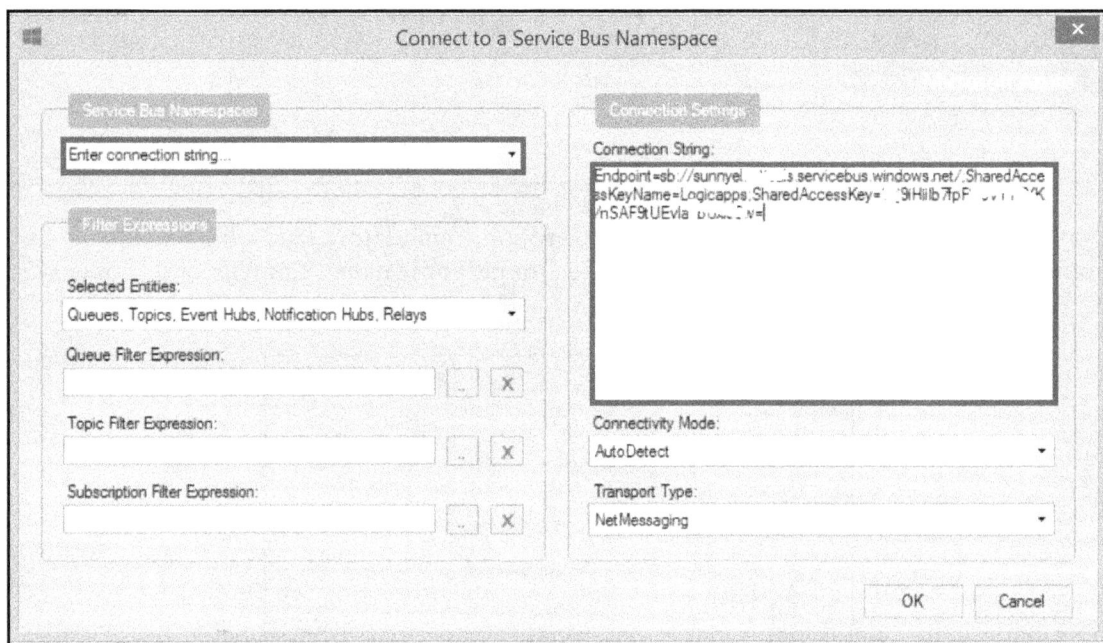

You need to post some sample request through Visual Studio test client or Postman, and you can verify the run result in Azure portal and Service Bus Explorer.

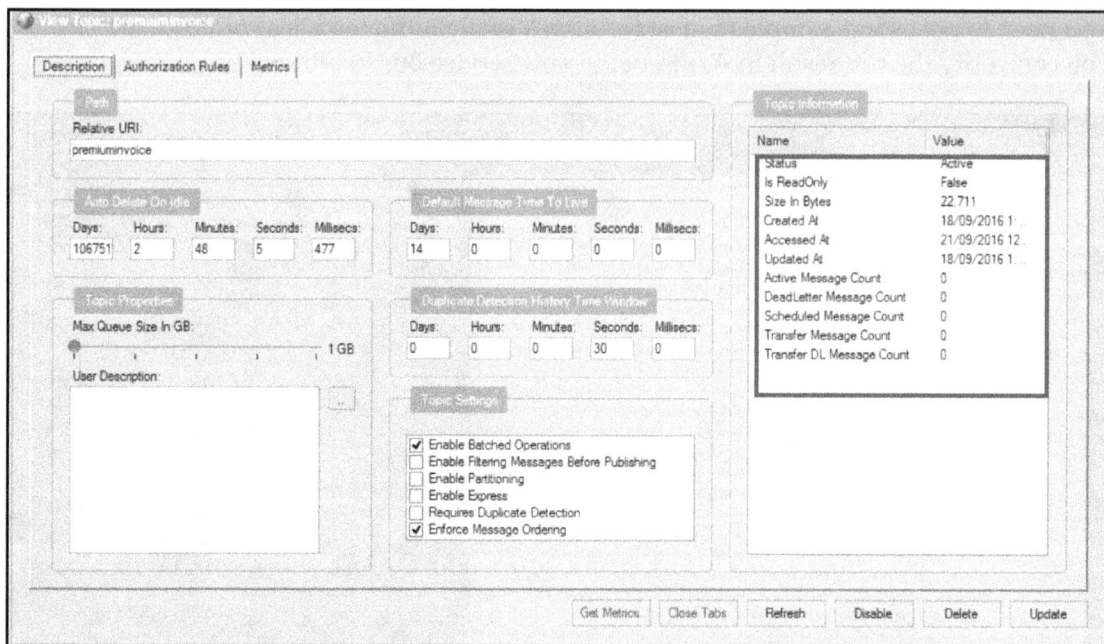

In the solution described so far, we have gone step by step through creating Logic Apps, Service Bus and creating different topics for Premium and general customers. We have also seen how to use Azure Service Bus Explorer. By doing this exercise, you now have some hands-on experience creating Azure Service Bus artifacts via Azure portal directly and also creating queues and topics. This sample also explains how you can use a Logic App to push data to Service Bus topics or queues.

In the next sample, we will be polling the *Premium* topic and doing some parallel processing on messages received from the topic.

In integration, the parallel action is one of the most common integration design patterns, which can be used widely and in different use cases.

Let's create a new Logic App with the name `GetPremiumCustomer` and associate the trigger on Service Bus topic.

Populate the Service Bus topic trigger with the correct topic name and subscription. You can fetch the list of parameters through portal using Azure PowerShell scripting.

After defining the trigger for Logic App, we have a set of two parallel actions that will be performed on the incoming message. First action is to send the message to the external HTTP listener endpoint and second is to store the premium customer details in the Azure SQL database.

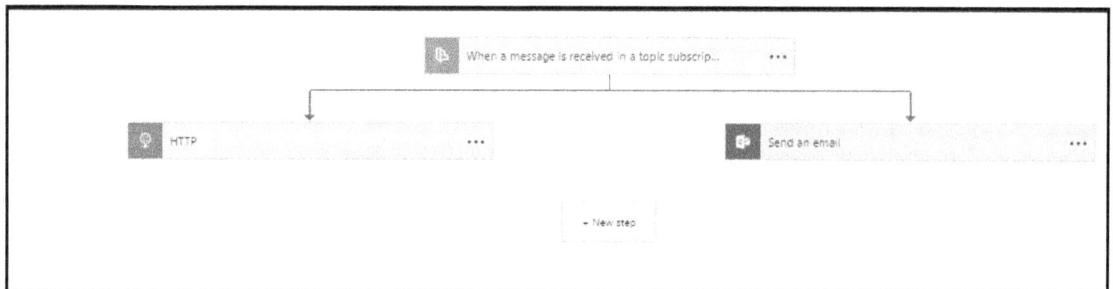

For the parallel processing of actions, you need to go through the code page of Logic Apps and define two actions in parallel, which will be invoked after the receiving message from service bus topic.

```
"actions": {
    "HTTP": {
        "inputs": {
            "body": "@json(base64ToString(triggerBody()?['ContentData']))?['Invocie']?['UserEmail']",
            "method": "POST",
            "uri": "http://requestb.in/1j1jvc71"
        },
        "runAfter": {},
        "type": "Http"
    },
    "Send_an_email": {
        "inputs": {
            "body": {
                "Body": "Hi \nThanks for purchasing from Sunny Electricals",
                "Subject": "Thank you for valuable Customer",
                "To": "@json(base64ToString(triggerBody()?['ContentData']))?['Invocie']?['UserEmail']"
            },
            "host": {
                "api": {
                    "runtimeUrl": "https://logic-apis-australiaeast.azure-apim.net/apim/outlook"
                },
                "connection": {
                    "name": "@parameters('$connections')['outlook']['connectionId']"
                }
            },
            "method": "post",
            "path": "/Mail"
        },
        "runAfter": {},
        "type": "ApiConnection"
    }
},
```

In this sample, we have used RequestBin: `https://requestb.in/` to intercept the web request.

To test this solution, you can verify the Logic App run and check requestbin for the HTTP intercepted request.

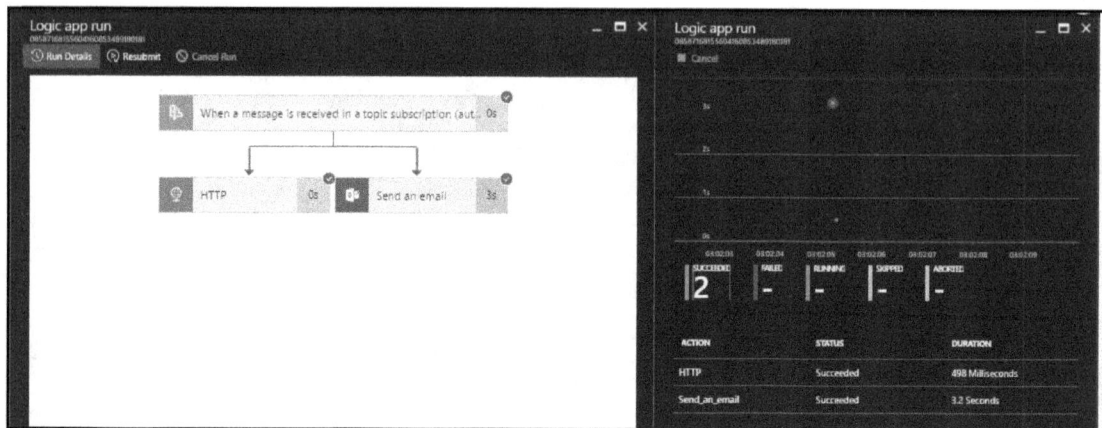

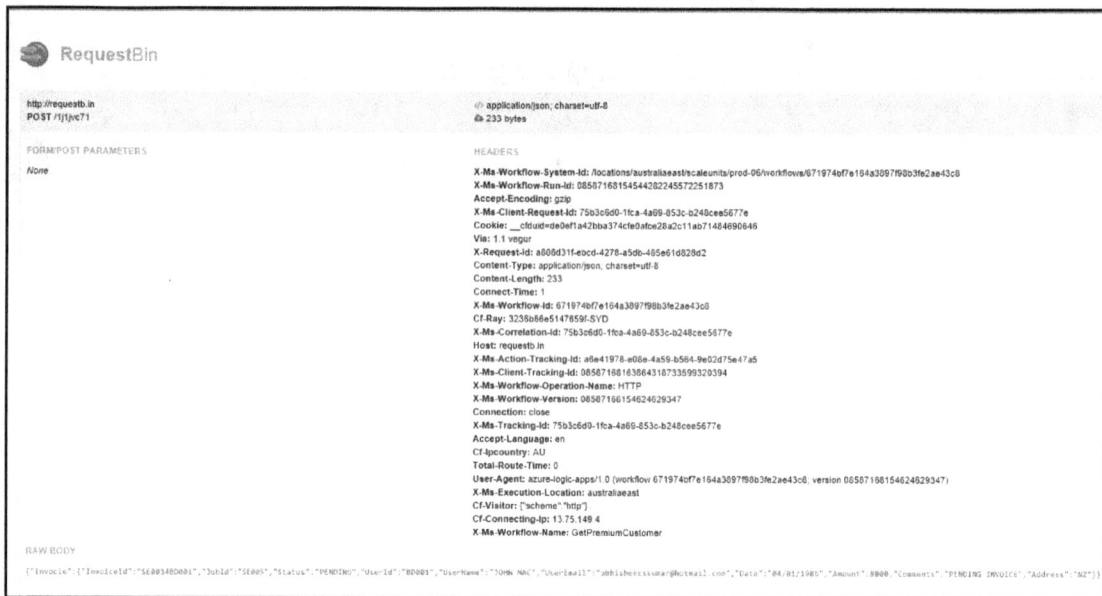

To verify the latency of the running logic apps, you can configure the matrix within the specified Logic Apps.

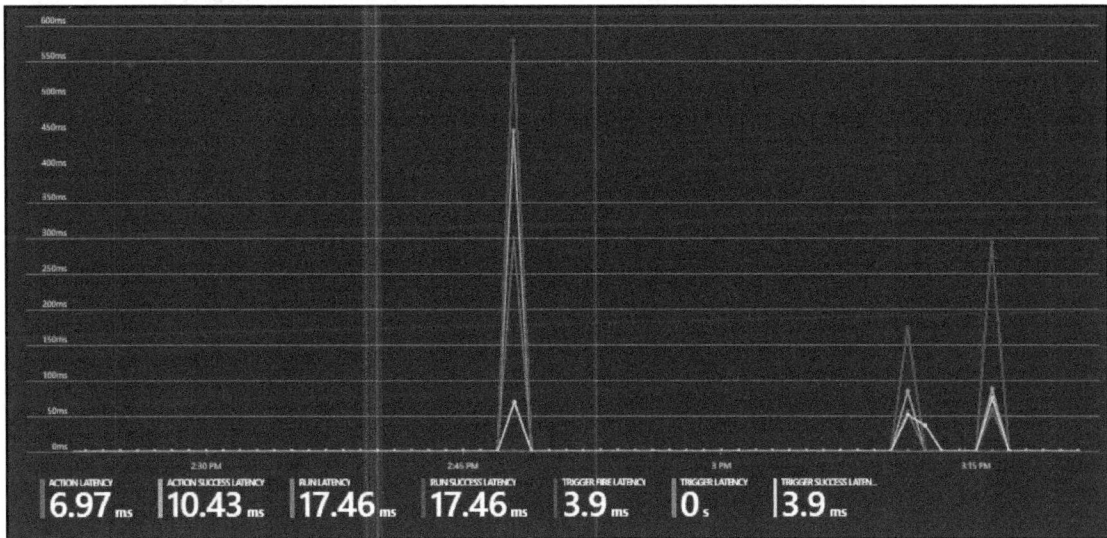

By doing the second sample, we have shown how you can trigger a Service Bus topic or queue from Logic App and can perform the parallel processing of multiple action within Logic Apps.

> You can extend the parallel processing to work with scatter gather pattern within Logic Apps.
> For more information refer to: http://www.enterpriseintegrationpatt erns.com/patterns/messaging/BroadcastAggregate.html.

Summary

Azure Service Bus provides a robust and scalable messaging infrastructure. It provides the framework to connect on-premise and cloud-based applications/services together.

Using topics with the Service Bus provides the framework to build scalable publish/subscribe message exchange patterns.

You learned how to wire up a Logic App to a Service Bus topic and how to subscribe to the messages using another Logic App.

In the next chapter, we will look at Event Hubs and IoT Hubs, which are another form of message queuing.

11
Connecting to Event Hubs and an Introduction to IoT Hubs

This chapter provides a brief review of Azure Event Hubs and provides an introduction to IoT Hubs. It will teach you how to connect to Event Hubs and consume data using partitions and how to connect devices to the IoT Hub. It will discuss the various security and connectivity options available today when connecting devices to the Internet.

In this chapter, you will learn the following topics:

- What are Event Hubs and IoT Hubs
- When to use either Event Hubs or IoT Hubs
- How to send and consume messages
- How to enable bidirectional communication with IoT Hubs
- Using an Azure IoT Hub in a simulated real-world example

An introduction to Event Hubs

Event Hubs are primarily designed to ingest large volumes of event and telemetry data in a high throughput manner from a variety of devices and services. They are similar in principle to Azure Queues and Azure Topics but with different characteristics and use cases. Although Azure Queues and Topics are used for enterprise messaging scenarios in which transaction support, dead-lettering, ordered delivery, and guaranteed delivery are of prime concerns, Event Hubs are biased toward very high throughput and event processing scenarios such as stream analytics.

Security in Event Hubs

When a device sends data to an Event Hub, it is normally to a virtual endpoint address defined by the publisher. A publisher requires a valid token to be passed with each message, which is a combination of a **shared access signature** (**SAS**) and a publisher name. The publisher name is normally the device's unique identifier.

Although it is not recommended, you can directly connect to the Event Hub endpoint by creating a token that provides this level of access. By doing so, you lose the throttling capability and the blacklisting of devices using this token.

You can also share the same token across multiple devices or services that share the same publisher.

Tokens can be generated using the following class available in the .NET Azure Service Bus SDK:

```
public static string
SharedAccessSignatureTokenProvider.GetSharedAccessSignature(string keyName,
string sharedAccessKey, string resource, TimeSpan tokenTimeToLive)
```

Here, `keyName` is the shared access policy name defined in the Azure portal. `sharedAccessKey` is the generated key from the Azure portal, and a resource is defined as `//[NAMESPACE].servicebus.windows.net/[EVENT_HUB_NAME]/publishers/[PUBLI SHER_NAME].tokenTimeToLive` is the TTL value of the token.

The Event Hub shared access policies can be managed in the Azure portal by selecting the Event Hub namespace, choosing the relevant Event Hub, and selecting the **Shared access policies** link.

```
SETTINGS

  🔑   Shared access policies
```

Event Hub streaming and partitions

The key technology that provides this high throughput is streaming using a partitioned consumer pattern. This pattern provides a mechanism where each consumer only reads a specific subset or partition of the message stream.

This differs from more traditional messaging solutions, such as Azure Queues and Azure Topics, which use a competing consumer model. In these solutions, if too many consumers target the same queue, it results in resource contention and scalability issues.

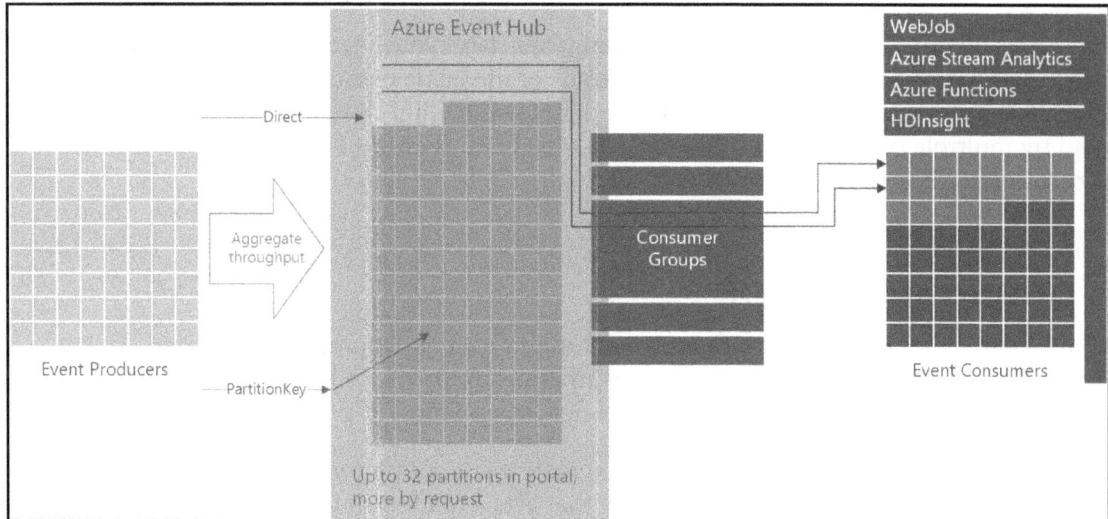

Messages sent to Event Hubs can be sent without setting a partition, in which case load is distributed evenly across the instance, or it can be forced to target specific partitions using a partition key. New messages are added at the end of the stream in the order in which they arrive. Each partition operates independently of other partitions and may have different growth rates and retention polices.

A good reason to use a partition key is that it ensures that messages are processed by the same downstream service. Although the ordered delivery cannot be guaranteed, because it depends on when a message is received across the Internet, it does mean that the backend service can make judgements based on the knowledge that messages have come from the same source.

At the time of creating an Event Hub resource, you have the option to specify between 8 and 32 partitions. The chosen number of partitions should be based on the number of downstream parallel consumers. The 32 partition limit can be increased by contacting the Microsoft Azure Service Bus team.

> Event Hubs are not intended to act as a permanent data store. They can only persist messages for up to 7 days in contrast to Azure Service Bus Queues or Topics, which have no limit.

Messages do not get deleted from the stream after they have been read by a consumer. Instead, the consumer is required to keep track of the last message read using an index. The index is based on either a timestamp or an offset value. This allows a single stream to be read by multiple consumers instead of each consumer getting a copy of the message, as in Azure Service Bus Queues/Topics.

Consumer groups

While creating an Event Hub, a default consumer group is automatically created. This is how consumers read the messages. A consumer group provides isolation from other consumers and allows a grouping of consumers by function or partition load.

Multiple consumer groups can be set up to create a fan out pattern. When a consumer reads from a consumer group, it creates an offset that acts a marker in the stream so that if an error occurs, the consumer can restart from the previous offset. This checkpointing can be handled automatically, as is used by Azure Stream Analytics, or set manually when using an `EventProcessorHost` instance.

Each consumer group manages its own offset and reads all the partitions at its own pace. You can create a maximum of 20 consumer groups for the standard tier Event Hub.

Reading from an Event Hub

An `EventProcessorHost` is a managed SDK class that reads from an event stream that can be run in either an Azure WebJob or an Azure Cloud Service such as a **Worker Role**.

When consuming messages from Event Hub with code, it is important to understand how load is distributed across a group of event processors. When manually reading from an event stream the number of partitions within the Event Hub should be a multiple of the number of event processors. For example, if an Event Hub is created with 10 partitions to support the throughput requirements of the solution, the number of processors would need to be 1, 2, 5, or 10. This ensures optimal performance as each processor is responsible for the same number of partitions.

In this scenario, each processor will maintain its offset and will periodically checkpoint the stream to provide a last read event in the event of a failure.

For example, if using a WebJob, you would configure a binding as follows assuming the inbound message was defined by the class Payload, deserialization is handled by the host:

```
public static void Trigger(
                [EventHubTrigger("MyHubName")] Payload x,
                [EventHub("MyHubName")] out Payload y)
{
    //Do Work
}

public class Payload
{
        public int Counter { get; set; }
}
```

When using a platform service such as Azure Stream Analytics for complex event processing, offsetting and checkpointing are handled by the service and the Event Hub stream merely needs to be assigned as an input to the Azure Stream Analytics job.

Other platform services support this automatic checkpointing and can be used as required. For example, if events need to be processed using some business logic rather than queried in a complex event processing solution, Azure Functions can be used.

Name your function

ProcessEventHub

Configure

Azure Event Hub trigger (myEventHubMessage)

Event Hub name ❶

telemetrydata

Event Hub connection ❶

motoralerts   ∨   *new*

Create

When using an Azure Function, the connection needs to be created or chosen. The connection string used needs to be the string for the event hub namespace and not the event hub instance itself. Once configured, clicking on **Create** brings up the development surface.

Replaying of messages

One of the benefits of the partition and checkpoint processes in Event Hubs is that you can replay messages for any period of time up to 7 days after they were first added to the event stream. This is achieved by changing the offset of the consumer to any point in the stream. When the connection is made, the reader will start processing the messages again from the checkpoint forward.

Since checkpoints are managed by the consumer in order to commit the current index position within a consumer group, there is a mechanism of marking events as being completed by downstream applications. When a consumer disconnects and reconnects at a later time, it will start to read from the last checkpoint. Reading before the checkpoint is still possible by providing a lower offset from the current checkpoint.

Poisoned messages

With Event Hubs, it is up to the receiver to handle invalid messages unlike Azure Service Bus Queues/Topics where messages can be rejected by placing them on the dead-letter queue, and can then be processed by another processor.

If you move the receiver index back before an invalid message, you will need to handle the corrupted message again.

Connecting to Event Hubs

You can connect to Event Hubs using HTTPS or **Advance Message Queuing Protocol** (**AMQP**). The main difference between the two protocols is that HTTPS provides short lived and low throughput messaging, while AMQP provides long lived and high throughput connections.

Event Hubs use AMQP 1.0, which maintains a session, is state-aware, and is by nature bidirectional. Due to this, creating the initial connection takes longer than HTTPS. However, once the negotiation process has completed, it is faster than HTTPS, which must obtain a new session after each request.

The main benefits of using AMQP are interoperability, reliability, and being based on open standards.

For further information about this protocol, see `http://www.amqp.org/`.

Introduction to Azure IoT Hubs

Connected things have been around for decades in the manufacturing, utilities, and resources industries and have solved the very real requirement of needing to know and understand how large-scale systems are operating; they have provided the **Operational Technology (OT)** to the more commonly talked about **Information Technology (IT)**.

An example of such a system is **supervisory control and data acquisition** (**SCADA**). Typically, a SCADA system consists of a large number of networked sensors reporting their data over proprietary protocols to a central resource that displays information and allow the decisions to be made. The data is stored in a large database known as a historian for ongoing analysis. These industrial control systems have existed for many years and are largely secure by default as they isolate the sensors and controls in a private network, for example, a process control network.

Because SCADA systems are largely proprietary or at least based on a few protocols with a low number of hardware and software providers, they are expensive to install and maintain.

With the invention of cloud computing and the dropping prices of microprocessors and sensors, it has become possible for everyone to be a device maker. The proliferation of things connected via the Internet has led to a true revolution where everything can communicate and real value can be derived for much lower cost. With devices such as the Raspberry Pi and a whole range of microprocessors, the development of Internet-connected solutions, more commonly named the Internet of Things, are in the hands of everyone.

However, with such opportunity comes inherent danger as companies develop and deliver solutions that are not secure by default and can lead to large scale compromise. There have been a number of cases where devices that are deployed as part of home automation have been used as bot networks to launch **distributed denial of service** (**DDoS**) attacks.

Given this, security in the Internet of Things has become a key battleground for future systems.

Microsoft Azure IoT Hub provides a cloud-based service for connected things. The background to the service and the way it has been developed can be found in a post by Clemens Vasters of Microsoft.

Service Assisted Communication for Connected Devices
https://blogs.msdn.microsoft.com/clemensv/2014/02/09/service-ass
isted-communication-for-connected-devices/

In the post, Clemens makes the case for strong security and trusted communication that is initiated by the device itself. This security is built in to the very fabric of the service to provide confidence and trust.

Before considering how to secure an IoT Hub, it is important to understand the basics and how to create one.

Getting started with IoT Hub

Azure IoT Hub is part of the Internet of Things set of platform services along with Event Hub, Notification Hub, Stream Analytics, and Machine Learning. It provides a mechanism for securely communicating from and to devices at scale using a range of open source protocols.

When you create an IoT Hub through the portal, the following items are important to understand:

- **Name**: This must be globally unique
- **Pricing and scaling tier**: This determines how many units you have available and the number of messages per day that the IoT Hub instance can scale to; you are allowed one free IoT Hub per subscription
- **IoT Hub units**: This is determined from the number of messages and devices that the IoT Hub is required to support
- **Device-to-cloud partitions**: These are similar to, but not fully functionally identical to Event Hub partitions

- **Enable Device Management**: At the time of writing this feature is still in PREVIEW

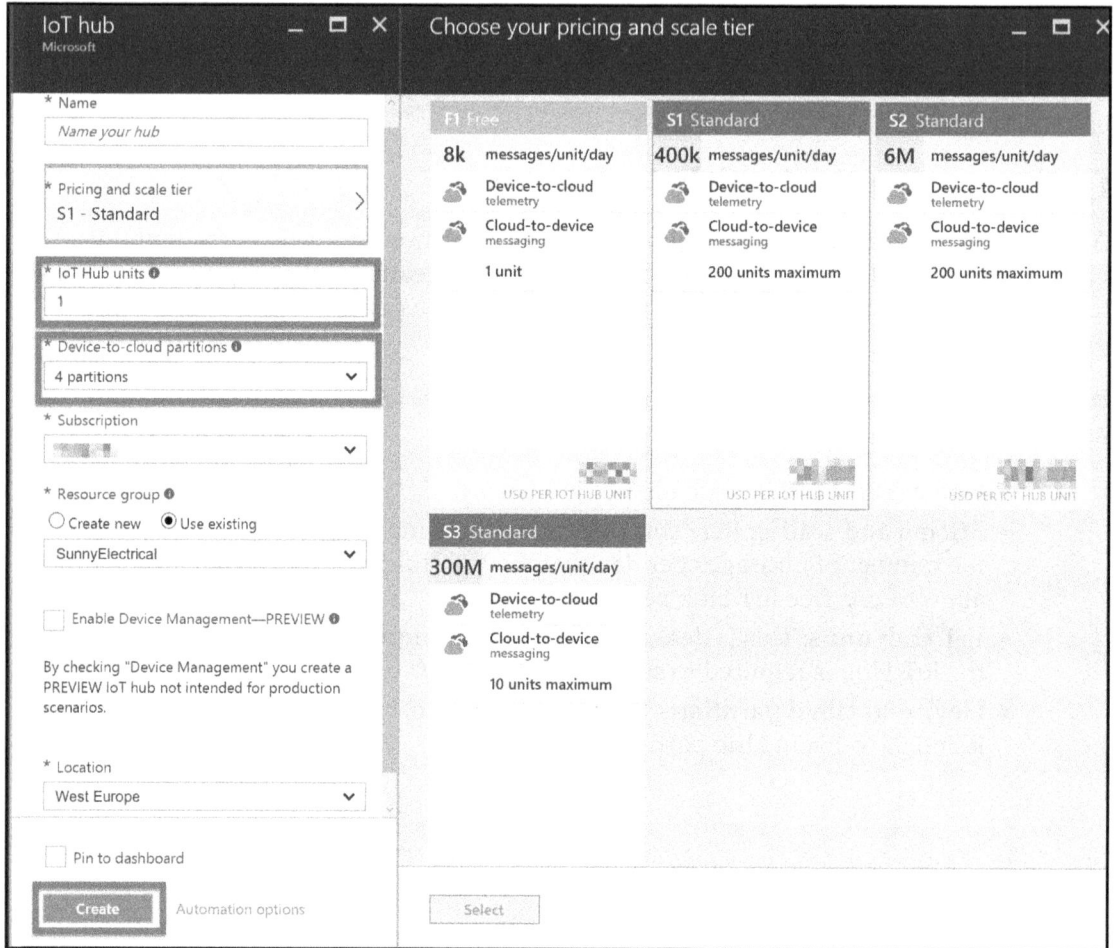

Once all information has been validated, clicking on **Create** creates the IoT Hub. Each Azure subscription can have a maximum of 10 IoT Hubs.

The pricing tier and IoT Hub units are used to determine the throughput and scale of IoT Hub, and it means that if not chosen correctly, your IoT Hub will throttle the messages being transmitted.

> For the pricing tier, the published throughput at the time of writing is as follows
> (see: `https://azure.microsoft.com/en-us/documentation/articles/iot-hub-scaling/`).

Tier	Sustained throughput	Sustained send rate
S1	Up to 1111 KB/minute per unit (1.5 GB/day/unit)	Average of 278 messages/minute per unit (400,000 messages/day per unit)
S2	Up to 16 MB/minute per unit (22.8 GB/day/unit)	Average of 4167 messages/minute per unit (6 million messages/day per unit)
S3	Up to 814 MB/minute per unit (1144.4 GB/day/unit)	Average of 208,333 messages/minute per unit (300 million messages/day per unit)

> For IoT Hub units, the throttling rules apply as follows
> (see: `https://azure.microsoft.com/en-us/documentation/articles/iot-hub-devguide-quotas-throttling/`).

Throttle	Per-hub value
Identity registry operations (create, retrieve, list, update, delete)	5000/min/unit (for S3) 100/min/unit (for S1 and S2).
Device connections	6000/sec/unit (for S3), 120/sec/unit (for S2), 12/sec/unit (for S1). Minimum of 100/sec. For example, two S1 units are 2*12 = 24/sec, but you have at least 100/sec across your units. With nine S1 units, you have 108/sec (9*12) across your units.
Device-to-cloud sends	6000/sec/unit (for S3), 120/sec/unit (for S2), 12/sec/unit (for S1). Minimum of 100/sec. For example, two S1 units are 2*12 = 24/sec, but you have at least 100/sec across your units. With nine S1 units, you have 108/sec (9*12) across your units.
Cloud-to-device sends	5000/min/unit (for S3), 100/min/unit (for S1 and S2).
Cloud-to-device receives	50000/min/unit (for S3), 1000/min/unit (for S1 and S2).

File upload operations	5000 file upload notifications/min/unit (for S3), 100 file upload notifications/min/unit (for S1 and S2). 10000 SAS URIs can be out for a storage account at one time. 10 SAS URIs/device can be out at one time.

After the creation of an IoT Hub, it can be scaled like a number of other platform services to ensure that it meets the need of the application.

> There is no autoscale facility so monitoring and alerts should be used to help understand the ongoing throughput and characteristics of the deployed solution.

To scale, you can either choose a new pricing tier or increase the number of IoT Hub units. Moving between the free tier and any of the paid tiers is not allowed.

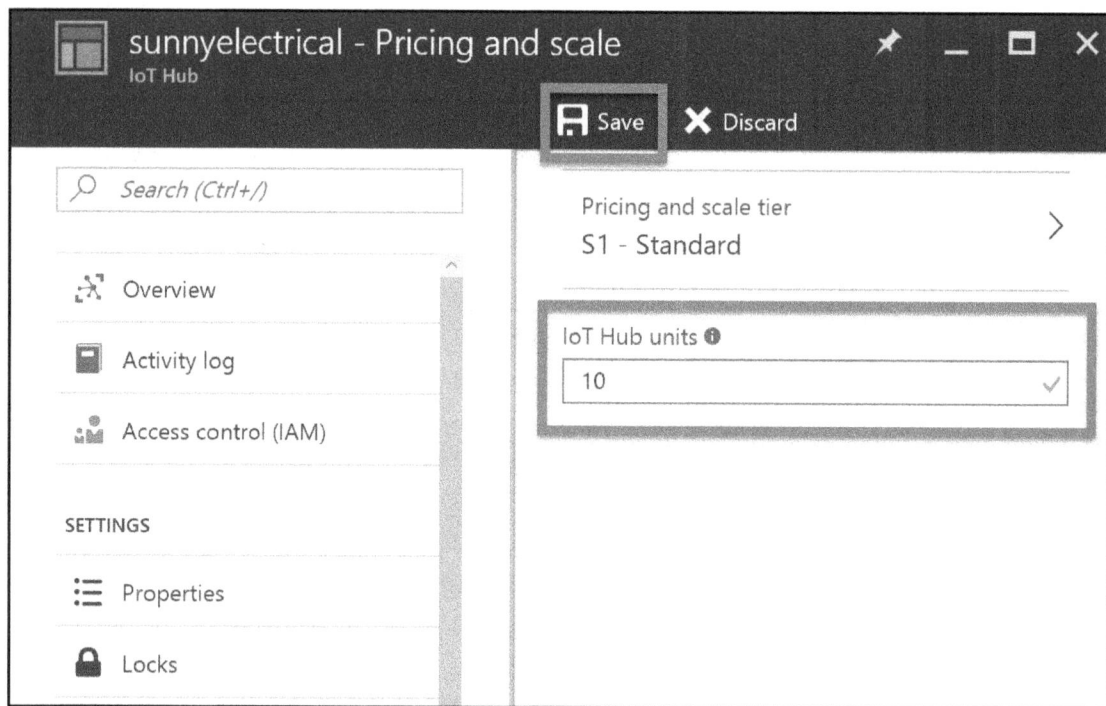

After making the necessary changes to either the pricing tier or the IoT Hub units, clicking on **Save** updates the configuration. IoT Hub units can either be increased or decreased to allow better tuning and cost management of the solution.

Communication mechanisms in a typical IoT solution need to support the following:

- **Telemetry**: Data ingestion from device to cloud at large scale
- **Query**: Device query to service backend for updates for example to configuration
- **Notification**: Cloud-to-device messaging to inform the device of environmental updates
- **Command**: control messages from service backend to device requiring confirmation

IoT Hub supports full bidirectional messaging between devices and cloud services, and this is reflected throughout the IoT Hub configuration.

When a device is registered with IoT Hub (see later in the chapter for details), message stores for both messages from devices and messages to devices are created; these message stores act like a mailbox to which messages are delivered and retrieved. To understand these processes, it is important to understand the following terms used within the portal and documentation that refer to this communication:

- **Cloud-to-device**: This is also referred to as C2D; this represents messages that are sent from backend services that are bound for a specific device. This service could be any compute resource
- **Device-to-cloud**: This is also referred to as D2C; this represents messages that are sent from an individual device that need to be processed by a backend service

IoT Hub has its roots in Event Hub, and this can be seen when looking at the**Messaging** configuration for an instance. The **Messaging** configuration is split across **Cloud-to-device** and **Device-to-cloud** settings.

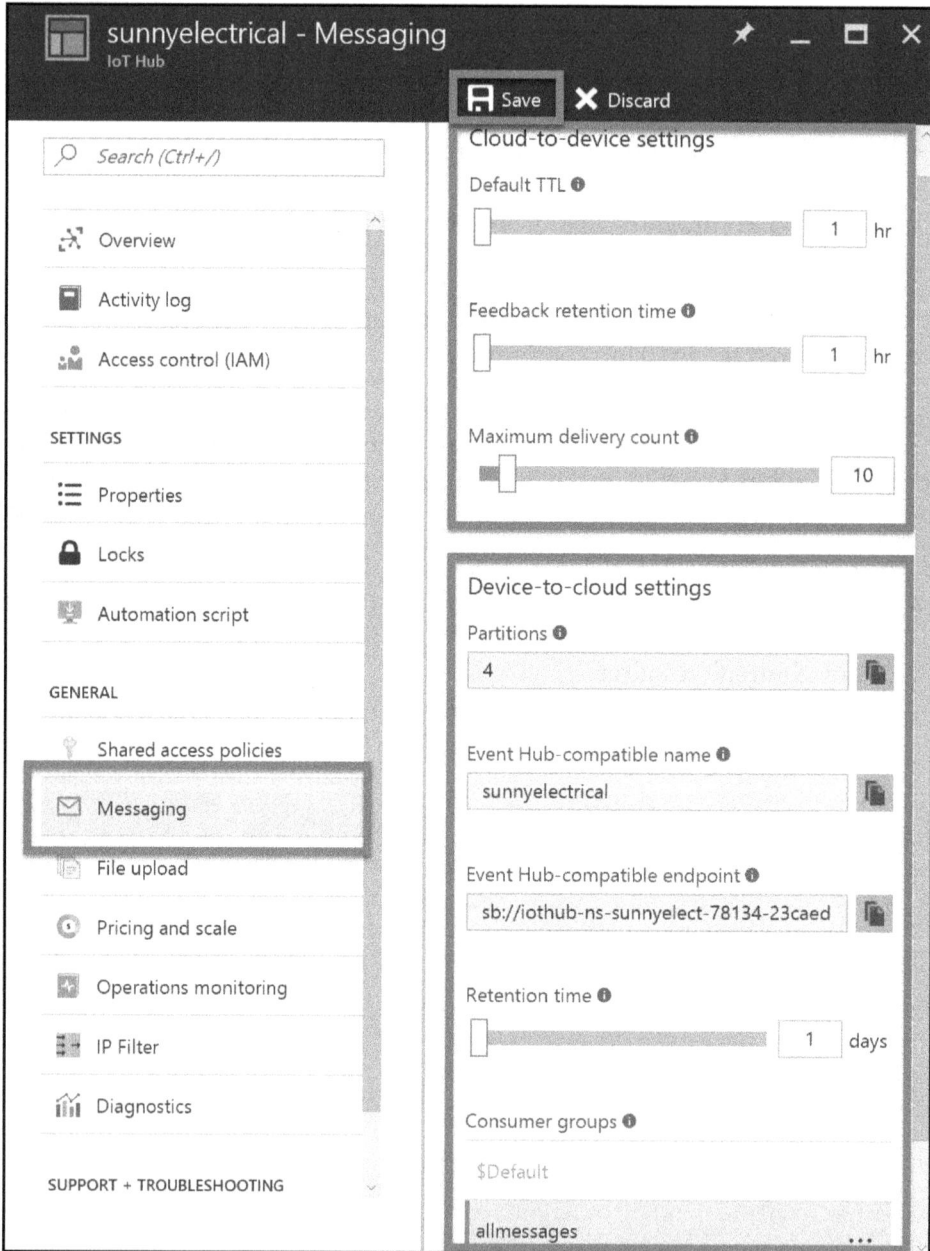

In the **Cloud-to-device setting** section, you can configure the following:

- **Default TTL**: This defines how long to retain messages for devices to consume before they are expired.
- **Feedback retention time**: When a message is sent to a device, an acknowledgement should be sent. This setting defines how long to retain these feedback messages in IoT Hub.
- **Maximum delivery count**: This defines how many times IoT Hub will attempt to deliver a message to a device.
- **Partitions**: This is read only and is set when the IoT Hub is created. This is similar in concept to partitions in Event Hub except for messages in IoT Hub you cannot set a partition key, so messages are distributed evenly across the partitions.
- **Event Hub-compatible name**: This shows the name of the Event Hub endpoint that can be used to consume device-to-cloud messages using, for example, Azure Functions.
- **Event Hub-compatible endpoint**: This shows the endpoint connection string for the Event Hub that is part of the instance.
- **Retention time**: This defines how long to retain device-to-cloud messages before they are expired.
- **Consumer groups**: Like Event Hub, this shows all consumer groups that are configured for the IoT Hub for message consumption; consumer groups in IoT Hub are functionally equivalent to those in Event Hub.

To support the rapid development of IoT Hub solution, there are SDKs for several languages.

> All the SDKs are open source and available for downloading;
> see: `https://github.com/Azure/azure-iot-sdks`.

At the time of writing, there are managed SDKs for C#, Java, JavaScript (that is, Node.JS), Python, and C. The SDKs are built on top of cross-platform C code that can be compiled and built on many other systems, such as microprocessors or simple devices, giving the broadest range of potential devices able to communicate with IoT Hub.

In addition to the managed SDKs, it is also possible to interact with IoT Hub through a set of HTTP APIs. These APIs allow control of many aspects of IoT Hub and devices and are available for:

- **Device identities**: These allow interaction with the device identity registry to create, delete, and manage devices in the IoT Hub
- **Resource provider**: This allows interaction with the resource management provider for an IoT Hub to allow creation, deletion, and the general management of the IoT Hub
- **Device messaging**: This allows messages to be sent to and received from the IoT Hub such as cloud-to-device or device-to-cloud

> For more information on the HTTP APIs and their use,
> see: `https://msdn.microsoft.com/library/mt548492.aspx`.

By providing programmatic access via HTTP/HTTPS, most aspects of both IoT Hub and device management and IoT Hub messaging can be handled over the Internet or by devices or services capable enough to support an HTTP protocol stack. See Endpoints later in this chapter.

Differences between Event Hub and IoT Hub

Event Hub and IoT Hub share a lot of similarities, and indeed the underlying infrastructure for IoT Hub is based on Event Hub.

However, it is important to understand the differences, so the correct choice can be made when required.

Area	IoT Hubs	Event Hubs
Communication patterns	Enables device-to-cloud and cloud-to-device messaging.	Only enables event ingress (usually considered for device-to-cloud scenarios).

Device protocol support	Supports MQTT, AMQP, AMQP over WebSockets, and HTTP/1. Additionally, IoT Hub works with the Azure IoT Protocol Gateway, a customizable protocol gateway implementation to support custom protocols.	Supports AMQP, AMQP over WebSockets, and HTTP/1.
Security	Provides per-device identity and revocable access control. See the *Security* section of the IoT Hub developer guide.	Provides Event Hubs-wide shared access policies, with limited revocation support through publisher's policies.
Operations monitoring	Enables IoT solutions to subscribe to a rich set of device identity management and connectivity events such as individual device authentication errors, throttling, and bad format exceptions.	Exposes only aggregate metrics.
Scale	Is optimized to support millions of simultaneously connected devices.	Can support a more limited number of simultaneous connections-up to 5,000 AMQP connections, as per Azure Service Bus quotas. On the other hand, Event Hubs enable you to specify the partition for each message sent.
Device SDKs	Provides device SDKs for a large variety of platforms and languages.	Is supported on .NET and C. Also, provides AMQP and HTTP send interfaces.
File upload	Enables IoT solutions to upload files from devices to the cloud. Includes a file notification endpoint for workflow integration and an operations monitoring category for debugging support.	Uses a claim check pattern to manually request files from devices and provide devices with a storage key for the transaction.

For further details,
see: https://azure.microsoft.com/en-us/documentation/articles/iot-hub-compare-event-hubs/.

From the table, it can be seen that one of the key reasons to choose between the two hubs is whether or not your devices are capable of bidirectional communication. However, even if your devices are only able to transmit telemetry data, IoT Hub is still useful when protocol support and greater security are required.

Security in IoT Hub

The most important thing to consider when creating an IoT solution is security. If a solution is not secure and gets compromised, the consequences could be potentially fatal.

Azure IoT Hub has security built in from the ground up and provides several mechanisms to ensure that any data transmission is safe, and full device life cycle management can be implemented to ensure that quick action can be taken in the event of a compromise of a device.

The device identity registry

IoT Hub uses a device identity registry to provide per device authentication and access control. Using device-initiated access control, per-device security, and trusted peer-to-peer communication between the device and IoT Hub, the attack vector to compromise devices is reduced.

Of course, devices themselves can still be physically compromised, but having a device identity registry allows quick remedial action to be taken to remove access to the IoT Hub and any backend services in the event of a compromise taking place.

It is not possible to create devices through the Azure portal directly; they need to be created either in a tool or via code. We discuss two tools for the simple management of devices and IoT Hub later in the chapter, but to create via code, you can use the RegistryManager class in the SDK:

```
static RegistryManager registryManager;
static string connectionString = "[IOT-HUB-CONNECTION-STRING]";

static void Main(string[] args)
{
    registryManager =
    RegistryManager.CreateFromConnectionString(connectionString);
    AddDeviceAsync().Wait();
    Console.ReadLine();
}
```

```
static async Task AddDeviceAsync(string deviceId)
{
    Device device;
    try
    {
        device = await registryManager.AddDeviceAsync(new
Device(deviceId));
    }
    catch (DeviceAlreadyExistsException)
    {
        device = await registryManager.GetDeviceAsync(deviceId);
    }
    Console.WriteLine("Generated device key: {0}",
device.Authentication.SymmetricKey.PrimaryKey);
}
```

To provision large volumes of devices at once, it is possible to import information in bulk.

> For more information on bulk imports,
> see: https://azure.microsoft.com/en-us/documentation/articles/iot
> -hub-bulk-identity-mgmt/#import-devices-example-bulk-device-
> provisioning.

Once created or imported, devices and their basic configuration can be viewed through the portal by clicking on **Devices** on the main IoT Hub blade.

In the resulting blade, information can be added to the view by clicking on **Columns** and choosing which information you wish to display.

Choosing a device opens a new blade that contains information such as shared access keys used to create shared access signatures and a connection string defined for the shared access key. It is possible to enable or disable a device from this blade.

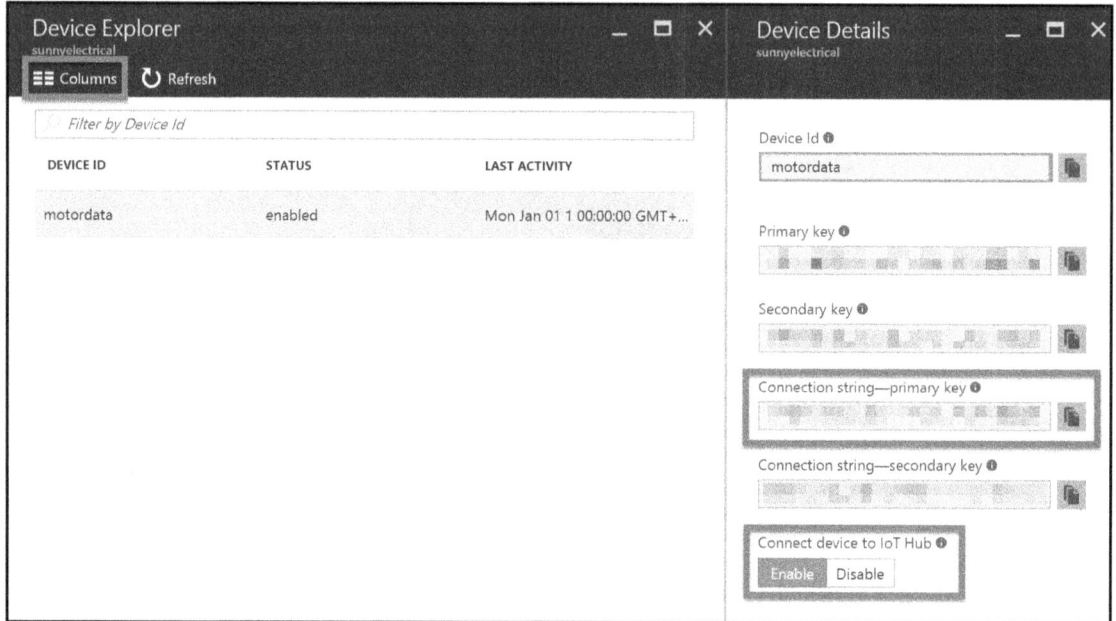

While the device information in the identity registry is important for the functionality of IoT Hub, in a real-world scenario, it is likely that further information is required to help define and administer a device, such as firmware version and commands that a device accepts. For this purpose, IoT Hub supports the concept of a **Device Twin**.

A device twin is a JSON document, stored, for example, in Azure DocumentDB, that contains additional metadata about a device that allows devices and backend services to synchronize device configurations, or it can be used to understand the state of any long-running operations that a device is reporting on. This metadata can include the following:

- Manufacturer information
- Firmware version
- Capabilities
- Valid commands

Device twins provide a mechanism to maintain the configuration state of a device using reported properties and desired properties:

- **Reported properties**: These are sent by devices to allow a service backend to query the current state of the device
- **Desired properties**: These are set by the service backend to allow configuration state change with the devices and can be used to notify a device of a state change in real time

Using device twins is an optimal way to manage device configuration, especially when physical access to the device is either limited or unavailable. By having a device *call home* to update itself either on a frequency or on restart ensures the state of the device is correct for the current operating scenario.

Shared access policies

IoT Hub supports the concept of **shared access policies** that are similar to the security within Event Hub. These policies can be used to create a **ature** (**SAS**shared access signature (SAS) that can be used for device-to-cloud and cloud-to-device communication.

When an SAS token is created, the time for which it is valid has to be provided. Creating timebound tokens for secure access reduces the attack vector for compromised devices and enhance the overall security of the solution.

When created, an IoT Hub has the following default policies:

- **iothubowner**: This has full permission to the IoT Hub
- **service**: This has permission for backend service components to send cloud-to-device messages
- **device**: This has permission for device to send device-to-cloud messages
- **registryRead**: This has permission to read the device identity registry
- **registryReadWrite**: This has permission to read and write to the device identity registry

These policies cover the operations that are possible in an instance, but it is possible to create new policies by clicking on the **Add** button on the **Shared access policies** page and choosing which permissions apply.

With this approach, it is possible to create boundaries between operations and between different parts of a more complex solution.

In the event of a compromise, it is important to maintain a strict security protocol.

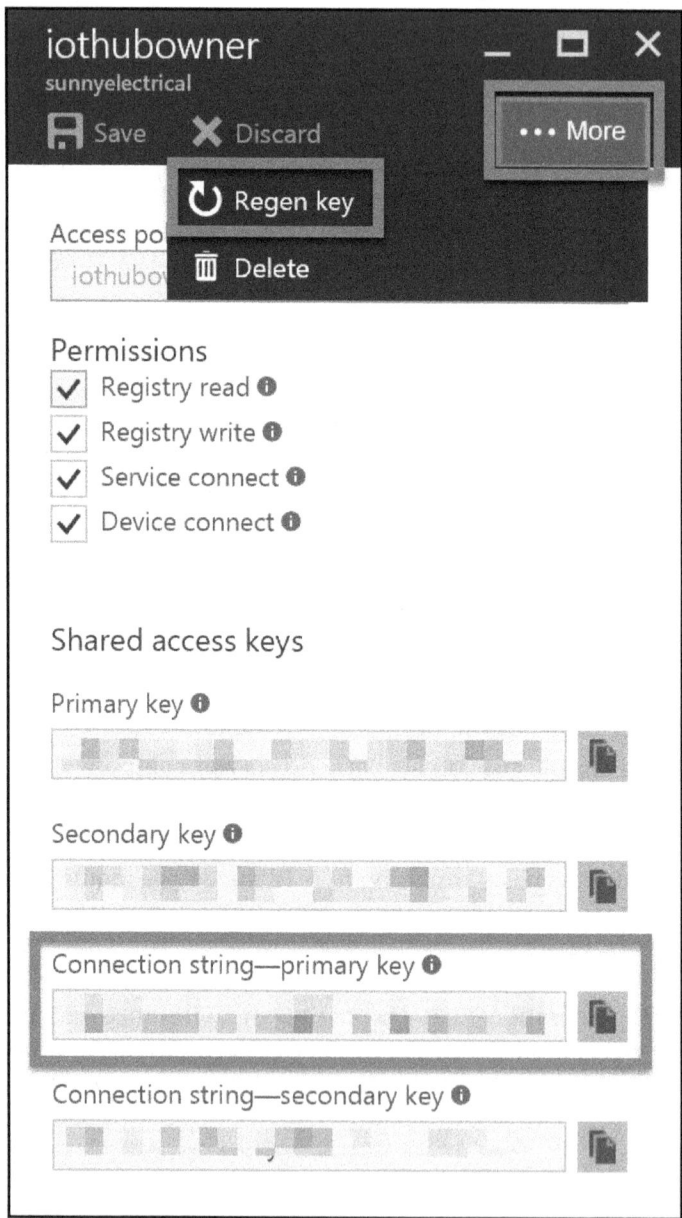

It is possible to regenerate the keys that are used for each policy, by clicking on **More** and then **Regen key**, to ensure that any device currently using it to sign SAS tokens can no longer connect without an update to the key. The connection string for a policy can be copied from the appropriate connection string text.

Shared access signatures

Shared access policies define the operations that are allowed by parts of an IoT solution, but shared access signatures should normally be used to perform the required operation.

Using SAS tokens adds an additional level of abstraction to the security protocol and ensures that keys are not sent across the wire.

SAS tokens are generated based on the device URI information, an expiry time, a cryptographic signature based on the device URI and expiry time, and a shared access policy name.

Because the token is based on an expiry time and shared access policy that defines the scope of access to IoT Hub, if a device connection string is obtained, the token can only be used for the time-period for which it is valid.

When using the managed SDKs, the creation of the SAS token is handled automatically at the time of the client connection.

X.509 certificates

If devices are capable of supporting full cryptographic certificate exchange, the security can be further enhanced through the use of X.509 certificates.

For IoT Hub, certificates can be obtained from a trusted certificate authority or self-signed. To create a self-signed certificate, you can use the `New-SelfSignedCertificate` PowerShell command.

IP filtering

The final part of the security that is supported by IoT Hub is the use of IP filtering.

IP filtering allows the creation of white lists (allowed devices or services) and black lists (denied devices or service) to further lock down and enhance the security.

IP filtering is applied by clicking on the **Add** button.

| ➕ Add | ↩ Undo | 🗑 Delete | 💾 Save |

If the table is empty or no rule matches, the connection is accepted. Rules are applied in order: the first matching rule decides the action. To change the order of the IP filter rules, hover over the row to drag and drop to the desired location in the grid

	IP FILTER RULE NAME	ACTION	IPV4 ADDRESS RANGE
	Non-company	Reject	10.10.0.0/24

An IP address range is defined in CIDR format and the range is either allowed or rejected.

> For more information on this key part of IoT Hub,
> see: https://azure.microsoft.com/en-us/documentation/articles/iot
> -hub-devguide-security/.

Monitoring your IoT Hub

A key part of any robust enterprise solution is the ability to look inside and understand the state of the running solution at any time. Monitoring provides this mechanism, and IoT Hub supports monitoring of many different parts of the solution.

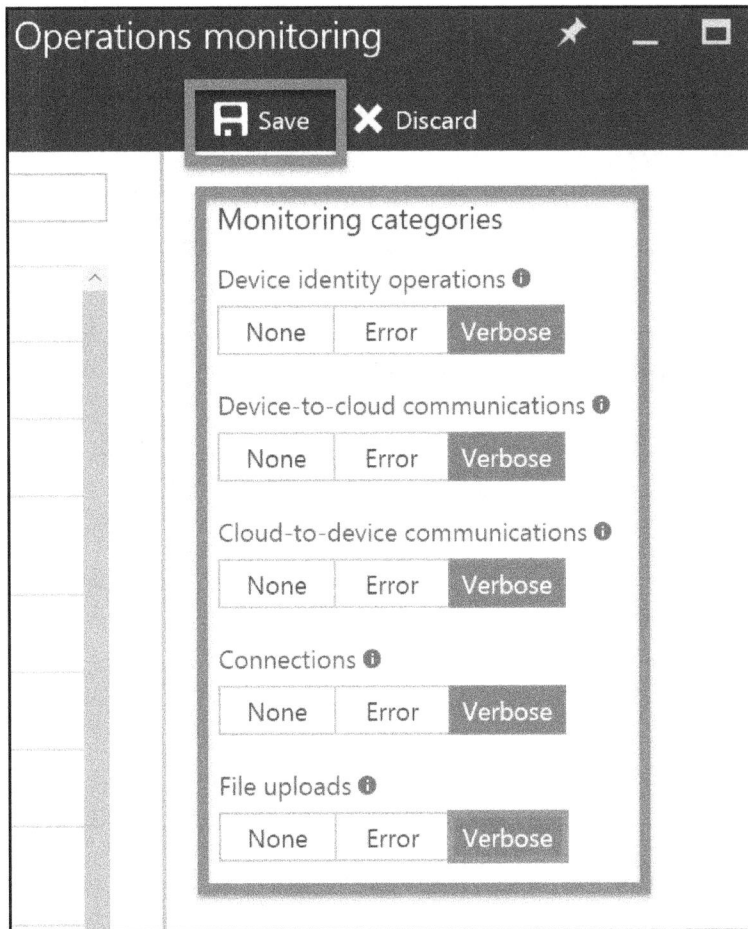

Monitoring events are generated for many operations in IoT Hub and should be configured to allow a fuller understanding of the health of a solution; error conditions should be monitored for communications including uploads, and further operational monitoring of connections could provide insight in to potential solution compromise.

Communicating with IoT Hub

Device communications in an Internet of Things solution needs to support more than just a telemetry channel as supported by Event Hubs. As mentioned previously, IoT solutions need to support four modes of communication: telemetry, query, notification, and command.

To facilitate this communication, it is important to understand how to build solutions that provide device-to-cloud and cloud-to-device messaging.

D2C messaging

Messages are sent from devices to IoT Hub to provide telemetry or to query a service backend or device twin. Sending messages can be done in several languages, including NodeJS, Python, C#, and C.

To send a message using the managed SDK for C#, a Nuget package needs to be installed, which contains the code for the SDK along with dependencies required for transport and security.

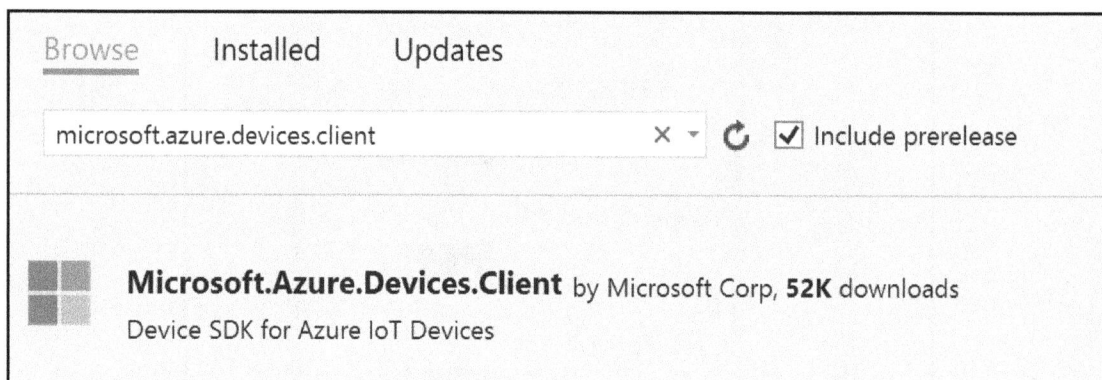

Browse	Installed	Updates

microsoft.azure.devices.client   × ▾   ↻   ☑ Include prerelease

Microsoft.Azure.Devices.Client by Microsoft Corp, **52K** downloads
Device SDK for Azure IoT Devices

Once installed, using the SDK to send a message is simple. First, you need to create a `DeviceClient` object and provide a connection string. The SDK takes care of generating a SAS token and uses the device connect shared access policy; the connection string should be the string for the specific device:

```
static DeviceClient deviceClient;
static string connectionString = "[DEVICE-CONNECTION-STRING]";

static void Main(string[] args)
{
    deviceClient =
    DeviceClient.CreateFromConnectionString(connectionString);
    while (true)
    {
        SendToIoTHub();
        Thread.Sleep(2000);
    }
}
```

```
static async void SendToIoTHub()
{
    Var myObject = new MyObject();
    var messageString = JsonConvert.SerializeObject(myObject);
    var message = new Message(Encoding.UTF8.GetBytes(messageString));
    await client.SendEventAsync(message);
    Console.WriteLine($"Sent message: {messageString}");
}
```

This code can be used to create a simulated device that sends messages every 2 seconds based on an object of type `MyObject()`.

Only a few lines of code are required to start sending messages to IoT Hub, and this makes it simple to start creating the infrastructure required for an entire solution while development and build of a device is ongoing.

C2D messaging

Once messages have been sent to IoT Hub, they can be processed using several services. However, once processed, it may be necessary to send messages back to the device. These messages could be notifications that the device wishes to know about or commands that instruct the device to perform a function or update configuration.

If using the managed SDK for C#, there is a NuGet package that needs to be installed in to a Visual Studio project to start interacting with the `ServiceClient` class. It is this class that allows communication with the service endpoint of the IoT Hub.

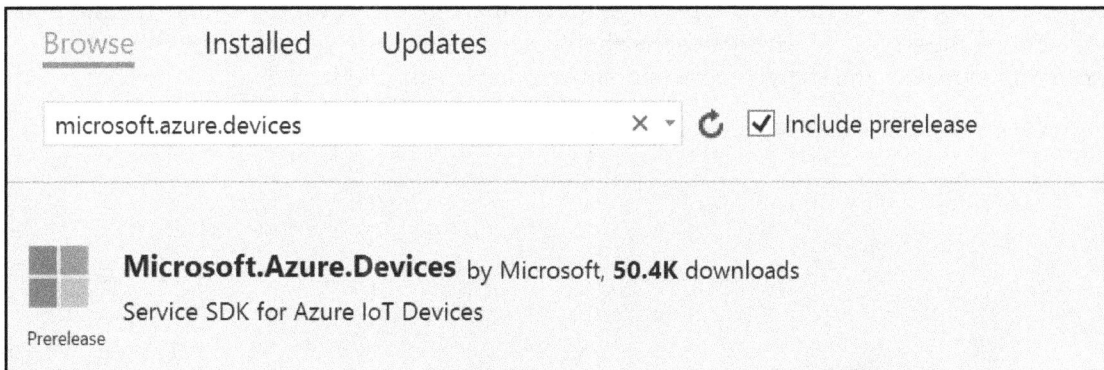

Browse	Installed	Updates

microsoft.azure.devices ✕ ▾ ↻ ☑ Include prerelease

Microsoft.Azure.Devices by Microsoft, **50.4K** downloads
Service SDK for Azure IoT Devices

Prerelease

Once installed, interacting with the service endpoint is as simple as D2C messaging:

```
static async void SendToIoTHub(object data)
{
    var messageString = JsonConvert.SerializeObject(data);
    var message = new Message(Encoding.UTF8.GetBytes(messageString));
    message.Ack = DeliveryAcknowledgement.Full;
    message.MessageId = Guid.NewGuid().ToString();

    var serviceClient = ServiceClient.CreateFromConnectionString("[IOT-HUB-
    SERVICE-POLICY-CONN-STRING");
    await serviceClient.SendAsync("[DeviceId]", message);
    await serviceClient.CloseAsync();
}
```

In this case, the `ServiceClient` class is created from a connection string that has the service connect policy associated with it. The outbound message has properties set for a `MessageId` and type of acknowledgement required from the device. In this case, `DeliveryAcknowledgement.Full` requests that the device sends an acknowledgement in the event of both success and failure of processing the message.

Receiving C2D messages

Once a message has been sent to IoT Hub from a service, it remains available for the device to pick up to account for scenarios when a device may only be occasionally connected.

To receive messages on a device, the `DeviceClient` class is used once again, and this requires installation of the NuGet package for the managed SDK for C#. Unlike the method for sending messages, which creates the shared access signature as part of the call, when receiving messages the shared access signature must be supplied:

```
static DeviceClient deviceClient;

static void Main(string[] args)
{
    deviceClient =
    DeviceClient.CreateFromConnectionString("[DEVICE-CONN-STRING-INCLUDING-
    SAS-TOKEN]");

    ReceiveIoTHub();
    Console.ReadLine();
}
private static async void ReceiveIoTHub()
{
    while (true)
```

```
    {
        Message receivedMessage = await deviceClient.ReceiveAsync();
        if (receivedMessage == null) continue;

    Console.WriteLine("\nReceiving message");
            var message =
            Encoding.UTF8.GetString(receivedMessage.GetBytes());
    Console.WriteLine("Message: {0}", message);

        await deviceClient.CompleteAsync(receivedMessage);
    }
 }
```

In this code, there is a loop that keeps polling the IoT Hub device endpoint for messages. Upon receiving a message, it can be processed as appropriate. Once it has been processed, `CompleteAsync` is called, which delivers the notification back to IoT Hub.

Again, the amount of code required to receive messages in IoT Hub when using one of the managed SDKs is very low and provides a quick route to build out a solution.

Processing D2C messages

There are several Azure platform services capable of processing a stream of data from IoT Hub, for example, Stream Analytics, Azure Functions, and HDInsight. Some of the decisions required when processing telemetry data is about the immediacy of insight.

Capturing data delivers no intrinsic value, but processing the data either in real time, sometimes named the **Hot Path**, or in batch processing, sometimes named the **Cold Path**, can deliver deep insight into a process or the potential outcome of a set of separate events. This data can be combined with data from other sources to build models and derive deep learning through services such as **Azure Machine Learning**.

Using Azure platform services allows a solution to be built out of building block services that are designed to be stitched together. This provides a mechanism to quickly build and prototype and solution to find out early if it can deliver real business value.

> For more information on cold and hot path processing of data, look at **Lambda Architecture** at: `https://www.mapr.com/developercentral/lambda-architecture`.

Uploading files

Messaging in the connected world can consist of large volumes of small messages or equally a large batch of messages or information stored within an external file.

To facilitate this latter use case, IoT Hub supports uploading of files in a way that is fully managed by the service.

Configuring the file upload process is performed through the **File upload** blade in the **IoT Hub** settings. Uploading files requires a storage account that acts as the landing place for files that are uploaded by the device. When configuring the process, the storage account is chosen along with whether you wish to receive notifications. Notifications can be consumed from the operational monitoring endpoint of the IoT Hub by Azure Stream Analytics in the same way as other operational monitoring information.

The file upload consists of three steps:

- Obtain a file URL that contains an SAS token valid for the time specified; the Azure Storage SDK uses this as the security authentication for the upload process
- Upload a file to the URI specified in the first step using the Azure Storage SDK
- Send a notification back to IoT Hub indicating success or failure of the file upload

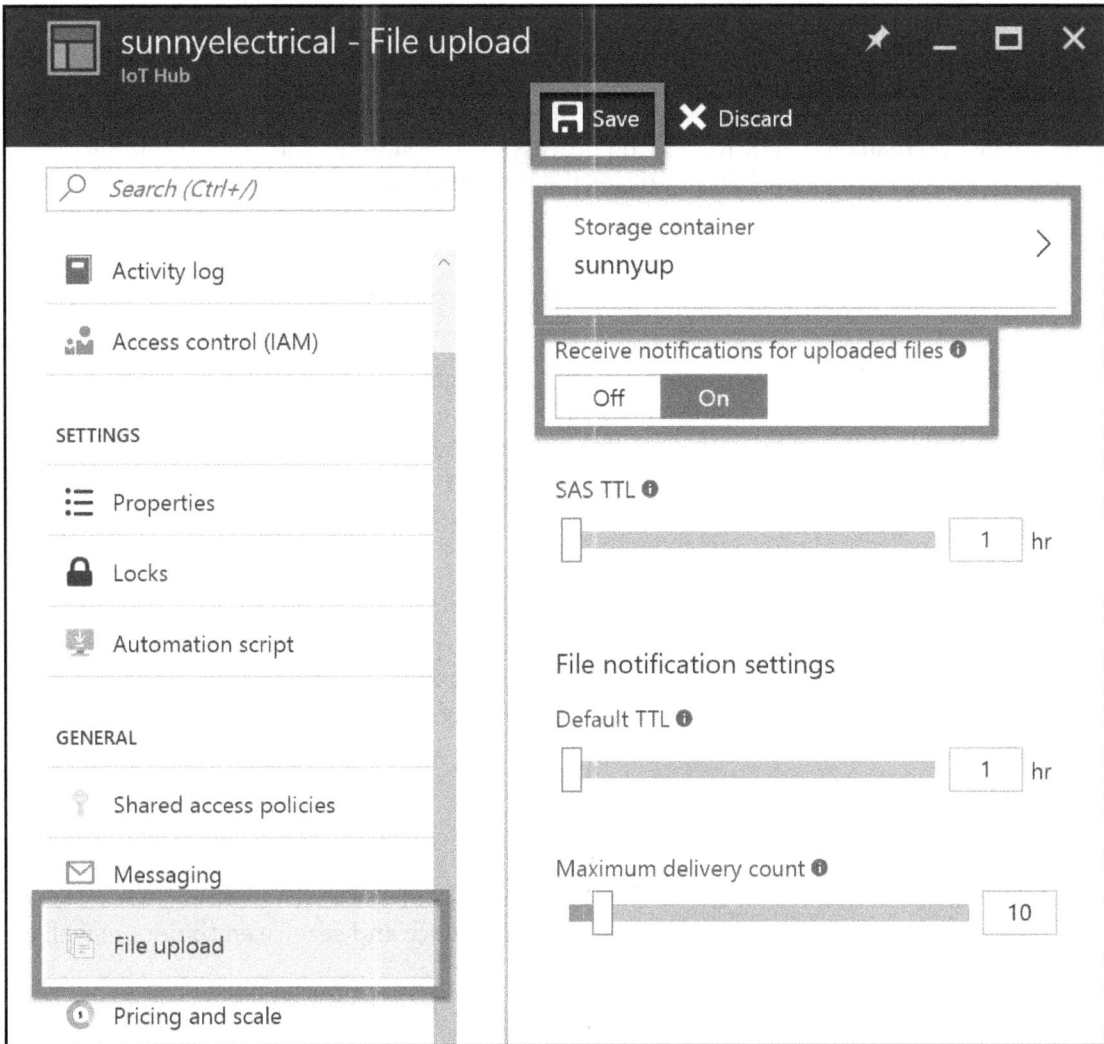

There are several other settings that relate to how long an SAS token is valid for and how long to keep notifications, along with the maximum number of times a notification is attempted to be delivered.

When using the managed SDK for C#, the process for uploading a file is simple and it consists of a single call as the SDK manages the three processes as an atomic unit of work:

```
using (var fs = new FileStream("MyFile.csv", FileMode.Open))
{
    await client.UploadToBlobAsync("MyFile.csv", fs);
}
```

Using the file upload process is a great way for a field gateway to gather incoming messages from many devices and then bulk upload on a schedule for further processing. The further processing can be performed by several other Azure services, for example, Azure Functions has a blob trigger that executes when new files arrive in blob storage.

IoT Hub tools

Like most Azure platform services, a lot of tasks can be performed within the Azure portal, such as changing scale and updating messaging information, but many tasks need to be performed outside the portal, such as device registration and shared access signature generation.

Device Explorer

One of the most useful tools for those starting with IoT Hub is Device Explorer. This provides an easy tool to use to interact directly with device and service endpoints as well as the device identity registry.

Once the IoT connection string has been entered on the **Configuration** tab and **Update** clicked, the application provides a mechanism to create, update, or delete devices, and to generate SAS tokens based on a configurable TTL. For devices in the **Management** tab, right-clicking opens a context menu that allows you to copy the device connection string.

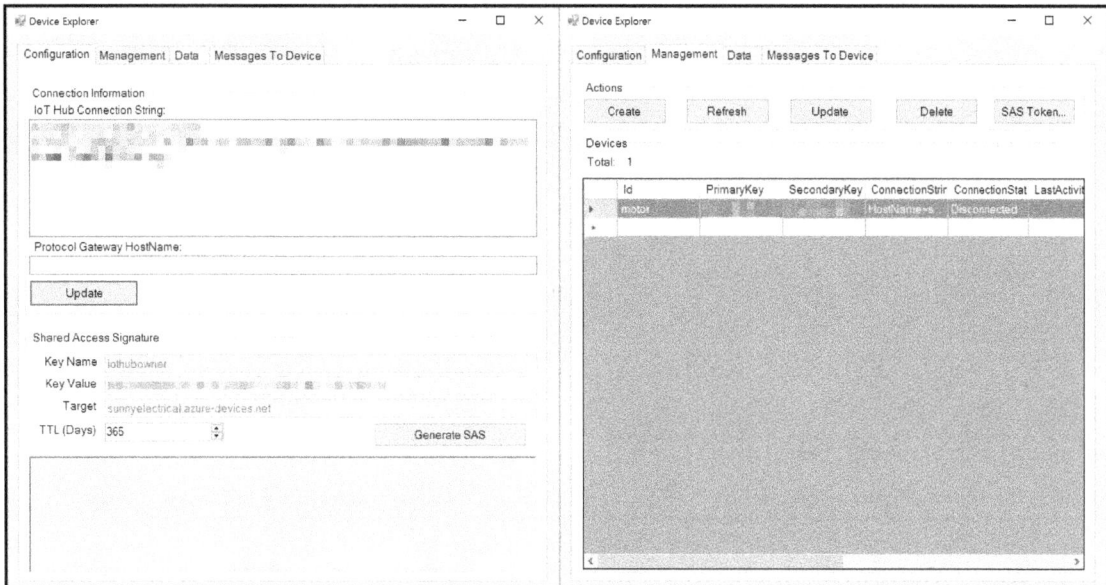

The **Data** and **Messages To Device** tabs allows the application to act as a message consumer service backend and a service backend sending messages to a device.

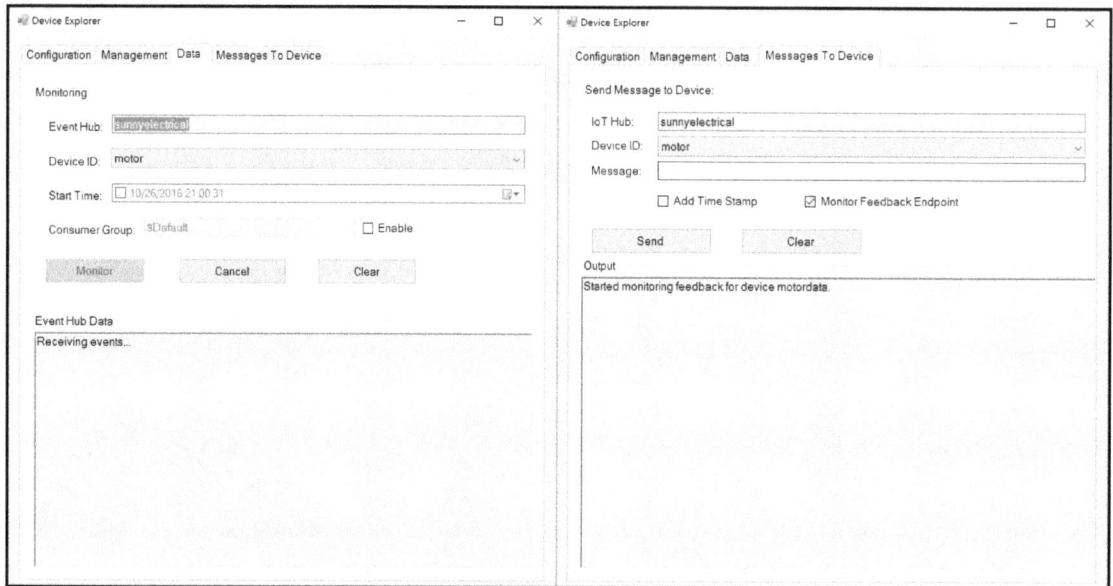

The **Data** tab is useful when checking the content of the data being sent by the chosen device and provides a mechanism to check the connectivity of the device to the IoT Hub. Likewise, the **Messages To Device** tab provides a mechanism to check the connectivity between the outbound message communication between an IoT Hub backend service and a device.

> For more information on Device Explorer,
> see: https://github.com/Azure/azure-iot-sdks/tree/master/tools/De
> viceExplorer.

iothub-explorer

For cross-platform support, there is a Node.js application that allows some management of IoT Hub and device identities.

With Node.js installed, iothub-explorer can be installed from the command prompt or terminal window with the following command:

```
npm install -g iothub-explorer@latest
```

Once installed, calling the application with the `--help` command switch shows all the commands and their functionality.

Using a PowerShell command prompt is convenient as it allows variables to be assigned for use within commands. For example, issuing the following command assigns the connection string to a variable that can then be used during a session:

```
$conn = [YOUR CONNECTION STRING]
```

Once stored, commands can be issued as necessary. Before performing any functions, a connection must be established with the IoT Hub instance:

```
iothub-explorer login $conn
```

Once logged in, commands can then be issued as normal without the need to pass in a connection string. For example, to list the `deviceId` and `connectionState` of all devices, you would issue the following:

```
iothub-explorer list --display="deviceId, connectionState"
```

The one exception to the rule for not having to supply a connection string once logged in is if you wish to monitor events for a specific device:

```
iothub-explorer $conn monitor-events [deviceId]
```

The iothub-explorer is a good tool if you are used to using a command line when working with resources. Although it is not capable of doing everything, it is a handy tool to have available.

> For more information on iothub-explorer and to contribute to its development, see: `https://github.com/azure/iothub-explorer`.

IoT gateways

In the Internet of Things, devices range in capability from simple sensors through to fully capable computers and from using proprietary protocols through to open standards.

Due to this, it is often necessary to deploy a gateway in the field to either do the actual communication to IoT Hub or to provide local compute resources.

IoT Hub protocol gateway

To overcome the issue when a device is unable to communicate using one of the IoT Hub-supported protocols, a protocol gateway must be used to act as a bridge between a device and IoT Hub.

Azure IoT Hub provides a sample protocol gateway that is open source. This gateway acts as a protocol translator and can run on capable devices that sit between deployed devices and IoT Hub or in a cloud service that is running in Microsoft Azure that can communicate with the devices.

The sample shows how to translate from MQTT. However, because MQTT is fully supported within IoT Hub, the sample is there as a means to show how to translate from a protocol that is available on low-powered and low capability devices.

A scenario would be simple sensors that are deployed and can communicate via protocols such as CoAP, which is a popular protocol on constrained devices, but for which no support currently exists within IoT Hub. In this case, a gateway could be deployed on a device in the field that can communicate with the devices via CoAP, and it could translate these messages to AMQP for delivery to IoT Hub.

> For more information on the IoT Hub Protocol Gateway, see
> `https://github.com/Azure/azure-iot-protocol-gateway/blob/master/README.md`.

IoT Hub gateway SDK

Another scenario where it is important to consider the deployment of a field gateway is when local computing resources are required to process messages before they are transmitted. This could include protocol translation, as possible with the IoT Hub protocol gateway, or could include more complex stream processing computing such as translation or data enrichment.

Having local compute resources also ensures that action can be taken by the gateway in the event of the Internet connection being unavailable.

Consider a scenario where a valve is reporting inlet pressure for a gas pipeline. In this scenario, imagine what the consequence would be if the only analysis of this data was performed in the cloud. It may be important to understand if the data is showing a trend that indicates the inlet pressure is increasing. In this case, it may be necessary to close the valve to protect equipment and life downstream of the valve. If the only analysis is done in the cloud and the connection is not available, damage to equipment or loss of life could occur. Having a gateway that is capable of making decision based on the streaming data becomes important in this case.

Fog Computing is the name given to local computing resources in this example and is increasingly important in the industrial and manufacturing sectors.

> For more information on the IoT Hub Gateway SDK,
> see: `https://github.com/azure/azure-iot-gateway-sdk`.

IoT suite

IoT Hub and the mechanism to create a system backend through analysis, processing, and decision making is a complex topic.

Microsoft Azure IoT suite (`https://azure.microsoft.com/en-us/suites/iot-suite/`) provides some sample solutions that can be used to gain an understanding of how the parts of the Microsoft IoT ecosystem can be used together.

They are full solutions that can be deployed in an Azure subscription for the purpose of testing, learning, and even if required production.

At the time of writing, there are two fully configured solutions.

- **Remote monitoring**: The solution provides a dashboard and can be used to provide the end-to-end monitoring of an IoT solution. With the solution, it is possible to provision devices that have a range of capabilities that then post their data to the dashboard. Devices can be simulated or real, and the solution allows the creation of rules and alerts, as well as the ability to send messages to the devices to update their configuration. It uses the concept of a **Device Twin** to store additional information about the devices in Azure DocumentDB. It is the IoT Suite solution with the widest level of service use within Azure and a good starting place to understand how to build out a full solution.
- **Predictive maintenance**: The solution uses Azure Machine Learning to predict the potential failure of aircraft engines based on a set of sample data. It is a good example of a truly large-scale industrial solution that uses and leverages an advanced analytics pipeline to predict an outcome.

> The solutions provision a lot of Azure resources using large-scale instances and therefore do incur a high cost when they are running. However, they can be downloaded from GitHub and tailored as required, both for provisioning and functionality.
> For more information,
> see: `https://azure.microsoft.com/en-us/documentation/articles/iot-suite-guidance-on-customizing-preconfigured-solutions/`.

Scenario – bringing it all together

In this scenario, Sunny Electricals manufactures industrial electric motors. To ensure that these motors are well maintained, Sunny Electricals has embedded piezo sensors near the bearing housing and temperature sensors in the stator windings. These sensors are then wired to a microcontroller that sends the telemetry data to an Azure IoT Hub every minute.

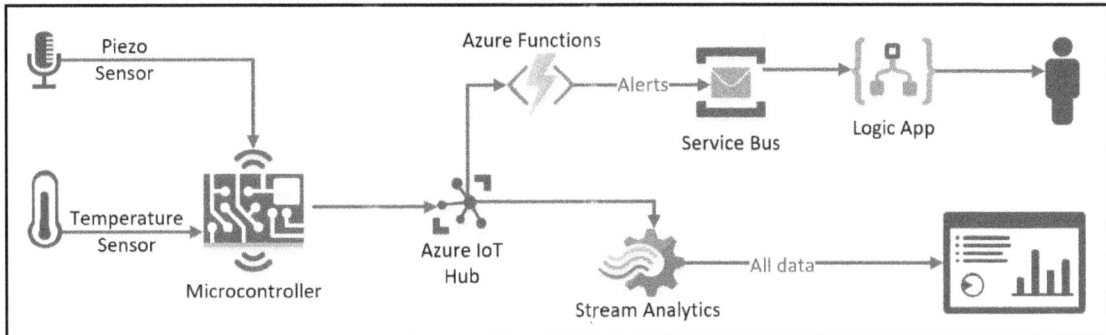

With this information, Sunny Electricals can tell their customers of possible bearing failure or if the motor is working under stressful loads.

For the scenario, the microcontroller and telemetry data are simulated and posted to a single device in IoT Hub named *motordata*.

Once received by IoT Hub, the telemetry data is processed by an Azure Stream Analytics job that pushes all data to a Power BI dashboard to show the current data in an easily consumable format. The data is also processed using an Azure Function that makes use of the Event Hub endpoint of the IoT Hub. This process checks for error conditions, such as high temperatures, and if encountered, posts an alert message to an Azure Service Bus queue. Messages on the Service Bus Queue are processed by a Logic App that sends an e-mail alerting a user of the condition.

The microprocessor simulation uses the C# SDK to send data to the IoT Hub. We create a new Console App project in Visual Studio and add the Nuget package required for device connectivity.

Once installed, a `DeviceClient` object is created, given the connection string required for our scenario IoT Hub:

```
static DeviceClient client;
static string connString = "[IOT-HUB-CONNECTION-STRING]";

static void Main(string[] args)
```

```
    {
        client = DeviceClient.CreateFromConnectionString(connString);
        while (true)
        {
            SendToIoTHub();
            Thread.Sleep(5000);
        }
    }
```

The `SendToIoTHub` method does the sending and calls another method to generate some random data:

```
static async void SendToIoTHub()
{
    var messageString = JsonConvert.SerializeObject(GenerateRandomEvent());

    var message = new Message(Encoding.UTF8.GetBytes(messageString));
    await client.SendEventAsync(message);
    Console.WriteLine($"Sent message: {messageString}");
}

static DeviceData GenerateRandomEvent()
{
    var rnd = new Random();
    var temp = 35.0 + rnd.NextDouble() * 6.0;
    var db = 10.0 + rnd.NextDouble() * 3.0;
    return new DeviceData
    {
            deviceId = "motor",
            eventTime = DateTime.UtcNow,
            temperature = temp,
            piezo = db
    };
}
```

The random number generator is used to create data points that provide values that are greater than the thresholds considered to be dangerous, in this case, a temperature sensor greater than 30 and a piezoelectric sensor reading greater than 12.

The `DeviceData` class is a simple class that is converted to JSON format for transmission.

The Azure Stream Analytics job simply passes through all data from the IoT Hub to a dashboard in Power BI for visualization:

```
SELECT * INTO [dashboard] FROM [telemetrydata]
```

In this case, `telemetrydata` is an input defined to read from the IoT Hub endpoint, and `dashboard` is a Power BI workspace where a report is created to show the live data.

The Azure Function reads from the Event Hub endpoint for the IoT Hub. To access this endpoint, the following format is required for the connection string, and it should use the information provided under **Messaging** blade of the IoT Hub settings:

```
Endpoint=[EVENT-HUB-CONNECTION];SharedAccessKeyName=[SERVICE-CONNECT-KEY-
NAME];SharedAccessKey=[MATCHING-KEY]
```

With the connection set, when telemetry data arrives each record triggers the function to process it. The processing checks for an error condition and if found, sends a message to a Service Bus Queue:

```
public static void Run(string myEventHubMessage, TraceWriter log)
{
    var connString = "[SB-QUEUE-ENDPOINT]";
    var queueName = "motoralerts";
    var client = QueueClient.CreateFromConnectionString(connString,
queueName);
    var msg = JsonConvert.DeserializeObject<DeviceData>(myEventHubMessage);

    var sendMsg = false;
    var outMsg = new DeviceAlert
    {
        deviceId = msg.deviceId,
        date = msg.eventTime.ToString()
    };

    // Test for alert condition and set sendMsg = true
    // <code removed for brevity>

    if (sendMsg)
    {
        var outString = JsonConvert.SerializeObject(outMsg);
        log.Info($"Service Bus Message: {outString}");
        var sbMsg = new BrokeredMessage(outMsg, new
DataContractJsonSerializer(typeof(DeviceAlert)));
        client.Send(sbMsg);
    }
}
```

There are two classes used to de-serialize the inbound message and serialize the outbound message:

```
public class DeviceData
{
    public string deviceId { get; set; }
    public DateTime eventTime { get; set; }
    public double temperature { get; set; }
    public double piezo { get; set; }
}

public class DeviceAlert
{
    public string deviceId { get; set; }
    public string alertType { get; set; }
    public string date { get; set; }
```

```
        public string value { get; set; }
}
```

The final part of the solution is a Logic App that reads messages from the Service Bus Queue and sends an e-mail containing the information about the alert using the content of the Service Bus message:

Once configured, the console application that is simulating the microcontroller and devices is started and posts the data to IoT Hub:

file:///C:/Users/Compe/onedrive/documents/visual studio 2015/Projects/SunnyMotor/SunnyMotor/bin/De... — □ ✕

Sent message: {"deviceId":"motor","eventTime":"2016-10-28T11:10:31.5616912Z","temperature":36.40
2185819764711,"piezo":10.404886910880398}
Sent message: {"deviceId":"motor","eventTime":"2016-10-28T11:10:36.7850115Z","temperature":38.64
6752615294773,"piezo":12.664020309999595}
Sent message: {"deviceId":"motor","eventTime":"2016-10-28T11:10:41.7863502Z","temperature":39.40
6178289282217,"piezo":12.943284160896802}
Sent message: {"deviceId":"motor","eventTime":"2016-10-28T11:10:46.787783Z","temperature":40.165
603963269668,"piezo":10.222548011794011}
Sent message: {"deviceId":"motor","eventTime":"2016-10-28T11:10:51.7888712Z","temperature":40.92
5029637257119,"piezo":10.501811862691218}
Sent message: {"deviceId":"motor","eventTime":"2016-10-28T11:10:56.790762Z","temperature":35.684
455311244562,"piezo":10.781075713588425}
Sent message: {"deviceId":"motor","eventTime":"2016-10-28T11:11:01.7927108Z","temperature":36.44
3880985232013,"piezo":11.060339564485634}
Sent message: {"deviceId":"motor","eventTime":"2016-10-28T11:11:06.7936706Z","temperature":37.20
3306659219464,"piezo":11.339603415382841}

The output of this is e-mails that contain the alert data.

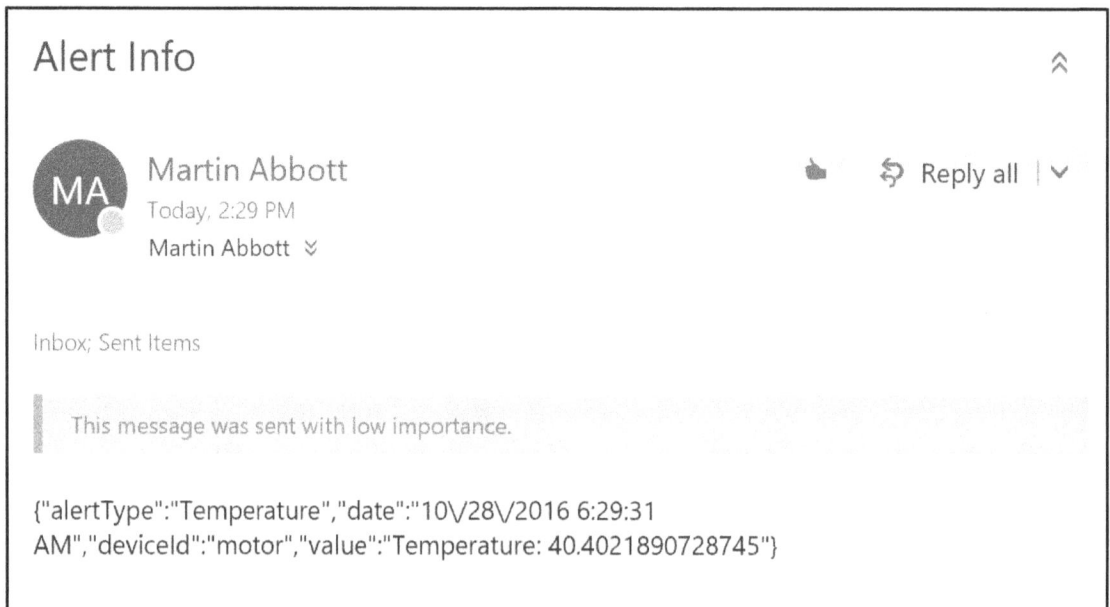

Alert Info ⌄⌄

MA

Martin Abbott
Today, 2:29 PM
Martin Abbott ⌄

👍 ⤺ Reply all | ⌄

Inbox; Sent Items

This message was sent with low importance.

{"alertType":"Temperature","date":"10\/28\/2016 6:29:31 AM","deviceId":"motor","value":"Temperature: 40.4021890728745"}

Finally, a Power BI dashboard displays the data stream being sent by Azure Stream Analytics to provide an easy-to-consume visualization of the data.

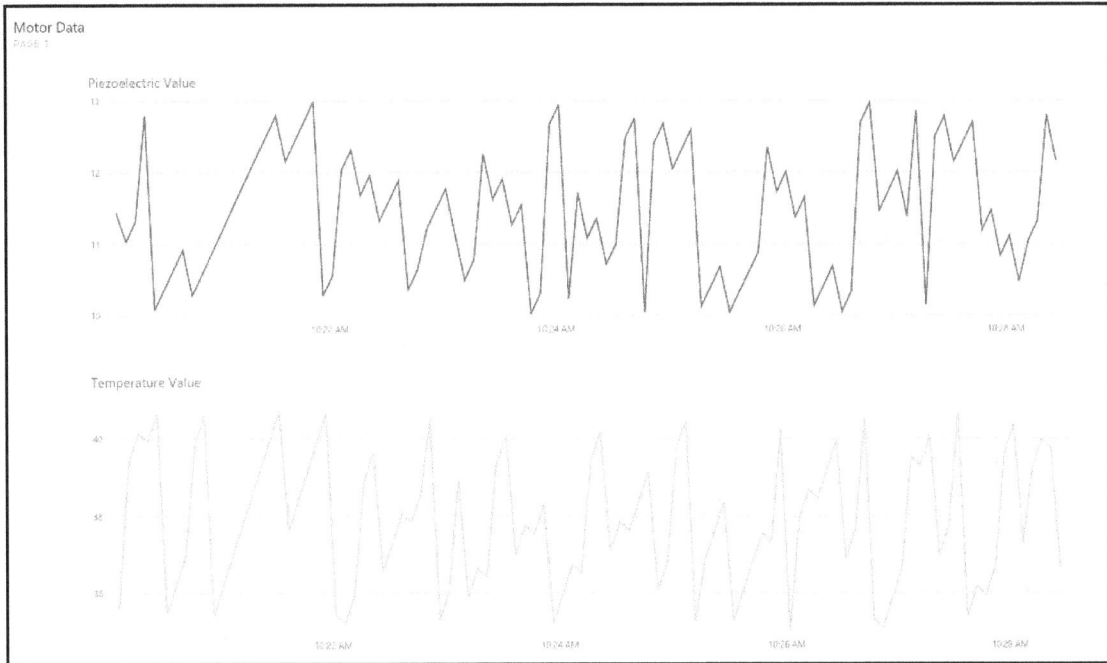

In this scenario, we have shown a basic end-to-end IoT solution using IoT Hub and some companion services that are part of the Azure platform.

In a real-world scenario, further analysis would likely be performed, such as using an Azure Machine Learning model to predict failure rather than just relying on a simple error condition check.

In a typical large-scale solution, a more pattern-based approach could be used to help drive governance and trust in the solution. One example of this is the Lambda Architecture described earlier.

Summary

In this chapter, we reviewed the functionality in Event Hubs to set the scene in order to take a deeper look at IoT Hubs.

The Internet of Things has been enabled due to the reduced cost of devices driven by a maker society and the advent of cloud computing.

This has driven a change in both cost and skills required to create a solution. By choosing cheaper hardware and standing up a simple pilot solution using Azure platform services, it is possible for organizations to understand the real value of a solution quickly, enabling them to move forward with confidence that the insights their IoT investment is delivering are valid and important.

Azure IoT Hubs are a key enabler to this process, providing a platform service that supports a near plug-and-play approach, while delivering trust in a secure solution that is difficult to compromise.

While physical devices can still be compromised, since they are outside the control of the Azure platform, having timebound and/or IP filtered secure access gives confidence to move forward with a key technology that can deliver previously unknown insight to a business.

In the next chapter, we discuss the enterprise integration and business-to-business capabilities within Logic Apps and create an end-to-end enterprise messaging scenario that showcases these capabilities.

12
EAI/B2B Integration Using Logic Apps

So far, we have looked at how anyone can get started with Logic Apps to build a standard workflow using Logic Apps in Azure. We also discussed how we can automate business process spanning across cloud and on premises in Logic Apps using on-premises data connector. All these we have achieved without any real client-side development.

Now in this chapter, we will build enterprise workflow using **Enterprise Integration Pack** for Logic Apps. We will also explore an **Enterprise Integration Tool**, which basically adds an integration project type to Visual Studio, and let you create XML schemas, Flat File Schemas, and maps to build an EAI /B2B integration solution.

This chapter introduces the following topics:

- What is the Enterprise Integration Pack?
- An Enterprise Integration Tool for Visual Studio 2015
- Enterprise Integration Pack connectors
- How to build the EAI/B2B app using the Enterprise Integration Pack in Logic Apps

Enterprise Integration Pack for Logic Apps

It is a cloud-based solution to develop Enterprise Integration workflows:

- **EAI**: Enterprise Application Integration
- **B2B**: Business-to-Business communication

The pack uses industry standard protocols, including **AS2** (`https://docs.microsoft.com /en-us/azure/logic-apps/logic-apps-enterprise-integration-as2`), **X12** (`https://do cs.microsoft.com/en-us/azure/logic-apps/logic-apps-enterprise-integration-x 12`), and EDIFACT (`https://azure.microsoft.com/en-us/documentation/articles/app -service-logic-enterprise-integration-edifact/`), to exchange messages between business partners. Messages can be optionally secured using both encryption and digital signatures.

Architecturally, the Enterprise Integration Pack is based on integration accounts, which is a container that stores the various artifacts you need for more complex business process workflow such as trading partner agreements, schemas for XML validation, and maps for transformation.

So currently, integration account can hold the following integration artifacts used for Enterprise Integration scenarios:

- **XML schemas:** You can use XML schema to define the message / document format that you expect to receive and send from source and destination systems respectively.
- **XSLT-based maps**: This can be used to transform XML data from one format to another format.
- **Trading partners:** Thisis a representation of a particular group within organization or partner you do business with. These are the entities that participate in **Business-To-Business** (**B2B**) messaging and transactions.
- **Trading partner agreements:** When two partners establish a relationship, this is referred to as an agreement (`https://msdn.microsoft.com/en-us/library/ee 920494.aspx`). Trading partner agreements is an understanding between two business profiles to use a specific message encoding protocol or a specific transport protocol while exchanging EDI messages with each other. Enterprise Integration supports three protocol/transport standards:
  - AS2
  - X12
  - EDIFACT
- **Certificates:** Enterprise Integration uses certificates for secure messaging of EDI data, which is achieved using **public and private keys**. Organization (Trading Partner) generates keys, distributes the public, and keeps the private secret. Data encrypted by the public key can only be decrypted by the private key.

Certificates are just electronic documents that contains a public key. These certificates are digitally signed by a trusted certificate authority (`https://en.wiki pedia.org/wiki/Certificate_authority`) and the signature binds owner's identity to the public key.

It is essential to create an integration account for a Logic App to use EAI and B2B capabilities. To create an integration account, log in to Azure portal and go to **New | Enterprise Integration**, as here:

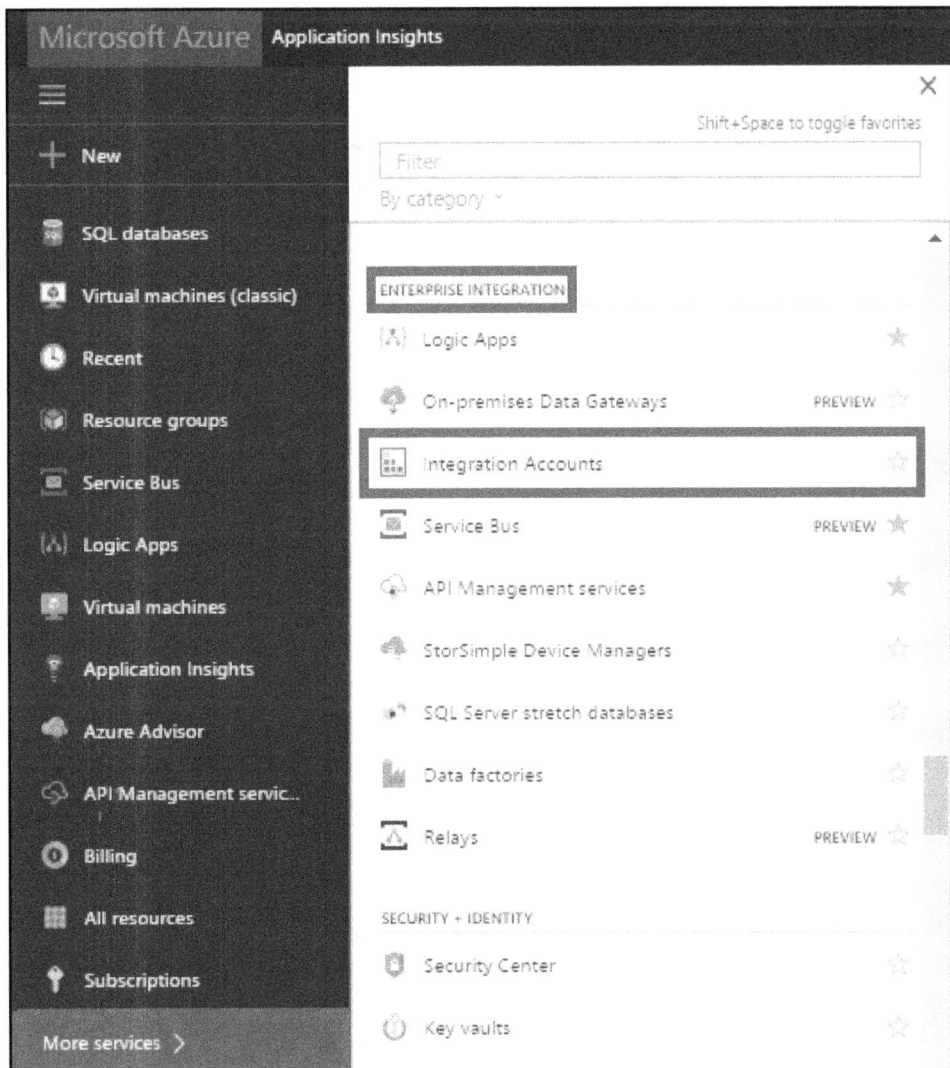

Now enter the **Name** for the integration account and select the**Subscription**, **Resource group**, and **Location**, as shown here. Click on the **Create** button.

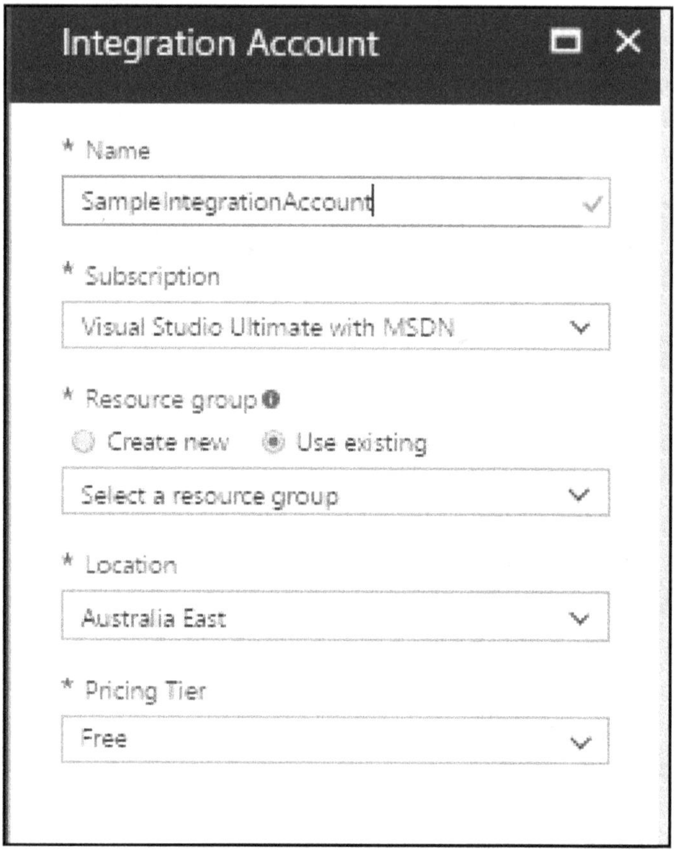

This is how the overview of the enterprise account created earlier look like.

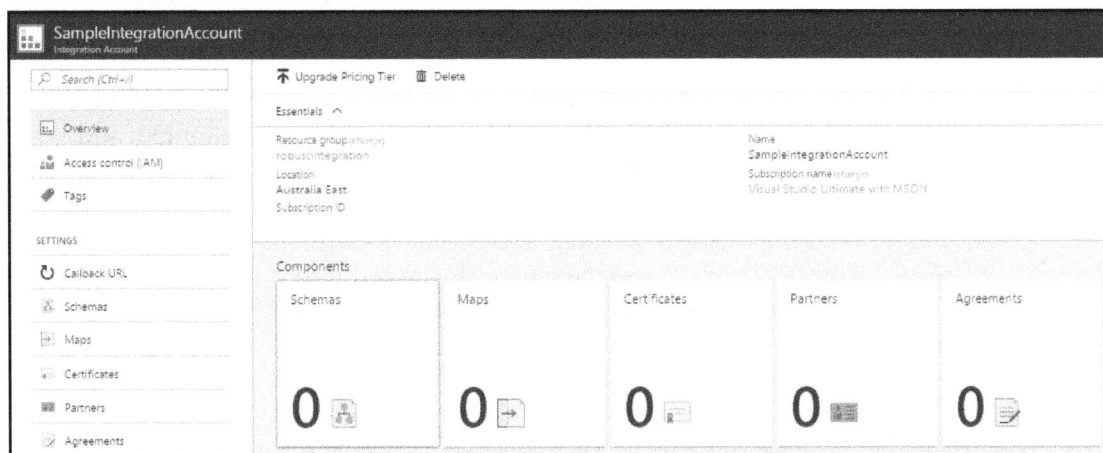

The earlier-mentioned artifacts can be used in Logic Apps to build Enterprise Integration workflows with EAI and B2B capabilities. We need to link the integration account to Logic App to use the artifacts stored in integration account. We will see how to link the integration account to Logic App in the later section.

Enterprise messaging in Logic Apps

The Enterprise Messaging in Logic App have the following features:

- **Flexibility in content types:** Logic Apps are flexible enough to support different content types, such as binary, JSON, XML, and primitives. Now you can receive different message types in Logic Apps and then convert them to JSON or XML format required for the downstream systems. We also have new BizTalk connectors, which can be used to push the message to the on-premise BizTalk server. More about BizTalk connectivity is explained in the next chapter.

  The Enterprise Integration pack provides XSD support in Logic Apps. So, you can upload your XML schemas to integration account and use them in Logic App workflow and further convert them to the binary or JSON format as per your requirement.

- **Mapping:** Now you can also create XSLT-based map in Visual Studio and use them in Logic App workflows. You can also leverage your existing assets-schema and maps by uploading them to integration account and using them in Logic Apps.
- **Flat file processing:** Now you can easily convert Flat files into XML and vice versa. Built-in connectors support Logic Apps to convert csv, delimited, and positional file into XML and then into JSON/base64.
- **EDI:** With Enterprise Integration Pack, Logic Apps now supports EDI processing for **business-to-business (B2B)** integration scenarioswith out-of-the-box X12 and EDIFACT support. You can use the integration account to store all the required artifacts, such as partners, agreements, and certificates along with schemas and maps.

Logic Apps Enterprise Integration Tool

The Enterprise Integration Tool is an extension for Visual Studio 2015, which can be downloaded from `https://www.microsoft.com/en-us/dow nload/details.aspx?id=53016`.

Basically, it adds an integration project type to Visual Studio 2015 and lets you create XML schemas, Flat File Schemas, and maps to build an EAI/B2B integration solution.

It uses the Logic App Schema editor, Flat File Schema generator, and XSLT mapper to easily create integration account artifacts. These artifacts, XSD and XSLT map files are uploaded to integration account so that you can use them for Enterprise Messaging in Logic Apps.

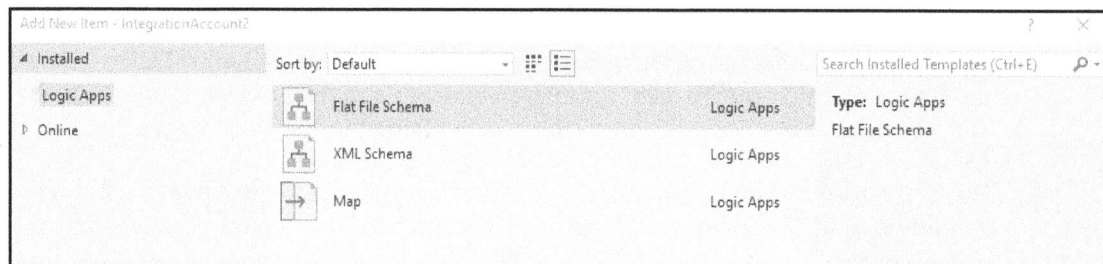

Enterprise Integration Pack connectors

The integration pack connectors enable you to easily validate, transform and process different messages that you exchange with different applications within your enterprise (EAI) or with your business partners (B2B).

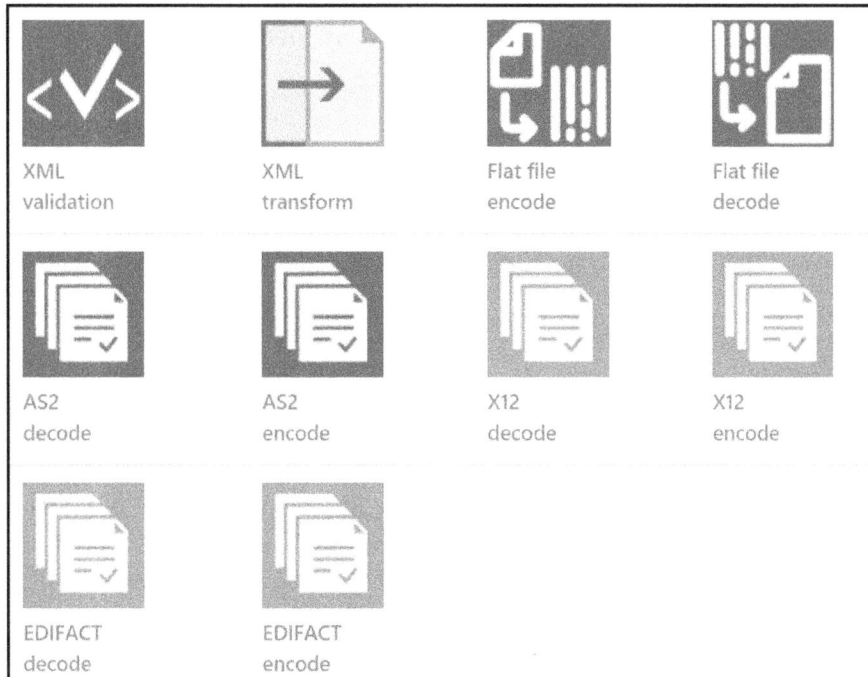

- **XML validation**: You can use the**XML validation** connector to validate documents against a predefined schema.
- **XML transformation**: It primarily converts data from one format to another format. For example, you may have incoming message that contains *FirstName*, *MiddleName*, and *LastName* fields and you need to transform to a destination message which only contains *Name* field. These kind of manipulation can be done using built-in functions. You can use different built-in functions to help manipulate or control the data, including string manipulations, conditional assignments, arithmetic expressions, date time formatters, and even looping constructs.
- **Flat file encode** and **Flat file decode**: The **Flat file encoding/Flat file decoding** connectors provide the ability to encode or decode a flat file to XML and vice versa.

Encoding XML content to EDI message before you send it to a business partner in a B2B integration is a very common scenario. You may also want to send the encoded data to line-of-business applications, such as Salesforce or Dynamic365 in your Logic App workflow. **Flat file encoding** connector can be used to encode XML content to flat file formats such as csv, delimited and positional files.

Also in case of receiving messages from different line-of-business applications or trading partners, **Flat file decoding** connector can be used to decode the flat file message content to XML content.

- **AS2 encode** and **AS2 decode** – AS2 is one of the most popular methods for transporting data, especially EDI data, securely and reliably over the Internet. **AS2 encode** and **AS2 decode** connector can be used to establish security and reliability while transmitting EDI messages. It provides digital signing, decryption, and acknowledgements via **Message Disposition Notifications (MDN)**.
- **X12 encode and X12 decode** – X12 is a standard protocol for interindustry electronic exchange of business transactions–**electronic data interchange (EDI)**.

  X12 encode connector validates EDI message and partner-specific properties. It also converts XML-encoded messages into EDI transaction sets in the interchange before sending the EDI message to trading partner. It can also be configured to request for a technical and/or functional acknowledgment.

  X12 decode connector also Validates EDI and partner-specific properties, generates XML document for each transaction set. It can also be configured to generate acknowledgment for processed transaction.

- **EDIFACT encode** and **EDIFACT decode** – The EDIFACT standard provides a set of syntax rules to structure data for EDI business transaction and is widely used across Europe. Same as X12, EDIFACT connectors also Validates EDI and partner-specific properties.

EDIFACT encode connector serializes the EDI interchange, converting XML-encoded messages into EDI transaction sets in the interchange. It can also be configured to request for a technical and/or functional acknowledgment.

EDIFACT decode connector generates an XML document for each transaction set for incoming EDI messages. It can also be configured to generate acknowledgment for processed transaction.

- In summary following enterprise features can be achieved by using **Enterprise Integration Pack (EIP)** connectors:
  - **EAI features**:
    - XML Validation
    - Transform XML
    - Flat File Encoding
    - Flat File Decoding
  - **B2B features**:
    - AS2 – Decode AS2 Message
    - AS2 – Encode to AS2 Message
    - X12 – Decode X12 message
    - X12 – Encode to X12 message by agreement name
    - X12 – Encode to X12 message by identities
    - EDIFACT – Decode EDIFACT message
    - EDIFACT – Encode to EDIFACT message by agreement name
    - EDIFACT – Encode to EDIFACT message by identities

Together all these features/capabilities enable customers to create end to end automated business processes that scale with the cloud connecting you to your business partners quicker than ever on Logic Apps. All the above features are in preview status at the time of writing this book.

Enterprise Integration templates

Logic Apps has rich set of pre-built template and few of them are for Enterprise Integration:

- EAI/B2B scenarios

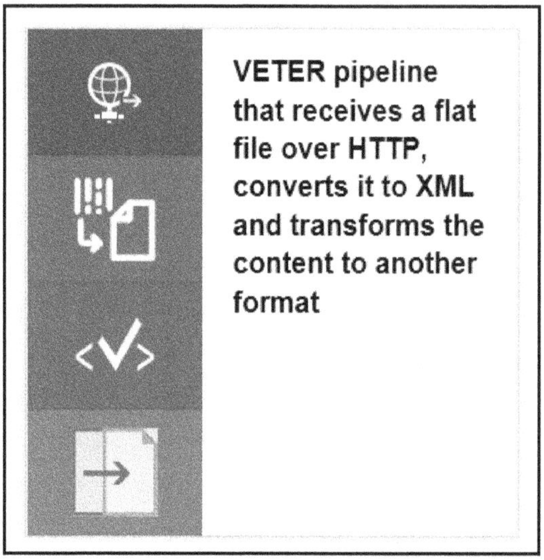

VETER pipeline that receives a flat file over HTTP, converts it to XML and transforms the content to another format

- EDI over AS2

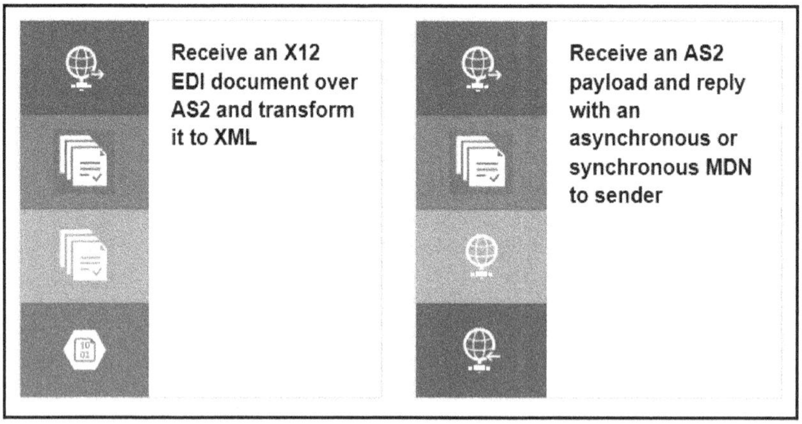

Receive an X12 EDI document over AS2 and transform it to XML

Receive an AS2 payload and reply with an asynchronous or synchronous MDN to sender

> We also have quick start template on github to try these scenarios. Here is the github link for VETER scenario: `https://github.com/Azure/azure-q uickstart-templates/tree/master/201-logic-app-veter-pipeline`.

Building your first Enterprise Messaging solution

In this section, we will try to build an Enterprise Messaging solution using Enterprise Integration Pack in Logic App.

> Here is the sequence of steps you need to take currently to develop the Enterprise Integration solution as described in Azure documentation: `http s://azure.microsoft.com/en-us/documentation/articles/app-servi ce-logic-enterprise-integration-overview/`.

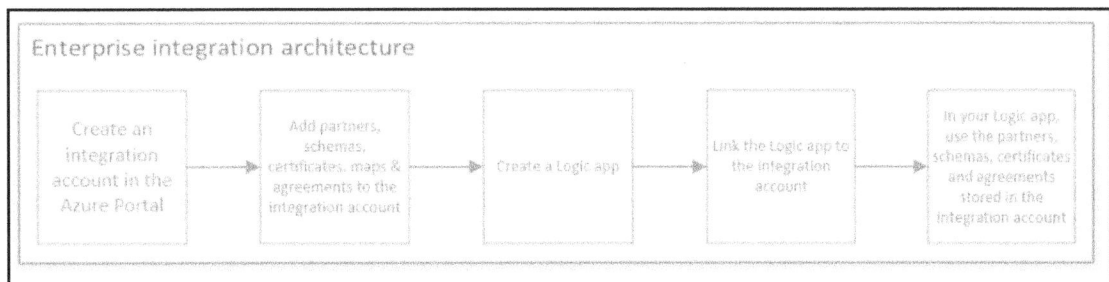

Enterprise integration architecture

Create an integration account in the Azure Portal → Add partners, schemas, certificates, maps & agreements to the integration account → Create a Logic app → Link the Logic app to the integration account → In your Logic app, use the partners, schemas, certificates and agreements stored in the integration account

Source: `https://docs.microsoft.com/en-us/azure/logic-apps/logic-apps-enterprise-i ntegration-overview`

Basically you do the following tasks to build your enterprise workflow in Logic Apps

- Create an Integration Account in the Azure portal
- Create schema and maps using **Enterprise Integration Tools** in Visual Studio 2015 and upload them to integration account you created in first step
- Add partner, agreement, and certificates to the integration account for B2B scenarios
- Create a logic app and link the logic app to the integration account
- Now build the enterprise workflow in Logic App using the artifacts stored in the integration account

- We will now use the preceding steps/tasks to develop our Enterprise Messaging solution in Logic Apps. Our Logic App will have an HTTP endpoint where we would send a comma-separated order payload (shown here) to an XML response.

OrderNumber	Item	Quantity	UnitPrice
1001	Pencils HB	100	1
1002	Highlighter	60	2

The workflow would use the Flat File Decoding, XML Validation, and Transform XML to produce the XML response with `TotalAmount` for each order as shown here:

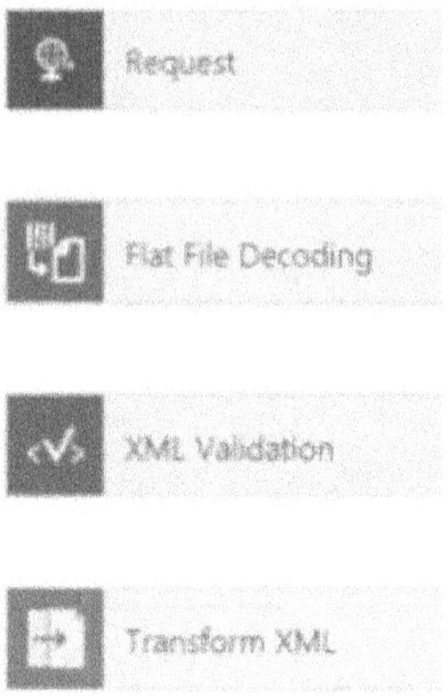

```
<?xml version="1.0" encoding="utf-8"?>
<ns0:Orders xmlns:ns0="http://EAIDemo.Orders_XML">
    <Order>
        <OrderNumber>1001</OrderNumber>
        <ItemName>Pencils HB</ItemName>
        <TotalAmount>100</TotalAmount>
    </Order>
    <Order>
        <OrderNumber>1002</OrderNumber>
        <ItemName>Highlighter</ItemName>
        <TotalAmount>120</TotalAmount>
    </Order>
</ns0:Orders>
```

Workflow would then iterate through each order record using `for each` connector and calls another child workflow to insert the order to the table `HighOrder` in Azure SQL, if the `TotalAmount` is equal or more than $100.

dbo.HighOrder [Data]

Max Rows: 1000

OrderNumber	ItemName	TotalAmount
1001	Pencils HB	100
1002	Highlighter	120

We would use the prebuilt template to start developing this solution. This template displays a message that an integration account would be required to use this template.

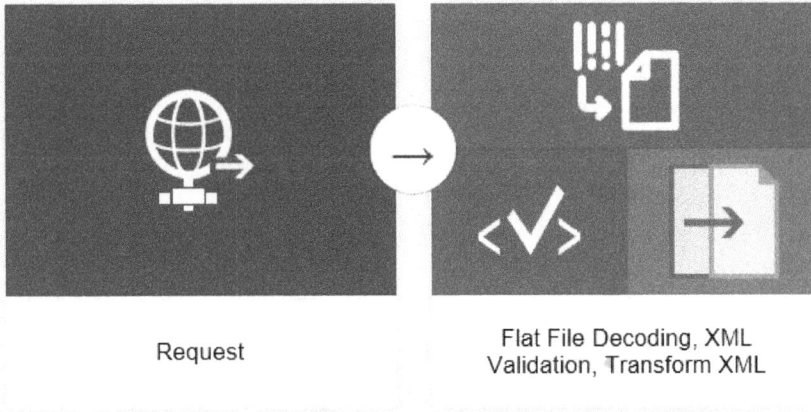

VETER pipeline that receives a flat file over HTTP, converts it to XML and transforms the content to another format

Request

Flat File Decoding, XML Validation, Transform XML

A VETER (validate, extract, transform, enrich, route) pipeline that receives a flat file over HTTP, converts it to XML and transforms the content to another format using an xpath() function to extract data from the message. An integration account is required to use this template. See here for details on how to create an integration account and add maps and schema to it.

Use this template

So, we would be using the `SampleIntegrationAccount`, which we created in the beginning of this chapter.

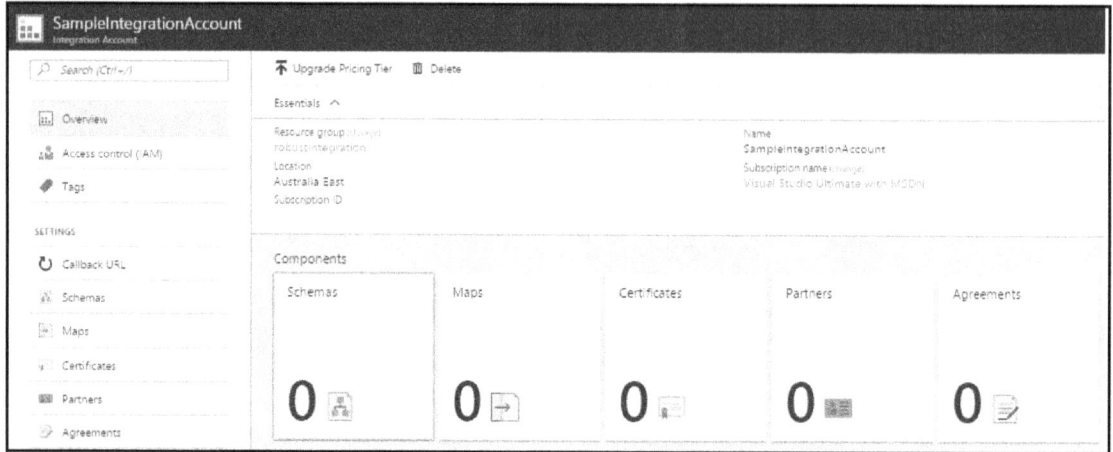

The next step would be to create schemas and maps for our solution and add them to integration account. This is where client-side development comes in. As explained earlier in this chapter, we need to use an Enterprise Integration Tool, which is really just Visual Studio extensions that give you the BizTalk schema editor and mapper in Visual Studio 2015.

You need to use **IntegrationFFSchema**, **IntegrationSchema**, and **IntegrationMap** in Visual Studio 2015 to create enterprise-class schemas defining an order–one Flat File Schema, one XML schema, and a map converting one format to another.

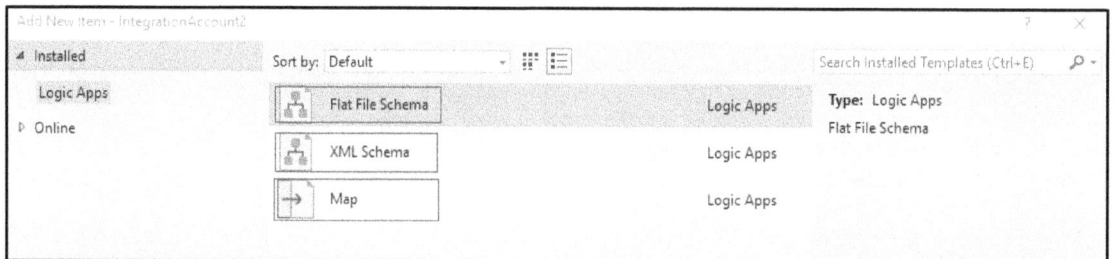

You would use **Logic App Flat File Schema Wizard** to develop the Flat File Schema. Please refer to this MSDN link for creating schemas using **Logic App Flat File Schema Wizard**.

For more information: `https://msdn.microsoft.com/en-us/library/aa 559306.aspx`.

Logic Apps Flat File Schema Wizard   ✕

Welcome to the Logic Apps Flat File Schema Wizard

Azure Logic Apps
Tools for Visual Studio

This wizard guides you through the steps to create a new flat file schema and define records and fields based on the specified document instance.

☐ Do not show this introductory page again.

| Help | | < Back | Next > | Cancel |

IntegrationFFSchema: Orders_FF

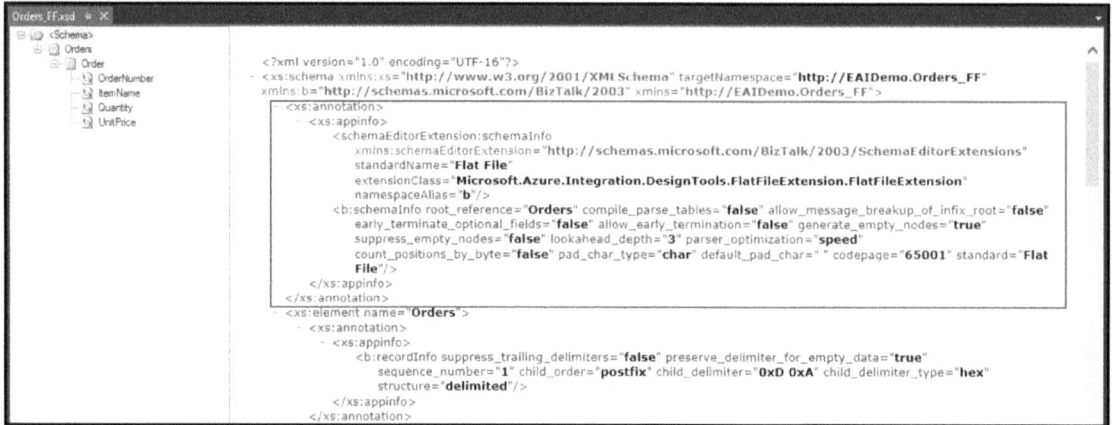

IntegrationSchema: Orders_XML

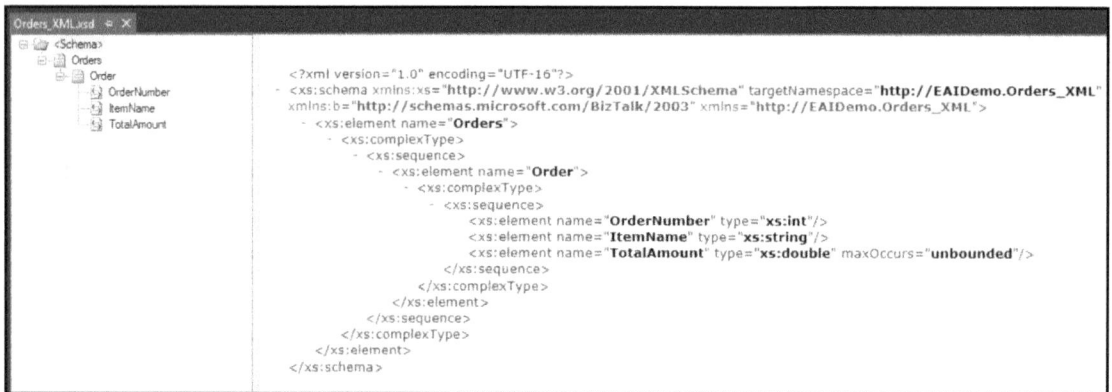

IntegrationMap: Map_Orders_FF_To_Orders_XML

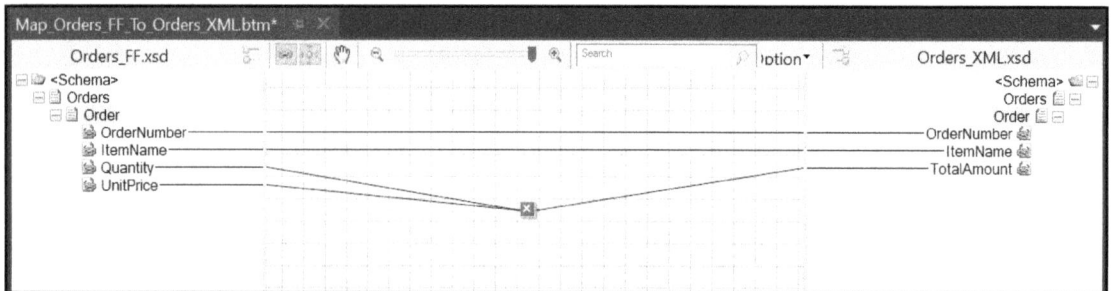

The map is very simple. It just multiplies `Quantity` and `ItemName` in the inbound message into the `TotalAmount` outbound field in the XML schema. And yes, as discussed before, the mapper includes the Functoids for basic calculations, logical conditions, and string manipulation.

Now we need to upload the schemas and map to integration account so that we can use them in Logic Apps. Integration account does not take the DLLs, so we need to upload the raw XSD and XSLT maps.

Schemas
SampleIntegrationAccount

➕ Add   ✏️ Edit   ⬇️ Download   🗑️ Delete

NAME	TYPE	CONTENT SIZE	CHANGED TIME
Orders_FF	Xml	3.5 KiB	11/6/2016 11:52 AM
Orders_XML	Xml	803 B	11/6/2016 11:53 AM

Maps
SampleIntegrationAccount

➕ Add   ⬆️ Update   ⬇️ Download   🗑️ Delete

NAME	TYPE	CONTENT SIZE	CHANGED TIME
Map_Orders_FF_To_Or...	Xslt	1.28 KiB	11/6/2016 11:43 AM

The next step is to create a Logic App and link the Logic App to the integration account.

So, I have created a Logic App–`EAIOrderMessaging`. To link it to the integration account, `SampleIntegrationAccount`, under **Settings** section of Logic App, click on **Integration Account**.

Now your integration account should show up in the drop-down menu. You select your intergation account and click on **Save**, as shown here:

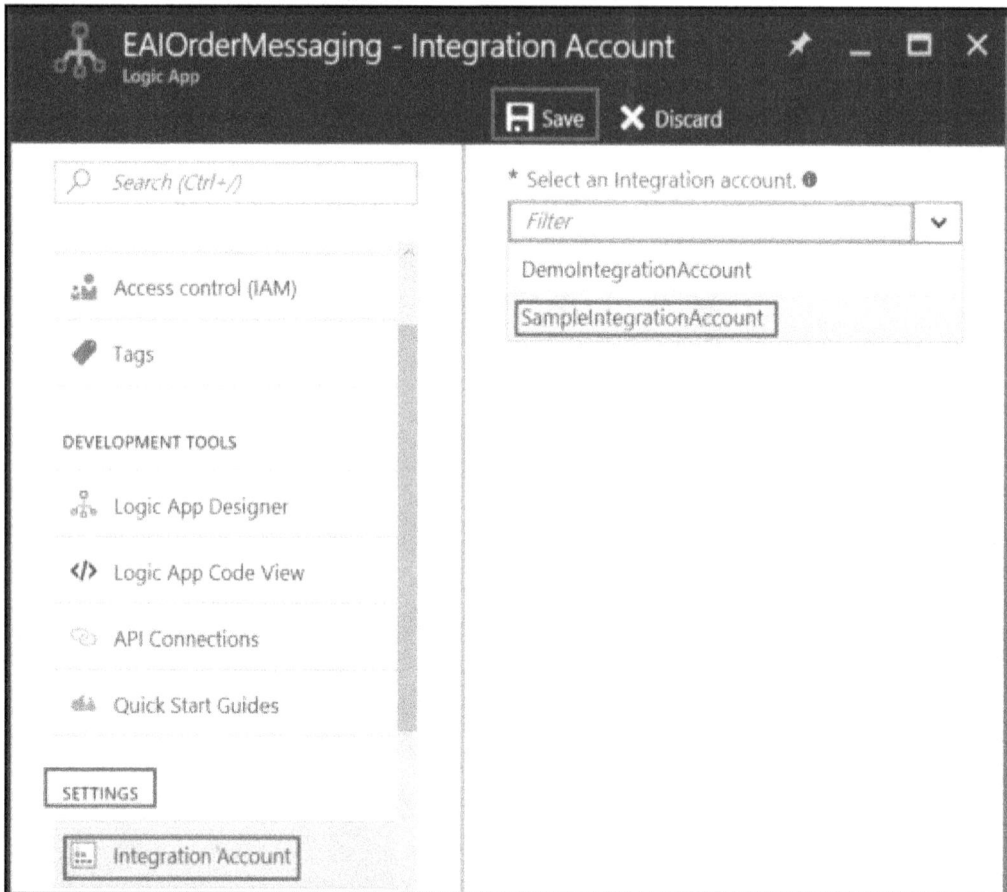

Now we can go back to Logic App and select the **VETER** template and start using the integration account artifacts there.

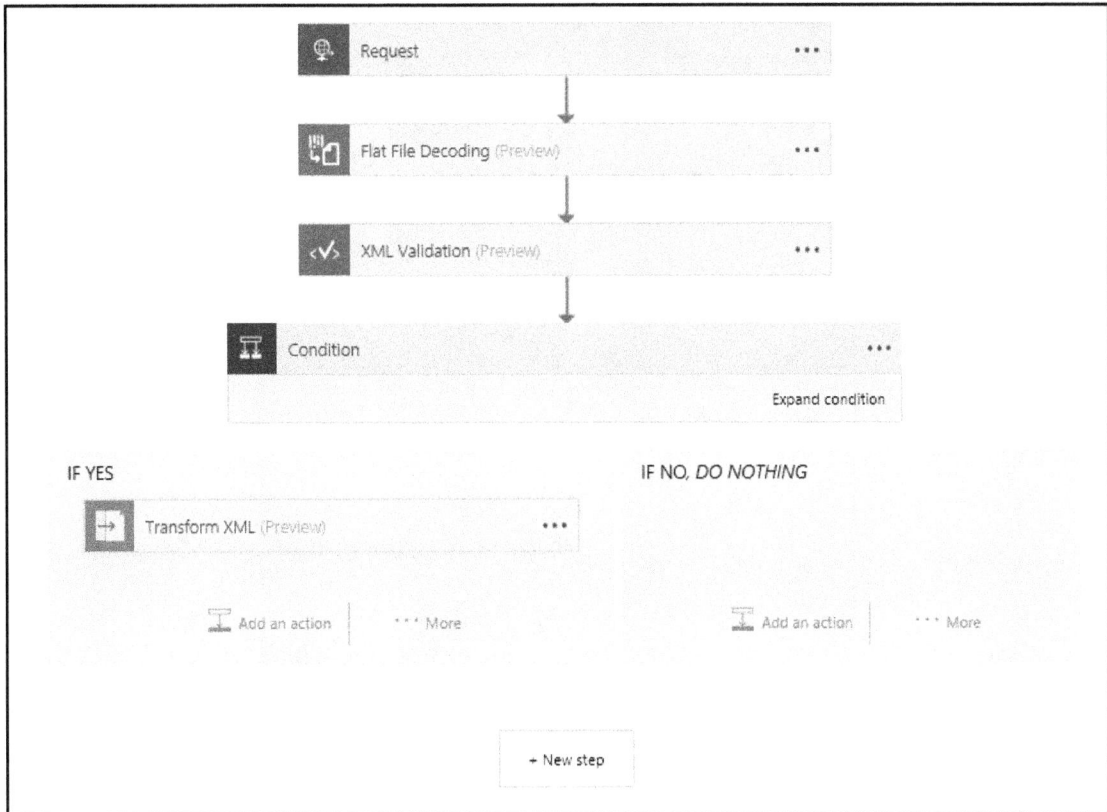

Select the `Order_FF` and `Order_XML` in **Flat File Decoding** and **XML Validation** actions respectively, as shown here:

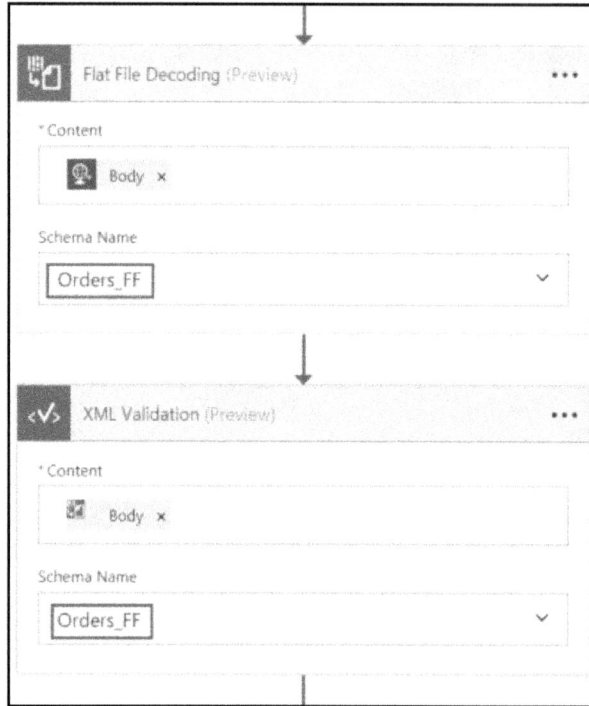

Once comma-separated order payload is decoded and validated, the next step would be to transform the order message using **Transform XML** action, as shown here:

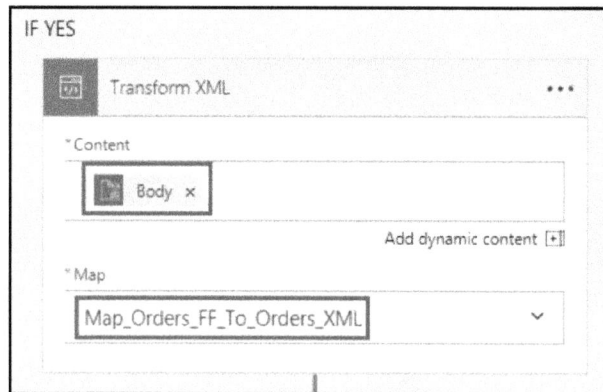

To get the XML response from the map, we are using the**Response** action, as follows:

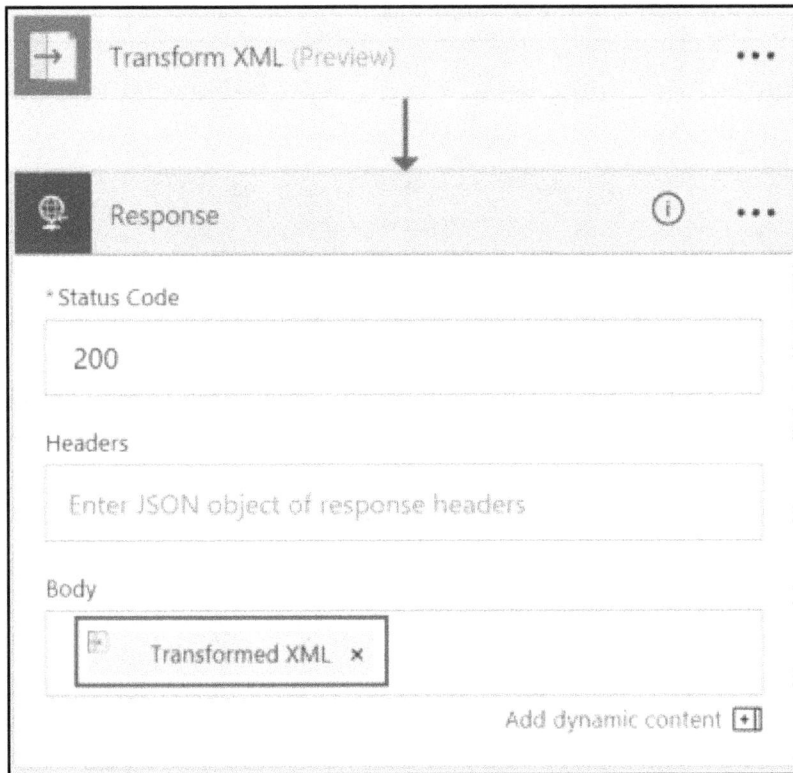

Now save the Logic App to create the URL endpoint in the **Request** trigger, as follows:

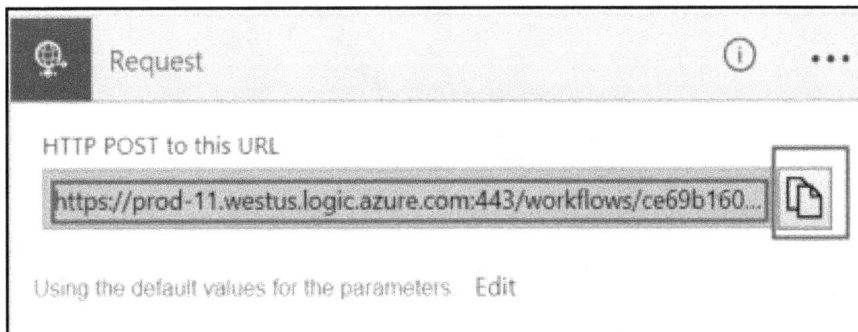

Copy the complete URL by clicking on the copy button as shown in the preceding screenshot. Now we can use this URL to test the workflow using the Postman application.

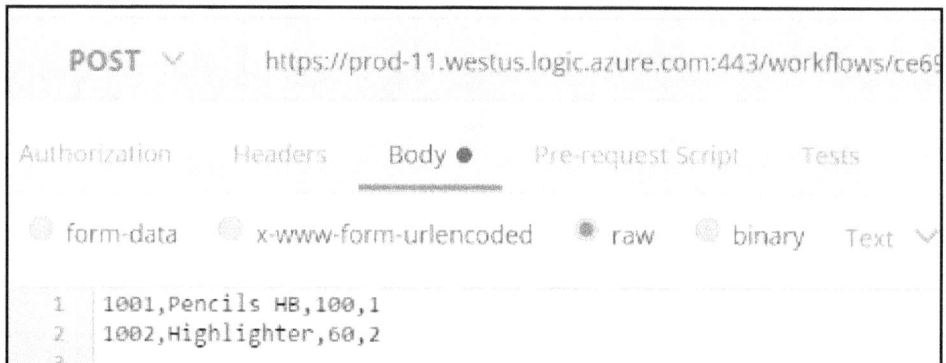

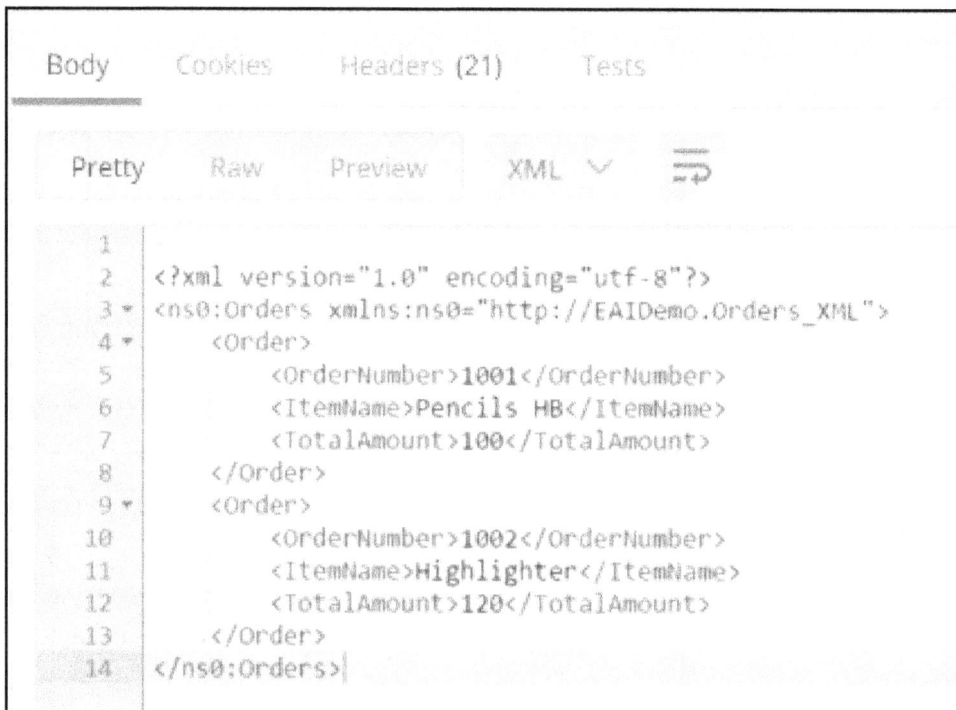

POST ∨   https://prod-11.westus.logic.azure.com:443/workflows/ce69

Authorization   Headers   Body ●   Pre-request Script   Tests

◯ form-data   ◯ x-www-form-urlencoded   ● raw   ◯ binary   Text ∨

```
1   1001,Pencils HB,100,1
2   1002,Highlighter,60,2
```

Body   Cookies   Headers (21)   Tests

Pretty   Raw   Preview   XML ∨

```xml
1
2    <?xml version="1.0" encoding="utf-8"?>
3    <ns0:Orders xmlns:ns0="http://EAIDemo.Orders_XML">
4        <Order>
5            <OrderNumber>1001</OrderNumber>
6            <ItemName>Pencils HB</ItemName>
7            <TotalAmount>100</TotalAmount>
8        </Order>
9        <Order>
10           <OrderNumber>1002</OrderNumber>
11           <ItemName>Highlighter</ItemName>
12           <TotalAmount>120</TotalAmount>
13       </Order>
14   </ns0:Orders>
```

So, here is my Logic App looks like till now. It takes in a flat file, validates the flat file using the Flat File Schema, uses a built-in check to see that it's a decoded flat file, executes my map within an Azure Function, and finally returns the XML response back.

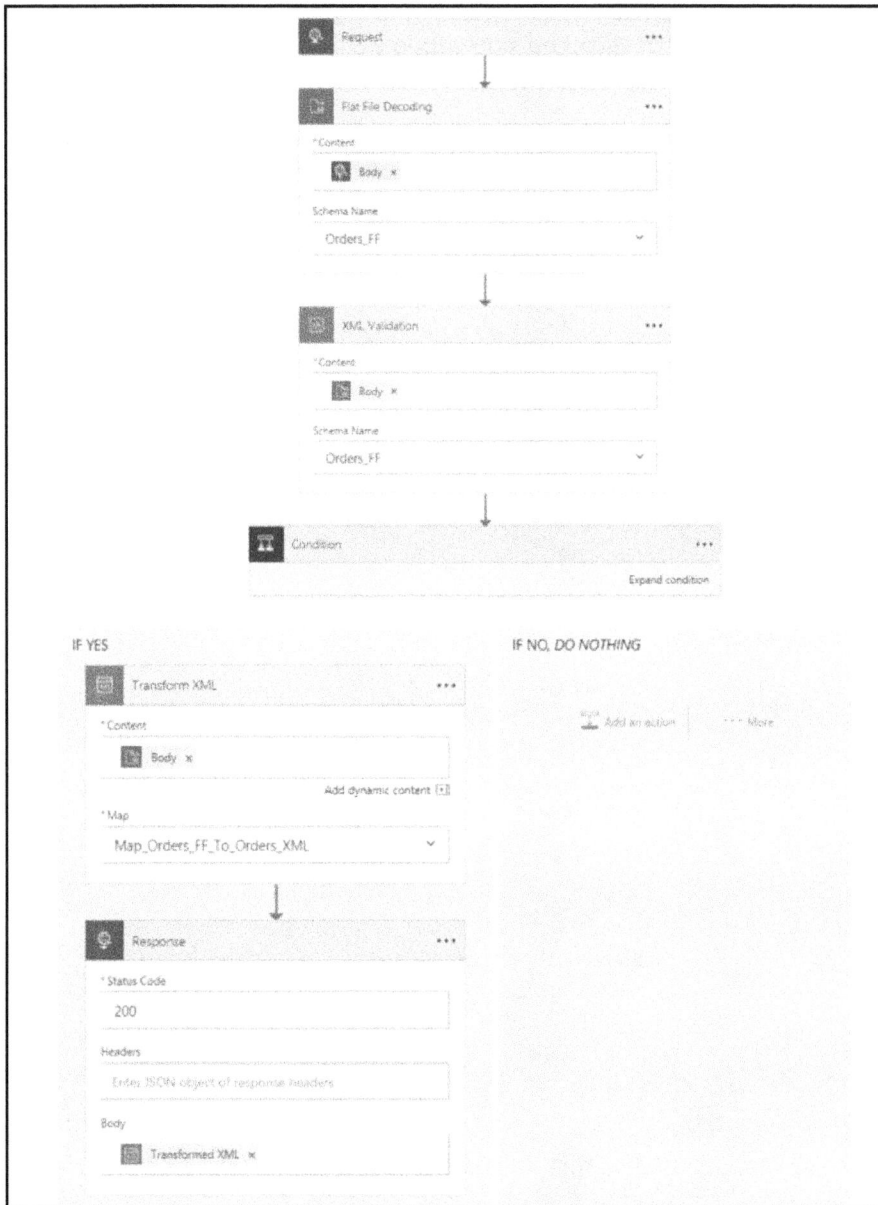

By now, we understand the concept of Enterprise Integration Pack and how it can enable us for Enterprise Messaging and integration scenario.

This Logic App now can be extended in various way. For example, instead of HTTP Request trigger, we can use FILE or FTP trigger, and the final XML response can be pushed to the Service Bus topic so that it can be subscribed by the on-premise line of business systems or any other downstream system.

As mentioned in the beginning of the section, we would now extend this app to iterate through each order record using `for each` connector and call another child workflow to insert the order to the table `HighOrder` in Azure SQL if the `TotalAmount` is equal or more than $100.

We need to add a **Compose** action to get the order records using the xpath function, which returns an array of xml nodes of Order. You can refer to more about the xpath function in Workflow Definition Language: `https://docs.microsoft.com/en-us/rest/api/logic/definition-language`.

Next, we would use the **For each** loop to iterate through the order records and send it to another Logic App by converting them into the JSON format.

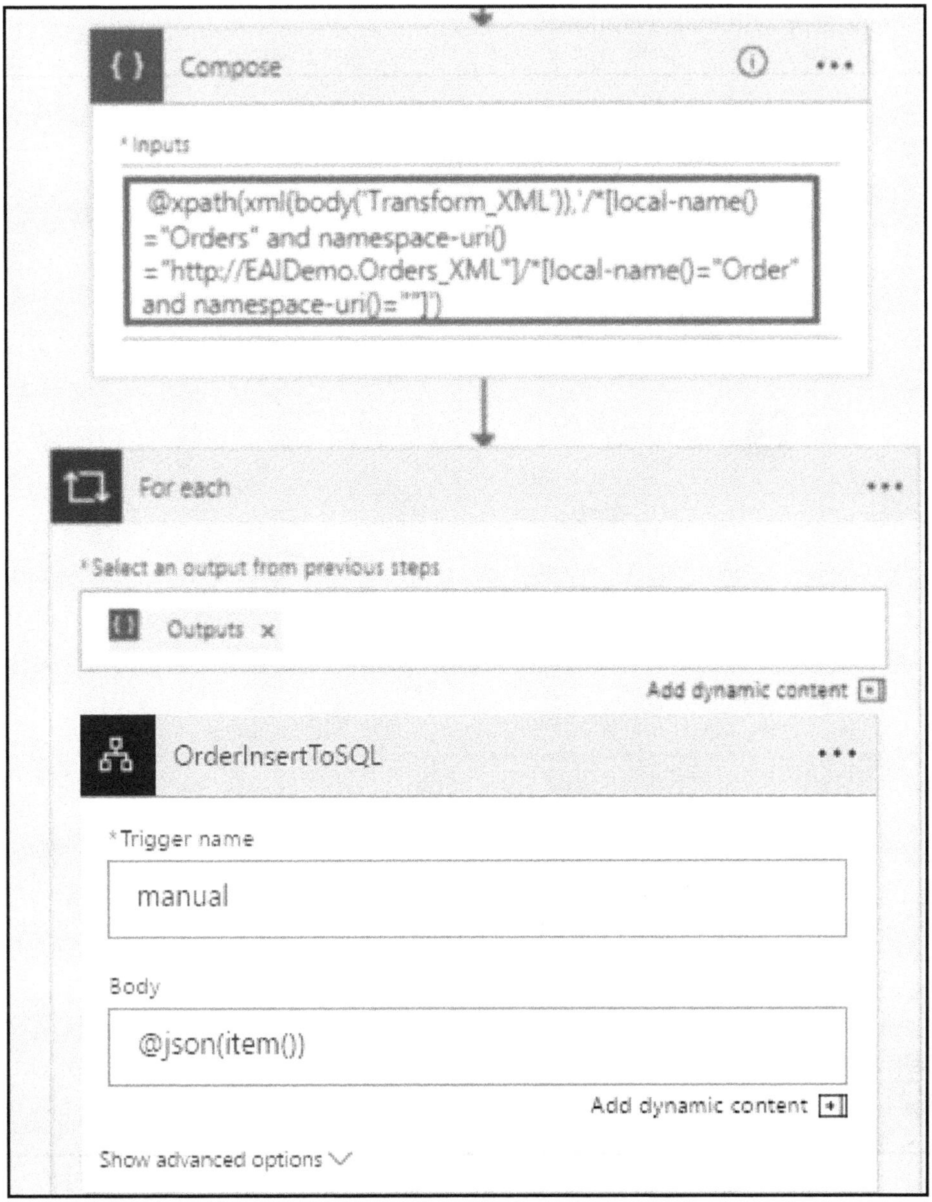

{ } Compose ⓘ •••

* Inputs

```
@xpath(xml(body('Transform_XML')),'/*[local-name()
="Orders" and namespace-uri()
="http://EAIDemo.Orders_XML"]/*[local-name()="Order"
and namespace-uri()=""]')
```

◻ For each •••

* Select an output from previous steps

[ ] Outputs ✕

Add dynamic content ⊡

뫔 OrderInsertToSQL •••

* Trigger name

manual

Body

@json(item())

Add dynamic content ⊡

Show advanced options ∨

Now the Logic App will look as follows:

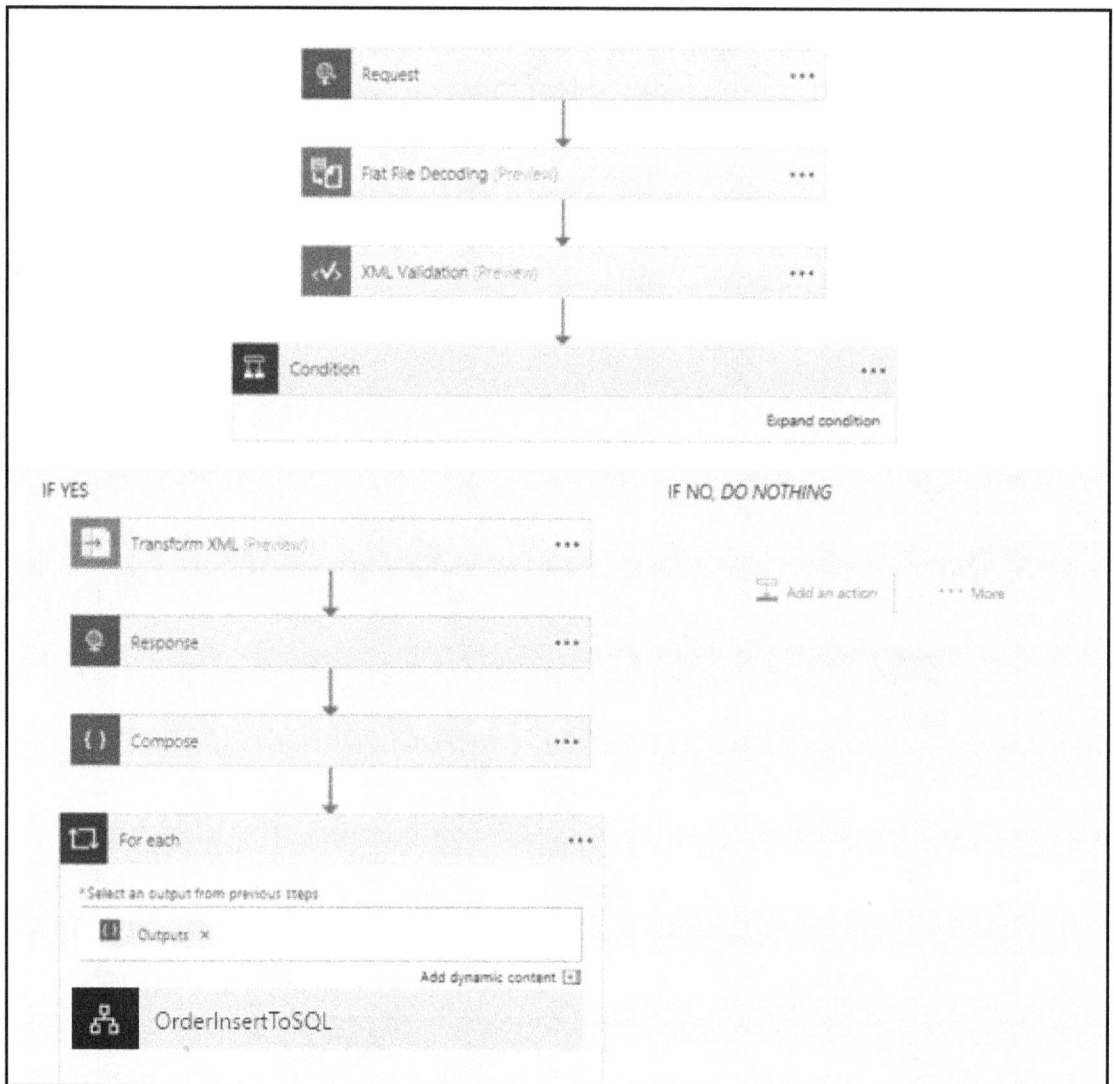

Child Logic App workflow is very simple as shown here:

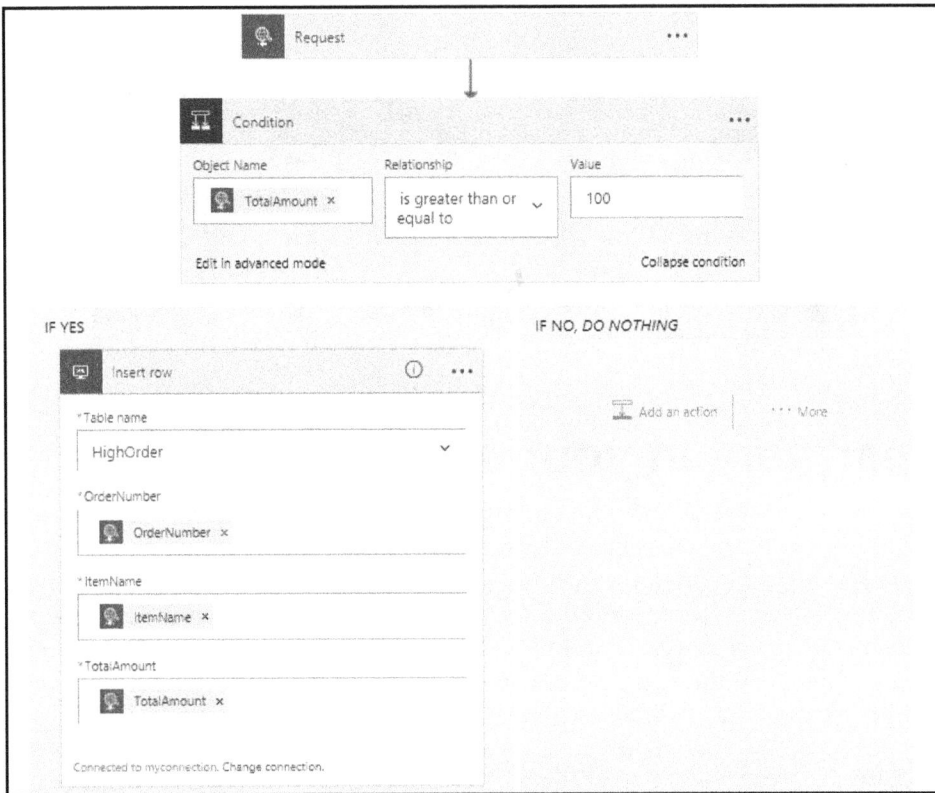

This workflow basically receives an order request as per the defined JSON schema as follows:

```
{
  "Order": {
    "OrderNumber": "1001",
    "ItemName": "Pencils HB",
    "TotalAmount": "100"
  }
}
```

Next, there is the condition to check the `TotalAmount` value. If it is greater or equal to 100, the record gets inserted into the `HighOrder` table of Azure SQL database using SQL server connector.

Add partners in your workflow

Partners are the key stakeholders who participate in B2B (**business-to-business**) transactions by exchanging messages. Before creating partners within an Enterprise Integration Account, you and your partner need to identify the protocol and messaging format used to make communication through an agreement. To create the agreement, one organization needs to act as a host partner and other will act as a guest partner. To learn more about partners and the agreement, you can refer to Microsoft documentation for the Enterprise Integration pack at https://docs.microsoft.com/en-us/azure/logic-apps/logic-apps-enterprise-integration-partners.

In the following section, we will walk through the process of creating the partner and agreement within the Enterprise Integration Account, which we have created in the preceding section.

Creating a partner within the Integration Account

To create a partner, we will perform the following steps:

1. Select the **Integration Account** within which you need to add a partner:

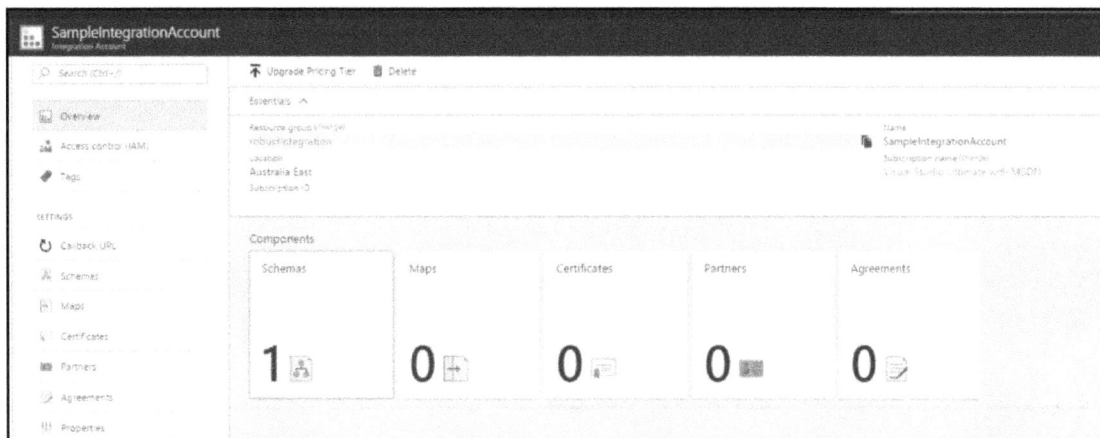

2. Select the **Partners** tile and choose **Add**. Enter **Name** for your partner, select **Qualifier**, and enter **Value** to help identify documents that come into your apps. Once required fields are populated, click on the OK tile to create the **partner.**

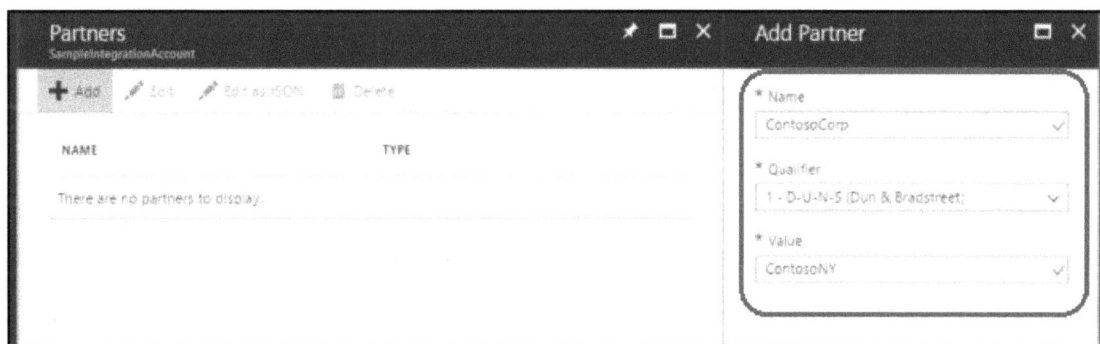

3. To confirm that your new partners were successfully added, select the **Partners** tile within the Integration Account.

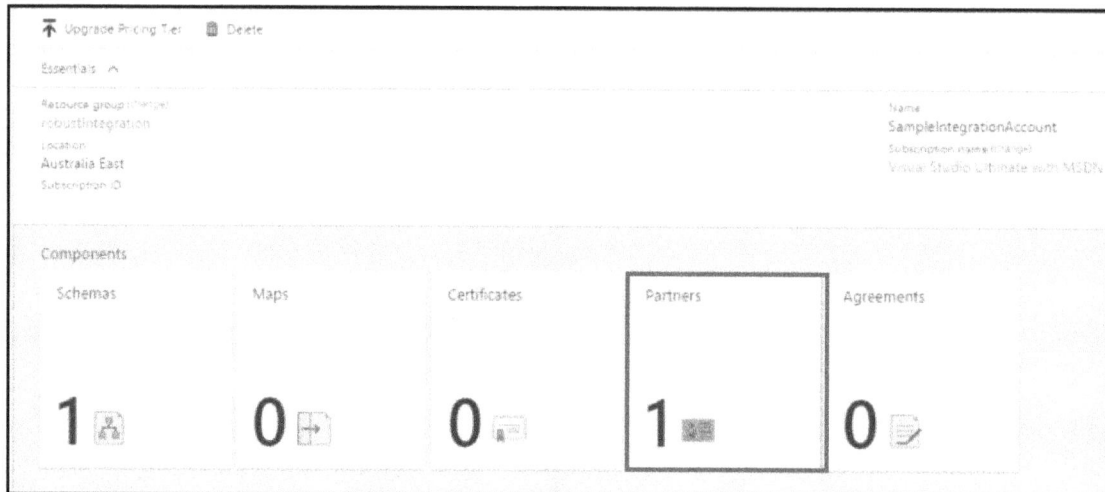

Once the partners are created, you can edit them as per your requirement through Integration Account:

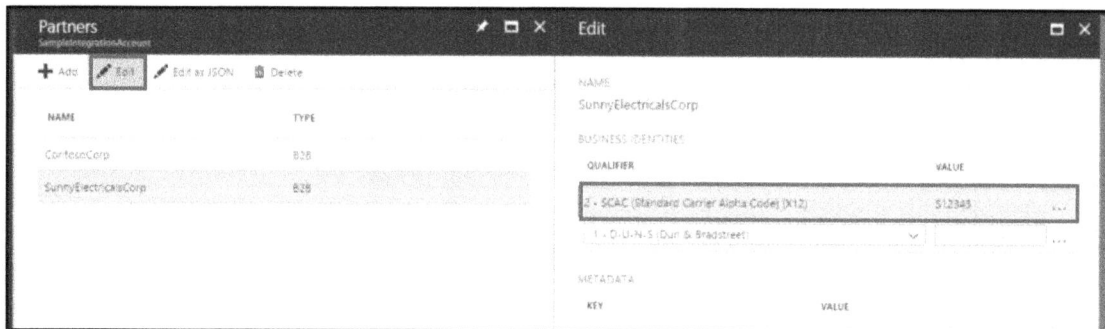

Enterprise Integration documentation has made it very simple to get started with the process. For more information, refer to the following MSDN link: https://docs.microsoft.com/en-us/azure/logic-apps/logic-apps-enterprise-integration-partners

Create an AS2 agreements

Trading partner agreements is an understanding between two business profiles to use a specific message encoding protocol or a specific transport protocol while exchanging EDI messages with each other.

Trading partners are the entities involved in B2B communications. When two partners establish a relationship, this is referred to as an agreement. The agreement defined is based on the communication the two partners wish to achieve and is protocol or transport specific:

- Select the Integration Account where you added the partner in the last section and Choose the **Agreements** tile.

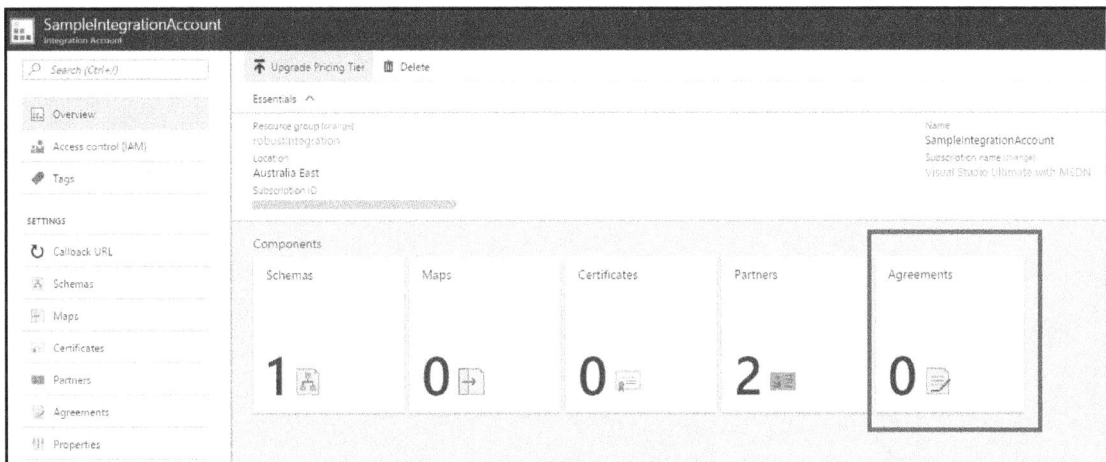

- In the **Agreements** blade that opens, choose **Add** and enter **Name** for your agreement. For **Agreement type**, select **AS2**. Select **Host Partner**, **Host Identity**, **Guest Partner**, and **Guest Identity** for your agreement.

Configure your agreement to handle receive messages

The next step would be to configure agreement properties; you can configure how this agreement identifies and handles incoming messages received from your partner through this agreement.

Under **Add**, select **Receive Settings**. Configure these properties based on your agreement with the partner that exchanges messages with you.

There is an option for you to override the properties of incoming messages by selecting **Override message properties**.

You need to select **Message should be signed** so that all incoming messages can be signed. From the **Certificate** list, select a public certificate in order to validate the signature on the messages. Otherwise, create the certificate if you don't have one.

Also, to encrypt all incoming messages, select **Message should be encrypted**. From the **Certificate** list, select an existing private certificate of the host partner to decrypt incoming messages or create the certificate if you don't have one.

- To compress the messages, select **Message should be compressed**.
- To send a synchronous **message disposition notification** (**MDN**) for received messages, select **Send MDN**.
- To send signed MDNs for received messages, select **Send signed MDN**.
- To send asynchronous MDNs for received messages, select **Send asynchronous MDN**.

After you're done, make sure to save your settings by choosing **OK**.

Now your agreement is ready to handle incoming messages that conform to your selected settings.

Configure your agreement to send messages

You can now configure how this agreement identifies and handles outgoing messages that you send to your partners through this agreement.

Under **Add**, select **Send Settings**. Configure these properties based on your agreement with the partner who exchanges messages with you.

- To send signed messages to your partner, select **Enable message signing**. For signing the messages in the **MIC Algorithm** list, select **host partner private certificate MIC Algorithm** and select an existing host partner private certificate.
- To send encrypted messages to the partner, select **Enable message encryption**. For encrypting the messages in the **Encryption Algorithm** list, select **guest partner public certificate algorithm** and select an existing guest partner public certificate.
- To compress the message, select **Enable message compression**.
- To unfold the HTTP content-type header into a single line, select **Unfold HTTP headers**.
- To receive synchronous MDNs for the sent messages, select **Request MDN**.
- To receive signed MDNs for the sent messages, select **Request signed MDN**.
- To receive asynchronous MDNs for the sent messages, select **Request asynchronous MDN**. If you select this option, enter the URL for where to send the MDNs.
- To require nonrepudiation of receipt, select **Enable NRR**.

After you're done, make sure to save your settings by choosing **OK**.

Now your agreement is ready to handle outgoing messages that conform to your selected settings.

After you finish setting all your agreement properties on the **Add** blade, choose **OK** to finish creating your agreement and return to your **Integration Account** blade.

Your newly added agreement now appears in your **Agreements** list.

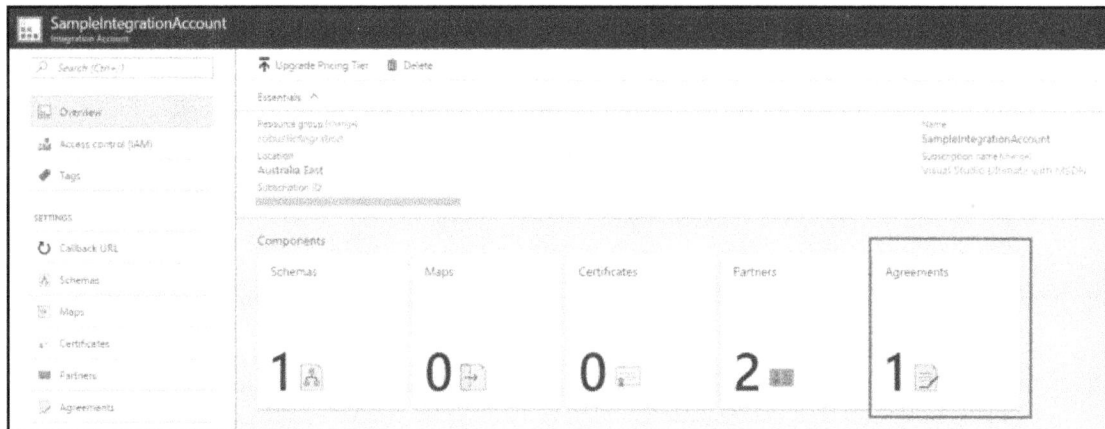

Further B2B scenario is very well explained in the following Azure documentation:

```
https://docs.microsoft.com/en-us/azure/logic-apps/logic-apps-enterprise-inte
gration-b2b
```

Store custom metadata information in Integration Accounts artifacts

With Enterprise Integration Pack, it is very much easy to add and retrieve custom metadata information within Enterprise Integration artifacts. For example, you can add metadata information for artifacts such as partners, schema, maps, and agreement. The next steps describe how you can easily add metadata information and retrieve it within the logic apps workflow.

Add Metadata information to Integration Account artifacts

In this walkthrough, we will go step by step to add metadata information in the uploaded schema. You can follow the same steps to add the custom metadata properties to other components such as partners, agreements, or maps.

- Create an Integration Account as being mentioned in the earlier sections or by following the Microsoft documentation at `https://docs.microsoft.com/en-us/azure/logic-apps/logic-apps-enterprise-integration-create-integration-account`
- Add sample schema to the Integration Account. The steps will be similar to partner, agreement, or maps

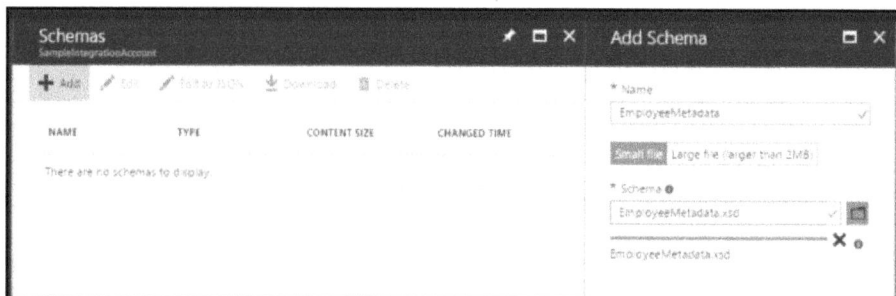

- Select the schema artifact, choose **Edit as JSON** to enter metadata details within the schema

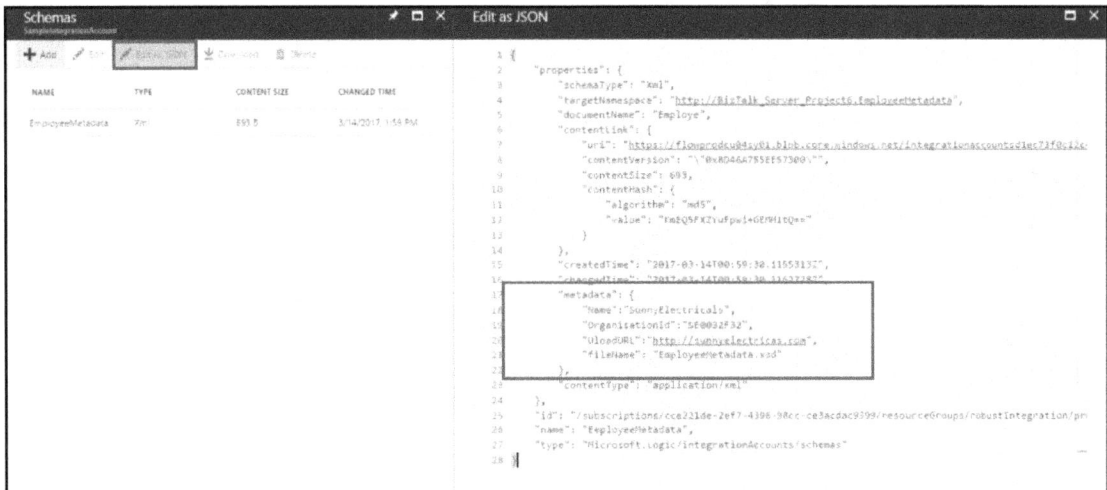

- Click on **OK** to add metadata information to the schema

Retrieve metadata from artifacts for logic apps

Logic Apps and Enterprise Integration pack make it very easy to integrate your B2B partners and to build a robust integration framework to connect your different business partners. In the following section, we will go ahead to retrieve the metadata information that we have added within the schema in the preceding section:

- Create a logic App and select the **Blank** Logic App template with the HTTP trigger

- In the next Step, **Add an action** for **Integration Account Artifact Lookup**

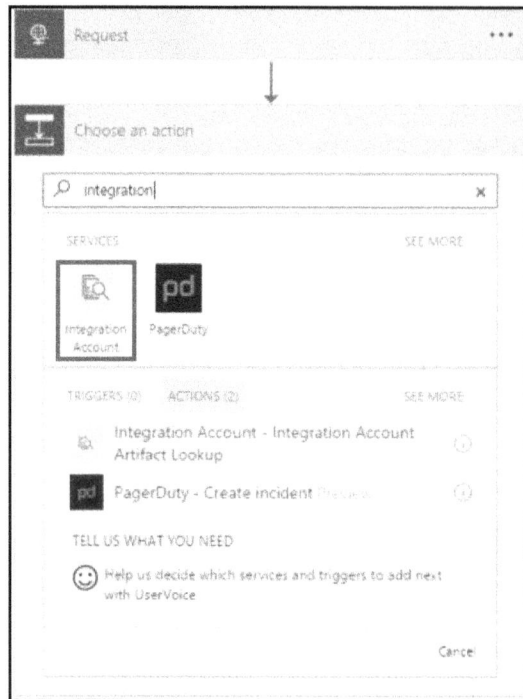

- The next step is to select the **Artifact Type** as schema and provide **Artifact Name** as the deployed schema.

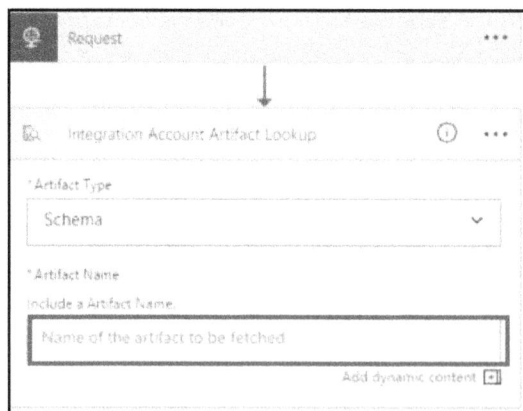

- To look for metadata information stored within schema, we will just use HTTP post operation. We are using `https://requestb.in/` to capture the metadata information. The Logic App code view for metadata lookup will be like the following screenshot:

- Now use a postman to trigger the request as explained before and then go to the **Overview** section of the Logic Apps and verify the details for the Logic App run.

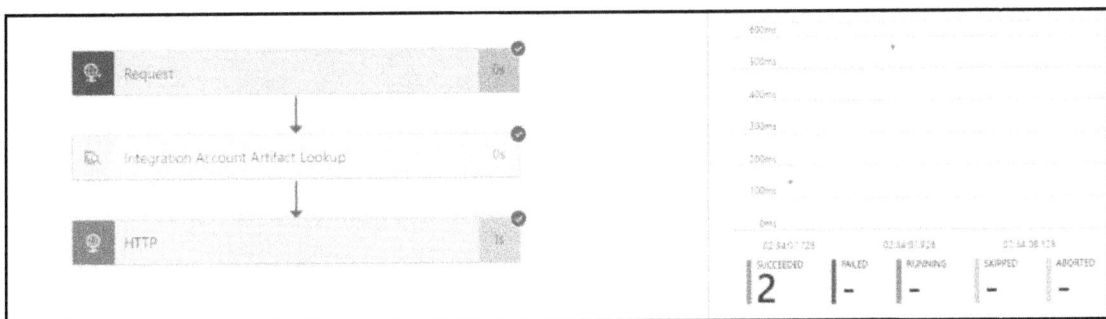

Summary

In this chapter, we explored Enterprise Application Pack for Logic Apps. We started with the concept of integration account and then how to create enterprise artifacts using an Enterprise Integration Tool.

We discussed about Enterprise Integration Pack connectors and finally developed an EAI messaging scenario from the scratch by creation schemas and map in Visual studio and using them in Logic App workflow.

In next chapter we will explore the tooling and monitoring of Logic App workflows.

13

Hybrid Integration Using BizTalk Server 2016 and Logic Apps

The best and most beautiful things in the world cannot be seen or even touched – they must be felt with the heart.
– Helen Keller

This chapter introduces the concept of Hybrid Integration and Microsoft BizTalk Server 2016, new capabilities toward cloud integration. It explains how we can create a bridge between an application running locally and cloud-hosted services, by taking the advantage of Logic Apps- and BizTalk Server-extensive integration capabilities.

This chapter discusses the following topics:

- The introduction to Hybrid Integration
- Why Hybrid Integration?
- Message Exchange Pattern
- What is BizTalk Server 2016
- Build demo from Logic App to BizTalk Server
- Demo from BizTalk Server to Logic Apps

Hybrid Integration

For many years, organizations have made huge expenditure to build custom applications and infrastructure running on premise. Most of this custom-built applications hold major portion of business-centric data. With shift toward cloud and global market, businesses are required to share the data in one or another form to the customers and the partners in a secure manner. The business is also making huge investments in cloud offerings looking at the benefits, such as auto-scaling, pay-as-you-use, multiple SaaS products, and PaaS offerings.

The challenges these organizations are facing is to bridge on-premise resources sitting behind a corporate firewall with the cloud. To solve this mission-critical issue, the term Hybrid Integration has gained popularity in recent times. In a hybrid cloud infrastructure approach, customers use cloud to deploy servers and platforms within an extended network connected to their local domain. Hybrid solutions span over cloud (public, private, or community) and on-premise resources. It is a key enabler to use the already existing systems and data with SaaS and PaaS offerings of the cloud. Hybrid Integration makes a robust way to innovate with existing data, take competitive advantage, and create a new business model:

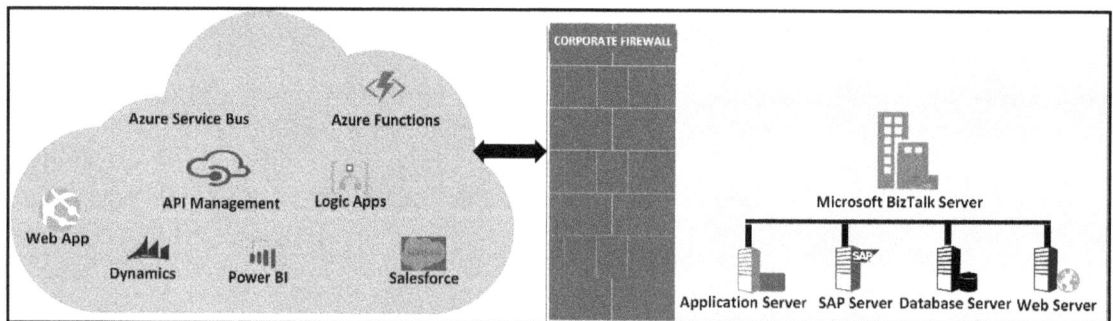

Why Hybrid Integration?

Data is more important than ever; organizations are heavily relying on the data for future innovation and expansion in the current market. In the journey of digital transformation, applications are spanned over cloud and on premises. Hybrid Integration provides a layer of abstraction between resources sitting on premise and the cloud.

Hybrid Integration provides a business opportunity to reach wider audience by leveraging the latest offerings whether it is within the organization firewall or in the cloud.

We will discuss some of the benefits of Hybrid Integration in the coming sections.

Maximize use of past/existing investment

Most of the business houses have invested in huge to build custom enterprise applications and store data relevant for their business. For industries, data is a key enabler for their future innovation, and in most cases, data resides within legacy system sitting on premise. With the advent of competitive market, business houses are taking advantage of cloud applications, which talk securely to the on-premises applications to give a new perspective toward future growth. Hybrid Integration provides a layer over legacy enterprise application to access to important data whenever and wherever required. Hybrid Integration provides benefits in terms of reduced cost, easy maintenance, geo redundancy, and so on.

Customer privacy and data security

There are multiple industries like healthcare, insurance, government agencies and so on. which are more concerned to store their sensitive information on the cloud. Hybrid Integration provides them the perfect solution to communicate with the resources sitting in the cloud, without making any compromise with the secured data within the corporate firewall.

Wider audience

With Hybrid Integration, businesses can reach to wide range of consumers by enabling the customer facing application running over cloud and in different regions. Most of cloud infrastructure can be auto-scaled based on the demand, which gives businesses the opportunity to expand.

Message exchange pattern

The **Message Exchange Pattern** (**MEP**) is an architecture design, which describes how two or more parties will connect and exchange messages amongst themselves. Understanding different MEP options is crucial to create correct architecture design for the Hybrid Integration solution.

There are three MEPs.

Datagram or one-way pattern

Datagram MEP uses one-way messaging pattern with fire and forget rule. In Datagram MEP, the message is sent with unidirectional and asynchronously without waiting for reply from the receiver. The number of message recipients can be single (point-to-point), a list of recipients (multicast), or a broadcast with a publish-subscribe mechanism:

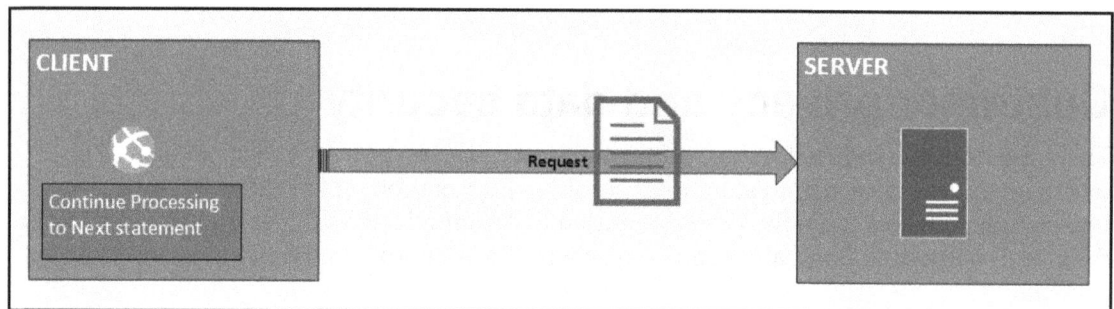

Datagram or one-way messaging communication is a powerful way to build more event-driven applications and take advantage of non-blocking service invocation patterns.

One-way messaging pattern is a fundamental concept, which can be extended within other transport protocol. It has multiple benefits that can be best used in an asynchronous design pattern within the solution.

Half-duplex or request-response

The request-response or half-duplex message pattern is the combination of two one-way messaging patterns. In the request-response pattern, both sender and receiver communicate on the same thread, based on the requestor data.

In the request-response pattern, a client sends a message to the processing system and wait for the reply on the same thread. This is a powerful messaging pattern and being used when the client requires to have synchronous communication with the downstream systems. This pattern is being widely used where systems are communicating with each other in real time. The examples are web service call, HTTP GET method, and so on.

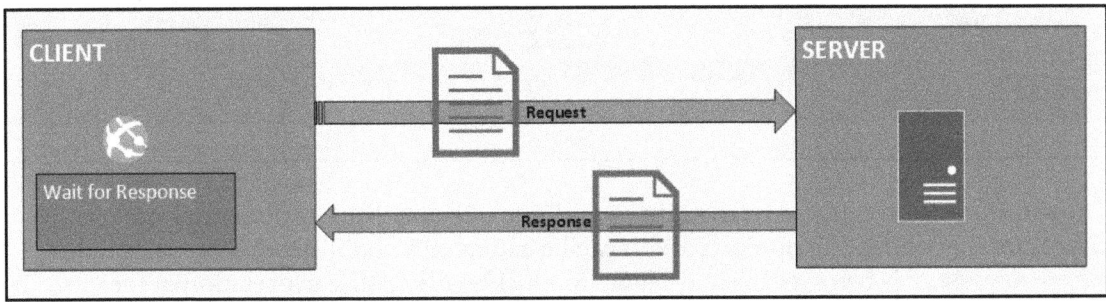

Request-response can be implemented asynchronously as well, with a response being returned at some unknown later time. This is referred to as **sync over a sync** or **sync/a sync**, and it is common in **Enterprise Application Integration (EAI)** implementations where slow aggregations, time-intensive functions, or human workflow must be performed before a response can be constructed and delivered.

> You can read more about the half-duplex messaging pattern on the MSDN link shared here: `https://msdn.microsoft.com/en-us/library/aa 480027.aspx`.

Duplex Message Exchange Pattern

The duplex MEP allows an arbitrary number of messages to be sent by a client and received in any order. In duplex MEP both client and server can initiate the call contrary to request-response and one-way MEP where the client is only responsible for initiating message exchange with the server.

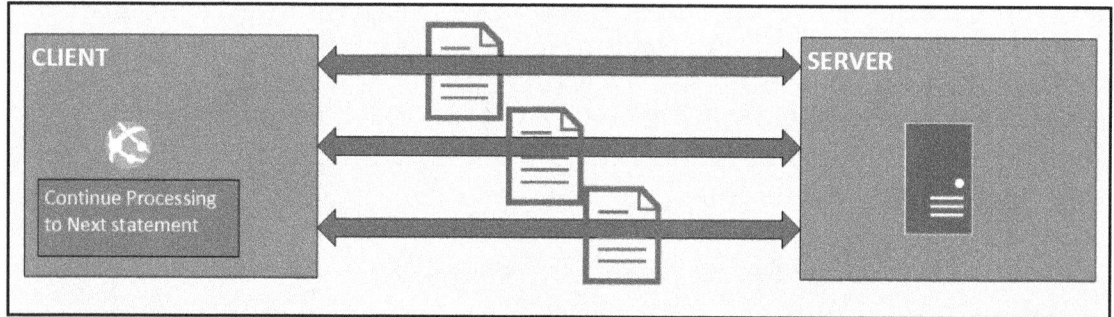

The duplex pattern can also be thought of multiple one-way MEP to communicate with the client and the server. The duplex pattern can be extended to publisher-subscriber model where a message is being published asynchronously without any expectation of the response. Based on message context properties, the message is then being transmitted to multiple subscriber parties. This publish subscribe MEP is being natively used in BizTalk Server and Azure Service Bus.

Each of three-message exchange pattern, discussed earlier, also support sessions. A session correlates all messages sent and received on a channel. The request-response pattern is a standalone two-message session, as the request and reply correlated.

> Refer to the following MSDN Link for more information: `https://msdn.m`
> `icrosoft.com/en-us/library/aa751829(v=vs.110).aspx`.

What is a BizTalk Server?

BizTalk Server is a Microsoft central platform for on-premise and Hybrid Integration. For a number of years, it has served as a mainstream integration platform for worldwide customers, and the latest BizTalk Server 2016 is the 10th release of the product. BizTalk Server uses adapter technology to connect disparate systems and enable message exchange between systems.

With BizTalk 2016, Microsoft has built a Logic App Adapter, which connects on-premise BizTalk Server with cloud-based Logic Apps integration workflow. This has eased the process to share the integration resources between both integration offerings (BizTalk Server and Logic Apps), such as connectors and schema. For example, now you can use a Dropbox connector or cognitive services connector within BizTalk Server using Logic Apps. We will discuss Logic App Adapter in detail in coming sections and will show how easily we can create a connection with Logic Apps and BizTalk Server and use power of both integration offerings to build a hybrid solution.

Traditionally, BizTalk Server used for the following:

- Enterprise Application Integration
- Business to Business
- Business process automation

In coming sections, we will discuss available options to make hybrid connections between Azure and on-premise BizTalk Server.

Azure Relay service

Azure Service Bus Relay is a cloud-based service that allows you to host an endpoint in the Azure cloud. The Service Bus relay service enables us to build hybrid applications that run in both an Azure and your own on-premises environment using WCF framework. In BizTalk Server, you can use the WCF adapters with the WCF relay bindings, which allow you to use BizTalk Server as the listening service on the relay endpoint.

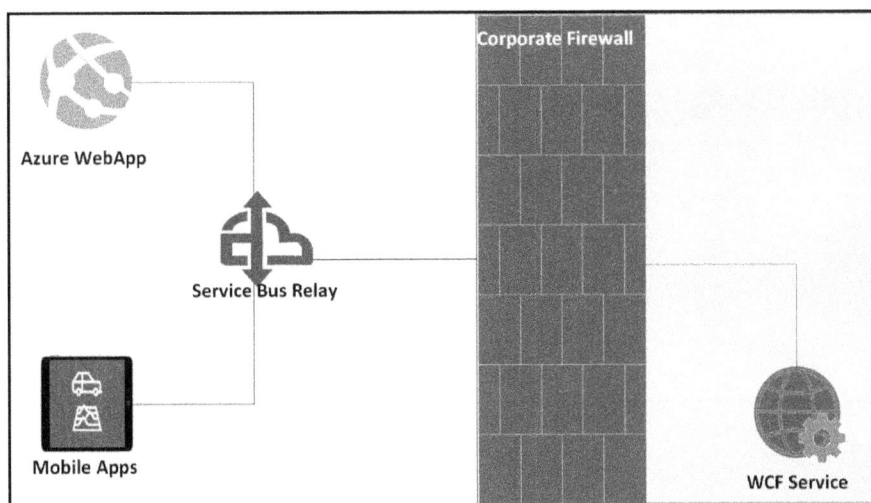

The **WCF-WebHttp**, **WCF-BasicHttp**, and **NetTCpRealy** adapters in BizTalk Server allow sending and receiving message through the Azure Relay service using BizTalk Server as the service broker between an on-premise application and the cloud-based applications.

> To go in detail, you can follow How to use the Azure Service Bus Relay service MSDN link: `https://docs.microsoft.com/en-us/azure/servic e-bus-relay/service-bus-dotnet-how-to-use-relay.`

SB-Messaging Adapter

SB-Messaging Adapter first shipped with BizTalk Server 2013R2 in order to connect Azure Service Bus entities. SB-Messaging Adapter can send and receive messages from Service Bus entities, such as queues and topics. You can use the SB-Messaging Adapters to bridge the connectivity between Windows Azure and on-premises BizTalk Server, thereby enabling users to create a typical hybrid application.

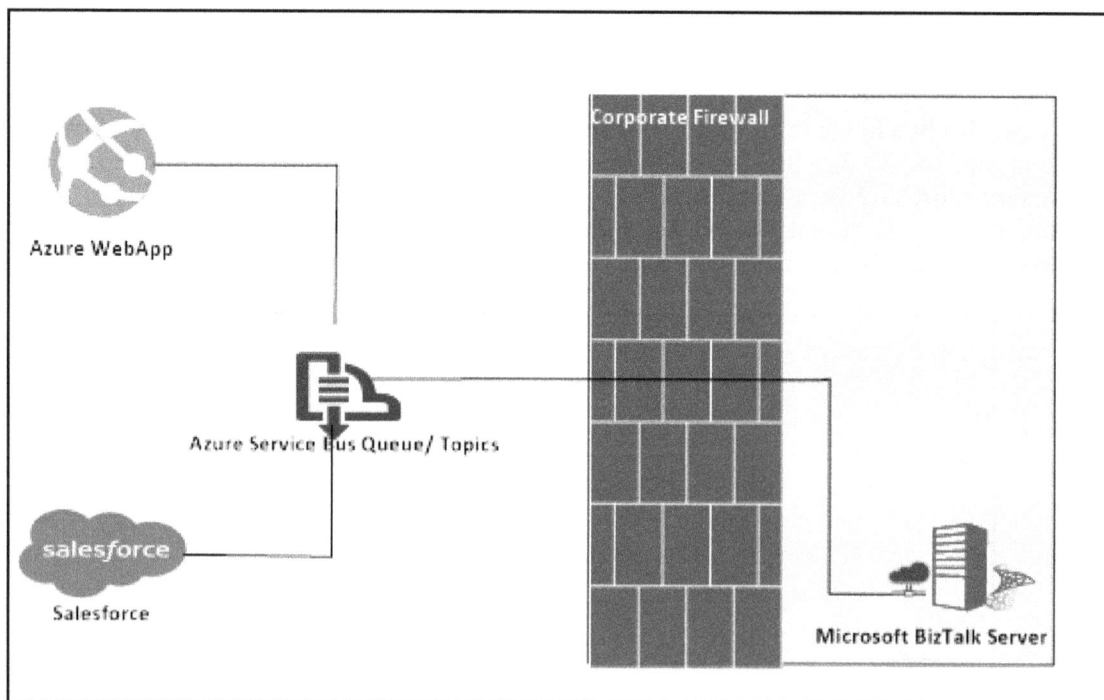

To configure BizTalk Server to use SB-Messaging Adapter, refer to the Microsoft documentation:

- `https://msdn.microsoft.com/en-us/library/jj572840.aspx`
- `https://msdn.microsoft.com/en-us/library/jj572838.aspx`

In this chapter, we will not go in detail about SB-Messaging Adapter and Service Bus Relay. There are already multiple articles existing on web, describing how you can use Relays and SB-Messaging adapter with BizTalk Server. We will discuss new ways to do Hybrid Integration with Logic App Adapter.

Logic App Adapter

With the latest release of BizTalk Server 2016, Microsoft has introduced Logic App Adapters used for communicating between BizTalk Server and Logic Apps workflow running on cloud.

BizTalk Logic App Adapter uses on-premise data gateway (discussed in `Chapter 8`, *A Deep Dive into Logic Apps*) to make hybrid connectivity with the workflow running on cloud.

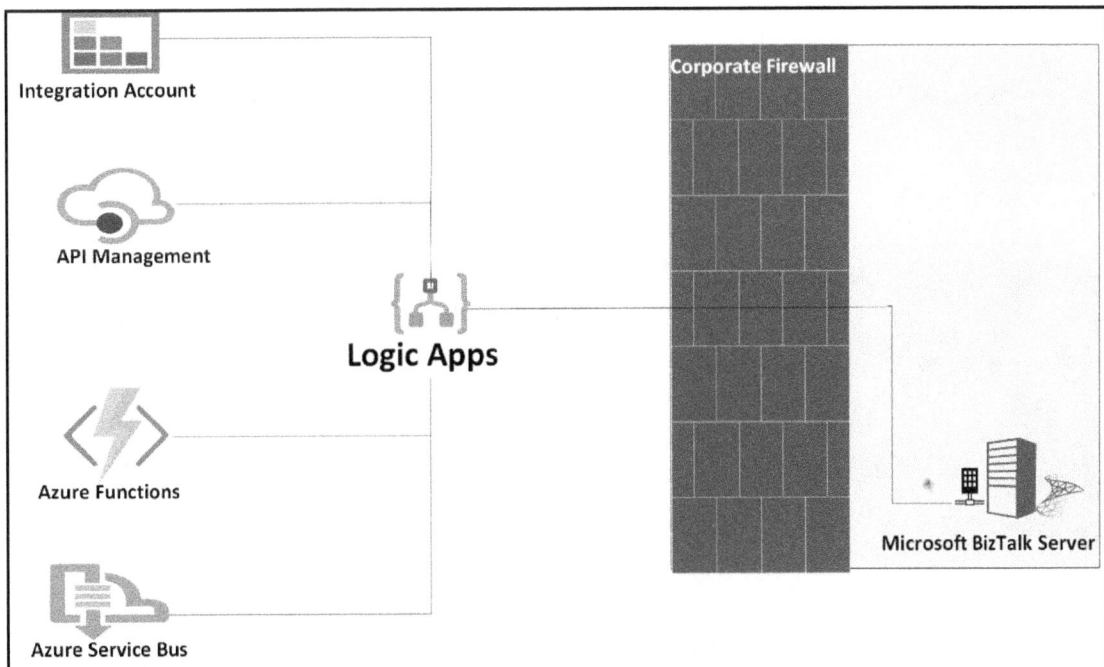

Logic App connectivity opened the gate to use multiple connectors available in cloud within BizTalk Server. For example, now it is possible to connect to cloud SaaS offering, such as Azure cognitive services, Drobox, and Slack with BizTalk Server without doing any custom coding or buying any third-party adapter.

Installing and configuring an adapter in BizTalk Server 2016

We assume that you have already installed and configured BizTalk Server 2016 along with Visual Studio 2015 and the appropriate version of SQL server.

With Microsoft BizTalk Server 2016 release, the Microsoft team has updated the **Line of Business** (**LOB**) adapters. To install LOB, follow these installation steps:

- Close any programs you have open. Run the BizTalk Server 2016 installer as administrator.
- On the **Start** screen, click on **Install Microsoft BizTalk Adapters**:

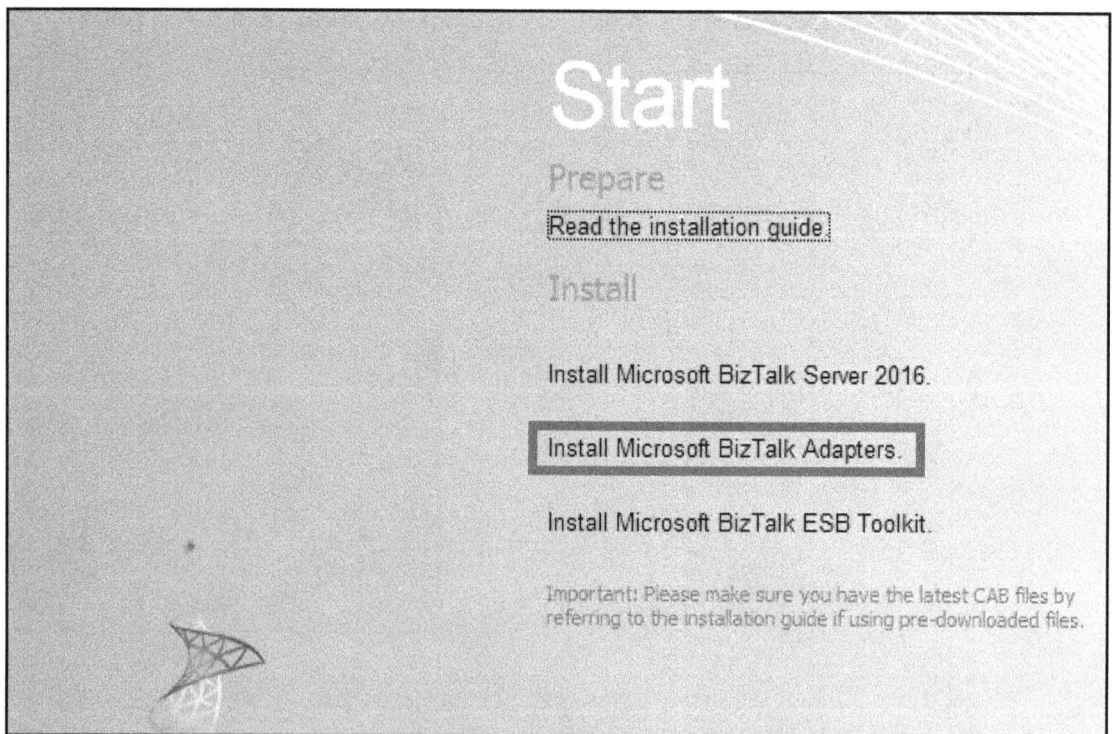

- In the next**Start** screen, the first step is to install WCF LOB Adapter SDK, select **Step 1: Install Microsoft WCF LOB Adapter SDK**:

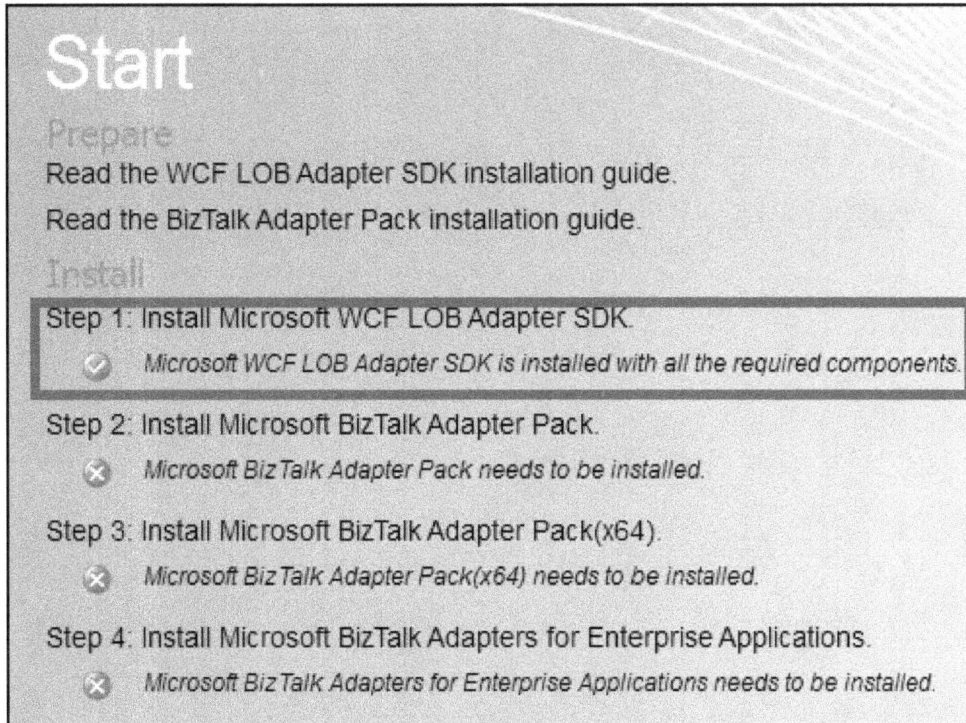

Start

Prepare

Read the WCF LOB Adapter SDK installation guide.

Read the BizTalk Adapter Pack installation guide.

Install

Step 1: Install Microsoft WCF LOB Adapter SDK.

   ⊘ *Microsoft WCF LOB Adapter SDK is installed with all the required components.*

Step 2: Install Microsoft BizTalk Adapter Pack.

   ⊗ *Microsoft BizTalk Adapter Pack needs to be installed.*

Step 3: Install Microsoft BizTalk Adapter Pack(x64).

   ⊗ *Microsoft BizTalk Adapter Pack(x64) needs to be installed.*

Step 4: Install Microsoft BizTalk Adapters for Enterprise Applications.

   ⊗ *Microsoft BizTalk Adapters for Enterprise Applications needs to be installed.*

- On the **Welcome to the Windows Communication Foundation LOB adapter SDK Setup Wizard** screen, click on **Next**.
- In the **Choose Setup Type** screen, select the installation type **Complete**.

- On the **Completed the Windows Communication Foundation LOB Adapter SDK Setup Wizard** screen, click on **Finish**:

Start

Prepare

Read the WCF LOB Adapter SDK installation guide.

Read the BizTalk Adapter Pack installation guide.

Install

Step 1: Install Microsoft WCF LOB Adapter SDK.

   ⊘   *Microsoft WCF LOB Adapter SDK is installed with all the required components.*

Step 2: Install Microsoft BizTalk Adapter Pack.

   ⊗   *Microsoft BizTalk Adapter Pack needs to be installed.*

Step 3: Install Microsoft BizTalk Adapter Pack(x64).

   ⊗   *Microsoft BizTalk Adapter Pack(x64) needs to be installed.*

Step 4: Install Microsoft BizTalk Adapters for Enterprise Applications.

   ⊗   *Microsoft BizTalk Adapters for Enterprise Applications needs to be installed.*

- On the **Welcome to the Microsoft BizTalk Adapter Pack Setup Wizard** screen, click on **Next**.
- On the **End-User License Agreement screen**, select **I accept the terms in the License Agreement** to accept the license agreement and click on **Next**.
- In the **Choose Setup Type** screen, select the installation type **Complete**.
- On the **Customer Experience Improvement Program** screen, select if you want to join the customer experience improvement program or not and click on **OK**.
- Back to the **Start** screen, the next step is installing the Microsoft BizTalk Adapter Pack (x64). Note that before you install this pack, you have to install x86 first and select **Step 3: Install Microsoft BizTalk Adapter Pack(x64)**. An installer of SDK is launched:

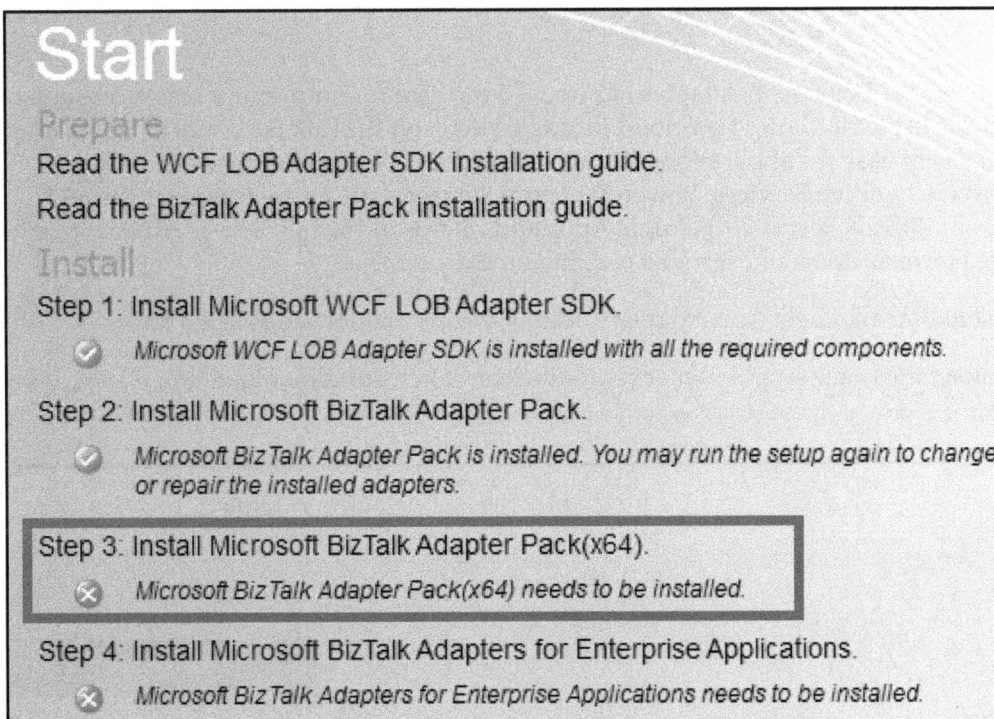

- On the **Welcome to the Microsoft BizTalk Adapter Pack(x64) Setup Wizard** screen, click on **Next**.
- On the **End-User License Agreement** screen, select **I accept the terms in the License Agreement** to accept the license agreement and click on **Next**.
- In the **Choose Setup Type** screen, select the installation type **Complete**.

- On the **Ready-to-install Microsoft BizTalk Adapter Pack(x64)**, click on **Install**.
- On the **Customer Experience Improvement Program** screen, select if you want to join the customer experience improvement program or not and click on **OK**.
- On the **Completed the Microsoft BizTalk Adapter Pack(x64) Setup Wizard** screen, click on **Finish**.

Installing the Logic Apps Adapter in BizTalk Server 2016

With release of Microsoft BizTalk Server, the Microsoft team has introduced a new adapter to communicate with Logic Apps and Microsoft BizTalk Server 2016 named BizTalk Logic App Adapter.

BizTalk Server Logic App Adapter has opened the gate for on-premise resources to use multitude of service hosted on cloud through Microsoft BizTalk Server 2016. For example, now it's very easy for applications sitting behind firewall to access services, such as Microsoft Cognitive Services, Power BI, Azure Storage, and Azure functions through Microsoft BizTalk Server 2016. Logic Apps and Microsoft BizTalk Server 2016 act as a bridge between cloud and services running on On-premise.

To install BizTalk Logic App Adapters, follow the installation steps listed later.

Download the Logic App Adapter setup file from Microsoft download link: `https://www.m icrosoft.com/en-us/download/details.aspx?id=54287`:

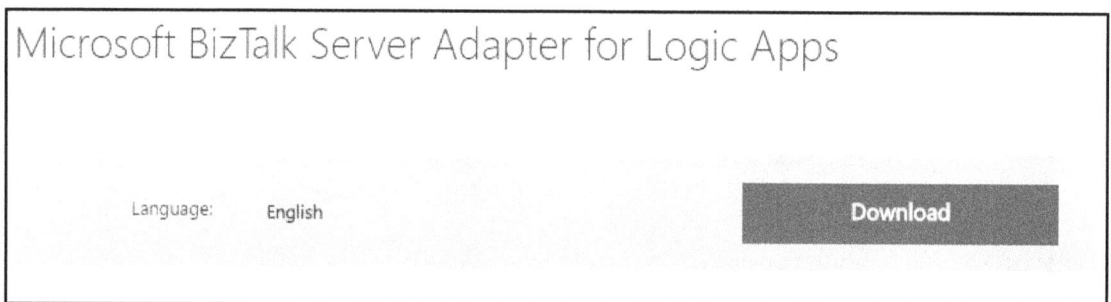

Microsoft BizTalk Server Adapter for Logic Apps

Language: English   **Download**

Installation steps:

- Close any programs you have open. Run the Logic Apps Adapter and set up installer as administrator
- On the Logic App Adapter setup welcome screen, click on **Next**

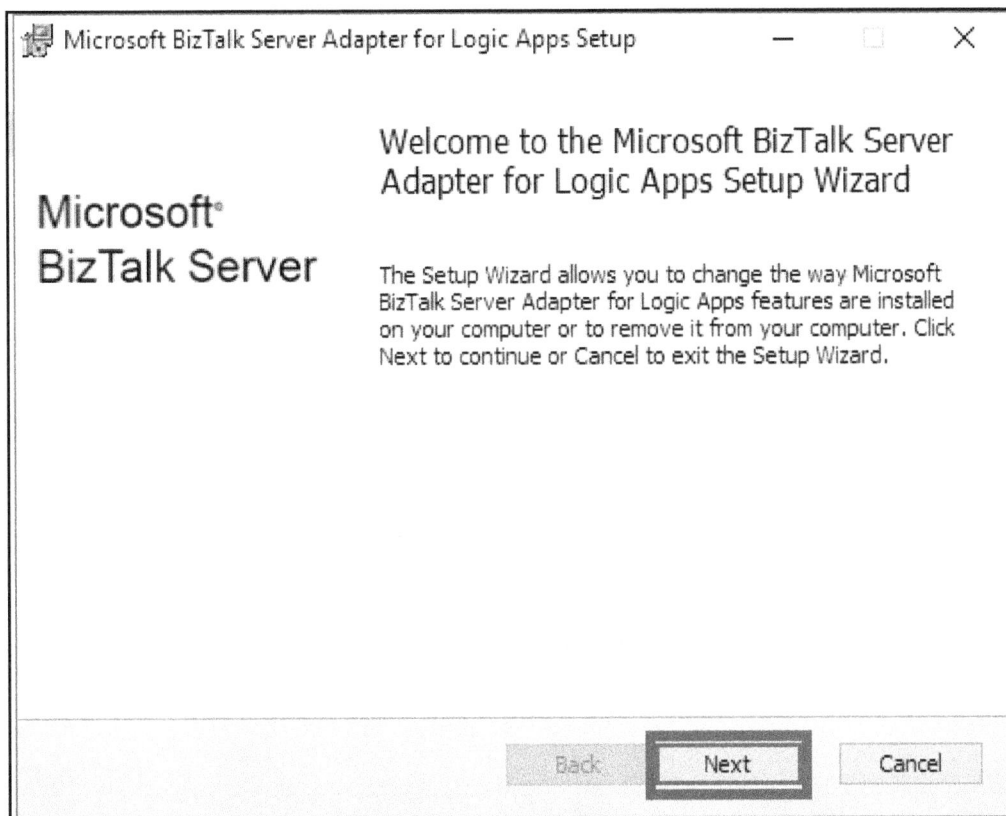

- On the next **End-User License Agreement** screen, accept the license agreement and click on next **Step 1: Install Microsoft WCF LOB Adapter SDK**:

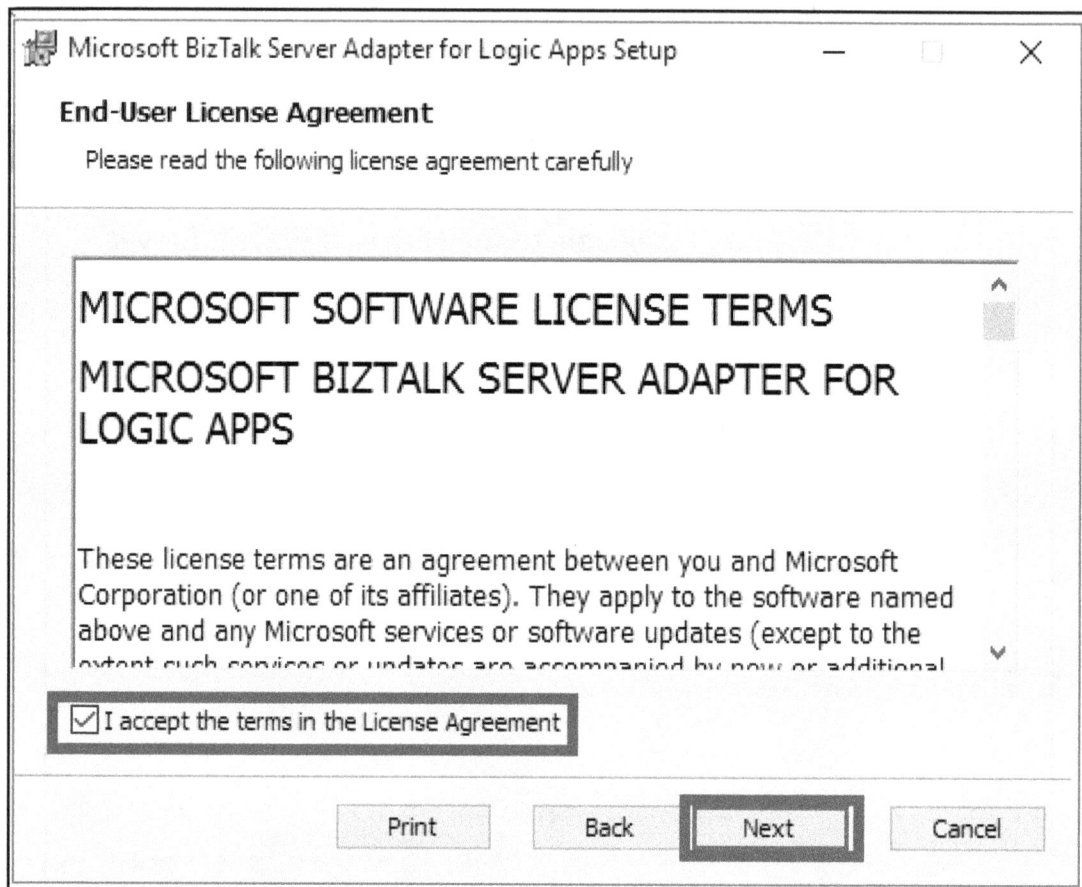

- On the **Ready to Install** screen, click on **Install**; this will install the Logic App Adapter on the BizTalk Application Server:

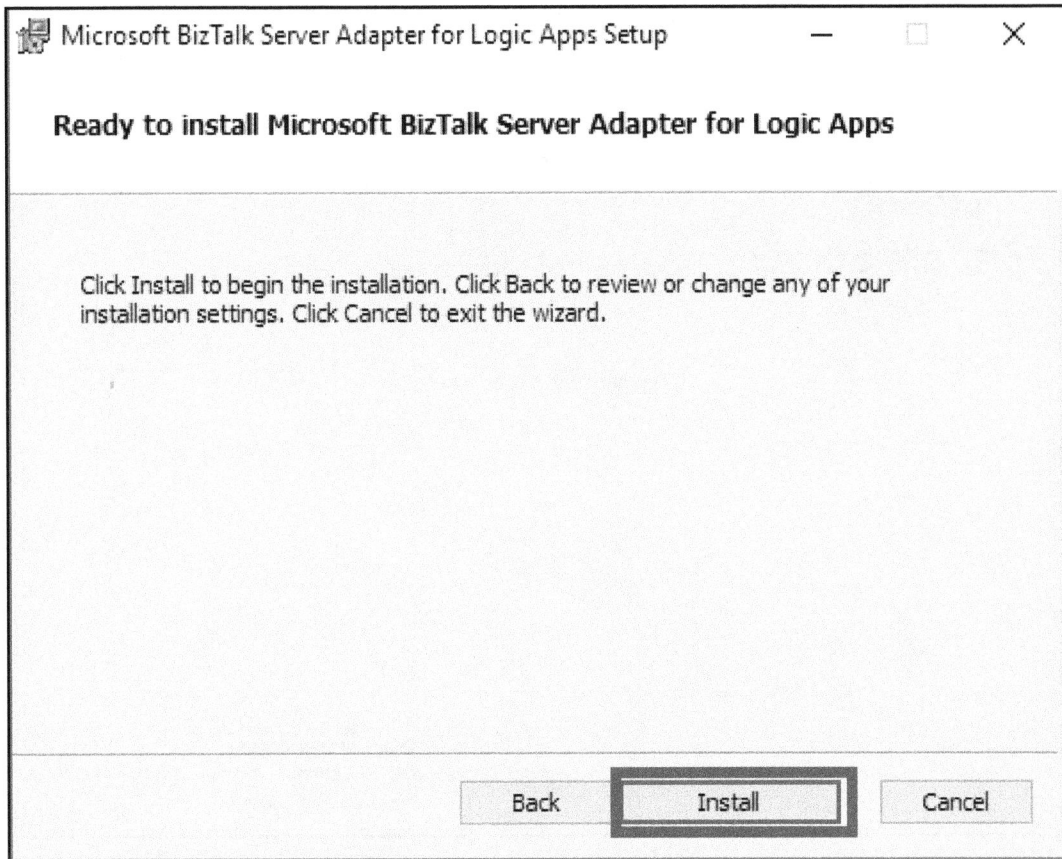

Microsoft BizTalk Server Adapter for Logic Apps Setup — ☐ ✕

Ready to install Microsoft BizTalk Server Adapter for Logic Apps

Click Install to begin the installation. Click Back to review or change any of your installation settings. Click Cancel to exit the wizard.

Back   **Install**   Cancel

- Click on **Finish** to complete the BizTalk Logic App installation:

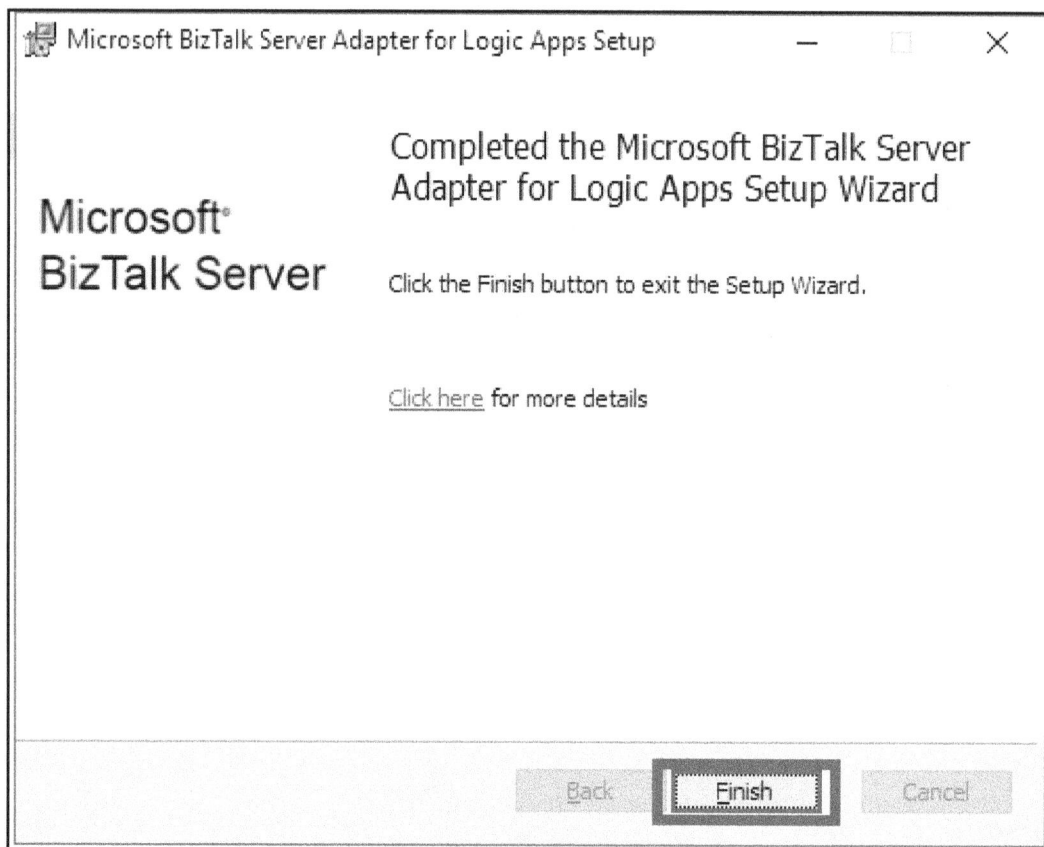

Connecting on-premise BizTalk Server 2016 with Azure Logic App

In this sample, we will use our fictitious company Sunny Electricals to do cognitive analysis done for a product based on the customer response once an item is sold, replaced, or serviced. We will be using the WCF-SQL adapter to poll the on-premise SQL server and get customer feedback data available for Logic App to perform cognitive analysis.

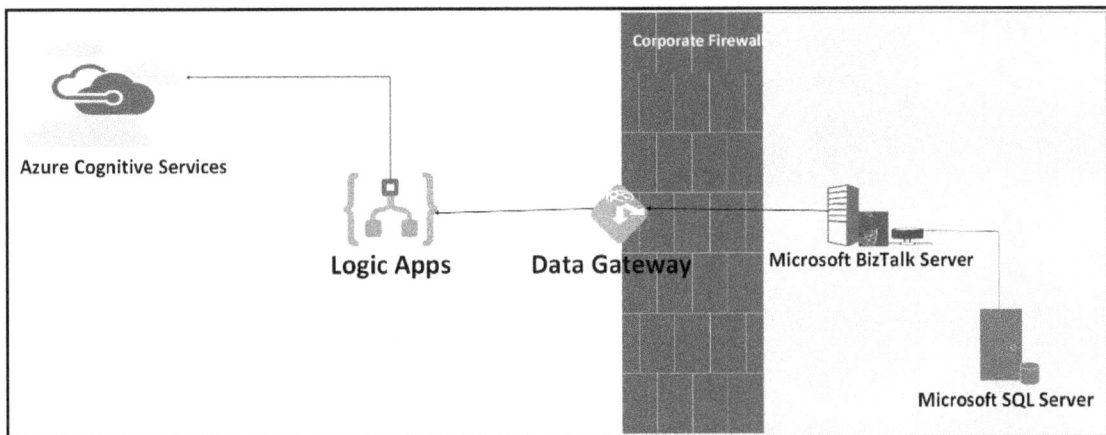

This solution requires the following components to be installed and configured along with Microsoft BizTalk Server 2016:

- The Logic Apps Adapter
- The WCF-SQL adapter

Step 1 – Creating Logic Apps for cognitive services

Azure Logic Apps provide cognitive services connector to be used in Logic App workflow. In the solution, we will show how to use Logic App that does sentiment analysis on sales data sitting on-premise. To perform sentiment analysis, we will use the **Text Analytics API** from cognitive services. To do this, in the Azure portal, you need to create cognitive services account:

Once cognitive service is created in Azure portal. Create a new Logic App with an HTTP request-response. This Logic App will use a sentiment analysis API over the requested data and send the response score to the caller:

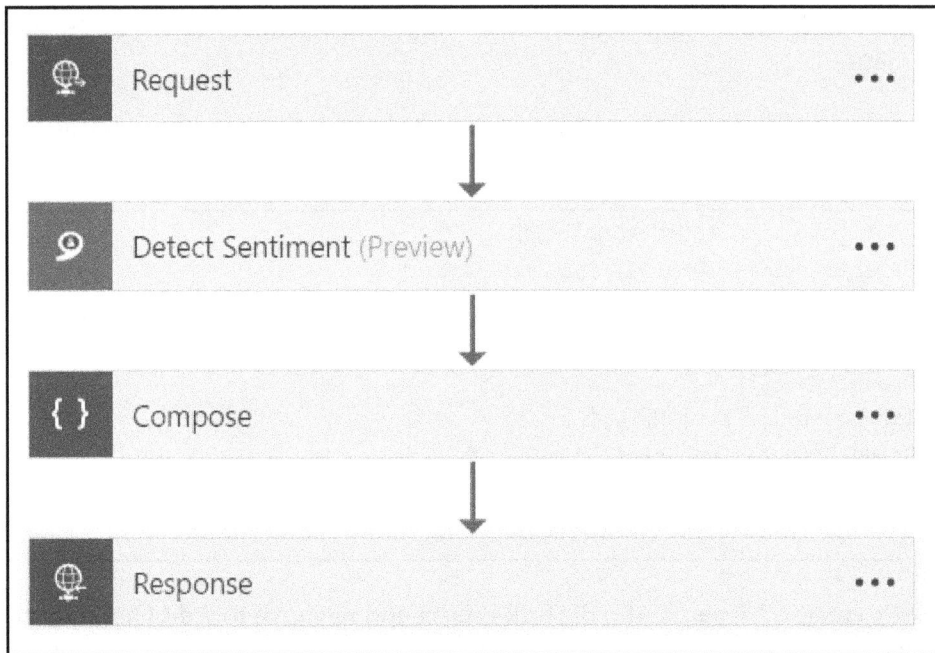

The next step is to create BizTalk Project with the request response Logic App port to make a request call to the cloud-hosted Logic App endpoint. In the exercise, we will be polling the SQL server to get the latest sales data and update each record with sentiment score.

Step 2 – Typed Polling with the WCF adapter

To poll for sales and product feedback data from SQL server, we will be using the WCF-SQL Adapter in BizTalk Server 2016. The adapter supports receiving polling-based messages, wherein the adapter executes a specified SQL statement, retrieves or updates the data and provides the result to the BizTalk Server receive location.

The WCF-SQL adapter supports three types of polling:

- Weakly Typed Polling (also named Polling),
- Strongly Typed Polling (also named TypedPolling)
- Xml-Polling polling using statements or procedures that include a FOR XML clause

For the purposes of this sample, we will be using the sales table of Sunny Electricals database. The table script is shown here:

```
CREATE TABLE [dbo].[SalesOrderTable](
    [SalesId] [int] IDENTITY(1,1) NOT NULL,
    [CustomerId] [int] NOT NULL,
    [Transationdate] [datetime] NULL,
    [ProductName] [varchar](50) NULL,
    [IsProcessed] [int] NULL,
    [ProductScore] [varchar](50) NULL,
    [CustomerProdcutFeedback] [varchar](max) NULL
) ON [PRIMARY] TEXTIMAGE_ON [PRIMARY]
```

To start with, create a Visual Studio BizTalk Project and navigate to **Add Generated Items** | **Consume Adapter Service** to generate XML schema for the Typed polling, which will return sales data based on date processed state:

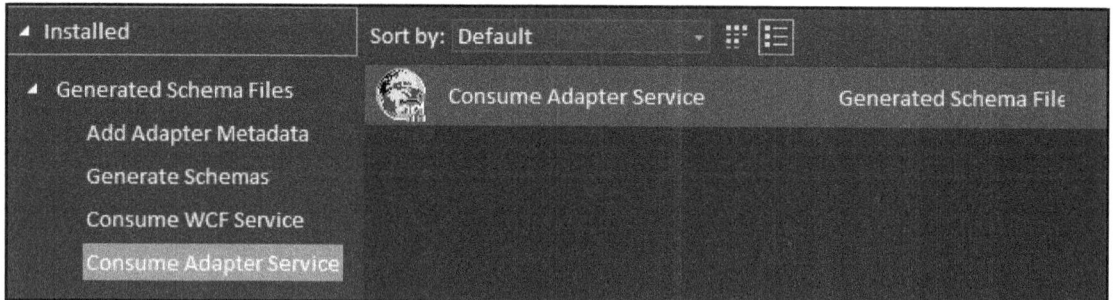

After selecting the **sqlBinding** as the adapter, populate the URI properties with server name, database name, and **InboundId**:

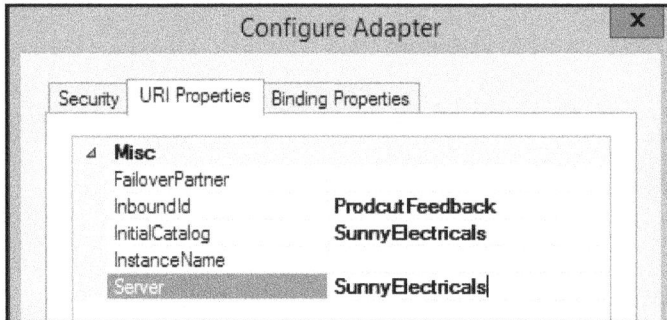

In the**Binding Properties** tab, set the adapter to use **TypedPolling** and populate the **PollingDataAvailableStatement** to a SQL statement that counts how many records match the Polling query. In the `PollingStatement` value to write query which will return records from Sales table where the IsProcessed flag is 0:

- **select count(*) FROM [SalesOrderTable] where IsProcessed= 0**
- **select * from [SalesOrderTable] where IsProcessed = 0;**
- **update [SalesOrderTable] set IsProcessed=1 where IsProcessed= 0**

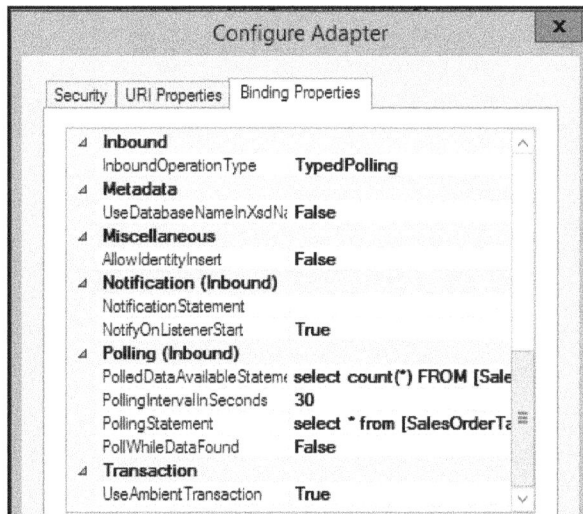

Connecting to the Sunny Electricals database

Click on **connect** to make sure that the URI configuration is correct. Select **Service (Inbound operations)** in the dropdown for the contract type. Choose **TypedPolling** and click on **Add** while selecting **Generate unique schema type**:

When the wizard is completed, it will end up with one new schema (and one binding file) added to the project:

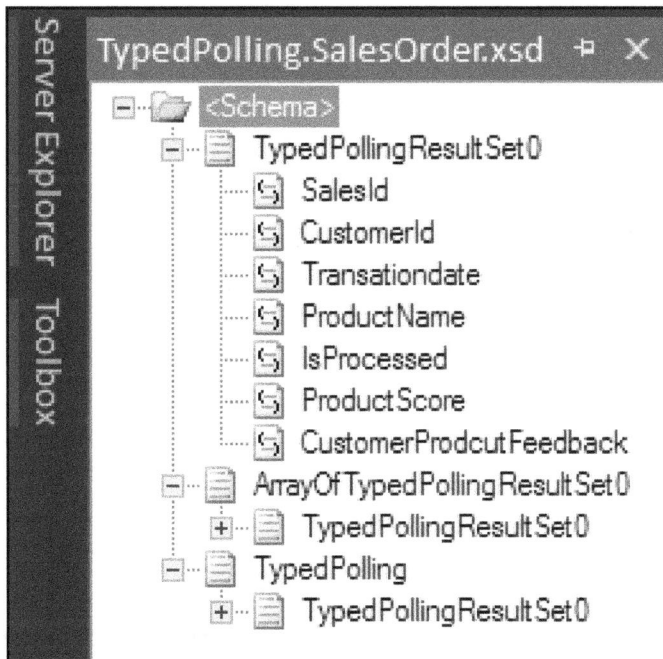

The final step is to split the polling data into separate distinct messages at the BizTalk pipeline stage. This can be done by setting the envelope property of the generated schema and the XPath of the repetitive node.

> If you require more information on how you can de-batch the sql message in Pipeline, you can refer to the following blog post: `https://seroter.wo rdpress.com/2010/04/08/debatching-inbound-messages-from-biztal k-wcf-sql-adapter/`.

Create orchestration, which will trigger with the sales data and call a two-way Logic Apps endpoint to get customer feedback sentiment analysis.

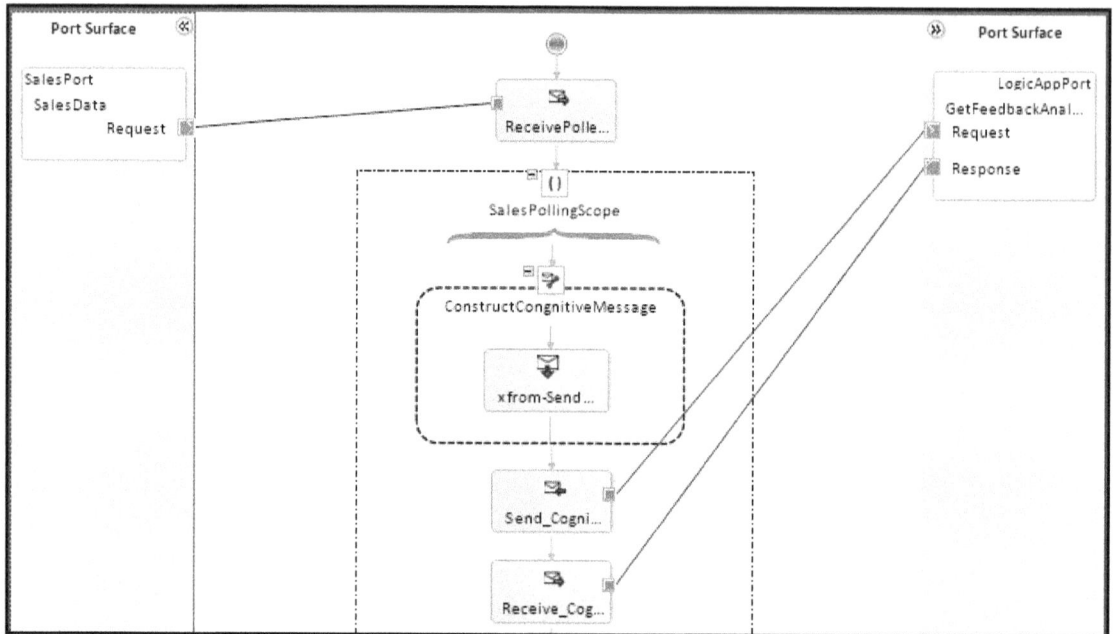

Once the sentiment analysis score is received in your orchestration, call the update sentiment analysis stored procedure to update the sales table.

Once the BizTalk orchestration workflow is completed, build and deploy the application within BizTalk administration console:

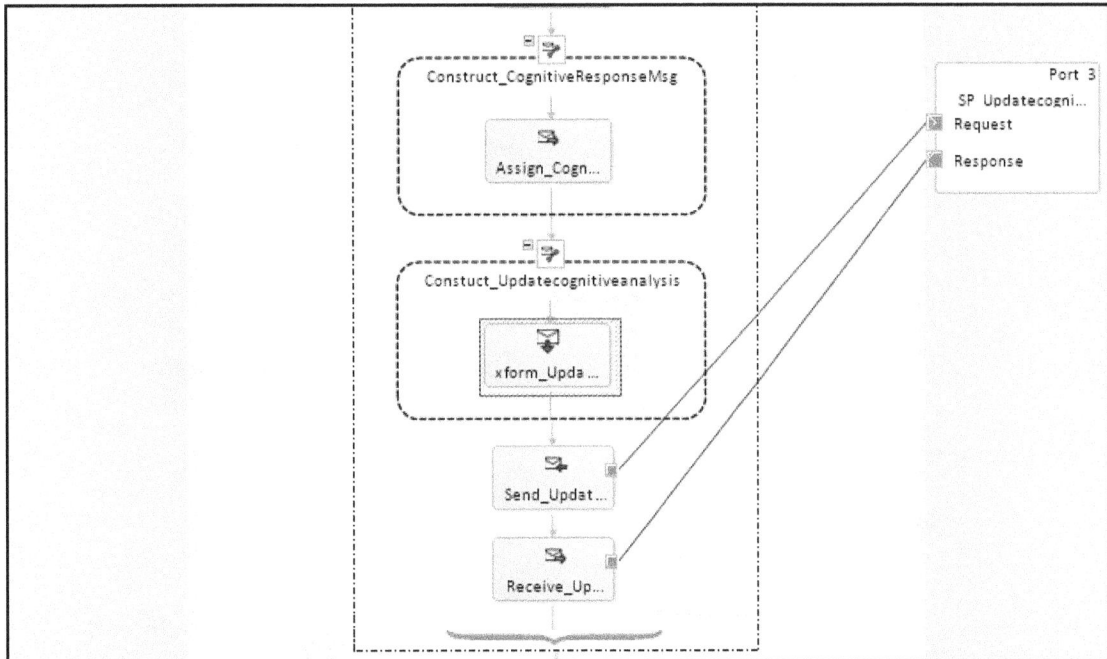

Creating a two-way send port for Logic Apps

From the BizTalk administrative console, navigate to the newly deployed BizTalk application. Expand the application, and on the send port, right-click to create a new two-way send port.

For configuration of two-way send port, select the Logic App Adapter as desired handler. On **LogicApp Adapter Transport Properties**, click on **Configure**. This will open a pop-up window. Enter your correct Azure subscription detailed under which sentiment analysis Logic App is deployed:

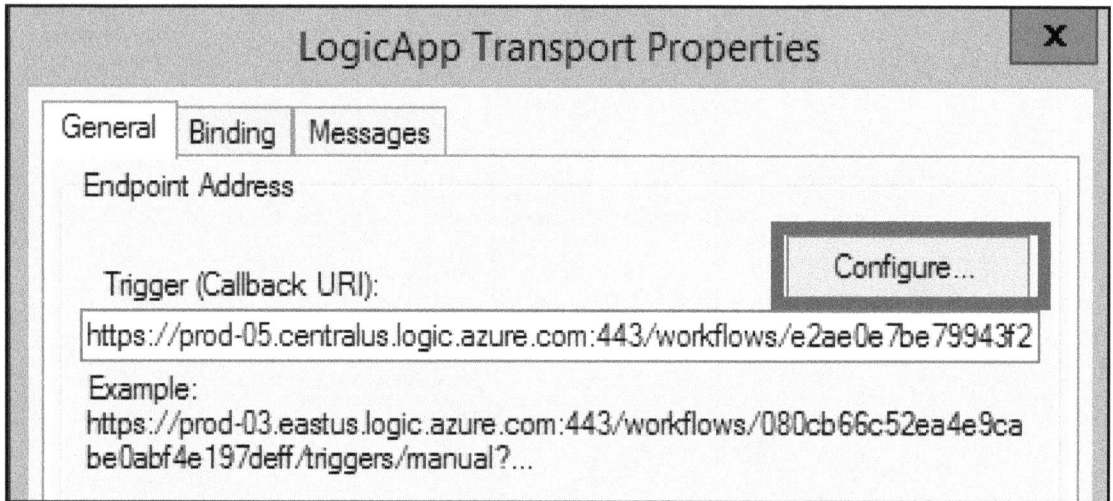

Once the BizTalk orchestration is correctly bounded with WCF-SQL and logic adapter, verify the run from the Azure portal and look at a sentiment analysis update on the sales table:

	SalesId	CustomerId	Transationdate	ProductName	IsProcessed	ProductScore	CustomerProd...
	1	1	2015-12-11 00:0...	FAN	1	0.9661295	Prodcut is good
	2	2	2016-09-11 00:0...	FAN	1	0.9937462	Awsome. but it ...
	3	1	2016-08-05 00:0...	AIRCONDITION	1	0.2740484	not good

BIZTALK2016.Sunny...o.SalesOrderTable

Connecting Azure Logic App with on-premise BizTalk Server 2016

In this code sample, we will call on-premise WCF Service from Logic Apps through BizTalk Server 2016. Here, WCF Service is responsible for getting account details for a specific Sunny Electricals customer. We will use **Consume WCF Service Wizard** to generate XSD schemas for the WCF Service and generate an IIS endpoint for Logic App to trigger.

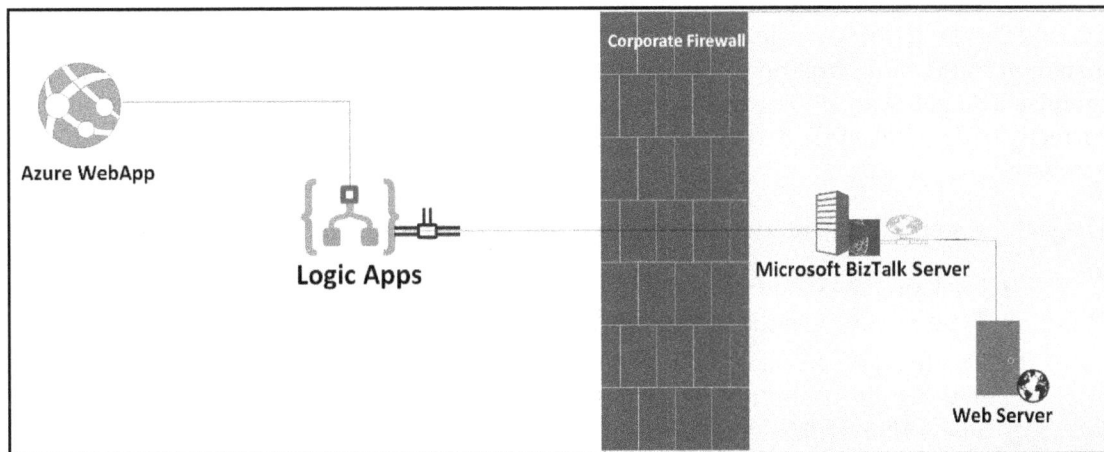

This solution requires the following components to be installed and configured along with Microsoft BizTalk Server 2016:

- On-premise data gateway
- IIS configuration for Logic App Adapter
- WCF-Basic HTTP adapter
- Logic Apps Adapter

We have already discussed in `Chapter 8`, *A Deep Dive into Logic Apps*, how to install and configure an on-premise data gateway using your Azure subscription. We will use the on-premise data gateway along with BizTalk Server and Logic App Adapter to make the hybrid solution.

IIS configuration for Logic App Adapter

We assume that you have already installed and configured an on-premise data gateway on BizTalk Server, if not, you can refer to `Chapter 8`, *A Deep Dive into Logic Apps*, for the installation and configuration of on-premise data gateway. Once you are done with the on-premise data gateway, you need to set up and configure the Logic App IIS endpoint correctly to access BizTalk Server environment from logic through an on-premise data gateway.

The step-by-step documentation to configure IIS for Logic App Adapter is as follows:

- Click on the Windows icon and type `run` to open up the **Run** command window. Type `inetmgr` in the search box and click on *enter*.
- Create an IIS Application Pool by right-clicking the **Application Pools** and select **new Application Pool**. Enter the desired name `LogicApp` and click on **ok** to add a new IIS Application Pool.

- In the **Advanced Settings** of newly created Application Pool, set the **Identity** property to the appropriate user who is a member of the BizTalk Server administrative group:

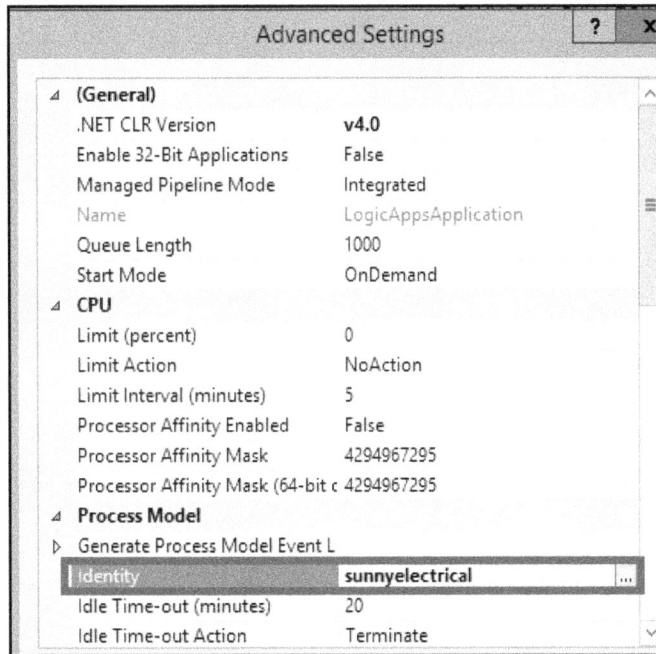

- Next, right-click on **Default Web Site** and click on **Add Application**. In the dialog that opens, enter a name for the application as `ManagementEndpoint`, and for the physical path, enter the installation path of Logic App `ManagementEndpoint`. The default path will be `C:\Program Files (x86)\Microsoft BizTalk Server 2016\LogicApp Adapter\Management`.

- For the newly created Application `ManagementEndpoint`, change the **IIS Application Pool** to **Application Pool** created earlier.

- Click on **test Settings** to confirm that the Application Pool identity passes the authentication and authorization tests.

- Open a web browser and go
  to: `http://localhost/ManagementEndpoint/Schemas?api-version=2016
  -10-26`. This will give a list of schemas deployed in the BizTalk Server
  Management database.

Consuming a WCF Service in BizTalk 2016

We move ahead to create a BizTalk solution, which will call a WCF Service hosted within
the corporate network. Create a Visual Studio BizTalk Project and use **Add Generated
Items** | **Consume WCF Service** to generate XML schema for the WCF Service, which will
return customer account details.

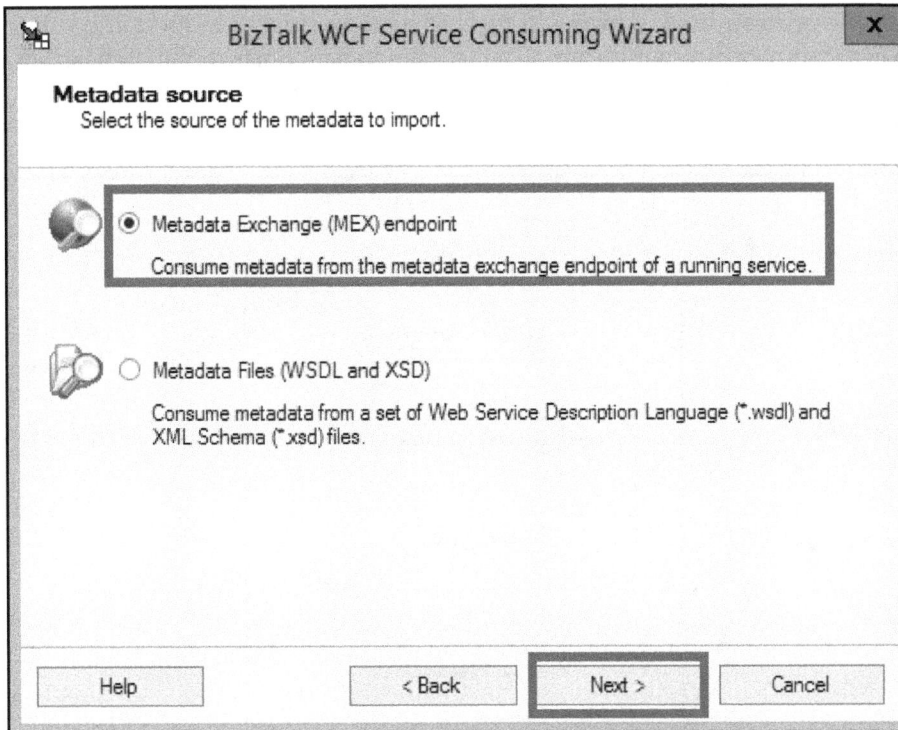

Enter the URL of the on-premise-hosted WCF Service to generate the WCF data contract, which will be used within the orchestration.

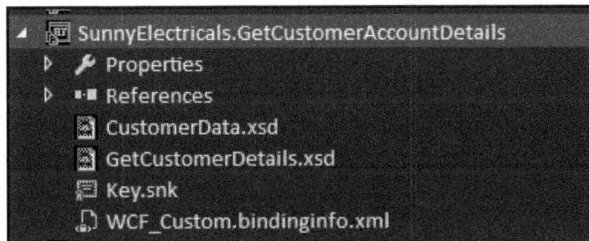

Create a simple orchestration, which will receive customerId as a request and call the WCF Service to get account customer information. All the logical ports in the orchestration are configured with a specify later binding. The solution containing the schemas and orchestration is signed with a strong name and deployed to the BizTalk runtime:

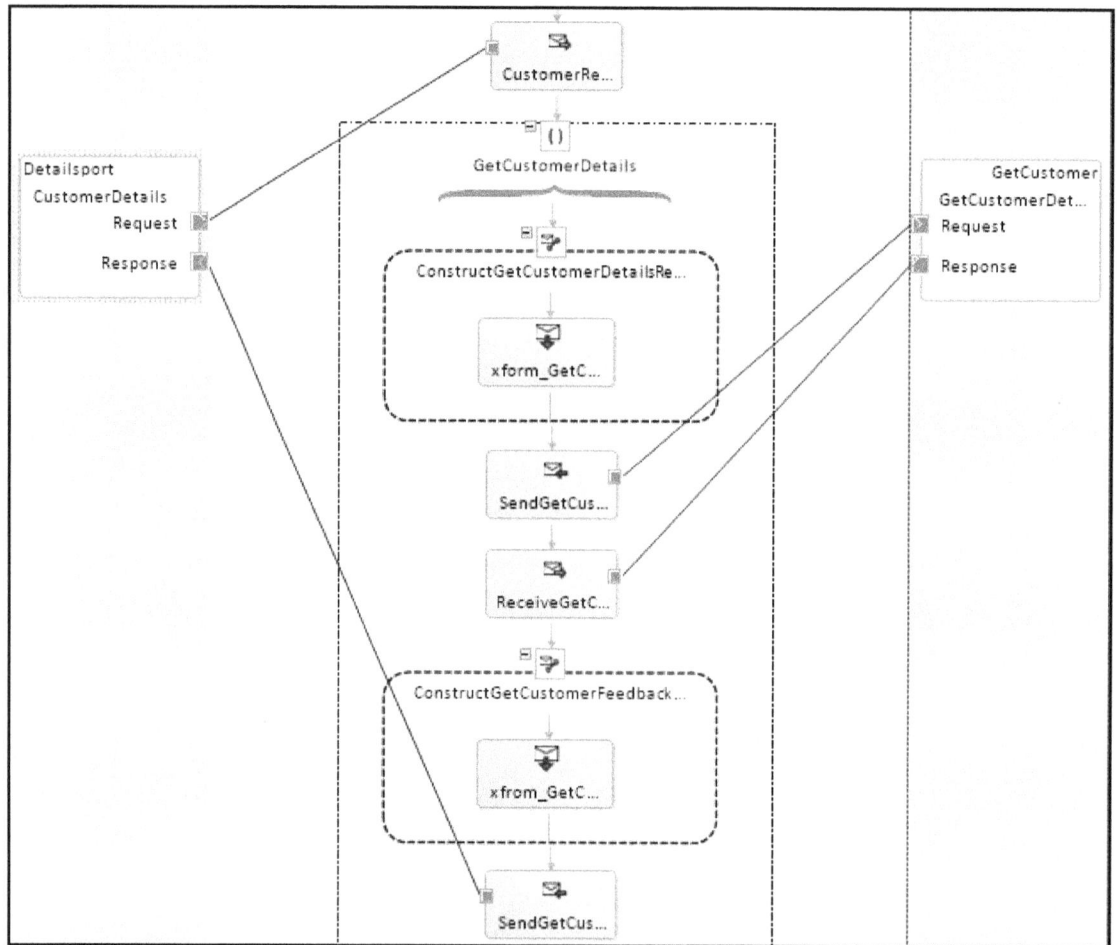

The configuration of the physical send and receive ports is done after the solution is deployed to the BizTalk Server administration console.

To create web port, import the binding file in the BizTalk solution, which is generated from the **Add Generate Item**. To create a request-response, receive a location for Logic Apps Create application within IIS for `GetCustomerDetails` and set the application poll same as of `LogicApp Management Endpoint`. Set the Application path for `GetCustomerDetails` to use `C:\Program Files (x86)\Microsoft BizTalk Server 2016\LogicApp Adapter\ReceiveService`.

In the BizTalk Admin console, create a request response port within the `GetCustomerDetails` solution, which will run under the Logic App adapter handler. The configuration details are shown in the following image:

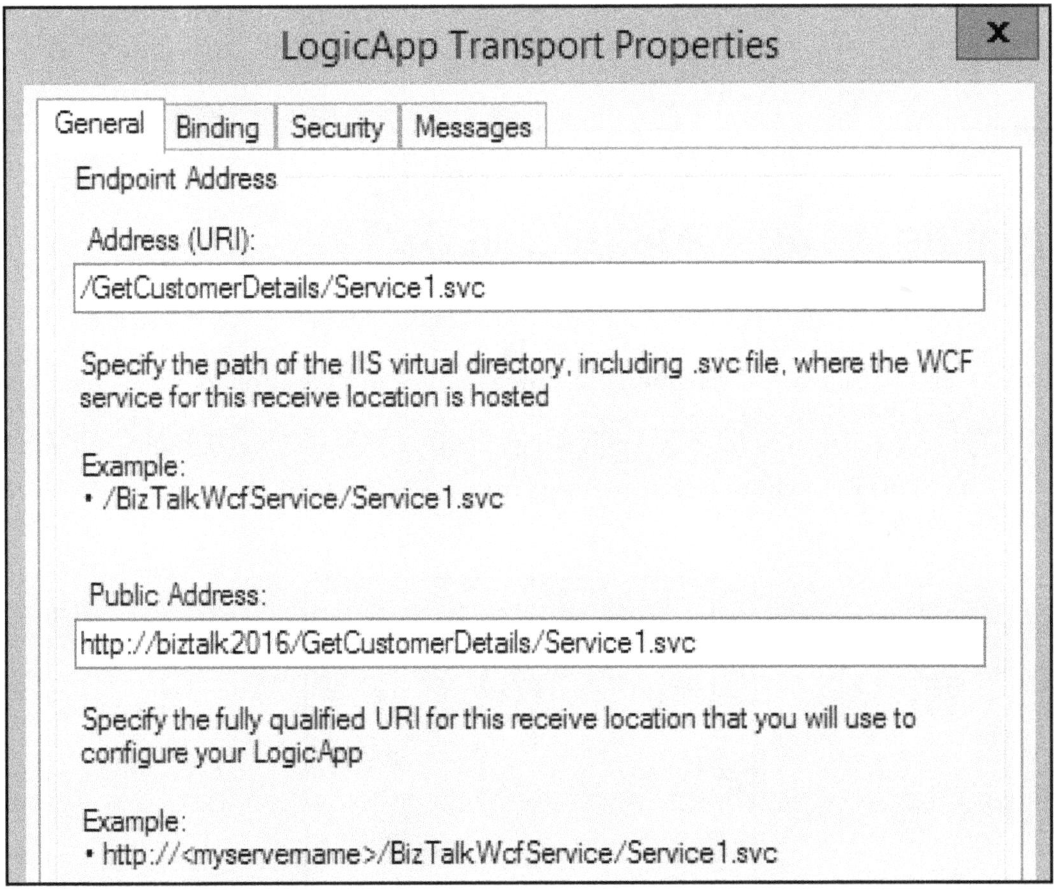

```
Service                    ×

←  →  C   ⓘ localhost/GetCustomerDetails/Service1.svc

Service

This is a Windows© Communication Foundation service.

Metadata publishing for this service is currently disabled.

If you have access to the service, you can enable metadata publishing by completing the following steps to modify your web or application c
file:

1. Create the following service behavior configuration, or add the <serviceMetadata> element to an existing service behavior configuration:

    <behaviors>
        <serviceBehaviors>
            <behavior name="MyServiceTypeBehaviors" >
                <serviceMetadata httpGetEnabled="true" />
            </behavior>
        </serviceBehaviors>
    </behaviors>
```

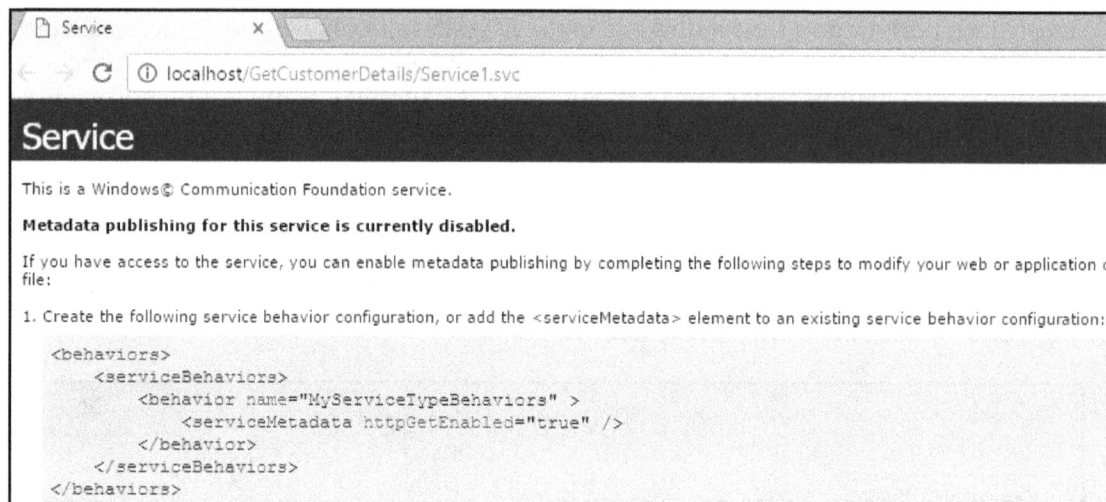

Creating a Logic App to call BizTalk

- From the Azure portal, click on **New**, search for a Logic App, and click on **Logic App**.
- Enter a **Name**, **Subscription**, **Resource Group**, and **Location** for your Logic App and then click on **Create**.
- Once new logic is created, design the Logic App workflow with the HTTP trigger and BizTalk actions (create message from XML and send message) and HTTP response.

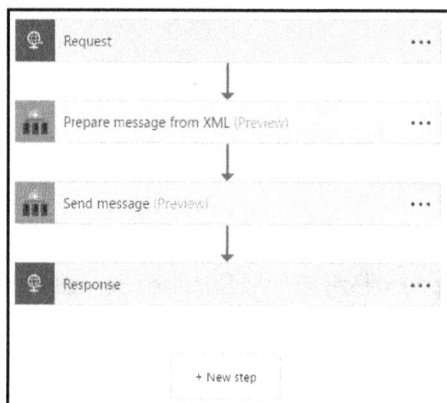

Once the Logic App design is completed and saved. Trigger the Logic App through the client application or any testing tool such as Postman.

We have used the Postman tool to make an HTTP post on created Logic App. The Logic App workflow calls to BizTalk endpoints through on-premise data gateway and gets the desired customer record into Logic Apps.

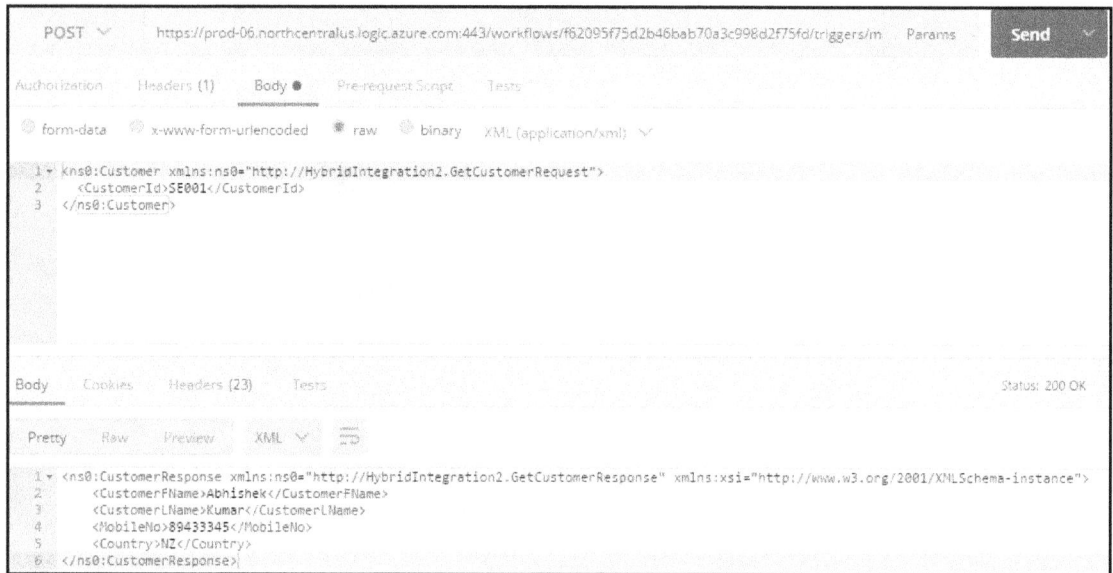

Summary

In this chapter, we explored the capabilities of Logic Apps and how they can be applied to typical Hybrid Integration scenarios using Logic App Adapter.

Logic Apps provide connectivity in on-premise applications. We showed how we can connect the on-premise BizTalk Server and wide variety of services, such as SQL and WCF services hosted within corporate network, with no access to cloud.

In the next chapter, we will discuss tooling and monitoring, which can be used within Logic Apps to monitor the cloud integration platform.

14
Tooling and Monitoring for Logic Apps

Being able to deploy a solution that consists of several resources and for different environments (Dev, UAT, QA, and Prod) in a repetitive and structured manner can be challenging without proper tooling in place.

In general, when a solution has been deployed to a cloud environment, you lose the capability to actively monitor, troubleshoot, and optimize your applications without the proper monitoring in place. Also, being able to view the current workload or being alerted of unpredicted loads can be another issue.

Another challenge is how do we actively monitor the consumption of resources and be alerted if we exceed the existing hosting plan.

In this chapter, you will learn the following:

- How to use the Azure Resource Manager templates to create resources and best practices
- Deploying Logic Apps either manually or using continuous deployments and using PowerShell scripts
- How to set up monitoring and alerting for Logic Apps

Tools to monitor Azure resources

With Azure, there are a set of APIs available to manage the provisioning of resources programmatically. There are two versions available; first, **Azure Service Management** (**ASM**) (For more information refer to: `https://azure.microsoft.com/en-in/blog/intro ducing-the-windows-azure-service-management-api/`), which was developed for the Classic portal and is used primarily for Azure v1 resource types. The second version is **Azure Resource Manager** (**ARM**), which is used to manage both v1 and the current version v2 of Azure resources.

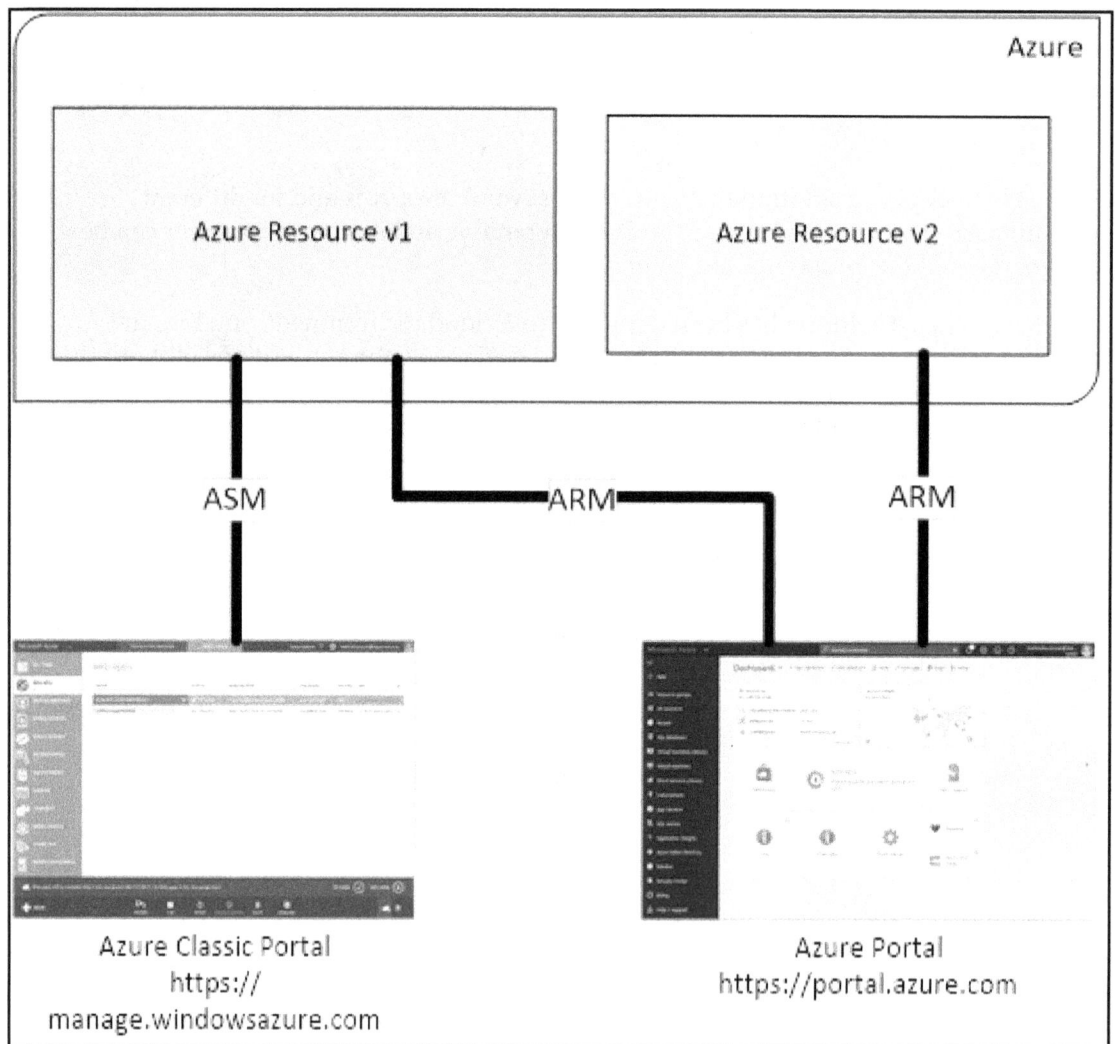

Note, however, that some of the resources provisioned using ARM cannot be viewable from the Classic portal.

Deployment options

There are several options available when deploying and provisioning Azure resources, and they are listed here:

- **Azure portal-based deployment**: Use the Classic or the new Azure portal to provision and manage resources individually and not as a group. You will need to manually set the order of provisioning and deletion of the required resources.
- **Azure PowerShell**: This provides a more automated way of provisioning resources to ensure that they are created in the correct order. Note that some resources may only be created or configured by using PowerShell scripts.
- **Azure command-line interface (CLI) tools**: This provides command-line tools to create, manage, and delete services via the command line. These tools are available for Windows, Linux, and OSX. These tools normally interact with the **Resource Manager** APIs and the **Service Management** APIs for the Classic portal.
- **Azure Resource Manager**: This is available in the new Azure portal. It provides the capability to deploy, update, or delete all resources pertaining to a solution in a single operation. Microsoft's recommendation is to use ARM templates for current and future deployments.
- **Visual Studio**: It allows you to deploy your solution directly from VS.
- **Continuous deployments**: It is available while using source code repositories such as BitBucket, GitHub and Visual Studio Team Services.

Azure Resource Management templates

A typical Azure solution normally consists of many components (SQL Server, Active Directory, App Svc and so on) and involves provisioning these resources independently using Azure Service Management APIs or PowerShell scripts. By using ARM (Azure Resource Manager) templates you now have the ability to group all these resources together and use a declarative style template written in JSON to manage the deployment of your cloud services and any dependencies. Using the same template, provides the capability to deploy repeatedly into different environments throughout the application lifecycle with the same consistent results.

The benefits of using ARM templates are as follows:

- Set up resource locks, this provides the option to prevent the deletion or modification of resources by other users
- View the rolled-up costs of the entire resources for a resource group as they can now be grouped together
- Use declarative templates that can be managed under a source control repository
- Set the sequence of provisioning resources by defining the dependencies in the template
- **Role-Based Access Control** (**RBAC**) is natively supported

Prebuilt templates are also community contributed and can form the basis to get you started by modifying an existing template that closely resembles your requirements. These templates are available from here: `https://docs.microsoft.com/en-us/azure/azure-res ource-manager/resource-group-overview`.

The basic structure of an ARM template is made up of six elements and is similar to the code segment shown here:

```
{
    "$schema": "http://schema.management.azure.com/schemas/2015-01-
    01/deploymentTemplate.json#",
    "contentVersion": "",
    "parameters": { },
    "variables": { },
    "resources": [ ],
    "outputs": { }
}
```

ARM template size is limited to 1 MB and each parameter file to a size of 64 KB. The 1 MB limit applies to the final state of the template after it has been expanded with iterative resource definitions and values for variables and parameters.

The following table describes the elements of the template in more detail:

Element name	Description
`$schema`	This is the location of the JSON schema file and is a mandatory value. The file sets the rules on how the template will be processed. Typically, this value will be set to: `https://schema.management.azure.com/schemas/2015-01-01/deploymentTemplate.json` until MS publishes a later version.
`contentVersion`	The version of the template you are authoring and can be any value (for example, 1.0.0.0) and is a mandatory field. Use this to help you keep track of the template version between deployments.
`parameters`	Provides the flexibility to collect user input for resource properties before starting the deployment.
`variables`	Variables are optional. They are used to simplify the template by reusing the same variable throughout the template. The value can be a simple data or a complex type such as another JSON object. Variables values can also be based on other values.
`resources`	This is a mandatory element, and it defines a collection of resources that you plan to deploy as a part of the template deployment. Note that at least one resource must be defined.
`outputs`	This is used to return data or objects after a deployment.

These elements are described in more detail in the following paragraphs.

Parameters

The parameters elements specified in the ARM template are complex objects themselves. The structure of a parameter is as follows:

```
"parameters": {
  "<parameter-name>":{
  "type" : "<type-of-parameter-value>",
  "defaultValue": "<default-value-of-parameter>",
  "allowedValues": [ "<array-of-allowed-values>" ],
  "minValue": <minimum-value-for-int>,
  "maxValue": <maximum-value-for-int>,
  "minLength": <minimum-length-for-string-or-array>,
  "maxLength": <maximum-length-for-string-or-array-parameters>,
  "metadata": {
      "description": "<description-of-the parameter>"
```

```
            }
        }
    }
```

Element name	Required	Description
parameter-name	Yes	The name of the parameter.
type	Yes	The data type of the parameter and can be any one of the following types: • String is any valid JSON string • secureString is any valid JSON string • int • bool • object: any valid JSON object • secureObject is any valid JSON object • array is any valid JSON array
defaultValue	No	Default value of the input parameter if no value is provided.
allowedValues	No	An array list of allowed parameters to select from.
minValue	No	The minimum value for the "int" type parameters and this value is inclusive.
maxValue	No	The maximum value for the "int" type parameters and this value is inclusive.
minLength	No	The minimum length for string, secureString, and array type parameters. This value is inclusive.
maxLength	No	The maximum length for string, secureString, and array type parameters. This value is inclusive.
description	No	The description of the parameter which is displayed in the custom template interface on the portal.

A secureString represents text that should be kept confidential, such as by deleting it from computer memory when no longer needed.

When you start to deploy the resources, you will be prompted for the input values of the parameters. You can also include the parameter values in another JSON file named `templatename.params.json`. This will allow you to have multiple versions of the input values for different environments.

Variables

The variable elements are in the following form and are defined as a JSON key/value pair and must follow the standard JSON syntax:

```
"variables":{
   "<variable-name>":"<variable-value>",
    "<variable-name>":{
       <variable-complex-type-value>
   }
}
```

The following is an example of two variables calling two different functions to obtain the resource group location and assigning a variable to a parameter. Functions are normally encapsulated in square brackets:

```
"location": "[resourceGroup().location]"
"sbVersion": "[parameters('serviceBusApiVersion')]"
```

Resources

This defines the resource to be deployed or provisioned. The configuration information can either be defined directly in the resource definition or populated from variables and or parameter values:

```
"resources": [
    {
       "apiVersion": "<api-version-of-resource>",
       "type": "<resource-provider-namespace/resource-type-name>",
       "name": "<name-of-the-resource>",
       "location": "<location-of-resource>",
       "tags": "<name-value-pairs-for-resource-tagging>",
       "comments": "<your-reference-notes>",
       "dependsOn": [
         "<array-of-related-resource-names>"
       ],
       "properties": "<settings-for-the-resource>",
       "copy": {
         "name": "<name-of-copy-loop>",
```

```
            "count": "<number-of-iterations>"
        }
        "resources": [
          "<array-of-child-resources>"
        ]
      }
    ]
```

The elements are described in more detail here:

Element name	Required	Description
apiVersion	Yes	The version of the REST API to use for creating the resource.
type	Yes	This a combination of the namespace and resource.
name	Yes	The name of the resource. The name must follow URI component restrictions defined in RFC3986.
location	depends	Supported geo-location for the resource. However, some types of resources do not require a location to be defined.
tags	No	Tags that are associated with the resource.
comments	No	User-defined notes.
dependsOn	No	ThedependsOnproperty is used to define dependencies among resources.
properties	No	Specific configuration settings for the resource. It can be set directly or through variables or parameters.
copy	No	The number of instances to create for a resource.
resources	No	An array of child resources that depend on the resource being defined.

Outputs

The structure of the output element is defined as follows:

```
"outputs": {
  "<outputName>": {
    "type": "<datatype-of-output-value>",
    "value": "<output-value-expression>"
  }
}
```

Element name	Required	Description
outputName	yes	The name of the output value. Must be a valid Javascript identifier.
type	yes	The datatype of the output value. Must be any one of the type listed here: • string: any valid JSON string • secureString: any valid JSON string • int • bool • object: any valid JSON object • secureObject: any valid JSON object • array: any valid JSON array
value	yes	The expression that will be evaluated and returned,

The output value can also be used to share state and data between nested template deployments.

Expressions and Functions

Apart from the default elements described earlier, the template can also be extended using expressions and functions. When using functions, it should be enclosed in square brackets.

A full list of the available functions is available from here: `https://docs.microsoft.com/en-in/azure/azure-resource-manager/resource-group-template-functions`.

They are grouped in the following categories:

- **Numeric**: for working with integers
- **String**: for working with strings
- **Array**: for working with arrays
- **Deployment values**: for getting values from sections of the template and values related to the deployment
- **Resource**: getting resource values

Parameter Files

These are files used to populate the parameters specified in the ARM template, and they are useful when provisioning Azure resources for different environments or configuration settings:

```
{
    "$schema": "https://schema.management.azure.com/schemas/2015-01-
    01/deploymentParameters.json#",
    "contentVersion": "1.0.0.0",
    "parameters": {
        "<name-of-parameter>": {
            "value": "<value>"
        }
    }
}
```

Element name	Required	Description
`<name-of-parameter>`	yes	The name of the parameters defined in the parameters section of the ARM template
`value`	yes	The value to be used for the parameter

Deploying templates

There are various options available when deploying these templates as listed here:

- **Azure portal**: Upload the JSON ARM template into the portal for deployment
- **Azure PowerShell**: You can use a local or external referenced templates for deployments using the **New-AzureRMResourceGroupDeployment** cmdlet
- **ARM REST API**: Use the APIs directly to manage the resources

- **Click to Deploy**: This provides the capability to deploy templates directly from GitHub
- **MS Visual Studio**: This directly deploys resources and groups from Visual Studio

Creating ARM Template using Visual Studio

Using Visual Studio 2015 or greater, it provides syntax and dependency checking as you type and allows you to use track changes using a source control repository. One of the most helpful features of using VS is the intellisense available when constructing a template. For this walk through, we will create a template to provision a Service Bus topic and a subscription.

Start Visual Studio and open a new Azure Resource Group project then give it a name. After adding the project name, you will be presented with a list of templates. Choose the option for a **Blank Template**; we will go through the steps of creating our own.

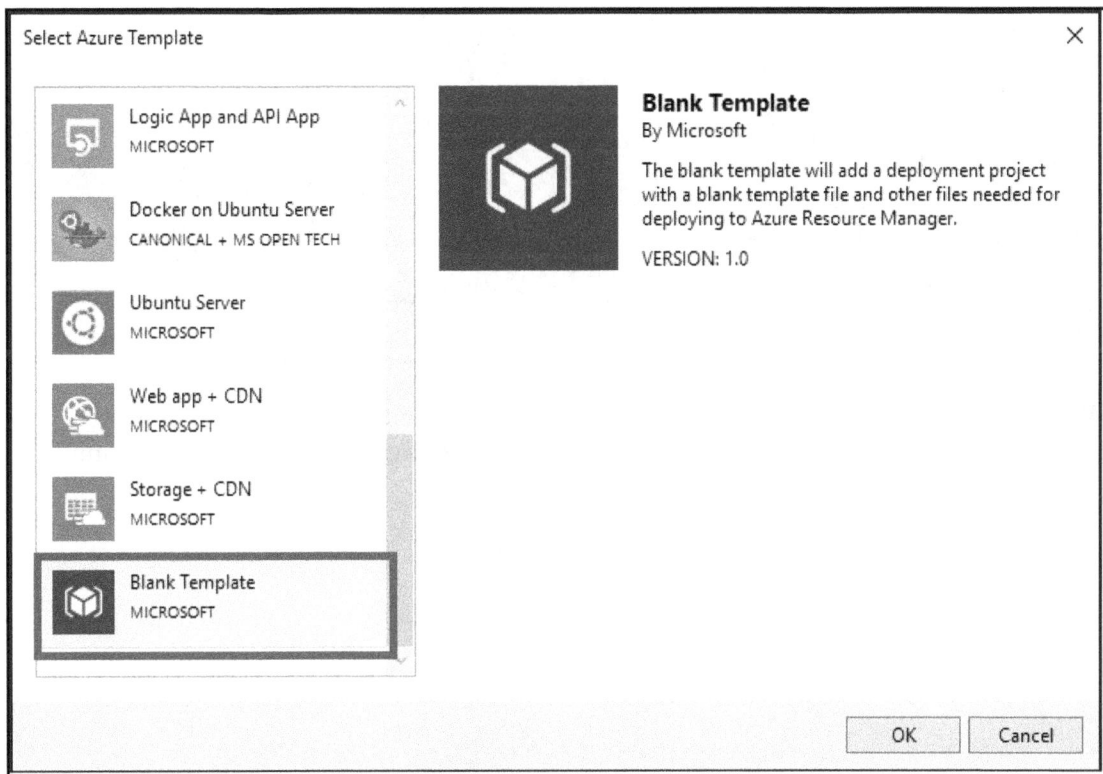

This will create a skeleton template project with two folders—a Scripts folder to hold PowerShell scripts for deployment, which contains a default deployment script, and `Templates` folder to hold your templates, which contains the resource template and a parameters file.

Go to the `Templates` folder, right-click and add a new item. Select **Azure Resource Mana... DeploymentProject** template as follows:

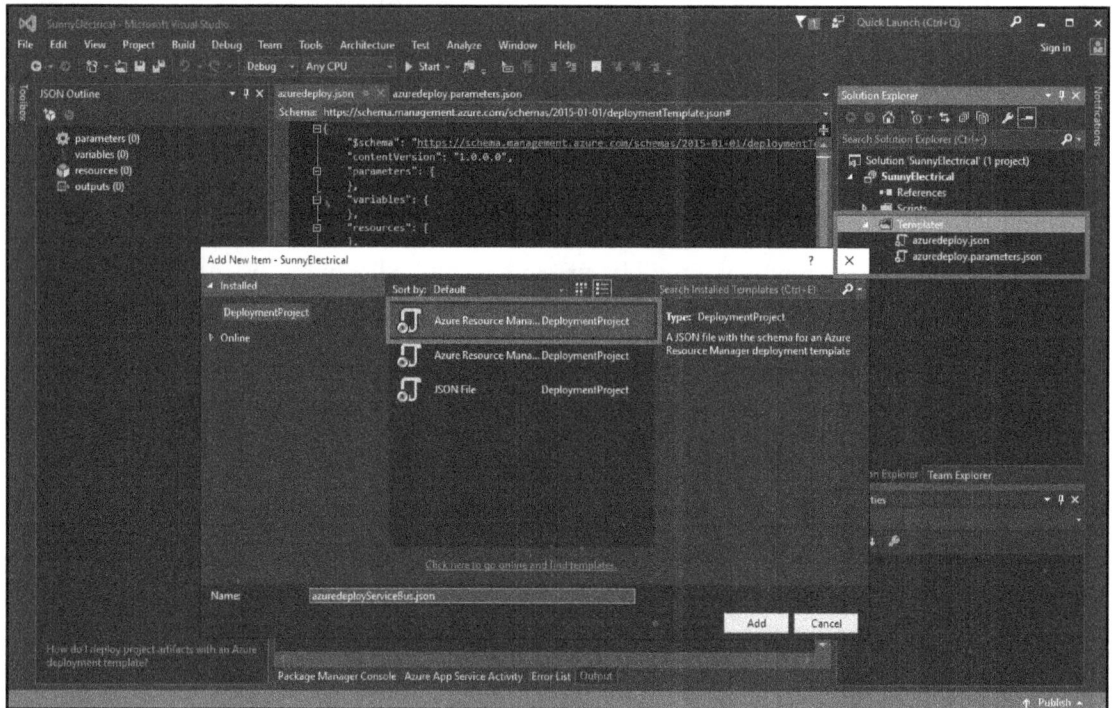

We can now start filling in the template sections, starting with the `parameters` section. The following input parameters listed here will be used to configure the resources at runtime:

- The name of the `serviceBusNamespace`
- The name of the `serviceBusTopic`
- The name of the `serviceBusSubscription`
- The name of the `serviceBusRule`
- Messaging tier for the Service Bus

The basic structure of the parameter section is shown later. Note that we have set the length of the `serviceBusNamespace` to be between 10 and 25 characters. The `serviceBusSku` also has a restriction list to allow a selection from predefined values with a default value being specified. Also, `serviceBusApiVersion` has been set to a default version of `2015-08-01`:

```
"parameters": {
    "serviceBusNamespace": {
      "maxLength": 25,
      "metadata": { "description": "Sunny Electrical Service Bus Namespace"
},
      "minLength": 10,
      "type": "string"
    },
    "serviceBusSku": {
      "type": "string",
      "allowedValues": [ "Standard", "Premium" ],
      "defaultValue": "Standard",
      "metadata": { "description": "Messaging tier for the service bus." }
    },
    "serviceBusTopic": {
      "type": "string",
      "metadata": {
        "description": "Name of the Topic"
      }
    },
    "serviceBusSubscription": {
      "type": "string",
      "metadata": {
        "description": "Name of the Subscription"
      }
    },
    "serviceBusRule": {
      "type": "string",
      "metadata": {
        "description": "Name of the Rule"
      }
    },
    "serviceBusApiVersion": {
      "type": "string",
      "defaultValue": "2015-08-01",
      "metadata": {
        "description": "Service Bus ApiVersion used by the template"
      }
    }
  },
```

The next section is declaring any optional `variables`. For provisioning a Service Bus, we will use the following variables here:

- `location`: This calls the function `resourceId()`, which returns the unique identifier of a resource
- `sbVersion`: This is set to the parameter value in the parameters section
- `defaultSASKeyName`: This has been hard coded to `"RootManageSharedAccessKey"`
- `authRuleResourceId`: This is the ID of the resource being created

The final code for the `variables` section is constructed as follows:

```
"variables": {
    "location": "[resourceGroup().location]",
    "sbVersion": "[parameters('serviceBusApiVersion')]",
    "defaultSASKeyName": "RootManageSharedAccessKey",
    "authRuleResourceId":
"[resourceId('Microsoft.ServiceBus/namespaces/authorizationRules',
parameters('serviceBusNamespace'), variables('defaultSASKeyName'))]"
    },
```

> **TIP**
>
> To debug a computed variable, use the Output section to display the evaluated value.

The next section is `resources`, which is mandatory and at least one resource must be specified. As we are creating a Service Bus Topic and a subscription, the following resource template will be used. Note that the **Subscription** resource has been created as a dependency on the **Topic** being created first by setting the `dependsOn` property to the `"[parameters('serviceBusTopic')]"` value:

```
"resources": [
        {
            "apiVersion": "[variables('sbVersion')]",
            "name": "[parameters('serviceBusTopic')]",
            "type": "Topics",
            "dependsOn": [
                "[concat('Microsoft.ServiceBus/namespaces/',
parameters('serviceBusNamespace'))]"
            ],
            "properties": {
                "path": "[parameters('serviceBusTopic')]"
            },
            "resources": [
```

```json
{
  "apiVersion": "[variables('sbVersion')]",
  "name": "[parameters('serviceBusSubscription')]",
  "type": "Subscriptions",
  "dependsOn": [
    "[parameters('serviceBusTopic')]"
  ],
  "properties": { },
  "resources": [
    {
      "apiVersion": "[variables('sbVersion')]",
      "name": "[parameters('serviceBusRule')]",
      "type": "Rules",
      "dependsOn": [
        "[parameters('serviceBusSubscription')]"
      ],
      "properties": {
        "filter": {
          "sqlExpression": "TransactionType = 'PO'"
        },
        "action": {
          "sqlExpression": "set FilterTag = 'true'"
        }
      }
    }
  ]
}
]
}
]
}
],
```

The final section is output. For the output, we will display the Service Bus connection string and the Shared Access Policy keys:

```json
"outputs": {
  "NamespaceDefaultConnectionString": {
    "type": "string",
    "value": "[listkeys(variables('authRuleResourceId'),
parameters('serviceBusApiVersion')).primaryConnectionString]"
  },
  "DefaultSharedAccessPolicyPrimaryKey": {
    "type": "string",
    "value": "[listkeys(variables('authRuleResourceId'),
parameters('serviceBusApiVersion')).primaryKey]"
  }
}
```

Now that the template is completed, we can now deploy it using Visual Studio. Right-click on the **project** and select **New Deployment**. This will bring up a dialog box where you can select your **Subscription:**, **Resource group:**, and templates.

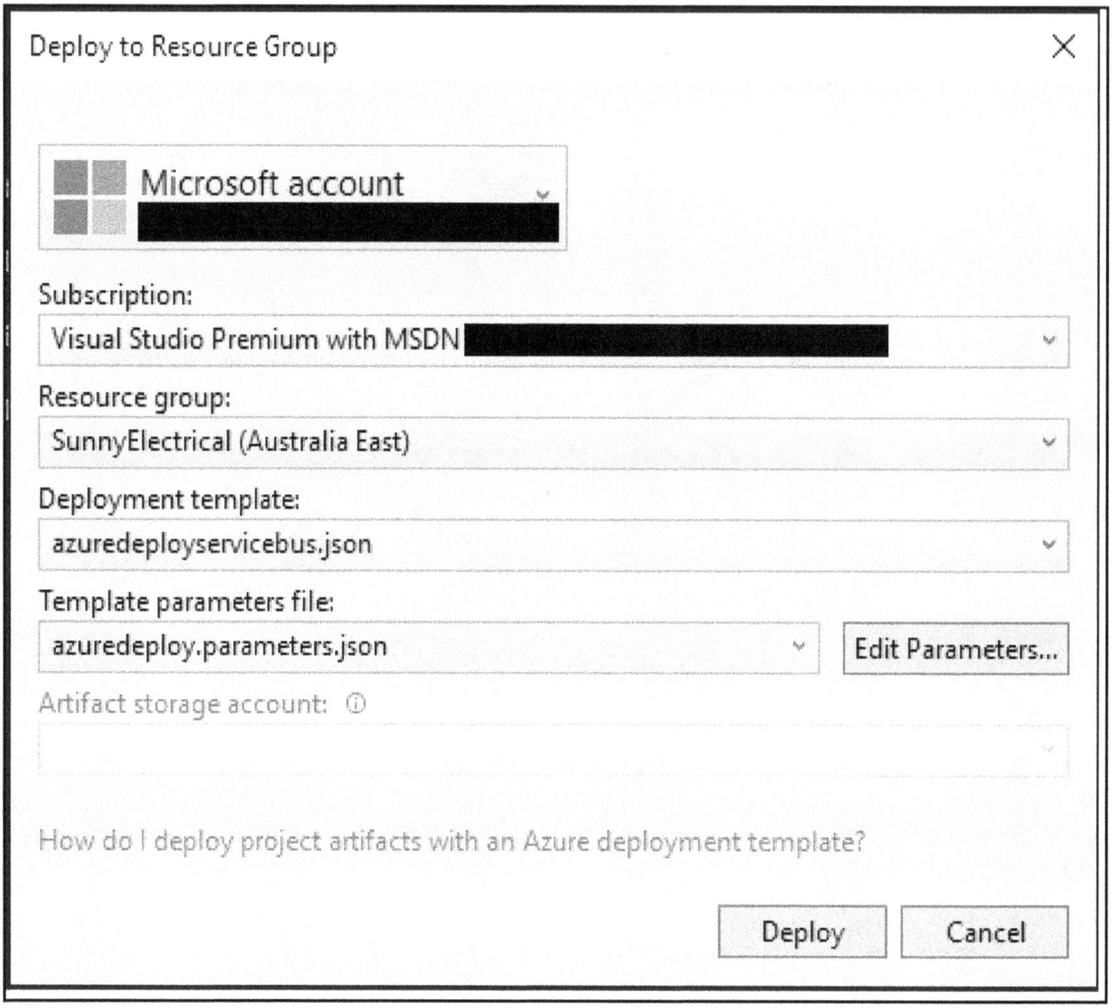

Deploy to Resource Group   ✕

Microsoft account ⌄

Subscription:

Visual Studio Premium with MSDN   ⌄

Resource group:

SunnyElectrical (Australia East)   ⌄

Deployment template:

azuredeployservicebus.json   ⌄

Template parameters file:

azuredeploy.parameters.json   ⌄   Edit Parameters...

Artifact storage account: ⓘ

       ⌄

How do I deploy project artifacts with an Azure deployment template?

Deploy   Cancel

Now click on the button **Edit Parameters**. This will open another dialog box that displays all the parameters that were defined in the template and allows you to add the values. Parameters that have **allowedValues** assigned are represented by a drop-down control.

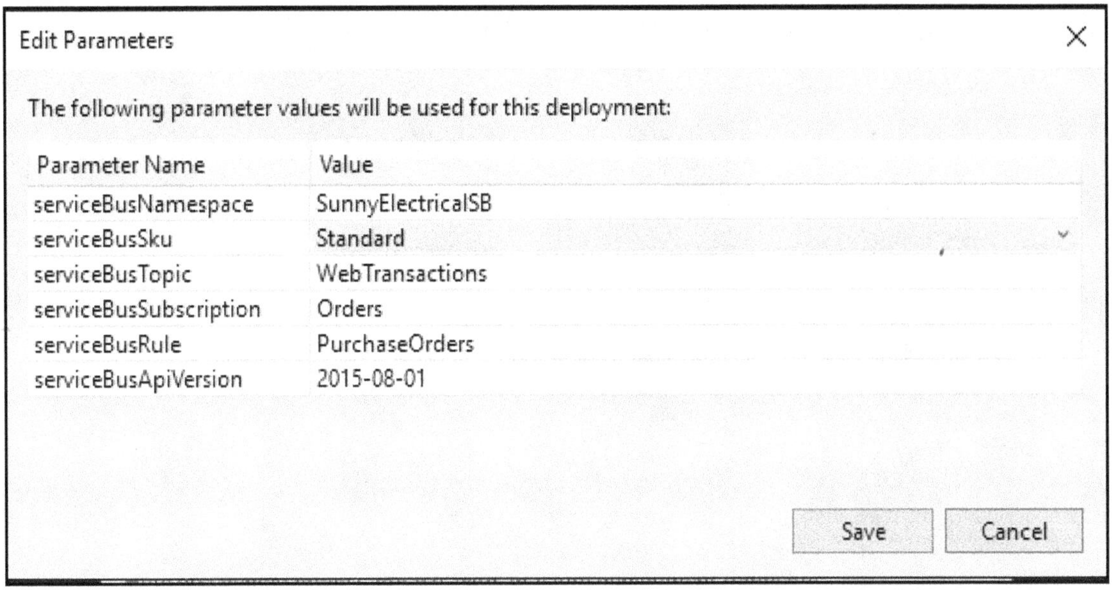

Edit Parameters   ✕

The following parameter values will be used for this deployment:

Parameter Name	Value
serviceBusNamespace	SunnyElectricalSB
serviceBusSku	Standard
serviceBusTopic	WebTransactions
serviceBusSubscription	Orders
serviceBusRule	PurchaseOrders
serviceBusApiVersion	2015-08-01

Save   Cancel

After saving the parameters, click on **Deploy**. This now starts provisioning the resources in Azure. Use the Visual Studio **Output** window and view the current status. Once completed, the **Output** window will display the message here:

If you open `azuredeploy.parameters.json` located in the `Templates` folder, it will now contain the values you had entered from the **Edit Parameters** dialog window as follows:

```
{
    "$schema":
"https://schema.management.azure.com/schemas/2015-01-01/deploymentParameter
s.json#",
    "contentVersion": "1.0.0.0",
    "parameters": {
        "serviceBusNamespace": {
            "value": "SunnyElectricalSB"
        },
        "serviceBusTopic": {
            "value": "WebTransactions"
        },
        "serviceBusSubscription": {
            "value": "Orders"
        },
```

```
    "serviceBusRule": {
        "value": "PurchaseOrders"
    }
  }
}
```

The same ARM template and parameters file can now also be deployed from a PowerShell console window using the following steps:

1. Open a PowerShell console window and log in to your account by executing the flowing script: `Add-AzureRmAccount`.

2. Before you can execute the ARM template, you need to have an existing resource group. If not, you will need to execute the script here to create the resource group first:

```
New-AzureRmResourceGroup -Name <name-of-resource-group>
-Location "<region-name-to-create-resource>"
```

3. The following script is then used to create the resources using the ARM template and parameters file:

```
New-AzureRmResourceGroupDeployment -Name ExampleDeployment
-ResourceGroupName ExampleResourceGroup
-TemplateUri <LinkToTemplate>
-TemplateParameterUri <LinkToParameterFile>
```

After successfully running the script, the following will be displayed in the PowerShell console:

Best practices

The new set of APIs available from Microsoft has revolutionized the deployment and management of Azure resources. Although there is a large number of quick start templates available, this should not discount you from the following best practices.

The following is not a complete list but a starting point of some best practices to follow:

- Use Visual Studio for authoring your ARM templates. It provides inbuilt **IntelliSense** and validation using the Visual Studio JSON editor, and you can visualize the resources and parameters using the JSON outline window. As with any best practices, using Visual Studio provides the capability to manage your artifacts and deployment templates using source control repositories.

- Increment the version number of the `contentVersion` element in the template file after any updates are made to the template to ensure that the correct template is being used for the various deployments:

```
{
    "$schema": "http://schema.management.azure.com/schemas/2015-01-
    01/deploymentTemplate.json#",
    "contentVersion": "1.0.0.3",
    "parameters": { },
    "variables": { },
    "resources": [ ],
    "outputs": { }
}
```

- Test your templates by predeploying them to ensure that there are no dependencies required. Don't rely on compiling the templates as this only ensures that it is syntactically correct.

- Decompose a large single template into smaller separate templates that are purpose specific. Use the **templateLink** property to link these together. More about linking templates can be found here: `https://docs.microsoft.com/en-us /azure/azure-resource-manager/resource-group-linked-templates`.

- If requesting passwords and secrets from the user in the `parameters` section of the ARM template, use the `securestring` type instead of normal string type. This will encrypt the entered text for privacy when being used and then delete it from the computer memory when no longer needed:

```
"parameters": {
    "secretValue": {
        "type": "securestring",
        "metadata": {
            "description": "Value of the secret to store in the vault"
        }
    }
}
```

- If deploying a resource that is dependent on other resources that must exist first, use the `DependsOn` property to specify the dependent resources. Use this property to define the deployment sequence of your resources also.
- Get into the habit of using the `outputs` element to return something when the deployment of the resources was successful. This could be the resource URL to visually check that the deployment was successful.

Manual deployments of App Services

Azure provides several options to deploy an Azure App Service, and each process has their own pros and cons. Note that these deployment options do not provision any required Azure resources, it is only for the application code.

FTP

Using FTP is simply a file transfer of the complied code and offers no versioning or file structure management.

MS Visual Studio

On the other hand, Visual Studio offers web deploy, which is an extensible client server tool for synchronizing content. It provides the capability to set security descriptors on the destination files and folders and has out-of-the-box support in order to publish databases including MySQL and Sqlite. The option to deploy only code differences between the source and target files. This will speed up the deployment time if there are a large number of files to transfer. Also, apply transforms on connection strings.

Synch

Another alternative of deploying an App Service manually is synchronizing with a cloud folder, such as OneDrive or Dropbox. This is known as **synch deployment**. It relies on the Kudu deployment engine (`https://github.com/projectkudu/kudu`), which is integrated into the Azure App Service. To use this option, you will need to set up the repository source from within the Azure portal first for the Logic App.

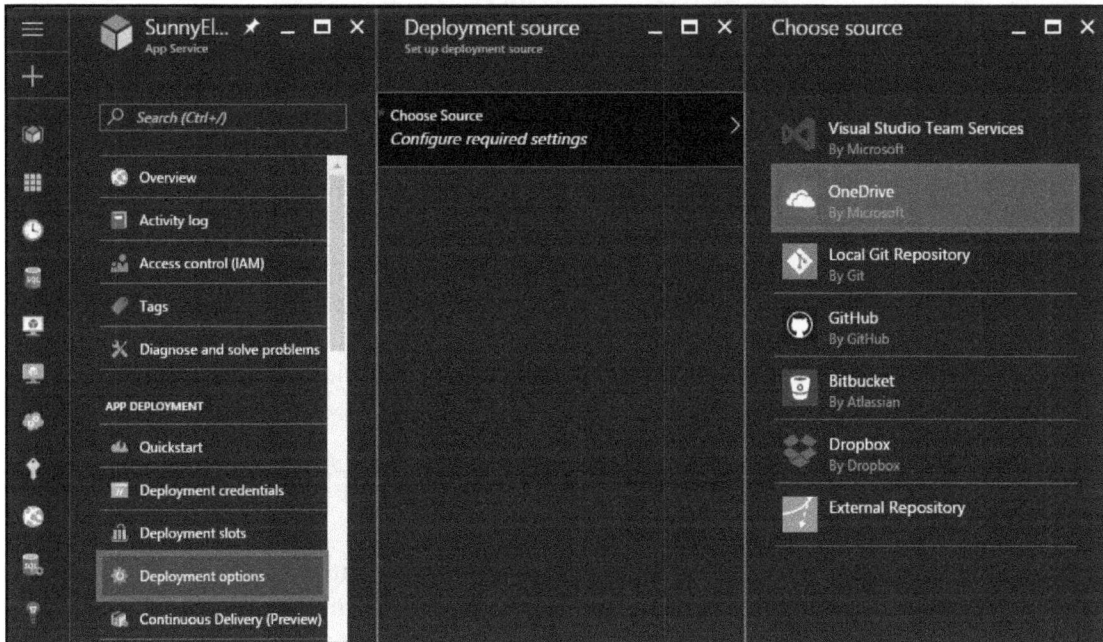

Once the credentials have been supplied, a new folder in OneDrive will be created under `Files\Apps\Azure Web Apps\<name-of-app-service>`. Once you have uploaded the deployment packages to your OneDrive folder, from the Azure portal, click on the **Sync** button to start the deployment.

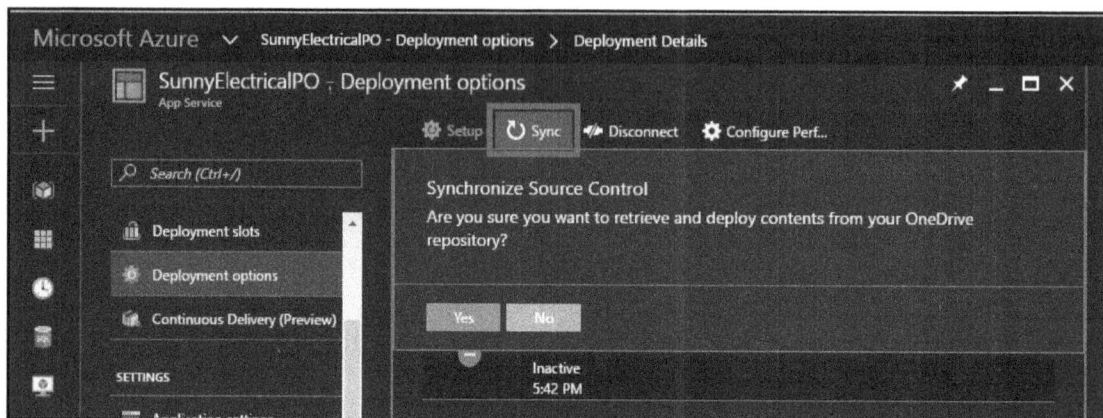

Using synch deploy does not provide version control for rollbacks and still requires a manual synchronization.

Local Git

Using a local Git repo provides similar benefits to MS Visual Studio. It provides version control rollback and deployment of different branches to different deployment slots. However, there is no turn-key solution for continuous deployments.

> A repository is often named a repo. It is a folder on your computer that Git uses to track code changes. These folders contain all versions of your code, including the current version you are working on.

When using a Git repo, you will need to add a `.gitignore` file to the root folder of the repository. This file is used by the Git repository to prevent Git from including unnecessary files that shouldn't be part of the solution, such as Visual Studio temp files and log files. More information about this can be found at: `https://www.visualstudio.com/en-us/docs/git/tutorial/ignore-files`.

> Visual Studio will automatically create the .gitignore file in your repo when youcreate a local Git repo for your project.

Continuous deployment

If your application has a frequent release cycles, then continuous deployment should be considered.

The advantage of using a continuous deployment strategy provides version control to roll back to a previous release and the ability to deploy from different branches to different deployment slots in Azure.

Continuous deployments for Azure App Services are available for cloud-based source code management repositories, such as Visual Studio Team Services and GitHub. Once you have set up the desired cloud-based repository, you simply publish your changes to imitate the build and deployment plus any load tests to be carried out.

At time of writing this chapter, the only build application types were only for ASP.Net and ASP.Net Core.

Setting up continuous deployments for these types of applications are made through the Azure portal under your **App Service** blade as follows:

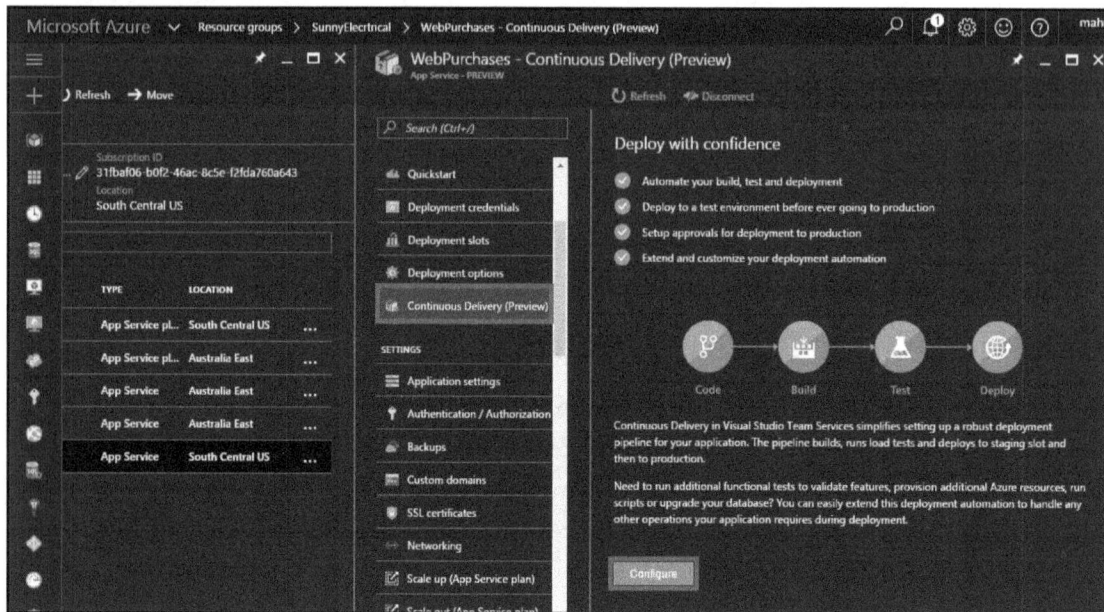

Clicking the **Configure** button starts a four-step wizard, the first step allows you to select either Visual Studio Team Services or GitHub as your code repository. Once you have selected which code repository to use, you then select the **Project**, **Repository**, and **Branch** to deploy from.

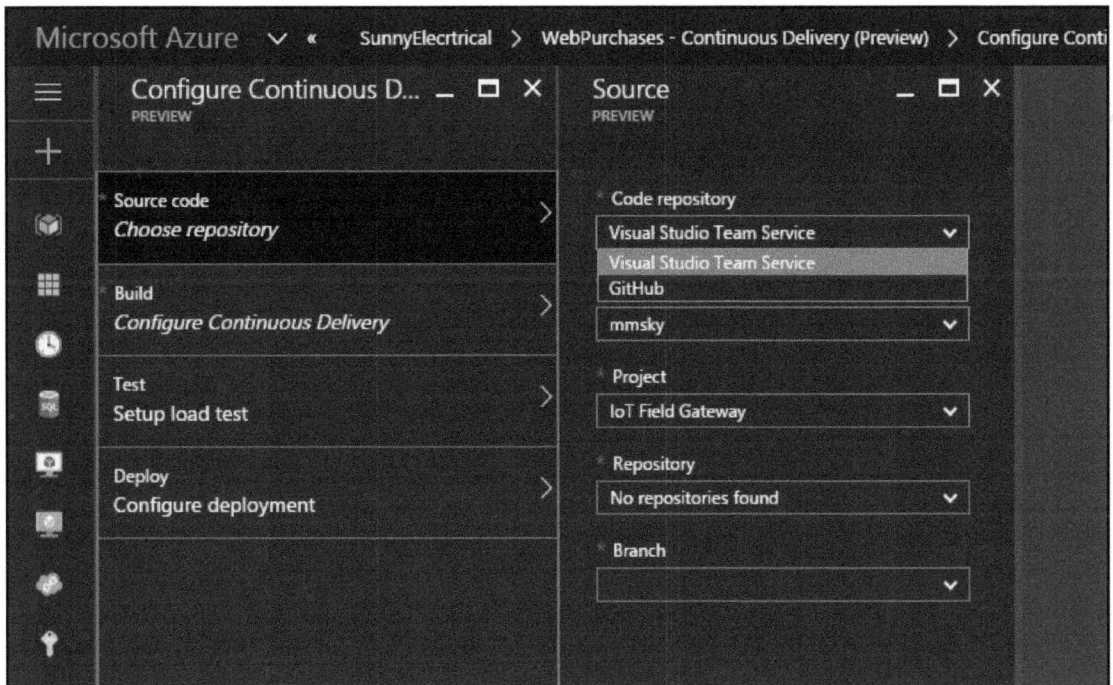

In the next step, you choose which application type you are deploying, which can either be ASP.Net or ASP.Net core. The last two steps are optional where you can choose to load test the application and choose a staging environment.

Opting in for load testing will spin up 25 virtual users to access your App Service for a duration of 60 seconds.

If you also opted for a staging environment, then the changes will be published to the staging slot first and then promoted to production.

Azure Function deployments

With Azure Functions, continuous deployments are possible using any one of the following supported repositories listed and are configured on a per function app basis:

- Bitbucket (`https://bitbucket.org/`)
- Dropbox
- Git local repo (`https://docs.microsoft.com/en-us/azure/app-service-web/app-service-deploy-local-git`)

- Git external repo
- GitHub (https://github.com/)
- Mercurial external repo
- OneDrive: (https://onedrive.live.com/about/en-us/)
- Visual Studio Team Services: (https://www.visualstudio.com/team-services/)

> Once continuous deployment is enabled, access to function code in the portal is set to read-only.

The source code needs to be in a folder structure similar to that of mentioned later with each function in a separate subdirectory from the wwwroot folder and the Host.json file at the root level.

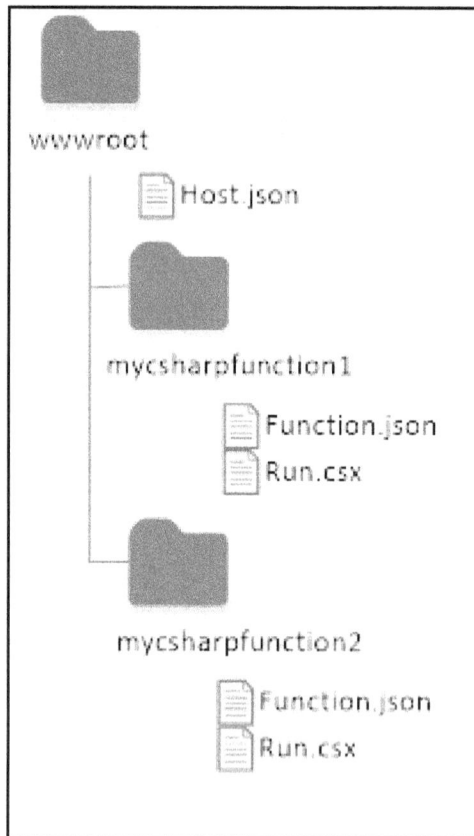

To set up continuous deployment on existing functions, go to the **Function app** blade in the Azure portal and click on the **Function app settings** link. Then, under **Deploy** section, click on **Configure continuous integration**.

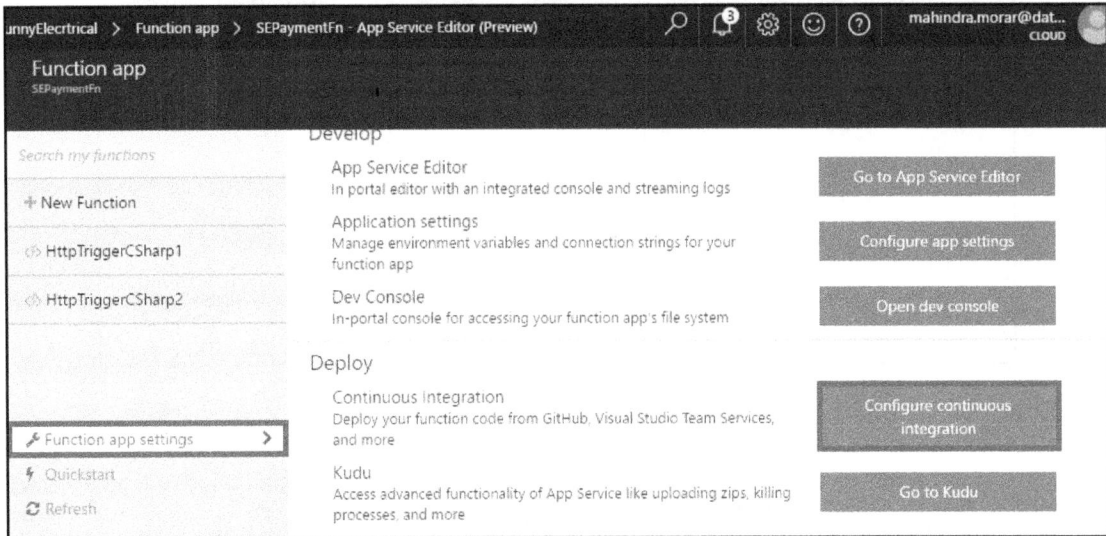

Once the **Deployments** blade opens, click on the **Setup** icon to configure the source. Just as we did before, we will configure the source as OneDrive.

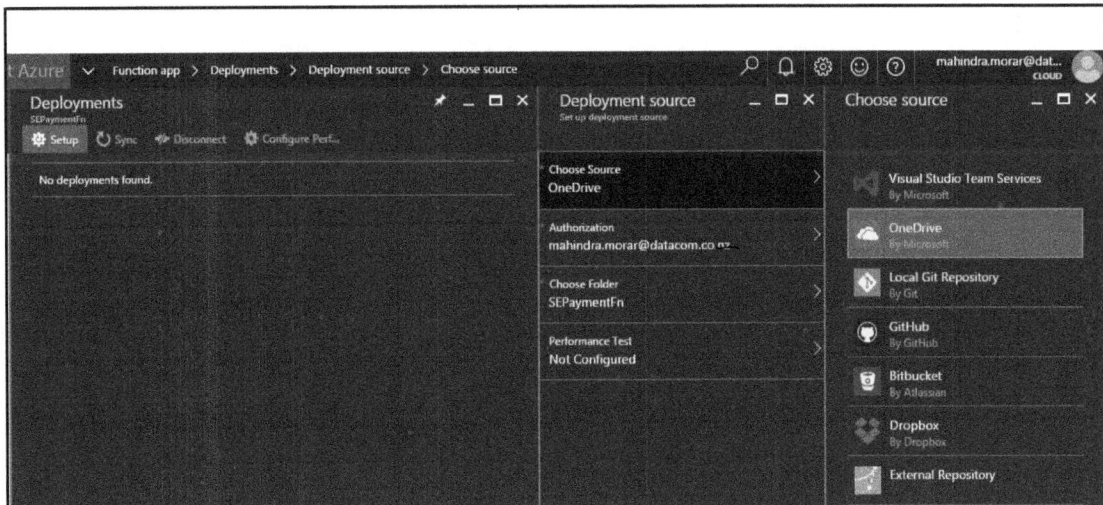

Once the configuration has been completed, you should see a new folder created in your OneDrive account under `Files\Apps\Azure Web Apps` as shown here:

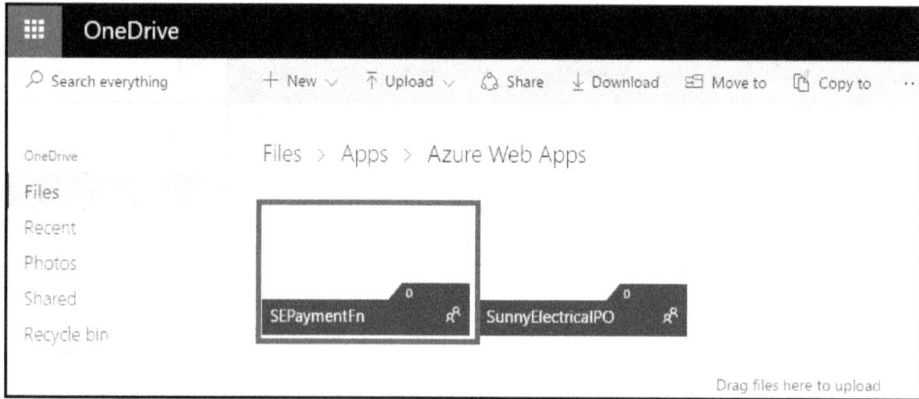

Now that the link between OneDrive has been created, we can now download the packages for your functions that you have created in Azure.

Go back to the main **Function app** blade and under the **age**Manage section, click on the **Go to App Service Settings** button. This will then open the **Function app** blade.

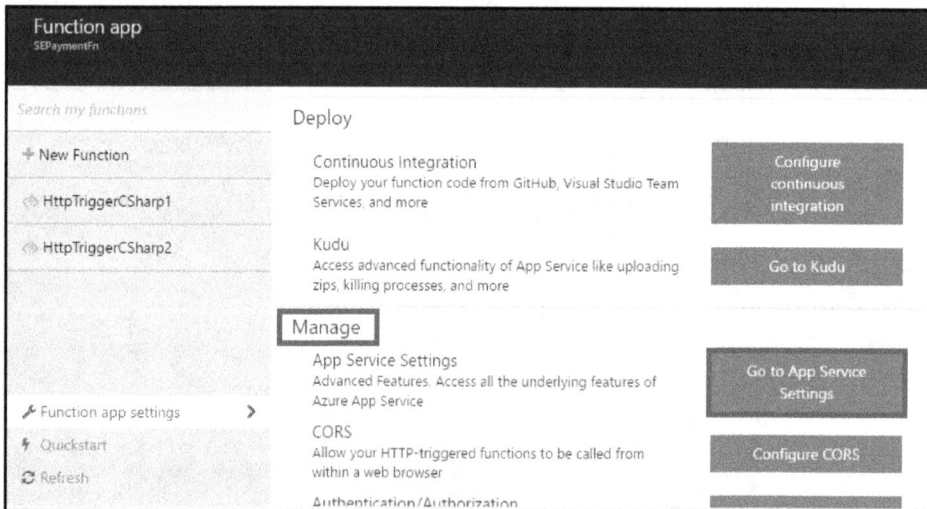

Scroll down and click on the **App Service Editor** link highlighted in the following image to open the **App Service Editor** blade:

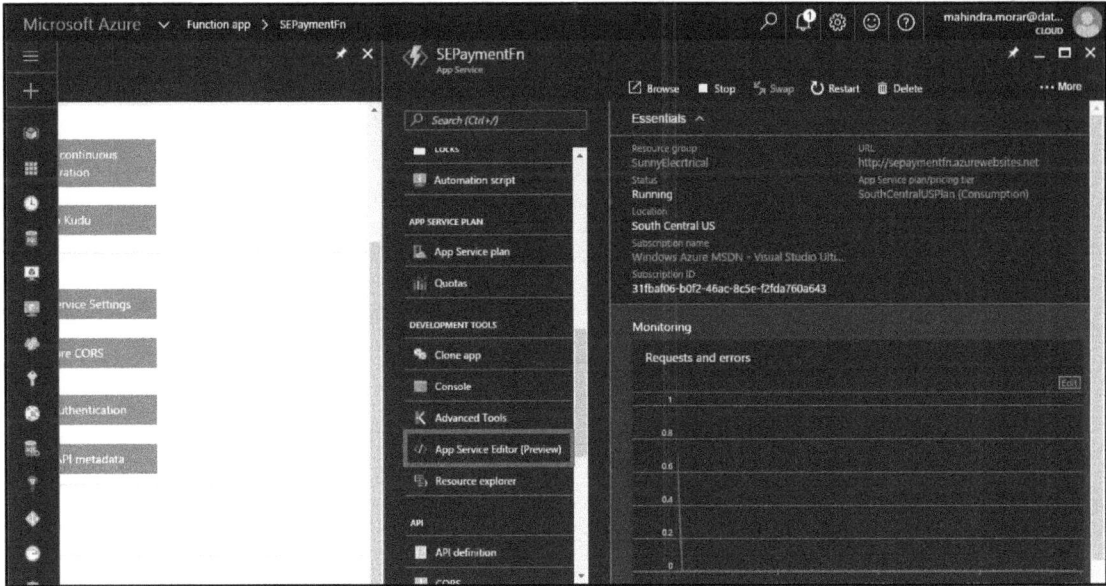

Once the **App Service Editor** blade has opened, click on the **Go** link to open a new browser tab, which shows all your functions.

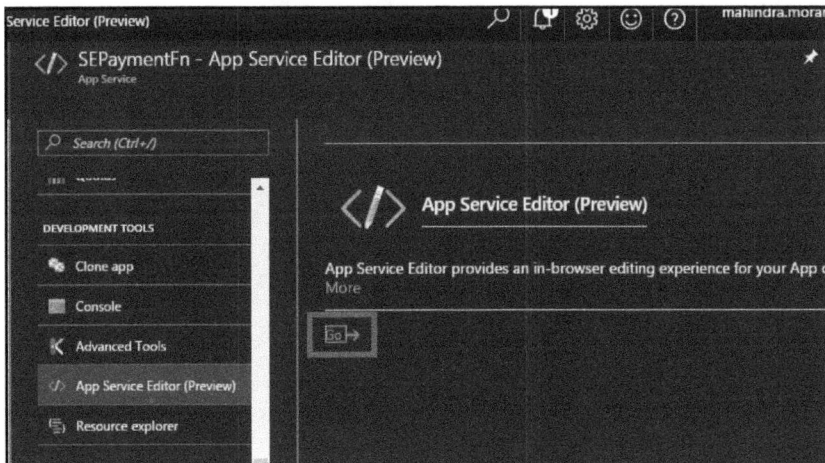

Hover your mouse over the **wwwroot** link and click on the ellipse (**...**) to bring up the context menu. Click on the **Download Workspace** link to download the wwwroot.zip file, as follows:

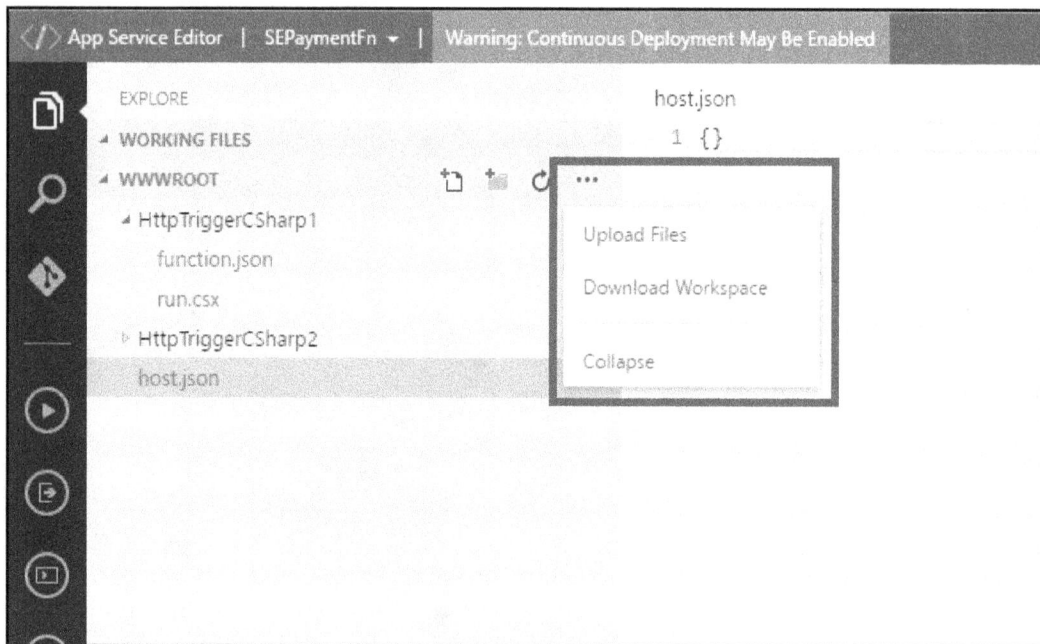

Now unzip the file and copy the whole contents to the function folder that was created in your OneDrive.

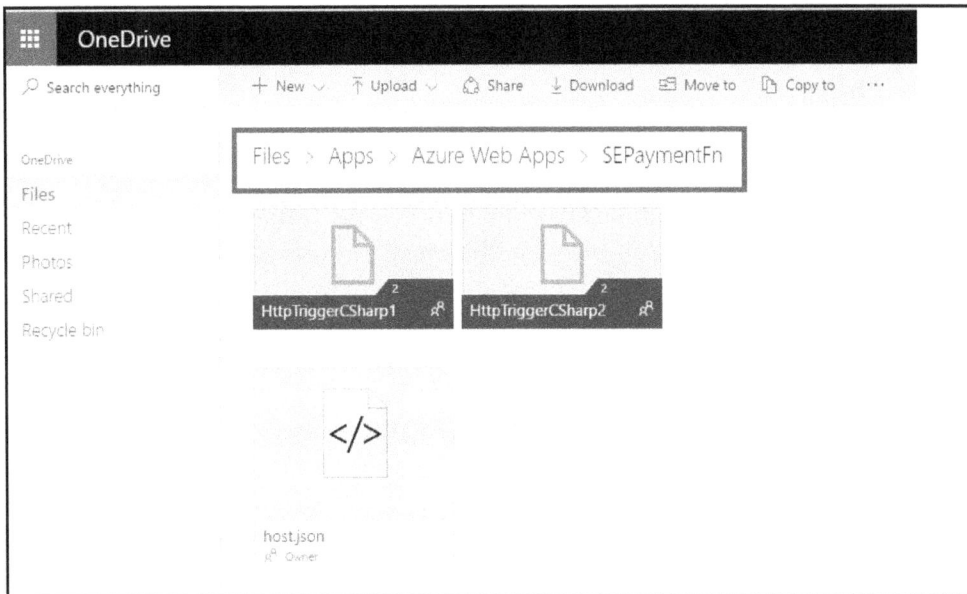

From the **Deployments** blade, you can synch deployments with your OneDrive folder contents and previous deployments.

If using cloud-based source code repositories such as Visual Studio Team Services or GitHub, any modifications to your source files are copied to the function app and a full deployment is triggered.

> When using Visual Studio Team Services as your deployment repository source and you cannot see your projects, it may be due to your VSTS account not being linked to your Azure subscription. See this link for the steps to set it
> up: `https://github.com/projectkudu/kudu/wiki/Setting-up-a-VSTS-account-so-it-can-deploy-to-a-Web-App`.

Managing solutions using PowerShell

PowerShell scripting is a great tool to automate the managed deployment for Azure resources. In this section, we will walk through the step-by-step process to create a PowerShell script, which can be used to deploy the Logic App definition and parameter JSON file into specific subscription and resource group. You can extend the PowerShell script as per your requirement.

There are certain prerequisites that need to be installed properly before you can get started with PowerShell Script and ARM template. The prerequisites are listed here:

- Install Microsoft Azure SDK for Azure
- Install Azure PowerShell and set `executionpolicy` to `unsigned`

We will divide the PowerShell script into different sections and add appropriate synopsis to explain them in detail. Let's now go in detail to develop the Script from start.

This PowerShell script uses modules such as `AzureRM`, `Resources` and `Azure.Storage` .We have defined a parameter, which will differ from environment to environment, such as subscription, resource group, and resource location. If you have not gone through the concept of earlier-mentioned parameters, we would suggest to go through `Chapter 2`, *What Is an Azure App Service?* for the detailed explanation.

```
.SYNOPSIS
    Powershell script to Deploy Logic App within specific
    subscription and resource group
.NOTES
    Created on:     20/11/2016
    Created by:     RobustIntegration
    Filename:       SunnyElectricals.ps1
#>

#Requires -Version 3.0
#Requires -Module AzureRM.Resources
#Requires -Module Azure.Storage
Param(
    [string] [Parameter(Mandatory=$true)]
    $SubscriptionID,
    [string] [Parameter(Mandatory=$true)]
    $ResourceGroupName,
    [string] [Parameter(Mandatory=$true)]
    $ResourceGroupLocation
)
```

After listing the necessary parameter for the PowerShell script, we start with defining appropriate functions to do the specific task such as register the resource group under a specific Azure subscription.

```
<#
.SYNOPSIS
    > Define SilentlyContinue and Set-StrictMode to gracefully
      complete the exceution of powershell script in exception.

    > Function RegisterResourceProvider to register the resource provider
      based on the Azure subscription

.NOTES
    Created on:     20/11/2016
#>
Import-Module Azure -ErrorAction SilentlyContinue
Set-StrictMode -Version 3
Function RegisterResourceProvider {
    Param(
        [string]$ResourceProviderNamespace
    )
    Write-Host "Registering resource provider '$ResourceProviderNamespace'" -ForegroundColor Green;
    Register-AzureRmResourceProvider -ProviderNamespace $ResourceProviderNamespace;
}
```

Next two functions perform actions to check the existence of resource group within the specified Azure subscription and to deploy the Azure resources such as Logic Apps, as follows:

```
<#
.SYNOPSIS
  > Function CheckDependentComponentStatus to check the resource group
   based on the Azure subscription
#>
Function CheckDependentComponentStatus
{
    param($dependencyComponent)
    foreach ($component in $dependencyComponent)
    {Get-AzureRmResource -ResourceGroupName $ResourceGroupName -ResourceName $dependencyComponent}
}

<#
.SYNOPSIS
  > Function DeployAzureComponent to deploy Azure resources
#>
Function DeployAzureComponent
{
    param($templateFilePath, $parametersFilePath, $componentName)

    Write-Host "Initialising deployment of $componentName Logic App Workflow..." -ForegroundColor Green;
    if(Test-Path $parametersFilePath) {
        New-AzureRmResourceGroupDeployment -ResourceGroupName $ResourceGroupName -TemplateFile
          $templateFilePath
          -TemplateParameterFile $parametersFilePath;
    }
    else {
        New-AzureRmResourceGroupDeployment -ResourceGroupName $ResourceGroupName -TemplateFile
          $templateFilePath;
    }

    Write-Host "Finished deployment of $componentName Logic App Workflow..." -ForegroundColor Green;
}
```

We have one more last function defined within the PowerShell script to give a user option to select the environment that will be used within the runtime:

```
<#
.SYNOPSIS
    > Function to select the Logical Environment within Logic App and releated articats
    are deployed.
#>

Function SelectEnviroment{
    Write-Host "Please select environment: 'P' for Production, 'U' for UAT, 'S' for Staging, 'D'
    for Development" -ForegroundColor Yellow
    $env = Read-Host
    IF(-not($env -eq "P" -or $env -eq "U" -or $env -eq "S" -or $env -eq "D"))
    {
        SelectEnviroment;
    }
    IF($env -eq "P"){
        Write-Host "Deploying using Production Settings..." -ForegroundColor Green;
        return "-Prod";
    }
    ElseIf ($env -eq "U"){
        Write-Host "Deploying using UAT Settings..." -ForegroundColor Green;
        return "-UAT";
    }
    ElseIf ($env -eq "S"){
        Write-Host "Deploying using Staging Settings..." -ForegroundColor Green;
        return "-Staging";
    }
    ElseIf ($env -eq "D"){
        Write-Host "Deploying using Development Settings..." -ForegroundColor Green;
        return "-DEV";
    }
    return "";
}
```

After you have successfully written the necessary function (in this PowerShell Script, we have four functions), you can use those functions definition within the script as follows:

```
Login-AzureRmAccount -SubscriptionId $SubscriptionID
# Register RPs
$resourceProviders = @("microsoft.web");
if($resourceProviders.length) {
    Write-Host "Registering resource providers" -ForegroundColor Green;
    foreach($resourceProvider in $resourceProviders) {
        RegisterRP($resourceProvider);
    }
}
$env = SelectEnviroment
#Create or check for existing resource group
$resourceGroup = Get-AzureRmResourceGroup -Name $resourceGroupName -ErrorAction SilentlyContinue
if(!$resourceGroup)
{
    Write-Host "Resource group '$resourceGroupName' does not exist.
    To create a new resource group, please enter a location."-ForegroundColor Green;
    if(!$resourceGroupLocation) {
        $resourceGroupLocation = Read-Host "resourceGroupLocation";
    }
    Write-Host "Creating resource group '$resourceGroupName' in location '$resourceGroupLocation'
    "-ForegroundColor Green;
    New-AzureRmResourceGroup -Name $resourceGroupName -Location $resourceGroupLocation
}
else{
    Write-Host "Using existing resource group '$resourceGroupName'"-ForegroundColor Green;
}

# Start the deployment
Write-Host "Starting deployment..."-ForegroundColor Green;

#Deploy SunnyElectricalsGetTweet Logic App
DeployAzureComponent .\SunnyElectricalsGetTweet\SunnyElectricalsGetTweet.json .\SunnyElectricalsGetTweet
\SunnyElectricalsGetTweet$env.parameters.json "SunnyElectricalsGetTweet"
Read-Host 'Press any key to continue..'
```

Monitoring

Logic Apps connect to various Application and Systems, which is distributed over cloud On-premise Applications. Monitoring deployed Logic Apps gives the enterprise view of integration point and health check of associated Applications. Within Azure, there are various ways to monitor developed Logic Apps. We will discuss them in the coming sections.

Metrics

The metrics section shows the chat view of all various actions, which is performed within the Logic App. There are the multitude of metrics that can be monitored using Azure metrics, such as **ACTION LATENCY, ACTION SUCCESS LATENCY, RUN LATENCY, RUN SUCCESS LATENCY, TRIGGER FIRE LATENCY** directly from the Azure portal.

To configure, click on the **Metric** within the **Monitoring** section of the **Logic App** blade and select on the required metrics, which you require to monitor within the specified interval.

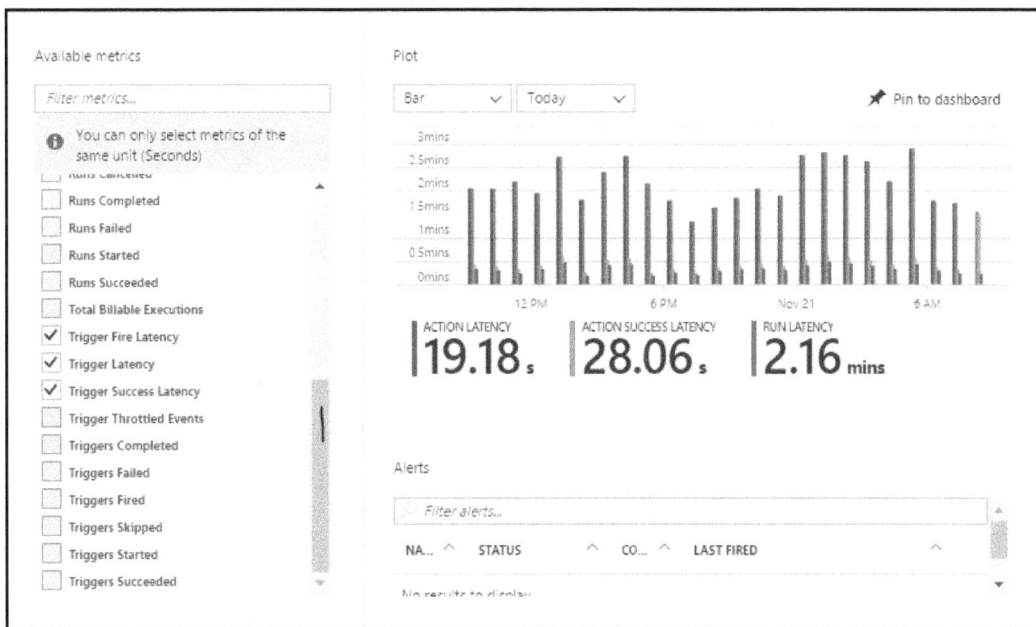

Add metric alert

The metric alert configuration is used as a notification service to send the health information of the Logic Apps. You can set the alert in case of Logic App workflow failure or specific threshold is reached. To configure a metric alert, follow these steps:

- In the Azure portal, click on the Logic App for which an alert needs to be set.
- Within the **Monitoring** section of the **Logic App** blade, click on **Metric**.
- Click on **Add metric alert** to populate the alert configuration blade.

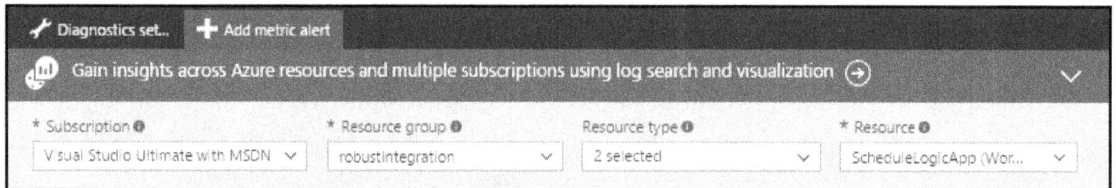

- Enter the alert **Name**, **Description**. Select the appropriate metric that needs to be monitored, populate the condition, and notify section.

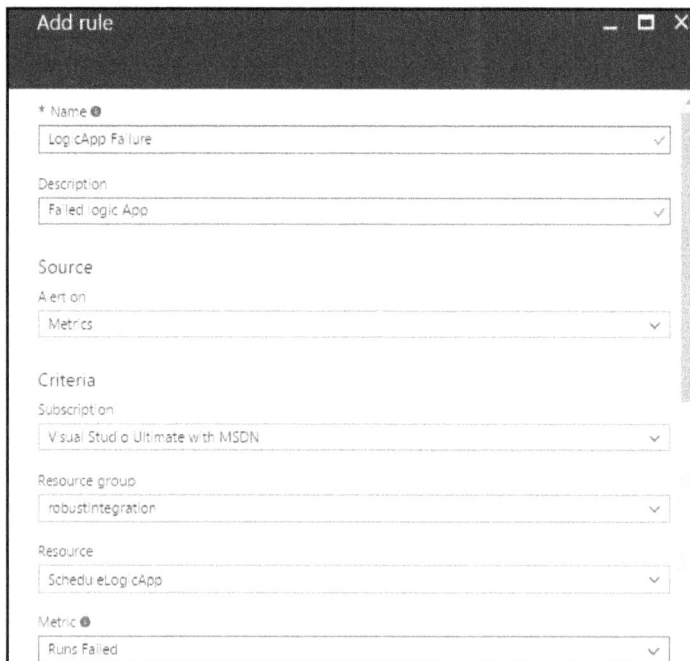

- If you have configured your e-mail as a notification option, then in case of failed metric, an auto triggered e-mail will be sent to the mentioned address.

Dear Customer,

⚠ 'RunsStarted GreaterThanOrEqual 1 (Count) in the last 5 minutes' was activated for schedulelogicapp

You can view more details for this alert in the Microsoft Azure Management Portal.

- You can also use the WebHook endpoint to send a notification message to a chat room, SMS, or any other action that you want to perform. For this, you need to enter the **Webhook** URL within the alert configuration page.

Notify via

Email owners, contributors, and readers

✓

Additional administrator email(s)

abhishel   @hotmail.com

Webhook ❶

HTTP or HTTPS endpoint to route alerts to

Diagnostics settings

You can configure Azure diagnostics to send the runtime log data associated with Logic App to storage account or event hub. These log data then can be used to get the runtime information of the logic app. To configure **Diagnostics settings**, follow these steps:

- In the Azure portal, click on the Logic App for which **Diagnostics settings** need to be performed
- Within the **Monitoring** section of the **Logic App** blade, click on **Metric**
- Click on **Diagnostics settings** to populate the required options, which is best suited for data emit and diagnostics

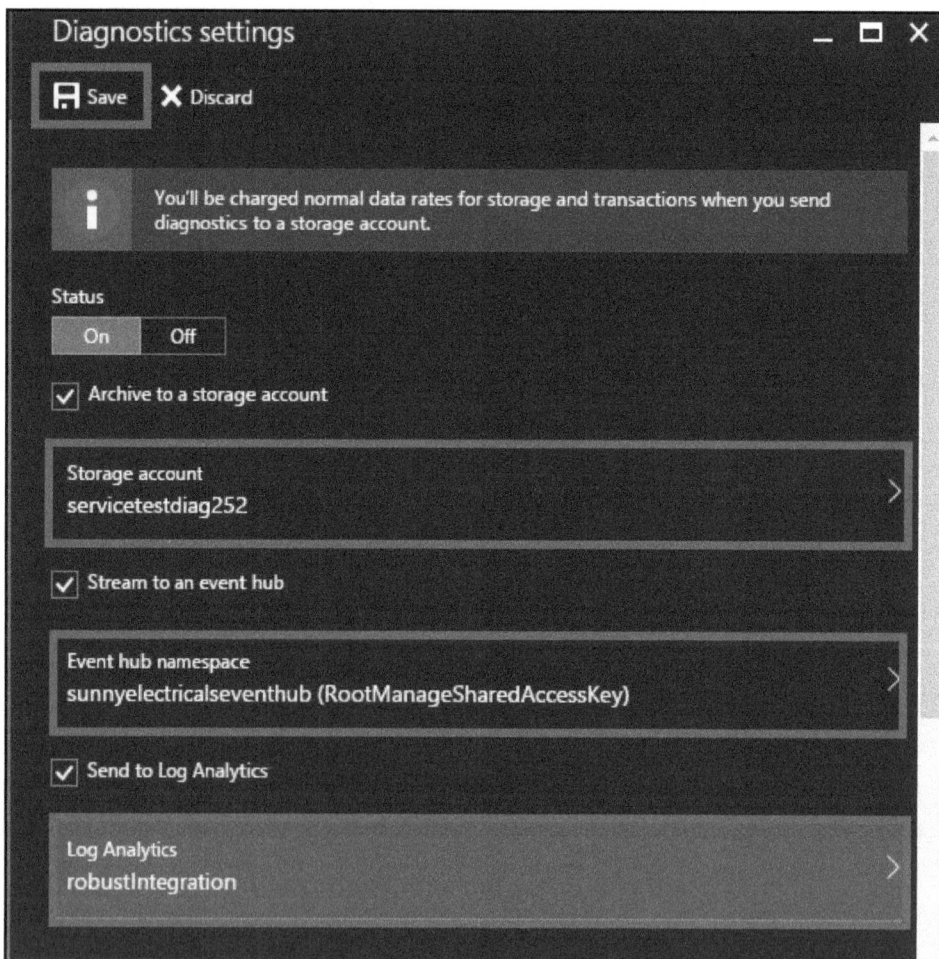

- To send a message to a storage account or Azure Event Hub, create a new Azure storage and Azure Event Hub for the Logic App to store Logic Apps telemetry data.

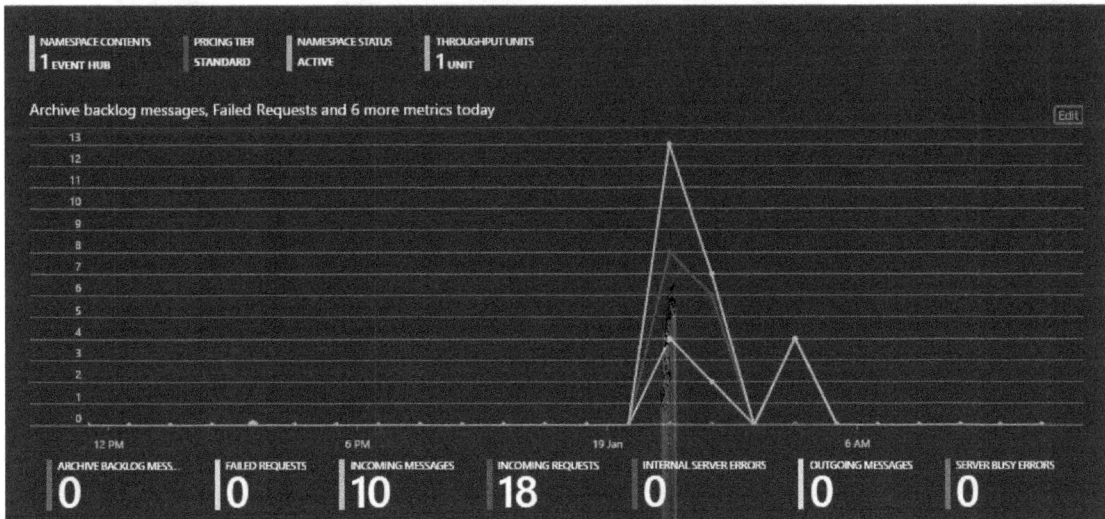

The OMS Portal

Microsoft operational Management suite (OMS) is Microsoft cloud-centric solution to monitor cloud and on-premise resources. Logic App has the inbuilt support to publish data through the **OMS Portal**. To configure the OMS portal from the **Logic App** blade, follow these steps:

- In the Azure portal, click on the Logic App for which the **OMS Portal** need to be configured.
- Within the **Monitoring** section of the **Logic App** blade, click on **Metric**.

- Click on **Diagnostics settings** and select the storage account along with options for the **OMS Portal**.

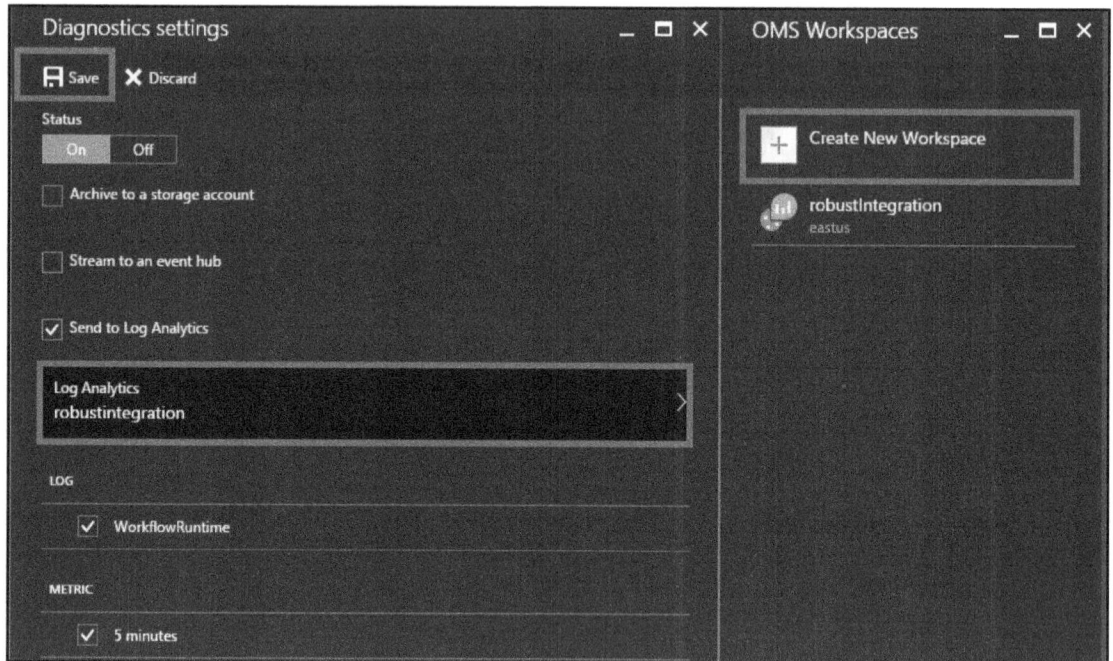

- Click on **Create New Workspace** and set correct name, subscription, resource group, and pricing tier. Click on **OK** to create a new workspace for the **OMS Portal**.

- To overview the OMS configuration, click on the appropriate resource group and navigate to the OMS configuration.

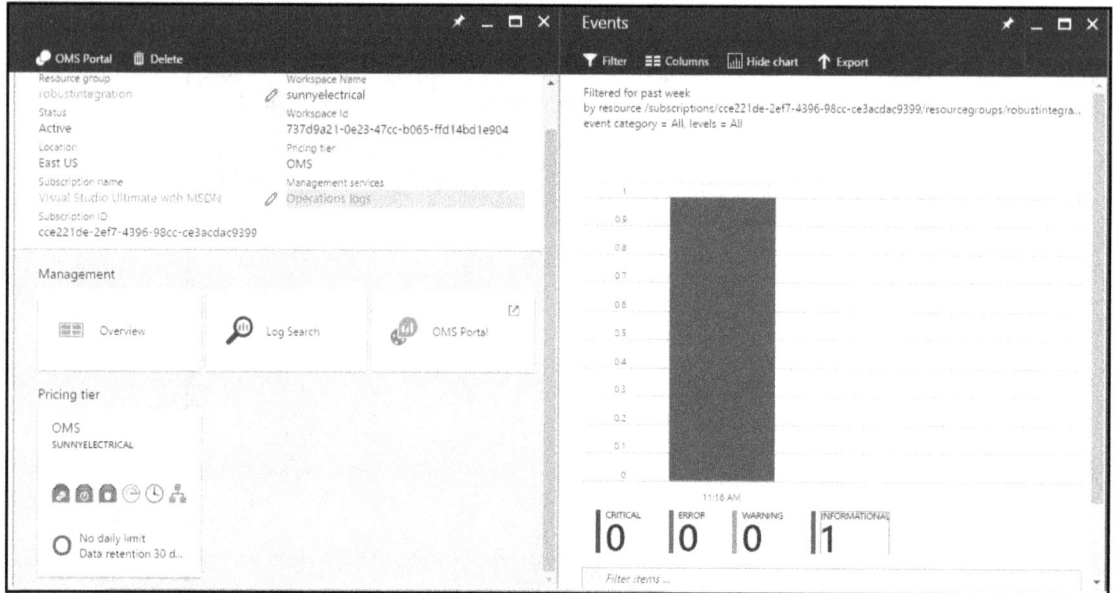

- You can set the alerts from the **OMS Portal** by monitoring the log files. The following MSDN documentation describes the process of setting alerts from the **OMS Portal**: `https://docs.microsoft.com/en-us/azure/log-analytics/log-analytics-alerts`.

Logic App monitoring

Run history

Logic Apps has inbuilt capability to get the run history of a specified workflow. You can get the run status of a workflow by clicking on the **Overview** section of the specified logic App.

The **Summary** section lists the run status of a specified Logic App workflow. To get the details of the workflow action, you can click on the respective action, and it will show the list of actions and triggers which have run during the workflow execution.

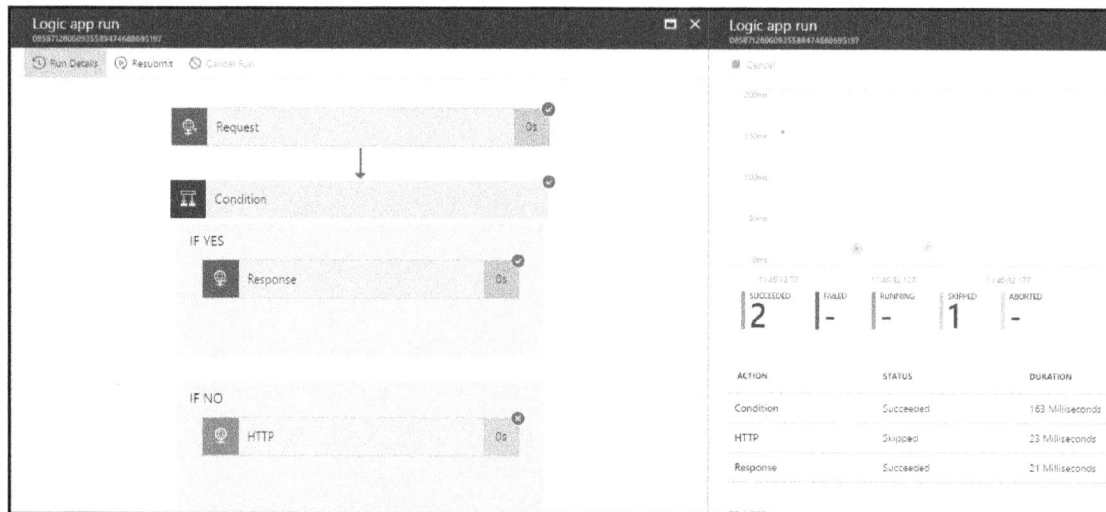

Run details specifies the status of each action and trigger within the Logic Apps. It also gives information about the actual time taken by each associated action.

Run details are important to troubleshoot any workflow or performance issues.

Trigger history

Trigger history specifies how many times logic apps is invoked or triggered. Trigger activity will have three values—Succeeded, Failed, and Skipped.

- **Succeeded:** The Logic App trigger is succeeded when the trigger has got the required data to run the logic App workflow.
- **Failed:** The Logic App trigger is failed when there is misconfiguration in the api connection and Logic App is unable to get the required connection to pull the data from downstream system.
- **Skipped**: The Logic Apps run is being when the polling connector does not find the processing data. This is very common scenarios while working with the recurrence and polling trigger, such as FTP, SFTP, and FILE.

Trigger History

| manual | ∨ | All | ∨ |

Callback url [POST]

https://prod-30.australiaeast.logic.azure.com:443/workflows/33852b494a9944

STATUS	START TIME	FIRED
⊘ Succeeded	3/6/2017, 11:48 AM	Fired
⊘ Succeeded	3/6/2017, 11:48 AM	Fired
⊘ Succeeded	3/6/2017, 11:48 AM	Fired
⊘ Succeeded	3/6/2017, 11:48 AM	Fired
⊘ Succeeded	3/6/2017, 11:48 AM	Fired

Logic App message logging with Azure Functions Application Insights

Application Insights is used to monitor application performance, logging, and detecting and diagnosing exception messages. In this section, we will discuss how we can write messages and logs within **Application Insights** using **Azure Functions** and **Logic Apps**.

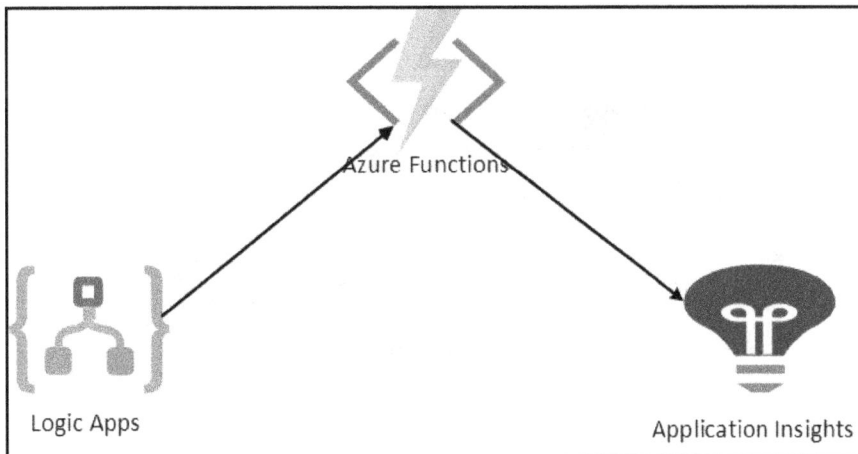

Azure Functions

Logic Apps

Application Insights

We will follow the step-by-step process of creating necessary artifacts for the solution.

Create the Instance of Application Insights in Azure:

- To add a new instance of Application Insights Log into Azure portal with the proper Azure subscription. Click on **More** and add **Application Insights**
- Populate the **Application Insights** with proper **Name**, **Resource Group**, **Application Type**

- Click on the newly created **Application Insights** and navigate to the **Properties** section to copy the **Instrumentation Key**

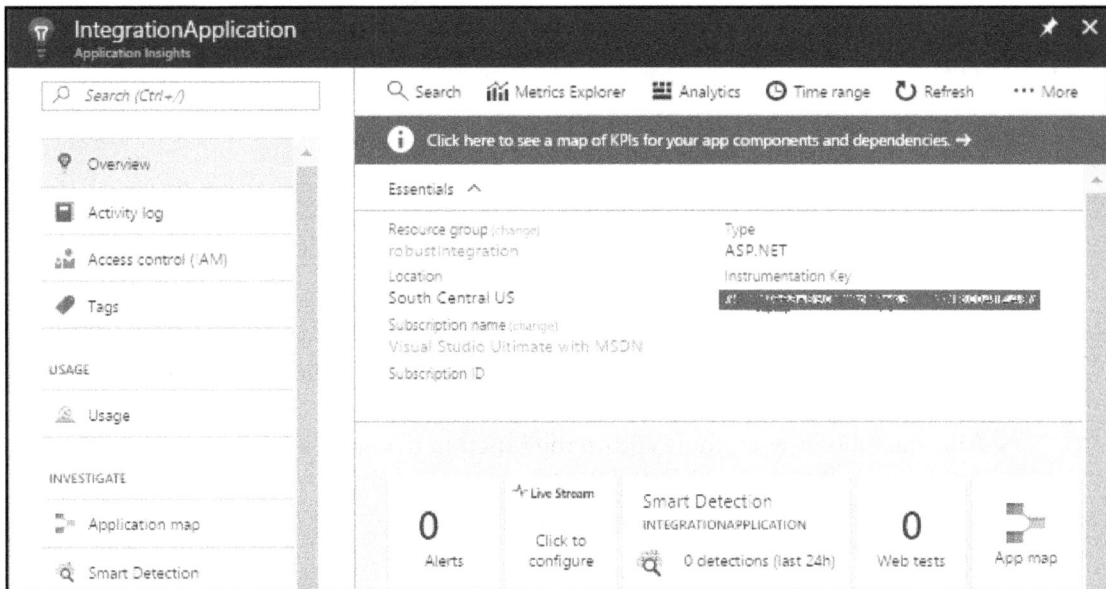

Add **Application Insights** to Azure Functions:

- Create New function `GetmessageLoggingFunApp` within Sunny Electricals Azure Function App
- Within the Function App, click on **Function App Settings** and Click on **Go to Kuddu**
- Inside Kuddu, navigate to the newly created `function` folder and click on **add new file** and add the `project.json` file

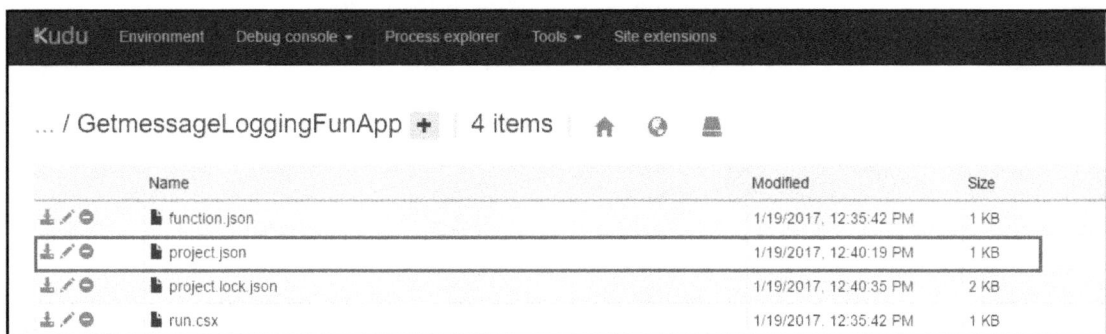

- Copy the following code to get the Application Insights NuGet Package installed in function App:

```
{
  "frameworks": {
    "net46":{
      "dependencies": {
        "Microsoft.ApplicationInsights": "2.2.0"
      }
    }
  }
}
```

- Click on save to download the Application Insights NuGet Package within the function. You can verify that the NuGet Package update through Function logs.
- In the next step, use the reference assembly for the Application Insights within the Function.
- Add the following method within the function to create a telemetry client for Application Insights within function:

```
using System;
using System.Net;
using Newtonsoft.Json;
using Microsoft.ApplicationInsights;
using System.Threading;

// references
public static async void Run(HttpRequestMessage req, TraceWriter log)
{
    var appInsights = GetTelemetryClient();
    string jsonContent = await req.Content.ReadAsStringAsync();
    dynamic expetionMessage = JsonConvert.DeserializeObject(jsonContent);

    appInsights.TrackEvent("LogicAppMessage", new Dictionary<string, string>()
    { { "Message", jsonContent } }, new Dictionary<string, string>()
    { { "LogicAppId", "LogicAppInstanceId" } });
}

// references
private static TelemetryClient GetTelemetryClient()
{
    var telemetryClient = new TelemetryClient();
    telemetryClient.InstrumentationKey = "7d8b1eea-b9d0-4376-8390-bf13c64124c7";
    return telemetryClient;
}

// references
private static void TrackException(Exception ex, string exceptiondesc, string LogicAppName)
{
    var appInsights = GetTelemetryClient();
    Dictionary<string, string> properties = new Dictionary<string, string>()
    { { "LogicAppName", LogicAppName }, { "Description", exceptiondesc }};
    appInsights.TrackException(ex, properties);
}
```

- In the next step, create a simple Logic App to send the logging information to Application Insights through the Azure Function.

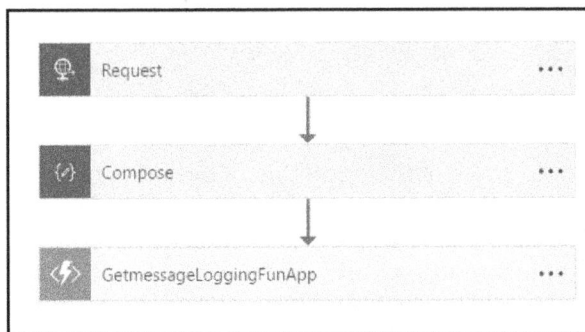

- Once the Logic App is being triggered, it will send the request and telemetry data to Application Insights. Now Go to Application Insights and verify the logs.

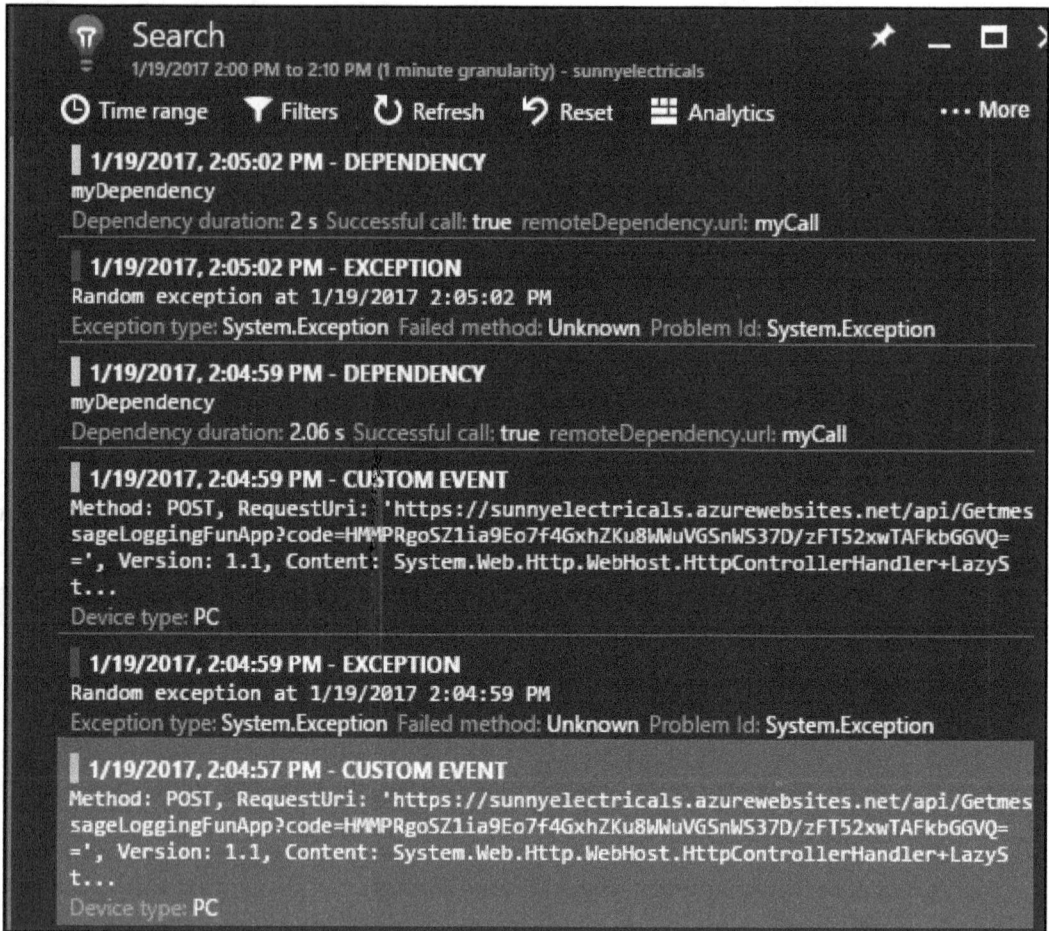

Summary

In this chapter, we explored some of the deployment options for Logic Apps and related components. We described Azure Resource Management templates, Deploying templates, and best practices. In this chapter, we also explored the Monitoring options available with the Logic Apps for real-time monitoring and auditing.

In the next chapter, we will look into What Next within the integration scope.

15
What's Next for Azure Integration?

Through this book, we have looked at the state of integration in Microsoft Azure. We have talked in depth about Logic Apps and discussed how we are moving to an increasingly connected world with IoT Hubs. We have looked at how we can leverage the huge investment in on-premises line of business applications by linking them with the cloud through the newest version of Microsoft's tried and tested integration platform, BizTalk Server 2016. By introducing BizTalk Server 2016, we have shown how to get the best of both worlds, on-premises security and business critical systems with cloud-based security, commodity, and scale.

On this journey, we have introduced our fictional company, Sunny Electricals, to help deliver the key messages about the how and why to use the array of options available in cloud integration with Microsoft Azure.

The pace of change for cloud computing in general, and Microsoft Azure specifically, means that this is a great time to be involved in solving technology problems with hybrid integration solutions.

Given this pace of change, it is as important to look at the horizon and see what is either just visible or may be coming soon.

This chapter gives an overview of what is coming next within the integration domain and in cloud-based services. It discusses Microsoft's integration roadmap and the industry trends that are driving transformation in the integration space. It examines how we can build integration solutions today that can support these future trends and, at the same time, remain relevant in a few years, by remembering the lessons from the past to build the next generation of successful applications.

- Microsoft's integration roadmap for on-premises and the cloud
- Lessons from the past and how they apply to building integration solutions today
- Introduction to PowerApps
- Introduction to Microsoft Flow

Here are the skills to be learned:

- How to navigate the maze of options to create applications that support extensibility and can cater for future trends and ideas
- Identifying currently available technologies in Azure and how they can be used in conjunction with one another to build a solution
- Understanding the past to build the solution of the future
- What factors should influence a design to provide a level of future proofing

An integration roadmap for the future

This book has introduced many technologies that affect the integration landscape of cloud computing, from API Management and Logic Apps to Azure Functions, BizTalk Server, and IoT Hubs. The current range of integration technologies is broad in reach and supports workloads in the cloud, on-premises, and between both.

None of us have a crystal ball, but it is possible to take a short look into the future and speculate on some of the ways these technologies may evolve:

- **Microservices**: So far, microservices have had only a limited impact in the enterprise, but it is safe to assume that they will become the new way to build agile and scalable integrated solutions of the future.
- **Azure Service Fabric**: This platform service is the basis for many other platform services, and it provides a good platform for highly scalable, highly distributed solutions. It supports both stateful and stateless applications as well as an ability to provide resilience and rolling updates. For more information, see `https://azure.microsoft.com/en-us/services/service-fabric/`.

- **Logic Apps**: The rate of change of Logic Apps since becoming generally available has been huge, and we can expect more connectors, more flow control, and more BizTalk-like capabilities built into the service. It has been indicated that Logic Apps will be the place where initial feature releases are made before they are moved to the core on-premises solution with BizTalk Server.
- **Azure Stack**: This data center for the masses solution provides a lot of core Azure features that can be run within your own data center, including Azure App Services. For more information, see
  `https://azure.microsoft.com/en-us/overview/azure-stack/`.
- **Azure Functions**: Since reaching general availability, it can be expected that additional language support and tooling will continue to make appearances in the core service.

Although integration is a key technology, it cannot be a technology in isolation and should deliver value to the business.

What and when of Microsoft Azure integration

When looking at hybrid integration and integration just within the Azure cloud environment, it can be difficult to know what to use and when. To provide some guidance, the following table aims to highlight the key strengths of each technology with an idea of when to use them.

Technology	Strengths	Weaknesses
Logic Apps	Provides a simple-to-use connector semantic that allows quick connection to a large variety of sources Contains the most common control flow options Has a simple-to-use JSON-based language accessible via a code view, which allows customization of the flow and any connectors	Lacks connectors to key on-premises line of business solutions, such as JD Edwards and PeopleSoft More complex control flows are difficult to model, and they can lead to the need to create many Logics Apps that need tying together
API Management	Provides a simple-to-use API governance tool providing policy-driven solutions	Cannot be used to create complex integration flows and flow rules

Functions	Simple-to-use serverless technology that is pay as you go and can provide HTTP API access to simple business rules processing Does not maintain state and so is very scalable Executes key business processing quickly	Lacks the expression language required by business users to articulate key rules Should only be used for short pieces of code that can execute quickly and not require state
Event Hub	Hyperscale ingestion of telemetry data from connected devices Partitioning and archiving provide additional functionality than simple ingestion Supported by many other Azure services	One-way communication only No device governance limits their use in true Internet of Things scenarios that require device life cycle No device management limits use in Internet of Things scenarios that require over-the-air updates
IoT Hub	Bidirectional communication providing full command and control Device registry and identity provides governance Security built in from device to cloud	More complex than Event Hub for telemetry ingestion scenarios
BizTalk Server	On-premises integration platform Many connectors to key business data sources Full orchestration engine Full business rules engine Supports complex messaging patterns	Not a platform service, so requires key skills Steep learning curve means that it is hard to get productive quickly
Microsoft Flow (discussed in detail later)	A lightweight version of Logic Apps that is similar in use to IFTTT (`http://www.ifttt.com`) and Zapier (`http://www.zapier.com`)	Basic flows only The limited number of connectors available Part of Office 365 or priced based on usage, including a free tier

A key aspect of any integration project is understanding not only how the technology has changed but also what mistakes have been made in the past and how to move forward.

A good example of this is service-oriented architecture, or SOA. This was supposed to become the ubiquitous approach to service and data provision for an enterprise and make the application architecture agile and easy to change. It never fully delivered on this vision for many reasons, including over-complexity and expectations that were simply too high. SOA services typically spanned many tiers in a multi-tier architecture and became monoliths themselves that sat in front of the large monolithic applications they were trying to mediate. Although solutions such as enterprise service buses introduced the ability to coordinate the interaction of these services, they added additional complexity, and the enterprise was often left with a tangled mess that was at least as bad as the application they were trying to replace.

Microservices are a new approach to service orientation and deliver smaller and more discrete solutions that are easier to change, easier to version, and much easier to manage. Only time will tell if they succeed where SOA failed, but for now, they offer a lightweight approach to service provision and an opportunity to use the best tools for the job for each service delivered. Typically, these services are going to be delivered as HTTP services via RESTful APIs and require stitching together to create a solution. By being agile, compact, and having a single responsibility, which are all important requirements for a microservice, it is possible to construct a solution that is itself agile and open to change, thereby removing the specter of monolithic applications that SOA solutions never eliminated.

However, when building solutions that communicate over HTTP and often over the public Internet, it is important to consider factors beyond just the creation of the solution. In these applications, the role of nonfunctional requirements becomes more important than ever.

Nonfunctional requirements, such as performance, latency, security, and reliability, need to move to the next level when the infrastructure on which they are built is no longer in the control of the organization. This infrastructure can be both at the network level, with modern workloads communicating over volatile Internet connections, and the machine level, with workloads constructed from platform services where the management of availability is controlled by a service-level agreements and service credits in the event of a problem.

This leads to several considerations that must be taken into account when building modern applications:

- **A design for connectivity failure**: Internet connections leverage network infrastructure that typically belongs to, and is maintained by, telecommunications companies. Although these companies do their best to keep service interruptions to a minimum, they do still occur. Any application or integration solution needs to take this connectivity issue into account to ensure some form of continuity. This could take the form of retry policies that may cope with transient outages or the use of the circuit breaker pattern (`https://msdn.microsoft.com/en-us/library/dn589784.aspx`) to account for longer term issues or through the use of Entity Framework Connection Resiliency (`https://msdn.microsoft.com/en-us/library/dn456835(v=vs.113).aspx`).
- **A design for hardware failure**: One of the strengths of cloud computing is cost and the use of platform services to build a solution; for cloud providers to keep these costs at a minimum, they typically use cheaper commodity hardware. To overcome the issues of hardware failures, platform services often have some form of redundancy built in. For example, **Azure Storage** makes three copies of files across different storage resources. However, depending on the service and the provision for failover of the service, any application or integration solution should still consider what action to take in the event of hardware failure. If the hardware in question is a virtual machine, the solution can be made more resilient using availability sets and balancing load between the instances of the application (`https://docs.microsoft.com/en-us/azure/virtual-machines/virtual-machines-windows-manage-availability`). If the hardware is providing platform services that you are not responsible for, then good application design, again perhaps using the circuit breaker pattern, can help relieve issues.
- **Design for geographically distributed services**: Azure data centers are globally distributed and provide most platform services across these data centers. For large-scale applications and integration solutions that need global reach, a solution needs to take in to account latency and experience of the end user by providing timely access to resources such as websites. This can be achieved using **Azure Traffic Manager** to ensure that local resources are accessed over those more geographically displaced (`https://azure.microsoft.com/en-us/services/traffic-manager/`), but the backend services also need to understand how to provide services using data replication, messaging, and eventual consistency.

Business productivity transformation

An artefact of the way that IT operations have evolved over the last 20 years is the idea of two-speed IT. Using this, the IT department is seen as not only a key enabler to adopt change but also a hindrance due to the speed at which they are able to execute. This has led to departmental decision makers using their own purchasing power to deliver the solutions required in a timeframe that is acceptable.

This notion of two speeds usually results in the IT department having to accept responsibility for purchasing decisions they did not make, or worse leaving it to departmental workers taking on the responsibility for IT delivery.

This approach does not provide a good outcome for the business as it pushes responsibility away from the IT department and a reliance on potentially unskilled personnel.

The business should be doing what the business does well, and the IT department should be responsible for enabling the business to achieve its outcomes without getting in the way.

Microsoft InfoPath was part of the Office suite that started this journey. By consuming XML web services and presenting forms-based access to data, it put the development of departmental solutions in to the hands of the people who knew and understood their processes, while leaving the IT department to manage the physical data access through the provision of the services. In the great vision of SOA, this type of solution showed real promise for business productivity improvement and transformation.

After InfoPath came Microsoft LightSwitch as a means to replace, or at least modernize departmental application access, particularly siloed data and simple workflow locked up in Microsoft Access databases. Microsoft Access, while useful for delivering quick solutions into the hands of the people who needed them, also creates a situation where there may be many instances of data and processes that govern that data can easily become decentralized.

Neither InfoPath nor LightSwitch truly delivered on the promises and expectations they were supposed to deliver.

As technology has moved forward, either with the ubiquity of APIs or varied data source types, such as NoSQL databases or data stored in Software as a Service solution, the requirements to drive business productivity through the use of these sources has grown. With that has come the need to connect to disparate endpoints and make sense of the data in a meaningful way to the business.

This need has introduced the concept of citizen integrators, business people who need and have the tools in their armory for building the business applications they require that are connected to the data sources and services that define and govern their business processes.

To solve this problem, Microsoft has introduced PowerApps and Flow.

An introduction to PowerApps

PowerApps is part of Office 365, although can be purchased separately, and provides a simple way to build powerful business applications by bringing in data from multiple sources. Data sources are made available using connections that are used to build forms-based applications that support not only standard create, read, update, and delete functionality, but also complex search and field validation. Since the service leverages the Logic Apps service, it provides a range of connectors out of box, including Office 365, Dynamics 365, Dropbox, Azure services, and social networks.

In this way, it is similar to both InfoPath and LightSwitch, but is much simpler and intended to be a tool that can target business users. Furthermore, applications built in PowerApps work immediately on tablets and phones to help deliver a truly digital experience quickly and easily.

An important aspect of any data processing is ensuring that the data structures used should be compliant to corporate rules and have a governance structure around them that ensures that proliferation of disparate types is avoided. This is akin to master data management, and Microsoft has introduced the Common Data Services, which includes the Common Data Model, to provide this structure and governance. For more information on these, see https://docs.microsoft.com/en-us/common-data-service/entity-reference/introduction.

As an example, let us introduce a scenario. In our scenario, our fictitious company Sunny Electricals wants to provide a process whereby new customers can call a helpdesk and request a change to their credit limit. For this, a customer service representative needs to be able to retrieve the customer details and update their credit limit as required. The responsibility for providing access to this data is the IT department, but they should not be concerned with the process of checking the limit.

For our scenario, we will keep things simple and use a basic database table, but this table exists in a SQL Server database that exists on premises:

```
CREATE TABLE [dbo].[CustomerCredit](
    [CustomerId] [int] IDENTITY(1,1) NOT NULL,
    [CustomerName] [varchar](255) NOT NULL,
    [CustomerContact] [varchar](255) NOT NULL,
```

```
    [CustomerEmail] [varchar](255) NOT NULL,
    [CustomerCreditLimit] [float] NOT NULL,
 CONSTRAINT [PK_CustomerCredit] PRIMARY KEY CLUSTERED
(
    [CustomerId] ASC
)WITH (PAD_INDEX = OFF, STATISTICS_NORECOMPUTE = OFF, IGNORE_DUP_KEY = OFF,
ALLOW_ROW_LOCKS = ON, ALLOW_PAGE_LOCKS = ON) ON [PRIMARY]
) ON [PRIMARY]
```

PowerApps is accessed by going to: `https://powerapps.microsoft.com/en-us/`. Once signed in, you can view any applications that have been built and can add or use connections that have been created.

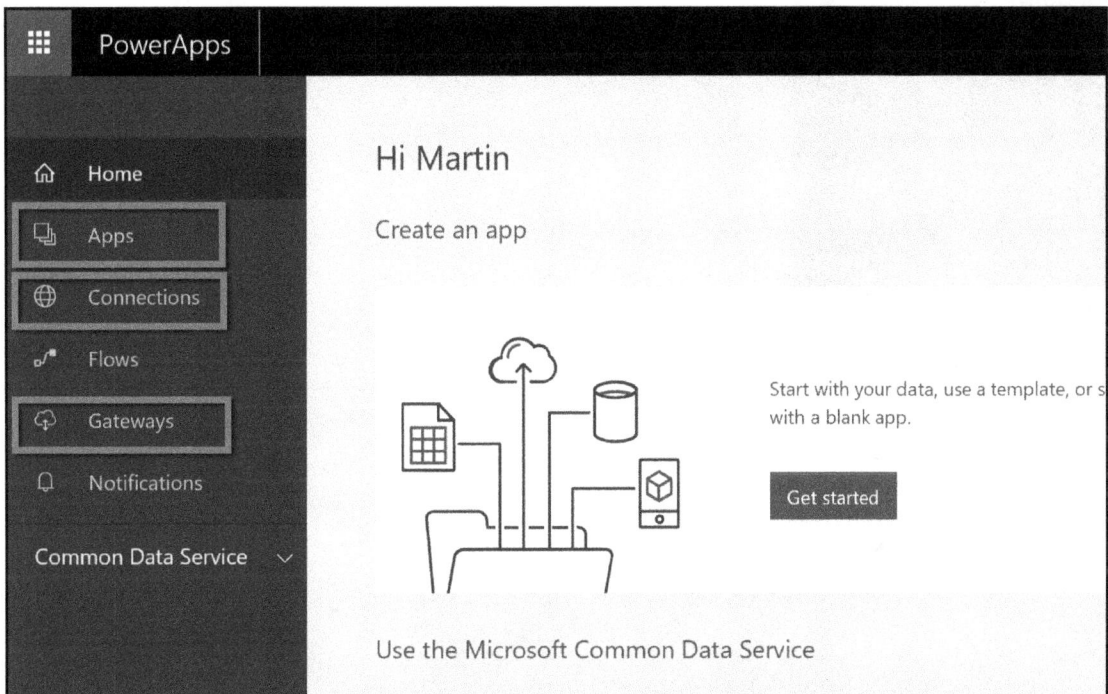

In our scenario, we wish to connect to an on-premises database containing the basic information about our customers and their credit limit.

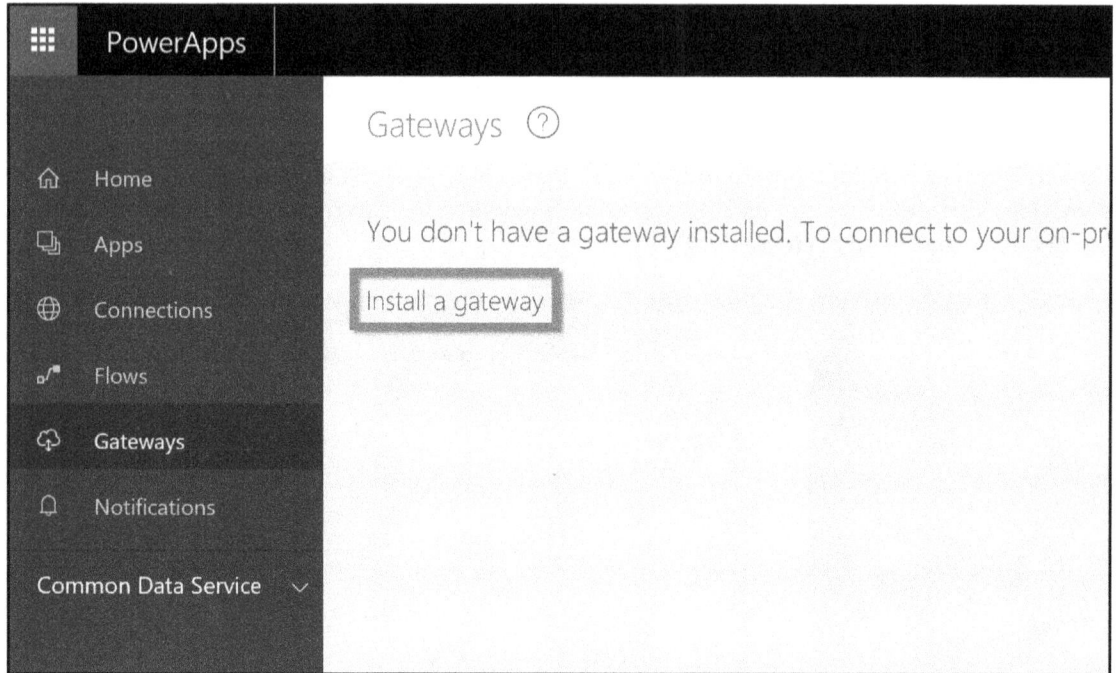

Clicking on **Install a gateway** downloads a small application that creates a Service Bus relay between your on-premises data source and PowerApps. When the installation is complete, you are prompted to sign in with an organization account that should match your PowerApps account. You can then configure the data gateway as required.

Clicking on **Configure** finishes the installation of the gateway, and if the connection is made successfully, you should see the following:

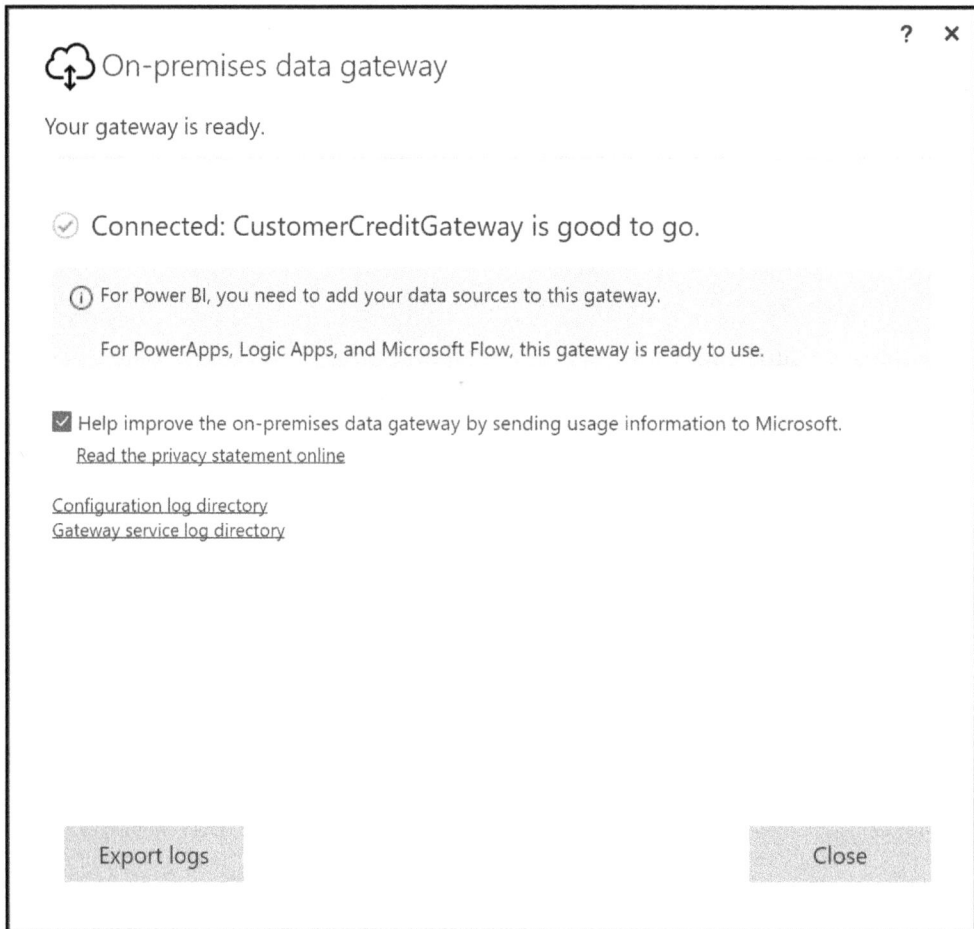

The gateway connection can be checked in the PowerApps portal and should have a status of **live**. At this point, we have a tunnel between our PowerApps solution and the machine hosting the gateway but we have not yet created a connection. To create a connection, we go to **Connections** and click on **+New connection**.

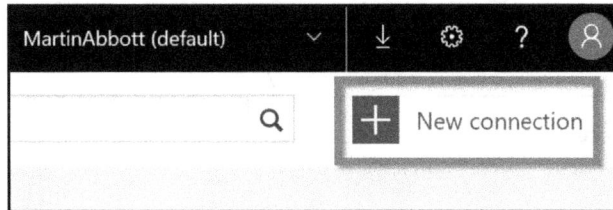

We search for SQL Server, since our on-premises data source is a SQL Server database, and we need to make sure that we choose to use our newly installed on-premises gateway.

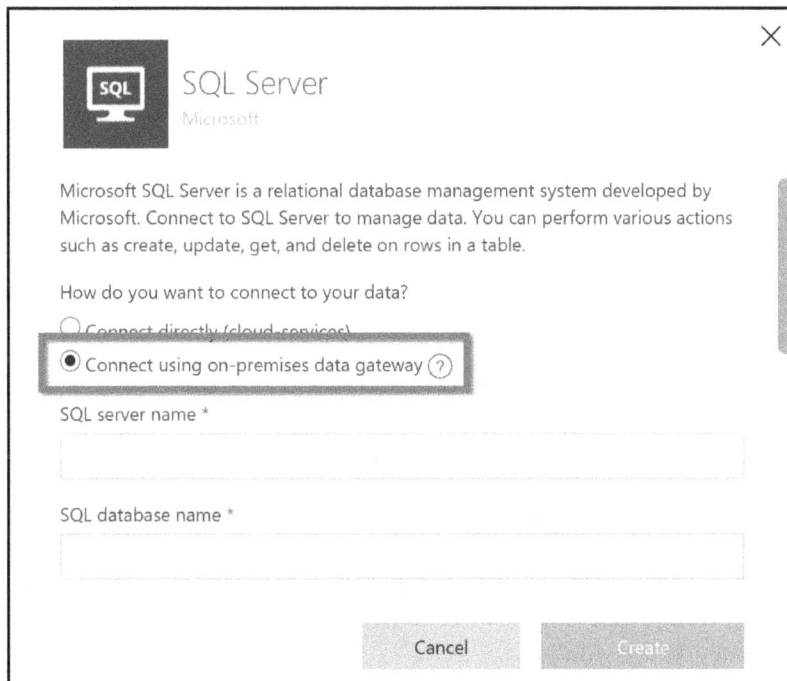

Once the details are entered, clicking on **Create** creates the connection. Once completed, the connection should show a status of **connected** in the PowerApps portal.

To provide this connection to others, for instance, if this connection had been created by an IT administrator and they wanted to make it generally available, the connection can be shared. Within a connections details, clicking on Share allows this sharing to be configured. For example, the connection can be shared with the entire organization within Office 365.

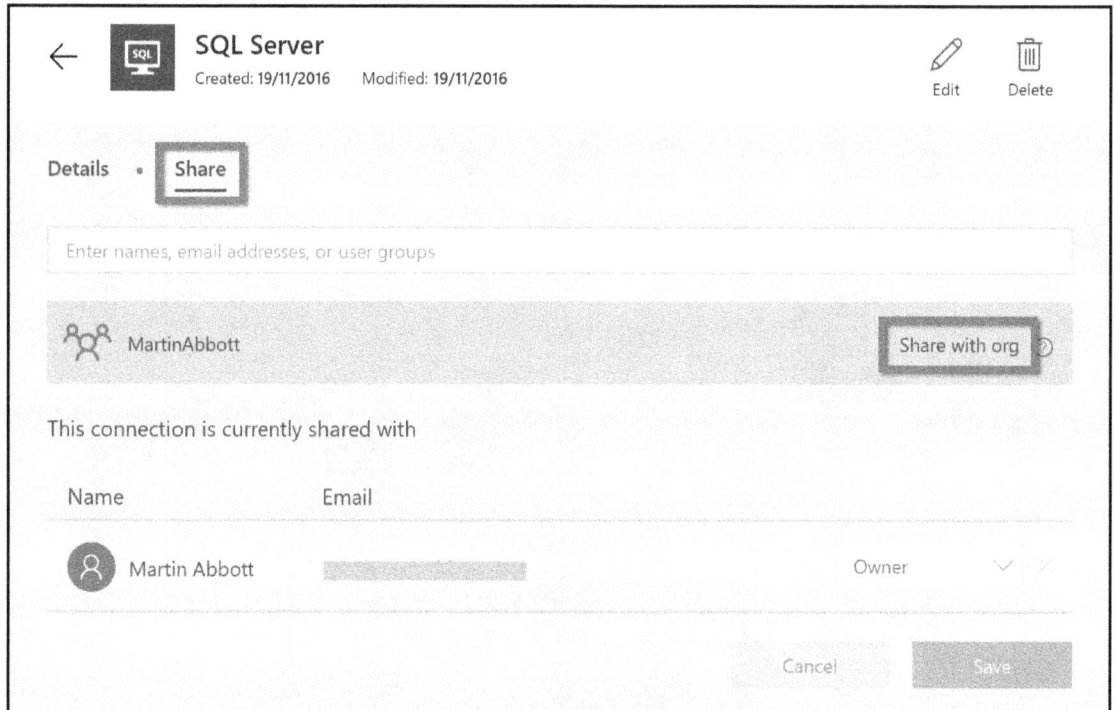

It is now time to create our simple PowerApp that allows updating of the information contained within the database. To create a PowerApp, you can use an application that can be installed from the Store or the PowerApps portal. Alternatively, at the time of writing, a web application creation experience is available in preview. Clicking on **+New app** in the PowerApps portal starts the process.

When the PowerApps application has opened, clicking on **New** allows the selection of the connection to be used to access the data. A list of standard connections is available to configure, or clicking on the right arrow allows selection of a custom connection.

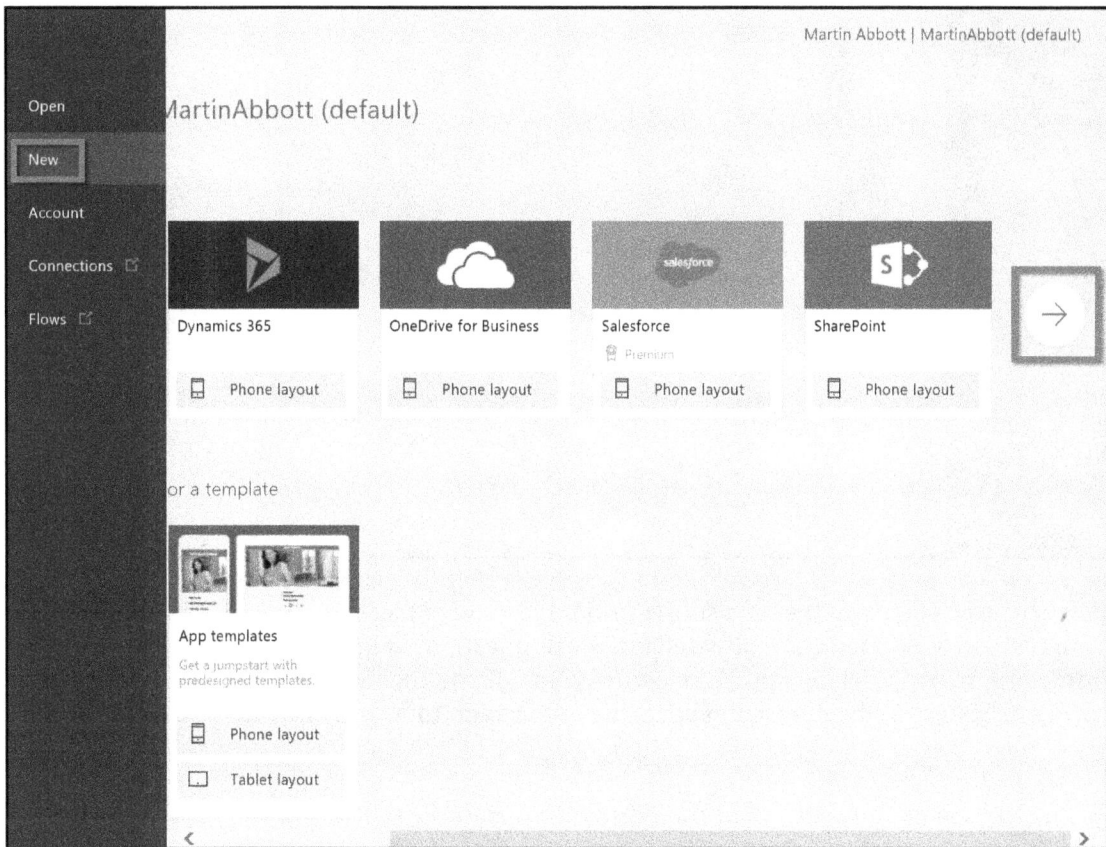

In our case, we want to connect to the CustomerCredit table we previously created, so we can view and update the information as required. Clicking on **Connect** completes the connection to the data source.

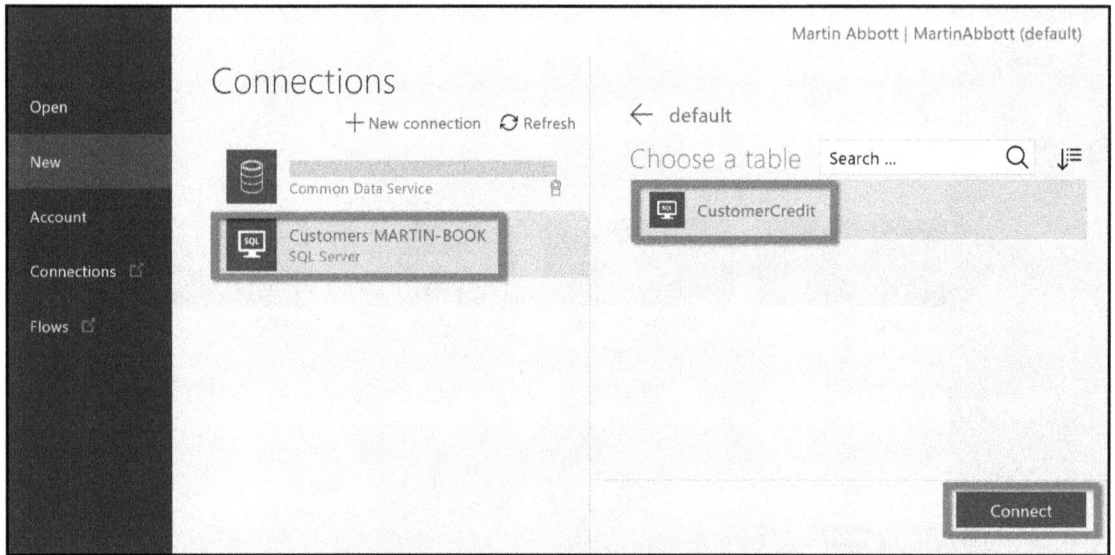

PowerApps connects to the data source and builds a very basic application that allows you to immediately be productive. By default, the application that is created has browse (including Search), detail, and edit views that contain all the information from the data source. Clicking on the play icon allows the application to be previewed.

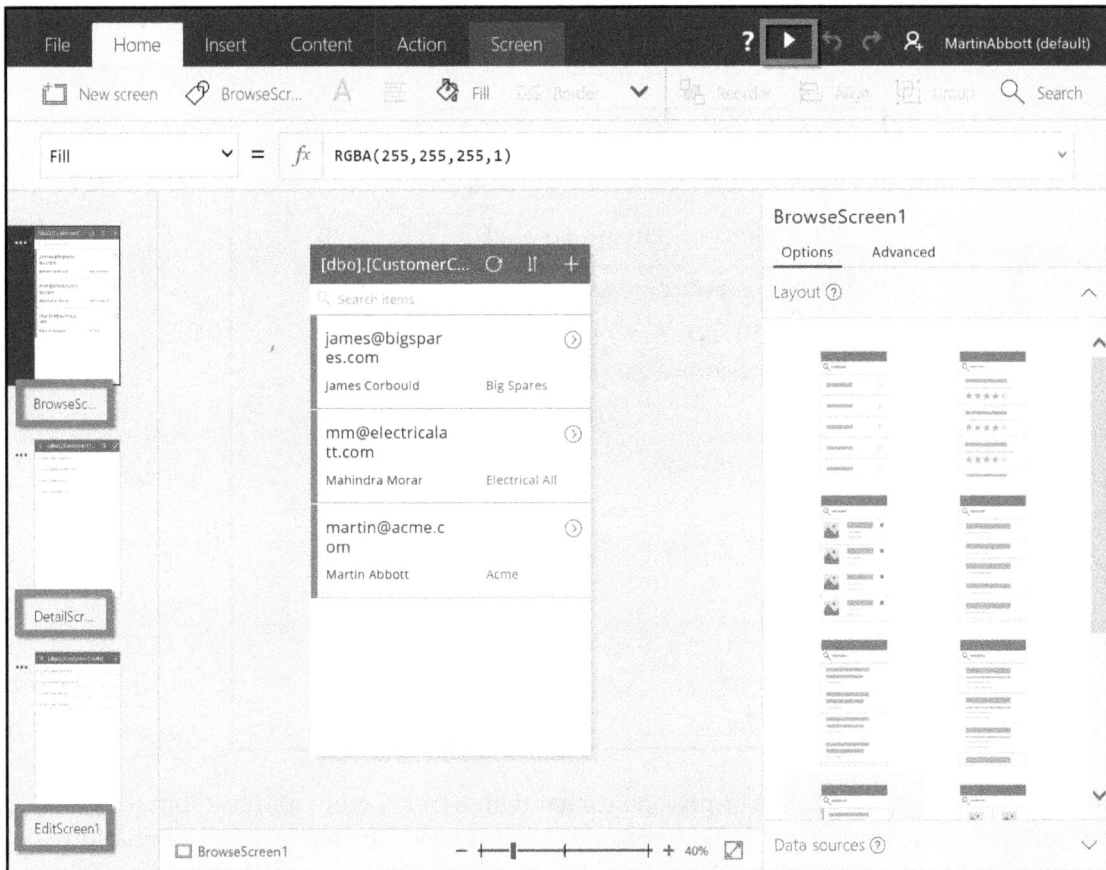

The application can be tailored to meet the specific needs of the people that need to use it. For example, layouts can be changed, along with colors; new screens and new data sources can be added. On the edit screen, validation is applied based on the incoming data requirements.

Validation and layout are locked by default for incoming data fields, but can be amended by clicking the padlock icon to unlock the field in the right hard dialog.

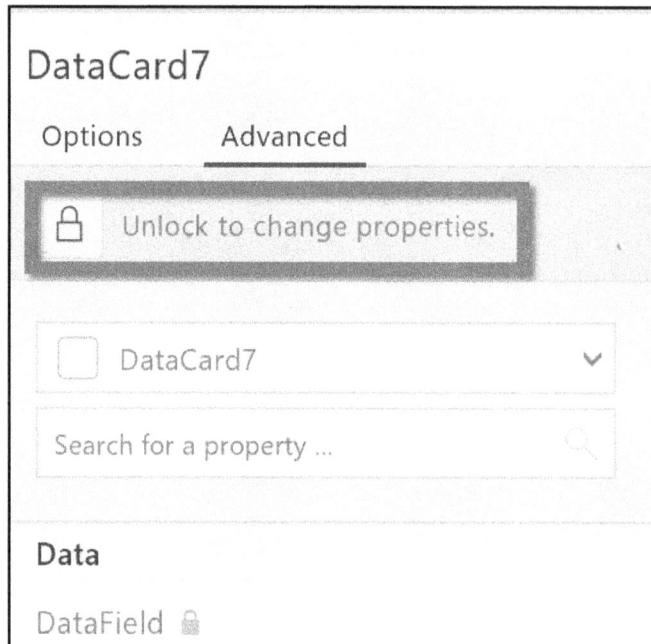

Most controls support a range of properties that define their layout and text, but they also support actions that can be tailored to provide, for example, the navigation or initiation of Flows. On the edit screen of our basic application, which contains a form named `EditForm1` and which posts the data back to the database, the confirmation icon has an action `SubmitForm(EditForm1)`. This submits the form to PowerApps, which understands that this action needs to post the data back to the database.

Once all updates have been applied, the application is previewed by clicking on the play icon. The emulator provides full control over both the screen flow and data, thereby providing a good mechanism to test the application, any validation applied, and the general flow and storage of data.

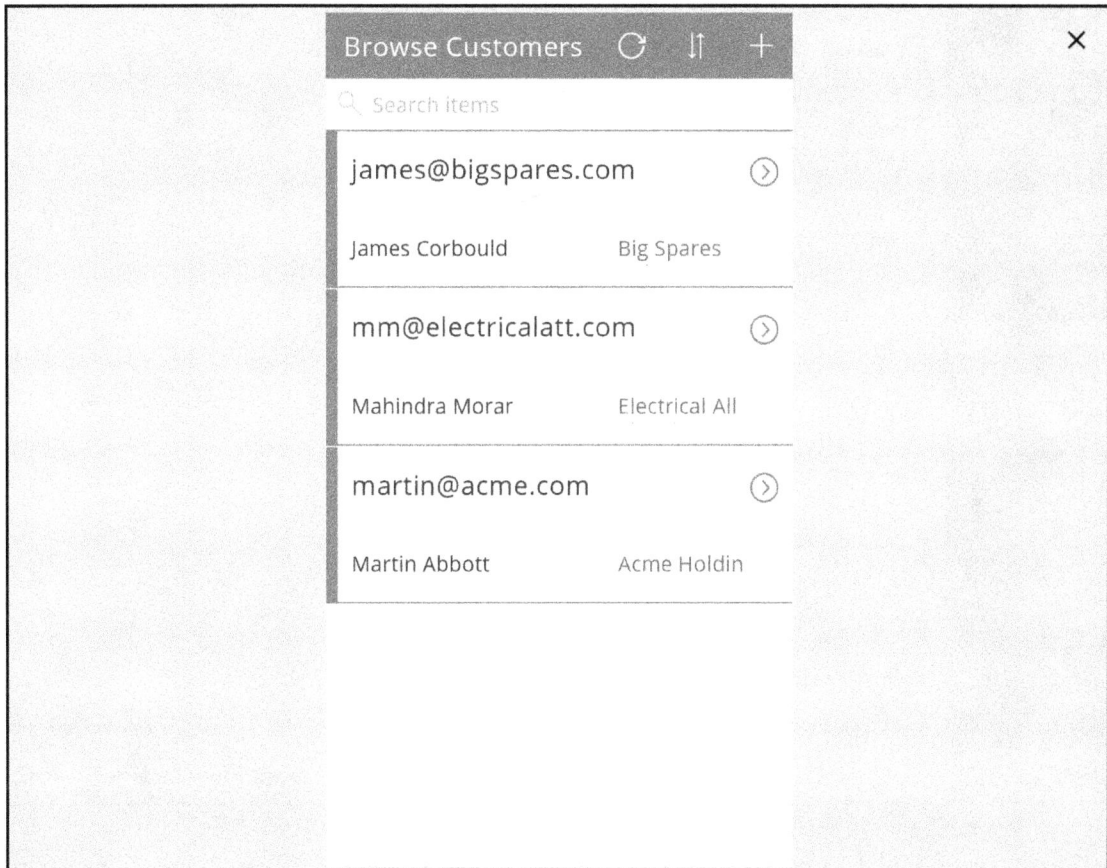

Once the application has been completed, it can be saved back to PowerApps, which then allows it to be used and shared by others.

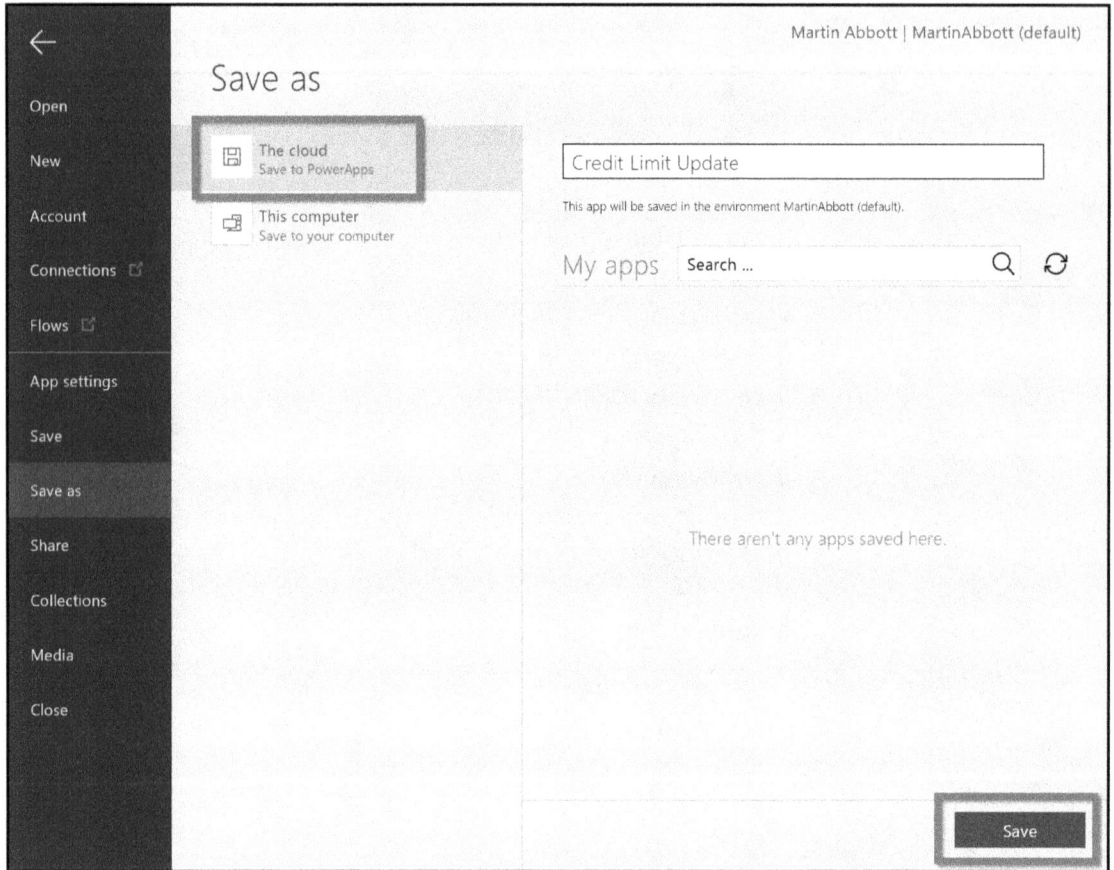

Once saved the application can be shared or amended as required, either back in the Windows 10 PowerApps application or online. The application can also be played, and now accessed from a mobile device that has the PowerApps application installed, available for Windows Phone, iOS, and Android.

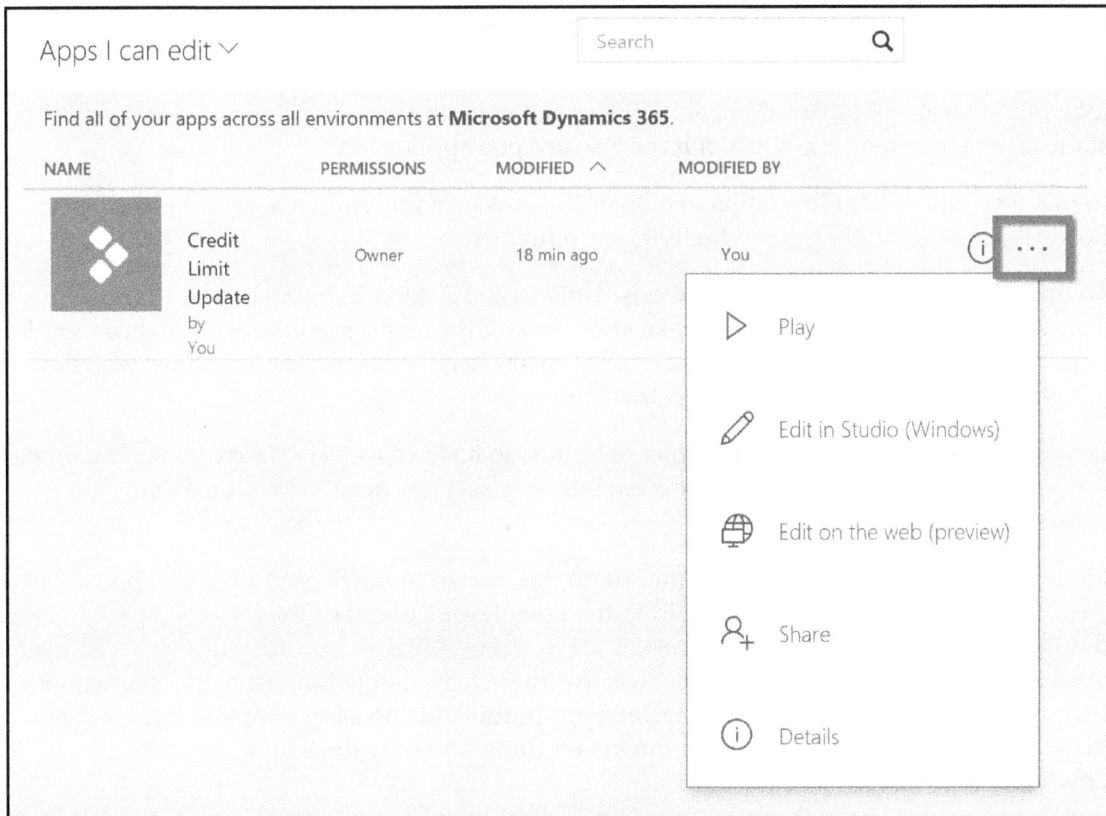

With this simple scenario, we have shown how easy it is to start creating applications that can deliver real business value quickly to the people who need them. By creating connections to data sources and sharing them across an organization or to individual users, business people that have access to PowerApps can create applications that meet their needs and demands to help boost their individual productivity.

To extend the use of PowerApps further, Microsoft Flow can be used to provide an experience similar to IFTTT (`http://www.ifttt.com`).

An introduction to Microsoft Flow

Although PowerApps provides an opportunity for business professionals to build just in time applications that expose their data sources in a meaningful way, it is still necessary to create governance and control over the flow and orchestration of that information. This is where Microsoft Flow play its part.

Microsoft Flow is a simple workflow engine that allows a sequence of events to be stitched together to create an integration solution that can combine inputs and outputs from several sources to help extend the reach of basic PowerApps applications.

In this way, Microsoft Flow helps to deliver the power of integration and orchestration to PowerApps to supercharge productivity even further.

To illustrate this, let us take our previous scenario and extend it. In the new scenario, when a customer service representative looks at increasing the credit limit, an approval process is performed and then the customer is e-mailed to let them know the result of their request and the database is updated to reflect this approval.

For the customer service representative to be able to have self-service to create this business process workflow, connections to external business services need to be set up and configured.

First, we need to create a new flow, and to do this, we go to the Flow portal. The portal can be accessed directly or via a link in either the PowerApps portal or the PowerApps designer. The Flow portal can be accessed via `https://flow.microsoft.com/`. If accessing via the PowerApps portal, you can choose to either create a new flow from blank or choose from a template. Accessing via the PowerApps portal and choosing template is a great way to get started as the list of templates shown are limited to only those that support PowerApps.

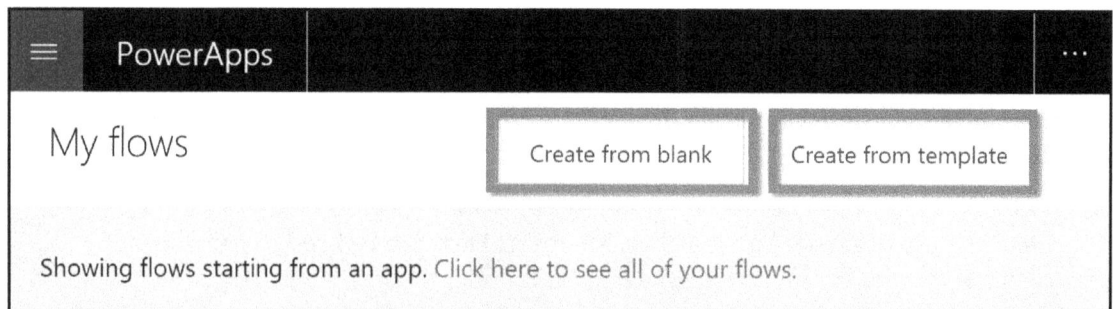

There are many templates to choose from that represent common tasks; for our scenario, we wish to have an approval process for when a credit limit change is requested.

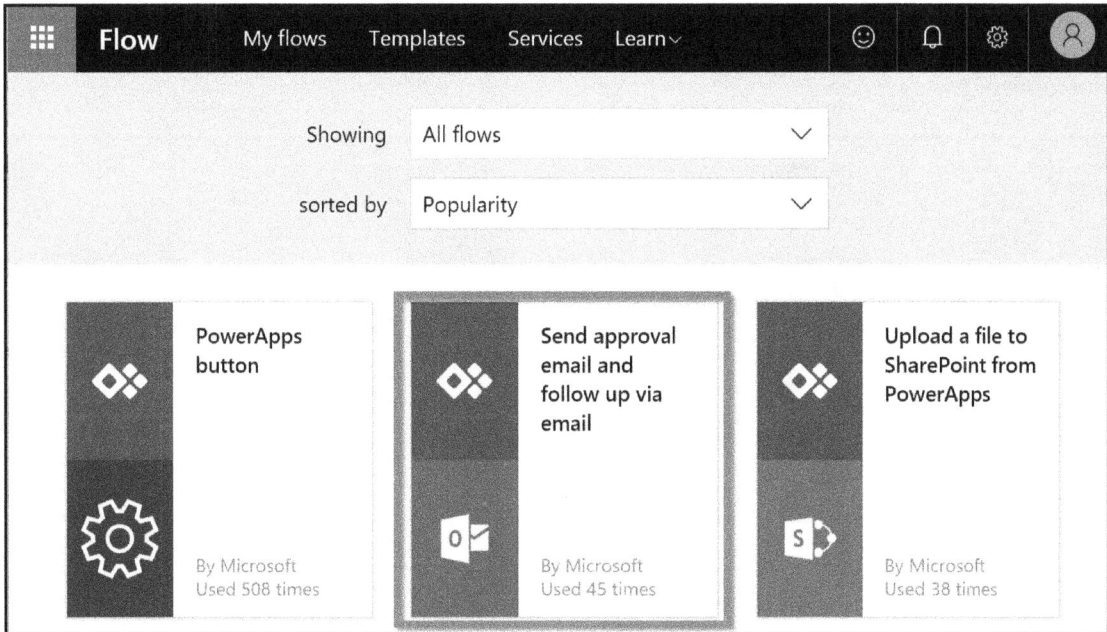

When we select the template, we need to provide some credentials for Office 365 as this is being used to deliver the e-mails. Like Logic Apps, on which Microsoft Flow is based, any credentials provided for a connection are stored securely. Once the template has loaded, we can see that we have a PowerApps trigger that then sends an e-mail. This e-mail contains options for approval or rejection, and a condition then sends an e-mail containing the outcome of the decision.

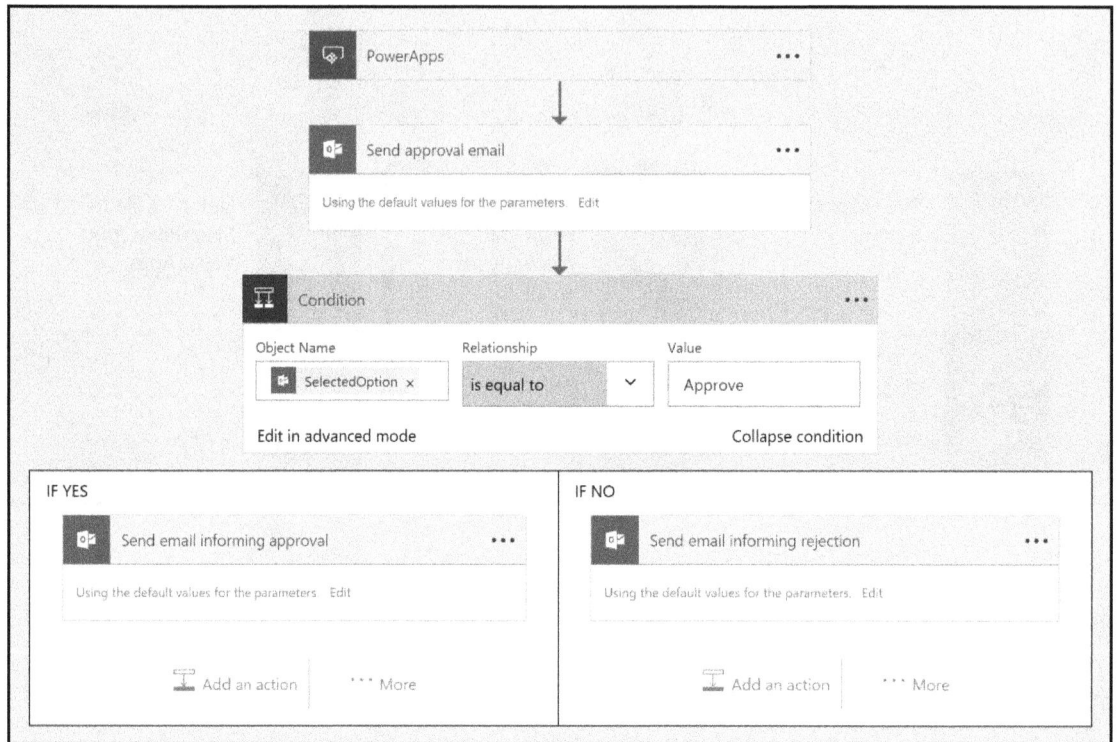

If we expand the e-mail controls, we can update them as required. One option that is available to us in the designer, is the ability to **Ask in PowerApps**. When we choose this option, a variable is created, and we can then provide the information directly from within PowerApps as part of an action. This means that we can pass information from our executing PowerApp directly to a new instance of a Microsoft Flow, making that instance contextually aware of the state of the PowerApp.

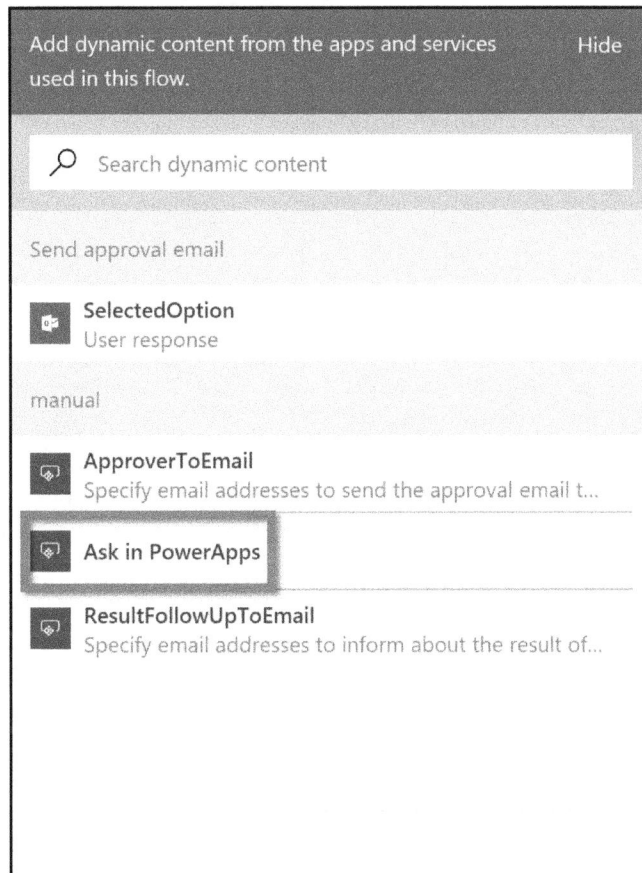

In our case, we will choose the e-mail addresses we want to send notifications to. In the previous scenario, we used the basic application to handle all communication to and from the database. This included using the default behavior on our edit screen that simply submitted changes back to the database. In our new application, there is a process that interrupts this transaction, waiting for an approval process, so we need to commit the changes to our database directly. We can do this using a SQL Server **Update Row** shape within our flow. Since the Microsoft Flow is still within the context of PowerApps, we can choose any table that is connected via a SQL connection, which is our case is our `CustomerCredit` table.

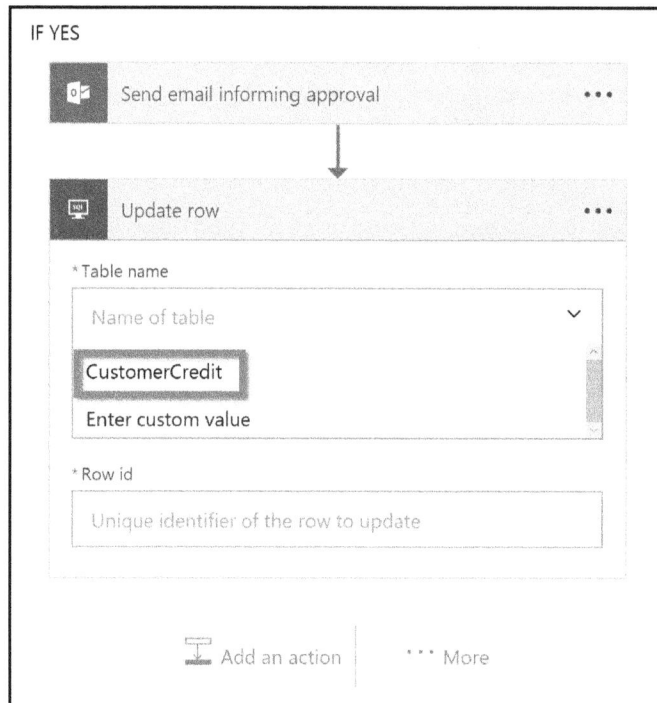

Once the designer has loaded, we have a list of the fields from the table and can again choose to **Ask in PowerApps**, so we can provide the information in the PowerApps designer when we update the appropriate action.

Once we have updated e-mail addresses and some e-mail content, and added our SQL Server update, we can create the flow so that it can be used in our application.

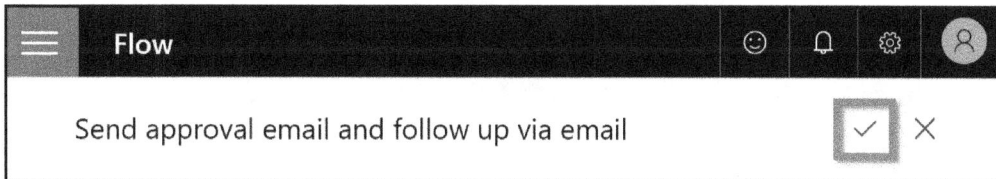

The Flow now appears in the PowerApps portal where it can be enabled and disabled, deleted or updated, which launches the Flow portal again. To make use of the flow, we need to go back to the PowerApps designer and update our previous application.

First, we add a new screen that will be the page to which the application will proceed once we have submitted our credit limit change request. This is just to provide some information to the user, we could equally navigate back to the browse screen.

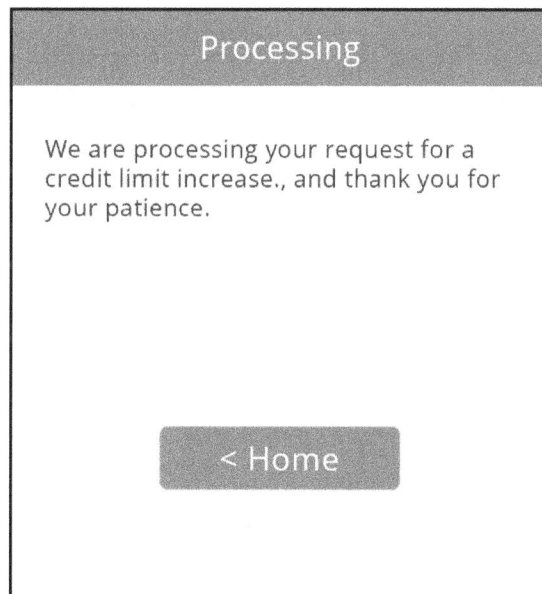

In the previous scenario, we accepted all the default behavior to quickly demonstrate the power of PowerApps. However, for our second scenario, things are more complex, and we need to update the default behavior and added new functionality based on our newly created Flow. In the example of our **Processing** screen above, we update the `OnSelect` action of the button to navigate back to the browse screen by setting the `OnSelect` action to `Navigate(BrowseScreen1, ScreenTransition.None)`.

On our browse screen, we need to update the navigation that takes the user to the details screen to reload the data from the database to ensure that the details are always up to date. We do this by setting the `OnSelect` action to `Refresh('[dbo].[CustomerCredit]');Navigate(DetailScreen1, ScreenTransition.None)`. This shows the ability to combine commands using a semicolon, and in this case, we are refreshing our data source and then navigating to the details screen.

Once we have done some simple changes to the layout, added a new screen, and changed some of the navigation, we then need to update what happens when we click on the confirmation button on our edit screen. Previously, this button submitted the form, but now, we need to initiate our instance of our flow. Before changing this, we need to be able to determine `CustomerId` of the record that is being edited. To do this, we simply add a new data card for the `CustomerId` data field. In our case, we set this to be hidden, so we can access the text of the field without it displaying. Once this is done, we can choose our button and go to **Action** in the ribbon and select **Flows**. This displays a list of flows that are currently available as well as offering an opportunity to create a new one.

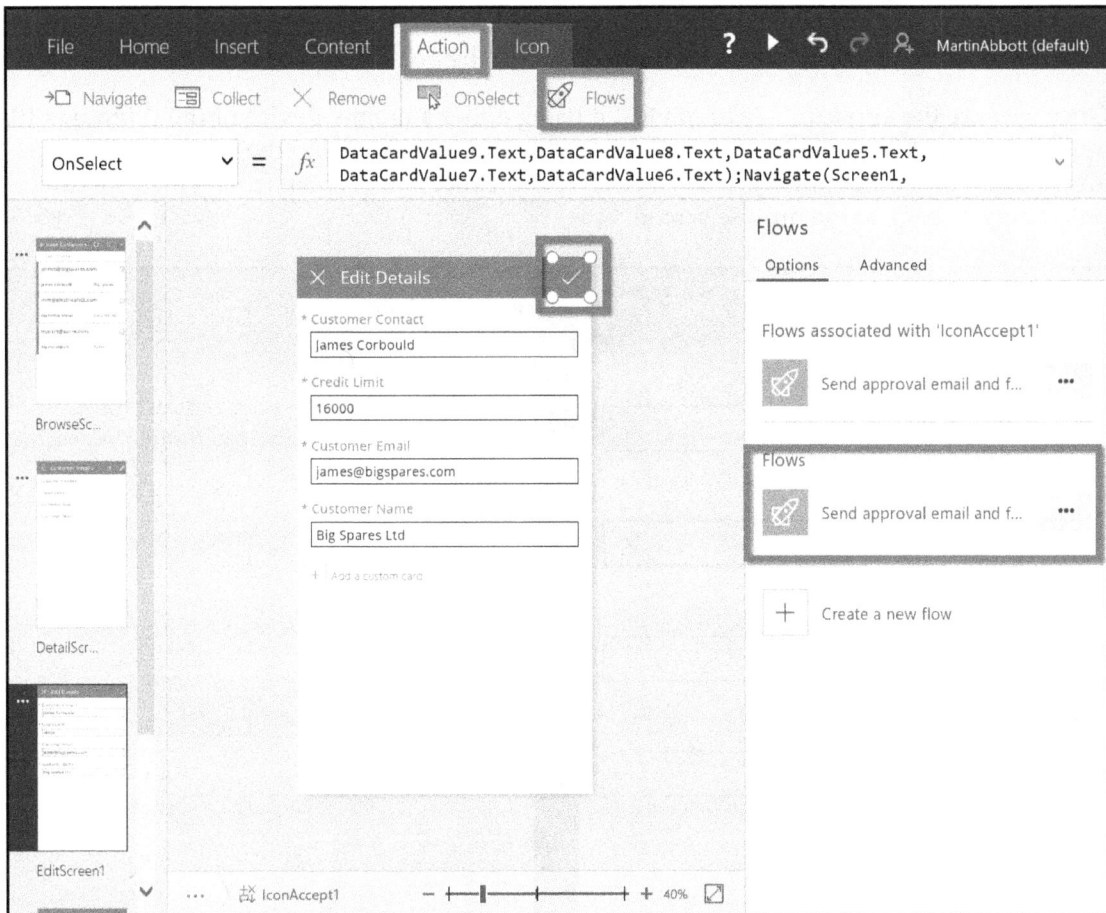

We chose to **Ask in PowerApps** when we created the Flow, so when we set the formula for the OnSelect action, we need to provide the values that will be passed to the Flow instance. The formula takes the form [FlowName].Run([Parameter List]). The parameter list is based on the values chosen as dynamic data within the Flow. For our case, we have e-mail addresses that we are sending e-mails to, and data values from our data source that we are using to update the record using our SQL Server connection. The expression used is as follows:

```
Sendapprovalemailandfollowupviaemail.Run("[ApproverEmailAddress]",DataCardV
alue7.Text,DataCardValue9.Text,DataCardValue8.Text,DataCardValue5.Text,Data
CardValue7.Text,DataCardValue6.Text);Navigate(Screen1,ScreenTransition.None
)
```

As can be seen, we use the values of the text fields taken from our edit form. The last part of the expression navigates to our screen that displays the helpful message about processing.

Once we save the application, we can test it using either a mobile device or the Windows 10 application. First, we update our credit limit, in our scenario, raising the limit to $17,000, and click on the accept button. This takes us to our **Processing** screen from which we can only navigate back to the browse screen.

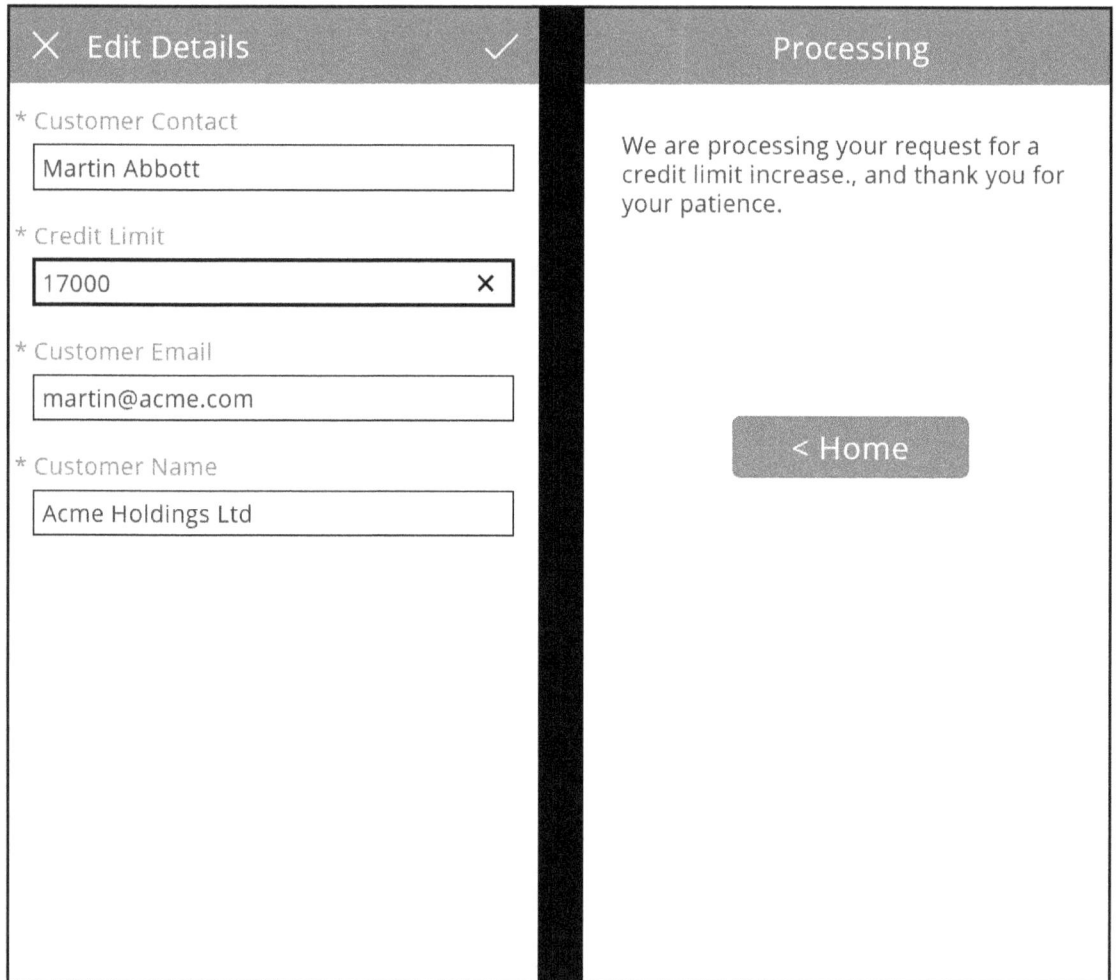

✕ Edit Details ✓	Processing
* Customer Contact	We are processing your request for a credit limit increase., and thank you for your patience.
Martin Abbott	
* Credit Limit	
17000 ✕	
* Customer Email	
martin@acme.com	
* Customer Name	< Home
Acme Holdings Ltd	

When we check our Office 365 mail, we see that we have received an e-mail asking us to approve or reject the increase.

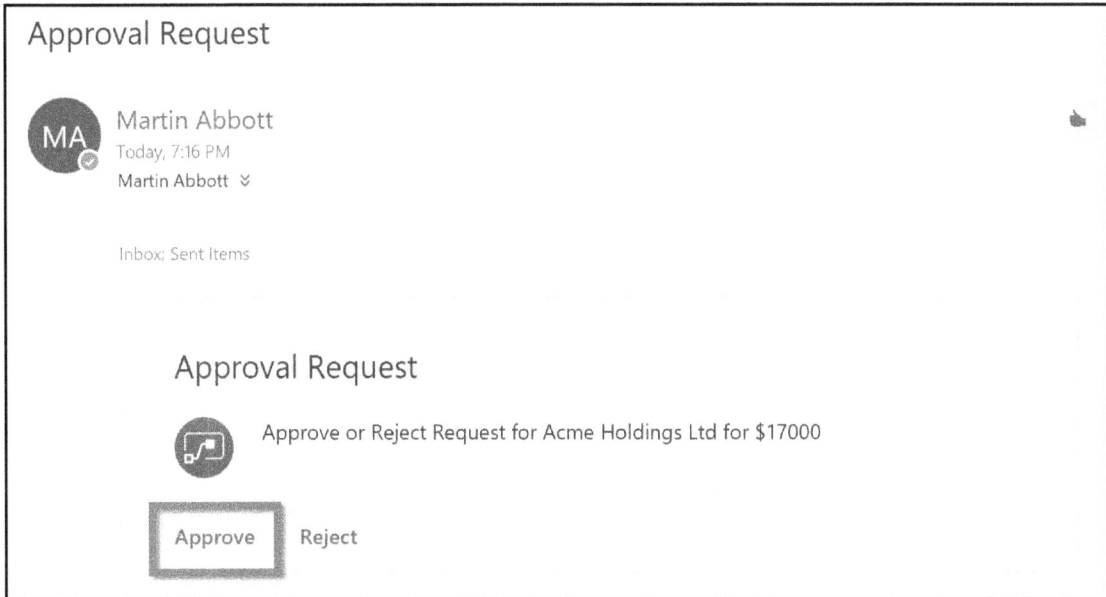

Clicking on **Approve** sends another e-mail to the person requesting the increase.

We can then either check our data source or look in the PowerApps application at the details for the record we have updated.

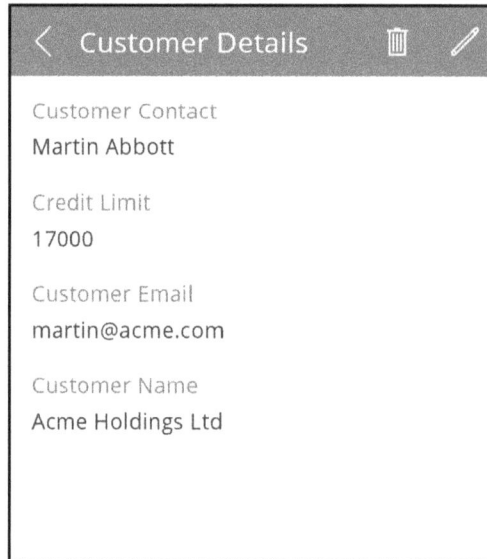

We can see that our Flow has run and completed. If we go to the PowerApps portal, we can go navigate to our flow and check the run history. To check the history, we click on the information button.

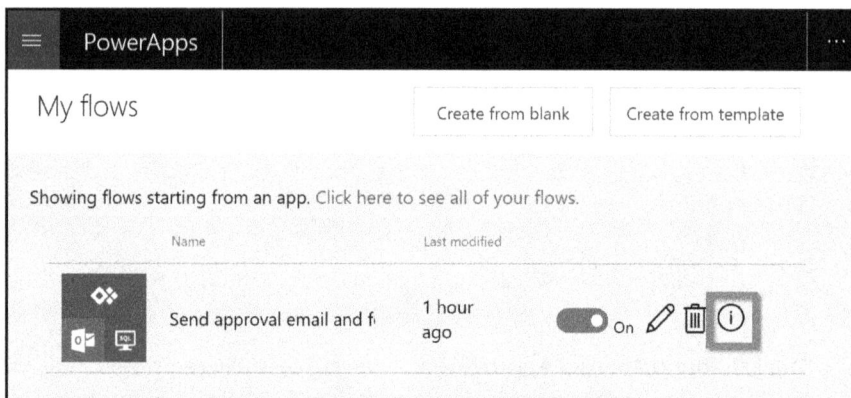

We then get a list of runs and their status, and we can filter the list to see specific types of runs.

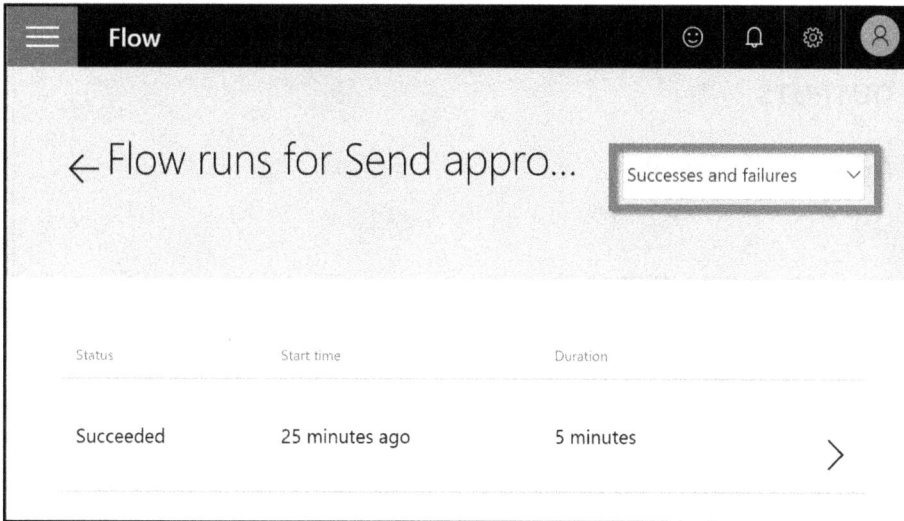

Clicking on a run allows us to view the Flow run and examine the details.

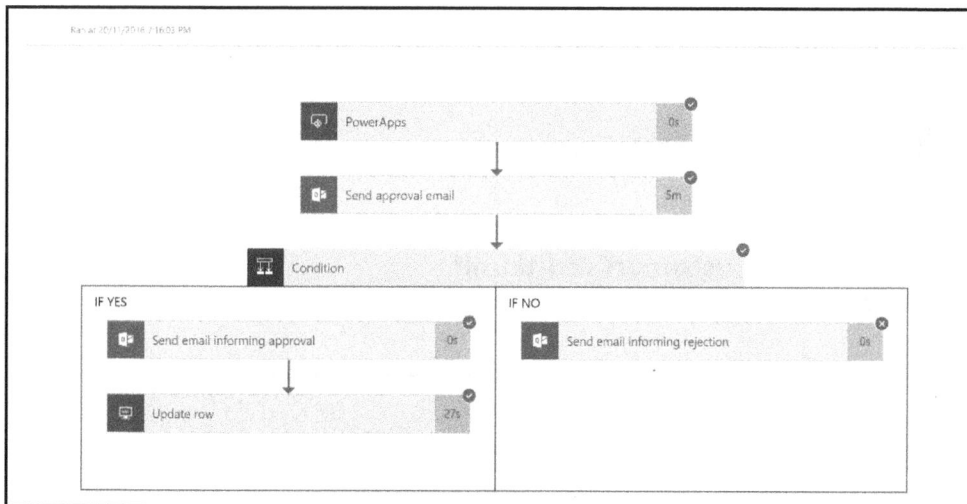

Clicking on any of the components opens up information about the inputs and outputs, and clicking on the **PowerApps** component shows the values that we passed out of the PowerApp to the flow instance.

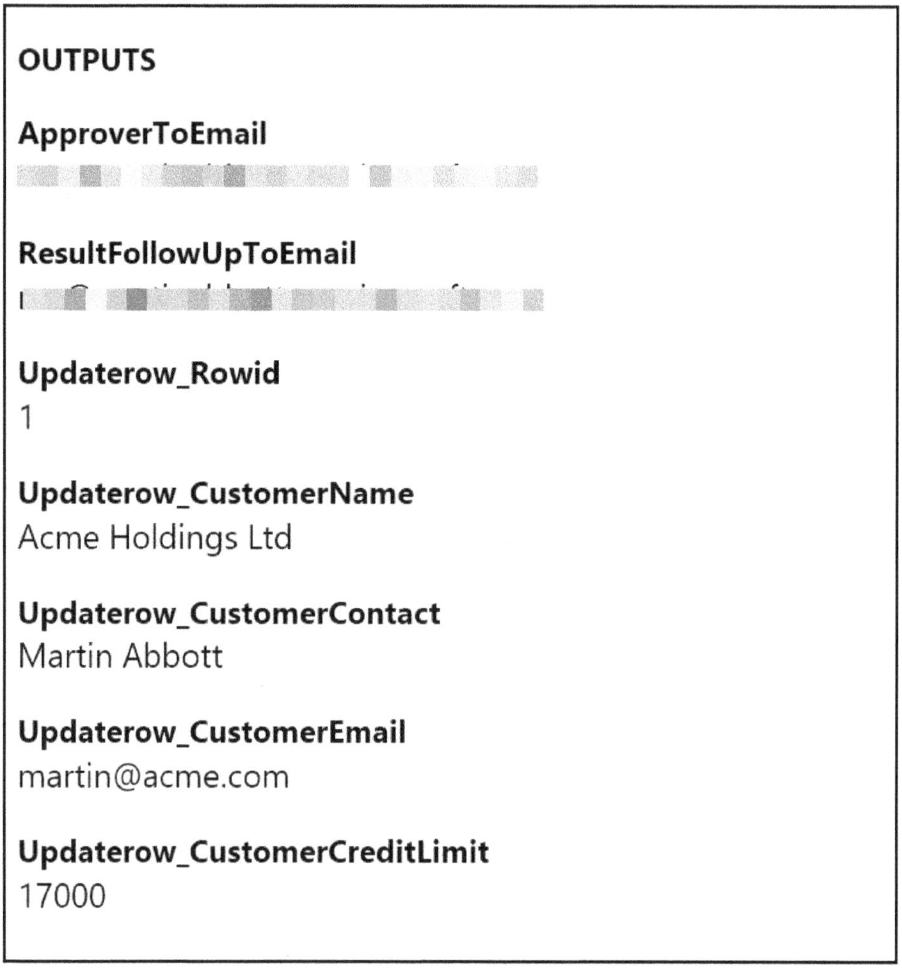

OUTPUTS

ApproverToEmail

ResultFollowUpToEmail

Updaterow_Rowid
1

Updaterow_CustomerName
Acme Holdings Ltd

Updaterow_CustomerContact
Martin Abbott

Updaterow_CustomerEmail
martin@acme.com

Updaterow_CustomerCreditLimit
17000

In this scenario, we have shown how to integrate a simple orchestration workflow for approval and database update in the context of our fictitious company. However, Microsoft Flow has capabilities beyond just PowerApps and has connections and templates available for building a range of other interactions.

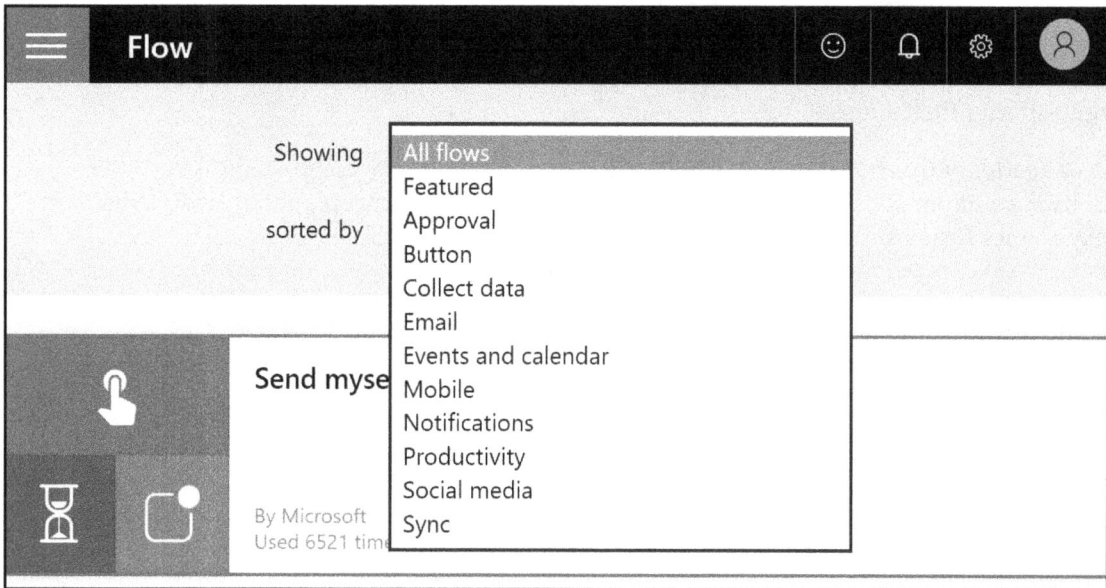

Microsoft Flow provides a first-class experience to create simple or complex workflows that are simpler to design than through the full Logic App design experience. By removing the need to look at a code view, integration is put in the hands of the citizen integrator, and when combined with PowerApps provides a great experience for creating business productivity applications that meet the specific needs of the individual.

Keeping up with the pace of change

The integration community is truly global and enriched by the people who contribute toward it. With the pace of change being as quick as it is, it can sometimes be a little daunting to keep up with things.

This is where the community plays a huge part. Through the Microsoft MVP program and the dedication of bloggers, the time between feature release and documentation or review is now shorter than ever.

As a reader of this book, you would be encouraged to take the contents, build on them, deliver solutions for the organizations for which you work, and play that knowledge and experience forward through blog articles or TechNet Wiki articles (see: `https://social.technet.microsoft.com/wiki/`).

Conferences and industry shows are another great opportunity to interact with the community of professionals, and one of the strengths of the Microsoft integration community is its openness and willingness to help.

Leveraging the community is a great way to stay current, but the strength of the community is in people getting involved; a community should grow and evolve to embrace the new technologies being released and the people willing to contribute to the body of knowledge held by it.

Final thoughts

It is an exciting time to be an integration professional. With the explosion of cloud computing and the real need for data governance and investment protection of expensive critical systems, the time for hybrid integration is firmly here and now.

We hope that you have found the book useful and that it has provided you with the confidence to take the next steps in your integration journey.

Index

www.ingramcontent.com/pod-product-compliance
Lightning Source LLC
Chambersburg PA
CBHW080343220326
41598CB00030B/4592